THE LIFE AND WORKS
OF
SAINT VINCENT DE PAUL

CARDINAL DE RETZ,
ARCHBISHOP OF PARIS

THE LIFE & WORKS
OF
SAINT VINCENT DE PAUL

Translated from the French of
PIERRE COSTE, C.M.

By
JOSEPH LEONARD, C.M.

VOLUME II

Published in the United States by New City Press
the Publishing House of the Focolare
206 Skillman Avenue, Brooklyn, NY 11211
©1987 New City Press, New York

Library of Congress Catalog Number: 87-61617
ISBN 0-911-782-57-5
Printed in the United States of America

NIHIL OBSTAT:
EDUARDUS J. MAHONEY, S.Th.D.,
Censor deputatus.

IMPRIMATUR:
✠ JOSEPH BUTT,
Vicarius generalis.

CONTENTS

CHAPTER XXIV

THE CONGREGATION OF THE MISSION IN ITALY. ROME —GENOA—TURIN 1

CHAPTER XXV

THE CONGREGATION OF THE MISSION IN IRELAND AND SCOTLAND 30

CHAPTER XXVI

THE CONGREGATION OF THE MISSION IN POLAND . . 41
Departure and arrival of the first band of Missionaries; Plague in Cracow and Warsaw; death of Father Lambert; departure and journey of Father Ozenne; the Queen's generosity; missions; reinforcements; the invasion of Poland; sickness and trials; death of Father Ozenne; peace.

CHAPTER XXVII

THE MADAGASCAR MISSION 51
Precursors; the first Missionaries in that island; the East India Company and the French Colony in Madagascar; Governor de Pronis; his successor, de Flacourt.
From the arrival of Father Nacquart till his death (December 4, 1648–May 29, 1650); the Mission is entrusted to the Congregation; Saint Vincent's advice to Father Nacquart; departure and arrival of Fathers Nacquart and Gondrée; the French Colony; religion of the Malagasies; their qualities and defects; state of Christianity on Father Nacquart's arrival; visit to the King of Antanosy; labours of Father Nacquart; death of Father Gondrée; new undertakings; baptisms; plans for evangelising the natives; misunderstandings with de Flacourt; a projected

CONTENTS

journey to France ; final labours of Father Nacquart ; his last illness and death.

From the death of Father Nacquart to the arrival of Father Bourdaise (June, 1650–August, 1654) ; wars in Madagascar ; difficulties in regard to sailing from France ; arrival of Fathers Bourdaise and Mousnier.

From the arrival of Father Bourdaise to the departure of Father Dufour (September, 1654–October 29, 1655) ; labours of Fathers Bourdaise and Mousnier ; fire at Fort Dauphin and the Church ; a hut is transformed into a chapel ; deaths of Father Mousnier and Governor de Pronis.

From the departure of Father Dufour to the death of Father Bourdaise (October 29, 1655–June 25, 1657) ; departure of Fathers Dufour, Prévost and de Belleville ; de Belleville dies at sea ; Father Dufour's zeal on shipboard ; arrival in Madagascar ; Feast of the Most Blessed Sacrament ; Fathers Dufour and Prévost on St. Mary's Island ; labours and death of Father Dufour ; death of Father Prévost ; labours and death of Father Bourdaise.

Unsuccessful attempts to help the Madagascar Mission ; Saint Vincent's exhortation on zeal ; arrival of de Flacourt in France accompanied by four young negroes who are educated in Saint-Lazare ; difficulties of the East India Company ; Fathers Herbron, Boussordec and Brother Patte are chosen ; shipwreck ; Saint Vincent's perseverance in the midst of trials and difficulties ; rivalry between the East India Company and the Duke de la Meilleraye ; Saint Vincent's embarrassment and attempts to reach an agreement ; departure of Fathers White, Arnoud, de Fontaines, Daveroult, and Brother Delaunay ; shipwreck ; preparations for a new embarkation ; annoyance of the Duke de la Meilleraye ; Saint Vincent promises him to have no further relations with the East India Company ; letter to Father Bourdaise ; voyage and return of Father Etienne and his confrères.

CHAPTER XXVIII

THE TUESDAY CONFERENCES 118

Organisation ; meetings ; members ; missions ; promotions to the episcopacy : Thursday conferences ; conferences in the Provinces.

CONTENTS

CHAPTER XXIX

RETREATS FOR ORDINANDS 150
    Grants and obligations ; preachers ; duties of the Community ; rules ; approbation of the work by the Holy See ; results ; retreats for ordinands in France and Italy, especially in Rome.

CHAPTER XXX

SEMINARIES 170
    Their spread ; seminary of the Bons Enfants, St. Nicholas, Saint-Sulpice, Saint Magloire, and Valence ; qualities of a Director ; training given at Saint-Lazare ; results.

CHAPTER XXXI

RETREATS FOR ECCLESIASTICS 192
    Paris, Alet, Narbonne, Genoa.

CHAPTER XXXII

THE REFORM OF PREACHING 197
    Preaching in Saint Vincent's day ; infatuation for pagan antiquity ; pedantic erudition ; frequent recourse to mythology and fable ; scriptural symbolism ; scholastic terminology ; silly phraseology ; theatrical descriptions ; abuse of antitheses ; play upon words ; grotesque comparisons ; buffoonery ; incursions into politics ; attacks on heretics.
    Preaching as Saint Vincent wished it to be ; an upright intention ; simplicity of matter, form and style ; the three points ; motives, nature, means ; charity.
    Training of future preachers at Saint-Lazare by teaching and example ; success of ' the little method.'

CHAPTER XXXIII

THE EPISCOPACY 226
    Saint Vincent's part in the appointments to Bishopric ; his intervention on behalf of certain candidates ; his advice to bishops.

CONTENTS

CHAPTER XXXIV

THE REFORM OF THE MONASTIC ORDERS . . . 237
Cardinal de La Rochefocauld is appointed Abbot of Sainte-Geneviève and Vicar General ; Richelieu's energetic measures ; chief reformers ; reaction on the death of Richelieu ; Benedictine reform ; Augustinian reform ; reform of the Order of Grandmont ; Dominican reform ; individual reforms.

CHAPTER XXXV

THE FOUNDLINGS 255
Welfare work for foundlings before the seventeenth century ; *La Couche ;* the Ladies of Charity help the children ; a modest attempt ; extension of the work ; children out at nurse ; alleged nightly expeditions of Saint Vincent ; advice to the Sisters of *La Couche ;* rules ; formation and education of the children ; hygienic precautions ; the 'Thirteen Houses' ; financial and other difficulties ; discourse of Saint Vincent ; Bicêtre ; fresh difficulties ; the state of affairs in 1657 ; the Foundling Hospital attached for administrative purposes to the General Hospital.

CHAPTER XXXVI

MENDICANTS 280
The fight against mendicancy in the first half of the seventeenth century ; the Hospice of the Holy Name of Jesus—its foundation ; the house ; selection of inmates ; Mlle Le Gras' suggestions ; installation ; the contract ; approbation ; organisation ; catechism ; plan for its extension.

The General Hospital ; the plan of the Ladies of Charity ; Saint Vincent's reluctance ; the *Salpêtrière* is given to the Ladies of Charity by the Queen ; works ; opposition ; the King's edict against begging ; administration of the General Hospital ; its inmates ; chaplains appointed by the edict ; a mission ; the King's edict is carried out ; Saint Vincent is attacked ; Chaplains appointed instead of the Priests of the Mission ; employments confided to the Daughters of Charity and to the Ladies of Charity ; begging at the gates of Saint-Lazare ; great services rendered to the General Hospital by the Ladies of Charity.

CONTENTS

CHAPTER XXXVII

PAGE

PRISONERS 305
Evils to which prisoners were exposed; solicitude of the Company of the Blessed Sacrament; prison work; the Confraternities and the Ladies of Charity assist prisoners; prisons within the Seignory of Saint-Lazare; house of correction at Saint-Lazare; Saint Vincent's charity towards his 'boarders.'

CHAPTER XXXVIII

THE GALLEY-SLAVES 315
The galley-slaves of Paris; at Saint Roch; transferred to La Tournelle; religious services; the Company of the Blessed Sacrament remedies abuses; convicts assisted by the Charity of Saint Nicholas; M. Cornuel's bequest; the Daughters of Charity and their work for galley-slaves.
The galley-slaves of Marseilles; convicts on the galleys; charity of John Baptist Gault, Bishop of Marseilles; mission to galley-slaves; death of John Baptist Gault; the hospital; the Missionaries of Marseilles are placed in charge of the chaplains to the galley-slaves; their services; Chevalier de la Coste; galley-slaves transferred to Toulon.

CHAPTER XXXIX

SLAVES 337
Slaves in Barbary; early days and difficulties of the Mission in Tunis; origin and trials of the Mission in Algiers; what the two Missions of Algiers and Tunis did for the slaves.

CHAPTER XL

SAINT VINCENT AND LORRAINE 366
Description of the famine; prayers and acts of penance at Saint-Lazare; Saint Vincent approaches Cardinal Richelieu; organisation of charity; alms given by the King, the Queen, and the Duchesse d'Aiguillon; famine and charitable relief at Toul, Saint-Mihiel, Bar-le-Duc, Pont-à-Mousson, Nancy, Metz, Verdun; Brother Mathew's charitable expeditions; distress in convents; depopulation; charity shown to refugees from Lorraine in Paris; help for the nobility of Lorraine.

CONTENTS

CHAPTER XLI

SAINT VINCENT AND THE RELIEF OF PICARDY AND CHAMPAGNE 398
Description of the state of these provinces; Saint Vincent, his missionaries and the Ladies of Charity intervene; the *Relations;* meetings of the Ladies; gifts; prayers; distribution of alms; the missionaries and the Daughters of Charity; a royal ordinance; barbarity of the troops; contributions; creditors' claims; famine; sickness; religious needs; alms; soup kitchens; asylums for orphans and young girls; establishment of hospitals; the Daughters of Charity; epidemics; relief of the clergy; recall of several missionaries and falling off in the supply of alms; Father Alméras; Brother John Parre; the Daughters of Charity nurse wounded and sick soldiers at Châlons, Saint Menehould, Sedan, La Fère, Stenay and Calais.

CHAPTER XLII

THE RELIEF OF L'ILE-DE-FRANCE 443
Political events of 1648 and 1649; arrest of Broussel, sedition, the Court at Rueil, the return to Paris and sojourn at Saint Germain-en-Laye; Paris threatened with a siege; sickness and poverty in its environs; Saint Vincent's efforts in favour of peace; his journey to the West; Villepreux, Valpuiseaux, Le Mans, Angers, Saint-Méen, Nantes, Luçon, Richelieu; return to Paris; Missions in reparation of sacrileges that had been committed; Mazarin and the Princes; risings in the provinces; Condé and Turenne; invasion of the Seminary of Saint Charles; massacres at the Hôtel-de-Ville; Saint Vincent again intervenes in favour of peace; the King enters Paris; extent of public misery; prayers and acts of penance; the Queen of Poland's gift; distribution of relief; missions to the refugees; asylums for nuns and young girls; appeals to the charitable public; the *Magasin charitable;* communities come to the assistance of those in distress; missionaries who fell sick or died; the Daughters of Charity at Étampes.

CHAPTER XLIII

THE SICK; LUNATICS; ORPHANS; THOSE DRIVEN FROM THEIR HOMES BY FLOODS; AND EXILES . . . 492

LIST OF ILLUSTRATIONS

Volume II

Cardinal de Retz, Archbishop of Paris	*Frontispiece*
	FACING PAGE
Cardinal Durazzo, Archbishop of Genoa	24
Fort Dauphin	51
Stephen de Flacourt	71
Island of Saint Mary	91
William de Lamoignon	111
Anthony Godeau, Bishop of Vence	130
Felix Vialart, Bishop of Châlons	149
Charles de Condren, Superior of the Oratory of France	175
Bossuet, Bishop of Meaux	221
Gregory Tarrisse, Superior of the Congregation of Saint Maur	242
La Salpêtrière	280
Tower and Gate of Saint-Bernard	316
Marseilles in the Seventeenth Century	336
Baron Gaston de Renty	376
Angelique Arnauld	396
Cardinal Mazarin	416
Madeleine de Lamoignon	450
Hippolyte Féret, Vicar General of Paris	480

SAINT VINCENT DE PAUL

CHAPTER XXIV

THE CONGREGATION OF THE MISSION IN ITALY
ROME—GENOA—TURIN

IN 1631, Saint Vincent, in order to put an end to the opposition which was retarding the approbation of the Congregation of the Mission in Rome, decided to have a representative there in the person of one of his first companions, Francis du Coudray. When the latter's mission was accomplished, after a sojourn of five years in that city, he was recalled to Paris. There may perhaps have been reasons of a personal nature, of which we are ignorant, for du Coudray's recall, because the permanent presence of a missionary in Rome, either to act as an intermediary between the Superior General and the Holy See, or to demonstrate on the spot, by the preaching of missions or retreats, the value of the new Institute, presented incontestable advantages. The place left vacant by Fr. du Coudray was filled, in 1639, by Louis Lebreton, a priest remarkable for his zeal and talents. Fr. Lebreton became the apostle of prisoners and sinners, and of the shepherds of the Campagna, visiting dungeons, sailing vessels and the humblest cabins of the poor. With the help of an Italian priest, John Baptist Taoni, he preached several missions.[1] He could have provided plenty of occupation for the one or two additional helpers whom he asked for, and whom

[1] *La Congregazione della Missione in Italia*, by S. Stella, oct., Paris, 1884, Vol. I, p. 4; notice on Fr. Lebreton in *Notices sur les prêtres, clercs et frères défunts de la Congrégation de la Mission*, 1st series, Vol. II, pp. 217–218.

Saint Vincent, indeed, was thinking of sending him, but in Lebreton's eyes, the acquisition of a suitable dwelling place was even more urgent. For this the Vice-Gerent's permission was necessary, and was, in fact, easily obtained.[2]

Hence a house of residence was sought for in Rome, in one of the healthiest quarters of the city, so that ordinands who went to make a retreat should be suitably accommodated. As the Fathers had only the modest sum of three or four thousand livres at their disposal, they had to moderate their ambitions. What Saint Vincent desired was a small house containing two or three rooms, on a site that could be extended in the course of time, and complete freedom from all obligations that might interfere with the work of giving missions and retreats.[3] It should be called 'The Mission,' and the chapel, which was to be subsequently built, should be dedicated to the Most Holy Trinity.[4] Fr. Lebreton received many proposals; he was offered Santa Bibiana, Our Lady of the Rotonda, Our Lady of Loretto, the little church of Saint John, the church of Saint Yves, and even Cardinal Bichi's palace,[5] but the prices were too high or the conditions imposed unacceptable. When he died on October 19, 1641, nothing definite had been settled.

Saint Vincent was deeply distressed at the rapid disappearance of a confrère on whom he had founded great hopes. In the following month, he wrote to Bernard Codoing, then Superior at Anneçy: 'Here is a piece of news that will grieve you. Our Lord had disposed of his servant, Fr. Lebreton, on his return from a mission at Ostia, to which he went in the month of October, for it is dangerous to go from Rome to Ostia and then return to the capital. Several persons have informed me of the wonders he wrought there, and the blessing which Our Lord bestowed on him. Fr. Le Bret wrote to tell me that their Eminences Cardinals Barberini and Lenti wept for him, as did also His Lordship the Vice-Gerent of Rome. He had obtained permission to erect an establishment in that city

---

[2] *Saint Vincent de Paul*, Vol. XIII, p. 282.
[3] *Ibid.*, Vol. II, pp. 27, 31, 386.
[4] *Ibid.*, p. 49.
[5] *Ibid.*, pp. 26, 27, 151, 262.

THE MISSION IN ITALY

in the hope of carrying on the work for ordinands. It is thought that there should be no delay in sending someone to Rome to make the foundation, and it seems as if Providence is turning to you to accomplish this work.'[6]

The generosity of the Duchesse d'Aiguillon, now enriched by the death of her uncle, Cardinal Richelieu, supplied the funds of which the house in Rome was in need if it was to increase and develop. Her first gift, in 1642, was an annual sum of 2500 livres derived from the Royal Postal Service, and on May 2, 1643, this was increased by an additional grant of 5000 livres. She asked, in return, that one Low Mass be said daily for the repose of the soul of her uncle, who had died on December 4, 1642, and, on the anniversary of his death, that all the Community Masses should be offered for the same intention, and a funeral service held ; the same obligations to be incurred for herself after her decease ; furthermore, ordinands should be admitted, at any time of the year, to prepare, by a preliminary retreat, for the fit reception of Holy Orders ; and finally, that a black marble tablet should be erected in a prominent and suitable position in the church, in memory of the foundress.[7]

Fr. Codoing arrived in Rome, accompanied by John Martin, then a student, and took up his residence in the Morone Palace near the Bridge of Saint Sixtus. As there was very little ready money in hand, the payment of a cook would have strained their funds, hence Brother Martin did the marketing and cooked for the community, to which John Baptist Taoni,[8] Father Lebreton's assistant, was now added. About the month of June, the little family was enlarged by the arrival of four new members : Nicholas Germain, William Ploesquellec, Thomas Berthe, a cleric, and a lay-brother, Francis. Shortly afterwards an Irishman, John Skiddy, arrived, and in July, 1643, two seminarists and another lay-brother, Brother Angeli, also formed part of the community. Two letters, one[9] written in 1643 and

[6] *Ibid.*, p. 204.
[7] *Ibid.*, pp. 271, 390 ; *Arch. de la Mission*, Ms. *des fondations*.
[8] Stella, *op. cit.*, pp. 6 ff.
[9] *Saint Vincent de Paul*, Vol. II, p. 362.

the other[10] in 1644, refer to a Father Boulier. Saint Vincent had intended to send Stephen Blatiron and John Joseph Brunet,[11] in 1642, but their departure was deferred, at the request of Father Codoing, who found it difficult to provide for the wants of his community in its actual condition.[12] When Father Codoing arrived in Rome, he did not know sufficient Italian to venture to preach in public, but at once set to work to study the language and to translate his sermons. In September, Fathers Germain and Taoni, in response to an appeal from Cardinal Lenti, set off to preach a three weeks' mission in the village of Norma, which subsequently supplied the Congregation with several apostolic labourers. The entire population, save two, attended the Mission, and it is related that one of the two hardened sinners was assassinated close to the Church a week after the missionaries had left. After Norma, they went to Cisterna, and then to Castel Giuliano, from which they returned to Rome to preach for two weeks to the old men and the sick in the Hospice of Saint Sixtus, of which Cardinal Lenti was protector.

We shall not follow the missionaries in their various apostolic journeys.[13] Cardinal Lenti, who had entire confidence in the Fathers, also requested them to train his clergy, and, to make a beginning, sent them his deacons and sub-deacons. Saint Vincent heard this last piece of news with the utmost satisfaction : ' I have heard,' he wrote to Father Codoing,[14] ' of the fruits which you tell me may spring from this new work if God be pleased to bless it, as I pray Him to do with all my heart, and I offer Him every beat of my heart as so many ejaculatory prayers to beg this grace from Him unceasingly.'

In 1645, Father Dehorgny was sent from Paris to enquire into the state of the Community ; he began his visitation early in July and finished it on the 20th. He recommended the priests to recite the Office attentively and devoutly, and to make the prescribed pauses at the asterisks. As the house, which was quite large enough for the Community,

[10] *Saint Vincent de Paul*, Vol. II, p. 462.   [11] *Ibid.*, p. 302.
[12] *Ibid.*, pp. 307, 361.   [13] Stella, *op. cit.*, pp. 7 ff.
[14] *Saint Vincent de Paul*, Vol. II, p. 376.

was much too small for retreats for ordinands, which were already well attended, he suggested that they should look out for a larger house.[15] The visitor, in order to obtain a fuller knowledge of the condition of the house and the work it was doing, and also perhaps to arrange some business matters with the Holy See, remained nine or ten months in Rome and shared in the labours of his confrères. He also thought it would be well to establish an 'internal seminary' so that the numbers might be increased.[16] Saint Vincent gladly supplied the priest, four clerics and three lay brothers that were asked for, and it was Father Dehorgny, who had returned to Paris in March, 1644, who brought them to Rome.[17] A great change had occurred since his departure, for Father Codoing had moved to the Palazzo Bufalo in the parish of Sant' Andrea delle Fratte. A second canonical visitation was begun early in August and ended on the 16th; the annual retreat was then held, and Father Dehorgny, following his bent for missionary work, immediately left for Sabina, accompanied by his confrères, and in four months they gave six missions.[18]

The house in Rome gradually grew in size and importance. Father Codoing, with his independent character and hasty, changeable and impetuous temperament, was not exactly the type of superior that was needed, and hence Father Dehorgny, who thoroughly understood the situation, was appointed to succeed him in October, 1644.[19] The new Superior encouraged missionary work, which indeed he could do all the more easily as the retreats for ordinands, owing to the financial state of affairs of the house, had fallen off, and, in addition, the external seminary had not proved a success. During an interregnum that lasted from Easter to September, Father Dehorgny and his confrères took up residence in the Abbey of Saint Saviour in Sabina where, in order to assist Cardinal Barberini, he took charge of the celebration of divine worship and the spiritual needs of the villages that depended on the Abbey.[20]

[15] Stella, *op. cit.*, p. 10.
[16] *Saint Vincent de Paul*, Vol. II, p. 456.
[17] *Ibid.*, p. 456.   [18] Stella, *op. cit.*, p. 11.
[19] *Saint Vincent de Paul*, Vol. II, p. 481.
[20] Stella, *op. cit.*, p. 12.

The arrival of Father Portail in 1647, on another canonical visitation, brought about a change in the government of the of the house. Father Dehorgny at this period was going through a spiritual crisis ; he had been won over to Jansenist ideas by John Bourgeois, one of the chief theologians of the party,[21] and had opened his mind on the subject to Saint Vincent. The authority which he enjoyed as Superior might have rendered him a source of danger to his confrères, and this perhaps was the reason why Father Alméras was appointed in his stead. From Superior, Father Dehorgny became Assistant, but he was still entrusted with the duty of keeping in touch with the Roman Congregations. Father Portail had never shown any inclination to bring his visitations to a close, although reproached more than once for this failing by Saint Vincent ;[22] this particular visitation dragged on from April 23 to the end of the year.[23] The visitor remarked that some of his confrères were rather slow in learning Italian, and laid down a rule that they should converse only in that language.[24]

Father Alméras, like his predecessors, saw that the question of a suitable residence was of capital importance for the progress of their works, but, like them, he too failed in all his efforts, although he was quite prepared to add to the purchase money from his own personal property.[25] When Father Dehorgny was re-appointed Superior in 1651, he had to be satisfied with a rented house.[26] As he was always away giving missions, he left the duty of transacting business with the Roman Congregations to his Assistant, Father Levazeux, which was most unfortunate, as the latter was deficient in the qualities requisite for such an important post. His line of action caused discontent and also displeased Saint Vincent ; hence Father Dehorgny was recalled, and in 1653, replaced by Father Berthe.[27]

[21] *Saint Vincent de Paul*, Vol. III, pp. 321, 362 ff.
[22] *Ibid.*, p. 113.
[23] Notice on Fr. Dehorgny in *Notices sur les prêtres, clercs et frères défunts de la Congrégation de la Mission*, 1st series, Vol. I, p. 176.
[24] Stella, *op. cit.*, p. 12.
[25] *Saint Vincent de Paul*, Vol. IV, p. 128.
[26] Cf. Stella, *op. cit.*, p. 18.
[27] *Saint Vincent de Paul*, Vol. IV, p. 541.

The new Superior would gladly have purchased the house in which he was living,[28] but the owner was unwilling to sell.[29] The Irish College, and then Saint John Mercatellis, were suggested, but the price demanded in each case proved too high.[30] The problem, no doubt, was very difficult, for few men were better equipped than Father Berthe to handle such an affair, and bring it to a successful conclusion. In him were combined in perfect harmony, prudence, discrimination, an affable and accommodating disposition, and a quick understanding of men and things. A favourite of the Cardinals[31] and especially of those who were most influential, he seemed to be just the man that was needed; everybody was delighted to think that he would be Superior for many a long day, when an unfortunate incident compelled him, two years after his arrival in Rome, to beat a hasty retreat to France. But to understand the matter fully, we shall have to retrace our steps a little.

After the public tumults of 1652, Louis XIV, once more master of his capital which was now at peace, was confronted by an impenitent malcontent, Cardinal de Retz. The turbulent co-adjutor defiantly and provocatively paraded the streets of Paris, surrounded by a large band of supporters. The King, irritated beyond measure, issued orders to have him arrested, alive or dead. The prelate was privately warned by his friends, but instead of going into hiding, continued to go abroad in public, convinced that no one would dare to lay a hand on him. On December 19, 1652, he was arrested in the Louvre by the Marquis de Villequier and taken to the Castle of Vincennes. The solitude of a prison was not at all to the liking of such an intriguer as Cardinal de Retz, but he had to spend the whole of the year 1653 in Vincennes, and was still chafing in durance vile when, on March 21, 1654, he heard of the death of his uncle, John Francis de Gondi, Archbishop of Paris, who had died that very day.

Mazarin had been impatiently awaiting the death of the Archbishop, for he hoped to deprive the de Gondi family of the position and to entrust it to a man thoroughly devoted

[28] *Ibid.*, Vol. V, p. 149. [29] *Ibid.*, p. 154.
[30] *Ibid.*, p. 459. [31] *Ibid.*, pp. 384, 466; VI, 19.

to his own policy : Peter de Marca, Archbishop of Toulouse. His plans, however, were upset, and Saint Vincent was one of those who rejoiced at his defeat, as may be seen from the following lines to his confrère, Father Ozenne : ' On last Saturday God disposed of His Grace the Archbishop of Paris, and at the same time His Eminence Cardinal de Retz took possession of this church by a Procurator and was received there by the Chapter, although he is still in the Wood of Vincennes. Providence had guided him, with this end in view, to appoint a Procurator and also to nominate two Vicars General a few days before his arrest, for he then intended to go to Rome and made these arrangements in case God should dispose of his uncle whilst he was travelling thither ; hence his Vicars General, both of whom are Canons of Notre-Dame, are now exercising their functions and we have ordinands here by their command. All are filled with admiration at such foresight . . . or rather at such governance by God, Who has not left this diocese without a Pastor even for a day at a time when certain persons were desirous of providing it with a Pastor other than its own.[32]

Although Mazarin felt this check severely, yet he never lost courage. He promised the Cardinal, as the price of his resignation, seven Abbeys, the revenues of which amounted to 120,000 livres, and this tempting offer was accepted. But the last word rested with the Pope, the sole judge of the validity of the proceeding. The prisoner, in the meantime, was transferred to the Castle of Nantes, where, under a more liberal régime, he led a gayer existence. The relations which he maintained with friends outside enabled him to plan and carry out an escape. When on August 8, 1654, he was once more at liberty, he withdrew his resignation, reached Spain by sea, and then moving on towards Italy, eventually arrived in Rome. Innocent X openly lavished marks of favour on de Retz, who was given 4500 gold crowns by the Pope as well as a promise of the hundred crowns customarily granted to poor Cardinals. A secret consistory was held on December 4, for the conferring of the Cardinal's hat. De Retz, preceded by a Master of Ceremonies, entered

[32] *St. Vincent de Paul*, Vol. V, p. 109.

THE MISSION IN ITALY

from a room at the back, to the great dismay of Cardinals Bichi and d'Este, protectors of French ecclesiastical affairs, who did not wish to meet him, and made a hurried departure so as not to be present at the ceremony.

The Pope had intended to provide de Retz with lodgings in the Vatican, at the risk of displeasing Mazarin, but on the advice of persons high in office, he abandoned the project and resolved to procure an asylum for the Cardinal with some French community. His choice fell on the house of the Congregation of the Mission. Father Berthe was summoned one day to the Vatican by Mgr Scotti, the Major-Domo of the Palace. 'Our Most Holy Father,' he began, 'requests you to render him a great service; it is to receive Cardinal de Retz.' Surprise and fear were reflected on Father Berthe's countenance as he replied: 'Monsignor, I am quite prepared to obey the Pope, but permit me to say that our house is very small for such a great personage as Cardinal de Retz, and moreover, there is not the slightest doubt that the King of France will not tolerate his presence in our midst.' 'It is the Holy Father's formal wish,' replied the Major-Domo, 'and there is nothing to be done save to obey.' Father Berthe then withdrew, and went off without delay to explain his embarrassing situation to Cardinal d'Este and to Guéffier who was acting for the French Ambassador in his absence. Both gave the same advice: he should refuse to admit Cardinal de Retz, and in case force were used, he should go elsewhere with his French confrères. 'If you act otherwise,' they added, 'your Congregation has everything to fear from the King's anger.' The poor Superior, caught between two fires, could only make a guess as to what would happen; he returned to the Vatican, thinking perhaps that no further steps would be taken in face of such a threat. Mgr Scotti was not perturbed; he merely remarked: 'The Holy Father means to be obeyed.'

In point of fact, orders had already been given, and when Father Berthe reached home he found the Cardinal's retinue and luggage installed; tapestries were being hung and the rooms furnished. There was no need, then, to search for a solution of his difficulties; he simply wrote to

Saint Vincent an account of what had occurred. On the same day, or the next, Cardinal de Retz took possession of his new domicile. Scarcely had he been installed than he put himself in the hands of Nicola, the most famous surgeon in Rome, for he had dislocated his shoulder by a fall from his horse. He had suffered agonies from this mishap, and all the efforts of two surgeons had only increased the pain ; Nicola proved no more successful, for though he tortured the patient, he did not improve his condition in the slightest. Another trial, of a different order, awaited the Cardinal, for on January 7, 1655, his protector, Innocent X, passed away. In anticipation of this event, Mazarin had sent to Rome, as Ambassador Extraordinary to the Princes of Italy, one of his creatures, Hugues de Lionne, who was commissioned to make preparations for the election of a Pope favourable to the Cardinal's designs, and to obtain from the newly elected Pope a command to Cardinal de Retz to appear before an ecclesiastical Court. Every precaution had been taken to expedite a trial. A formidable indictment had been drawn up and was ready to be despatched from France, containing the life story of the Cardinal, from his youthful peccadilloes to his duels, amorous adventures and treasonable offences.

As de Retz, protected by his Cardinal's purple and by the authority of the Sovereign Pontiff, could not be directly attacked, his enemies were only too glad to strike at those who, directly or indirectly, had come to his assistance. The news that a French religious community (so far the particular one was unknown) had afforded an asylum to the fugitive, caused the greatest excitement at Court, and on January 1, the King interrogated the Ambassador and issued most rigid instructions. 'It only remains for me,' he said in conclusion, ' to remind you that you are to speak with the gravity and dignity befitting the Minister of the King of France, the successor of those rulers who increased the temporalities of the Church, gave it the sovereignty of Rome and the rights of a King, and to act in such a uniform manner as to lead the Pope to fear, and the Sacred College to hope, for everything, so that the present line of conduct may be changed.' When the whole truth became known at Court, there was an outburst of rage against the Missionaries. ' They are filled with anger against the Priests of the Mission who received the Cardinal into their house,' wrote Count de Brienne, Secretary of State for Foreign Affairs. ' The Jesuit Father who paid him a visit has been looked on as being out of his senses, and the Fathers of the Society were the first to accuse him of having gone. Judge from this the attitude of our Court towards the Cardinal.'

Lionne arrived in Rome on January 20 and quickly showed himself to be Mazarin's docile instrument. When the French colony arrived to pay their respects, he ordered one of de Retz's suite, the Abbé Charrier, who was waiting in an ante-room, to be turned out of the house. ' I have acted in the same way with the Superior of the Mission,' he wrote to de Brienne, ' who had also come and insisted on speaking to me in order, as he said, to justify his conduct, on account of the express order that had been given him by the Pope to receive the said Lord Cardinal. . . . I sent word to him again that I would not see him, and this second reply was accompanied with the sharpest reprimand I could think of in connection with such a matter.'

On February 3, an order arrived from Paris to expel from Rome all Priests of the Mission of French nationality, and the Ambassador informed Father Berthe of the fact. ' Here is a letter,' he said, ' in which the King commands you to leave Rome and return to France. Read it.' After Father Berthe had read the document, he declared in writing that he received it with all the respect due to His Majesty and signed his name at the foot of the copy presented to him. ' The original belongs to you,' the Ambassador added, ' keep it. Will you leave to-day ? ' ' I cannot,' replied Father Berthe. ' Give me time to put my papers in order, and to give instructions to whichever of the four Italian priests takes my place. My French confrères will leave to-morrow ; I will follow them as soon as my presence will no longer be required.' On the following day, the 4th, Fathers Legendre, Pesnelle and Bauduy left Rome ; the latter for Genoa, where the Congregation had a house, and the others to Our Lady of Loretto, to labour in the neighbouring dioceses under the authority of the bishops, whilst waiting for definite instructions as to their final destination.

Father Berthe hesitated as to where he would go. 'I am preparing to leave and go I know not where,' he wrote to Saint Vincent on February 5. ' Some advise me to return straight to France, as the command expressly directs; others, friends of mine, think I should withdraw to some secret spot, outside Rome, until I receive a new order from you. But such a secret place is hard to find, and moreover I should not be fully obeying the King's orders if I remained in Italy. If I do remain here, it may be thought at Court that I consider myself guilty, since I am not returning to France in conformity with the command, and if I go to Paris, I know not if you will approve.'[33] Saint Vincent had too much respect for the King's order to think of any other solution than that of obedience. Instead of lamenting the cruel blow that had fallen on his house in Rome, he showed an entirely supernatural joy, happy, as he said himself, to see his Congregation afforded an opportunity of practising two great virtues : submission to the Pope and the King, and gratitude to a benefactor.[34]

Lionne, for his part, was filled with pride at his inglorious victory. He wrote to Paris : ' It has produced resounding effects in this Court, and will prove advantageous to the King's service.' The rage caused by his powerlessness in regard to the fugitive only rendered him all the more vindictive towards those who came under his lash ; he struck out savagely at all de Retz's entourage, resolved to isolate the man whom he could not touch. All Frenchmen were forbidden to have the slightest relations with the Cardinal, whose friends and domestics were ordered to leave Rome.[35] Saint Vincent refused to be intimidated. He went to Mazarin and explained the whole business ; the Cardinal listened, and if he did not fully approve of

[33] *St. Vincent de Paul*, Vol. V, p. 271.
[34] *Ibid.*, p. 336 ; Vol. XI, p. 172.
[35] For further information on this incident, which aroused the animosity of the French Court against the Missionaries, see *Saint Vincent de Paul et les Gondi* by Chantelauze (Paris, 1882, oct., pp. 340-364) and *Le Cardinal de Retz* by Louis Batiffol (Paris, oct., pp. 161-162).

THE MISSION IN ITALY

Father Berthe, at least he allowed his place to be taken by another French priest, Edmund Jolly.[36]

The new Superior's past life had prepared him for the duties with which he was now entrusted. In his youth, he had studied Law and the procedure of the Court of Rome, and under the name of M. le Haignon, had visited the Eternal City with the Marquis de Fontenay-Mirail, the French Ambassador, whose confidence he won, as also that of Cardinal de Valençay. Both of them entrusted him with a secret and important mission to the King of France, which he discharged with all the skill of a professional diplomatist. As he was employed at the Datary he might have looked forward to a professional career, but his piety opened up another road, and during a retreat made in the Missionaries' House in Rome, he discovered what was his true vocation. On April 3, 1646, he left Rome, settled some business matters in Paris, paid a visit to his family in his native place, and then, on November 13, at the age of twenty-four, entered the novitiate at Saint-Lazare. Eighteen months of the 'internal seminary,' in proximity to the holy Founder, initiated him into the practices and customs of the Company. He subsequently returned to Rome where he made his ecclesiastical studies and was ordained priest on May 1, 1649 ; he became the adviser and right-hand man of the three Superiors who in succession were appointed to rule that house : Fathers Alméras, Dehorgny and Berthe. Ten months at Saint-Lazare as Director of the Internal Seminary, completed his training, and when he returned to Rome as Superior, he had every qualification to enable him to succeed in the duties with which he was entrusted.[37]

The approbation of the vows of the Company had been in a state of suspense for fifteen years ; the most urgent and most pressing attempts to secure it had remained without effect ; in two months and a half Father Jolly succeeded in obtaining the long awaited favour. As he was a highly intelligent and energetic man, he refused to consider any

[36] *Saint Vincent de Paul*, Vol. V, p. 366.
[37] Notice on Fr. Jolly in *Notices sur les prêtres, clercs et frères défunts de la Congrégation de la Mission*, 1st series, Vol. III, pp. 387 ff.

obstacle as insurmountable, and every difficulty gave way before him. At his request, the Holy See decided on the interpretation of the vow of poverty that had been proposed by Saint Vincent ; the Pope commanded ordinands in Rome to prepare for Holy Orders by making a retreat with the Priests of the Mission, and united to the Congregation four priories : those of Saint-Lazare, Saint Pourçain, Coudres and Bussière, as well as one conventual revenue, that of the Abbey of Saint-Méen. It should be admitted that the successful issue of these negotiations was rendered easier by the succession of Alexander VII who was much more friendly towards religious communities than his predecessor, Innocent X. Father Jolly also succeeded in settling the question of a residence, which had exhausted the patience of all his predecessors. This, however, was not accomplished without some difficulty. His attention was called in the first instance to a property of which the Pope wished to dispose ' for some work of piety,'[38] but the conditions imposed proved unacceptable. Cardinal Bagni suggested that he should accept apartments in the Palace of Saint John Lateran ;[39] the noble family of Mattei proposed their town-house ;[40] Cardinal Maldachini a building outside the city,[41] and there were also fruitless negotiations in regard to a house situated in the district of Saint Nicholas.[42]

Saint Vincent both feared and hoped for the success of Father Jolly's endeavours ; hoped, because the works might then be developed ; feared, because poverty and discomfort are of more value to the soul than worldly goods.[43] On October 25, 1658, he wrote : ' We shall be very much mistaken if we do not rightly appreciate the happiness we enjoy in Rome of resembling Our Lord when He said He had not a place whereon to lay His head. It is no slight humiliation to be poorly lodged, in the house of another, in a great city which thinks very little of communities that are not well housed ; we should, however, love to be

[38] *Saint Vincent de Paul*, Vol. V, p. 635.
[39] *Ibid.*, Vol. VII, pp. 27, 33.
[40] *Ibid.*, p. 391.
[41] *Ibid.*, p. 615.
[42] *Ibid.*, p. 253.
[43] *Ibid.*, p. 312.

THE MISSION IN ITALY

unknown and neglected as long as God may be pleased to keep us in such a state, and God may perhaps utilise our love of abjection, if we possess it, to provide us with a suitable residence. Oh ! if God were pleased to establish such a foundation of humility in us, we should have great reason to hope that our house would be a house of peace and benediction !' In 1659, his confidence was rewarded. Cardinal Durazzo's credit and generosity, together with that of two or three Genoese noblemen who were his relations, enabled them to purchase, at little expense, the palace of Cardinal Bagni, situated in Montecitorio, one of the healthiest quarters of the city.[44] Henceforward the works of the Congregation, and especially that for ordinands, developed magnificently, as we shall see later. The Missions continued their beneficent work in poor country districts, and externs in even greater numbers than before, came to Montecitorio for a few days' spiritual retreat. The 'Internal Seminary' was re-established in 1657[45] and proved highly successful. Father de Martinis, a Priest of the Mission, had acted since 1656 as Spiritual Father to the Propaganda College in which Father Jolly also gave conferences and preached retreats.[46]

The plague of 1656, which first broke out in the Propaganda College, found the Missionaries prepared to prove their devotion. Father de Martinis remained within the College the better to assist its inmates ;[47] Father Jolly fell victim to the plague and his life was despaired of ;[48] he recovered however, but not completely, for his legs proved a source of trouble to him for the remainder of his life. The House in Rome benefited by his intelligent activity, but the services he rendered to the whole Congregation as Procurator to the Holy See, subsequently as Assistant to Father Alméras, and finally as Superior General for twenty years, cannot easily be estimated.

[44] Notice on Fr. Jolly in *Notices, etc.*, 1st series, Vol. III, p. 400.
[45] *Saint Vincent de Paul*, Vol. VII, p. 41.
[46] *Ibid.*, Vol. VI, p. 124 ; Vol. VII, p. 376 ; Vol. VIII, p. 172 ; Vol. XII, p. 65.
[47] *Ibid.*, Vol. VI, pp. 116, 138 ; Vol. XX, p. 365.
[48] Notice on Fr. Jolly in *Notices, etc.*, 1st series, Vol. III, p. 399.

The labours and success of the Missionaries in Rome inspired several Cardinals with a profound esteem for the Congregation, and Cardinal Durazzo, Archbishop of Genoa, one of an illustrious family which had given several Doges to the Republic and several prelates to the Church, expressed a desire to utilise, for the good of his flock, the services of apostolic labourers animated with the same spirit and zeal. He wrote to Saint Vincent, and whilst waiting for the labourers he needed, kept Father Codoing by his side from January to August, 1645. Codoing had been recalled to Paris and was passing through Genoa; he now evangelised several parts of the diocese, and the Archbishop declared : ' He has everywhere laboured with much fruit and benediction for the service of God, the salvation of souls and to my own special satisfaction.'[49] To supply a staff for this new establishment, Saint Vincent despatched two priests and one lay-brother from France, and begged the Superior of the House in Rome to sacrifice two of his best members : Fathers Blatiron and Martin. Father Dehorgny was reluctant to surrender two confrères for whom he had the highest regard ; he was willing enough to let Father Blatiron go, for he was to be the new Superior and the post required a man of the highest gifts ; but why, he asked, should Father Martin be removed from Rome ? Was Rome not as important a place as Genoa ? Father Dehorgny's reluctance to obey brought him a severe reprimand from Saint Vincent, who wrote,[50] on March 2, 1646 : ' I have seen by your last letter that you have at length sent Father Martin to Genoa. May I now venture to tell you, Sir, that it is far more important than I can express that you should give yourself to God to carry out exactly all the General's orders, whatever they may be, even though repugnant to your own ideas, and no matter what pretext you may have for doing something better, because no greater inconveniences can arise than those which would follow from such disobedience. . . . I assure you, Sir, that two or three Superiors who would act in such a fashion, would be enough to ruin the Company, and that if I did not know your dear heart as well as I do, I should

[49] *Saint Vincent de Paul*, Vol. II, p. 544. [50] *Ibid.*, p. 566.

THE MISSION IN ITALY

be compelled to adopt another line of action.' Whilst the Missionaries were waiting for a house near the sea which the Cardinal had proposed to give them, they rented a building that proved to be very unsuitable for their various employments.

Scarcely had they settled in than they began to preach missions in all directions. Saint Vincent, though delighted at their zeal, trembled for their health; ' Be moderate, be moderate,' he constantly advised them in a tone in which tenderness and admiration were equally blended. Those two great Missionaries—Fathers Blatiron and Martin—held a great place in his heart. He thanked God for having given them to him, and whenever he thought of their virtues and successes it was to God he always turned. ' O God, my Saviour,' we read in a letter[51] to Father Blatiron, dated September 7, 1647, ' be Thou, if it so please Thee, the bond that unites their hearts; show forth the results of all those devout sentiments which Thou hast led them to conceive, and increase the fruits of their labours for the salvation of souls. Bedew this house with Thy eternal blessings as if it were a tree newly planted by Thy hand; strengthen these poor Missionaries in their fatigues, and finally, Oh, my God ! be Thou Thyself their recompense and by their prayers extend Thy immense mercy to me.' Fathers Blatiron and Martin assisted each other by their sermons and catechetical instructions, and the felicitations which Saint Vincent addressed to them for this reciprocal charity ended with this beautiful prayer: ' O Divine Goodness, thus unite all the hearts of the little Company of the Mission, and then command what Thou pleasest; suffering will then be sweet and every labour easy; the strong will comfort the weak, and the weak will love the strong and obtain for them from God an increase of strength, and thus, O Lord, Thy work will be accomplished to Thy own satisfaction and the welfare of Thy Church, and Thy workmen will be multiplied, attracted by the sweet odour of charity.'[52]

In the Saint's addresses to his confrères in Saint-Lazare, the example of those two apostolic men naturally rose up

[51] *Ibid.*, Vol. III, p. 239.   [52] *Ibid.*, p. 256.

before his mind, and he once admitted to Father Blatiron : 'When an opportunity arises for stimulating the community of Saint-Lazare to seek after its perfection, I speak to them of the example afforded us by your house ; I tell them of your prolonged labours despite the illness of some, of your patience under trials, of your charity and mutual forbearance, and of the gracious welcome, the honours paid and the services rendered by each of you to externs. From this you may see, Sir, how the honey from your hive trickles even as far as this house and serves to nourish its children. Ah ! What a motive of consolation for the entire Company !'[53] The Missionaries in Genoa had moreover an excellent model before their eyes in the person of their Archbishop, Cardinal Durazzo, who frequently travelled with them on their missionary journeys, sharing in their labours, recreations and retreats, living their lives, assisting at their spiritual exercises and following their rule. Urged on one occasion by a nobleman to accept a present, he declined, alleging as an excuse that it was the custom of the Company never to accept a gift in the course of a Mission.[54]

When a novitiate was opened towards the end of 1646, it became even more evident that the house was not large enough to serve as a residence, and that it was high time the building in course of construction should be completed. In the course of the following year, the workmen had finished, but before the Missionaries took up residence, it was essential that the Senate should grant them rights of citizenship, and before they presented their petition, certain formalities, such as the foundation contract, had to be concluded. This agreement, which had hitherto been neglected, was signed on November 4, 1647, by Cardinal Durazzo, Canons Baliano Raggi and John Chrysostom Monza, on the one hand, and Father Blatiron on the other, and was ratified[55] by Saint Vincent on the 27th. The Senate, which was naturally enough somewhat mistrustful

[53] *Saint Vincent de Paul*, Vol. III, p. 275.
[54] *Ibid.*, Vol. III, p. 187.
[55] *La Congregazione della Missione in Italia dal 1640 al 1835*, Paris, 1884, oct. p. 15.

THE MISSION IN ITALY

of foreign priests, did not reply to the petition for two years, and the delay would have been even longer were it not that some of the city's most illustrious residents addressed a petition to the Senate on behalf of the Missionaries. The signatories to the document say: 'We . . . desirous of the universal welfare of our most serene Republic and more especially of the salvation of the souls of all, especially of those of the poor inhabitants of country and mountainous districts who are deprived of the abundant helps enjoyed by those living in cities, having seen the great fruits produced by the Priests of the Congregation called the Mission, and having considered the still greater good that may be hoped for in the future by the efforts of the said Congregation, not only for the good of souls, but also for the universal welfare of the entire State, inasmuch as by this means the people will become more obedient and submissive to their Superiors and be at peace amongst themselves, especially if instructed and trained by persons of this country, of whom several have presented themselves for acceptance and only await the establishment of the Congregation in this city, subject to the good pleasure and approbation of the Most Serene Senate ; we have resolved to unite our desires and supplications to those of the said Dom Stephen Blatiron and his companions to beseech Your Serenity to be good enough to approve of the said Missionaries and permit them to establish themselves and to reside within the city and the city walls, so that they may be able to exercise their functions and carry out their exercises for the good of priests and clerics and also for poor country folk, according to their Institute.'[56]

The number of Missionaries in residence at this time was about seven or eight, and it is certain that in 1650 there were actually eight in the house: five Frenchmen, Fathers Blatiron, Martin Gabriel Damiens, Francis Richard and Michel Gerard ; two Irishmen, Patrick Walsh and John Henry, and one Italian, Stefano Baccigalupo.[57] Their time was devoted to four important duties: preaching missions and retreats, training novices and scholastics, and

[56] *Notice on Fr. Blatiron* in *Notices, etc.*, 1st series, Vol. II, p. 158.
[57] *Ibid.*, p. 159.

finally giving conferences for ecclesiastics. The Missions did immense good both in the country round Genoa and in Corsica, and we shall return to this subject in another chapter. The Missionaries were so much in demand that Father Blatiron could not meet all the requests for their services ; hence his desire for an ' internal seminary ' that would provide him as quickly as possible with numbers of apostolic workmen. The little community often knelt in prayer for this intention before a picture or statue of Saint Joseph.[58] Father Blatiron's reflections on the best method of increasing his numbers had led him to the conclusion that it would be well to admit to his seminary devout children who would be trained and taught, and whose minds, in the course of their studies, should be unceasingly directed towards the ideal connoted by the word ' missionary.'

Saint Vincent had had too many disappointments, first in the Bons-Enfants and later at Saint Charles, to share this opinion. ' The means you suggest for increasing the number of children in your internal seminary,'[59] he wrote to Father Blatiron, on March 3, 1656, ' is very slow and very risky, because children admitted before they are old enough to make a choice are liable to change ; they will say readily enough that they wish to be missionaries, and will even submit for a time to discipline, so that they may be able to study, but as soon as they are capable of doing something useful, they change their tune, say they have no vocation, and leave. How many such have we not had ! ' The project of an Apostolic School was soon quashed for reasons of another order. Very shortly afterwards, a rumour spread that the plague had appeared in Genoa and was rapidly spreading. As soon as Father Blatiron heard this, he went to the Archbishop to place himself and his two confrères, Fathers Lejuge and Luc Arimondo, at the Cardinal's disposal.

Saint Vincent was profoundly affected by this step. ' Sir,' he wrote on July 28, 1656, ' what a generous and

[58] Notice on Fr. Blatiron in Notices, etc., 1st series, Vol. V, pp. 102, 145, 462.
[59] Ibid., Vol. V, p. 563.

sublime resolution have you not taken ! One heroic deed such as this is quite sufficient to render you perfect in your state of life, because there is no greater act of charity than to give one's life for one's neighbour . . . Nevertheless, the matter is so important and I see so many reasons against it, at least in your own case, that I dare not either give my consent or oppose your determination. I trust that God may make known His Will to you either through his Eminence the Cardinal or through Himself.'[60] Saint Vincent was not satisfied with one letter ; after much prayer and reflection, he felt himself in a position to send definite instructions both to Father Blatiron and to the Superior of the house in Rome. 'It is quite right for your priests there,' he wrote, ' to render assistance to the plague-stricken ; it is just that the members should expose themselves for the preservation of the head ; nature dictates that ; but it is not true to say (except on certain occasions that are not so important or of such a nature as this) that the head should be the first to begin, for when it is a question of some grave crisis in which Superiors should give orders, like generals of armies in combats and battles, then they are, and should be, the last to put themselves in danger. Some member of your family will volunteer, and others will imitate his example. I beg you, Sir, to bring them together and tell them what I have just written to you, although I have written briefly as I am in a hurry.'[61]

Scarcely had his instructions reached Genoa when one of the chief benefactors of the house, Cristoforo Monza, took to his bed, stricken down by the dread disease. Father Blatiron, seeing the position of the invalid, thought it his duty to run the risk of infection, but Cardinal Durazzo did not agree. Father Lejuge then volunteered, but Monza refused to let anyone approach him and died the following night.[62] In a short time nothing was to be heard in Genoa but accounts of the dead and dying. The Missionaries' residence, like all other large buildings, was requisitioned by the authorities for an hospital, and Father Blatiron and his companions, not content with handing over their house,

---

[60] *Saint Vincent de Paul*, Vol. VI, p. 48.
[61] *Ibid.*, p. 58.   [62] *Notice de Blatiron*, p. 191.

volunteered to serve.[63] Father Luc Arimondo was the first to be selected ; as soon as he heard the good news, he went on retreat, after which he left, full of courage, for the ' Consolazione' Fever Hospital. After twelve days of devoted service and three days' illness, he rendered up his soul to God ;[64] the grief of his confrères was mingled with sentiments of a noble envy, and Saint Vincent had some difficulty in restraining their zeal. 'It will be quite enough,'[65] he wrote to Father Duport on July 13, 1657, ' for you to renew the offer made to the Cardinal by Father Blatiron of the whole family and each of its members to give spiritual succour to the sick, whenever His Eminence may think it fitting to give them such employment. You should say and do all that you can. God does not ask for more. He knows your dispositions and will certainly know how to summon you by name when the hour comes for Him to employ you in the present circumstances. I beseech you not to anticipate the time without a special order. Whatsoever people may say on the matter should not be considered, and to behave otherwise would be to yield to human respect, on the pretext that someone would be scandalised by not seeing you in danger, as if it were the right thing for all priests and religious to be in peril at the same time.'

The moment for making the great sacrifice was close at hand. The Missionaries, surrounded by the sick and dying, went from one patient to another, bringing the help and consolations of religion. At the end of July, a letter reached Paris to say that several of the plague-stricken had died two or three days after they had gone to confession to Father Blatiron and received Holy Viaticum from his hands.[66] No part of the city was immune from danger ; the plague found an entrance into every home ; in the

[63] *Notice de Blatiron*, p. 193.
[64] *Ibid.*, p. 193. *Saint Vincent de Paul*, Vol. VI, p. 151. *La vie du Vénérable Serviteur de Dieu Ant. M. de Saint-Bonaventure, Augustin déchaussé*, gives some details of Fr. Luc Arimondo's death (cf. *La Congregazione della Missione in Italia dal 1640 al 1835*, pp. 30–31.).
[65] *Notice de Blatiron*, Vol. VI, p. 354.
[66] *Saint Vincent de Paul*, Vol. VI, p. 375.

streets, one had to turn aside at every step to avoid treading on corpses or on the dying; passers-by fell down in a state of exhaustion, and in a few moments their terrible death-agony began; five or six thousand inhabitants died of the plague every week.[67] A ship filled with provisions sailed away after depositing its cargo on the quays; nobody heard the shouts of the crew, and when it returned some days later the stores were in the same place.[68]

A miracle would have been needed to preserve the Missionaries, and nearly all of them died during the month of July. Saint Vincent heard the news from Rome, and his grief-stricken heart gave vent to his feelings in the presence of his confrères on September 23, 1657. 'We have lost,' he said,[69] ' the chief support and the main prop of our house in Genoa; Father Blatiron, who was the Superior of that house and a great servant of God, is dead. But that is not all. Dear Father Duport, who laboured so joyfully in the service of the plague-stricken, who had so much love for his neighbour and so much zeal and fervour in furthering the salvation of souls, has also been carried off by the plague. One of our Italian priests, Father Domenico Bocconi, a most virtuous and good missionary, as I have been told, has also died in a lazaretto to which he went to serve the poor plague-stricken country folk. Father Tratebas, who was also a true servant of God, a really good missionary, remarkable for every virtue, is also dead. Father Francis Vincent, whom you knew and who was in no way behind the others, is dead. Father Henry, a wise, devout and exemplary man, is dead. It is quite true, Gentlemen and my Brethren, that this contagious disease has deprived us of all these excellent labourers; God has taken them away from us. Of the eight that were there, only one remains, Father Lejuge, who, having been attacked by the plague, recovered and is now tending the other sick. O Jesus! my Saviour! What a loss! What an affliction! Now we are in sore need of resigning ourselves to whatsoever God wills; for otherwise, what should we do but lament and grieve in vain for the loss of those great zealots for the glory of God?

[67] *Ibid.*, p. 411.   [68] *Ibid.*, p. 450.
[69] Abelly, *op. cit.*, Vol. II, Bk. III, Ch. V, sect. II, p. 48.

But together with this resignation, after allowing a few tears to fall for this separation, let us raise ourselves to God, let us praise and bless Him for all those losses, since they have happened in accordance with the dispositions of His most holy Will.'

To weep is a natural consolation, but tears will not provide for the future, and it was essential to fill up as rapidly as possible the places made vacant by Death. Prudence, no doubt, demanded that no one should be sent to Genoa before the epidemic was over, but time could be saved by selecting confrères to replace those who were gone and sending them to Italy, where the Congregation had two other residences, so as to familiarise them as soon as possible with the language of the country. There was a long delay, for the plague might break out again at any moment during the winter; as a matter of fact, one missionary was attacked by it early in 1658.[70]

In the month of August, the house was re-established under the direction of Father James Pesnelle; it resumed its former works and the 'Internal Seminary' began to admit postulants. The memory of Father Blatiron and his companions, who had died so gloriously in the cause of Charity, stimulated the zeal of the new arrivals and helped them to bear their heavy burthens.

Many of them, before arriving in Genoa, had worked with Father Martin in Turin, in which there had been a house of the Congregation since 1655. Saint Vincent declined the first proposal to send his priests to that city; the request had come from an ecclesiastic who had no special right to make it, and in the Saint's eyes, the voice of a private individual was not the call of Providence which he desired to hear before making a new foundation.[71]

Towards the end of 1654, the Marquis de Pianneza, First Minister of State in the Court of Savoy, expressed a wish to have two Missionaries. His letter was soon followed by another in which he asked not merely for two, but for six priests. They were to take charge of the Church of the Blessed Sacrament in Turin; other priests would be added,

[70] *Saint Vincent de Paul*, Vol. V, p. 164.
[71] *Ibid.*, p. 164.

CARDINAL DURAZZO,
ARCHBISHOP OF GENOA

as soon as funds were available, who should be employed in giving Missions. Saint Vincent did not like the proposal; the duty of acting as chaplains did not fall within the Congregation's sphere of action, and in this particular case, all other functions were excluded, at least in the beginning. Hence the proposal, as made, was unacceptable; but the Prime Minister was not a man who would refuse to alter a jot of his preliminary suggestions, and there was no reason for not discussing the matter with him.

Father Blatiron was sent to the Marquis, and Saint Vincent thus formulated his instructions: ' I beg you . . . to explain the object of our Institute to him, and say that we cannot accept foundations save on condition of giving missions in country places, and, should the occasion arise, accepting ordinands, in case Their Lordships should so desire; and that otherwise we should be going against God's designs in our regard; but . . . if the matter can be so arranged that one can be done without omitting the other . . . we will strive to do so. . . . If it could be arranged that of the six priests for whom he asks and for whom he has the funds . . . three were allotted to missionary work in the country, whilst the others laboured in the city, in that case we would do what Our Lord and the Marquis ask of us. You might then tell him about ordinations, seminaries, and the other works of the Company.'[72]

The Marquis di Pianneza gladly accepted Father Blatiron's explanations, but it is doubtful whether he grasped them fully. The draft contract forwarded to Paris some time afterwards was not, in one point, in conformity with the customs of the Company; it was stated that the six priests asked for should preach and hear confessions in the city. Saint Vincent begged the Marquis to allow the Missionaries to live in accordance with their Rule. ' We are completely devoted to the service of poor country-folk, and to procuring the spiritual advancement of the ecclesiastical state; and, so as not to be hindered or diverted from these employments by any others which would keep us in cities, we have an express rule not to preach or hear confessions in cities where a bishopric or presidial Court is

[72] *Ibid.*, p. 250.

established, except in the case of ordinands and other ecclesiastics or seculars who will make retreats in our houses ; all the more so because in large towns there are, as a rule, plenty of good preachers and confessors, whereas in the country, there are very, very few . . . We shall always be quite prepared to render services to the diocese of Turin in the manner permitted by our rule, namely, to go and instruct country folk, to hear their general confessions, to bring about reconciliations, to put an end to disputes and to make arrangements for the poor to be assisted when ill, both in body and soul, by establishing a Confraternity of Charity. Such, My Lord, are our works during missions, and having done so in one village, we go on to another and do the same, the whole being done at the expense of the foundation, for we have given ourselves to God to serve the poor without payment. Some of our priests are employed in this manner, whilst others, in cities, are put in charge of seminaries, ordinands, and persons making retreats, if there be any ; these others go on missions in turn so as to afford an opportunity to the first to return for a period of recollection to the house, where they then carry on the work that the others have been doing. I very humbly beseech you to be pleased that we may act in this way, and to induce those who, with you, have done us the honour of summoning us, to agree to this arrangement.'[73]

This letter is dated May 4, 1655, and in the month of October all preparations had been made for the arrival of the Missionaries. Four set out for Turin and they were to be joined by a fifth in the following year. With such a Superior as Father Martin, who had been parish priest in Sedan for a year, they were bound to succeed.

Saint Vincent advised him to begin modestly ' by giving a little mission,' and he added, ' It may seem annoying to you to begin in such a quiet way, because it might appear that if you are to be esteemed, you should make some display by giving a complete and splendid mission which would reveal the fruits of the spirit of the Congregation. May God guard you from entertaining such a desire ! What accords both with our poverty and with the spirit of Christianity is

[73] *Saint Vincent de Paul*, Vol. V, p. 371.

to fly ostentation and to hide ourselves, to seek after contempt and humiliations, as Jesus Christ did ; and then, if you resemble Him in this, He will co-operate with you.'[74] The Missionaries imitated Christ in another point ; they were, like Him, lodged in poor and cramped quarters. The question of finding a suitable home was as acute in Turin as it was in Rome, if we are to judge from the difficulties they encountered in their search for a habitation. They moved two or three times without succeeding in finding a suitable residence. They were offered the Church of the Blessed Sacrament ;[75] the Marquis di Pianneza suggested they should move to Savigliano,[76] and took steps to secure for them a palace which had been placed at the disposal of the Pope ;[77] a nobleman begged them to accept a small church and a set of chambers ;[78] there was also question of uniting the Abbey of Sant Antonio to the Congregation, which would have settled every difficulty, but all these various projects failed.[79] During all this time, Saint Vincent continually advised them to trust to Providence. On August 27, 1660, he wrote to Father Martin :[80] ' One must be patient about the delay in finding a house. God will give you one when the time comes and when you have sufficiently honoured the poverty of Our Lord Who had none, and not even a stone on which to lay His head. Our family in Rome lived for eighteen or twenty years in hired houses. Provided yours is faithful to its employments and its rule by firmly establishing the Kingdom of God and His Justice in itself and others, it will want for nothing.'

Nothing, indeed, was wanting, not even calumny. Some malevolent persons disseminated a rumour that the Missionaries had encouraged the people not to pay taxes. The Senate was informed of the charge, and deliberated on their expulsion as ' disturbers of the public peace.' An enquiry was ordered which resulted in their justification.[81]

[74] *Ibid.*, p. 471.   [75] *Ibid.*, pp. 251, 638.
[76] *Ibid.*, Vol. VI, pp. 466, 480, 504, 542, 563.
[77] *Ibid.*, Vol. VIII, p. 97.   [78] *Ibid.*, p. 209.
[79] *Ibid.*, Vol. VI, p. 542, etc.
[80] *Ibid.*, Vol. VIII, p. 402.
[81] *Ibid.*, Vol. VI, pp. 1, 26.

This trial was not useless, for it taught them the need of prudence. If there had been any need to re-habilitate themselves in the eyes of the public, their Missions would have sufficed. They were called the *Padri santi* and Father Martin was generally known as ' The Apostle of Piedmont.' His sermons were so powerful and convincing that even the most stubborn were gained. He never sought for recondite considerations or fine language, for his sole aim was the salvation of souls, and to attain it, he aimed chiefly at making himself understood ; he was not afraid of using current barbarisms and plain, downright language when such methods rendered his sermons more intelligible and convincing.[82]

In Italy, as in France, the Missions would have produced no lasting fruits if the people were not provided with good, zealous priests, and there was no means of supplying them save by seminaries. Hence, from the first year of his sojourn in Turin, Father Martin conceived the idea of adding this work to that of the Missions. Saint Vincent gave his approval, but did not urge him on. ' Wait,' he wrote, ' until the proposal is made to you.'[83] The Marquis di Pianneza and the Archbishop of Turin were in favour of the project, but means to carry it out were wanting, for a house, furniture and subjects were needed.[84] They relied on obtaining from Rome the Abbey of Sant Antonio, which the religious were unwilling to relinquish.[85]

Father Martin never succumbed to the fatigue caused by his labours, and this is fortunate, for we owe to this fact some touching letters of Saint Vincent which enable us the better to understand the treasures of tenderness that filled his heart. This kind father wrote to the brother who was cook in Turin : ' Continue your care and charitable services to dear Father Martin during the missions and wherever he may have the greatest need of them, and do not cease from making chicken soup to nourish and sustain him when physically exhausted, as often as the Assistant

[82] Notice on Fr. Martin in *Notices, etc.*, 1st series, p. 284.
[83] *Saint Vincent de Paul*, Vol. V, p. 594.
[84] *Ibid.*, Vol. VI, pp. 120, 588.
[85] *Ibid.*, Vol. VIII, pp. 57, 97.

thinks fitting, no matter what others may say about it. You know that the preservation of this good servant of God is important for the service of souls and is most dear to the Company.'[86] Good Brother Gautier's chicken soup no doubt helped Father Martin to recover from the effects of his labours, for this valiant Missionary lived to be seventy-four, dying in 1693, having occupied successively the position of Superior in Turin, Rome, Genoa and Perugia.

[86] *Ibid.*, Vol. VIII, p. 36.

CHAPTER XXV

THE CONGREGATION OF THE MISSION IN IRELAND AND SCOTLAND

IRELAND, SCOTLAND, THE HEBRIDES, THE ORKNEY ISLANDS

THE evangelical labourers sent from France to Italy were at work in a country which possessed the faith, and in which the religious issue was not at stake; the conditions of their confrères in Ireland and Scotland were quite dissimilar.

The Missionaries were sent to Ireland in 1646. The ignorance of the people and the dangers to which they were exposed, living as they did in the midst of heretics bent on proselytising, touched the heart of Pope Innocent X, and in February, 1645, Vincent de Paul received orders from Propaganda to send some priests there.[1] The project was not realised until the end of the following year, when five priests were chosen: John Bourdet, Gerald Bryan, Edmund Barry, Francis White and Dermot Duggan; one or two clerics: Philip Le Vacher and perhaps Thaddeus Lee;[2] and two lay brothers, Peter Leclerc and Solomon Patriarche.[3] In all, eight or nine Missionaries, of whom five were Irish, three French and one, a lay-brother, from Jersey.

Saint Vincent called them together before leaving, to bid them farewell and give them some advice. He insisted on the necessity of union: ' Be united . . . and God will bless

---

[1] *Saint Vincent de Paul*, Vol. II, p. 505.
[2] Thaddeus Lee certainly went to Ireland before 1650, but it cannot be definitely affirmed that his departure took place at the very beginning of the Mission.
[3] *Saint Vincent de Paul*, Vol. III, p. 82.

you, but let your union be through the charity of Jesus Christ . . . A union not cemented by the blood of this divine Saviour cannot last. It is . . . in Jesus Christ, by Jesus Christ and for Jesus Christ you must be united. The spirit of Jesus Christ is a spirit of peace and union ; how could you draw souls to Jesus Christ if you were not united to one another and to Him ? It could not be done. So, then, be of one and the same mind, one and the same will. . . . It would be rather as if horses were . . . yoked to the same plough, and one started to pull in one direction and the other in another ; they would spoil and ruin everything. God is calling you to labour in His vineyard ; enter it then, having only one and the same heart, one and the same intention in Him, and by this means you will return with fruit from His vineyard.'

Union amongst themselves and union with the Supreme Head of the Church. After Saint Vincent had given some practical advice as to how they should behave during and after the journey, he gave them his blessing as they knelt devoutly at his feet.[4] At Nantes, they waited for John Bourdet who had not been able to make up his mind to go and even found excuses for remaining in France.[5] In his place, Saint Vincent selected Peter Duchesne, of whom there was no news for three weeks or more.[6] They spent their time usefully in Nantes in visiting the sick in the hospitals, teaching catechism to the poor and instructing the Ladies of Charity on the best methods of assisting the destitute.

A Dutch vessel was to take them to Saint Nazaire, and whilst waiting for it to sail, they gave a mission to the passengers, one of whom, an English gentleman, abjured his heresy. This was their first victory. Three days later, the neo-convert was the victim of a fatal accident and died manifesting to his last breath his attachment to the Catholic Church.

The voyage was painful and dangerous ; painful from the bitter hostility of some heretics, and dangerous from a series of violent storms that more than once placed them in imminent danger of shipwreck.

[4] Abelly, *op. cit.*, Bk. II, Ch. I, sect. VIII, p. 145.
[5] *Saint Vincent de Paul*, Vol. III, p. 104.   [6] *Ibid.*, p. 127.

The Missionaries, on their arrival, formed two bands, of which the first placed itself in the hands of the Archbishop of Cashel, whilst the second set off to work in the diocese of Limerick. They began in a small way : first, by teaching the catechism, next, by giving a course of sermons, and finally, by preaching real missions. Their preaching attracted large crowds who came from great distances and awaited their turn to go to Confession ; sometimes they waited from morning till night and often even whole days. As soon as the Nuncio heard of the good effected by the Missionaries, he expressed his profound satisfaction, and this, of course, was a source of great encouragement to them.

The increasing violence of the religious persecution put an end too soon to these wonderful manifestations of faith. The priests, hunted and tracked down, were forced to fly and conceal themselves. Some of the Missionaries returned to France in August, 1648, bearing two letters, written in Latin, to Saint Vincent, one from the Archbishop of Cashel and the other from the Bishop of Limerick. ' The departure of your Missionaries,' wrote the former, ' affords me an opportunity of expressing to you my humble gratitude . . . for having, in your great charity, deigned to succour . . . the little flock committed to me by God ; and this help was rendered at a time when their services were most useful, or rather, absolutely necessary. The people are now more inclined to devotion, and their fervour increases daily. Despite difficulties without number, these good priests and indefatigable workers have gloriously extended the worship and reign of the Most High . . . God, the Almighty and good God, will Himself be your ample reward, and theirs ; I will beg Him to preserve you for the good and welfare of His Church.'

Some of the Missionaries soon left Ireland, leaving behind them the four Irishmen, Fathers Bryan, Barry, and a third whose name is now lost, and the cleric, Thaddeus Lee. The heretics, now masters of the countryside, drove the Catholics into the cities, and Limerick overflowed with poor villagers. Three scourges—war, pestilence and famine—threatened the inhabitants with destruction, and as the Bishop thought that a mission would prepare the people for every eventuality, he asked the three Missionaries to preach one with him. It was early in 1650, and the mission began under very unfavourable conditions; so much so indeed that the prophets foretold failure. They were deceived: 'God,' wrote the Bishop subsequently, 'has made use of the weak to confound the strong.' Not one of the 20,000 Catholics in Limerick failed to make a general confession, and some even did public penance for their sins. The chief citizens were the most assiduous in attending the exercises of the mission, and the authorities took severe measures against public scandals, cursing and blaspheming.

Abelly gives two incidents, the authenticity of which we shall not venture to guarantee.

In the market-place of Thurles, a butcher blasphemed the holy name of God in the presence of a Missionary who reprimanded him for his sin; the man admitted his fault and penitently replied: 'It is true, I have sinned, I deserve to be put in irons, take me yourself to prison.' One of his relations who was present cried out: 'No, no, not that, do you wish to disgrace your family?' and, collecting some stones, he threatened the priest who was encouraging the blasphemer to persevere in his intention. Immediately the man's arms became paralysed, and his tongue protruded from his mouth, quite black and hanging out like a dog's. The people began to pray for him; holy water was sprinkled and the tongue resumed its normal position.

In the open street in Rathkeale, a gentleman on horseback publicly blasphemed, and on being advised by a friend to kiss the ground, replied with sneers; on seeing the other kneel down and, despite the mud, put his lips to the pavement, he held him up to ridicule. On his way home, he fell from his horse, rolled on the ground and injured himself. He profited by the lesson, made a good general confession and lived an exemplary life for the future.

The Bishop of Limerick was in a better position than any to appreciate the value of the Missionaries' labours: 'Never within memory,' he wrote, 'we have heard it said, was there such great progress in the faith, and such improvement as that which we ourselves have witnessed during these last few years, and all this is due to their industry, piety and assiduity.' The parish priests who had had the Missionaries in their Churches, signalised themselves during the Cromwellian persecutions by their faith and courage ; not one apostatised, not one abandoned his flock ; all were condemned to death or banishment.

Amongst the ecclesiastics who came to Limerick to make a few days' retreat, the Missionaries had remarked one of angelic piety, who, animated with a most special devotion to the Passion of Our Saviour, desired to reproduce it in his own life. His prayers were heard. One night, whilst administering the sacraments to the sick, he was recognised and massacred by the heretical soldiery. A Missionary had heard his annual confession on the previous day, in a peasant's cabin, at the foot of a mountain.

A few days after the Limerick mission, Father Bryan wrote to Paris to say that he and his three companions had determined to remain in the midst of the dangers that threatened them, and Saint Vincent congratulated him on their resolution. ' Since the Gentlemen,' he wrote, ' who are with you also intend to remain, in spite of the dangers of war and famine, we think they should be allowed to do so. How do we know what God wishes to accomplish ? He certainly has not inspired them in vain with such a holy resolution. Oh ! my God, how unsearchable are Thy judgements ! Behold, at the end of one of the most fruitful and perhaps necessary missions of which we have ever heard, it would seem as if Thou hast arrested the flow of Thy mercies on this penitent city to lay Thy hand even more heavily upon it, adding to the evils of war the scourge of pestilence ! But this is only to garner souls who are already well disposed and to store up the good wheat in Thy eternal granaries. We adore Thy designs, O Lord ! ' In Limerick, eight thousand died of the plague ; amongst them was the Bishop's brother, who contracted it whilst tending the sick. The people suffered with resignation and died in peace. The Bishop was filled with admiration at their holy dispositions and said with tears : ' Alas ! even if M. Vincent had done nothing else for the glory of God save the good he has wrought for those poor people, he should consider himself happy.'

The series of calamities was not yet ended. Limerick experienced the horrors of a siege and capture; it had also its martyrs, amongst whom was Thomas Strich, the Mayor of the city. This great Christian had begun his year of office by making a retreat with the Missionaries, and when the keys of the city were placed in his hands, preceded by the chief citizens, he carried them with great ceremony to the Church, where he placed them in the hands of the Blessed Virgin. On his return, in a speech vibrating with the spirit of Faith, he recommended the people to be for ever loyal to God, the Church and the King, even to death if it were necessary. When Limerick was taken, he was arrested with three other prominent citizens. All four had previously made a retreat with the Missionaries, and now they met once more to face death together. They put on their robes of state before going to the place of execution, and in moving language which drew tears from all eyes, they protested that they were giving their lives for confessing and defending the Catholic religion.

Thaddeus Lee, who was still only a cleric, was massacred before his mother's eyes. The executioners cut off his feet and hands and then battered in his head.[7] In 1652, Fathers Bryan and Barry succeeded in escaping in disguise to France; part of the expenses of their voyage was defrayed by the Duchesse d'Aiguillon. The third priest succeeded in concealing himself, and, as Abelly states, 'gloriously terminated his life whilst engaged in missionary work.'

The Missionaries had spent only six years in Ireland and yet it is computed that they had heard eighty thousand general confessions. Father Bryan proposed to write a history of the Mission but Saint Vincent said : ' It is enough that God knows the good that has been done ; the Little Company should honour the hidden life of Jesus Christ. Let us put our confidence in the martyrs ; their

[7] *Saint Vincent de Paul*, Vol. IV, p. 343. It is most surprising that Abelly, who gives a most detailed account of the Mission in Ireland, says nothing of the Martyrdom of Thaddeus Lee, whose name is not even mentioned. For an admirable account of Edmund O'Dwyer, Bishop of Limerick, see Sir Michael O'Dwyer's *The O'Dwyers of Kilnamanagh* (London, Murray 1933, Ch. XV, pp. 200–220).

blood will be the seed from which new Christians will spring.'[8]

The abandonment of the mission in Ireland did not entail that of the mission to Scotland and the Hebrides, where three Missionaries had arrived the year before.[9] Father Dermot Duggan and his two companions left Paris in 1651, disguised as merchants, and in Holland met a newly converted Scotch laird named Glengarry. As soon as they reached Scotland their arrival was made known by an apostate priest who had become a minister. The informer, Abelly relates, soon met with the punishment he deserved; he was seized with violent pains in all his limbs and almost entirely lost the use of the senses of sight and hearing. Suffering led him back to the right path; he sought out Father Duggan, and in the latter's presence, abjured his heresy.

The Missionaries accompanied Glengarry to his house where they met the Laird's father, a fine old man aged ninety suffering from a mortal disease; they joined their petitions to those of his son, and at length had the consolation of seeing him abandon heresy. Several domestics and some of his friends were also converted. After this first missionary effort, Father Duggan and his companion separated; the former went North and crossed over to the Hebrides, whilst the latter took to the mountains.[10] In the following year, their hearts were gladdened by the arrival of two more Missionaries from France: Fathers Thomas Lumsden and Francis White.[11]

Amongst the cold and barren mountainous districts of the Hebrides lived an ignorant and neglected people, made

---

[8] Abelly, *op. cit.*, Bk. II, Ch. I, sect. VIII, pp. 146 ff.

[9] Saint Vincent, on October 7, 1650, had suggested to Propaganda the names of Dermot Duggan and Francis White (*Saint Vincent de Paul*, Vol. IV, p. 92), Father White certainly did not go in 1651, for on January 19, 1652, he was still attached to the house in Genoa (cf. *Saint Vincent de Paul*, Vol. IV, p. 305).

[10] Abelly speaks of three missionaries (*op. cit.*, Bk. II, Ch. I, sect. XI, p. 201) and yet one of Father Duggan's letters seems to limit the number to two.

[11] *Saint Vincent de Paul*, Vol. IV, p. 494; Abelly, *op. cit.*, pp. 206, 208.

in 1651-1652, between eight and nine hundred persons. On Uist, in which there was scarcely a Catholic before 1651, there were close on twelve hundred in 1654. Clanranald, one of the two Lairds, to whom the island belonged, helped to bring about the conversion of his wife, his son, his family, and all his clansmen save two. The priest's stay in Skye was equally consoling. The inhabitants of Moidart, Arisaig, Morar, Knoidart, Glengarry and the island of Barra, all abjured heresy or waited for the arrival of the missionary to renounce their errors. 'It was quite enough,' wrote Father Duggan after visiting the island of Barra, ' to teach one child the *Pater*, *Ave* and *Credo* for the whole village, great and small, to know these prayers in two or three days.' Towards the end of his life, Father Duggan meant to penetrate the ' strange and terrible ' island of Pabbay ; he obtained the Governor's consent to land, the date of his sailing was fixed and one of his confrères was invited to go with him. He wrote from the island of Uist, on May 3, 1657 : ' Despising danger and death itself, we will set out with the grace of God to Whose Will I commit myself.' The valiant missionary had not reckoned on illness ; twelve days later he was dead, and was buried where he expired. A chapel still recalls his memory and bears his name.[12]

Father Lumsden, for his part, evangelised the Orkney Islands and Moray, Ross, Sutherland and Caithness with a zeal that was recompensed by daily returns of heretics to the true faith. On Easter Sunday, 1654, he said Mass in the house of a Laird and gave Holy Communion to fifty persons, of whom twenty were recent converts. ' The great success of our missions,' he wrote a few days later, ' has mightily aroused the jealousy of the ministers, who are more deficient in power than in will to sacrifice us to their passion. . . . We trust in the goodness of God Who will, if He so pleases, always be our protector.' Father Lumsden was accustomed, after hearing a general confession, to defer the reception of Holy Communion for some time. In the interval, he used to instruct his penitents, stir up their fervour and devotion, and purify their souls still more by

[12] *Les relations de Saint Vincent de Paul avec l'Irlande*, by Patrick Boyle, *Annales de la Congrégation de la Mission*, 1907, No. 3, p. 355.

up in great part of heretics who had not even been baptised and who were utterly negligent of all religious practices. The conditions of existence were painful in the extreme, less so indeed for the inhabitants than for the Missionaries who had been accustomed to a more civilised form of life. ' We sometimes spend whole days without food,' wrote one of them, ' especially when we have to cross barren and uninhabited mountains.' They had, as a rule, only one meal a day, and what a meal ! A little cheese or salted butter spread on oat cake or barley bread. Meat was scarce ; occasionally they were given some in the houses of gentlemen who lived far from the sea, but it was so dirty that their gorge rose at it. The meat was dragged along the ground over the scanty straw that served ' as table and chair, tablecloth and napkin, dish and plate.' There were no butchers' shops in the district and meat was not sold in small quantities ; whoever wished to have meat had to buy a whole sheep or ox. The Missionaries could not afford such luxuries, as they were continually on the road in the performance of their duties. As for fish, there was no use in thinking of that, because the lazy and shiftless population was as yet ignorant of the art of fishing.

Apart from such discomforts, which put their spirit of mortification to the test, the Missionaries found a soil favourable to conversion in the naturally religious spirit of the people. They had, moreover, very little opposition to face because nearly all the ministers had long since abandoned the islands, on account of the prevailing poverty and discomfort. For nearly a century no one had been baptised ; a state of such profound ignorance existed that the people did not know to what religion they belonged, they merely suspected that concubinage was a sin and had almost completely abandoned the practices of religion. Father Duggan, on his missionary journeys, was accustomed to take two men with him, one of whom rowed or sailed the boat from island to island and, when on land, carried the requisites for Mass and the luggage, whilst the other, who was better educated, used to teach Catechism and serve Mass. Crowds followed the Missionaries as if they were saviours. In the islands of Eigg and Canna alone, Father Duggan converted,

a second confession. God, as he said, multiplied wonders in his path. Holy Water produced marvellous results; Baptism brought peace again to persons troubled by ghosts or evil spirits. Five individuals in a state of mortal sin were unable to withdraw their tongues after they had received the Eucharist, but when the Host was removed, three of them recovered, and after a good confession, were able to receive Holy Communion without difficulty.

Father White evangelised the Highlands and rivalled Father Lumsden in his zeal for converting heretics and strengthening Catholics in the Faith. He endured the same dangers, labours, fatigues and privations. Fishermen had the greatest confidence in the efficacy of his prayers, and when their efforts were fruitless it was to Father White they turned. On one occasion, after he had sprinkled Holy Water on the sea and prayed to the Most High, the weather became fine and the nets were filled.

The ministers ended by obtaining an edict from Cromwell commanding all judges and magistrates in Scotland to search out priests, to cast them into prison, and to apply remorselessly all the laws enacted against them.

Father Lumsden, pursued by the minister of Brechin[13] with a pitiless hate, remained for a long time in hiding. His confrère, Father White, surprised in the Castle of the Marquis of Huntly, in February, 1655, along with a Jesuit and another ecclesiastic, was imprisoned in Aberdeen. Saint Vincent was deeply moved at the news: 'Behold!' he said to his community, 'behold this dear Missionary on the road to martyrdom. . . . As for me, I confess that according to nature I am deeply afflicted, and my sorrow is intense; but according to the Spirit, I think we should bless God for it as a most special grace.' Father White was released after five or six months' imprisonment, as it could not be proved that he had said Mass or exercised any of the functions of his ministry. The witness who had denounced him hesitated, contradicted himself and finally withdrew his

---

[13] *Saint Vincent de Paul*, Vol. XI, pp. 173–174. (In the text the phrase *ministre de Bredonique* is given. I have been unable, even after consulting Major Hay, to identify the locality and have inserted Brechin as a guess. J.L.)

charge. When the magistrate released Father White, he said threateningly : ' For this time, we set you free, but if you are again caught preaching, instructing, baptising or administering the other Sacraments, you will be hanged without further trial.'[14] Father White was not deterred by the threat of the gallows, though it taught him to be more prudent. He resumed his apostolic journeys in the Highlands with a courage that was all the more meritorious since he was well aware he was more closely watched and exposed to danger. He died in 1679, and with him the mission to Scotland came to an end. Several reports to Propaganda testify eloquently to his apostolic zeal. His portrait was long venerated in Invergarry Castle in a room called ' Father White's Room.'[15]

[14] Abelly, *op. cit.*, Bk. II, Ch. I, sect. XI, pp. 200 ff.
[15] Boyle, *op. cit.* We should like to refer in conclusion to Father Boyle's excellent book : *St. Vincent de Paul and the Vincentians in Ireland, Scotland and England*, A.D. 1638–1909, London, 1909.

CHAPTER XXVI

THE CONGREGATION OF THE MISSION IN POLAND

THE year 1651 saw the beginnings of two missions: those of Scotland and Poland. The latter, sought for and requested by Queen Louise Marie de Gonzague, was at first supplied with two priests: Lambert aux Couteaux and William Desdames; two clerics: Nicholas Guillot and Casimir Zelazewski, and one lay-brother, James Posny.[1]

The Superior, Father Lambert, was in the prime of life and as he was only forty-five, he gave hopes of a long career. It was not without some hesitation that Saint Vincent consented to deprive himself of one whom he regarded as his eye and his right hand.[2] He could have made no better choice in laying the foundations of a mission whose beginnings promised to be especially difficult.

The Missionary band of five arrived at their destination during the first fortnight of November. The Queen secured lodgings for them near the Palace and also purchased a small house and garden near Holy Cross Church.[3] She proposed, moreover, to establish them in the diocese of Vilna on one of her estates, where they would direct a seminary in which the future clergy of Poland would be trained.[4] The project fell through owing to the opposition of a powerful religious Order, who, seeing the friends on whom the new arrivals relied, suspected them of some tendency towards Jansenism.[5] Some other work had to be found, and the idea of entrusting the Fathers with a German

[1] *Saint Vincent de Paul*, Vol. XIII, p. 360.
[2] *Ibid.*, Vol. III, p. 158.
[3] *Mémoires de la Congrégation de la Mission en Pologne*, p. 10.
[4] *Saint Vincent de Paul*, Vol. IV, p. 272
[5] *Ibid.*, Vol. IV, p. 405; *Mémoires*, p. 10.

Church was entertained for a while, but after some days' consideration it was abandoned.

The Queen, accordingly, waited until an ecclesiastical benefice to which the King had the right of presentation should fall vacant, intending to bestow it on the Congregation. Such an opportunity was not long delayed, for in 1652, Father Lambert accepted, in the name of the Company, the parish of Sokolka, a little village in the Palatinate of Grodno in Lithuania, on condition of establishing therein as soon as possible the works of the Congregation. Father Desdames at once took up residence, but his Superior and Father Guillot chose another field of action.[6] For six months, they laboured amongst the plague-stricken of Cracow with the noblest disdain of their own safety.[7]

Father Lambert fell ill, and the state of his health clearly demanded a long period of convalescence, but as soon as he had heard that the terrible scourge had fallen on Warsaw, he made a great effort and travelled to that city. The Queen wished him to reside in the royal palace and in the King's own rooms. 'I hear news of him every day,' she wrote to Saint Vincent,[8] ' and every day I urge him not to expose himself to danger. He has all that he needs to take him here, as soon as he has established order, and I keep on urging him to hasten to me as soon as he possibly can.' But Father Lambert could not hasten, for, as public sanitation was utterly unknown in Warsaw, he had to create the whole system. ' All the citizens who could do so have fled,' we read in one of Saint Vincent's letters,[9] '. . . There is scarcely any order, nay rather, on the contrary, everything is in a state of disorder. . . . No one buries the dead ; they are left in the streets and devoured by dogs. As soon as anyone in a house is stricken with this disease, the others put him out into the street where he must die, for nobody will bring him anything to eat. Poor workmen, poor men and women servants, poor widows and orphans are entirely abandoned ; they can find no employment or anything to eat because all the rich have fled.'

Father Lambert cleared the streets and houses of the

---

[6] *Mémoires*, p. 12. [7] *Ibid.*, p. 10.
[8] *Saint Vincent de Paul*, Vol. IV, p. 487. [9] *Ibid.*, p. 535.

corpses with which they were encumbered, set up hospitals for the plague-stricken, collected the poor and needy into special hospices and organised the distribution of assistance and medical stores. As soon as his presence in Warsaw became less essential, the Queen recalled him, believing that Father Guillot was quite well able to carry on the good work. At this time war seemed to be imminent, for Charles Gustavus, King of Sweden, was hastening on military preparations. The Ukranian Cossacks, who had revolted against their own nobility, placed themselves under the protection of Alexis, Czar of the Muscovites, who was collecting a large army on the Lithuanian frontiers. King Casimir marched against him, and was followed by the Queen as far as Grodno, where she remained. Father Lambert accompanied her, and they both interviewed the Archbishop of Vilna, when the question of the seminary again came up for discussion ; but nothing was settled, and the project was not realised until thirty years later.

Sokolka, where Father Desdames was living, was only six leagues from Grodno, so Father Lambert paid him a visit, but fell ill there, and after three days' suffering, died a holy death on January 31, 1653. He was buried in the village church in front of the high altar, but in 1686, his remains were removed and placed in the vault of the Church of the Holy Cross in Warsaw. The Queen felt his death intensely and wrote with her own hand to Saint Vincent a long letter ending with the words : ' If you do not send me a second Father Lambert, I do not know what I shall do.' It would have been somewhat difficult to send her a second Father Lambert. ' It would be hard,' wrote Fleury, the Queen's confessor, ' to find a more accomplished priest or one better fitted for the work of God. Of him if may be said : *Dilectus Deo et hominibus, cujus memoria in benedictione est.* He sought after God alone ; no one, in so short a time, has ever gained the good graces and esteem of the King and Queen than this dear priest, and no one was more universally esteemed, for wherever he went he spread the good odour of his virtues.'[10]

[10] *Mémoires*, Vol. I, pp. 12 ff. : *Saint Vincent de Paul*, Vol. IV, pp. 561-562.

Father Lambert's death created a great void, and Saint Vincent asked himself who was best fitted to fill it; his choice fell on Father Ozenne, Superior of the house in Troyes. On August 9, 1653, Father Ozenne, with his confrère, Nicholas Duperroy, a cleric, some nuns from the Visitation Monasteries of Anneçy and Troyes, who were to be the nucleus of the future Convent of Warsaw, and their director, Father de Monthoux, left Paris. On the 20th, they set sail from Dieppe in a Hamburg vessel.[11] Scarcely had they left port than the ship was attacked and captured by an English pirate; the passengers were robbed even of their luggage and personal belongings and brought to Dover, but two long weeks passed before they reached that port. It would be impossible to describe what they suffered physically and morally. Both man and the elements seemed to enter into a conspiracy against them. Once such a fearful storm arose that shipwreck seemed inevitable, and on another occasion the vessel nearly took fire. The nuns were confined to a narrow cabin and sought for consolation in prayer. From time to time a pirate would enter demanding money.

Their trials were not ended when they reached Dover. They were kept there for six weeks during which Parliament first and then the Board of Admiralty debated whether the ship was a lawful prize of war. Parliament decided that it was not, and the Admiralty that it was. The Visitation nuns, who were charitably assisted by some English ladies, turned their house into a monastery. Of all their privations they suffered most acutely from the want of Holy Mass and Communion. Their ingenious piety found one consolation, for the Superioress, Mother Anne Frances de Pra, established perpetual adoration before a statue of the Holy Child Jesus at Whose feet each of the nuns prayed in turn. Although some points in dispute remained to be decided after the Admiralty had given its verdict, still the prisoners were

---

[11] The *Mémoires* (p. 15) are, on this point, in conflict with the notice on Mother Anne Frances de Pra in the *Année Sainte des religieuses de la Visitation Sainte-Marie;* they state that the travellers passed through the Low Countries in order to take ship on a Hamburg vessel.

THE MISSION IN POLAND

now at liberty, and decided to return to Calais, from which they would set out, either by land or sea, for Warsaw. On October 5, they disembarked on their native soil.[12]

As the weather was bad, Saint Vincent advised them to put off their departure, but Father Ozenne and his companions, impatient to reach their post, departed without waiting for the Visitation nuns, who were detained in Calais by illness, the result of their sufferings and imprisonment. They arrived in Warsaw towards the middle of January, 1654, just a year after the death of Father Lambert. The plague was still raging, and Father Ozenne resolved to remain in the city and assist in combatting it. The Queen gave the new Superiors proofs of her kindness, for she induced the parish priest of Holy Cross, Warsaw, to resign the benefice in favour of Father Ozenne, and at the end of the year, the parish was transferred to the Congregation. Moreover, at her request, the Prince Bishop Czartoryski granted the Missionaries full liberty to exercise their sacred ministry, and the Superior General was given the right of presentation to the cure on condition of fulfilling parochial obligations. The Queen also extended the garden surrounding the Church, and by various donations, generously contributed to a fund for the maintenance of the Community. Father Desdames, who was buried away in his little village in Lithuania, rejoined his confrères in Holy Cross, and the parish of Sokolka passed into other hands.

On May 3, 1654, the Congregation received another benefice, that of Skuly, and it was here that the first mission was preached in Poland. It lasted from October 25, to November 1; Father Desdames was in charge, and the only preacher was Father Zelazewski, who was the only one who could speak Polish. Their zeal had its reward; with few exceptions, all who had been leading scandalous lives were converted and purified their consciences by a good General Confession. The benefits of the Mission were extended to other places, for people from all around flocked in to follow the exercises.[13]

[12] *Année sainte des religieuses de la Visitation Sainte Marie*, Vol. IV, pp. 104 ff.
[13] *Mémoires de la Congrégation de la Mission en Pologne*, pp. 15 ff.

The future seemed full of promise. The Bishop of Posen was talking of sending his ordinands to Holy Cross to make a retreat preparatory to Orders ; the Queen was thinking of establishing a seminary ; three of the best young clerics from Saint-Lazare, named Simon, Eveillard and Durand, and a lay-brother, had arrived. Father Guillot, it is true, had returned to France after passing through a phase of discouragement, but scarcely had he reached home than he recognised his error and returned to Poland. The newcomers were studying the language with the greatest earnestness. The parish services were attracting the faithful who were delighted at the manner in which religious worship was carried out. Saint Vincent, by his letters, was maintaining the rules and customs of the Company. Father Ozenne, induced by the example of members of other communities and strongly encouraged by his confrères whom he consulted, had thought he was acting wisely in accepting invitations to public banquets, but a letter reached him from Paris which left him with no desire to do so again.[14] The Missionaries' labours were beginning to bear fruit ; a mission given in Holy Cross was followed by the baptism of a Jewess and the abjuration of two Lutheran ladies ; the ladies of Vilna requested Father Ozenne to establish the Confraternity of Ladies of Charity ; Prince Wielopolski offered a house on his estates near Danzig as a mission centre.[15] The future, in fact, looked very bright if only the numbers could be increased. In the month of August, 1655, Saint Vincent sent a new colony, composed of two lay-brothers and three Daughters of Charity, under the guidance of Father Berthe, who had been entrusted with the mission of studying the situation of both communities on the spot and seeing what were the prospects of development. The little band was about to set out from Rouen when orders came to go back to Paris, for bad news had come from Poland.[16]

Whilst the Muscovites, who had been called on by the Ukranian peasants for support, were moving into

[14] *Saint Vincent de Paul*, Vol. V, pp. 344 ff.
[15] *Mémoires*, p. 20.
[16] *Saint Vincent de Paul*, Vol. V, pp. 406, 412, 417.

Lithuania, Charles Gustavus, King of Sweden, declared war on King Casimir and advanced on Warsaw at the head of a formidable army. Saint Vincent, fearful for the French communities who were in danger, at once wrote to the French Minister in Sweden to ask for the protection of King Charles Gustavus on their behalf. At the approach of the Swedes, Father Ozenne, the Daughters of Charity and the Visitation nuns followed the Court to Silesia ; Fathers Guillot, Simon, Eveillard and Durand received orders to return to France, and only Fathers Desdames and Duperroy remained in Warsaw, for by this time Father Zelazewski and Brother Posny had left the Congregation.[17]

The more critical the situation became, the more did the Queen turn to Heaven for assistance. 'She begs us in all her letters,' said Saint Vincent to the Community of Saint-Lazare, ' to pray to God for this poor Kingdom, which is in such great need of help, that God may look on it with an eye of pity, because it is being attacked on all sides.'[18] His fears were realised, for on August 30, 1655, the Swedes entered Warsaw. Driven out, they returned the following year and avenged their former defeats by abominable acts of cruelty. They pillaged the whole city, sparing no building, sacred or secular, and amongst those that suffered were the Church and presbytery of Holy Cross. Father Duperroy ventured to protest but was seized by the soldiers, beaten and left for dead. He owed his life, it was said, to some charitable women of the district who, as soon as the pillagers were gone, hastened to his assistance.[19]

Such news filled Saint Vincent's heart with pride and sorrow ; with pride, for the courage of his confrères was not deficient in beauty, and sorrow, for he must have wept over such a tale of repeated disasters. ' Ah ! Gentlemen,' he said to his disciples,[20] ' how happy are they who spend every moment of their lives in the service of God and offer themselves to Him in a becoming manner. What consolation shall they not receive at the end of their life ! Think,

[17] *Mémoires*, p. 21.
[18] Abelly, *op. cit.*, Bk. II, Ch. I, sect. X, p. 196.
[19] *Mémoires*, p. 35 ; *Saint Vincent de Paul*, Vol. VI, p. 79, note.
[20] *Saint Vincent de Paul*, Vol. XI, p. 364.

for instance, of Fathers Desdames and Duperroy who are in Warsaw and of what they have done. Neither cannon fire, pillage, plague, nor any other danger and risk to which they were exposed could make them leave or abandon their post or the post in which Divine Providence had placed them, for they much preferred to expose their own lives than to fail in the practice of the beautiful virtue of compassion.' To cannon and plague were added calumny and sickness; Father Desdames was vilely calumniated, and Father Duperroy fell ill. The former had to defend himself, before the Bishop of Posnamia, against an infamous charge of which he was proved innocent.[21] The latter was attacked by an abscess in the stomach and to his great regret, had to leave Warsaw. He was taken to Opelln, where Father Ozenne chanced to be, and carefully nursed by the Daughters of Charity; he was operated on by a surgeon who, in accordance with the custom of the time, cauterized several bones.[22] The patient, convinced that he could never fully recover, asked to return to France, and waited until he should be sufficiently well to undertake the journey. He regained strength, however, and thereupon lost all desire to leave Poland.[23]

Father Desdames remained alone in Warsaw; he believed his proper place was amongst his parishioners, and not even the repeated demands of the Queen herself could induce him to move.[24] The danger, nevertheless, was very great. On the morning of July 6, 1657, having a presentiment that the Swedes would force the gates of the city on that day, he was happily inspired to withdraw to Connart, and by doing so, saved his life. The enemy appeared at midday and began to plunder and murder. The Recollets lost three of their Fathers. 'The Guardian,' says Father Desdames, 'was so maltreated that his whole body was black from the blows; the others fled as well as they could to the city; you may judge from that what happened in the suburbs, the numbers of those murdered by those barbarians, and the number of

---

[21] *St. Vincent de Paul*, Vol. VI, p. 277.
[22] *Ibid.*, Vol. XI, pp. 408, 410.
[23] *Mémoires*, pp. 36–37.
[24] *Saint Vincent de Paul*, Vol. VI, p. 431.

those wounded and tortured, etc. . . . At Skuly, they killed the parish priest, set the church on fire, as also our brew-house, stables, and five small houses of the villagers. . . . In our quarter, everything, from the gardener's house in which the Sisters lived, right up to Madame Bridzicka's, has been destroyed by fire. . . . Our house and garden, as well as the stables, were burnt. I had taken the utmost care to close the garden on all sides, but the fire made a large gap. . . . I have no consecrated chalice and had much difficulty in borrowing one, for every Church has only the chalices it needs.' The fire destroyed the whole of the new city, the Church of the Bernardines, the suburb of Kosno, the beautiful Ossolinski palace and a number of other buildings.[25]

Father Ozenne withdrew with the Court to Silesia, first to Glogau and then to Oppeln, where he kept up the courage of the Daughters of Charity and the Visitation Nuns. In the end, the advance of the Polish army entailed the departure of the King and Queen. Father Ozenne followed them to the camp in Cracow and there with the help of the Daughters of Charity nursed the sick and wounded; finally, after Warsaw was taken in October, 1657, he returned to his parish of Holy Cross.[26] What a change! Of the eight houses belonging to the Company, three in the city and five in the country, not one remained, and his eyes filled with tears. 'It is certainly a great disaster,'[27] Saint Vincent wrote to him on December 7, 1657, 'but it would not be just if you were exempt from public affliction, and God, who has permitted it, will have the goodness, if He so pleases, to repair these losses in time.' The era of trials, however, was not over; the Bishop of Cracow refused to authorise the foundation of a house in that city where a Polish gentleman named Falibowski had offered a house and garden.[28] In July, 1658, Father Ozenne felt violent pains in the legs. On August 9 he had a severe attack of fever and on the 14th, he died in his forty-sixth year. He was buried in the parish cemetery and his remains were

[25] *Mémoires*, pp. 27-29.   [26] *Ibid.*, pp. 21-22.
[27] *Saint Vincent de Paul*, Vol. VII, p. 5.
[28] *Mémoires*, p. 22.

afterwards removed and placed beside those of Father Lambert in the vault of Holy Cross Church.[29] His funeral oration may be found in a line from Saint Vincent's pen : 'He always fled from evil and did good unceasingly and with fruit.'[30]

Fathers Desdames and Duperroy were now alone, and, aided by a Polish priest who felt an attraction for the works of the Congregation, continued to give missions.[31] Paris could not come to their assistance whilst wars were going on and armies were on the move. The long expected peace was at length made at Oliva on May 13, 1660, and as soon as the news reached Saint-Lazare, an appeal was made for volunteers ; four Missionaries and three Sisters of Charity were chosen from those who volunteered for Poland. They had not set out before a still more painful sacrifice was entailed, not only on the Mission in Poland, but on the whole Congregation, for its founder, Vincent de Paul himself, succumbed to a prolonged illness.

[29] *Mémoires*, p. 23.
[30] *Saint Vincent de Paul*, Vol. VII, p. 266.
[31] *Mémoires*, p. 22.

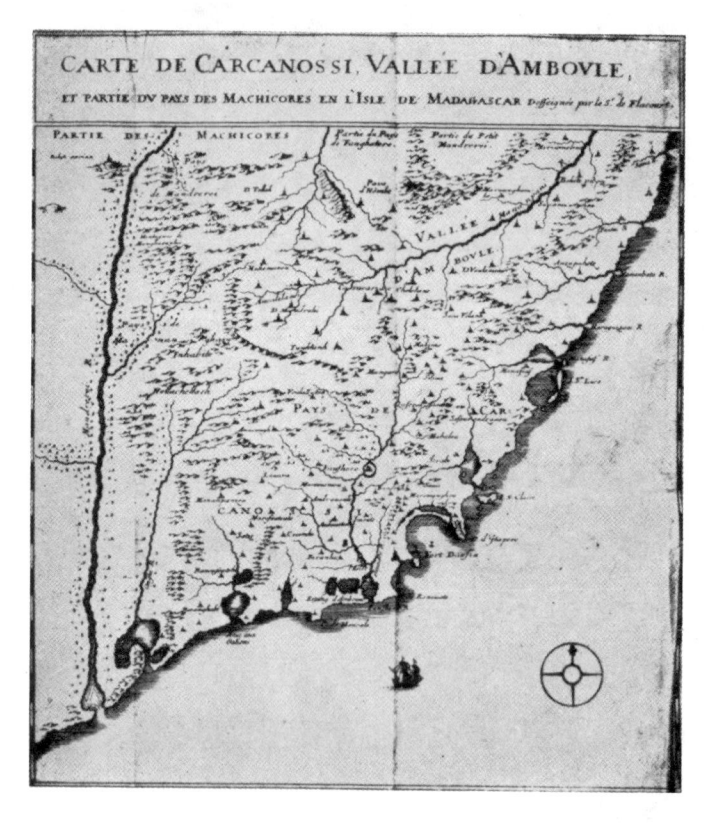

FORT DAUPHIN

(From a Map by de Flacourt)

CHAPTER XXVII

THE MADAGASCAR MISSION[1]

SAINT VINCENT looked farther afield than Poland; his mind frequently turned towards those vast lands inhabited by infidels for whom Jesus Christ had shed His blood and who had never even heard of their Saviour. He was well aware that zeal should be boundless and often called to mind that his Divine Master had not said to His disciples : ' Remain in Judea and convert it,' but, ' Go ye into the whole world and preach the Gospel to every creature.' He saw many Communities, both old and new, Franciscans, Dominicans, Capuchins, Carmelites, Jesuits and others, going out to all the nations of the earth to spread the Kingdom of God. How then could he remain idle whose heart was so large and so full of charity ?

He was not satisfied with his own efforts to stir up the zeal of his priests. By his orders, the life of the great Apostle of the Indies, Saint Francis Xavier, one of the saints whom he most admired, was read in the refectory of Saint-Lazare, and also the printed ' relations ' sent home by Jesuit and other Missionaries. Whenever a religious, home from a distant mission, came to Saint-Lazare, he was asked by the Saint to address the Community. The accounts that he heard stirred up feelings of noble emulation in his heart, but however great his desire to go forth and extend the Kingdom of God, he knew how to moderate it. Faithful to his

---

[1] This subject has been dealt with by M. Henri Froidevaux (*Les Lazaristes à Madagascar au XVIIe siècle*, Paris, s.d., duodecimo), Malotet (*Saint Vincent de Paul et les Missions de Madagascar*, 1900, pp. 369, 510, 575) and an anonymous writer (*Histoire de la Mission fondée à Madagascar par Saint Vincent de Paul*, 1895, quarto).

customary practice, he waited for the call of Providence. At length the call came, and it was to places in Africa, as far apart from each other as Barbary and Madagascar.[2]

We shall say nothing about Barbary here, because the work on behalf of slaves took up all the time and energy of the Missionaries who went there, and we shall devote a special chapter to this subject later on. We shall deal here only with the Madagascar Mission.

The history of the evangelisation of this island before 1600 is both defective and obscure. Madagascar was discovered by Diego Diaz on August 10, 1500 (and on that account called the Island of Saint Lawrence), and was explored in 1508 and 1509 by Lopez de Siqueyra. During the sixteenth century, ships occasionally cast anchor in its ports, either on the look-out for shipwrecked men who might have landed there, or to trade with the inhabitants or to plunder them. These pillages, often accompanied by massacres, had inspired the natives with a hatred for all strangers. In 1548, in the province of Antanosy, several sailors were taken by surprise and put to death. About the same time, near the village of Emoro, seventy Portuguese, including several religious, were invited to a village to take part in the customary festivities after a new house had been built. They were treacherously attacked in the middle of the feast and all perished. A Dominican, Brother John of Saint Thomas, was poisoned on the north-east coast in 1584, after labouring for some time at the evangelisation of the negroes.

In the beginning of the seventeenth century, Portugal resolved to exploit commercially the natural wealth of the island, and a fleet was sent from Goa in 1613. Two Jesuit Fathers, Pedro Freire and Luiz Mariano, accompanied it as chaplains. After a voyage of eight months, the captain discovered some descendants of the Portuguese in the port of San Lucas, where he remained for a considerable time and made a treaty with Tsiambany, the King of Antanosy. In the meantime, the Fathers established themselves in the island of Santa Cruz where a presbytery and wooden church were built for them in ten days. The captain found it difficult to come to terms with Tsiambany, who was loth

---

[2] Abelly, *op. cit.*, Bk. II, Ch. I, sect. VII, pp. 91-92.

THE MADAGASCAR MISSION

to bind himself definitely in any way, but in the end his resistance was overcome and he consented to make a treaty, whilst quite prepared to break it at the first favourable opportunity. It was arranged that his eldest son, Ramaka, a boy fourteen years old, should proceed to Goa for his education, after which he would be sent back to his family. As a guarantee, two Missionaries and four Portuguese were to remain as hostages on the island of Santa Cruz, which, by a deed of gift signed by the King, was to become the property of the Jesuits who received permission to preach the Christian religion, to carry out public worship and to build churches there. The King, who was deeply attached to his son Ramaka, at the last moment refused to carry out his engagements although he had sworn to do so. As neither promises nor threats could bend him, the captain gave orders to a sailor to seize the lad when he and his father had come to the seashore. The King, taken by surprise, uttered loud cries of grief and terror, and the natives ran down prepared to use their spears, but as the ship's boat was moving rapidly away from the shore, all they could do was to vent their anger in shouts and threats.

The fleet, after forty-three days' stay at the fort of San Lucas, continued the exploration of the coast. On August 14, 1614, it sailed from Madagascar to Goa, arriving only on October 16 at that port, which Father Freire and Ramaka had reached five months previously. During the long voyage, the Fathers had the consolation of instructing and baptising a certain number of natives. Ramaka was handed over to the Jesuits in Goa, and remained in their college for two years. The Viceroy took much interest in his progress and expressed his delight at the lad's excellent dispositions. On the feast of Saint John the Baptist, 1615, the Archbishop of Goa solemnly baptised Ramaka in the presence of the Viceroy, who expressed a wish to act as godfather and to have the youth placed under the protection of his own patron, Saint Andrew. When it was decided that Ramaka was sufficiently educated, the Viceroy sent him home laden with presents and honours. Two ships, a caravel and a small man-of-war, the former commanded by Captain Juan Cardoso de Pina and the latter by Pedro de Almeida Cabral, set sail from Goa on February 7, 1616, with four Jesuits on board : Fathers Manoel de Almeida, Luiz Mariano, Custodia da Costa and Antonio de Azevedo, and after two months at sea, they reached the port of San Lucas. The King of Antanosy and his wife shed tears of joy on hearing that their son was one of the passengers. They hastened to see him, but the Portuguese captain had no intention of handing over Dom Andrew to his parents without obtaining in exchange sufficient guarantees for the success of negotiations which he had received orders to open. Tsiambany was reluctant to give guarantees and took the first opportunity of escaping with his son, but the Portuguese pursued him and he had to consent to leave two of his nephews as hostages before he obtained permission to take Dom Andrew home. Thanks to this precaution, the Portuguese succeeded in overcoming his opposition to the departure of his nephew, Andrian Sambo, for Goa, and two Jesuits were allowed to reside on the little island of Santa Cruz and to teach their religion in the kingdom of Antanosy. The captain had asked for further concessions ; he wished to take the King himself to Goa, and that the four Fathers should evangelise Antanosy together, but those already given were considerable, and he contented himself with what he had obtained. Fathers Mariano and de Azevedo had to leave, and departed to Sadia, which accordingly became a second mission centre.

The sojourn of Fathers Antonio de Azevedo and Custodia da Costa in Santa Cruz was nothing but a prolonged series of sufferings and privations. Plagued by the climate, persecuted by the powerful and despised by the natives, they had not even the sole consolation they sought on this ungrateful soil—the conversion of souls. Tsiambany forbade his people, under penalty of death, to have any communication with them, or to supply or sell them food. His fear of the return of the Portuguese prevented him from making a direct attempt on their lives, but he had spells cast around their house to bring all sorts of evils upon them. His people obeyed him loyally because they regarded him ' not only as a great King worthy of all respect, but also as the chief fakir or sorcerer in the country.'[3] Hence all the Fathers' efforts came to nothing. 'We have not found,' wrote Custodia da Costa, ' one single person, man or woman, noble or slave, to pay any attention to our sermons or to believe in them, for they have all shown themselves more animal than the beasts themselves.'[4] The same failure was experienced in Sadia. The Malagasies told the Missionaries they preferred to go to Hell with their own folk than ' to follow the Fathers into Paradise.'[5] ' Not only,' says Father Mariano sadly, ' have we not saved the least little innocent soul, but we have no hope of greater success in the future.'[6]

Nobody in Goa had the slightest idea of all the difficulties the Missionaries in Madagascar had to face. Andrian Sambo, Tsiambany's nephew, was instructed and baptised there and given the name Jeronimo ; he too, like Dom Andrew, was a godson of the Viceroy. Early in February, 1617, Captain Manoel Freire de Andrade set sail for Antanosy, taking Jeronimo with him. He was entrusted with magnificent presents for the King of that region and his son, and besides a hundred soldiers, had on board two Jesuit Fathers, Paulo Jovio and Pedro Carreiro, who were to assist the Missionaries in Santa Cruz.

At the end of April, the ship cast anchor in San Lucas and great was the joy of the two Jesuits on seeing two of their confrères. They held a council and resolved to leave Santa Cruz and join forces with the Missionaries in Sadia. The captain himself could bear witness that the Fathers were not exaggerating, for the Malagasies, coming down the beach as friends, fired stones and spears at the Portuguese, who replied with musket shots. He hanged several natives on trees near the shore, set fire to the village and carried off Dom Jeronimo and one of his brothers. The two Missionaries in Sadia, for their part, had made up their

[3] A. Grandidier and others, *Collection des ouvrages anciens concernant Madagascar*, Vol. II, p. 160, extract from a letter of P. Custodia da Costa.
[4] *Ibid.*, p. 169.
[5] *Ibid.*, extract from a letter of P. Mariano, p. 235.
[6] *Ibid.*, p. 237.

minds to go elsewhere as soon as they should find a vessel, and hence when the caravel, *The Discovery*, arrived from San Lucas, they persuaded their confrères to abandon the idea of establishing themselves in Sadia. Accordingly, the whole band left for Mozambique.

Thus ended the first attempt at evangelising the island by Portuguese Jesuits. They had arrived there in 1616 and now, a year later, left it after labouring fruitlessly for the conversion of a people obstinate in their errors ; or rather, after meriting by their sufferings and privations, that God, in a still distant future, would grant other Missionaries the joy of beholding a magnificent harvest springing up from its soil.[7]

On January 29, 1642, the twenty-four shareholders of the East India Company obtained from Cardinal Richelieu a trading monopoly for ten years with Madagascar and the adjacent islands. The Royal warrant imposed an obligation to maintain one or more priests in the colony to attend to the spiritual interests of the French and to preach the Gospel to the infidels. The Company had already made arrangements to sail, and during March, the *Saint Louis* left France, carrying on board the new Governor de Pronis, and fourteen colonists, almost all of whom were Huguenots. After a six months' voyage, the ship arrived at the port of Manafiaf, in Antanosy territory, in the south-eastern end of the island. With the permission of the King, Andrian Ramaka, the little colony established itself there, and in the following May, a vessel cast anchor in the bay of Saint Lucy and disembarked seventy men, twenty-two cannon, and all tools and implements necessary for the building of houses and the cultivation of the soil. Amongst the newcomers was a deacon.

Scarcely had the French established themselves in Manafiaf than they were forced to leave, owing to the unhealthy climate ; in less than two months half of them died from sickness. They moved down the coast for about twenty leagues, and on a more healthy site on the borders

---

[7] The Jesuits made renewed attempts to establish themselves in Madagascar in 1619, 1620 and 1630. See Grandidier, *op. cit.*, Vol. II, pp. 307, 322, 325 and 431.

of the sea, built a fort which was called Fort Dauphin. The havoc wrought in their ranks by death and massacre was compensated, in 1644, by the arrival of ninety French colonists.

With a wise and prudent Governor, firm and conciliatory, ready to forget himself and to further the welfare of all, the colony might have prospered despite the difficulties of food supplies in a region deficient both in cattle and rice. De Pronis had neither the mind nor the heart of an organiser; he failed to win either the esteem or the affection of his compatriots, still less those of the natives. The harshness of his character, the excessive work he imposed on his subordinates, his waste and extravagance, turned all minds against him. The French were deprived at times of meat and even of rice, whilst the relatives of his concubine wallowed in abundance. The sermons which he preached to his ten fellow-Protestants could be overheard in the Catholic Chapel and disturbed their devotions. The discontent went so far that in the end the colonists rebelled, and on February 15, 1646, put de Pronis in irons. He was in jail six months when the *Saint Lawrence*, under Captain Roger de Bourg, arrived with a priest, M. de Bellebarbe, and forty-four colonists on board. De Pronis was released, arrested twelve of the chief rebels and after making them apologise in their shirts, with their heads and beards shaven and a rope around their necks, deported them to the island now known as Reunion.

When de Bourg returned to France, he made a report of the whole regrettable occurrence. De Pronis could not be allowed to remain on the island, and it was decided to send Stephen de Flacourt, one of the chief shareholders of the Company. The new Governor was forty years old; he had travelled in Italy, Germany, Holland and England, and during his travels, had completed his studies in chemistry, medicine and botany. He possessed a powerful constitution, an open, cultivated mind, a firm, upright will guided and directed by a great love of order and justice. Prudence and reflection tempered his courage, audacity and energetic disposition; besides these qualities he had certain defects of character which will be more evident later on when he comes to play a chief part in our history. Like all absolute and imperious people, he would neither brook opposition, tolerate discussion, nor admit any infringement of his rights, though he thought it no harm to infringe those of others. All had to bow before him ; otherwise his pride was hurt and he became passionate and vindictive. De Flacourt had the same colonial policy as his contemporaries : to make as many conquests as possible, if needs be, by fear and terror. A Governor who extended the boundaries of a colony confided to his administration was regarded as an excellent ruler, no matter what means he employed to attain his end. This was an axiom ; and officials most anxious to be regarded as just men thought they were doing no wrong in following it.

The superseding of de Pronis by de Flacourt was not the only reform decided on by the East India Company, for it also resolved to improve the state of religion in the colony by entrusting it to the members of a community. M. de Bellebarbe had proved a failure ; he was without zeal, and certain faults of character deprived him of any influence over the colonists. He made others unhappy and was unhappy himself, and there were certain advantages to be found in replacing him by a religious community. The East India Company, perhaps after several fruitless attempts, consulted Nicholas Bagni, the Papal Nuncio in Paris, who chose the Congregation of the Mission. Bagni was then unaware of the fact that Propaganda had selected the Discalced Carmelite Fathers for Madagascar, but as the vessel was about to sail and as there was no time to apply to Rome and obtain a reply, the Nuncio took it on himself to settle the matter and to grant the necessary faculties. Saint Vincent, urged at the same time by the East India Company, in which he had many friends, and by the Sovereign Pontiff's representative in Paris, could do nothing but comply.

A few days later he wrote to Charles Nacquart, a young missionary in Richelieu : ' His Eminence the Nuncio, by the authority of the Sacred Congregation of Propaganda, of which our Holy Father is head, has chosen the Company to go and serve God in the island of Saint Lawrence, otherwise

THE MADAGASCAR MISSION

called Madagascar, and the Company has cast its eyes on you as its best victim to be offered as a homage to our sovereign Creator. . . . O my more than dearest Father, what does your heart say to this news ? Does it experience the shame and confusion appropriate to the reception of such a grace from Heaven ? A divine call as great and adorable as that of the greatest apostles and saints of the Church of God ! Eternal designs accomplished in time in your person ! Humility, Sir, is the only means of supporting such a grace ; and then perfect abandonment of all that you are and can be, with an overflowing confidence in your sovereign Creator, will be sure to follow. Generosity and heroic courage are needed, and you also need a faith as great as that of Abraham ; you stand in great need of the charity of Saint Paul ; zeal, patience, courtesy, poverty, solicitude, discretion, moral integrity and a great desire to sacrifice yourself entirely for God, are as suitable for you as they were for the great Saint Francis Xavier.'[8]

After exalting the vocation of the future apostle of Madagascar, the Saint goes on to give some practical advice : ' You should make it your chief study, after labouring to live . . . in the odour of sweetness and of good example, to help the poor people, born in the darkness of ignorance of their Creator, to arrive at a knowledge of the truths of our faith, not by subtle theological arguments, but by reasonings drawn from Nature. We will send you some pictures of all the mysteries of our religion which will be a wonderful help in enabling those dear people to grasp what you wish to teach them ; and they always take delight in looking at them.'[9] He was speaking from experience, for he had himself given catechism lessons to a twenty-year-old negro who was staying at Saint-Lazare after arriving in France from Madagascar in one of the East India Company's ships, together with another Malagasy who had been detained at Nantes ; the Saint's personal observation had taught him that teaching by means of pictures was best understood and most enjoyed. The very day on which Saint Vincent wrote to Father Nacquart (May 22, 1648)

[8] *Saint Vincent de Paul*, Vol. III, pp. 278–279.
[9] *Ibid.*, pp. 281–283.

had been selected by the Nuncio for the baptism of the young man, and one may well imagine the fervour of the Saint's prayer, whilst the water was being poured over the head of the new Christian, for the conversion of the infidels to whom he was sending two of his best priests.

Father Nacquart did not leave France alone; he was accompanied by a Missionary twenty-eight years old, Nicholas Gondrée, a 'humble, charitable, kindly and zealous' priest. At La Rochelle they went on board the *Saint Lawrence*, on May 21, 1648, Ascension Thursday, together with de Flacourt, two negroes and seventy-six colonists, all of whom were Catholics. They had a good passage, and during the six months' voyage, Fathers Nacquart and Gondrée never forgot they were priests, and that a priest should unite zeal and good example in his person. They regarded the ship as their parish and carried out the duties of pastors of souls. They took occasion of the Jubilee to preach a little mission which was devoutly attended both by sailors and passengers. The Feasts of Pentecost, Ascension, Corpus Christi and All Saints were celebrated as they would have been in any French parish and the most fervent Christians on board again approached the Sacraments. During their leisure hours, the two Fathers, with the help of two young Malagasies, studied the language of the country they were about to evangelise, so that they might get to work as soon as possible at the conversion of the people. At Cape Verde, the *Saint Lawrence* fell in with a ship returning to France and Father Nacquart gladly seized the opportunity of sending Saint Vincent an account of their experiences. On December 4, after a six months' voyage, he stepped on shore with a heart overflowing with joy and confidence.

What did they find on this island, the scene of their brief apostolate? In the first place, a group of their own fellow-countrymen, but, apart from a few exceptions, what a group! Those who had responded in France to the summons of the East India Company were, for the most part, young men attracted by a life of adventure in an uncivilised land, who hoped to make their fortunes easily and rapidly, or who were glad to get away from their families for a life of independence for which they craved. They found in Madagascar, if not a life of independence, a life of immorality. At their age, in such a climate, in a country where the women were ignorant of the dictates of modesty, they succumbed to the temptations of the flesh. The licentiousness of their lives was almost a result of the melancholy thoughts that invaded their minds and threw them into a state of discouragement. They were, in fact, profoundly unhappy, and the illusions they had cherished on leaving France vanished before the harsh realities of existence. Madagascar was not the earthly Paradise of which they had dreamed and which had been promised them. They were compelled to suffer the severest privations, the most painful labours and an unendurable heat, so that even the strongest felt their strength give way. Death struck blow upon blow, and each might well ask himself: 'Will it be my turn tomorrow?' Hence there was but one desire: to go home. They counted the days that separated them from the termination of their contract, and when it arrived thought themselves happy if there was a ship in the harbour to bear them to France. As a general rule, they had to wait months and sometimes years, for as we shall see, relations between France and Madagascar were not at all good, owing to a variety of unfortunate circumstances. A Missionary's words ran great danger of making little or no impression on minds such as these, disappointed, embittered and inclined to curse their fate. Again, his influence on the natives met with obstacles of another kind; first of all, a strong and lively attachment to their superstitions which from habit had in a manner become a second nature.

The Malagasy religion was that of the Indonisian races, mingled with various infiltrations in which the influence of Judaism could easily be recognised.[10] In the Heavens reigned God, Creator and Omnipotent, utterly indifferent to all that took place on earth. Under him were demi-gods or genii, many of whom were maleficent. The most intelligent natives had vague notions, in which partial truths were mingled with grotesque and childish fables, on creation,

[10] These races inhabited some of the islands in the Malay Archipelago.

sin, a future life, Adam, Eve, Abraham, Isaac, Moses, Solomon, Mahomet and Jesus Christ. There were no temples or altars in the country, and God, it may be said, was held in little honour. It is true that sacrifices were offered to Him, just as they were offered to demons and the shades of their ancestors, but the largest part of the victim was always set aside for the devil. 'His Lordship the Devil,' as he was respectfully designated, was more truly worshipped than God, because he was more feared. Idol worship also played a great part in Malagasy life. These idols, called *olis*, were not invisible beings; the natives wore them constantly in their belts, in the shape of simple pieces of wood, covered with powder and oil, on which were engraved human figures. These idols enjoyed very extensive supernatural powers in Malagasy eyes: they regulated fine weather and rain, preserved their wearers from sickness and averted dangers. The natives, before crossing a river, asked their *olis* to protect them from the teeth of the crocodile. Whenever seed was sown, they brought out an *oli* to which they sacrificed an animal, and then sprinkled the field with the blood of the victim. If a swimmer were devoured by a crocodile or the harvest proved a failure, confidence in the *oli's* power was in no way diminished; they simply thought a bad one had been selected.

The manufacture and sale of *olis* was reserved to a class known as *ombiases*; men who had a certain amount of education, who could read and write Arabic, and whose name signified 'scribes.' They combined the functions of priests, doctors, diviners, and sorcerers, presided over ceremonies and saw to the maintenance of customs and superstitions. Every public festival was accompanied by sacrifices, and no sacrifice could be offered without an *ombiase*. They alone had the right to slay oxen; their books inspired the natives with respect mingled with fear, and yet contained nothing very terrifying: a few passages from the Koran, the words 'God is great,' and, in far greater number, badly drawn figures which, the *ombiases* declared, they employed to cure the sick, to foretell the future, or to discover lost objects. These men had considerable moral influence over both the people and the chiefs, and they utilised it to enrich themselves at the latter's expense, for the slightest service had to be rewarded by gold, fowl or bullocks. A further source of revenue, in addition to the sale of *olis*, was the circumcision of children and other ceremonial rites. The *ombiases* always reserved for themselves the greatest part of all victims immolated to the gods, and sacrifices were frequent. They took part in the customary rites at the funeral of a chief, on the taking possession of a newly built or repaired house, and at marriages, for the people believed there was no more efficacious means of appeasing evil spirits; the sick were advised to go to the *ombiases* for a cure, and those haunted by evil dreams that the dangers with which they were threatened might be averted.

The Malagasies offered sacrifices not only to good or evil gods, but also to the shades of their ancestors who, they believed, continued to live a mysterious life, ever ready to intercede on behalf of their descendants with the divinities, whenever they were invoked. Hence, they sought to win the good graces of these shades by bringing to their graves the first fruits of the season, and by never touching fruit that grew on trees planted around their tombs. Every month and even every week they might be seen placing rice or little jars full of wine on the sepulchres of their dead.

Amongst other causes that influenced their lives for weal or woe were the stars. They had also lucky and unlucky days, and fathers and mothers had everything to fear from a child born during the night between Saturday and Sunday; hence it was abandoned, or made the slave of its brothers.

Women were bought and sold, and a man married as many wives as he desired and could purchase. Some of the natives, who were called 'the whites' on account of their lighter complexions, were accustomed to observe a fast which, for two months of the year, entailed abstinence from wine and beef. This fast, however, was not very severe, for the prohibition ceased between sunset and sunrise, fowl could be eaten instead of beef, all other drinks, including spirits, were permitted, and the obligation could be fulfilled by inducing a negro, by means of a present, to promise to observe the fast. Such were the superstitions and religious observances that Fathers Nacquart and Gondrée had to combat in order to bring about the reign of Jesus Christ, and to these superstitions and observances the *ombiases* were attached from motives of interest, and the people from custom.

The Missionaries had to attack another and an equally formidable enemy, if they were to sow the seed of the Gospel : the vice of immorality. In Saint Vincent's letter to Father Nacquart announcing his selection for the mission he writes : ' I am aware how deeply your heart loves purity. You will need to practise it there in a very high degree seeing that these races, vitiated in many respects, are especially so in this.'[11] They were, indeed, so completely vitiated in this respect that an immoral act was, if not a virtuous, at least an indifferent one. Parents taught their children to be vicious from their infancy, and instead of correcting, encouraged them, with results that may be imagined.

On the other hand, the natives had quite a number of good qualities ; they were charitable, gentle, hospitable, docile, temperate, respectful to the old, obedient to their chiefs, and possessed in a high degree the domestic virtues. They had a profound respect for all that concerned religion, even for a religion different from their own. If, in the sixteenth and seventeenth centuries, Europeans had acted with kindness and justice, they could easily have ruled, and even have absorbed them, but their plunders and massacres had rendered the natives suspicious and treacherous.

Before de Flacourt's arrival, the fact that both the Protestant and the Catholic religions were practised on the island had interfered with the progress of the latter. The return of de Pronis and most of his co-religionists to France, and the abjuration of five others during Father Nacquart's first days in Madagascar reduced the number of Huguenots to a minimum. A great obstacle was thus removed, and the zeal of the new Missionaries was to benefit by this altered state of affairs.

[11] *Saint Vincent de Paul*, Vol. III, p. 282.

Apart from the French and the two negroes who had returned from France, the only baptised persons on the island were three little girl slaves taken from enemies in the course of an expedition, a little girl found wandering in the woods, a little boy, the illegitimate offspring of a Frenchman and a native woman, and four others converted by the Jesuits, namely, an old woman and her daughter, Andrian Ramaka, and another native, but the two latter had long since fallen back into their old superstitions.

Andrian Ramaka lived in the village of Fanshere, a day and a half's march from Fort Dauphin. The excellent account which Father Nacquart had heard of Ramaka led him to believe that if he were authorised by the King, he could proceed more quickly in the work of evangelisation. Accordingly, six days after his arrival on the island, he set off to visit the King who showed him the greatest kindness. Ramaka, quite pleased to show that he had not forgotten the lessons learned in his youth, made the sign of the Cross on his forehead, lips and heart, repeating the words: *Per signum sanctae crucis de inimicis nostris libera nos.* He then recited in Portuguese the *Pater*, *Ave* and *Credo*. Father Nacquart, thus encouraged, said: 'Since you love Jesus Christ, why do you not tell your people about Him, so that they too may know and love Him?' He replied: 'They would not be able to understand me. Moreover, if they had no priest living with them, how could they practise the Christian religion? Remain with us. The people will love you and be converted.' The priest then said: 'I have come to teach them. Are you willing to allow me, and even to help me?' The King replied: 'I am content, quite content. I promise to join in the prayers you will offer up in my village.'

Father Nacquart visited the other chiefs of the district and everywhere found the same good dispositions. His presence in Fanshere especially excited the curiosity of the children who followed him about, and crept up beside him, when he had the Breviary in his hands, to see how he prayed to God. The Missionary petted the children and distributed little glass bracelets, of which he had an ample supply, amongst them. He was soon on terms of intimate familiarity with those who understood that the priest who called them ' my children ' deserved the name of ' Father ' which they at once gave him.

Father Nacquart returned from his trip more confident than ever of the future of the Mission. He felt that the sound doctrines of the Faith would easily take root amongst the natives whose simplicity charmed him. On the Feast of the Epiphany, he had the further consolation of baptising some children in Fort Dauphin. Several of their elders asked for a similar favour, but his first duty was to instruct and prepare them, and to this both he and Father Gondrée devoted themselves with the assistance of an interpreter. The Malagasies, owing to a peculiar sense of humility to be explained by the methods of the *ombiases*, were convinced they could never learn to pray to God, and that they were too stupid to assimilate His teachings. The first thing was to disabuse them of this idea and nothing proved easier. The Missionary, taking them by the hand, moved it from the forehead to the breast and then to the left and right shoulder, telling them to repeat the words ' In the name of the Father, and of the Son and of the Holy Ghost.' When this was done they looked at each other in astonishment, quite delighted to find that they could do what had seemed so impossible a moment before. At times, fear was added to this false idea of humility. Father Nacquart on one occasion terrified the bystanders by making the sign of the Cross over one of them ; they all fled except the master of the house, but when the others saw him putting his hand to his forehead without incurring any mishap, they took courage, returned, and even ventured themselves to make the sign of the Cross.

Once their fears and timidity were overcome, they never grew weary of hearing religion spoken of, and many of them were far more interested to hear of the mysteries of the next life than to learn the causes of natural phenomena. Accordingly, they gave Father Nacquart their undivided attention and he, for his part, satisfied their curiosity with a zeal that nothing could diminish. If they came to Fort Dauphin to see the Governor or for any other reason, he invariably took them to the Chapel, and, whilst explaining the use and symbolism of the various religious objects that met their eyes, gave them a little course of religious instruction. Those who wished to attend divine service found the door always open, and as everything they saw was new and strange, they were astonished and delighted. They plied the Missionary with questions every time they met him, and some of their queries were amusingly simple. One thing surprised them above all, namely, that when the priest had sung, all the French, without previous arrangement, replied in the same terms. 'Don't be surprised at that,' said Father Nacquart, 'we Catholics are all agreed in asking God for what we need, and we all sing His praises in the same way.'

When Easter was over, he returned to Fanshere, where he received the same kindly welcome as on his first visit. Andrian Ramaka begged him to dwell in the village, and even promised to pray to God, as he had once done, as soon as ever he had a *Book of Hours* in Portuguese; he added, however, one condition to his promise, which spoiled its value, and that was that the King of France should send him a fine present. The King of Antanosy evidently was not as yet up to the standard desired by Father Nacquart, who hoped that Ramaka's over-worldly mind would be gradually purified by a deeper knowledge of the Gospel teachings, and cherishing this hope he returned to Fort Dauphin. The Missionary was already well known in the villages along the road, and gladly devoted some time to the natives, speaking to them of Jesus Christ. He was asked to pay a visit to one of the village chiefs who had been attacked by a severe illness from which neither the *olis* nor the superstitious rites of the *ombiases* could deliver him, and who hoped that the God of the foreigners might be more favourable. Father Nacquart encouraged him. 'God,' he said, ' protects those who honour Him and who embrace His religion. If you wish to recover your health, begin by learning what He has taught us and prepare to receive Baptism.' The sick man, with no other thought than that of a speedy cure, declared that he submitted in advance to all the Missionary's wishes, and even agreed that the villagers should be invited to come and hear the Catechism lesson. The negroes required no second invitation and the priest, in the midst of a profound silence, began to speak. At the end, his hearers gave naïve expression to their satisfaction. 'Your words,' they said, 'are more precious than silver and gold. Thieves may steal what we possess, but they shall never rob us of what you have told us; we are sure to find your words again in our hearts after we have slept.' The sick man's wife added : ' We have had recourse to God for many a long day. In all that we do, especially when we plant and harvest the rice, we say to Him, with eyes raised to Heaven : " It is Thou Who hast made our fields to ripen; if Thou hast need of what I have gathered I will give it to Thee. This rice shall not be for myself alone; I will distribute it amongst the French who may visit my house and amongst the poor slaves."' Whilst his wife was speaking, the sick man made signs of agreement and added : ' My heart is comforted. I believe what I have just heard. I am moved at the thought that the Son of God suffered and died for me. I thank Him for it and will never forget Him. His power is great; can He cure me?'—'Certainly,' said Father Nacquart, ' provided you believe in Him and are prepared to receive Baptism.' The sick man regarded this as an invitation, had water fetched and said to the Missionary : ' Baptise me.' ' No, not now,' was the reply, ' it would be too soon. You do not love God as you should if you love Him only for the sake of your health. I will come back when you are cured. If you will then agree to complete your religious instruction, I will baptise you.' It was a prudent reply, for as soon as the village chief had recovered, he showed less eagerness for baptism and contented himself with asking the Missionary to instruct and baptise two of his children. From the moral point of view, his conduct henceforward was irreproachable, and if he did not realise the full extent of his obligations, it was because he was afraid of the frowns of the great; human respect deterred him, as it has done so many others. Young girls were more courageous than the chief, and Father Nacquart baptised two of them on Whit Sunday, and a few days later the two new Christians married the two negroes who had been instructed in France.

In the midst of these consolations, Father Nacquart's heart was oppressed with grief at the thought that his confrère was battling against an illness that threatened to carry him off. Some days previously, Father Gondrée had accompanied de Flacourt to Fanshere. The journey, made on foot, under a burning sun, and with no food save a little boiled rice, had exhausted him; he was suffering from a violent attack of fever accompanied by intolerable pains in all his joints. The end was near. He received Extreme Unction with sentiments of the tenderest devotion, recommended the French to fear God and be devout to His Mother, manifested the utmost gratitude for having been chosen amongst so many to labour at the conversion of infidels, and then, on May 26, in the flower of his young manhood, after a fortnight's illness, he expired painlessly with a smile on his lips. The negroes mingled their tears with those of the French and were loud in their praises of his kind heart and gracious character.

One may easily imagine Father Nacquart's grief and disappointment. Alone amidst that vast untilled field, for M. de Bellebarbe had retired to St. Mary's Island waiting for an opportunity to return to France, he saw all his plans for evangelising the people melt away. He had dreamed of penetrating farther into the interior, and now he had to be at Fort Dauphin every Sunday and Feast day to look after his parish. Hence, he could never be absent for longer than six days, but he resolved to make the best use of his time by instructing such negroes as came to see the Governor on business.

In June, he returned to Fanshere and found the King of Antanosy in great grief, for his grandson, attacked by a severe illness, seemed to be at his last gasp. 'Cure him,' said the King to the Missionary, 'Cure him, I beg you; give me back my grandson.' 'God alone can cure him,' said the priest, 'but He asks you to have the child baptised and, once baptised, to live like a good Christian.' 'I give him to you,' said the King, 'do what you like with him; you shall be his father and mother when he grows up.' The holy water was poured over the head of little Jerome, as he was called, and shortly afterwards he recovered. This cure increased Andrian Ramaka's friendly dispositions towards the Missionary and his religion. He himself taught the commandments of God to his people, and thanks to his efforts, the Catholic faith was more and more favourably received in all his territory. Even the chiefs asked for Baptism. The women alone seemed indifferent, for it was commonly believed that instruction was not suitable to their sex, and even that the level of their intelligence was too low to permit of their aspiring to the knowledge of supernatural truths. They were quite astonished when Father Nacquart told them that in France women were taught just as well as men, and often even served God with more devotion and intelligence.

Divine Providence seemed to take pleasure in supporting Father Nacquart's zeal. Death respected the children he baptised and carried off those whom their parents preferred to hand over to the *ombiases* for circumcision. Refusals from some of the fathers of families, which he sometimes met with, were usually, if not always, due to their fear of the *ombiases*. On one occasion, when he had vainly urged one of these timid individuals to have recourse to the water that saves the soul and, in addition, may bring health to the body, he added : ' If you do not listen to me, your child will die.' Shortly afterwards, the father and mother came to him bathed in tears. 'Why,' they cried aloud, 'did we not follow your advice ; our son is dead.' Such providential coincidences strengthened the priest's authority. Wherever he went, the meetings, held at the end of the day to explain the Catechism, were better attended. The whole village was present, except the *ombiases* and the sick, to hear his sermons and gaze at his pictures, for he always took care to take with him on his missionary journey, large pictures which spoke more eloquently to the eye than the tongue to the ear, representing in lively colours, the Last Judgement, Hell and Heaven. 'I have come,' he said to the crowd, ' so that your eyes may see and your ears hear the tidings of your salvation.' The crowd gathered around and the lesson began. He first explained the chief truths of our religion and then, coming down to particulars, spoke of the duties laid on us by the moral law. When he had finished,

STEPHANVS DEFLACOVRT BISET INDIARVM ORIENT. COLON
GALL PRÆFECTVS. Natus Aurelius Deuexit Peregrinus in Occeano Anno
Salutis. 1660 Die decima junii Ætatis Suæ 53.

*Per mare per terram porque auras Astra secutus
Elatus mediis ignibus Astra tenet*

P. Du Vergier

STEPHEN DE FLACOURT

he took a picture and unrolled it in the midst of the greatest excitement. Everybody came closer in turn to have a better view. Then, beginning again, he said : ' Choose now. Do you want to go above or below, to Heaven or to Hell ? , There was a unanimous reply. No one wanted to go to the devil ; all preferred the company of God. In case of a new-comer arriving after the picture had been folded up, there were cries on all sides ' Oh ! you missed it,' and the Missionary, out of pity, seeing his disappointment, would unroll the picture and begin his explanations over again, interrupted, as at first, by the comments of his hearers. ' If I had you,' said one, pointing to the devil, ' I would burn you.' Another cursed our first parents : ' Wretches ! It was you then who deprived us of the happiness of Paradise. It is because of you we are obliged to labour, suffer and die ! '

Father Nacquart's unselfishness charmed the Malagasies just as much as his pictures. When they saw him leave without asking for anything, rewarded for his labours by the pleasure he had had in teaching them, they could not but think of the demands of the *ombiases*, always so ready to profit by their alleged services, and the *ombiases* began to fall into disrepute which developed into systematic opposition. Father Nacquart would, indeed, have gladly gained them, for he felt that without their help and that of the chiefs, all his effort would be in vain. Hence, he went amongst them as he did amongst the people, but here he was not so successful, for he had to conquer a formidable enemy, temporal interest, against which so many priests, armed with the zeal of the apostles, have found their weapons break in their hands.

None of the chiefs was so favourable as the King of Antanosy, Andrian Ramaka. ' If we could only bring the Kinglet back to his former state,'[12] wrote Father Nacquart, ' all the other chiefs would follow him, and one's arms would grow tired from baptising.' Ramaka, speaking in a tone that could not but be regarded as sincere, contented himself with a promise that he would abandon his superstitions on the day when a priest came to live in Fanshere

[12] *St. Vincent de Paul*, Vol. III, p. 573.

and a church was built there. Whilst waiting for that day which never arrived, the Missionary was at full liberty to preach and baptise in the district, but he was forbidden to speak against circumcision.

At one end of the island, two days' journey from Fort Dauphin, lived Andrian Madamboro, the eldest brother of the chief of that district, a most superstitious *ombiase* to whom the people attributed the power of bringing and banishing locusts. He suffered from gout and begged the Missionary to cure him. 'God alone,' said the priest, 'can give you what you ask. If you wish that all may be well with you, believe in Jesus Christ, His Son.' Madamboro listened to the priest reading an account of the life of Our Saviour, gazed for a long time at a picture of Christ, and, after kissing it, pressed it to his heart. Father Nacquart had long wished to know the contents of the *ombiases*' books. The kindness shown him by Madamboro emboldened him to ask the latter for his own books which he readily gave. When he was about to take them, those who stood by, moved by superstitious fear, plucked him by the cassock and said: 'What are you doing? You will bring misfortune on us. Wash your hands and your mouth.' The books were fumigated; when Father Nacquart saw some roughly drawn figures in the books he asked what they represented, and was told they were the names of planets. 'Names of planets,' he cried, 'say rather they are signs meant to deceive the people. Abandon all these falsehoods and superstitions. Why not serve God instead of the devil?' 'I have no intention of serving the devil,' said the chief, 'my ancestors had their customs and I am following them. If I have done wrong, I will give them up. You shall instruct me. Come and see me frequently. My house is yours. I will see you every day except Friday.' 'Are you very busy then on Fridays?' said Father Nacquart. 'Oh, no,' said Andrian, 'but it is an unlucky day; misfortunes befall all those who speak to me on that day.' 'You are mistaken,' said the priest, 'it was on a Friday Jesus Christ died and redeemed us. I will return to let you see that that day is no more unlucky than any other.' Whereupon the Missionary left after asking Andrian to make the sign of the Cross.

He went to the village in which the chief's son-in-law, Andrian Machicore, resided. He, too, was an *ombiase* who fostered the belief amongst the people that he had magical powers over the weather. They were so convinced of this that on one occasion, after several days' waiting, when the rain began to fall, they offered him oxen in gratitude for the favour. When Father Nacquart visited the chief it was obvious, from a look at the fields, that the rice crop was in danger from a prolonged drought. ' Will it rain soon? ' Andrian asked his visitor. Father Nacquart looked up at the sky in which a pale moon shone through the clouds and said : ' I think you will have rain soon ; but God alone knows, for none but He disposes of the weather. Now why do you, who claim to have the same power, allow the rice to fail, your own as well as the rest?' 'I am not the master,' was the reply, ' but my *olis*.' ' Your *olis*,' said the priest, ' are only grotesque figures invented by sorcerers, and when you honour them, you are honouring devils ; you attribute a power to them that only God possesses.' The respect felt by the natives for Father Nacquart enabled him to speak as freely as this to the chiefs as well as to the people who regarded him as the priest of the Most High God Who would take vengeance on anyone who dared to lay hands on him.

Some time afterwards, he went to preach Jesus Christ in the valley of Amboule, where four thousand people lived under a King who, when he saw the pictures, was filled with admiration which quickly turned to fear when the priest pointed out the damned in the fire of hell : ' That,' said he, ' is the punishment reserved for polygamists : you, too, will burn, if you keep your five wives.'

Wherever the Missionary went, he found the same desire for Baptism ; the poor people crying out to him, with tears in their eyes : ' Where is this water that cleanses souls, the water you promised us ? Bring it here.' If he had listened only to his own kind heart, he would gladly have given a favourable reply to their prayers, but prudence demanded precautions. Instruction was needed as well as desire, and after instruction, guarantees of perseverance. In places **remote from Fort Dauphin, and therefore seldom visited** by the Missionary, it was very much to be feared lest, in the interval between two visits, the baptised, left to themselves, or rather once more under the influence of the *ombiases*, might return to their superstitions. Little children escaped this danger for a while, but the Father asked himself anxiously how long it would be possible to distinguish between the baptised and the others. Hence, he contented himself with baptising the dying.

Around Fort Dauphin, such problems did not exist, and yet here, too, there was need for great prudence. Amongst those who wished to be baptised, many were ignorant of what they asked for and the obligations entailed; they longed for the water that cures the body, or brings material advantages, but not for that which ' damps the fire of concupiscence and springs up into eternal life.' Again, the young people were so dissolute that it was prudent to defer the administration of Baptism until they were about to be married. Hence, there is no reason to be surprised at the fact that, despite the large number of requests, Father Nacquart baptised only seventy persons from his arrival on the island to his death, a period of eighteen months.

On February 16, 1650, he wrote to Saint Vincent:[13] ' You sent me to cast out the nets; so far, the catch has amounted to only fifty-seven fishes, all small, except three; but there are so many ready to be taken, I have no doubt that you will send to sea those who will fish so well that they will break the nets.' If the number of Missionaries were increased, the number of Christians would increase ten or even a hundred fold, hence Father Nacquart cried out, like another Saint Francis Xavier: ' Where are all those doctors who are wasting their time in academies, whilst so many poor infidels *petunt panem, et non est qui frangat eis*? The Lord of the harvest truly desires to provide for them.'[14]

After a year in Madagascar he had acquired sufficient knowledge of his surroundings to form a clear idea of the needs of the mission and the most suitable means for securing the success of the work. He had a plan, and even though

[13] *St. Vincent de Paul*, Vol. III, p. 607.
[14] *Ibid.*, p. 576.

THE MADAGASCAR MISSION 75

it was on too large a scale to be immediately put into execution, nevertheless, he hoped to see it realised by degrees. In the first place, a secular priest should be stationed at Fort Dauphin to minister to the spiritual needs of the French, and a church built in place of the poor little chapel that served as a place of worship. A community of twelve priests should be established in the Matatane district, inhabited by an intelligent tribe, well disposed to receive the Faith. At Fanshere, where the King of Antanosy resided, another community of six Missionaries, and a seminary for children. Some Daughters of Charity should be sent to look after young girls ' who were, in all districts, shameless from childhood, as much as or even more than the boys.' There should be two carpenters, a cabinet maker and four lay-brothers capable respectively of fulfilling the duties of surgeon, tailor, school-master and bursar, who would look after the temporal side of the mission.

In a country where five pennyworth of rice was sufficient ' to feed a hundred men a day '[15] and a cow was worth a crown, it would not be difficult to maintain a seminary, for the children would be more comfortable in it than in their own homes. For a bed, the ground; for food, rice and roots, and for clothing, a simple ' tunic made of drugget.'[16] In order to render the spiritual means of the apostolate more efficacious with the chiefs and *ombiases*, he thought it would be well to satisfy their greed by attractive presents such as olive-shaped pieces of crystal ; silks, silver cups or clasps, grains of gold, artificial pearls and pieces of coral. In Father Nacquart's eyes the Missionaries who would be most likely to succeed were not men conspicuous for their knowledge but men of solid virtue. He did not desire them to be either too young or too robust, but fairly strong and healthy, and from thirty-five to fifty years old, because foreigners of that age were better able to endure the heat of the climate. In his own life-time, only one element of this big scheme was begun : the building of a church at Fort Dauphin, of which he laid the foundation on February 2, 1650.

[15] *Ibid.*, p. 285.   [16] *Ibid.*, p. 589.

If the zealous Missionary had such rosy dreams for the future of Madagascar, the present was not always so attractive, for here, as elsewhere, there were crosses to be met with as well as consolations.

His chief difficulties arose from the conduct of a large number of the colonists. As he was obliged to live amongst them in Fort Dauphin (for, despite his repeated requests, the Governor refused to allow him a separate dwelling), he was forced to witness their disorderly conduct and felt entirely out of place in their society. He was disgusted by their vicious lives; their lewd conversations offended his ears, and hence he wished for another priest to take his place and to be left free to work for the natives. ' It would be very pleasant,' he wrote to Saint Vincent,[17] ' not to have to look after such people with whom, as a rule, one only wastes one's time, and who reward one only with ingratitude and calumny, just as lunatics behave towards the physician who tries to cure them, and grow angry with him instead of taking his remedies.'

De Flacourt closed his eyes to all this, and made no attempt to punish the guilty. He may have thought that such offences were of a private and not a public character, and that he was not called on to interfere, or he may have been unwilling to render the lives of his subordinates less unbearable, for their lives were hard enough as it was, or he may have simply thought it would be useless to interfere. However that may be, such toleration seemed to Father Nacquart to be simple indifferentism, and he was revolted by it. It was not the only point on which the Missionary and the Governor did not see eye to eye. ' The generous, enthusiastic and unselfish character of the young priest,' as Malotet well remarks,[18] ' did not harmonise with the shrewd, thoughtful, practical character of this elderly Governor. Their ideas, plans and interests were as opposed as their natures. Territorial conquest, military glory, honour, dignities, were what de Flacourt dreamed of whilst Father Nacquart's sole aim was the conquest of souls and their eternal happiness. One aspired to play the rôle of conqueror and had nothing so much at heart as to please

[17] *St. Vincent de Paul*, Vól III, p. 587. [18] *Etienne de Flacourt*, p. 127.

the King and Court; the other desired to walk in the footsteps of Saint Francis Xavier, and his chief thought was to satisfy his Superior and to please God. . . . Flacourt was guided by his desire to serve the material interests of the Company, Nacquart by the spirit of abnegation and charity; one wished to carry on the work of an administrator, the other that of a Missionary; the first represented worldly interests and temporal power; the other, religious interests and spiritual power.'

The Governor was a business man, and had been sent to Madagascar by the East India Company to look after its interests. This preoccupation dominated every other consideration and led straight to avarice; despite the guarantees given to Father Nacquart, he refused to provide him with the necessary food, clothing and lodging, and he also refused to provide his sick countrymen with the remedies they needed. They were forced to work on Sundays, and any act of generosity, such as giving a present to a native, was frowned on and severely blamed. Father Nacquart obviously needed an interpreter to instruct the negroes and to learn the language himself; for a long time the Governor refused, from motives of economy, to let him have one. If he insisted, he was made to feel he was not necessary in Madagascar and that if he left, there were plenty of other religious prepared to take his place. In addition, the Governor had as little respect for the law of abstinence as he had for the Sabbath rest.

A trifle was enough to annoy de Flacourt. The bell for Mass, for instance, was rung too early; it was at the prescribed time in fact, but as the Governor had not finished dressing, the entire congregation had to wait. Again, the Missionary was given a piece of crystal by a negro, which he intended to fashion into a little cross for the Church; he was reprimanded for trafficking with the natives. If he intervened in the mildest way to turn the conversation from lewd or slanderous topics, he was looked on as a kill-joy. But the chief source of Father Nacquart's grief was the attitude adopted towards the natives. The Governor preferred military methods to a policy of peaceful penetration. From time to time, armed bands left Fort Dauphin, advanced far into the interior, massacred the inhabitants and seized their cattle, which they led back in triumph to the Fort to feed the colonists. De Flacourt, by a strange aberration, persuaded himself that by such a bloodthirsty expeditions he was even serving the interests of religion. Father Nacquart, trained in the school of Jesus Christ ' who did not command His apostles to take up arms to establish the Christian religion, but to be as lambs amongst wolves ' rightly declared that such conduct was that of brigands and not of civilised men.

These disagreements brought about a coolness in the relations of the priest and the Governor. Matters were in this state when de Flacourt announced his intention of returning to France on the *Saint Lawrence* which was due to sail on February 19, 1650. As soon as Father Nacquart heard this, he took up his pen to let Saint Vincent have his views on the situation, and to put the Saint on his guard against what the Governor might have to say. The latter, after making all preparations to sail, changed his mind, and it now occurred to Father Nacquart that it would be just as well to go home himself. The presence of de Bellebarbe in Fort Dauphin (he had returned from St. Mary's Island) enabled him to leave without causing too great an inconvenience. De Flacourt's consent was necessary, and Father Nacquart called to see him and spoke out quite openly. ' I must be at liberty to say what I think quite freely to my Superior. . . . There are only two things to be done and you can decide which is the better : either I go to France to say what I think, before God, is necessary for His glory in this country, or write with an assurance that I am not suspected ; or on the other hand, if I remain here, I must be provided with essentials . . . for instance, as I need to have confidence in you, you should have confidence in me ; you should help me and I will help you ; in short, you should give me permission to withdraw a hundred yards from the Fort, away from all its turmoil, with an interpreter, so that I can live by myself and carry on the duties of a poor Missionary, such as I am,'[19] De Flacourt advised him to sail, and Father Nacquart bade good-bye to

[19] *Saint Vincent de Paul*, Vol. III, p. 605.

THE MADAGASCAR MISSION

the colonists at Vespers on Septuagesima Sunday, and on the following day his luggage was taken on board. Both the French and the natives were deeply affected when they heard he was about to leave, and from all sides he was urged to remain. The negroes threw themselves on their knees and begged him with tears and tender reproaches not to leave them. ' What,' they cried, ' you are going away ! Who then will make us pray to God ? ' He could not but be touched, and did in fact change his mind. He wrote to Saint Vincent :[20] ' This put shackles on the feet of my will, which remained a prisoner to the Will of God made known to me by the voice of the people ! ' He remained, and de Bellebarbe sailed to France.

This incident was productive of good ; de Flacourt realised that he must be more amenable ; he granted the interpreter which the priest had demanded, and promised to build a prebystery close to the Church.

The proof of affectionate attachment which Father Nacquart had just received from his flock, redoubled his zeal for the salvation of their souls. Lent was about to begin and he spent the whole of it at Fort Dauphin preparing the entire population, black and white, for their Easter Communion. He preached three times a week. The native servants of the French, almost all young boys or girls to the number of twenty, had special instructions which they never failed to attend, and they were also taught their catechism and prayers. He was satisfied with their progress and baptised six or seven at the end of Lent. A few days after Easter, two adults aged eighteen were also received into the Church. On April 25, the Feast of Saint Mark, three of the newly baptised were married to three young Christian women. On the second Sunday after Easter, Father Nacquart read the following passage from the Gospel at Mass : ' And other sheep I have that are not of this fold : them also must I bring,' and like the Good Shepherd, he prepared to go in search of them. He evangelised the country round Fort Dauphin for a radius of ten leagues, and this new journey enabled him to see that

[20] *Ibid.*, p. 606.

everywhere the ground was ready for the good seed. His sole regret was his inability to baptise all who asked for the sacrament. From May 9, to the 19, he baptised nine little children and an old man who was dying.

He was very much fatigued by this journey through mountainous country and on his return home he took to his bed, suffering from a violent attack of fever. The feast of the Ascension fell that year on May 26, and in order that the faithful might not be deprived of all religious service on that great feast, he rose to say Mass and preached on the words of our divine Saviour : ' I command you to love one another.' This display of energy was unwise ; he went back to his bed utterly exhausted by his effort. Death was at hand and he beheld its approach without fear, but not without anxiety as to what would happen after his death to the native Christians who had given such great hopes ; and then there were the colonists who, deprived of divine worship, sermons and the sacraments, were in danger of falling into religious indifference and immorality. In the evening, he summoned a Frenchman who seemed by his piety to be best qualified to fill the place of a priest towards his fellow countrymen, gave him a copy of Bonnefon's *Charitable Christian*, and said : ' This is an excellent book to prepare the sick for death ; use it until the Missionaries arrive.'

All the colonists came to see him on his death-bed. He exhorted them to fulfil their duties as men and Christians, urged them especially to help the sick and to love one another, and then added : ' Should circumstances ever compel you to abandon the Fort, do not forget to bring away the Tabernacle, or at least the holy ciborium.' He asked de Flacourt as a special favour to allow his body to be buried in the ground on which the future Church was to be built, and that the coffin containing the remains of Father Gondrée should be placed in the same grave. When he had made these arrangements, he lost consciousness and the death-agony began. His noble soul took flight to Heaven on Sunday, May 29, whilst everyone in Fort Dauphin was sadly meditating on the loss they had suffered. His body, clad in the sacred vestments, was exposed in the Church, and on the following day, after chanting the Office

THE MADAGASCAR MISSION

for the dead, the French bore him to the spot he had selected for his grave.

Father Nacquart was deeply and sincerely regretted, and de Flacourt, who had not always seen eye to eye with him, felt his loss more than any. 'He was,' he wrote,[21] 'a very intelligent man, zealous for religion, and he led an exemplary life; he had acquired sufficient knowledge of the language to instruct the inhabitants of the country, and took the greatest pains to be constantly engaged in that work. He was deeply regretted by us all; and the more so, seeing that many French people who endeavoured to imitate him and to lead a good life, have since, for want of instruction, allowed themselves to fall into the most common sin in this country, that of the flesh.' One of the native chiefs said, more briefly and imaginatively: 'the spirit of the French has departed; their light is extinguished.' Words of praise, indeed, but well deserved!

Father Nacquart died on the eve of grave events. On June 11, 1650, Fanshere was in holiday mood; the children were being circumcised and the ceremony was attended with the customary rejoicings; twelve Frenchmen from Fort Dauphin, to show that they shared in the general rejoicings, resolved to fire a volley with their muskets. A piece of lighted wadding fell on a hut which took fire; at once there were loud cries for help, and although those who were shouting had no other idea than that of summoning help to extinguish the flames, others imagined they were being attacked. Four thousand natives ran up to massacre the foreigners, but luckily Andrian Ramaka was able to interpose in time; not indeed that he was animated by any friendly feelings for the French, but prudence dictated this act of kindness.

At the very time when he thus saved twelve Frenchmen from death, he was maturing a plan to annihilate all the colonists; he was making arrangements with the other chiefs, hatching plot after plot and skilfully fostering the hatred of the natives for the colonists. It became more and more dangerous for the French to stray from Fort Dauphin.

[21] *Histoire de la grande isle Madagascar*, Troyes, 1660, quarto, p. 275.

One of them was assassinated. Lieutenant Laroche, at the head of twelve fellow countrymen, was attacked, near Ivoule, by six thousand Malagasies armed with spears and muskets. The little band fell back on the Fort, closely pursued by the enemy, who killed one of the party and wounded another. When the Malagasies reached the Fort they began to make preparations for an assault, but were dispersed by a discharge of artillery.

Unfortunately, all the French were not protected by the cannons of Fort Dauphin. Lieutenant Leroy had led a band of nineteen colonists to look for crystals; he was warned by a messenger of the dangers he was incurring and took with him an escort of black troops, who betrayed him, treacherously massacring the Lieutenant and all his companions at Maropia.

Andrian Ramaka did not despair of capturing the Fort. He gathered an army of ten thousand men and approached it on January 22, 1651. As before, a salvo of artillery was enough to damp the warlike ardour of his troops who fled in dismay. However, this did not discourage the chief for, calling one of his followers, he said : ' Do you wish to be of service to your King ? ' ' Certainly,' said the man. ' Very well, you know several of the servants of the French ; find out the one in whom you can put the greatest trust ; tell him to set fire to the huts in Fort Dauphin on such a day, at such a hour, and promise him a rich reward from me. Whilst the foreigners are engaged in putting out the fire, I will surprise them with an army and massacre them all, Go, and fear nothing.'

It was not a bad stratagem, but like all other military operations, success depended on the discretion of those to whom the secret had been entrusted. The servant, instead of lending himself to Ramaka's plan, revealed his designs. De Flacourt seized the King's emissary, cut off his head and put it on a pole. Ever since the Governor had begun to fight against the native chiefs, he was finding greater and greater difficulty in procuring supplies. In order to escape from this embarrassment, he captured Ramaka on May 12, 1651, and before setting him at liberty, demanded a ransom of a hundred head of cattle and a hundred baskets of rubber.

As the conspiracies continued, de Flacourt resolved on a policy of 'Blood and Fire.' He sent the French out to burn, pillage and massacre the inhabitants without distinction of age or sex. Ramaka and one of his sons were murdered, and in a short time, within a wide range of territory, the villages were nothing but deserts, devoid of inhabitants, flocks and herds. From all directions the chiefs began to pour in to Fort Dauphin to surrender, which was just what the Governor had hoped for; he imposed harsh conditions on the vanquished and made them take an oath no longer to live as enemies, but as allies.

Whilst de Flacourt, by violent methods, was putting an end to the difficulties that were multiplying in his path, what was happening in Paris?

As we have already seen, when Fathers Nacquart and Gondrée left for Madagascar, no one in the capital was aware that Propaganda had already selected the Discalced Carmelite Fathers for that mission, and had granted them the faculties given by the Nuncio to the Priests of Saint Vincent de Paul. The Sacred Congregation could not reasonably withdraw the powers granted to the Carmelites, and requested that every facility should be afforded for sending the Fathers to Madagascar. In case they renounced their rights—but in that case only—it would re-erect the Mission, and place it under the authority of Father Nacquart as Prefect Apostolic. As it might take time before the matter was definitely settled, the two Missionaries were granted power to administer the Sacraments. The withdrawal of the Carmelite claims put an end to this ambiguous situation.

After the departure of his confrères, Saint Vincent remained for two years and a half without news from Madagascar. In October, 1650, the *Saint Lawrence* brought him simultaneously five letters from Father Nacquart, one of which brought tears to his eyes; that announcing the death of Father Gondrée. Another gave him full particulars of the country, its climate, population, resources and customs, the labours of the Missionaries, the obstacles encountered and the results already obtained. The Holy Founder had copies made and distributed, especially amongst his own houses. He would gladly have yielded to requests to have the letters published if he had not feared he might be sinning against humility by divulging the blessings God had bestowed on his Congregation.

Father Nacquart was now alone and asking for help, so the Saint at once set to work to prepare collaborators. He intended to send three or four priests and two lay-brothers, but as at the last moment some of those on whom he counted might be unable to go, he applied to Rome for the faculties of missionary apostolic for seven of the priests: Fathers Duport, Dufour, Villain, Deschamps, Mousnier, Maillard and David. One of the brothers he had in his eye—René Forest—was already acquainted with the country, for he had lived in Madagascar as a colonist before joining the Congregation. Father Dufour had asked as a favour to be employed in the conversion of infidels, and Saint Vincent was all the more willing to grant the request inasmuch as he hoped in this way to divert this priest's mind from the thought of joining the Carthusians. When writing to tell Father Dufour that his name was on the list, the Saint said: 'There are many Carthusians who would wish to go and who could go, or at least we may say that it would be desirable they should leave their cloister for such an important work.'[22]

The departure of the vessel, first fixed for January, 1651, then for the Spring, and later for the Autumn of the following year, was finally put off indefinitely. These successive adjournments perturbed Propaganda and it was suggested to Saint Vincent from Rome that he should have his priests sent on Portuguese or Dutch vessels. His reply to the second letter addressed to him by the Cardinal Prefect on this matter points out the drawbacks of such a proposal (August 15, 1652). 'I have, my Lord, just seen one of the shipping agents to Madagascar. I tell Your Eminence with grief that he is doubtful as to whether they will sail in September, as arranged. So far, they have not a ship, and they are in no hurry to fit out one. The cause of this, My Lord, is the present state of France which has forced some of the shareholders to leave Paris, and made the others chary about

[22] *Saint Vincent de Paul*, Vol. IV, p. 104.

incurring essential expenses. I am deeply afflicted at this delay, because for the last three years we have had one of our priests alone on that island and have had no tidings whatever of him on account of commerce being interrupted. I have made enquiries as to whether we could send them by any other route, and have been told that the Portuguese have now no communication with the island. As for the Dutch, they hold the Island of Saint Maurice, which is only a hundred leagues distant, and they sometimes go to Madagascar, but only to that end of the island where there are no French, who live at the other extremity, some hundred and twenty leagues away, and there are great difficulties to be encountered in traversing the island. But the greatest difficulty, My Lord, would be to travel there on Dutch vessels, because the Dutch are doing their utmost to make themselves masters of the Indies and to drive out the French; and it is even feared that they are paying a pension to one of these gentlemen to induce them to abandon the enterprise, so that, instead of helping us to go there, they would rather hinder us. Nevertheless, My Lord, I shall see if we cannot find some means of sending labourers to this nascent Church, and if I do, I shall inform the Sacred Congregation.'[23]

In March, 1653, Saint Vincent believed for a moment that the long expected opportunity had arrived, but he was again disappointed and had to wait another year. The Missionaries finally selected were Brother Forest, Toussaint Bourdaise and Francis Mousnier, for whom he requested the faculties of a Prefect Apostolic, should Father Nacquart be dead. The two travellers left Saint Nazaire, on March 8, 1654, on two vessels, one of them commanded by De Pronis, and arrived in Madagascar after a voyage of five months.

When the new Missionaries set foot on the island, the Christians there had been living without a priest for more than four years. As a result, there was not only great indifference for all religious practices, but also considerable moral laxity. Father Nacquart's little Christian community had sadly degenerated, and his successors had much to do to regain lost ground.

[23] *Ibid.*, p. 454.

Before they could bring the colonists to frequent the Sacraments, they had to induce them to lead better lives. As persuasion produced no effect, the two priests, with the Governor's approval, went into the huts of Fort Dauphin, armed with whips, and drove out the prostitutes. They succeeded in regularising several unlawful unions, after first baptising the wives. Little by little, the Missionaries brought the lost sheep back to the fold. Father Bourdaise, a year and a half after his arrival, noted with satisfaction that only four of the French had remained deaf to his appeal, and that three out of the five heretics in the colony had been converted. The Fathers were even more successful with the natives whose good dispositions, already observed by Father Nacquart, had not altered. Father Bourdaise succeeded in converting, on their death beds, three of the chiefs who lived near Fort Dauphin ; ' the most powerful lords in the whole country,' he writes, ' most feared by all, and most attached to their superstitions.' They died after Baptism, and were buried in the Christian cemetery, amid a great concourse of negroes who had come ' to see those whom they had once looked on as gods laid in the earth.' [24] An old man, long regarded as a wizard, joined the other negroes who were being taught their catechism and prayers ; he promised, when better instructed, to go himself and teach the natives in their villages.

Father Bourdaise did not neglect human means to attract and convert the natives, such as little presents or medicines for the sick. Thanks to some medical knowledge and a small medicine chest furnished with supplies brought from France, he worked some cures which prepared the way for the action of divine grace on their souls. For instance, a negro had been unable to sleep for three months ; his leg was enormously swollen, and when Father Bourdaise saw it, he diagnosed an abscess. He made an incision with a lancet at the right spot and drained off a large amount of pus. In three days the man was quite well. Again, every year for three months an epidemic of dysentery, due to bad food, caused frightful ravages ; but with the help of a little theriac, Father Bourdaise put more than a hundred patients

[24] *Saint Vincent de Paul*, Vol. VI, p. 231.

on their feet. On another occasion, he was called to see a native woman who had been frightfully wounded by fifteen thrusts of an assagai, and by means of ointments he succeeded in healing the wounds. The poor woman did not know how to show her gratitude. She brought him her three children. 'Baptise them,' she said, 'I beg you; they are your slaves; I give them to you.' The Missionary was satisfied with making them servants of God by instructing and baptising them, for such were his methods of profiting by the good dispositions of those whom he healed.

The hut purchased to receive and instruct neophytes was never empty throughout the whole day. Whilst the Missionary was addressing them, ' their spirit soared aloft' to use their own expression to indicate that their thoughts had risen above earthly things. When the priest withdrew to the Church to read his Breviary, the little children would not leave him in peace; they followed him in, knelt down in front of him and waited until he made them recite the *Our Father*; after which they ran out, quite happy to be able to tell everybody that they had been praying to God. In the case of many, this was not simple curiosity or mere caprice, for they had already an exalted idea of prayer. A child said to one of his little comrades, not so devout as himself: 'You are no good; you don't pray to God; He is the master of the whole world.' And a grown girl, pained at seeing one of her companions distracted during prayer, reproached her severely: 'You have a wicked heart; it does not speak with your tongue; don't laugh, it is wicked.'

The Missionaries were soon so overwhelmed with the number of neophytes that it became impossible to instruct them individually; it was found necessary to form them into groups and to give lessons to classes. The village of Tholanghare, in which Fort Dauphin was situated, set the example. All the women and most of the men asked to be baptised and married. 'Send us two or three priests,' Father Bourdaise wrote to France, ' and in a year almost the whole of Antanosy, although a large district, will be baptised.'[25] When the bell rang for evening prayer it was a pleasant sight to see all those poor people leave everything

[25] *Ibid.*, Vol. V, p. 520.

aside and go to Church where their devout attitude and recollection edified all. When their husbands were away fighting, the native women were accustomed to dance every day, to obtain, as they said, victory. One evening, when the bell rang for prayers, they hastened to Church from the dance, insufficiently clad, but a reprimand from Father Bourdaise taught them a lesson and they never repeated the offence.

There was one thing in particular that greatly impressed the natives, and this was that the house of God was open to all; all were there treated on an equal footing; all recited the same prayers and received the same blessed bread. Even the infidels were allowed to attend Church during divine service, and the Missionary invited them to come in. On one occasion, Father Bourdaise saw a sick man who was listening at a distance and went up to him. 'Oh! I just listen,' said the poor fellow when the priest questioned him, 'I have smallpox; I am ashamed to enter God's house.' 'God,' said the priest, 'only looks at the soul; He is not like men who pay attention to bodily beauty.' 'Then,' said the man, 'teach me how to pray.' Another time, a cripple who could only drag himself along on his hands, was waiting at the Church door. 'I am poor and a cripple,' he said, 'I cannot enter the house of God.' 'God's house,' said Father Bourdaise, 'is for everybody. In Heaven, the poor will be the greatest, if they have been baptised and pray devoutly to God. There will be no more crippled limbs there. Their bodies will be beautifully formed and will shine like the sun.' 'That's fine,' said the poor man, 'that's fine,' and ever afterwards he was faithful to his prayers; in fact, he learned the whole of them in a month.

All, however, did not show the same perseverance. Some did not return after seven or eight visits. Father Bourdaise, as a rule, required two or three months' attendance at Catechism from those who asked to be baptised. He shortened the period for old men and lengthened it for those who did not learn quickly enough or did not show sufficiently good dispositions.

There can be no real love of prayer without the frequentation of the Sacraments. The faithful, docile to the instructions of their pastors, often approached them to seek the graces they needed, either to be made more pure or more strong. Little children, before reaching the age for Holy Communion, often came to be absolved from their sins. At every Feast, even those of the second class such as the Purification, the Missionaries had the happiness of seeing a fairly large number approach the Holy Table. Communions were more frequent whenever a scourge, such as war, drought, or a plague of locusts, fell upon the island. Whilst the infidels were seeking to calm the rage of the devil by sacrifices, the converts implored the mercy of God by approaching the Sacraments ; and among the latter, many came on foot from places far distant to satisfy their devotion.

In one of the friendly conversations which Father Bourdaise often had with his negroes, he had the curiosity to ask what were their thoughts after Communion. A woman answered and said that she was delighted and felt her heart warm. Others told him of the words they interiorly addressed to God : ' O, my God, I believe Thou art here, because Thou hast said it,' or, ' I love Thee with all my heart,' or, ' I promise never more to offend Thee.' Such was their desire for the Eucharist that the delays imposed before receiving their first Holy Communion drew tears of regret from their eyes. A woman, recently baptised, was being prepared for the Sacrament ; Pentecost was at hand and she hoped to kneel at the Holy Table on that Feast. Unfortunately, she was not sufficiently instructed, but still she asked the Father's permission to go to Holy Communion. ' You have not been sufficiently instructed,' was the reply, ' you will go later on.' ' Then teach me what I do not know, so that I may not have to wait,' said the woman. ' Oh ! First Holy Communion is only given on the great festivals. So be patient and wait until your religious instruction is finished,' Father Bourdaise replied. ' I will do so,' she said, ' since you wish it.' She waited, and on the day appointed, she had the double satisfaction of receiving Holy Communion herself and of seeing her husband, a Frenchman, at her side.

Some of the recently converted native women gave

magnificent examples of Christian virtue. One of them was married to a drunken, debauched and brutal colonist who, in his mad fits of rage, used to drag her by the hair of the head along the ground and kick her mercilessly. Her sole reply to his blows was meekness and tears. The man fell ill and had to depend on his wife's care and attention; she did not let him want for anything; showed him the greatest affection and devotedness, and not only succeeded in curing his body but won his affections.

The Missionaries sought to influence the chiefs the better to reach the natives. Andrian Mananghe, Chief of Mandrare, 'a most intelligent, wise, discreet and courteous' man, who had allowed his four children to be baptised, seemed to be one on whom they could most easily rely. On a visit to Fort Dauphin, he called on Father Bourdaise. 'May my children,' he asked, 'have several wives?' 'No,' was the reply, 'God forbids it; He wishes that the woman should be baptised and that the marriage should be celebrated in Church in presence of a priest. If the woman dies, then He allows her husband to take another wife, but never two at the same time.' 'That is quite right, quite right,' said Andrian, who had brought his children, except the eldest, with him. He looked at the third. 'Did you understand? You want two wives; you can have only one; are you not baptised?' The second son improved the occasion, by adding: 'You have a perverted heart. No longer desire what is evil.' Mananghe wished to be present at Mass. 'It is beautiful,' was his comment, 'beautiful; it is a good thing to pray to God.' He prayed himself and withdrew, making such excellent remarks that Father Bourdaise hoped to be soon able to enrol him amongst the Catholics of the island.

Andrian Machicore, who had been kept for some time in Fort Dauphin as a hostage, lived in a hut with his wife and children, one of whom was baptised, and his slaves. The Missionary had frequent conversations with the chief, and one day invited himself and his family to visit the Church. When they saw the vestments and sacred vessels they uttered loud cries of admiration, but when they stretched out their hands to touch the latter Father Bourdaise

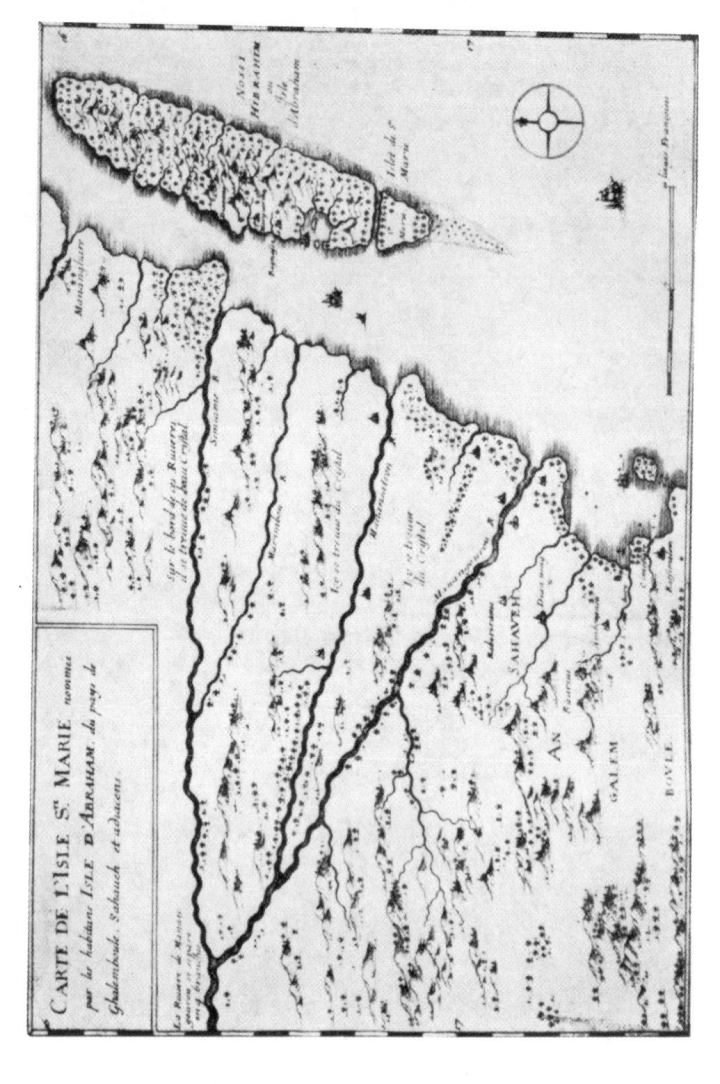

ISLAND OF SAINT MARY
(From a Map by de Flacourt)

restrained them, saying : ' Only priests may touch what is sacred.' To show them that this was not because the vessels were made of gold, he handed them a silver gilt cup which they took in turn, placed on their heads, kissing it and crying out ' It is grand ; it is grand.' ' No,' said the priest, ' it is very little ; nothing but yellow clay. This cup has no mind, it cannot move of itself. We must not seek after either gold or silver, but think only of Him Who made them, God, our sole Master. If we honour these vessels (pointing to the chalices) it is not because they are made of gold, but because they are consecrated to God.' The chief's wife nodded approval. She came for eight days with her children and slaves to pray to God, and her example brought Machicore himself. As he could only walk with difficulty, Father Bourdaise went and taught him his prayers in the hut. He was much moved at the sight of the King kneeling in the midst of his family in the devout attitude of a Christian deeply penetrated with the truths of Faith, and thought the moment had come to speak to him of Baptism. ' I am too old,' said the chief, ' but if you like, baptise my wife and children.' The Missionary had not time, for shortly afterwards, Machicore was allowed to return to his village.

Father Bourdaise was very proud of his Church, his pictures, vestments and laces, and gladly showed them to the natives who came to Fort Dauphin and were, of course, filled with admiration. Hence one may well imagine his grief and surprise when he heard, on February 20, 1655, at nine o'clock in the morning, that a fire, after burning down a hut, had reached the Church and threatened to reduce it to ashes. He ran as fast as he could, and, as the entrance door was in flames, jumped through a window to save what was most precious. Chests, vestments, books, chandeliers, were quickly thrown out, and, as the fire had by now become dangerous, he took the Tabernacle and handed it to a Frenchman who bore it away. Two or three beautiful pictures hung in the Church, but it was too late to save them. Father Bourdaise seized the antependium and altar linen and dashed through a window. He was caught by a nail, made a struggle, tore his clothes, and just succeeded in escaping as the flames reached him. Favoured by the wind, the fire began to spread; it reached the Governor's house and the stores of provisions; next came the powder magazine, and, with a roar like thunder, the barrels exploded. There was a general *sauve-qui-peut*, and in less than half an hour, the Fort with its forty or fifty inhabitants was nothing but a blazing furnace.

It did not take long to rebuild the Fort and huts. Father Bourdaise had purchased a hut, just outside the Fort, in which he used to instruct his negroes, and this had remained intact; he now moved the Tabernacle, which had been placed on the ground in a courtyard, into the hut, which he enlarged and decorated, thus providing a new home for the Blessed Sacrament. There was a house in front of the hut which obscured the view of the Church and partially blocked the entrance to it; he went to the old woman who lived there, and said to her: 'Your house is out of place in front of the house of God.' 'Quite true,' said she, 'Zanahary (God) is a great Master,' and without more ado, she took up her residence farther away.

Father Mousnier did not see the disaster that had befallen the Church for he had left Fort Dauphin the preceding Monday to accompany forty French and two hundred negroes on an expedition to the Imaphalles, twenty-five days' march from the Fort. Father Bourdaise had not seen him depart without anxiety, but it was all in vain that he pointed out to his confrère the great distance, the difficulties of obtaining supplies, and the rough nature of the road which had to be traversed bare-footed. The thought that the French were going into danger, and that many of them had not been to confession for six years, outweighed, in Father Mousnier's mind, the objections of his colleague. The expedition was expected back in Fort Dauphin at the end of April, but none of its members had appeared early in May. The little colony now began to grow uneasy, and soon became nervous and anxious. On May 23, at three o'clock in the afternoon, a Frenchman at last appeared in the distance. The news spread from mouth to mouth and the crowd that hastened to meet him listened in gloomy silence to his story. The French had secured very few cattle; they had lost several negroes in fights with the natives; a

Frenchman had died of sickness; twelve others, including Father Mousnier, were lying ill in a village and unable to continue their journey. Father Bourdaise was filled with consternation when he heard Father Mousnier's name mentioned; he felt that his place was beside his confrère, made hasty preparations for the journey, and on the next day, May 24, at nine o'clock in the morning, he was standing by his bedside. Father Mousnier was unconscious and his death agony had already lasted over two days; at three o'clock in the afternoon, he received the last Sacraments and passed without a struggle from this life to a better one. He was a Missionary of tried virtue, devout as an angel, zealous as an apostle, austere as an anchorite and so mortified that on fast days he would eat nothing but a little rice boiled in water and a scrap of cheese. He believed that zeal was not enough to win souls to God, and sought by the use of the discipline, vigils and acts of mortification of all kinds, to supplement the sufferings he endured from without.

Some days later, de Pronis fell ill of nephritis. He had been placed at the head of the little colony by de Flacourt, who left the island on February 12, 1655, to return to France; ripened by age and profiting by experience, he had shown much more wisdom, toleration and prudence than during his first period of administration as Governor. He had been on excellent and even affectionate terms with Father Bourdaise, and, were it not that the difference of religion had produced a bad effect on the natives and slackened the movement towards conversion, the Missionaries would have congratulated themselves on being under his authority. His death followed closely on that of Father Mousnier. A few hours before he expired, in the middle of the night, he called for Father Bourdaise to dictate to the priest his final arrangements and to entrust him with the care of his little daughter. The Missionary hoped that at this supreme moment the Governor would abjure his Calvinism and die a Catholic, but he was disappointed. 'Let us leave all that alone,' said the dying man, 'it is too late.' And those were his last words.

Father Bourdaise, in his grief and isolation, often thought of France. 'When,' he asked himself, 'will some zealous priests come here to labour for the salvation of souls, who are being lost in such great numbers ? ' Indeed, he was not forgotten, for Vincent de Paul was well aware of his needs and was preparing to send him help.

If the assistance for which Father Bourdaise had waited so long was slow in coming, this was certainly not the fault of the holy Founder of the Mission. The East India Company was disinclined to proceed with an enterprise that was a greater source of expense than of profit. Internal divisions and disputes, the death of some of its most influential members, the resignation of a number of others, and universal discouragement, explained the Company's inertia. The Duke de la Meilleraye resolved to act alone ; he fitted out four vessels : *The Duchess, The Marchioness, The Armand* and *The Lady Admiral*, and placed La Roche Saint André in command. Saint Vincent was told a little later that there was room for two of his priests, who should be in Nantes on September 4. He selected Fathers Feydin, Gicquel, Dufour, Prévost and de Belleville, for he hoped that at least two of the five would be able to reach that port in time. The three last named priests were finally chosen, and Saint Vincent wrote to them on the eve of their departure : ' You know your health will be in danger in this foreign climate until you have grown a little accustomed to it, and hence I warn you not to expose yourselves in the sun, and to do nothing for some time except to apply yourselves to the study of the language. Just act as if you were children and were being taught to talk, and in this spirit, allow yourselves to be ruled by Father Mousnier, who will take the place of a father in your regard, or in his absence, by Father Bourdaise. I beg you to regard them in Our Lord and Our Lord in them ; and even if you are deprived of them both, you will not want for God's special assistance, for He has said that even if the mother should forget the child of her womb, He Himself will take care of it. How much more, then, are you bound to believe that He will be good to you, my dear Fathers, and that He will take pleasure in training defending and providing for you, who have abandoned yourselves into His hands and have placed all your confidence in His protection and power ! So then, Gentlemen, love one another and you will help one another ; bear with one another and be united amongst yourselves in the spirit of God, Who has chosen you for this great design and will preserve you for its accomplishment.'

The three Missionaries, fortified by these wise words of advice, embarked at La Rochelle on October 29, 1655. Amongst the passengers were du Rivau, who was to take over the government of the colony, Father Couderon, a Dieppe priest, ' one of the most learned men in France in both the theory and the art of navigation,' and another ecclesiastic. A chaplain was placed on board each of the vessels to facilitate the practice of religious worship for both sailors and passengers. Father Prévost went on board *The Duchess*, Father de Belleville on *The Armand*, and Father Dufour on *The Lady Admiral*. An accident cast a shadow over the travellers quite early in the voyage ; Father Couderon fell from the bow of the vessel into the sea and was drowned. Father de Belleville next fell ill ; he had been suffering from fever ever since the ship left Nantes, and he died in the harbour of Sierra Leone on January 18, 1656, after receiving the consolations of religion. He was a great loss to the Madagascar Mission, for his zeal, piety and gentleness had aroused great hopes for the future. The ascendancy he had acquired over the sailors was shown on two occasions : he induced them to make restitution of certain objects stolen from a small English ship, and succeeded, by asking the admiral to replace an unpopular lieutenant, in re-establishing peace amongst the crew, which had split up into two factions. ' I have travelled,' said the ship's third officer, ' in Italy, Spain and France, but I have never met such a gracious man ; I have never seen a man who caused saintly courtesy to be so highly esteemed or who practised it better.'

On reaching the Cape of Good Hope, the vessels separated. *The Armand* sailed for Fort Dauphin, whilst *The Duchess*, *Marchioness* and *Lady Admiral* made for Saint Mary's Island, where a new colony was to be established. Father Dufour left his own ship for *The Armand*, and on Passion Sunday began a Mission to prepare his fellow-travellers to fulfil their religious duties. His sermons attracted to the confessional sinners who had been absent from it for ten or even sixteen years. On Good Friday, the idea occurred to him to establish a Confraternity for the salvation of the negroes of Madagascar. He drew up a set of rules, intending to propagate the association in France and even 'throughout Christendom,' and to obtain from Rome, together with canonical approbation, certain religious favours, such as Indulgences. In the meantime, there was a certain amount of uneasiness on board. It is not a long journey from the Cape of Good Hope to the south coast of Madagascar, and yet, after sailing a month and a half, land was not yet in sight. Fresh water began to grow scarce; the number of sick kept on increasing, and there were already eighty lying ill. All were uneasy; only Father Dufour was confident. 'If you promise to do what I ask you,' he said, 'you will see land in fifteen days.' All said: 'We promise.' 'Swear it,' he said, and all cried aloud: 'We swear.' 'Very well, then,' said the priest, 'make a vow to go to confession and to Holy Communion within the fortnight.' The vow was made and kept, with only two exceptions. At dawn on the fifteenth day, Sunday, May 28, all eyes searched the horizon. No land in sight. 'Let us pray to God, my children,' said the Missionary and went off to say Mass. The morning passed away, and as far as the eye could reach, there was nothing but a limitless expanse of sea. After the midday meal, Chevalier de Sourdis and his first officer approached Father Dufour and said: 'We are lost; you promised us land to-day, and, though it is now far spent, we do not see it.' 'Gentlemen,' was the reply, 'the day is not yet done; let us go to Vespers.' He was about to intone the *Magnificat* when a cry arose: 'Land! Land!' and one may imagine with what joy they sang that hymn of praise.

On June 13, the ship entered the harbour of Fort Dauphin. Father Bourdaise shed tears of joy on seeing Father Dufour. 'He seemed to me like an angel from Heaven,' he wrote,[26] 'He was as red as a rose, but that was merely the result of the fire of his zeal, for even then he was ill; his legs were black and much swollen, and yet he concealed the fact; to see his serene countenance, one would say he was in the best of health.' The following day, the Feast of Corpus Christi,

[26] *Saint Vincent de Paul*, Vol. VI, p. 212.

THE MADAGASCAR MISSION 97

Mass was celebrated in Fort Dauphin with the ceremonies customary in France. Nothing was wanting : neither the altar of repose, nor the procession, the flower-strewn routes, the altar boys, delighted to swing a censer or scatter blossoms before the priest, nor the congregation carrying lighted tapers. The highest officials in the colony gladly accepted the places of honour assigned to them. De Sourdis held the chasuble ; Guelton, the Governor of Fort Dauphin, and his Lieutenant carried the canopy. When the procession, at which three hundred neophytes assisted, left the Fort, cannons and musket shots rang out. Nothing was better fitted to give the natives an idea of the greatness of God than manifestations such as these, and nothing could have made a better impression on Father Dufour.

The latter devoted himself at first to the sick on board *The Armand* whom he visited even before he had said Mass. He continued to practise in Madagascar the austerities he had adopted in France. He slept on a mattress spread on the ground. The sight of the hut in which the Blessed Sacrament was kept filled him with grief and he urged his confrère to build a Church. As he was a strict observer of the rubrics and rules, he reminded Father Bourdaise that a lamp should be kept constantly alight before the Blessed Sacrament, that it would be better not to allow women enter the courtyard of the house, to have their meals in silence whilst a book was read, and to avoid, as far as possible, taking meals outside the house.

Eight days had not elapsed after the arrival of *The Armand* before Father Dufour began to talk of leaving ; he was in a hurry to go to Father Prévost at St. Mary's. Father Bourdaise vainly begged him to remain, pointing out that there was enough work for two on the island, and that a stay at Fort Dauphin would be of greater advantage both for learning the language and acquiring some knowledge of his new duties. Father Dufour persisted ; he promised to return and even to bring back Father Prévost with him, as soon as possible. He could not, in fact, have kept such a promise. The climate of St. Mary's was so bad that Father Bourdaise feared for the lives of his two confrères, and accordingly he begged them both, one in person and the other by a letter (June 21, 1656), to take every precaution.[27] 'I advise you,' he wrote to Father Prévost, ' to eat no fruit, but only rice, meat and fish, and to drink wine made from honey or fresh sugar. No milk. It would be imprudent to fast; abstinence would be quite enough. I also advise you to be purged and bled every two months.' It would have been too great a penance to ask Father Dufour to take care of his health. Surrounded by the sick, he took no thought of self. He established ' a sort of hospital ' for which he begged. He ate little, so as to have more to give to others and sometimes fasted until evening. To the duties of chaplain he added those of preacher, catechist and even compiler of a Malagasy dictionary. He was not satisfied with all this; he conceived the idea of planting twelve crosses in honour of the twelve apostles, in the twelve chief villages of the island, and set off accompanied by a little negro boy. Want of food, and more especially, the habit of allowing his clothes to dry on him after they had been soaked with rain or with water from rivers which he had to cross, reduced him to such a condition, that after planting eleven crosses he was forced by an attack of fever to seek his lodging. In eighteen days the fever gained the victory over a body already worn out by austerities. (August 18.)

The news of his death fell on Father Bourdaise, as he says himself, ' like a thunder-bolt.' He was well aware of what he had lost. ' He was always regarded,' he writes,[28] ' as a real model, a mirror of innocence, and his life was a tissue of good works. I never remarked any fault in him unless the excessive virtue and mortification, which he displayed in particular at Saint Mary's, is to be regarded as such.'

In a letter announcing the death of Father Dufour, written on August 25, Father Prévost added : ' I am still very weak from tertian fever and an waiting for the sixth attack of it this evening. . . . God will do what He pleases. I beg you affectionately to pray for me and to offer up the Holy Sacrifice of the Mass, which will benefit me alive or dead.'[29] The zealous Missionary could not endure both

[27] Arch. de la Mission.
[28] *Saint Vincent de Paul*, Vol. VI, p. 219.
[29] Arch. de la Mission.

THE MADAGASCAR MISSION

the deadly climate of Saint Mary's and his labours for the large number of sick of whom he had charge; he gradually grew worse and died in September.

Father Bourdaise now had none to rely on but God alone. He never lost confidence, and if he had severe trials to face, consolations were not wanting. In September or October, 1656, a small expeditionary force set out from Fort Dauphin, under the command of Guelton and de Champmargou, looking for cattle. As the party was to pass near a village in which a Frenchman lay sick, he made up his mind to accompany it. He was charmed with the discipline and piety of the soldiers. 'Good order reigns throughout,' he wrote,[30] 'particularly in regard to prayers, which are recited morning and evening. . . . What most edified me was that when we arrived in the Antanosy district . . . several Frenchmen, about to set out on expeditions to Manamboule, did not wish to leave until they had gone to Confession and received Holy Communion. When we arrived at Imoro, a review was held; after supper, the drums beat in a large open space and when all were assembled, I offered up prayers before a crucifix. There were nearly two thousand negroes . . . around us. Next day, I erected an altar in the middle of the open space; several went to Confession . . . and I afterwards celebrated Mass in presence of the whole army. I could not, at that time, speak in public . . . I just contented myself with seeing the soldiers in their hut and said a few friendly words of encouragement to each. When this was over . . . we separated.' When he returned to Fort Dauphin he set about preparing his flock for the Feast of All Saints which was approaching, and he had the happiness of hearing the Confessions and giving Holy Communion to the majority of his native Christians.

Amongst the latter were several who aided him in his apostolic labours. A woman, eighty-nine years old, often sent pagans to him to be instructed; her eight slaves were baptised, and she gathered them round her every evening for prayer and succeeded in introducing this custom into several families. Again, a negro at Fort Dauphin,

[30] *Saint Vincent de Paul*, Vol. VI, p. 222.

dangerously ill, begged for and received Baptism. He could not be happy without Father Bourdaise and asked for him night and day; in the midst of the convulsions that racked his frame, he frequently said: ' My God, I love Thee in spite of all.' The pagans themselves manifested a piety not always to be found in those who have the Faith. Ambassadors from the Mahafalles tribe, who came to treat with the Governor, desired to pray to God, and to hear Him spoken of during their stay in the Fort. They followed Father Bourdaise's example and dipped their fingers into the holy-water stoup on entering the Church. When one of the slaves spoke during prayers, his master said to him severely: ' You talk in the house of God! Have you any intellect at all!'

On another occasion, Father Bourdaise had to go to Ikombo to give the last Sacraments to a sick Frenchman. In the evening, he gathered together all the French in the village for prayers. The negroes came around the hut to listen, and when he had finished, several asked him to begin all over again with themselves. ' You pray with the French,' they said, ' why not also pray with us?' Touched by their entreaties he went into another hut and recited aloud the usual evening prayers.

On February 19 he was happy to announce to Saint Vincent that the Catholic population of Madagascar consisted of thirty-five families, twelve negro and twenty-three French. But his rejoicings over the results obtained were equalled by the sufferings he endured from the obstacles in his way, of which the presence of a group of Huguenots in Fort Dauphin was not the least. ' If my desire to see a band of Missionaries come out here is intense,' he wrote,[31] ' my wish to see the Huguenots depart is no less so. Father Dufour converted two; God has made use of me to touch the heart of another and there is one more on the point of abjuring his heresy; but alas! there are still fifteen who severely try our patience. In the name of God . . . *capite nobis vulpes parvulas, quae demoliuntur vineas*; they are ruining all the new plants in the Lord's vineyard; they even have had the temerity to hold their prayer-meetings when the

[31] *Saint Vincent de Paul*, Vol. VI, p. 233.

French are at prayer; they discourage our poor neophytes from marrying by holding out hopes to them of greater liberty by tolerating their polygamy; they speak contemptuously of the Holy Sacrament of the Altar and thus cause *nomen Dei blasphemari inter gentes*. In the name of God make another effort, set us free from this evil leaven that is capable of corrupting the good mass which we have here; speak, cry aloud into the ears of him who you know can remedy this great evil, and do not cease until he is pleased to give orders for these people to be recalled to France.'

Father Bourdaise did not live to see his wish realised. Shortly afterwards, on returning from a visit to de Champmargou, who had fallen ill in a fort in the valley of Amboule, two or three days' journey from Fort Dauphin, he had a severe attack of dysentery and died on June 25, 1657. His death was a real disaster to the Madagascar Mission, for more than six years elapsed before any other priests arrived on the island, and during that time certain influences were at work which in great part ruined his labours. Saint Vincent de Paul did all in his power to prevent this misfortune, but his plans were constantly hampered by untoward circumstances.

Whilst waiting for an opportunity, which came only too rarely for Saint Vincent's liking, to send helpers to the Missionaries in Madagascar, he was accustomed to stir up the zeal of his disciples in private conversations and in the familiar discourses he addressed to the community at Saint-Lazare. On July 24, 1655, he said:[32] 'The Missionaries in Madagascar preach, hear confessions and catechise continually from four o'clock in the morning until ten, and then from two o'clock in the afternoon to nightfall. The rest of the day is spent in reading the Divine Office and visiting the sick. These, indeed, are labourers! These are real Missionaries! May it please God's goodness to grant us the spirit that animates them—a great and noble heart! *Magnificat anima mea Dominum*: Our souls should magnify, praise and glorify God, and if we are to do so, God should magnify our souls, give us a great breadth of mind by which we shall thoroughly grasp the grandeur, the range of God's

[32] *Ibid.*, Vol. XI, p. 203.

power and goodness, so that we may know the extent of the obligations we are under to serve and glorify Him in every possible manner ; and a greatness of will, to seize on every occasion for procuring the glory of God. If we can do nothing of ourselves, we can do all things with God. Yes, the mission can do all things, because we have within us the germ of omnipotence. We shall always have more strength than we need, especially when the occasion arises ; for when the occasion comes, we shall feel ourselves renewed.'

When Saint Vincent was exhorting his followers to glorify God by extending His Kingdom, he certainly knew that on the preceding June 26, de Flacourt had landed at Saint Nazaire with four little negroes, all of whom had been baptised except the eldest, a lad fifteen years old. One of them was the son of a powerful Malagasy chief, Andrian Theron. Three months later they were in Paris, and the Saint would hear of no other home for them than Saint-Lazare. At the ' repetition of prayer ' following their arrival, he recommended the community to give them good example and not to smile at their simple ways. ' I do not know,' he said in substance,[33] ' whom to select to instruct and guide them ; an angel would be needed, for, as far as I can judge their natural disposition, it will be very difficult for them to give themselves, as we must desire, to the practice of Christian virtues. Are they to study ? Are they to learn a trade ? God has not yet given me light on these points. The Jesuit Fathers do not admit to Holy Orders Indians born of an Indian father and mother. They do not think that such people are as a rule endowed with the qualities needed in a priest.

He trained the four little Malagasies, for several years ' in the spirit of Christianity ' hoping that they would afterwards exercise a beneficial influence on their fellow-countrymen and serve as interpreters and catechists to the Missionaries. The eldest was baptised and showed such excellent dispositions that Saint Vincent said, three years later, ' he was a marvellously good convert.'[34] The sight of these four children, thus gained to God and disposed to serve Him

---

[33] *Saint Vincent de Paul*, Vol. XI, p. 298.
[34] *Ibid.*, Vol. VII, p. 75.

subsequently with their compatriots, whilst bringing consolation to the Saint's heart, produced a certain amount of uneasiness. Three troublesome questions rose up before his mind. Had the unhealthy climate of Madagascar claimed another victim? Would the East India Company continue for any length of time to be in a position to trade? Would the Company not be annoyed if his Missionaries sailed on the Marshal de la Meilleraye's ships, and would not the latter be displeased if they went on the Company's ships?

On February 26, 1656, Saint Vincent had a visitor who came with good news: the Marshal and the Company had reached an agreement. The Company proposed to send a ship to Madagascar every year and to establish several colonies in various parts of the island; and the Marshal had advised them to apply to Saint-Lazare for whatever Missionaries were needed. Saint Vincent, not to be taken unawares, hastened to ask Rome for Missionary Apostolic powers for Fathers Herbron and Boussordec. Whilst waiting for the vessel to depart, a ship from Madagascar arrived with a letter from Father Bourdaise with the news of Father Mousnier's death (July, 1656). It was a severe blow, and his desire to come to the relief of Father Bourdaise grew all the stronger.

The East India Company, unfortunately, had not succeeded in overcoming the difficulties that were paralysing its activities. The Government grew alarmed and on August 10 the Council charged Oliver Lefêvre d'Ormesson and Michel de Marillac to establish a new Company, and the members of the old Company were asked to say if they wished to join the new one (September 19). William de Lamoignon, Stephen de Flacourt and some others agreed to join, and Cazet was appointed Director.

The Company, now constituted under the name of ' The Company of the Island of Madagascar, other islands and the coasts adjoining,' received from the King all the rights enjoyed by the old Society and also inherited its possessions: munitions, stores of food, forts and other establishments. It also incurred the same obligations: it was bound to send, at its own expense, as many Missionaries, artisans and soldiers as were needed to convert the people, teach the natives useful arts and trades, and bring them under the King's authority. Cazet, in order to get things done quickly, acknowledged the agreement made between the Duc de la Meilleraye and some members of the old Company. In virtue of this agreement, the Duke was bound to carry in his ships all merchandise entrusted to him by the Company for purposes of trade. Ignoring his engagements, the Duke gave orders to his Captain to set sail.

The Marshal had not forgotten the Missionaries, and as it had been suggested that only one was available, he cried out : ' What ! Does M. Vincent mean thus to abandon the twelve thousand souls who are waiting for priests to be converted ? ' The number was then raised to three : two priests, Fathers Boussordec and Herbron, and a lay-brother, Christopher Delaunay. The three Missionaries had been waiting for at least a month at Nantes for their ship to sail, when a tragic accident placed them in the sad necessity of abandoning the voyage. Here is Saint Vincent's account of the matter given to the Community :[35] ' On All Saints' Day, Fathers Herbron and Boussordec said Mass on board the vessel, which was in the harbour, with great difficulty on account of a strong wind which was blowing all that day. On the next, All Souls' Day, the storm grew worse, and to avoid the danger, the ship was taken down the river Nantes opposite Saint Nazaire. When they reached there, these Gentlemen had a great desire to say Mass on that day, thinking of their friends and relations who are perhaps in Purgatory, crying aloud : *Miseremini mei, saltem vos amici mei* ; whereupon, seeing the devotion they had to say Mass on that day, well, whereupon, as I have said, they made up their minds to leave the ship, and go to Saint Nazaire about a quarter of a league off, to say Mass. So off they went to celebrate Mass. When Mass was over, they returned to go on board with the Captain of the vessel who had also gone ashore. When they were on the bank of the River Nantes, in which the vessel was riding, they could not find anyone willing to row them out to the vessel, because the storm was very great and the sailors did not dare venture

[35] *Saint Vincent de Paul*, Vol. XI, p. 373.

to expose themselves in such a gale, so there they were, high and dry on shore, unable to get on board. Seeing this, and as the tempest had lasted all day, they went back to Saint Nazaire where they slept.

'Well, then, that night, about eleven o'clock, the storm, redoubling in fury, drove the ship on to a sandbank where she foundered. God, however, gave some of those on board an inspiration to make a sort of raft—they lashed some planks together. How was it done? As yet, I do not know. But sixteen or seventeen persons got on to it and committed themselves to the mercy of the waves and to the mercy of God. Amongst these sixteen or seventeen was our poor brother, Christopher Delaunay, who, crucifix in hand, began to cheer up his companions. "Courage," said he to them, "let us have great faith and confidence in God; let us hope in Our Lord and He will save us from danger." And he began to spread out his cloak to serve as a sail. I do not know if the others had cloaks: however that may be, he spread out his own, one end of which he may perhaps have given some one to hold and the other end to another; and in this way they reached land. God having preserved them by His goodness and special protection from the danger in which they lay; all arrived alive on shore, except one man who died of the cold and fright he had gone through.'

Of the hundred and sixty-four passengers, only those were saved who had remained on shore or were with Brother Delaunay on the raft, thirty-four in all.

It was an incident calculated to damp the ardour of those who felt attracted to the Madagascar Mission. Saint Vincent realised this, and he added: 'No, Gentlemen, no, my Brethren, do not be astonished at this and let not those to whom the Divine Majesty has given a desire to go to Madagascar be a whit discouraged by this accident, for the ways of God are so hidden that we do not see them. And let no one say that God does not will the conversion of those poor people. Even though He has permitted this disaster, He has done so for reasons unknown to us. Perhaps some sins had been committed on that ship which God would endure no longer. Father Herbron told me, two or three weeks ago, that the bad conduct was so great and the curses, blasphemies and vilenesses committed so horrible as to fill one with grief. There were several on the ship who had been taken forcibly aboard to be carried over-seas. . . . Alas ! because this accident has occurred, would it be reasonable for men to whom God has given a desire to go to foreign parts to behave now like bedraggled hens because, forsooth, a ship has gone down ! No, I should not like to think there were any such men as that in the Company. . . . If we consider the grace bestowed on those of the Company who have been saved from shipwreck, would you not all agree that God has, in a special manner, protected this poor little Congregation and these Gentlemen ? And this should more and more encourage us to give ourselves to God in the best possible manner, that we may finish His great work.' Saint Vincent's appeal was heard, and accordingly, when three months later there was talk of another ship sailing to Madagascar, several of his priests volunteered. Gabriel Laudin and Marand Ignatius Arnoul were selected.

Nevertheless, the Saint had further trials to meet ; he learned in August that Fathers de Belleville, Dufour and Prévost were dead. His courage was not shaken, as we may see from the address given to his community on this occasion : ' Somebody in the Company may say, perhaps, that Madagascar should be abandoned ; flesh and blood may say that no more men should be sent there, but I feel assured that the spirit speaks with another voice. What, Gentlemen ! shall we leave our dear Father Bourdaise there, all alone ? The death of these Gentlemen, I feel sure, may surprise some. God drew out of Egypt six hundred thousand men, without reckoning women and little children, to lead them into the Promised Land ; and yet, out of that great number, only two entered it—even Moses, the leader of them all, did not enter. God has called our confrères to that country, and yet, behold ! some die on the way and others shortly after their arrival. Gentlemen, at this we must bow the head and adore the admirable and incomprehensible ways of Our Lord. Were they not called by God to that country ? Who can doubt it ? . . . Would it be really possible for us to be so cowardly of heart and so effeminate as to abandon this vineyard of the Lord, into which His Divine Majesty has called us, merely because four or five or six have died ! Now, would not that be a fine army which, because it had lost two or three, four or five thousand men . . . abandoned the fight ! Such an army of poltroons and runaways would be a nice sight ! Let us say the same of the mission : the mission would be a fine Company if, because five or six had died, it were to abandon God's work ; a cowardly Company, attached to flesh and blood ! Oh, no, I do not believe there is a single man in the Company who has so little courage, and who is not quite prepared to go and fill the place of those who are dead. I have no doubt that Nature may shudder a little at first ; but the spirit, which holds the upper hand, says : " I will do it ; God has given me the desire ; no, that will not make me abandon this resolution." '[36]

The disciples were worthy of their master. Although they had faced death at the very port of embarkation, Fathers Boussordec and Herbron and Brother Delaunay wrote at once to Saint Vincent to say they were quite ready to set out on a new voyage. Brother Delaunay, in his letter, says that he used sometimes to ask himself : ' Do you love the Will of God better here or in Madagascar ? ' and the reply was always the same, ' I love it better in Madagascar.' Such sentiments as these edified the holy Founder and gave him the certainty that when the day again came for him to ask his followers to face death to spread the Kingdom of Jesus Christ, he would not ask in vain.

At one time, it almost seemed as if God was about to rest content with their good will. The ceaseless rivalry between the East India Company and the Duc de la Meilleraye placed Vincent de Paul in a very delicate position, and hence he did all in his power to bring about an agreement between them. Both sides wished for an amalgamation, but the difficulty was on what terms it should be made. Early in 1658, the members held several meetings to reach the basis of an agreement, and the results were discussed at another meeting attended by William de Lamoignon and the Marshal de la Meilleraye. The latter rejected the settlement,

[36] *Saint Vincent de Paul*, Vol. XI, p. 240.

because he was annoyed by what he considered an impertinent question.

Negotiations were resumed a little later. In the course of November, 1659, Saint Vincent received a memorandum from the Marshal, to be conveyed to Cazet, in which he still maintained his claims. The members of the Company considered, on November 28, that the new proposals constituted a manifest infringement of their rights and that it was essential to revert to the old ones. In the midst of all these bickerings, Saint Vincent needed all the gifts of a perfect diplomatist to avoid offending either the members of the Company or the Marshal, who was an imperious, headstrong and touchy man, prompt to take offence and slow to forgive. At the end of 1657, relations were strained. Marshal de la Meilleraye had come to believe that Saint Vincent preferred the East India Company to his own, and had not shown sufficient zeal in maintaining his interest before the members of that body. It was even said that the Marshal had asked the Capuchins for twelve of their Fathers. The Saint wrote to him to see if there were any foundation for this rumour, but the Marshal did not reply. Saint Vincent then wrote to several of the nobleman's associates who could give him no information. He was quite ready, in case de la Meilleraye carried out the project attributed to him, to recall Father Bourdaise from Madagascar. 'Our maxim,' he declared to one of his confrères, 'is always to give place to others, believing that they will do better than us.' The Saint wrote to the Duke, who replied in a letter full of complaints; Vincent de Paul felt the need of explaining his position and wrote again on January 12, 1658 :[37]

'My Lord, I did myself the honour to inform you in two letters that the former India Company met once and that it was to meet again, through the efforts of MM. de Lamoignon and Cazet, to come to a decision about the proposed union. Now, My Lord, I may say at once that as I have had a fall and have injured my head, I have been unable to continue my appeals, and that M. de Lamoignon, having undertaken to write and tell you what those gentle-

[37] *Saint Vincent de Paul*, Vol. VII, p. 43.

men had decided, told me this morning that he would do so to-day.

'I have had a letter from M. Couplier to say that he had been negotiating with you, My Lord, about going to establish a dwelling on the Island of Madagascar and he wishes me to send him a priest and a lay-brother who will travel there with his own people. Whereupon I told him I would very willingly do so if you, My Lord, were willing that we should send, at the same time, one or two other priests to Madagascar. The manner in which we were called there to labour for the salvation of those poor people, which was not by our own choice, but rather by that of His Holiness, the losses we have sustained there of six good ecclesiastics, together with the expenses incurred for this mission which amounts to from seven to eight thousand livres, the aid it is essential to give the Missionary now living on the island, the knowledge of the country and of its language which he has acquired, and some blessings which God has been pleased to bestow on him, all these, My Lord, lead me to hope that it may be your good pleasure for us to continue with this good work, or on the other hand, if you are unwilling, that we may recall Father Bourdaise who is still there.

'You have done me the honour to write and tell me that our people have shown greater affection for the old Company than for you. I beg you, My Lord, to allow me to tell you that that is an ill-office done us in your regard. As for myself, I have never considered anything else than the service of God in this employment, and I think they too were of the same mind. In truth, My Lord, we were all well pleased that the Providence of God had turned to you for the establishment of His Kingdom in those countries, and we have prayed to God, and often do so still, to bless your person and this design. If the reply which M. de Lamoignon is commissioned to convey to you, My Lord, does not fall in with your wishes, I deeply regret it, and I very humbly request you to believe that I have done all in my power, and that it is only my sins that have rendered me unworthy to serve you efficaciously in this affair, in accordance with your desires.

'If then, My Lord, you are pleased to do us the favour to agree that we should still carry on our little services to God in Madagascar, and to supply a passage for the labourers we have set aside for that purpose, I very humbly request you, My Lord, to let me know as soon as possible so that we may send them away at once.'[38]

De la Meilleraye was disarmed by the Saint's courtesy and humility. He accepted the proposal, and on March 14, Fathers Le Blanc, Arnoul, de Fontaines, Daveroult, Brother Delaunay and another lay-brother, with two young negroes educated in France, took ship at Nantes for Madagascar. Yet again, God was content with the good will of the Missionaries. The day after their departure, the sky became overcast, a storm burst and the ship was driven before the gale for a week; the masts and rudder were broken and the Captain forced to put into Lisbon. When the necessary repairs had been effected, the vessel again put to sea, but only to meet with danger of another kind. An Ostend ship fell upon it and captured it, and landed the passengers in Spain. Saint Vincent, after recounting the story, added:[39] 'Here, now, is another motive for adoring the ways of Providence and subjecting our poor reasonings to them.' Father Le Blanc returned to Paris in July and was rejoined there, two months later, by Fathers Arnoul and de Fontaines. Brother Delaunay, after staying for a while in Saintes and then in Mans, arrived at Saint-Lazare in December. Father Daveroult who, very probably on account of the state of his health, had not gone aboard ship with his confrères at Lisbon, was still in that city on June 16, 1659.

Such a chapter of accidents would have discouraged any one else except Saint Vincent; they did not disturb the serenity of his soul in the slightest. When there was talk of a new voyage in the spring of 1659, he did not hesitate to promise three priests. Marshal de la Meilleraye was negotiating with a Dutch Company for a vessel, but as no agreement was reached, the voyage was postponed until autumn. Saint Vincent sent word to that effect to Father

[38] *Saint Vincent de Paul*, Vol. VII, p. 45.
[39] *Ibid.*, p. 196.

WILLIAM DE LAMOIGNON

Herbron who was waiting to set out with Father Turpin and another confrère, and he added : ' I do not know as yet whether there may not be another delay. Man proposes and God disposes ; and Providence has already so often brought their plans to nought and hindered this design that no promise can be made. However, as far a we are concerned, we should always be prepared to proceed with this enterprise, in so far as it concerns the glory of the Master we serve, Who often rewards perseverance with the success He did not bestow on first attempts, and Who is pleased to try His labourers severely before entrusting them with difficult employments, so that they may merit, by the practice of faith, hope and love, the grace to go and spread these virtues in souls that have them not. I give thanks to God, Sir, that these three lamps are not only always alight in you but that they burn more and more brightly with desire to go and enlighten these nations who are living and dying in the darkness of infidelity.'[40]

On the approach of autumn, Saint Vincent took measures in connection with the voyage. Several Missionaries volunteered, and from them he chose four priests, Fathers Boussordec, Daveroult and Feydin (the name of the fourth is missing), a cleric, Etienne, who was to be ordained before leaving, and Brother Patte, who had a certain amount of surgical knowledge. Father Etienne was appointed to act as Superior during the voyage, and Rome was asked to appoint Father Bourdaise Prefect of the Mission, or, in case of his death, the Nuncio's nominee.

On August 18, Saint Vincent, surprised at Marshal de la Meilleraye's silence, again asked himself what were the latter's intentions. His anxiety is revealed in a letter to de Flacourt : ' The Marshal's steward,' he wrote,[41] ' says that this good nobleman's ship will sail on October 24. I hope to have some news of it shortly, in case he consents that we go. If not, what are we to do ? Do you think, Sir, that the Gentlemen of the Society are sending a vessel of their own ? Will you be one of the party ? In this case, when does it sail ? ' Saint Vincent's fears were not realised. As soon as he was assured that the Marshal would take his

[40] *Ibid.*, p. 510.   [41] *Ibid.*, Vol. VIII, p. 155.

Missionaries, he wrote on October 10 : ' We will send three Missionaries on the fourth of next month. I would have sent a fourth, My Lord, were it not that I have given my word to these gentlemen to let them have two, for they had decided to send a ship to Madagascar whilst it was doubtful whether you, My Lord, during your severe illness would send yours.'[42]

Father Etienne, accompanied by Fathers Daveroult, Feydin and Brother Patte, went straight to Nantes, and, acting on instructions received, paid a visit to Marshal de la Meilleraye who lived there. The Marshal gave him a very bad reception, and manifested his displeasure at seeing Saint-Lazare still making use of the East India Company ; he declared that Saint Vincent must at once and openly break with him or with the Company. When the Saint heard the result of the interview from Father Etienne he was not surprised, for an angry letter from the Duke had clearly shown the state of exasperation produced by his own. He hastened to reply (November 22) : ' My Lord, immediately I received the letter you were pleased to do me the honour to write me, I sent to M. Cazet to ask him to be kind enough to come and see me and I begged him to make my excuses to the members of his Company because I was unable to let them take any of our priests, seeing that you, My Lord, do not approve of my having bound myself to let them take them ; and I added that we were obliged to side with you, My Lord, because our confrère, Father Bourdaise, is in your hands as are also the Christians for whose conversion God has been pleased to make use of our little Company and whom we are obliged to assist ; also because of the special avowal I have always made of being your very humble servant, which I desire to remain until death. To which he replied that he would convey this information to the Gentlemen of his Company and that he thought they would be quite satisfied at my acting in this way. Hence, My Lord, you may see that we did not hesitate to take your side and to break with these Gentlemen to whom, My Lord, I have given my word that I will not let them take any priests in future, either

[42] *Saint Vincent de Paul*, Vol. VIII, p. 83.

priests of our own Company or others, and I have written to Father Etienne to have nothing more to do with them or with their people. I very humbly request you, My Lord, to rest assured that we shall carry out things as I have said.'[43]

Saint Vincent hoped that after this assurance de la Meilleraye would no longer talk of exacting an oath of fidelity from the Missionaries. If the Marshal should persist in this resolution, Saint Vincent wrote to Father Etienne,[44] ' tell him that as you are children of obedience, it is enough for you to know what are the intentions of those who send you for you never to act to the contrary, and that that is your oath.'

The virtue displayed by the Saint all through these proceedings ended by extorting the Marshal's admiration. He frequently invited the Missionaries to his table, and kept Father Etienne for hours in his room conversing on devotional topics or explaining his plans for the colonisation of Madagascar. He also gave orders to his captains not to undertake anything of importance at sea without consulting the priest, and when he bade the latter good-bye, he embraced him tenderly and shed many tears.

Before Saint Vincent allowed Father Etienne to set out on his journey, he could not but remember Father Bourdaise who, as he thought, was still alive. He wrote to encourage him and to express his regret at not having come sooner to his assistance. ' We have wept,' he said,[45] ' for your sorrows and for your losses by the death of Fathers Dufour, Prévost and de Belleville. . . . It would seem as if God were treating you as He treated His Son. He sent Him into the world to establish His Church by His Passion, and it seems as if He is unwilling to introduce the Faith into Madagascar save by your sufferings. . . . We have deeply regretted the death of those great servants of God. . . . He knows that we have gladly kissed the hand that smote us, although we were unable to understand the reasons for the early deaths of men who gave such promise in the midst of a people that asks to be instructed, and after all the

[43] *Ibid.*, p. 174. [44] *Ibid.*, p. 176.
[45] *Ibid.*, p. 156.

marks of a vocation to christianise this people which were manifest in them. . . . You would not have been so long without help were it not that two attempts to sail turned out badly. . . . It has not pleased God that any help or consolation should reach you from here, but it was His Will that they should come directly to you from Himself; it was His Will that He should be your first and second helper in the divine and apostolic work to which He has applied you in order to show that the establishment of the faith is His own affair and not the work of men. It was in this way He acted in the beginning of the establishment of the Universal Church, selecting only twelve apostles who went one by one throughout the world to announce the coming and the doctrine of their Divine Master. But when this holy seed had begun to sprout, His Providence arranged that the number of labourers should increase, and it will do the same for your nascent Church, multiplying it little by little; and it will gradually be provided in the end with priests who will live to cultivate and extend it. . . . The fears you have entertained that our dear dead ones hastened their death by labouring too hard should oblige you to moderate your zeal.'

Saint Vincent must certainly have given that last piece of advice to Father Etienne and his companions before they left Paris, and to it he added other counsels not less useful. When he was asked by Brother Patte how he should behave towards the heretics who were to be his fellow-travellers, he said: 'All sorts of disputes and abuse must be carefully avoided; you should be patient and genial towards them, even when they may attack yourself, your beliefs, and your devotional practices. Virtue is so beautiful, so lovable, that they will be compelled to love it in you if you practise it well. It is to be desired that in the services you will render to God on board ship (by practising his art as a surgeon) you will make no distinction of persons and let no difference appear in your dealings with Catholics and Huguenots, so that the latter may know you love them in God.'[46]

At Nantes, the Missionaries heard that the vessel was to

[46] *Saint Vincent de Paul*, Vol. VIII, p. 183.

sail from La Rochelle, and Father Etienne decided that he and Brother Patte would go there by sea and the others by land. He left Nantes on December 6. The vessel, driven out of its course, was hugging the Gironde coast when a north-westerly wind struck her, smashed the main-mast, and drove her towards a sand-bank near Soulac. Father Etienne was sea-sick; the pilot came, with tears in his eyes, to ask him to give absolution to the whole crew, for all hope was gone. When he had done so, a sudden change of wind saved them from the impending danger. The vessel was now driven towards the coast of Spain, and then back to the mouth of the Gironde. Waves were constantly breaking over the bridge which none dared to mount. On December 15, they all made a vow to go to Confession and Holy Communion, and to provide clothes for twelve poor persons; Father Etienne, in addition, promised to say twelve Masses. It was necessary to make land at all costs, for, as provisions were by now exhausted, all were suffering from both hunger and thirst. The ship was lightened by throwing overboard all merchandise and baggage, and at length, on the 21st, after fifteen days of anguish and suffering, whilst they were pitching about helplessly some distance from San Sebastian, a passing fishing-boat came to their aid and landed them at Saint Jean de Luz.

They were no longer expected at La Rochelle, and in most of the communities of that city, a Requiem Mass had been sung for the repose of their souls. Hence, when Father Etienne arrived on November 29, the surprise of the people was general. The news of his death had been sent on to Saint-Lazare and carefully concealed; only four persons were aware of it. A new Superior was chosen and the moment for his departure had come. He was having a meal and Saint Vincent, on his side, was preparing in haste to send a few words to the Missionaries who had remained at La Rochelle, when the door of his room was thrown open and several bundles of letters placed on the table. He looked at them and two addresses caught his eye, for the writing resembled Father Etienne's.[47] He opened the letters and found that they were indeed from that

[47] Abelly, *op. cit.*, I, III, Ch. XXI, p. 312.

unfortunate traveller who had written from Bayonne and Bordeaux ; it was without any apparent emotion that the Saint revealed the contents of the letters to his assistant and secretary who were present, and who were in the secret.

On January 18, the *Lady Marshal* weighed anchor, and reached the Canary Islands on February 5. She made the port of Rufisque on the 20th and remained there until the 28th. On March 29, they crossed the line. The weather was calm and everything promised well for the remainder of the voyage. The weather changed on May 7. As the wind was driving the ship on to a rocky coast two or three leagues distant, the Captain felt obliged to cast anchor next day in Table Bay. Unfortunately, one anchor broke, the cable of another snapped, and the vessel once more was heading for the reefs. During the night of the 19th-20th, the situation seemed desperate. Passengers and crew prepared for death by going to Confession and saying their prayers. The first gleam of dawn showed that they were out of danger. The vessel, buried deep in the sand, was unable to move, and there was no use whatever in thinking she could be repaired or re-floated. Thanks to help sent by the Dutch Governor of the Cape of Good Hope, the shipwrecked passengers and crew were able to land. Their stay at the Cape was prolonged to six months, but at length they were taken aboard some Dutch vessels, arrived in Holland, and, after passing through Belgium, reached Paris in July, 1661. Saint Vincent was not there to receive them, for God had taken him to Himself on September 27, 1660.

His successor, Father Alméras, was too conscious of the admirable tenacity of the holy Founder to abandon a mission that had cost so many sacrifices and tears. He found opportunities, in 1663, 1665 and 1666, to send Missionaries to Madagascar, and eleven priests and seven brothers went there whilst he was Superior General. Brother Patte was poisoned, and Father Etienne, Brothers Gallet and Pilliers massacred on the island. The others, for the most part, died in the prime of manhood, victims of the climate. Their sacrifice was not in vain, for the progress made by the Gospel in our own days, in those regions

THE MADAGASCAR MISSION 117

only too long peopled with infidels, is due to those valiant soldiers of Christ.

The mission of Fort Dauphin which had to be abandoned in 1674, owing to the departure of the French colonists, was resumed, in 1896, by the sons of Saint Vincent. It has now its own Vicar Apostolic, and the Daughters of Charity are there to assist the poor and sick. Some of the natives have become priests and are labouring for the conversion of their fellow-countrymen. Besides the Vicariate of Fort Dauphin there are five others under the jurisdiction of the Jesuits, the Spiritines and the Fathers of La Salette ; the Missionaries of these different communities rival each other in zeal for one common end—the glory of God by the conversion of souls.

To procure the glory of God by the conversion of souls was also the aim of another society of ecclesiastics founded by Saint Vincent—the members of the Tuesday Conferences at Saint-Lazare.

CHAPTER XXVIII

THE TUESDAY CONFERENCES

WE have already related the origin of the first Tuesday Conference established in Paris in 1633. Saint Vincent was in no hurry to give it a definite organisation; at first, he simply determined its essential features. As usual, he began with a temporary set of rules which were gradually modified in the course of time by the lessons of experience before attaining their final shape.[1] The first clause defines the end; the members of the Conference propose ' to honour the life of Our Lord Jesus Christ, His eternal Priesthood, His holy family and His love for the poor; and therefore, to imitate Him by procuring the glory of God in the ecclesiastical state, in their own families, in the poor and even in poor country folk.' All the members were priests, deacons or sub-deacons, and admission was preceded by a rigorous enquiry. Those who were not leading an exemplary life were refused admission, as were all who belonged or even had belonged to any other society.[2] The fortunate individual who had secured admission went to Saint-Lazare to make an eight-day retreat, during which he prepared himself for his new life by a general confession.

The associate rose ' early in the morning,' spent half an hour in mental prayer, recited the ' Little Hours ' and then said or heard Mass. He read every day, kneeling and bareheaded, a chapter of the New Testament. His daily exercises of piety comprised, in addition to spiritual reading, a ' particular examination ' of conscience before the two principal meals, grace before and after meals, a general

---
[1] The definitive set of rules is given in *Saint Vincent de Paul* Vol. XIII, p. 128.
[2] *Saint Vincent de Paul*, Vol. VII, p. 569.

examination of conscience, and after night prayers, the reading over of the points of meditation for the next day. He went to Confession once a week, or more frequently, if impelled to do so by devotion. Deacons and sub-deacons received Holy Communion on Sundays and the principal Feasts. All the members met every Holy Thursday for a touching ceremony, when they renewed their baptismal vows, the vow taken on becoming sub-deacons, and the good resolution to observe the rules of the Company till death.

The mere fact of belonging to the same Confraternity established amongst the members a spirit of brotherhood that entailed certain duties. 'They shall,' says the rule, 'call to mind that Our Lord has united them by a new bond of His love, and unites them in a most perfect manner; hence they shall love, visit and console one another in their troubles and illnesses, and shall attend the funerals of those who die; each priest shall say, if possible, three Masses for the repose of the soul of departed members; and the others shall go to Holy Communion once for the same intention.'

The Conference was governed by a Director, a Prefect and two Assistants.

According to the rules, the Superior General of the Congregation of the mission was always to be the Director, and in case of absence, he should depute one of his Missionaries to take his place. Saint Vincent wished to establish a permanent bond between the two societies; God had made use of one to give him the other; it was God who had united them, and no man could take it on himself to break this bond. He said one day:[3] 'If there are any persons in the world obliged to make use of and profit by Conferences, it would seem as if the Priests of the Congregation are thus bound, because it is to them that God has turned to introduce this particular manner of holding conferences of ecclesiastics on the special duties of their state. When I came to Paris, I had never seen conferences of this sort—at any rate conferences on the virtues proper to the ecclesiastical state and on the means of leading a virtuous life in

[3] *Ibid.*, Vol. XI, p. 13.

that condition. There were, indeed, plenty of Academies in which the clergy conferred on various points of doctrine, and in some places, on cases of conscience. About fifty years ago, Cardinal de Sourdis introduced into his diocese of Bordeaux this method of dealing with certain points in moral theology; he brought together parish priests and others so as to enable them the better to instruct one another, and he did so with success. But until we began, there were no conferences of ecclesiastics, like ourselves, on the virtues proper to their state; at least, I myself never saw or heard of any. It is quite true that several good religious still maintain this holy practice, as did the ancient monks in former days. But however that may be, it was to this poor little Congregation that God was pleased to turn, in this century, to establish and extend the practice, not only as an excellent remedy for good priests, exposed in the service of souls, to the corrupt atmosphere of the world, but also to assist them to perfect themselves in their own profession.'

'It is the Congregation of the mission, then, which was inspired by God to take an interest in, and cultivate a love for the practice of these virtues, by means of conferences in which we treat of the motives to acquire them, their nature, specific acts, the means of putting them into practice, and finally, the obligation of our state both in regard to God and our neighbour. Such, then, is the object of these Conferences.'

'Now, what would become of us if we were the first to neglect them? What an account should we not have to render to God if we ultimately came to despise so useful and efficacious a means and one which the Fathers and anchorites of old embraced so ardently, as Cassian tells us in his Conferences? I must confess, speaking from my own experience, that there is nothing so touching, nothing that moves me so deeply, nothing of all that I hear, read or see that goes to my heart like these conferences.'

In Saint Vincent's eyes the Conferences were not a personal work but one proper to the Congregation of the mission. The title of Director given to the Superior General entitled him to preside at the meetings, to collect opinions and to sum up; nothing was proposed, nothing

THE TUESDAY CONFERENCES

determined, nothing carried out without his advice. After him came the Prefect, who was chosen from the members of the Conference and consulted with the Director, before the meetings, as to what advice was to be given, what proposals put forward. He was also charged with the duty of seeing that the rules were observed, and hence was bound, in this as in all other matters, to be the first to give good example. Those of the Prefect's confrères who had committed a fault were reprimanded by him, and in case a member fell ill, it was he who arranged that the patient should be visited ; if necessary, it was the Prefect who told those who were ill that they should receive the last Sacraments. Nicholas Gedoyn, Abbé de Saint-Mesmin, was Prefect in 1658. The Prefect had two Assistants whose duty it was to assist, and in case of necessity, take his place ; the instruction and training of new members was a specially important part of their obligations. There was, in addition, a Secretary who drew up the minutes of the meetings and attended to correspondence.

The office-holders met every three months and the most usual topics for discussion were fidelity to the rules, preservation of the primitive spirit and the means of advancing in virtue. If a member had failed to carry out his duties, the others sought means to remedy this failure. At the quarterly meetings, the various duties were assigned according to the taste, capacity and leisure of the members. Some were appointed to hear the confessions of the sick in the Hôtel-Dieu, others to visit and exhort prisoners, others to give missions, if there were any in prospect, both in cities and country places. The resolutions adopted were read at the next weekly meeting and each was asked to ' give his consent.'

The Company kept in touch with the members wherever they went and was informed when one of them left Paris. Those who were absent were requested to send news of themselves from time to time, and especially to mention in their letters ' what they may have done or suffered for God ' and also to behave everywhere in such an edifying manner that all should see in them ' most worthy members of the Company.'

The Tuesday Conferences were so called from the day on which the meetings were held. Every Tuesday, at three o'clock in the afternoon from All Saints' Day to Easter, and at half-past three from Easter to All Saints', they met either at Saint-Lazare or the Collège des Bons Enfants. Those who could not come wrote to explain their absence or, if that was impossible, made their excuses at the next meeting. Absence did not dispense members from the duty of edifying their associates, for they were requested to write down what they would have said at the meeting and to forward the letter to the Director or Prefect.[4]

The meeting began with the recitation of the hymn, *Veni Creator*, with its versicle and prayer, followed by one of the anthems of Our Blessed Lady. The subject of the conference, announced on the previous Tuesday, was either one of the liturgical Feasts, or the lessons to be drawn from contemporary occurrences or any abuses noticed in the Society. Every year, at the beginning of Lent, a conference was devoted to the best method of employing that holy season.[5] All-Saints recalled to mind the eight Beatitudes and the practical lessons to be drawn from them; occasionally the Beatitudes were dealt with in turn, during the weeks following that Feast.[6] The death of a member afforded an opportunity for a conference on his virtues.[7] In 1659, fifteen conferences were devoted to an enquiry into the sources of 'the wretched state of the Church, and of ecclesiastics so attached to the goods of this world and so desirous of amassing them.'[8]

The distinguishing features of these meetings were their humility, simplicity and charity; no member ever contradicted another, or demeaned himself by making unkind, personal remarks. All spoke simply and modestly, in accordance with 'the little method.' If any member forgot himself, or if it were noticed that a member was showing a desire to display his knowledge or indulge in fine lan-

[4] *Saint Vincent de Paul*, Vol. X, p. 700.
[5] *Ibid.*, Vol. XI, p. 89.   [6] *Ibid.*, Vol. VII, p. 390.
[7] *Ibid.*, Vol. XI, p. 393.
[8] *Ibid.*, Vol. XII, p. 374. Other subjects dealt with, in 1650 and 1651, are mentioned in Ms. 457, Bibl. Mun. Chartres.

guage, the others became uncomfortable, and a discreet hint was conveyed to the offender that he was not observing the usual forms of procedure.[9] Adrian Gambart, who was a member of the Conference, went to the trouble of taking notes of what was said at the meetings. His manuscripts, bequeathed to Saint-Lazare with permission to have them published, would have enabled us, if they were still in existence, to appreciate the charm of those familiar discourses of apostolic men whose minds were endowed with the rarest and most beautiful gifts of nature and grace.[10]

Of all the members of the Conference the one most eagerly listened to was Saint Vincent himself, and when he was unable to speak at the close of a session, owing to want of time, all were disappointed. As a general rule, he added a few words, and though he did not usually say anything novel but contented himself with a commentary on an idea already expressed that had most appealed to him, his remarks penetrated his hearers' minds and hearts by their charm, unction and power. On this point we have the unimpeachable evidence of Bossuet himself:[11] ' After our ordination to the priesthood, we were associated with that Company of devout ecclesiastics who met every week to confer together, under his direction, on divine things. He was its founder and its soul. We heard him with the utmost eagerness, clearly recognising that in him was realised the words of the Apostle : " If any man speak, let his words be as the words of God." ' When a bishop was present, he was invited by Saint Vincent to bring the meeting to a close. On one occasion, when several bishops were present, the senior said :[12] ' M. Vincent, you must not, in your humility, deprive the Company of the good thoughts God has communicated to you on the subject with which we have been dealing. There is an inexpressible unction of the Holy Spirit in your words which touches each of us, and therefore, all these gentlemen beg you to let them share your

[9] *Ibid.*, Vol. II, p. 233.
[10] Arch. Nat. S. 6708, dossier de Noyon.
[11] Postulatory Letter, August 2nd, 1702.
[12] Abelly, *op. cit.*, Bk. III, Ch. iv, p. 30.

thoughts, for one word from your lips will produce more effect than all that we could say.'

The Tuesday Conferences soon rapidly developed, and the foremost priests in Paris regarded admission to its ranks as an honour. 'There was scarcely an ecclesiastic of merit in Paris,' wrote Lancelot, 'who did not desire to belong to it.'[13] The list of members admitted before October 1, 1660, comprised more than two hundred and fifty names ; names which recall all who were most remarkable for nobility of birth, wisdom, intellect and piety in the contemporary Church of France. In its ranks were more than forty Doctors of the Sorbonne or the College of Navarre and twenty-two bishops, amongst others, Nicholas Pavillon, Anthony Godeau, Francis Fouquet, Louis Fouquet, Felix Vialart, Henry de Maupas du Tour, Francis Perrochel, Stephen Caulet, John de Maupeou, Philibert de Brandon, Francis Paul de Gondi, Cardinal de Retz,[14] Louis Abelly and Bossuet. Others became founders of religious communities, Vicars General, Officials, Archdeacons, Superiors or Visitors of religious houses, or devoted pastors of country or city parishes. The first two Rectors of the General Hospital belonged to the Society. Amongst other names it is enough to recall those of the Venerable M. Olier, founder of Saint-Sulpice, Francis Pallu, co-founder of the Foreign Missions, Louis de Chandenier, Abbé de Tournus, Claude de Chandenier, Abbé de Moutiers-Saint-Jean, Claude de Blampignon, Vicar General of Bayonne, Omer de Champin, Dean of Saint Thomas du Louvre, Adrian Gambart, Director of the Daughters of Providence of Saint Joseph,[15] Nicholas Gedoyn, Superior of the Ursulines of Saint Cloud, Francis Renar, Director of the Nuns of Saint Thomas, de Saint Jean, Almoner to the Queen, Claude Tristan, Vicar General of Beauvais, the Abbé de Saint Floran, Councillor

---

[13] *Mémoire touchant la vie de M. de Saint-Cyran*, Cologne, 1738, 2 vols. du decimo, Vol. I, p. 287.

[14] 'I played a little at being devout, and went to the Saint-Lazare Conferences.' (*Œuvres* du Cardinal de Retz, éd. Hachette, II Vol., oct., 1870–1920, Vol. I, p. 167.)

[15] Migne has published an account of Adrian Gambart in the *Collection intégrale et universelle des orateurs sacrés*, Vol. LXXXIX, pp. 10–26.

THE TUESDAY CONFERENCES

to the Parlement, Bourdin, Archdeacon of Noyon, and Michel Alix, parish priest of Saint Ouen l'Aumône.[16]

The name of Cardinal de Retz, then Abbé de Buzay, comes as a surprise in this list, and perhaps it was not without some hesitation that he was admitted. The adventures of the gallant Abbé were too recent to have been forgotten by the clergy, but Saint Vincent knew that he had before him the future Archbishop of Paris. He preferred to shut his eyes to the past, hoping that intercourse with the devout ecclesiastics of the Conference would not fail to make an impression on a mind more inclined to the world than to devotion. Moreover, the Abbé de Buzay, as he himself admits, was shrewd enough to conceal his real thoughts : ' I began to lead a more regular life,' he says, ' at least in appearance. I lived in great retirement and no longer let the choice of a profession seem problematic ; I studied a great deal and carefully established contact with learned and devout persons ; I almost turned my rooms into an Academy and began, without affectation, to treat with respect the canons and parish priests I naturally met at my uncle's. I did not play the devout, because I could not feel sure I should be able to keep it up for long, but I did esteem devout persons very highly ; and that, in their eyes, is one of the great marks of piety. I even accommodated my pleasures to this mode of life. ·. . . Finally, I succeeded so well that really I became quite the fashion amongst those of my profession, and even the devout used to repeat, after M. Vincent, who had applied the words of the Gospel to me : that though I was not sufficiently pious, still I was not too far away from the Kingdom of God.'[17] In this company of devout ecclesiastics, the Abbé de Buzay was an exception. ' Amongst the gentlemen of the Conference who meet here,' Saint Vincent used to say, ' there is not one who is not an exemplary man ; they all labour with unparalleled success.'[18]

Amongst their conspicuous virtues were two that chiefly

---

[16] Lancelot tells us (*op. cit.*, Vol. I, p. 287) that de Secq and Singlin were members of the Tuesday Conferences.
[17] *Œuvres* de Cardinal de Retz, éd. Hachette, Vol. I, pp. 177-180.
[18] *Saint Vincent de Paul*, Vol. XI, p. 10.

attracted public attention : their zeal and piety. It was the custom of the members on entering a Church, whilst the office was being recited, to put on a surplice and assist in choir.[19] When they arrived too early at Saint-Lazare, they used to take out their breviaries and recite the Divine Office in groups of two.[20] They were concerned, indeed, about their own salvation, but did not forget that of their neighbours. Saint Vincent knew he could rely on their good-will, and whenever he was in need of preachers for retreats—retreats for ordinands or retreats for ecclesiastics, in Paris or the provinces—he had them ready to his hand.

Zeal is a virtue that cannot remain concealed ; men are bound to see and admire it. A book, published in 1643, that is to say twenty-one years before the first biography of Vincent de Paul, gives a description of their work and invites the clergy of France to make them their models. 'This Company,' wrote Bonnefons,[21] ' is composed of a large number of learned and zealous ecclesiastics, amongst whom are Abbés, parish priests, Doctors of the Sorbonne, Bachelors of the University, in short, men perfect in doctrine and piety, all of whom have no greater desire or pretention than to teach the first principles of Christian doctrine to rich and poor. Hence they may be seen on Sundays teaching Catechism to the young after Vespers in their parish church, and some of them also select one day in the week to instruct, above all, numbers of poor persons whom they gather together in church ; they distribute alms spiritually by teaching the truths of Faith, and corporally by little sums of money. There are others who, not content with these exercises, fervently undertake to preach missions in those quarters of Paris farthest removed from churches and chiefly inhabited by the poor. They select a house or a large room in some wealthy person's house, and there assemble three or four hundred poor people of the parish twice a day, for the space of a week. They instruct them on the truths necessary for salvation, and afterwards divide

[19] *Saint Vincent de Paul*, Vol. V, p. 194.
[20] *Ibid.*, Vol. XII, p. 231.
[21] *Le Chrestien Charitable*, by Amable Bonnefons, 1643. We have been unable to discover the first (1637) edition of this work.

them into groups and question each individual in turn. When the instruction is over, they give a regular alms, usually a loaf of bread or three or four *sols*. For five or six days they continue these instructions, and on the seventh or eighth day, confessions are heard and Holy Communion administered in sight of the whole parish. O holy and divine exercise which gives honour to the Church, instruction to poor ignorant people and great consolation to those who are taught! Would to God that those He has called to the ecclesiastical state imitated the majority of those who thus labour in Paris! France would thereby be a better cultivated vineyard of the Lord.'

In 1641 and 1642, these zealous Missionaries preached two missions in the church at La Chapelle to refugees from Lorraine, to prepare them to receive their Paschal Communion. With the same end in view they gathered together the King's Guards, and on several occasions rendered a similar service, during the men's free time, to the masons of the city of Paris who were working at the vast and numerous buildings then in course of erection. They also gave missions in the chapels of hospitals and hospices, not only to the sick, the nursing staff and the servants, but also to such of the public as cared to attend.

One of their first missions, perhaps the first, was that preached in 1633, in the hospice known as the *Quinze-Vingts*, to the blind inmates and their relations. Six years later, a mission was given in the Hôtel-Dieu in which all took part—the sick and the staff, including the Augustinian nuns, to whom special conferences were given three times a week. At the *Petites Maisons*, which consisted of a number of small, detached houses for lunatics, another mission was given, in the course of which *The Christian Exercise* was composed. This little leaflet proved such an amazing success that, in response to the demand both from France and abroad, millions of copies were distributed. The spiritual welfare of girls and women who had been leading disorderly lives, and were confined in the refuge of *La Pitié*, as also the poor in that hospital, the galley slaves of La Tournelle and beggars in hospices was also attended to. These missions were given frequently and one was preached almost every year in the General Hospital ; even then the Missionaries' zeal was not satisfied ; they frequently went to the Refuge and the General Hospital, especially on Sundays and Holidays, to visit, preach, hear confessions and administer the Sacraments.[22] The Hôtel-Dieu was the chief centre of their activities. At first, they visited the Hospital daily, in a body, to prepare and dispose the sick to make General Confessions, but later on they came to the conclusion that it would be sufficient to depute some members in turn to pay the daily visit, and on Fridays to exhort and teach Catechism to the convalescents.[23]

Amongst the missions given by the members of the Conference were some that created a great deal of public attention, such as the famous mission preached in 1641, in the Faubourg-Saint-Germain, Paris. The Faubourg had then a deplorable reputation, from both the moral and religious standpoint. 'At this time,' wrote Abelly,[24] ' it was, as it were, the sink of vice not only of Paris, but almost of the whole of France, and served as a refuge for all libertines, atheists, and those who led impious and disorderly lives.' A lady of great virtue (the Duchesse d'Aiguillon in all probability), who knew what a powerful means missions were to lead souls back to God and to rekindle fervour, had the idea of applying this remedy to those who resided in her quarter. She saw M. Vincent, but the latter, surprised at the request, did not dare to undertake it himself. If, with God's help, success did not seem to be impossible, he might, he thought, find men sufficiently confident and resolute not to be frightened at the difficulties before them. The lady returned, made even more urgent entreaties, and finally had her way. Saint Vincent promised to convey her proposal to the members of the Tuesday Conferences.

---

[22] Bossuet preached at the General Hospital on June 30, 1657 (Feast of Saint Paul) and on April 4, 1659 (Feast of the Compassion of the Blessed Virgin) ; at the Incurables on September 8, 1659 (*Œuvres oratoires* de Bossuet, éd. Urbain-Levesque, Paris, 1914–1916, 7 vols., oct., Vol. II, pp. 376, 562 ; Vol. III, p. 51).

[23] Abelly, *op. cit.*, Bk. II, Ch. III, pp. 255 ff.

[24] *Ibid.*, sect. IV, p. 261. See Faillon, *op. cit.*, 4th ed. Vol. I, p. 434.

He spoke at the next meeting, but his appeal met with no response ; all the ecclesiastics present begged to be excused, as the task seemed beyond their powers. During the week, Saint Vincent prayed fervently to God for help, and at the next meeting he repeated his request. Again he was refused. He returned to the attack ; some ecclesiastics present manifested impatience at the obstinate way in which he kept on making an appeal which had been so persistently refused. He perceived this at once, and falling on his knees, asked pardon for his stubbornness, saying : ' I am only a proud and wretched man ; I cannot surrender my own views ; pray forgive me, but I thought God was urging me to propose this work to you.' This act of humility proved more efficacious than all his arguments. All opposition ceased and the project was unanimously adopted. Perrochel undertook to act as Superior to the mission, and some of the members, only one of whom is known to us (Claude de Blampignon), promised to assist.

The Missionaries were to be faced with quite a different type of congregation from that to which they were accustomed, and wondered whether they should not adopt a new method. When Saint Vincent was asked, he replied : ' Hold fast to the simplicity which you have found so successful in other missions. The spirit of the world, with which this district is saturated, can neither be fought nor conquered successfully save by the spirit of Jesus Christ. Let the sentiments of Jesus Christ be yours. Seek, like Him, the glory of God and not your own : be prepared, like Him, to embrace abjection and contempt and even to suffer opposition and persecution, if God so permits ; preach, as He did, simply, familiarly, humbly and charitably ; when you speak thus, it will not be you who are speaking but Jesus Christ speaking through you, the instruments of His mercy and grace, and you will touch the most hardened and convert the most rebellious hearts.'[25]

They listened to his advice and ' the little method ' had one of its most glorious victories, as we are told by M. Olier who was to become, in the following year, parish priest of Saint-Sulpice, which formed part of the Faubourg-Saint-

[25] *Ibid.*, Bk. II, Ch. III, sect. IV, pp. 261 ff.

Germain. 'M. de Perrochel,' he wrote,[26] 'preached last year in the Faubourg-Saint-Germain with as much energy as man can display, and for a long time exhorted his hearers to penance with marvellous efficacy. He brought an amazing number of persons to Confession, so that people came to tell me of these wonders and to say that the hearts of men, most hardened and most attached to sin, were now as pure as those of little children, who were also the object of his zeal. The hearts of all were filled with delight at the sight of these poor little innocents going to Holy Communion and walking in procession. Paris went out from its gates in crowds to hear M. de Perrochel, who was preaching in the Abbey of Saint-Germain (the Church of Saint-Sulpice was too small), and he earned such a reputation that he is now called the Apostle of Paris. Not only did the people go in crowds, but also priests and prelates, who all bore testimony and were resolved to imitate him, confessing that that was the right way to preach.' Abelly adds, more briefly but just as expressively, 'If one had to state in detail all the good accomplished by this mission, all the conversions, reconciliations, acts of restitution, etc., that were made, one would have enough matter to fill a volume.'[27]

A citizen of Paris who had witnessed the success of the Missionaries, called on them one day and said : 'I am alone, my wife and children are dead ; I have an income of from seven to eight thousand francs ; I will give you my fortune and place myself at your disposal for the rest of my life on the day you form a community to continue in other places the good you have begun here.'[28]

The number of missions given in the provinces by the members of the Conference, either alone or with the Priests of the Mission, is beyond reckoning. Francis Renar evangelised Poitou, Touraine, Saintonge, Auvergne, Champagne, Burgundy, 'and almost every province of France,' says his biographer.[29] Premature illnesses and

---

[26] *Vie de M. Olier*, par Faillon, *op. cit.*, Vol. I, p. 468.
[27] Abelly, *op. cit.*, Bk. II, Ch. III, sect. IV, p. 261 ff.
[28] *Ibid.*, p. 263.
[29] *L'idée d'un véritable prestre de l'Eglise de Jésus-Christ et d'un fidèle directeur des âmes, exprimée en la vie de M. Renar, prestre, directeur*

ANTHONY GODÉAU
BISHOP OF VENCE

weakness compelled him to desist and he died at the age of forty-nine. Olier, one of the preachers at the Refuge in 1636, evangelised several parts of Auvergne, Velay and Vivarais; he preached in Montdidier, Amiens, Mantes, Illiers, Chartres and a multitude of other places. In 1634, he suggested to his fellow-members to give a series of missions in the districts depending on his Abbey of Pébrac; Perrochel, Renar and de Barault accompanied him, and Saint Vincent also sent one of his most experienced Missionaries. They rivalled each other in zeal, and preached the good tidings to the inhabitants of these places, oblivious of fatigue and rejoicing at their success, for God had profited by their labours for souls.[30] Olier's mind was still filled with memories of these fruitful missions when he returned two years later to Auvergne, accompanied by five or six priests from Saint-Lazare. From May 25 to June 15 they made Saint-Ilpize their headquarters, and for three weeks it was a centre to which all the people of the neighbouring villages poured in. They came in such numbers that the church could not contain them; doors and windows were crammed with people, and the crowd overflowed as far as the boundaries of the cemetery. As the summer was prematurely and oppressively hot, one may imagine the weariness of these poor people, especially on days when the ceremonies were prolonged. Numbers fainted outright and wine was sent round to those who needed it to recover their strength. Crowds gathered round the Confessionals. Many of them, says M. Olier: 'spent whole nights in the Church, sleeping even on the threshold, and waited for three or four days in succession for an opportunity to go to Confession.' Priests from the neighbourhood were called in; many responded to the invitation and there were twelve or thirteen confessors at work.

des religieuses du monastère de Saint Thomas, par Abelly, Paris, s.d. duod. p. 54. Francis Renar also did much work in Paris; he was one of the priests who gave missions at the *Quinze Vingts*, the *Pitié*, the *Refuge*, and at La Chapelle for the Lorraine refugees. At the last mission he gave the longer instructions on the Catechism; a hæmorrhage of the lungs carried him off whilst still hard at work.

[30] Faillon, *op. cit.*, Vol. I, pp. 92–93, 96–97.

Olier was delighted, and when the mission was over he wrote to tell the members of the Conference in Paris of the graces God had showered down on the mission. There is, perhaps, a touch of reproach for those who had not accompanied him, in the concluding words of his letter : ' Paris, Paris, thou holdest back some who might convert many ! Alas ! how many fruitless works, how many false conversions and holy discourses wasted for want of dispositions that God scatters in abundance elsewhere ! Here, a word is a sermon, and nothing seems wasted. . . . All these poor people, with very little instruction, may be seen to be filled with God's graces and blessings.'[31] Saint Vincent read the letter and promised to help his friend. Four or five Priests of the Mission were about to leave for Pébrac, when Louis XIII asked the Saint for chaplains to accompany the troops sent to Picardy against the Spanish armies marching on Paris. Olier had to be satisfied with two new helpers, both of them remarkable men : Caulet and Meyster.

Wherever the Missionaries went, similar fruits were gathered : nothing was heard of but acts of restitution, reconciliations, general confessions, conversions of heretics and sinners, and the reparation of sacrileges. Confraternities of Charity and Ecclesiastical Conferences were established, and the parish clergy, now better instructed in their duties, carried out more faithfully the obligations of their ministry. The fourth mission, in which eight priests took part, ended on January 25, 1637. Two thousand General Confessions and the conversion of five Huguenots rewarded the Missionaries' labours. The people poured in from places twenty-five miles distant to assist at the exercises ; they brought food for three or four days, and when not in church, withdrew to outhouses and barns where they usually discussed the sermon amongst themselves, or what they had been taught at the Catechism lesson. When the mission was over, the faithful, in their turn, became Missionaries ; Olier writes : ' peasants and their wives may be seen giving a mission in their own families, and shepherds and labouring men chanting the commandments of God in

[31] *Saint Vincent de Paul*, Vol. I, p. 333 ; Faillon, *op. cit.*, Vol. I, pp. 170–171.

THE TUESDAY CONFERENCES

the fields, asking, questioning one another about what they have learned during the mission.'[32]

When he returned to Paris after a sojourn of some months in Auvergne, he went to give an account of his labours to Saint Vincent, who had already been informed of them by others. 'I do not know how you do it,' said the Saint, 'but the blessing of God follows you wherever you go.' 'It is quite true,' replied Olier, 'and I can certainly say to the sole glory of my Master, that these missions in Auvergne, where we were only poor little men of straw, of no virtue, have been marvellously blessed; these blessings were quite different from those which God bestowed on our other labours, although we then had with us men of learning and piety.'[33]

The mission at Saint Germain-en-Laye in 1638, for which the King himself had asked, was one of the most difficult, for it was attended by all the Court. Louis XIII, to set a good example to his courtiers, went to hear the preacher on several occasions; the sermons on the necessity of thinking seriously of one's salvation and on the small number of the elect, made a deep impression on all. Pavillon had the greatest success with the Queen and her Ladies-in-Waiting, and his indignant protests against immodest dress put an end for a time to the fashion of low-necked costumes. He pointed out that the ladies, instead of wasting their time, as they only too frequently did, might usefully devote some of it to the poor, and was so successful in convincing them that they were no longer to be seen present at the frivolous amusements of the Court. A Confraternity of Charity was established which was joined by a large number of the Ladies-in-Waiting who encouraged one another to visit and help the poor. Such a change, as one may well imagine, was not to the liking of the courtiers, who did everything in their power to counteract the efforts of the Missionaries. They were suddenly seized with great anxiety about the Queen's health, and enquired most solicitously whether those who came into such close contact with Her Majesty might not be in danger of communicating to her some of the infected atmosphere which they encountered in the

[32] Faillon, *op. cit.*, Vol. I, pp. 172-185.   [33] *Ibid.*, p. 201.

VOL. II.—K

hovels of the poor. They succeeded in making Louis XIII uneasy, but Anne of Austria had no great difficulty in meeting the mild remonstrances of her husband; she simply said that the Ladies and Maids-in-Waiting were well aware of how to combine prudence and charity. The courtiers did not abandon the fight. To see them listening so attentively to the preacher, one might imagine that they too were beginning to be influenced by the words of the Gospel. Such was not the case, at least in regard to a large number; they were not thinking about the salvation of their souls, but were on the look-out for an imprudent or ambiguous phrase which would enable them to discredit the preacher in the King's eyes. One day, Pavillon compared Louis XIII with the Beast in the Apocalypse; the comparison as developed by the preacher was in no way offensive, quite the contrary, but the courtiers pretended to be indignant and loudly protested that it was scandalous.

On another occasion, the preacher declared that the King's Musketeers should not demand anything from those on whom they were billeted, but should rest content with their pay. He may not have known that their pay was insufficient to meet absolutely necessary expenses, but the remark touched the King indirectly and thus afforded another opportunity of abusing the Missionary. Pavillon was summoned before the King to explain his language; he promised to state his doctrine in writing and asked that it be submitted to the judgement of the Sorbonne. As the theologians declared there was nothing reprehensible in what he had said, Pavillon did not lose the royal favour.[34]

Opposition such as this brought down God's blessings on the labours of the Missionaries. Three days before the close of the mission, on February 21, Saint Vincent wrote: 'The mission at Saint-Germain is drawing to a close blessed by God, though in the beginning there was occasion to exercise the holy virtue of patience. Few of the King's household have omitted to do their duty; the people too have fulfilled it, and all with a devotion that is most edifying. Firmness in the matter of low-necked dresses supplied an

[34] *Un prélat indépendant au XVIIe siècle, Nicolas Pavillon, évêque d'Alet*, par Étienne Dejean, Paris, 1909, oct., p. 15, note I.

opportunity for exercising the virtue of patience. The King told M. Pavillon that he was very well pleased with all the exercises of the mission, that this was the way men should labour, and that he would testify to the fact wherever he went. I had great difficulty in sending anyone there whilst the Court was in residence, but as His Majesty told me that such was his desire, we had to lay aside our objections. The Ladies who experienced most difficulties at first have now become so fervent that they have joined the Charity, serve the poor day and night, and have collected money in the town going about in four groups.'[35]

The memory of the mission at Saint-Germain is now almost forgotten, and yet it was marked by an event of permanent interest to the Church of France, for it was at Saint-Germain, on February 10, 1638, that Louis XIII placed his Kingdom under the protection of the Blessed Virgin; he then consecrated himself in person, his crown and his subjects, to Our Lady, and instituted a solemn annual profession on August 15 in her honour.[36] Was the idea of this consecration one of the results of the mission, or did Louis XIII ask for the mission to prepare the Court for the ceremony? However that may be, it would be interesting to have an account of what happened on that day, and by what ceremonies Mary was honoured as the Queen of France.

Saint Vincent attributed the success of the Missionaries to 'the little method.' He said one day:[37] 'The little method is . . . good for the Court. . . . It has had a good reception there. . . . All opposition was overcome by the little method.' 'Let us all, then,' he concluded, 'make use of this little but powerful method.' It did, in fact, prove most efficacious; another instance of its value was given in a large town of which Abelly does not give the name. Deplorable abuses that had taken root there, due to arrangements between the officers of justice and the local tavern-keepers, who were very numerous, were eradicated. These officers met litigants in the taverns, on

[35] *Saint Vincent de Paul*, Vol. I, p. 450.
[36] Arch. Nat. fonds Joly de Fleury, Ms. 2429, f⁰ 206.
[37] *Saint Vincent de Paul*, Vol. XI, p. 282.

Sundays and Holidays as well as on week-days, during the hours of divine service as well as at other times, and then proceeded to deal with their affairs. They cared little whether justice was meted out ; all that interested them was how much profit they could extract from their profession. The Missionaries were not satisfied with denouncing this abuse from the pulpit ; they held conferences with the chief of police, the Provost, the public prosecutors and the police. When they left the town, order had been restored. A police proclamation commanded all taverns to be closed on Sundays and Holidays, during the hours of divine service, under penalty of fines and other punishments for tavern-keepers and their customers ; the Provost decided to use his authority against all officers of justice who arranged meetings in taverns, prolonged law-suits through pure chicanery, or abused their powers in any other way ; and the attorneys and police promised to carry out the proposed regulations. The Missionaries were all the more readily obeyed as many of them were related to the Presidents and Councillors of the Parliament, and hence would readily find support in high places for the execution of their reforms and the punishment of the guilty. The Provost, who was the son of an attorney, set an example by fining his own father, who was convicted of chicanery and of prolonging law-suits to obtain still larger fees.[38]

No mission, perhaps, brought together so many members of the Conference as that preached at Metz. Anne of Austria, during a sojourn of six weeks in that city with the Court, in September and October, 1657, saw for herself the number of dangers to which the faith of Catholics was exposed, living as they did in the midst of a larger and most energetic population of Jews and Huguenots. By a strange abuse, the title of Bishop of Metz had been held since 1607 by an illegitimate son of Henri IV and the Marquise de Verneuil, Henri du Bourbon, who never took Holy Orders and never had any intention of doing so, and who finally married the daughter of Chancellor Séguier. The diocese had been administered for half a century by suffragan bishops, the last of whom was Peter Bedacier, titular

[38] Abelly, *op. cit.*, sect. IV, pp. 258 ff.

Bishop of Augustus, who was zealously and energetically supported by Bossuet, but did not meet with similar assistance from the clergy, particularly from the Chapter.

Shortly after the Queen's return to Paris, she sent two prelates to Saint Vincent to say that she wished to speak to him. ' Monsieur Vincent,' she said, ' I have, as you know, just come back from Metz. There is much good to be done in that city ; I think a mission would be most useful. Can you send some of the priests of your Congregation there ? ' He replied : ' Your Majesty is perhaps unaware that the poor priests of the mission are only for poor country folk ; but we have another Company of ecclesiastics, who meet at Saint-Lazare every Tuesday, and who would be well able, if Your Majesty consents, to carry out that work better than we could.' ' I did not know,' the Queen went on, ' that your Congregation debarred itself from all work in cities. I should be very sorry, indeed, to interfere with its customs. As there is nothing to prevent the members of the Tuesday Conferences from preaching in Metz, I rely on you and on them ; Lent is not far off : let everything be ready for Ash Wednesday.'[39]

At the next meeting, Saint Vincent gave the members the substance of his conversation with the Queen, and there was, of course, nothing to be done but to fall in with a wish coming from such an exalted source. Metz was divided into sixteen parishes ; hence, a large number of Missionaries was required, and sixteen or seventeen were chosen.[40] The names of the following have been preserved : Claude de Blampignon, Omer de Champin, Nicholas Gedoyn, Claude de Chandenier[41] and his brother Louis, who had the general direction of the mission. Saint Vincent added one of his own priests and two lay-brothers to attend to

[39] *Saint Vincent de Paul*, Vol. XII, p. 4.
[40] *Ibid.*, Vol. VII, p. 92 ; Saint Vincent says elsewhere, eighteen or twenty. (*Ibid.*, Vol. VII, p. 76.)
[41] The presence of Claude de Chandenier at Metz, denied by Maynard (*op. cit.*, Vol. II, p. 86, note 1), is attested by Saint Vincent (*Saint Vincent de Paul*, Vol. VII, pp. 109, 121 ; Vol. XII, p. 17). Maynard's mistake arose from the fact that he confused M. de Saint-Jean, the Queen's almoner, with M. de Moutiers de Saint Jean.

their material wants.[42] Bossuet, who was then in Metz, had to make all arrangements for the sojourn of the Missionaries and to do what he could to make the mission a success ; he had more than one difficulty to surmount.

In principle, wherever the members of the Conference went to give a mission, they alone should occupy the pulpits ; it was an excellent idea, intended to prevent all rivalry and jealousies amongst the preachers. Now, a Dominican Friar, Father Anthony Guespier, doctor of the Sorbonne, had long been engaged to preach that Lent in Metz, and was then actually in the city. To dispense with his services would have been adding insult to injury, all the more so as he had declined an offer to preach in Angers in order to accept the invitation of the Bishop of Augustus. No one knew what to do. The Suffragan suggested that the Dominican should preach in the Cathedral on Mondays, Tuesdays and Thursdays, and the Missionaries during the rest of the week, but this solution did not appeal to Saint Vincent.[43] An attempt was then made to induce the Friar to agree that in the general interest it would be better for him not to preach at all during that Lent. He replied that, far from injuring the success of the mission, he would contribute to it because he would strongly exhort the people to render themselves worthy to gather its fruits. The public were fully aware of a state of things which might easily, owing to the influence of certain individuals, have developed into a dispute and even a scandal, thus destroying in advance the work of the Missionaries.

No one knew how to cope with the situation, but in the end Saint Vincent found a solution. He went to the Queen, informed her exactly of the state of affairs and asked her to intervene. His diplomacy succeeded in settling the matter without displeasing anybody. Bossuet wrote to him :[44] ' God, Who provides for all things, has brought peace to us all through the order communicated to the Syndic of this city to inform the Bishop of Augustus and M. de la Contour that the Queen would be gratified if the preacher would entirely abandon his claim and accept one

[42] *Saint Vincent de Paul*, Vol. VII, p. 92.
[43] *Ibid.*, Vol. VII, p. 63.   [44] *Ibid.*, p. 96.

hundred crowns, given by Her Majesty, in addition to the usual fees, and also if he should be engaged to preach next year.'

In the meantime, Saint Vincent was making preparations to instal the Missionaries, and with this end in view, sent Nicholas Demonchy, Superior of the house in Toul, with instructions to Metz. He had to exercise his ingenuity to provide board and lodging for all with the meagre sum at his disposal. Baron Moussy la Contour, the King's Lieutenant, lent the Hôtel de la Haute Pierre, where the Kings of France resided whilst staying in Metz. The city provided furniture, beds, mattresses, linen and bed-clothes. Some private individuals generously made up for whatever else was needed. Bossuet found it difficult to provide table linen and kitchen utensils ; he wrote to Father Demonchy:[45] ' It would be a great relief to have a cook who would provide all that is wanted.' He looked out for one, but those he approached demanded forty *sols* a day, which seemed to him excessive. ' It is for you,' he added in his letter, ' to take measures accordingly ; in the meantime, I will continue to make enquiries, as to what can be done to make the best and most economical provision.' Even this point was settled at last, for Saint Vincent sent one of the cooks of Saint-Lazare to Metz.

Lent was approaching ; the Missionaries set off in bitterly cold weather which was followed by a thaw and disastrous floods, from which even the capital suffered : ' In many streets in Paris,' Saint Vincent wrote on March 1, 1658,[46] ' more boats are to be seen than carriages. No one has ever seen the waters rise so high. All Paris has been terrified by the floods which have caused much damage both inside and outside the city. We have just been told that four whole arches of Saint Mary's bridge were carried away by the flood to-night, as well as the houses built on them. . . . This extraordinary inundation will have surprised the gentlemen who are on their way to give a mission at Metz.' Saint Vincent's uneasiness was shared in Metz, but the arrival of Brother Mathew Régnard, who was used to

[45] Bossuet's *Correspondance*, Hachette's edit., Vol. I, p. 18.
[46] *Saint Vincent de Paul*, Vol. VII, p. 94.

braving perils, calmed their fears. On March 2, Bossuet wrote to Saint Vincent : ' Brother Mathew who has arrived here almost by a miracle, in the midst of a flood which is encircling us on all sides, will give you an account, Sir, of the preparations that have been made for these gentlemen. We are now almost ready to make a beginning ; time will settle everything, and assuredly everything possible will be done to satisfy these servants of Jesus Christ. . . . Nothing now remains but to pray that God may soon open a path through these floods for His servants, that He may render fruitful their labours and make their words efficacious.'[47]

At length, on March 4, the travellers reached their destination, and the mission opened on the following day in every parish of the city. Blampignon and Gedoyn preached in the Cathedral and Bossuet also spoke there occasionally. He had reserved for himself the small Church of Saint John of the Citadel where his congregation consisted for the most part of soldiers and workmen ; he preached a sermon and gave a conference daily and a catechetical instruction twice a week. On April 2, he preached on scandal ; on the 9th, on sacramental satisfaction, and amongst the other subjects treated were penance, honour and brotherly love.[48]

As may be imagined, the announcement that a mission was to be given disturbed the Consistory which forbade Huguenots to attend the sermons. One of them disobeyed, and on returning home, he spoke of what he had heard to his wife who, touched by divine grace, was converted and publicly abjured her errors in presence of the suffragan Bishop, Bossuet, Blampignon, the King's Lieutenant, and other persons of rank. The solemnity given to the ceremony had no other object in view than to promote conversions.

Some days after her act of abjuration, the woman fell ill and was confined to bed. She asked for the Holy Viaticum which was brought to her in solemn procession, the priests

[47] *Saint Vincent de Paul*, Vol. VII, p. 96.
[48] Lebarcq has published the text or at least the sketch or notes of these five sermons. (*Œuvres Oratoires* de Bossuet, éd. Urbain-Levesque, Vol. II, pp. 421 ff.)

and chief personages of the city following the priest, bearing lighted tapers in their hands. The invalid manifested a touching devotion, and on beholding the Sacred Host, protested her love for her Saviour and her sorrow for the past. ' I renounce,' she said, ' all affection for earthly things and all human interests which might have led me, whilst among the Calvinists, to form a number of plans regarding either my husband or my children. I place my daughters, who are Catholics, in the hands of Divine Providence and I ask on their behalf the protection and prayers of all those worthy persons here present. Ah ! too long did I shut my eyes to the lights which God was pleased to give me from time to time and resisted the inspirations which drew me to the true Faith. I believe, I love and hope with all my heart.' The procession returned to the church, chanting the *Te Deum*. The author of the *Account*[49] from which these details have been taken adds : ' The heretics who, like owls, fled from the God of light, hastened to shut themselves up in their houses when they saw all those gleaming tapers and torches approaching them at eight o'clock in the evening ; whilst the Catholics ran to the Church from every quarter to stir up their devotion and to render thanks to the Lord for all His mercies.' The sick woman was also confirmed. The vexation of the ministers can easily be understood, and also their desire to recover ground by bringing this lost sheep back to the fold. Bossuet, however, was on the watch ; he frequently visited the woman during her illness to strengthen her more and more in the Faith.

This conversion greatly contributed to the success of the mission. ' Grace and piety,' says a contemporary account,[50] ' triumphed in the hearts of the Governor, his wife and all the officers and soldiers.'

Louis de Chandenier kept Saint Vincent informed of the progress of the mission and the latter, in turn, encouraged the Abbé to husband his strength. The Saint was accustomed to read, at the Tuesday Conferences, the letters from

[49] *Relation d'un fait mémorable arrivé dans le cours de la mission de Metz*, published in *Bossuet's Correspondance*, Hachette's edit., Vol. I, p. 28, note 5.
[50] Quoted by Maynard, *op. cit.*, Vol. II, p. 99.

Metz with the intention of stirring up the zeal of those who had remained in Paris. On one occasion, the Queen's Almoner, M. de Saint Jean, after listening attentively to some extracts from the letters recounting the results of the mission, asked if he might have a copy for the Queen, for he rightly thought she would be consoled to hear of the many blessings bestowed by God on the labours of those sent to Metz by her orders. He saw her the following day, and Anne of Austria was much moved when she heard the letter read. ' Her joy,' wrote Saint Vincent, ' was so great and abundant as to be manifested even in her countenance, and her Almoner perceived this immediately.' She asked for the letter, so that she might be able to read it again in private, and manifested special satisfaction at all that had been done in Metz for the temporal and spiritual welfare of the poor. ' I desire,' she said, ' that alms should continue to be distributed, and if money is wanting, let me know and I will supply it.'[51]

The Missionaries, however, were not numerous enough for the work and Louis de Chandenier asked for help. Three priests arrived from Paris during Holy Week. Saint Vincent, announcing their departure, added : ' If you are in need of any more priests, Sir, I think you should not hesitate to select some from amongst the local seculars and regulars, the Jesuits, for instance. I sincerely hope our house in Toul may be able to send you one, but I am very much afraid it cannot.'[52] The number of evangelical labourers was increased from twenty or so to forty, which was not too great for the sixteen parishes of the city.[53]

As was said above of the Saint-Germain mission, it would need a volume to recount the effects of divine grace as revealed in the people of Metz during this period. The Missionaries influenced their hearers not only by word but by example, for Saint Vincent tells us :[54] ' They went in pairs, vested in surplices, from their lodgings to the

[51] *Saint Vincent de Paul*, Vol. VII, p. 120.
[52] *Ibid.*, p. 121.
[53] Postulatory letter of Henri-Charles de Coislin, Bishop of Metz, for the introduction of Saint Vincent's cause, 1706.
[54] *Saint Vincent de Paul*, Vol. XII, p. 17.

church and from the church to their lodgings, without uttering a word, and so profoundly recollected that all who saw them were filled with admiration at their modest demeanour, never having seen anything like it.'

The mission lasted two months and a half. When Louis de Chandenier returned to Paris, he brought a letter from Bossuet to Saint Vincent, dated May 23 :[55] ' I cannot see those dear Missionaries depart,' wrote the great Archdeacon of Metz, ' without bearing witness to the universal regret and marvellous edification they have left behind them. It is so great, Sir, that you have every reason in the world to rejoice in Our Lord, and I too would joyfully abound on this subject were it not that the results far too greatly exceed what I can say. Nothing better organised, nothing more apostolic, nothing more exemplary than this mission has ever been seen. What news should I not have to tell you of the individual members, and most especially of the leader and the others who have preached the Gospel to us in such a holy and Christian manner, if I did not believe that you were more fully informed by more important eye-witnesses and from your own personal knowledge, and in addition, the fact that I am not unaware of the pain endured by their modesty at being praised ? They have captured all hearts here and are now returning to you, fatigued and exhausted in body, but rich in spirit, with the spoils they have snatched from Hell and the fruits of penance which God has produced by their ministry.' What Bossuet was unable to say in this letter, he said many years later in his petition to Clement XI for the introduction of the cause of his saintly friend, for the success of the mission was due in part to the prayers and exhortations of Vincent de Paul.

When the mission was over, people began to realise that its memory should be preserved by a permanent establishment which would perpetuate its fruits. The Queen gladly co-operated with the project by giving 60,000 livres to found a community of Missionaries in Metz, some of whom would preach missions in the surrounding districts, whilst others would devote themselves to the training and education of the diocesan clergy. Bossuet's father willingly

[55] *Ibid.*, Vol. VII, p. 155.

placed himself at Saint Vincent's disposal to purchase a suitable site, and selected the Hôtel de Montgomery, a very large establishment consisting of five distinct groups of buildings, with courtyards and garden, the entire property being surrounded with walls. It was here the first seminary of Metz was established in 1663, and called the Seminary of Saint Anne, after the Queen.

The mission at Metz produced another result: the creation of a conference for ecclesiastics on the model furnished by Paris. Bossuet wrote to Saint Vincent to tell him of the foundation of the new conference and added: 'It promises itself the honour of having you for its Superior, for we have been led to hope for the favour of being associated with that of Saint-Lazare. . . . I have been asked, Sir, to request this favour and do so with all my heart.'[56]

As the preceding pages show, the Tuesday Conferences happily completed the work of the Congregation of the mission. With the help of these two societies, Saint Vincent was enabled to realise in all their fulness the words of Jesus Christ: *Evangelizare pauperibus misit me*, which he adopted as the device of his Company. The poor are not only to be found in country places, but also in cities, and Jesus Christ preached both to townspeople and villagers. The holy priest, who had the noble ambition to imitate his Lord in all things, was therefore bound to extend his field of action in every direction, and this he did, like a military commander directing his troops, by means of the two groups of Missionaries at his disposal.

The apostolic zeal of the members of the Conferences at Saint-Lazare did not escape Cardinal Richelieu's attention. His niece, the Duchesse d'Aiguillon, had often spoken of them to him, and as everything that related to ecclesiastical reform greatly interested the Cardinal, he asked Saint Vincent about the organisation, membership and works of the Society. This first meeting was followed by several others, and Richelieu conceived the highest idea of the holy priest's virtues. 'People have frequently spoken to me about M. Vincent,' he told his niece, 'but what I now know myself far surpasses all I ever heard of his virtue.' The Cardinal

[56] *Saint Vincent de Paul*, Vol. VII, p. 156.

THE TUESDAY CONFERENCES 145

one day said to the Saint : ' Monsieur Vincent, could you give me the names of those of your priests who in your estimation are worthy of the episcopate ? ' The latter, though at first surprised, mentioned some names which the Cardinal immediately wrote down lest he should forget them.[57] Some months later, on January 8, 1638, Vincent de Paul wrote to a friend : ' The Assembly of the Ecclesiastics of this city continues to grow better and better. Three bishops have just been selected from it : M. Godeau for Grasse, M. Fouquet for Bayonne, M. Pavillon for Alet, and M. Barreau has just been nominated by the King Co-adjutor Bishop of Sarlat.'[58]

Pavillon, dismayed at the responsibilities attached to the office of a bishop, fell ill and long refused to give his consent. In the end, in order to induce him to yield, it became necessary to threaten him with the wrath of God, and to tell him that the souls of the diocese of Alet would rise up against him at the Day of Judgement. The ecclesiastics of the Conference had the happiness of assisting at his consecration in Saint-Lazare on August 22, 1639. Anthony Godeau had not time to bid good-bye in person to his fellow-members before leaving Paris, but contented himself with a farewell letter : ' I regard it as a special blessing,' he wrote,[59] ' to have been admitted into your ranks. The remembrance of the good example I have seen, and the excellent teachings I have heard there, will rekindle my zeal whenever it grows cold, and you will be the models on which I will strive to form good priests. Continue your holy exercises, then, in the same spirit, and faithfully respond to the designs of Jesus Christ on you, for He wishes, no doubt, to renew by your means the grace of the priesthood in His Church.' In 1640 and 1641, the Conference lost two more of its members, Felix Vialart and Henri de Maupas du Tour, who were chosen by Richelieu for the bishoprics of Châlons and Puy respectively. All these selections were excellent, and hence Saint Vincent could write on April 17, 1643 : ' Those who were trained here stand out from the other prelates in

[57] Abelly, *op. cit.*, Bk. I, Ch. XXVII, p. 125.
[58] *Saint Vincent de Paul*, Vol. I, p. 373.
[59] Abelly, *op. cit.*, Vol. II, Ch. III, sect. V, p. 268.

such a way that everyone, even the King himself, remarks how different they are.'[60] He wrote these lines on the day after Louis XIII, who was lying gravely ill at Saint Germain-en-Laye, had sent his confessor, Father Dinet, to ask for a list of names of those who seemed to be worthy of the episcopate. Amongst the names given were those of Francis Perrochel and Stephen Caulet; in the following year, the former was consecrated Bishop of Boulogne and the latter Bishop of Pamiers. Other nominations followed, namely, Philibert de Brandon, Bishop of Périgueux (1648); Louis Fouquet, Bishop of Agde (1658); John de Maupeou, Bishop of Chalon (1658); Francis de Nesmond, Bishop of Bayeux (1662); Louis Abelly, Bishop of Rodez (1662) and Bossuet, Bishop of Meaux (1668). Saint Vincent had nothing to do with the three last appointments for he died in 1660; neither had he anything to do with that of Cardinal de Retz (1654) who, being co-adjutor, succeeded his uncle, John Francis de Gondi, Archbishop of Paris.

These episcopal nominations presented one grave difficulty; there was a risk that ambitious priests might join the Tuesday Conferences, under a mask of piety, and with no other intention than that of reaching an episcopal throne. Saint Vincent saw the danger, and to avoid it, employed the utmost discretion. In presence of the members, he never uttered a word that could lead them to suppose that he had the slightest intention of proposing them for ecclesiastical dignities. On the contrary, he exhorted them to shun honours and taught them to rest content in their own abjection and lowliness.[61] Were it not for this sentiment of humility which he inculcated so strongly, the list of twenty-eight bishops selected from the members of the Tuesday Conferences would have been much longer, for some, such as the Venerable M. Olier and Louis de Chandenier, refused episcopal sees.

When Saint Vincent saw the marvellous fruits produced by the Tuesday Conferences, it naturally occurred to him to create similar institutions in other places. In 1642, six voluntary chaplains were added at his request to the

[60] *Saint Vincent de Paul*, Vol. II, p. 387.
[61] Abelly, *op. cit.*, II, Ch. XXVII, p. 125.

regular staff attached to the Hôtel-Dieu who were unable to carry out all their duties.[62] Whilst these ecclesiastics were making a preparatory retreat at Saint-Lazare, in view of their new functions, he gathered them together to point out the best methods of fulfilling their duties, and to exhort them never to forget their personal sanctification. On his advice, they adopted the rules of the Tuesday Conferences with the difference that their meetings should be held on Thursdays at the Collège des Bons Enfants so as to allow the students, on their free day, to take part in the assemblies. This Thursday Conference was, like its prototype, composed exclusively of ecclesiastics.[63]

Moreover, Conferences were not established in Paris or France alone, but beyond the frontiers. Wherever the Priests of the Mission or the members of the Conference gave a mission, they encouraged the clergy to form similar associations; they also aided them to do so by supplying the regulations and by taking part at one or more meetings to show how they should be carried out. Father Codoing established Conferences in Dauphiné;[64] Father de Sergis in Languedoc;[65] Father Dufour in Saintes;[66] Father Get in Marseilles,[67] Pavillon in Alet,[68] Bossuet in Metz,[69] Father Blatiron in Genoa,[70] and Father Martin in Turin. Angers and Bordeaux had their own Conferences and also many other cities.[71]

The Conferences of Puy, composed of the Cathedral Canons, were established by Olier. Its members were chiefly distinguished from other ecclesiastics by their great love of the poor. They catechised children, visited the sick in hospitals, and gave missions in places dependent on the Chapter.

Bourdin, the Archdeacon of Noyon, induced the Canons

[62] Arch. Nat. LL. 267, f⁰ 278 V⁰.
[63] Abelly, *op. cit.*, Bk. I, Ch. XXVII, p. 126.
[64] *Saint Vincent de Paul*, Vol. I, p. 537.
[65] *Ibid.*, p. 537.
[66] *Ibid.*, Vol. II, p. 604.
[67] *Ibid.*, Vol. VII, p. 286; Vol. VIII, p. 545.
[68] *Ibid.*, Vol. II, pp. 491, 563.
[69] *Ibid.*, Vol VII, p. 156.
[70] *Ibid.*, Vol. IV, p. 225; Vol. VII, p. 398.
[71] Abelly, *op. cit.*, Vol. II, Ch. III, sect. V, p. 267.

of the Cathedral there to imitate those of Puy, but their obligations did not permit them to adopt the Paris regulations in their entirety. After they had made the necessary alterations in the rules, they forwarded them to their confrères in the capital. 'When they have been submitted to your judgement,' says the accompanying letter, ' we shall follow them all the more readily and confidently.' They added : ' Permit us, Gentlemen, . . . to ask you for a written account of one of your Conferences on the special spirit of your Company that we may be the better able to clothe ourselves in this spirit, without which we could never succeed in our enterprise.'[72]

The provincial Conferences regarded that of Paris as their source and model ; they had recourse to the same lights and were inspired by the same sentiments which were, in fact, those of Saint Vincent de Paul whose words were listened to as the words of God. The Conference of Pontoise wrote to him : ' We are as yet but infants in virtue, not strong enough to support and guide ourselves. . . . We beg you to be pleased to send us from time to time some of the ecclesiastics of your Company, who will teach us how to carry out with greater confidence, the exercises which we are now so courageously beginning.' The same sentiments animated the Conference of Angoulême, as may be seen from a letter to Saint Vincent : ' Our Company thinks that it should no longer delay to pay you its respects, and to bear testimony to the fact that it deems itself unworthy of the honour you have done it by coming to its assistance in all things that concern its advancement and perfection. It very humbly requests you, Sir, to allow it to regard you as its grand-father, for it was one of your children whom God made use of to bring it to life, and also that you would add this other favour to the first, namely, not to regard it as a stranger but as your grand-daughter and to arrange that this noble and illustrious Company of Paris, which is, as it were, your eldest daughter, may not disdain to regard it as a sister, although inferior to it in every respect.'[73]

[72] Abelly, *op. cit.*, Vol. II, Ch. III, sect. V, p. 265.
[73] *Ibid.*, pp. 264 ff.

FELIX VIALART,
BISHOP OF CHALONS

THE TUESDAY CONFERENCES

The association established by Saint Vincent under the name of the Tuesday Conferences continued to expand up to the end of the eighteenth century.[74] It was swept away in 1792 by the tempest that brought ruin on all French Catholic institutions. Nevertheless, the idea that had given rise to the establishment of the Conferences was too good to be abandoned, and hence, associations of priests multiplied during the nineteenth century. Under different forms, they all tend to the same end : to band priests together for mutual edification, by word and example, the better to fulfil all their duties ; duties towards themselves by labouring unceasingly at their own perfection, and duties towards souls by devoting themselves unselfishly to win or to preserve them for God.

Laymen have also been influenced by Saint Vincent's central idea, and the establishment of Conferences by Ozanam in 1833 corresponds with the Saint's concern for the preservation of morals and religion and the exercise of charity towards our neighbour ; we cannot therefore but applaud Ozanam's idea in placing his Society under the patronage of Saint Vincent de Paul.

[74] Collet bears witness to its vitality in 1748 (*op. cit.*, Vol. I, p. 203).

CHAPTER XXIX

RETREATS FOR ORDINANDS

THE preceding chapters have enabled us to see who were Saint Vincent de Paul's helpers : the members of the Charities, the Ladies of Charity, the Daughters of Charity, the Priests of the Mission, the Ecclesiastics of the Tuesday Conferences ; the time has now come for us to enter into some detail on his sacerdotal or religious undertakings, his works for aiding his fellowmen in body and soul.

We shall begin with the retreats for ordinands.

From 1631 to 1642, there were six retreats for ordination every year, either in the Collège des Bons Enfants or in Saint-Lazare. In 1643, the mid-Lent ordination was suppressed, as the episcopal council had come to the conclusion that if ordinations were held at longer intervals, the clerics would have more time to make a better preparation for Holy Orders. The number of ordinands on each occasion varied from eighty to a hundred ; they were boarded and lodged gratuitously for eleven days.

No matter how heavy a burthen this imposed on the house, Saint Vincent fully intended that those on retreat should be properly looked after. Devout men and women were interested in the work ; the Ladies of Charity, for instance, undertook to defray part of the expense of providing lodgings and furniture ; the wife of President de Herse gave a thousand livres for each ordination, and this sum covered all the expenses. Anne of Austria generously helped the work during the next few years, and the Marquise de Maignelay was also conspicuous for her munificence. A number of ecclesiastics proposed to unite their priories to the house of Saint-Lazare so as to consecrate their revenues to this laudable purpose; Abbé Ribier offered that of Bruyères-le-Chatel,[1] Abbé Louis de Chandenier that of Saint Pourçain;[2] M. de Saint Aignan ceded one of his, and on his advice, a friend did likewise.[3] The sum total of all these revenues would have extricated Saint-Lazare from all embarrassment if the good will of the donors had not been thwarted. Unfortunately, only one union, that of Saint Pourçain, was effected, and that only in 1659; even then, to obtain the consent of the bishop of the diocese, Saint Vincent had to bind himself to give a mission every five years in that locality.[4]

By means of charitable donations, the work was carried on without too much difficulty up to 1647, but from then onwards, and especially during the Fronde, when prices soared beyond all bounds and Saint-Lazare received only a negligible portion of its revenues, difficulties grew greater and greater. The Bursar, who did not know where to turn to find money to support the community, never ceased from groaning. Vincent de Paul sought to console him by talking of confidence in God, but the Bursar was not convinced. One of the lawyers of the Parliament, on seeing the large number of externs present in the refectory, wondered how the house was able to stand the strain. He expressed his surprise to Saint Vincent, who said: 'The treasure of divine Providence is indeed very great; it is well to cast one's cares and thoughts on Our Lord, Who will never fail to supply us with food as He has promised.' He then quoted the words of the Psalmist: '*Oculi omnium in te sperant, Domine, et tu das illis escam in tempore opportuno; aperis tu manum tuam et imples omne animal benedictione.*'[5]

The retreats for ordinands attracted to Saint-Lazare men remarkable in various ways, such as Noël Brulart de Sillery, an ex-Ambassador; Olier, the founder of Saint-Sulpice; Abbé de Rancé, the reformer of La Trappe; Bossuet, whose eloquence shed such lustre on the Christian pulpit, and Abbé Fleury, one of the great historians of the Church.

[1] *Saint Vincent de Paul*, Vol. III, p. 233.
[2] *Ibid.*, Vol. VII, p. 298.   [3] *Ibid.*, Vol. II, p. 249.
[4] *Ibid.*, Vol. VII, p. 299.
[5] Abelly, *op. cit.*, Bk. III, Ch. III, p. 13.

John Francis Paul de Gondi, the future Cardinal de Retz, also went there and has left us a disconcertingly cynical account of his retreat :

'As I was obliged to take Orders, I made a retreat at Saint-Lazare where I behaved in the usual fashion, as far as externals are concerned, but inwardly my mind was much and deeply preoccupied with the line of conduct I should adopt in future. It was very difficult. I saw the Archbishopric of Paris degraded in the sight of the world by the baseness of my uncle, and rendered desolate in the sight of God by his negligence and incapacity. I foresaw infinite difficulties in its re-establishment, and was not so blind as not to recognise that the greatest and most insurmountable obstacle was myself. I was quite well aware of the need of a moral code for a bishop . . . and felt, at the same time, that I was incapable of it, and that all the obstacles that I could oppose to a disorderly life, such as a sense of duty and a desire for renown, would prove to be very uncertain barriers. After six days' reflection, I made up my mind to do evil with my eyes open, which is, without comparison, most criminal in the sight of God, but without doubt, the wisest in that of the world ; for when a man acts thus, he always takes precautions for partial concealment and so avoids the most dangerous form of ridicule that can be met with in our profession, namely, an unseasonable mingling of sin and devotion. Such was the holy disposition in which I left Saint-Lazare. Nevertheless, it was not wholly or completely bad ; for I made a firm resolution to carry out exactly all the duties of my profession and to be as good a man for the salvation of others as I was bad for my own.'[6] The retreat, then, of the future Cardinal de Retz was not wholly without fruit. If grace produced no stronger effect on this rebellious nature, at least nothing had been spared to procure its future triumph.

Saint Vincent took particular care in his selection of preachers and allotted two for each retreat : one for the morning and one for the evening discourse. He invited some of the priests of the Tuesday Conferences, or bishops

---

[6] *Mémoires du Cardinal de Retz*, éd. Chantelauze, Paris, 11 vols. oct. 1870–1920, Vol. I, pp. 216 ff.

RETREATS FOR ORDINANDS

who had formerly belonged to the Association, and occasionally, members of his own Congregation.[7] Amongst those who preached retreats were Perrochel, Bishop-elect of Boulogne ; Sevin, Bishop of Sarlat ; Caulet, Bishop of Pamiers ; Laurence Bouchet, afterwards parish-priest of Nogent-le-Roi ; Louis Abelly, parish priest of Saint Josse, Paris ; Bossuet, afterwards Bishop of Meaux ;[8] Hopille, Vicar General of Agen ; Hobier, who was praised by Balzac for his wisdom and good sense ; Andrew Guignard, Principal of the College of Navarre ; Charles Camus de Baignolz, Doctor of the Sorbonne ; Claude de Blampignon, Abbé de l'Aumône ; Francis Renar, director of the nuns of Saint Thomas.

Saint Vincent asked them above all else to speak simply, without any striving after rhetorical effect. 'Simplicity,' he said one day to his followers, 'edifies the ordinands ; they congratulate one another on it and come here looking for nothing but that ; the truths taught them are well received when presented in this guise and are more efficacious when so naturally adorned.'[9] A good preacher, in his eyes, is also clear and practical ; he enters into detail and has no other thought than the interest of souls. He can only be simple after conquering vanity which would incline him to speak of 'lofty and noble things.' Those who surrender to this failing destroy instead of building up. If one wishes to do the right thing, one should raise oneself to God to receive His inspirations. 'God is an inexhaustible source of wisdom, light and love. It is from Him we should draw what we say to others ; we should annihilate our own spirit and our own particular ideas and feelings to make

---

[7] It was not without a certain repugnance that Saint Vincent sought preachers from outside ; circumstances rather than his own inclination compelled him to do so. (See *Saint Vincent de Paul*, Vol. II, p. 284.)

[8] Bossuet gave the morning instructions during the retreat from April 3 to April 12, 1659, and the evening ones from May 13 to May 22, 1660. (Cf. *Œuvres oratoires*, éd. Urbain-Levesque, Vol. II, p. 234.) After Saint Vincent's death he was invited to give the evening instructions on two occasions, May 10–19, 1663, and June 6–15, 1669.

[9] Abelly, *op. cit.*, Bk. II, Ch. II, sect. III, p. 222.

room for the operations of grace which alone enlightens and inflames hearts. One must leave oneself to enter into God ; He must be consulted if we are to learn His language and we must beg Him to speak in and by us ; He will then do His work, and we shall not spoil anything.'[10] Such was Saint Vincent's teaching, and he fully lived up to it.

The March retreat of 1656 was a great success. The cause of this was sought and it was easily discovered that the good results were due to the fidelity with which Nicholas Sevin, Bishop of Sarlat, had conformed to the programme 'without adding far-fetched ideas or new-fangled language.'[11] In 1658, Sarlat was again asked to give the June retreat. After one of the discourses, Saint Vincent went to him and said : ' My Lord, you converted me to-day.' ' How is that ? ' asked the Bishop. ' You spoke so simply and so well that I am touched to the heart, and I cannot prevent myself from praising God for it.' To this Sarlat replied : ' My language might, it is true, have been more polished and elevated, but I should have offended God, if I had not spoken simply.'[12] Saint Vincent was sometimes disappointed in his expectations. He speaks in one of his letters of preachers ' who have spoiled everything because they would not come down to the usual simplicity and the little method, or confine themselves to appropriate subjects.'[13] ' I was obliged,' he adds, ' during an ordination retreat, to kneel twice at the feet of a priest to beseech him not to wander away from the straight and beautiful path.' The priest in question was one of his own Missionaries, who remained deaf to the Saint's entreaties. It was obvious that he was not made for the Congregation and he ultimately left it.

The preachers received in advance a manuscript copy of a work entitled *Discourses for Ordinands*,[14] with a request

[10] Abelly, *op. cit.*, Bk. II, Ch. II, sect. IV, pp. 228–229.
[11] *Saint Vincent de Paul*, Vol. V, p. 572.
[12] *Ibid.*, Vol. XII, p. 23 ; Abelly, *op. cit.*, Bk. III, Ch. XV, p. 244.
[13] *Ibid.*, Vol. V, p. 572 ; Vol. XII, p. 24.
[14] Ms. copies of these *Discourses*, or rather only afternoon *Discourses*, are extant ; one in the Bibliothèque Sainte Geneviève, Paris, Ms. 2946, the other in the Bibliothèque de Beaune (Ms. 85).

to follow the subjects, order and plan of the sermons or lectures. It was the joint work of Olier, Perrochel, Pavillon and some other devout persons who had been induced by Saint Vincent to compile it about the year 1631. The names of the authors are a sufficient testimony to the value of the book. 'These discourses,' he said, 'were composed . . . and found to be quite sufficient. Other material has never been employed. I once made enquiries, even from Doctors of the Sorbonne, if a person with a good grasp of these *Discourses* would be qualified to hear confessions in villages and elsewhere, and they all replied that such a man would even be capable of hearing confessions in Paris.'

Saint Vincent imprinted on this particular form of retreat the stamp of his own genius for organisation which anticipated and made regulations for all points even in the smallest details. He was too well aware of its importance not to establish it upon a firm foundation. Apart from the two preachers who were to give the morning and evening discourses, there was also a general director of the retreat; priests appointed to preside at the repetition of prayer held after the meditations and instructions, and at the practice of ceremonies for the conferring of Holy Orders ; clerics to instruct the ordinands and look after their wants ; and brothers to cater for their material needs. Vincent de Paul selected all this staff from the community of Saint-Lazare, with the exception of the preachers, who were frequently from outside.

In 1647, during the December retreat, he appointed Firmin Get, who was then only a cleric, to preach the morning instruction ;[15] encouraged by the result of this experiment, he realised that the young should not be debarred from major employments. In 1650, he wrote : ' In the past our ordinations have always been directed by our older members, but we have made up our mind on this

Laurence Bouchet, a devout and prolific author, gave the morning instructions during the February, 1655, retreat. The manuscripts containing his lectures are in the municipal library of Chartres (Mss. 453 and 454) ; we can gather from them some idea of what the first part of the *Discourses for Ordinands* was like.

[15] *Saint Vincent de Paul*, Vol. III, p. 258.

occasion to allow Father Dufour, who is quite young, to take charge, and to entrust the care of the first academy to two young priests, one of whom has been ordained only a month or two, and the other two years. We shall not stop there.'[16]

When the time arrived for a retreat, Vincent de Paul did not fail to give advice to those who had any duty to fulfil in respect to the ordinands. He recommended them to be full of respect, courtesy and cordiality ' to foresee their wishes and desires,' ' to anticipate their wants and supply them ' as far as one reasonably could.[17] He insisted above all on humility and the pure intention of pleasing God, virtues essential to combat the natural desire for the esteem of others and the wish to appear learned.[18] He had no difficulty in showing what an unfortunate impression would be made on the ordinands by a Missionary full of his own importance. ' They are not won by knowledge, nor the beautiful language in which they are addressed ; they are more learned than we are ; several are bachelors and some licentiates in theology, others are doctors of Canon Law, and there are few who have not studied philosophy and a little theology ; they dispute on these matters daily. Scarcely anything we can say to them is new ; they have already either read or heard it ; they say themselves that this is not what affects them, but the virtues they see practised here.' And who are we ? ' Deficient in knowledge, deficient in intellect, deficient in rank. Alas ! how is it that God has chosen us for such a great work ! The reason is that God, as a rule, makes use of the humblest materials for the extraordinary operations of His grace ; as, for instance, in the sacraments where He makes water and a few words serve as a channel to confer His greatest graces.'

Such was the advice given by Saint Vincent to those of his confrères who were selected to deal with the ordinands. The other members of the community had also special duties to perform during the retreats. They too could contribute to the success of the exercises by their prayers, acts

[16] *Saint Vincent de Paul*, Vol. IV, p. 114.
[17] Abelly, *op. cit.*, Bk. II. Ch. II, sect. IV, p. 229.
[18] *Ibid.*, p. 226.

of self-denial, Holy Communions, and good example. Human means availed little if they were not accompanied by supernatural ones, especially prayer. 'Saint Theresa, who saw the need in which the Church of her own day stood of good labourers, besought God to be pleased to grant it good priests, and she also wished that the daughters of her Order should often pray for this intention; perhaps the change for the better in the ecclesiastical state at the present time is due in part to the devotion of that great Saint.'[19] In the same way, the success of an ordination might be due to the prayers of a humble brother who, without interrupting his daily work, would raise his heart to God to beg Him to bestow His blessing on the retreat.[20] But Saint Vincent insisted above all on good example. He wished to create an atmosphere about the ordinands conducive to devout sentiments and good resolutions. He never omitted to call the attention of the community to its liturgical obligations. 'I recommend attention to the ceremonies,'[21] he said one day, 'and I beg the Company to avoid the faults that might be committed at them. Ceremonies, indeed, are only shadows, but they are shadows of great truths, and it is essential that they be carried out with the greatest possible attention, and practised in a religious silence and with great modesty and gravity. How will these gentlemen observe them, if we do not perform them well ourselves? The chanting should be done quietly and modestly; the Psalms should be sung devoutly.'

Repeated exhortations such as these helped to prepare the environment in which ordinands were to spend their ten days' retreat; they formed part of the work of preliminary organisation.

When the ordinands arrived at Saint-Lazare they were requested to write down their names, official status and rank. Their luggage was then collected, and they were brought to their rooms, in each of which a printed card was placed indicating the order of day. The guide then withdrew, after requesting the ordinand to observe silence and the other rules and to practise modesty and recollectedness.

[19] *Ibid.*, p. 232.   [20] *Ibid.*, p. 230.
   [21] *Ibid.*, p. 226.

Seven hours and a half were allotted for sleep, after which the ordinands had a very full day ; half an hour for mental prayer ; recitation of the Office in common, with a pause at the asterisks ; during meals, a chapter from the Bible was read and also a work *On the dignity and holiness of the priesthood* by Molina, a Carthusian ; two hours a day were allotted to devout conversation ; an hour after each meal.

After mental prayer and after each lecture, the ordinands divided up into groups (based on the extent of their previous education) called 'Academies.' Each 'Academy' consisted of some twelve or fifteen persons, placed under the guidance of a Priest of the Mission, so that all might confer on the subject matter of the meditation in order to learn how best to apply its lessons to themselves, or on the lecture which they had just heard, that they might the better remember and profit by it. They were trained every day in the functions of the sacred order they were about to receive, and taught how to make a general confession of all sins committed since their last general confession or from the time they had reached the use of reason.

The instructions lasted an hour. The preacher, faithful to the plan laid down in the manuscript entrusted to him, spoke in the morning on matters concerned with Moral Theology, and in the evening, on the virtues demanded of ecclesiastics, on their duties, and the functions of each of the Holy Orders.

On the first morning, censures in general ; on the second, particular censures ; on the third, the sacrament of penance, its institution, form, effects, and the duties of a confessor ; on the fourth, the dispositions of the penitent—contrition, confession and satisfaction—and indulgences ; on the fifth, divine and human laws and on sin in general ; the circumstances, species, causes, effects, degrees of sin and of their remedies ; on the sixth, the first three commandments of the Decalogue, namely, those which determine man's duties towards God, and especially the three theological virtues, the virtue and acts of religion ; on the seventh, the remaining seven commandments, that is to say, our duties towards our neighbour ; on the eighth, the sacraments in general, Confirmation and the Eucharist as a sacrament; on the ninth, the sacrifice of the Mass, Extreme Unction and Matrimony; on the tenth, the Apostles Creed; what a priest is bound to know, and what he should do to teach others with fruit.

Prayer was deliberately placed first in the evening instructions, for as the practice of mental prayer was carried on daily, it was important that the ordinands should be at once taught how to make it. On the second evening, vocation to the ecclesiastical state; the dangers of embracing it if not called by God; its nature, signs, the means of recognising and faithfully corresponding with it; on the third, the ecclesiastical state; the need a priest has of this spirit, its nature, marks, and the means of acquiring and perfecting it; on the fourth, Orders in general, their institution, necessity, matter and form, specific differences, and the disposition requisite for their reception; on the fifth, clerical tonsure : the ceremony, obligations contracted by the ordinand, the qualities demanded by his state, the requisite dispositions, and solutions to any objections that might be brought forward; on the sixth, minor Orders : definition, matter, form, functions, and virtues of the state; on the seventh, the Sub-Diaconate, and the virtues essential to a sub-deacon, especially chastity; on the eighth, the Diaconate and the virtues proper to that Order, especially charity towards one's neighbour; on the ninth, the Priesthood and the knowledge priests are bound to acquire; on the tenth, the holiness of the ecclesiastical life : the duties clerics have to be more holy than the laity; means of sanctification.

Wednesday was the day fixed for General Confessions, and on Thursday, general Holy Communion during High Mass; the ordinations were held on Saturday. With this the retreat was over, but the ordinands remained at Saint-Lazare until after High Mass on Sunday to thank God in a body for the graces received.[22]

During the retreats, as we may see, piety went hand in hand with instruction. A good priest is at one and the same time an angel and a doctor; it does not suffice for him to pray to God; he is bound to pray according to the

[22] *Ibid.*, Bk. II, Ch. II. sect. III, pp. 218 ff.

regulations of the Church and is also bound to teach, and on occasions to defend his religion.

Bourdoise profited by the retreats he made at Saint-Lazare to spread the custom of reciting certain prayers, such as the *Benedicite* and *Thanksgivings* which he published as leaflets in 1636.[23]

Saint Vincent at first did not venture to entrust the direction of retreats for ordinands to his own Missionaries. After creating the Congregation to give missions in country places, he was doubtful as to whether this work might not suffer if he were to undertake other engagements, and it needed all the authority of the Archbishop of Paris to make him enter on this new road. Once the will of God was made known to him, he resolutely set to work, and it was at his own request that Urban VIII, in the Bull of Foundation, mentions the preparations of clerics for Orders by means of a general Confession and a retreat for fifteen days, as one of the works of the Congregation. Later on, another official act of the Holy See arrived further to inspire his zeal ; this was the Brief of Alexander VII (March 1, 1659) which granted special indulgences for retreats to ordinands.[24]

Saint Vincent had not to wait long to see the beneficent effects of these retreats. Not only did they inspire a large number of ecclesiastics with the desire to live well-regulated lives in which piety and charity found a place, but they were also the source from which two other important works derived : the Tuesday Conferences and spiritual retreats for all conditions of men and women. This is clear from one of his letters written in 1633 to Father du Coudray :[25] ' It has pleased the divine Goodness to bestow a most special and unimaginable blessing on the exercises of our ordinands. . . . All those who have made them here, or at least the majority, are leading such lives as good and perfect ecclesiastics should lead.' Even ' many individuals, conspicuous for their birth, or for other qualities bestowed on them by God, are living as regular lives at home as we do

[23] Courtin, *op. cit.*, p. 522.
[24] *Saint Vincent de Paul*, Vol. VII, p. 480.
[25] Abelly, *op. cit.*, Bk. II, Ch. II, sect. V, p. 233.

here, and are as much and even more spiritual men than many of us, or at any rate, than myself. They have their rule of life, their mental prayer ; they celebrate Holy Mass and examine their consciences every day like ourselves ; they visit hospitals, prisons and colleges where they catechise, preach and hear Confessions, with God's very special benediction. . . . There are twelve or fifteen in Paris who live in this way and who are men of rank, and the public are beginning to be aware of it. Now, during the past few days, one of these, referring to the mode of life led by those with whom he had been on retreat, suggested to the others an idea that had occurred to him, namely, that they should band themselves together in an association or company. . . . He did so, and all the others expressed a quite special satisfaction with the proposal. And as God has blessed the retreats made here by several parish priests of this diocese, these gentlemen wish to do likewise, and in fact, have begun to do so.' Ten years later, he wrote again : ' Everyone here recognises that the good that may be seen to-day in Paris chiefly comes from that.'[26]

The decorum of the ordinands, the order observed during the exercises and the excellent manner in which the ceremonies were carried out, attracted devout persons in search of edification to the Priory Church. Queen Anne of Austria had the curiosity to go and hear Perrochel ;[27] the Archbishop of Paris on more than one occasion attended the retreats ;[28] eight or ten bishops were present at some of the lectures.[29] The Prior of the Charterhouse of Mont-Dieu remained at Saint-Lazare for a whole day, and his emotion whilst the Pontifical was being explained indicated the intensity of his feelings. Before leaving, he wished to express his satisfaction to Vincent de Paul, and did so in such terms that the latter, when referring to the interview, excused himself for not repeating the Prior's words ' so laudatory were they.'[30]

[26] *Saint Vincent de Paul*, Vol. II, p. 361.
[27] Abelly, *op. cit.*, Bk. II, Ch. II, sect. II, p. 217.
[28] *Saint Vincent de Paul*, Vol. I, p. 480.
[29] Courtin, *op. cit.*, p. 474.
[30] *Saint Vincent de Paul*, Vol. III, p. 202.

Amongst other valuable results of these retreats for ordinands must be reckoned that of eliminating from the ranks of the clergy men who had no qualification whatever for the ecclesiastical state. Saint Vincent was very determined on this point; in 1657, three days before the September ordination, he called the attention of the Paris Chapter to a person on retreat who gave no signs of a vocation.[31]

The success of the Paris retreats induced a number of bishops in the provinces to introduce them into their dioceses. To the work of giving missions or training ecclesiastics, the Vincentians now added that of retreats for ordinands. Cardinal Richelieu made it obligatory on the house of the Congregation in Richelieu; the Bishops of Troyes, Saintes, Cahors, Mans and Agen asked the Missionaries residing in their episcopal cities to do likewise. Similar clauses may be found in the contracts signed by founders or benefactors of the Congregation of the Mission for the houses in Creçy, in the diocese of Meaux (1641), and La Rose, in the diocese of Agen (1643).

Lambert aux Couteaux, when Superior at Richelieu, once wrote to Saint Vincent to express his delight at the good example given by the ordinands: 'The people who see them reciting the Divine Office cannot restrain their tears on beholding the order, decorum, and devotion with which they carry it out, so much so that these good folk say that they seem not to be looking at men but angels of Paradise' (June, 1642).[32]

In 1643, Saint Vincent, at the request of the bishops, sent some of his priests to preach retreats at Reims, Noyon and Angoulême. They met with the same success everywhere, and the Bishop of Angoulême, so as to be sure of having preachers in the future, resolved to establish a house of the Congregation in his diocese.

At Noyon, several ordinands went to the retreat most unwillingly, because they had been ordered to; they had fully made up their minds either not to make a general confession or to select any confessor but a missionary. The lectures touched their hearts and modified their dispositions

[31] *Saint Vincent de Paul*, Vol. VI, p. 476.
[32] *Ibid.*, Vol. XI, p. 117.

so that they told their fellow-clergy that they felt quite transformed. The members of the Conference at Noyon, witnesses to the effects of grace on souls, sent a joint letter to Saint Vincent to express their joy and gratitude.

In 1644, whilst two Fathers went to render the same service to the ordinands of Chartres, two more responded to the call of the Bishop of Saintes. ' Our ordinands,' wrote the latter, ' are being marvellously blessed, and at present there is as much anxiety manifested to be admitted to the exercises as formerly there was difficulty, in certain cases, to get them to attend.'

Retreats for ordinands spread over almost the whole of France.[33] Several communities, such as the Oratory, the Nicolaites and the priests of the Most Holy Sacrament, took up the work. The Bishop of Valence required twenty days' residence in the seminary before each ordination. Devout writers composed books for the use of ordinands.[34] Saint Vincent was unable to meet the demands of several bishops for retreats, as he had not sufficient priests at his disposal.[35] However, he recommended Superiors of houses to hold themselves at the disposition of the bishop, in case the latter desired to send them ordinands of their dioceses, and to prepare candidates for Orders during ten days, according to the method employed at Saint-Lazare. He would have wished that all ordinands were admitted without payment, but his houses were not sufficiently well endowed to meet the expense.

The custom of holding these retreats spread from France to Savoy and Italy. Juste Guérin, Bishop of Geneva, in a pastoral letter of September 8, 1641, gave orders for his ordinands to spend the ten days before ordination in the Missionaries' house at Annecy. This establishment had been founded by Commander de Sillery and was obliged by the Commander to devote any surplus funds to defraying the expenses of retreats. A man who had made a retreat,

[33] *Ibid.*, Vol. VIII, p. 308.
[34] Francis Hallier, a disciple of Bourdoise, published in 1631, *Monita ad ordinandos et ordinatos*, duodecimo, reprinted in 1664. In 1639, appeared *Instructio spiritualis ordinandorum*, Parisiis.
[35] Abelly, *op. cit.*, Bk. II, Ch. II, sect. V, pp. 233-237.

touched by grace, threw himself at the feet of the Superior and said :[36] ' I am a sorcerer ; if I desired to enter the sanctuary it was that I might be able to pile horrible sacrilege on sacrilege ; I renounce the ecclesiastical state, for I am not worthy of it.' He made a general confession with tears in his eyes.

Cardinal Durazzo, Archbishop of Genoa, was one of the first prelates in Italy to understand the importance of this exercise. He had, it is true, the advantage of possessing a house of Missionaries in his episcopal city. Their Superior, Father Blatiron, wrote to Saint Vincent after an ordination : ' Our ordination was small in numbers but abundant in graces, God having plentifully showered down His blessings on it. The rules were exactly carried out ; such silence and seemliness reigned throughout the house during the exercises, especially at meal times, that the ordinands might have spent all their lives in our house.' He admired the fervour of his guests, especially at prayer and at the lectures ; he perceived by their tears that their hearts had been touched ; they were filled with regrets for past offences and fully prepared to correspond with God's graces. Nobody rejoiced more than Cardinal Durazzo at the good dispositions manifested at the close of this retreat. He maintained the custom of holding retreats in his diocese, and was rewarded for his zeal by the gradual transformation that took place in his clergy.

In Rome, the retreats for ordinands began in 1642, as a result of a generous donation from the Duchesse d'Aiguillon. Clerics who felt a desire to prepare for Holy Orders met in the house of the Congregation. Pope Alexander VII, than whom none more fully realised the excellence of this practice, wishing to extend it requested the Cardinal Vicar to impose an obligation on all clerics in Rome about to receive Holy Orders, to prepare for them by a ten days' retreat in the house of the Priests of the Mission. The order was promulgated in November, 1659, and a few days later, Father Jolly, the Superior, wrote to Saint Vincent : ' We are about to make preparations, in our own little way,

[36] *La vie de Mgr. Juste Guérin*, par Maurice Arpaud ; Bk. II, Ch. X, p. 242.

to be of service to the ordinands. Our confidence is in God who reveals Himself all the more clearly as the author of this work inasmuch as no one knows how this resolution to adopt it was arrived at, or who was its instigator. . . . I may say *a Domino factum est istud* and so we may hope that *qui coepit ipse perficiet.*'

The ordination was held during the December Quarter-Tense, and the preparatory retreat was carried out according to the programme of Saint-Lazare. The two brothers, Louis and Claude Chandenier, at that time guests of Father Jolly, edified all by their modesty and piety. Louis celebrated High Mass daily, in presence of the ordinands, whilst his brother acted as acolyte and thurifer. The lectures were given by two Italian confrères. Alexander VII took a lively interest in the proceedings, and wished to be kept fully informed as to how the retreat was progressing ; the news he received filled him with joy, and he gave expression to his satisfaction at the next Consistory.

There were two retreats for ordinands during Lent. Cardinals and other prelates mingled with the clerics to listen to the instructions. No one was exempt, no matter what his rank ; Cardinal Mancini's nephew, a Canon of Saint John Lateran's, and Count Marescotti, a Canon of Saint Peter's, were obliged to attend as well as everybody else. Whilst the third retreat was in progress, Father Jolly wrote to Saint Vincent : ' The ordinands whom we had at the beginning of Lent and those who are here with us now are so punctual at all the exercises and carry them out with such devotion, that we are all surprised. I may say that, as far as silence and decorum are concerned, it seems to me there is little or nothing to be desired. . . . Our Lord wishes thereby to let us see in a sensible manner, that . . . He alone . . . is the author of all these good things.'

A Spanish gentleman of the diocese of Placencia was present at one of these retreats and was perturbed by some of the discourses. The priesthood, for which he was quietly preparing, now seemed to him such a holy calling that he asked himself in dismay whether God had given him a vocation. It needed all the authority of his director to set his mind at rest. After the ordination he saw his bishop, then Ambassador Extraordinary of the King of Spain at the Court of Rome, and communicated his admiration for the retreats for ordinands to that prelate. 'The bishop,' Father Jolly wrote to Saint Vincent, ' wishes to come here during the next ordination and asks if, after he has returned to Spain, we can let him have some of our priests ; in the meantime, he wishes to send a report to his diocese of what is done here during an ordination so as to have a beginning made at home.'

The Bishop of Placencia kept his word ; he followed all the exercises at the next ordination, and all that he saw confirmed him in the design to extend this exercise to his own clergy, and even to invite the Priests of the Mission to his diocese to carry on this work and to give missions. Saint Vincent was in no hurry to meet the Bishop's views ; he was afraid lest Father Jolly, instead of allowing Providence to do its work, had influenced the Bishop, and advised Father Jolly to be discreet : ' As for this good prelate . . . no matter what desire he manifests of having our priests, hold out no hopes to him, but at the same time, do not utterly discourage his desire ; nay, rather, respectfully and thankfully listen to all that he may have to say to you on the matter. Do not even give him the notes for which he asked you, though you may do so later. . . . We should be on our guard against thrusting ourselves into places where we have no house and into employments we have not already adopted.'[37]

The Congregation of the Mission had barely begun to exist. The obligation imposed on all ordinands in Rome to go to one of its houses and prepare for the reception of Holy Orders aroused jealousy in an older and more distinguished religious Order. One of its members stated publicly, during the examination for ordinands, that it was unbecoming to oblige persons of rank to make a retreat with the Missionaries, and that the Pope would withdraw his command. Those who were dissatisfied won over some influential personages to their side, but their attempts to convince the Cardinal Vicar and the Holy Father himself proved all in vain, for both of them resisted all intrigues

[37] *Saint Vincent de Paul*, Vol. VIII, p. 279.

and held fast to their decision. Nothing could have been more admirable than Saint Vincent's conduct in the circumstances. After reading out to his assistants the letter written by Father Jolly to inform him of the opposition with which he was meeting, the Saint added : ' How would human prudence and wretched nature behave in such circumstances ? One would go and complain to the members of this Society, to their friends and to our friends ; one would take sides against this body. That is what the maxims of the world demand of us. But as these maxims are of shifting sand and those of Jesus Christ so many little rocks, it is to the latter that the Company should attach itself. Let us resist human nature, and let us remain steadfast. Now, if we listen to Jesus Christ, we shall not say a word about the matter to this body, either to their or our friends ; not only shall we do nothing against the Order, but we will take its part, we will praise it and be happy that it is praised ; we will help it every time an opportunity occurs of doing so. The Father Examiner thought he was at liberty to say what he said ; he found it hard to persuade himself that strangers like us—quasi gentiles in Rome, for we live so far away from it—could succeed at this employment. If we act uprightly, we shall have all men on our side. Gentlemen, let us pray to God that we may act uprightly in all places, in Rome and elsewhere, and hold so fast to our rules and the maxims of Jesus Christ that the world cannot find anything to blame in our conduct, and remember that it was said of Jesus Christ : *Posui te in signum cui contradicetur.* But, Oh ! wretched man that I am. What a comparison ! O my Saviour, forgive me ! So then let us hold fast, Gentlemen ! '[38]

Alexander VII, instead of listening to the opposition party, extended the regulation, in 1662, to the clerics of the six suburbicarian bishoprics ordained in their diocese, and lest any should escape by underhand means, he declared that the rule applied to clerics ordained outside the accustomed times, and reserved the right of dispensation to himself. Following the Pope's example, Cardinals granted

[38] *Ibid.*, Vol. XIII, pp. 175-177. (The opposition came from some Jesuit Fathers. Vol. XIII, p. 175.)

their patronage to the retreats given in the house of the Congregation in Rome. Amongst those who took part in the exercises were Cardinals, Superiors General of Orders, and other persons of distinction. Cardinals Barbarigo, Albici, and de Sainte Croix even accepted invitations to deliver some of the lectures.

The example given by Rome proved contagious. In 1662 the Priests of the Mission gave a retreat in Bergamo. About the same time, the Archbishop of Naples, at the suggestion of one of his priests who had followed the exercises in Rome, established retreats in his dicoese, and the custom has been followed by innumerable dioceses in Italy ever since.[39]

When Saint Vincent reflected on the choice God had made of his young Congregation for ' such a holy eminent and heavenly work,'[40] he could not refrain from admiring the divine Goodness and humbling himself in God's sight. ' It is to us,'[41] he once said to his confrères, ' that God has granted such a great grace as that of re-establishing the ecclesiastical state. God did not turn for that . . . either to theologians or to the many Communities and religious Orders full of knowledge and holiness, but to this poor wretched Company, the last and most unworthy of all . . . O, Gentlemen! faithfully preserve this grace . . . If, through our negligence, we leave it unused, God will take it away from us and bestow it on others to punish us for our unfaithfulness. Alas! which of us will be the cause of such a great misfortune? Which of us will deprive the Church of such a great boon? Will it not be my wretched self? Let each of us put his hand on his heart and say to himself: " May I not be this unfortunate man? " Alas! all that is needed is just one such wretch as myself who, by his abominations, will turn away the favours of Heaven from a whole house and bring down on it the maledictions of God.' At these words he raised his eyes to Heaven and said : ' O Lord, who beholdest me entirely covered and filled with sins that weigh me down, do not on that account

[39] Abelly, *op. cit.*, Bk. II, Ch. II, sect. VI, pp. 237-244.
[40] *Ibid.*, sect. IV, p. 223.
[41] *Ibid.*, p. 224.

deprive this little Company of Thy graces ; grant that it may still continue to serve Thee with humility and fidelity, and that it may co-operate with the design Thou seemest to have of making through its ministry a last effort to re-establish the honour of Thy Church. . . . O Lord ! grant us the spirit of Thy priesthood, such as the Apostles and the first priests who followed Thee possessed ; grant us the true spirit of that sacred character which Thou hast stamped on poor sinners, on the working folk and poor people of those days when Thou didst communicate to them this great and divine spirit.'[42]

This spirit was all the more needed for the Priests of the Mission inasmuch as divine Providence, after confiding to them retreats for ordinands, was on the point of calling them to the direction of seminaries.

[42] *Ibid.*, p. 223.

CHAPTER XXX

SEMINARIES

THE seminary for ecclesiastics, set up in the Collège des Bons Enfants in February, 1642, was begun at the same time as that in Vaugirard by M. Olier, who had admitted the first three seminarists in the preceding month.[1] For some time previously there had been a strong tendency in the episcopacy to encourage such seminaries, of which, as du Ferrier tells us,[2] de Condren on his death-bed was strongly in favour, and which several bishops wished to confide to the direction of the Priests of the Mission. Saint Vincent refers to this in a letter written on February 3, 1641, to the Superior of the house in Rome :[3] 'Their Lordships the Bishops all seem to wish to have ecclesiastical seminaries for young men. His Lordship the Bishop of Meaux, who is willing to have a foundation made in his diocese, desires this. His Lordship of Saintes has made us a similar offer.' He then proceeds to rejoice at the thought of the good his Missionaries were being called on to accomplish for the welfare of the Church. 'God will make use of this Company ; in regard to the people, by missions ; in regard to those about to be priests, by ordinations ; in regard to those already priests by refusing to allow those who have not made a retreat nor been instructed in a seminary to accept benefices or curacies ; and in regard to those who hold benefices, by spiritual exercises.'

The Bishop of Geneva, Juste Guérin, was also thinking of establishing an ecclesiastical seminary in his diocese, but unlike the Bishops of Meaux and Saintes, he did not intend

---

[1] *Saint Vincent de Paul*, Vol. II, p. 225.
[2] *Vie de M. Olier*, par Faillon, 4ᵉ ed. Paris, 1873, 3 vols. oct., Vol. I, p. 292.
[3] *Saint Vincent de Paul*, Vol. II, p. 153.

to exclude children. The Priests of the Mission had a house in Anneçy and it was to them he wished to entrust his seminarists; Saint Vincent therefore was justified in pointing out to the Bishop the difficulties of such a project. 'The plan of His Lordship of Geneva,' he says in the letter already quoted, ' seems to me to be good taken as a whole, except that he wishes to have children educated in it; for up to the present I have never heard anyone say that a seminary of this kind proved successful, as far as the welfare of the Church is concerned; experience teaches us the contrary as far as those of Rouen, Bordeaux and Agen are concerned. I shall write my own little ideas on the matter to the holy prelate, or at any rate to Father Codoing; but pray do not raise the difficulty there' (i.e. at Rome).

Father Codoing was Superior of the Missionaries at Anneçy and shared his bishop's views; Saint Vincent advised him not to admit ' any but priests or persons ... in Orders, and not to teach the latter the theological sciences but the practice of them, as is done with the ordinands,'[4] When he wrote this letter on September 15, 1641, the Bishop of Geneva had already begun his seminary. In the pastoral charge published on this occasion, he declares that the seminarists shall follow in the public College ' classes in grammar, rhetoric and philosophy.' The establishment was open, on principle, not merely to clerics in Orders but also to aspirants to the priesthood who had not received Tonsure, that is to say, to children.[5] As far as one may guess from Saint Vincent's letters, the Priests of the Mission had nothing to do with this section of the seminarists, but only with the ecclesiastics, who certainly formed a group apart, from 1641 onwards, as in the Bons Enfants; that is to say a real ' great seminary.' This is certainly implied in a letter of Saint Vincent to Father Codoing (February 9, 1642) : ' You have begun a seminary at Anneçy; His Lordship of Alet who has some of our priests is doing the same; His Lordship of Saintes has a similar design, and

[4] *Ibid.*, Vol. II, p. 188.
[5] *La Vie de Mgr. D. Juste Guérin,* par Maurice Arpaud, Anneçy, pp. 247–251.

we are about to make a beginning here in Paris with twelve students.'[6]

The seminary at Alet admitted ordinands for the diocese, and was in full swing on October 20, 1641, for on that day Nicholas Pavillon, the Bishop, wrote to Saint Vincent : ' The extreme ignorance of candidates for Holy Orders and the slight hope of their acquiring greater knowledge in the future has compelled me to summon them to Alet and to keep them here as long as it may be necessary to teach them the minimum required to gain admittance. I am employing Father Blatiron at this work, and any other ecclesiastics we have at hand, to help on this little project, which is, so to say, just an experiment.'[7] After some further attempts, the Bishop of Alet began in 1645, but without the help of the Priests of the Mission, a ' great seminary,' which contained twenty-five pupils[8] on February 5, 1646, and from eighteen to twenty[9] on February 15, 1660.

Alain de Solminihac, Bishop of Cahors, was too zealous a bishop to allow himself to be forestalled by other prelates in the establishment of seminaries. Scarcely had he arrived in his diocese when he convoked a Synod (April, 1638) and declared his intention to open a seminary so as to assure the formation of the clergy of his diocese. This declaration was received somewhat coldly, for those who held benefices foresaw pecuniary sacrifices. The Archdeacon even ventured to state openly, what all were thinking : ' Take care, the clergy are very poor.' The Bishop was indignant at the remark ; he spoke of the beauty and value of the work, and the duty of all to collaborate with him, as it was not a personal but a diocesan affair ; he then pointed out that there were many in his diocese who were wasting the patrimony of the Church and of the poor in profane and scandalous ways. He asked how such money could be better employed than in helping to educate ecclesiastics, and spoke so eloquently that the adversaries of the project were convinced.

Fortified by the Synod's approbation, Alain de

[6] *Saint Vincent de Paul*, Vol. II, p. 225.
[7] *Ibid.*, p. 195.   [8] *Ibid.*, p. 563.
[9] *Ibid.*, Vol. VIII, p. 244.

Solminihac rented a private house for the reception of his ordinands; he himself took charge of the retreats and he selected one of his parish priests and a religious from Chancelade to give the instructions. One of his biographers writes: 'Such were the feeble beginnings of a small, regular community in which everything was carried out in an orderly fashion and in which the most edifying and beautiful sight was that of our prelate kindling the fires, laying the tables in the refectory, and cheerfully performing the humblest duties.'[10] The Bishop unfortunately could not always be present; the administration of his vast diocese frequently called him elsewhere. There was need of a man on the spot capable of taking the bishop's place and such a man was not to be found. 'Deprived of the fruits for which he had hoped,' as he says himself, he called the Priests of the Mission to his assistance in 1643, and took occasion of their arrival to re-organise the seminary completely. He bought an enclosed piece of property, in the finest quarter of the city, where he erected a seminary, and annexed to it the cure of Saint Bartholomew so as to afford the seminarists opportunities of becoming acquainted with parochial functions, endowed it by a union of simple benefices, established six burses for young clerics, and made a rule that no one should be ordained subdeacon unless he had spent six months in the seminary. This period was prolonged for those who desired to be dispensed from the prescribed canonical intervals. On April 14, 1646, a further period of six months' residence was added before a candidate could receive ordination to the priesthood.

The seminary at Cahors took a new lease of life with the arrival of the Priests of the Mission. In 1647, there were thirty seminarists;[11] the maximum number was rapidly reached, with the result that all places had to be reserved for clerics of the diocese.[12] It was not without a certain amount of pride that in 1649 Alain de Solminihac wrote to

[10] *Vie de M. Alain de Solminihac*, par le P. Léonard Chastenet, p. 215.
[11] *Saint Vincent de Paul*, Vol. III, p. 143.
[12] *Le premier grand séminaire de Cahors et les prêtres de la Mission*, par M. Foissac, 1911, oct., p. 29.

Saint Vincent of his seminary : ' Those of your priests who have seen it say that it is the finest in the kingdom, and a short time ago I was told that order is better maintained in it than in those of Paris.'[13]

James Raoul, Bishop of Saintes, was, like Alain, a friend of the Saint's ; hence he was one of the first bishops to take thought of the training of his clergy. As far back as 1633 or 1636, he had induced his clergy to allocate a grant of two thousand livres for a seminary. For a long time he was doubtful where to lodge his seminarists, and after much hesitation, he selected a ruined edifice in the suburbs, the Priory of Saint Vivian, which he fitted up to the best of his ability. On March 18, 1644, he officially announced the opening of a seminary for young ecclesiastics, and in the same year, he united it to the Congregation of the mission. This part of France had long been given over to heresy, and hence vocations were few.[14] In 1656, there was not even one pupil in the seminary ; there were three in 1657,[15] and four or five in 1658.[16]

The number of seminaries directed by the Priests of the Mission increased as its Founder grew older. In 1645, Mans and Saint Méen were added, and later, Marseilles, Tréguier, and Agen (1648), Périgueux (1650), Montauban (1652), and Narbonne (1659). On April 9, 1647, Saint Vincent thus reviewed the seminaries confided to his Congregation : ' We have sixty priests in the Collège des Bons Enfants, forty young seminarists in the seminary of Saint Charles and thirty ecclesiastics in the seminary at Cahors . . . In Anneçy, there are eight, who are also making a good beginning, as many in Mans and twelve or fifteen in Saint Méen.'[17] In the following year, he mentions in a letter that his Company took charge of seminaries for ' those who are ready to take Holy Orders . . . others are for young children who aspire to the ecclesiastical state, like the " little seminaries " in Saint-Lazare, Saint Méen, and Mans, and both together are about to be started in Agen.'[18]

---

[13] *Saint Vincent de Paul*, Vol. III, p. 167.
[14] *Ibid.*, Vol. V, p. 628.   [15] *Ibid.*, Vol. VI, p. 424.
[16] *Ibid.*, Vol. XII, p. 66.   [17] *Ibid.*, Vol. III, p. 167.
[18] *Ibid.*, p. 379.

CHARLES DE CONDREN,
SUPERIOR OF THE ORATORY OF FRANCE

The Marseilles seminary prepared candidates for Orders. Owing to the civil wars of the Fronde, it lost all its sources of revenue and was closed in less than a year after it had been opened. When re-opened in 1656, it was almost solely to admit novices from the Abbey of Saint Victor, who continued their classical studies, and who had to be removed in 1658 for disciplinary reasons.

The Montpellier seminary also did not last very long.

Saint Vincent recalled his priests from the Périgueux seminary some months after their arrival, because, as he wrote to the Vicar General, ' God has not been pleased to grant us the grace to be of service to His Lordship and his diocese.'[19]

He was not discouraged by a few failures; they, too, just as much as successes, were in the order of Providence. With his eyes fixed on the future of the Church of France, he thought himself happy to be one of those who were preparing for it. ' Our little functions,'[20] he wrote, ' have been seen to be so beautiful and useful that they have stirred others to emulation, and they now devote themselves, like us, and more successfully than us, not only to giving missions but also to directing seminaries, which are multiplying greatly in France.'

France had never perhaps seen such a galaxy of apostolic men. They had an acute comprehension of the needs of their time, and all, or almost all, clearly perceived that their first duty was to devote their efforts to the restoration of ecclesiastical order. Their zeal proved the more efficacious as they had at hand, ready to march at the first sound of command, disciples trained in their schools and animated by their spirit: Bérulle, de Condren and the Oratorians; Bourdoise and the Nicolaites; Olier and the Sulpicians; Saint John Eudes and the Priests of Jesus and Mary; Christopher d'Authier de Sisgau and the Priests of the Most Blessed Sacrament.

Besides these founders of religious communities, occupying a higher rank in the ecclesiastical hierarchy, but obliged by their position to confine their activities within a narrower

[19] *Ibid.*, Vol. IV, p. 168.
[20] *Ibid.*, Vol. VIII, p. 510.

compass, there were saintly bishops whose chief preoccupation was to provide their flocks with clergy fitted to instruct and edify them; men such as Sebastian Zamet of Langres, Augustin Potier of Beauvais, Charles de Montchal of Toulouse, Alain de Solminihac of Cahors, James Raoul of Saintes, Juste Guérin of Anneçy, Charles de Leberon of Valence, Nicholas Pavillon of Alet, Francis Stephen de Caulet of Pamiers, Francis Perrochel of Boulogne, and Anthony Godeau of Grasse.

It would be unjust to omit the name of Cardinal Richelieu. The Prime Minister of Louis XIII encouraged all these men of good will to the best of his ability. Vincent de Paul, as we have seen, received one thousand crowns from the Cardinal to establish a 'great seminary' at the Bons Enfants; Bourgoing, the Superior of the Oratorians, three thousand crowns for seminaries at Saint Magloire in Paris, Rouen and Toulouse. At his command, his niece, the Duchesse d'Aiguillon, gave fifteen hundred livres to Saint John Eudes to establish a seminary in Caen. He graciously offered his castle at Rueil to M. Olier, who did not accept it, for the seminarists of Vaugirard. He encouraged Christopher d'Authier de Sisgau, endeavoured to bring him to Paris to establish a seminary there, and endowed the seminary of the Priests of the Most Blessed Sacrament in Valence by uniting two cures. Bourdoise also would have had a large share in his benefits if he had not, by his unmannerly conduct towards the Duchesse d'Aiguillon, wounded her uncle's susceptibilities.

As a result of this movement and these generous endowments of the Cardinal Minister, the chief evolution in the history of French seminaries was brought about in 1642 by united action. It was in this year that Olier and the Superior of the Oratory opened their first seminaries for ordinands, the former in Vaugirard and the latter in Saint Magloire, Rouen and Toulouse. It was also in 1642 that Saint Vincent, by creating an ecclesiastical seminary alongside one for students in the Collège des Bons Enfants, actually established the distinction between a 'great' and a 'little seminary. The year 1642 marks the beginning of the movement that was to give rise to the Congregation of Saint

John Eudes, the transformation of the College of Saint Nicholas-du-Chardonnet and, in a general way, to the establishment of ecclesiastical seminaries in the form in which we now know them.

The single type of seminary, in which the lower forms were composed of children who proceeded upwards step by step until, if they persevered, they reached the priesthood, more and more tended to divide into two separate parts. It was no longer one, but two seminaries that were in existence, sometimes housed in the same, sometimes in different buildings : the 'little' and the 'great' seminary. In addition to those who passed from the little to the great seminary, we find in the latter type, clerics educated outside any seminary, who wished to receive Orders. They either entered voluntarily to acquire the necessary knowledge or were sent there by a bishop who made residence in a 'great' seminary a condition for ordination. Some 'great' seminaries, such as the Bons Enfants, also contained within their walls young priests desirous of receiving a training they had not obtained before ordination. This type of seminarist obviously tended to disappear as time went on, for a time did come when no one could be raised to the dignity of the priesthood unless he had gone through a seminary ; then the 'great' seminaries were only seminaries for ordinands where students prepared for Holy Orders by a more or less prolonged sojourn.

Bourdoise established a special type of seminary—the parochial. The seminary was simply an extension of the presbytery ; it was placed under the jurisdiction of the parish priest, and prepared solely for the exercise of parochial functions. The teaching was of a purely practical character. It was not a diocesan seminary as the term is now understood. Parochial seminaries either became useless when true diocesan seminaries were established, or were transformed into the latter by the authority of the bishop who brought them under his own jurisdiction. The seminary of Saint Nicholas-du-Chardonnet was of this special type. In the beginning, it admitted as residents, clerics, priests, children, young men, and before 1641, even persons with no inclinations for the clerical life.

Students went there to carry on their classical education, to see if they had a vocation, to make a retreat and to prepare for Tonsure, Holy Orders and the Priesthood. Newly ordained priests were bound to go to Saint Nicholas to learn the ceremonies of the Mass and the rubrics of the Breviary and Missal; if priests came from other dioceses they had to pass an examination. Of the ten members who made up the community in 1627, one was in charge of students who pursued their work in the University; three were employed in elementary schools for boys, and the others assisted the rector to fulfil his parochial obligations. From 1637 to 1642, a special 'Clerical Fund' enabled Bourdoise to give board and lodging, education and training, to one hundred and eighteen poor ecclesiastics for the space of about a year. Parish priests were admitted in preference to others, and priests in preference to clerical students. Between 1631 and 1644, more than five hundred priests passed through the seminary of Saint Nicholas. In 1631, the Archbishop of Paris gave it verbal approval, and on April 20th, 1644, it became the diocesan seminary.[21]

The Venerable Olier was a worthy rival of Bourdoise. Sometime in January, 1642, the first three seminarists arrived in Vaugirard where Olier and his first collaborators, Caulet and du Ferrier, then resided. His intention was to admit only such clerics as had completed their classical studies. This was not the only modification Olier made of the plan of the Council of Trent. The seminary was not open to poor young men unable to pay a pension, and when it was transferred to Saint-Sulpice (August, 1642), as it was on territory under the spiritual jurisdiction of the Abbot of Saint-Germain-des-Prés, who gave it his approval in 1645, it was exempt from episcopal jurisdiction.[22] Theiner and Degert have called attention to this fact, and the latter rightly adds[23] that the exceptional condition of the diocese

---

[21] *Histoire du séminaire de Saint Nicholas-du-Chardonnet*, par P. Schoenher, Paris, 1909, 2 vols., 8vo, Vol. I, pp. 65 ff.

[22] *Histoire des institutions ecclésiastiques*, translated from the German by J. Cohen, Paris, 1840, 2 vols., 8vo. Vol. I, p. 316.

[23] *Histoire des séminaires français jusqu'à la Révolution*, Paris, 1912, 2 vols. 16's, Vol. I, p. 191.

of Paris dispensed M. Olier from the obligation of slavishly following out the plan proposed by the Council of Trent. This seminary was greatly influenced by Bourdoise's parochial type. When one reads the various lives of M. Olier one cannot but feel how the latter, whilst paying more attention to theoretical teaching, was influenced by Bourdoise, who remained for some time in Vaugirard to point out the road to be followed.

When in 1620 Cardinal de Retz united Saint Magloire to the Oratory, he laid down a stipulation that a seminary should be established there and that twelve students of the diocese should be provided with free board, lodging and education. Years passed before this stipulation could be carried out; Saint Magloire did not establish regular courses in theology until October 10, 1640, and was not really constituted a seminary until 1642, as the result of a grant made by Cardinal Richelieu. On April 16, 1642, De Blois, the Superior of the Oratory, wrote to de Chavigny, Secretary of State : ' I went to Lyons on the first Sunday of Lent . . .[24] Before I left Paris I had made a beginning, in our house of Saint Magloire, of an institution for young ecclesiastics in accordance with His Eminence's intentions and commands. There are only fourteen, carefully selected ; but several who have made application, whilst remaining on a waiting list for a year or two, give much promise of being useful to the Church.'[25] Bourgoing, after stating the subjects that were taught at Saint Magloire—moral theology, preaching, method of catechising, ritual, administration of the sacraments, sacred chant, and ceremonies—adds : ' A course of studies carried out in the same manner has been begun in Rouen. . . . We hope, as soon as possible, to establish a similar institution in Toulouse.' The seminaries at Rouen and Toulouse had only an ephemeral existence, and even Saint Magloire itself carried

[24] March 9.
[25] This letter was published in full by Mgr. Prunel in *Etudes*, the organ of the Jesuit Fathers, in February, 1909, pp. 349-350. Further information on the early organisation of the seminary of Saint Magloire may be found in the Arch. Nat. M.228^B, February, 1642.

on with great difficulty and was ultimately abandoned. In 1658, the Oratorians petitioned the Archbishop of Paris for authorisation to open their seminary on July 1, 1660, and in the meantime, to admit six ecclesiastics selected by themselves. The seminary was begun again in 1660, in virtue of a decree of Cardinal de Retz.

This establishment was not very flourishing when, on September 18, 1660, a week before his death, Saint Vincent, passing in review the four seminaries of Paris, gave the following curious appreciation of each : ' Here, in Paris, are four houses engaged in the same work : the Oratory, Saint-Sulpice, Saint Nicholas-du-Chardonnet and the wretched Bons Enfants.[26] Those in Saint-Sulpice tend and direct all their efforts to raise men's minds and hearts from things of earth and all earthly affections, to lead up to great spiritual enlightenment, to lofty, elevated thoughts and feelings, and we see that all who have been there attach great importance to all this ; in many instances, this state of mind and heart increases or diminishes ; I do not know if they study scholastic philosophy and theology there. Those in Saint Nicholas do not aspire so high ; they concern themselves with the work of the vineyard, in turning out hard-working men for ecclesiastical duties, and to that end insist on : (1) practical work always and everywhere, and (2) lowly employments such as sweeping, washing dishes, brushing . . . lowly employments ; they can do so because most of the people there are admitted without fees. . . . The Oratory, let us leave it alone and not talk about it. Of all these four houses, the most successful is, incontestably, Saint Nicholas, in which there are so many shining little suns ; I have never seen anything there to complain of, but always matter for edification. So Saint Nicholas then, is the most useful, and we should aim at that, or at least strive to imitate them. You know that scholastic (philosophy and theology) is never taught there, only lessons in moral theology and practical matters.'[27]

---

[26] This was a term of humility and not of contempt ; Saint Vincent might have referred, in the same way, to ' our poor little Company.'

[27] *Saint Vincent de Paul*, Vol. XIII, p. 185.

Whilst the founders of the new communities were inclined to establish by preference seminaries for ecclesiastics alone, Christopher d'Authier de Sisgau, founder of the Priests of the Most Holy Sacrament, remained faithful to the old Tridentine ideal. His plan for a seminary contains the following passages: 'Clerics admitted to the seminary shall study Hebrew, Greek and Latin; they shall then take up the study of Literature and Philosophy; after which, they shall study Positive Theology, Scholastic and Moral Theology, and also Canon Law; subsequently, they shall be trained in controversy. At the same time, they shall be taught Sacred Music or the Chant sung in Church, holy Ceremonies, and the worthy administration of the sacraments. But they shall study above and beyond everything else to conform their conduct to the laws of ecclesiastical discipline and to raise up their minds to the heights of their sublime vocation. Hence, conferences shall frequently be held on the sacrament of Orders and on the excellence and dignity of the priesthood. Poor persons who show good dispositions for the ecclesiastical state shall be admitted to the seminary. The Institute will provide, at its own expense, for their board and maintenance; it shall teach and train them until they are fitted for the priesthood by age, virtue, and knowledge.'[28] According to d'Authier, the seminary was not meant to exclude retreats for ordinands, for the two works were complementary. His priests, who were entrusted with the direction of the seminary at Valence, received and prepared ordinands for a period of twenty days before ordination.

Charles de Leberon, Bishop of Valence, provided for the maintenance of twelve young clerics in his seminary during his whole episcopate. At first, the seminary went on so well that d'Authier never doubted of its success, but Saint Vincent, who had learned from experience, did not share his optimism. 'M. d'Authier and M. Le Bègue,' he wrote,[29] 'are certain that theirs will succeed. Now, I have no doubt that in their case this will prove true in the beginning,

---
[28] *Histoire des séminaires du diocèse de Valence*, par le chanoine Nadal, 1895, oct., p. 20.
[29] *Saint Vincent de Paul*, Vol. II, p. 460.

but undoubtedly . . . it is greatly to be feared that the fruits will never ripen and that the various accidents I have mentioned will spoil them.'

When Saint Vincent saw how seminaries were multiplying, he thanked God that the Church of France was at last about to enter on a new era. No one realised better then he the absolute necessity of clerical training; hence he made it one of the principal ends of his Congregation which had been primarily instituted to give missions. He attached equal importance to both works, and, as he said, a man who desired to be engaged in one and was unwilling to take up the other was only ' half a missionary.'[30]

He had the loftiest idea of what a director in a seminary should be. ' Oh ! how happy you are,' he wrote to one of them,[31] ' to serve as one of Our Lord's instruments for fashioning good priests, and to be such an instrument as you are who enlighten and animate at the same time ! In this you are performing the office of the Holy Ghost to Whom alone it pertains to enlighten and inflame hearts; or rather it is this Spirit, holy and sanctifying, Who effects that through you; for He resides and operates in you, not only to make you live by His divine life, but also to establish His very life and operations in these gentlemen, called as they are to the loftiest ministry on earth, by which they are bound to exercise the two great virtues of Jesus Christ, namely, religion in regard to God, and charity in regard to man. Reflect then if there is any employment in the world more necessary and more desirable than yours; as for me, I know of none.'

If this office is one of the noblest, it also needs special qualities for its worthy fulfilment. A good director should be a devout and interior man, mistrustful of self and full of confidence in God, humble and modest, firm without rudeness and gentle without mawkishness. He is placed in a seminary chiefly to train students in virtue, and if his words are accompanied by example they are bound to prove of untold influence. ' It is not enough,' Saint Vincent wrote to the Superior of a seminary,[32] ' to teach them the chant,

[30] *Saint Vincent de Paul*, Vol. VII, p. 561.
[31] *Ibid.*, Vol. VI, p. 393.   [32] *Ibid.*, Vol. IV, p. 597.

the ceremonies and a little moral theology ; the principal thing is to train them to be solidly pious and devout. Now to do this, Sir, we should first be filled with piety ourselves, for it would be almost useless to give instruction and not example. We should be like reservoirs of water to be poured out on others, without suffering any diminution in ourselves, and we should possess the spirit with which we desire them to be animated, for no man can give what he does not possess.' We should avoid behaving ' like masters to those under our charge ' ; we should dis-edify them ' if we wish to be over polished and fastidious, treat ourselves too comfortably, seek to make ourselves honoured and esteemed, are on the look-out for amusements, spare ourselves and have too much communication with externs. One should be firm but not rude in one's government, and an insipid sort of gentleness that serves no good purpose should be avoided.'

The director should unite knowledge of the subject he teaches to virtue. Although Saint Vincent's type of mind was practical, he had the highest esteem of knowledge and learned men. His diplomas of Bachelor of Theology and Licentiate in Canon Law, his close relations with doctors of the Sorbonne, and of the College of Navarre, such as Andrew Duval, Nicholas Cornet and John Coqueret, and still more his writings against the errors of his time, clearly prove this fact, against which Jansenist calumnies will ever prove unavailing. But what is true, and this cannot be levelled as a reproach, is that virtue was in his eyes superior to knowledge ; virtue played a greater part in the conversion of heretics than theological learning, and knowledge without virtue was practically sterile and even dangerous. 'Knowledge is essential,' he said to his disciples, ' and woe to those who do not employ their time profitably ! But let us fear, let us fear, and I even venture to say let us tremble a thousand times more than I can express ; for those who are intellectual have much to fear ; *scientia inflat* ; and those who are not intelligent are in even a worse plight if they be not humble.'[33]

Saint Vincent prepared his young men in Saint-Lazare

[33] *Ibid.*, Vol. XI, p. 128.

for the office of teaching in seminaries by several years devoted to study. The priests themselves, both young and old, attended lectures on Moral Theology, Sacred Scripture, preaching and catechising, the administration of the sacraments and casuistry. At this time, the course of studies in a diocesan seminary was limited to a few months, or a year or two at most. What students chiefly sought in a seminary was practical instruction; they were taught how to celebrate Mass, to administer the Sacraments, recite the Divine Office, preach, chant, catechise and solve cases of conscience. Those who wished to make a thorough study of Philosophy, Dogmatic Theology, Sacred Scripture, Canon Law and other branches of clerical studies, attended lectures at the University. During the period passed in a seminary, the students had not sufficient time for the speculative sciences; they had to be taught essentials, and the essentials were practical as opposed to theoretical knowledge.[34] Saint Vincent admired the method adopted in Saint Nicholas-du-Chardonnet and advised his disciples to follow it. 'As there is no better way of learning than to see how a thing is actually done,'[35] he said in one of his conferences, 'they are accustomed at Saint Nicholas-du-Chardonnet not to allow a priest to baptise until they have brought him a child on whom he performs the ceremonies observed in Baptism. The same holds true for Confession; one of the seminarists behaves as if he were at confession, says out aloud sins that may possibly he committed, and the priest who is listening, if the student does not accuse himself properly, interrogates him. The same thing is done for Holy Communion.'

The seminarists of Saint Nicholas had the advantage of being able to carry out ecclesiastical ceremonies in the parish church to which they and their directors were attached. Hence they made greater and more rapid progress than those trained within the four walls of a lecture

[34] Some days before his death, Saint Vincent, speaking of the Bons Enfants Seminary, said that he would suppress the chair of scholastic theology because it was of little or no use and also because it was easy to follow courses of Theology in the Sorbonne or the College of Navarre.

[35] *Saint Vincent de Paul*, Vol. X, p. 625.

room. Saint Vincent had observed this, and as a result, though he had long refused to accept parishes in cathedral cities, he came to wish that wherever a seminary was established, a parish church should be united to it, so that the students might be initiated into all the works of the ministry.[36] He even went further; he did not hesitate to send advanced students on the mission, at least for some time, and this, too, was his motive for wishing to have a few Missionaries on the staff of every seminary.[37] In accordance with the same principle, he recommended the practice of controversy; one student stating objections and the other answering. At Saint-Lazare such exercises were carried out with a certain amount of ceremony, on account of the rank and position of those invited to attend. Several famous controversialists, such as Francis Véron, Girodon and Beaumais, were present from time to time, and gave the students valuable lessons in the art.

The teaching, therefore, was primarily practical, but not exclusively so; theoretical teaching cannot be dispensed with in a seminary; but here, too, Saint Vincent had a method of his own. A class, as he conceived it, should go through three phases: first, the professor explained to the students a few pages of a good text-book; next, the pupils repeated the substance of the professor's explanations, either that evening or the following morning; and finally the students were allowed a certain amount of time to ask further explanations of any points they had not fully grasped.[38]

He strongly insisted on keeping to a good text-book, and a professor who yielded to the temptation of dictating a course of lectures or even simply giving notes, was severely reprimanded when the fact became known in Saint-Lazare. In his eyes, such dictation of notes or lectures was unnecessary, and he put forward excellent reasons for his objection to the practice. 'There is such an abundance of authors . . . who have mapped out their matter so well that one need only have recourse to a good casuist in case of need.' The doctrine taught ' will be more certain, as it is

[36] *Ibid.*, Vol. VII, p. 253.   [37] *Ibid.*, Vol. IV, p. 43.
[38] *Ibid.*, Vol. II, p. 212.

the teaching of an approved master, than the writings of a private individual.' The seminarists 'will much prefer an approved author than the writings of a young man who has given no proof of his theological knowledge in the schools.' A large number of members of the Congregation are quite well able to explain an author; very few are qualified to compose courses of lectures. To prepare such courses the subject should be studied profoundly, many books should be read, and this can only be done by men who devote themselves exclusively to study and authorship. But in seminaries, professors have several other duties to perform and therefore have not sufficient time at their disposal. If they become too much absorbed in writing books, they will not have sufficient time for anything else. 'Who,' he asks, 'will instruct the seminarists on the interior life? Who will teach them to catechise and preach and who will see that order is observed? A large staff would be needed for each seminary; who would maintain them, and what would become of the missions?' Hence there should be no dictated courses of lectures, but good text-books such as Binsfield or the smaller edition of Bécan should be employed.[39]

Such were Saint Vincent's instructions to his professors. In our time 'great seminaries' are not what they were in his; students now remain several years, professors are more numerous and specialise far more in the subjects they teach, and a much greater part is assigned in the curriculum to speculative branches of learning. Yet, despite the difference in time, there is still much that is valuable in the Saint's advice to his disciples. Lectures and class work develop a student's intellect, but instruction is only part of what a seminary is supposed to do; the will should be trained and developed, as well as the intellect; a priest stands in even greater need of the natural and supernatural virtues than he does of knowledge; the ecclesiastical spirit must be formed—that is to say, the student is bound to acquire habits of piety, respect for the hierarchy, and zeal which will incline him to sacrifice all, even life itself, for the glory of God. The acquisition of such a spirit is fostered and

[39] *Saint Vincent de Paul*, pp. 231 ff.

maintained by retreats, mental prayer, spiritual conferences, exhortations, the reading of devotional works, devotion to the Blessed Sacrament, the frequentation of the Sacraments of Penance and the Holy Eucharist, good example and obedience to rule. The rules of a seminary are concerned with each of these exercises and indicate the necessary dispositions for their suitable observance.

Devotional exercises and study took up most of a seminarist's day, and we shall now supply some details of seminary life in Saint Vincent's time. Students rose at half-past four and then went to morning prayer; Matins and Lauds were recited standing; next came mental prayer for half an hour, kneeling, preceded or followed by Prime, according to the season of the year; after this a chapter of the New Testament was read in private. At seven o'clock, they attended Mass in the parish church; before setting out, they washed their hands, meanwhile praying to God to wash and purify their souls; a procession then started, the students walking two by two, the juniors going first. When Mass was over, the senior student gave the signal for departure, and they moved off without showing any undue haste. When they reached home, they were free to go to the refectory or remain fasting. If the weather was very cold, the student who was appointed to light the fire did so, and then each withdrew to his room to prepare for class. At half-past eight, Terce, explanation of the ritual, and a lecture which was brought to a close at ten o'clock by the recital of the antiphon of Our Lady. Then followed half an hour's reflection by each student in his own room on what he had heard in class. At half-past ten, from October to Easter, half an hour's manual labour carried out in silence: the house was swept, the garden tended, fire-wood cut and stacked; on Saturdays and the eve of Festivals, the church was swept and decorated; after Easter, a lesson was given in Plain Chant. At eleven o'clock, Sext, the midday meal, and a cheerful and gay period of recreation during which two faults were to be avoided: over-seriousness and levity. Each student was free, if he so wished, to play billiards, bowls, or any other game consistent with ecclesiastical decorum.

At one o'clock, preparation for the next lecture, after a few moments spent in recollection in the prayer hall. At two o'clock, None and class. From October to Easter, a class of Plain Chant was held. At four o'clock, study. At five, Vespers. At half-past five, spiritual reading, bareheaded and kneeling, from the New Testament, and in preference, from the Gospels; if anyone so desired, he was also free to add a passage or so from the *Imitation*. After Easter, the class in Plain Chant was discontinued; Vespers and spiritual reading were advanced half an hour so that the half-hour's manual labour, omitted in the morning, might be carried out before supper. At six o'clock, particular examen in the prayer hall, then the evening meal and recreation. At eight, prayer, Compline, and the subject of the following morning's meditation was read. At half-past eight, bed, and lights out by nine o'clock.

There was a special order of day for Sundays and Festivals. Rising was at four, and at half-past the students came down vested in surplices. Then came morning prayer, meditation, after which they attended divine service in the parish church. If the Bishop was to be present, the students proceeded to his residence and accompanied him to church; if not, they were obliged not to leave the Choir until the faithful had departed. After service, they returned to the seminary where each student remained in his room until the last bell had rung for the parochial Mass. If the bell had not rung before eight o'clock, Terce was recited, but if it had, this canonical hour was recited after returning from church. Next came breakfast and study. At eleven o'clock, Sext, the particular examen, the midday meal and recreation. At one o'clock, study and reading of the Bible. At half-past two, they went back to church for afternoon devotions. On their return, the Gospel or rubrics were studied. Spiritual reading followed at five and at half-past, the litany of the Holy Name of Jesus was recited and they meditated until six o'clock. The remainder of the day was spent in the usual way save that Compline had been recited in church.[40]

[40] *Le premier grand séminaire de Cahors*, par Adrien Foissac, Cahors, 1911, oct., p. 15.

This order of day observed in the diocese of Cahors was, so the biographer of Alain de Solminihac tells us, the same as in all seminaries directed by the Priests of the Mission.[41]

The Bons Enfants had a special set of regulations drawn up by Saint Vincent himself.[42] Two retreats were prescribed: the first, on entering the seminary, and the second on leaving; the latter retreat, in the case of those who were clerics, being the retreat before ordination. Mass was to be celebrated every day by the priests;[43] the clerics were to be present, and with their director's permission, to go to Holy Communion at least on Sundays and Festivals. Divine Office should be recited in common. The students should consult their directors on their spiritual progress at least once a month. To honour the Passion of Our Lord, the evening meal on Fridays should consist only of one dish of herbs or vegetables. Each student should in turn wait at table. During meals, which should be taken in silence, a book should be read. There were certain regulations regarding students' rooms: they should not be locked; they should be swept twice a week; fellow seminarists should not enter the room but should transact all necessary business at the door; each student should make his own bed every morning. They are recommended to observe clerical simplicity and modesty in regard to their clothes, beards and hair, and to avoid, when abroad, 'taverns, tennis courts and bowling greens as poisonous resorts.' It is stated that on this last point, no permissions will be granted and no excuses taken. It is clear from one clause that all courses of lectures were not given in the seminary, and

[41] *La vie de Mgr Alain de Solminihac*, par le P. Léonard Chastenet, nouv. éd. Saint-Brieuc, 1817, duodec., p. 224.

[42] This rule is certainly anterior to 1680, for the 9th article states: 'They shall sedulously attend the Divine Office, which shall be said in common according to the Roman Breviary,' and the diocese of Paris abandoned the Roman Breviary in 1680. The form and substance clearly reveal the hand of Saint Vincent. Several clauses reproduce word for word the rules given to his Missionaries. This rule was printed, with some modifications, after 1680, (Bibl. Maz. A 15, 451, piece 24) and reprinted in 1720.

[43] At least in the beginning, the priests went every day to say Mass in Notre Dame. (*Saint Vincent de Paul*, Vol. II, p. 535.)

from another, that towards the end of the time, permission would be given to go on missions.

Clauses 13, 14 and 15 deal with abuses long since dead, and from which happily modern seminaries are completely free. 'They shall above all strive strenuously to repress that over-eagerness for the reception of Holy Orders, manifested by so many and shall leave this matter entirely in the Superior's hands. And as *extra tempora* are, in the case of most of those who avail themselves of them, an abuse rather than a dispensation, no one shall make use of them without express permission, in case of urgent necessity and after having prayed, during some days of retreat, for the dispositions that should precede ordination. Newly ordained priests shall endeavour to say their first Mass in the seminary; in which case, they shall not introduce an extern ecclesiastic to assist at the ceremony, save with the Superior's consent; and they shall avoid, as far as possible, inviting lay-folk, especially women, to be present. And in complete opposition to the usage of this corrupt century which turns occasions of piety into motives for sensual indulgence, they shall not be at pains to make any other preparations than that of a good retreat during three or four days. They may, nevertheless, after Mass, detain five or six of their nearest relations or friends to dine with the community. The 37th clause advises seminarists to return home to their own dioceses, on the completion of their stay, ' both to reside in their benefice, if they have one, and to ask to be employed.'

Saint Vincent had the consolation of seeing the Church of France renewed, thanks to the spread of seminaries. Discipline flourished once more, the standard of ecclesiastical science and virtue was raised, holders of benefices renounced such as they were forbidden to retain by the Councils, parish schools multiplied and the zeal of ecclesiastics was greatly stimulated. They began again to wear the cassock, cut off their flowing locks, gave up hunting, kept out of taverns and met together periodically to discuss liturgical questions and points of moral theology; in some places they even lived together under the same roof to help each other to lead a virtuous life; parish priests became more assiduous in teaching their flocks by preaching and catechetical instruction.

As an inevitable result, the faithful, better instructed and encouraged by the example of their pastors, were more zealous in observing their religious duties. ' Oh ! Gentlemen,' said Saint Vincent one day, ' what a great thing is a good priest. What cannot a good ecclesiastic accomplish ! What conversions can he not effect ! The welfare of Christendom depends on the priests ; for when good parishioners see a good ecclesiastic, a charitable pastor, they honour and obey him ; they try to imitate him. How should we not strive to make them all good, since it is our duty, and the priesthood is so exalted.'[44]

If Saint Vincent had merely striven to train the clergy, he would not have fully attained his object ; for they had not merely to be trained but the fruits of their formation had to be preserved. Amongst the means of preservation that occurred to him were two in particular : first, the creation of ecclesiastical associations, and second, an annual retreat in common. The associations which he organised were known as Conferences, of which we have already spoken ; we shall now deal with retreats for ecclesiastics.

[44] Abelly, *op. cit.*, Bk. II, Ch. V, p. 298.

CHAPTER XXXI

RETREATS FOR ECCLESIASTICS[1]

AS we shall see in another chapter, there was not a single day in the year when at least twenty externs, including laymen as well as ecclesiastics, might not be seen on retreat at Saint-Lazare. Such private retreats produced good results, but collective retreats for persons in the same state of life with the same objects in view, presented more favourable opportunities, since they enabled all the meditations, lectures and sermons to be directed towards a common end. This was the motive of Saint Vincent's desire to introduce annual retreats for ecclesiastics.

The first attempt was made in 1633. Several parish priests of Paris voluntarily met at Saint-Lazare to make a retreat, and God blessed their devotion. The members of the Tuesday Conferences, who constituted the élite of the Parisian clergy, shortly afterwards followed this example and afterwards kept up the custom.[2] It is hard to know why the practice of holding ecclesiastical retreats was so long restricted to such a small group, when one bears in mind their value for the entire clergy. As the matter really depended on the Archbishop of Paris, it is probable that the question of expense was the chief obstacle to the custom being adopted.

What Saint Vincent was unable, to his great regret, to realise in Paris was established in the provinces by his disciples. Nicholas Pavillon, Bishop of Alet, and Francis Fouquet, Archbishop of Narbonne, both former members of the Paris Conference, worked a reformation amongst

---

[1] The matter of this chapter has been taken almost entirely from Abelly, *op. cit.*, Bk. II, Ch. IV, sect. IV, pp. 286 ff.
[2] *Saint Vincent de Paul*, Vol. I, p. 205.

RETREATS FOR ECCLESIASTICS

their clergy by means of ecclesiastical retreats.[3] They had all the greater merit for introducing and keeping up this practice inasmuch as many of their priests, and these not the least influential, openly opposed the project and fomented discontent amongst the clergy, and also because the prelates put themselves to personal inconvenience by throwing open a portion of their residences for those who were making a retreat.

The success of the first retreat in Narbonne, given by a Priest of the Mission, surpassed all expectations. Those on retreat, brought face to face with their consciences, enlightened as to the gravity of their past sins and the greatness of their ministry, realised, perhaps for the first time, the full extent of their obligations. The tears that flowed from their eyes bore witness to the sincerity of their repentance. Most of them made confessions of their past lives as far back as the days of their youth. Those who had been compelled to attend, went home rejoicing, and publicly expressed their satisfaction; whilst those who had congratulated themselves at not having had to make the retreat, felt their joy turn to regret.

Prejudices were overcome, and as a result, invitations to make a retreat were in future gratefully accepted. As on the first occasion, hearts were opened to admit the grace of God.

One of the most striking conversions was that of a priest who had hitherto dishonoured the sanctity of his state by a life that was by no means exemplary. He was gradually influenced by the force and conviction of the preacher's instructions, the order and regularity of the exercises, the modesty and recollection of his confrères, until he at last began to feel ashamed of himself. Nevertheless, he found it extremely difficult to go to Confession and, after putting it off to the evening before the day fixed for Communion, could not even then make up his mind. He went to bed without having made his peace with God, but the thought of confession did not cease to haunt him; he began to tremble all over; a cold sweat broke out over his body and

---

[3] *Saint Vincent de Paul*, Vol. II, p. 491; Abelly, *op. cit.*, pp. 286–287.

he grew terrified. He thought that God was about to strike him dead for this want of docility to Divine Grace. One of his fellow priests was sleeping in the same room; he woke him up and said: ' I am going to die; hurry off and bring me the Missionary.' The priest arrived. It was midnight when he began to hear the man's confession, which lasted for four hours, interrupted by spells of sobbing and fainting fits that almost seemed as if they would carry him off completely. After the penitent had recovered peace of mind, he rapidly regained bodily strength. He went to Holy Communion and when the retreat was over he was a completely reformed man. ' My sins were public,' he repeated, ' and I am bound to make public reparation for them.'

After the retreat, many priests, realising how little fitted they were for the guidance of souls, asked permission to spend some time in a seminary to become acquainted with their duties and to learn how to lead a devout life.

When the time arrived for the annual retreat, they continued to express their readiness to attend, and in order to surmount obstacles arising from want of sufficient funds, they made contributions to meet all necessary expenses.

Cardinal Durazzo, Archbishop of Genoa, should be reckoned amongst the prelates who chiefly distinguished themselves by their zeal for ecclesiastical retreats. He set the example by making a retreat every year either in his own palace or with the Missionaries in their house in Genoa. He was present every morning at prayer, kneeling devoutly from the first moment to the last; if compelled by fatigue to rise for a few minutes, he humbly asked permission to do so from Father Blatiron, the Superior. He made his repetition of prayer just like the others, and was present with the Missionaries in the chapel, the refectory, and at all the exercises; the only difference between the Cardinal and the Missionaries was his greater simplicity, humility and devotion. At the end of the retreat, when the Superior requested him to bless the Missionaries, he replied that he would gladly receive the Superior's blessing.

A prelate who realised so fully in his own person the value of a spiritual retreat, could not but advise others to adopt the practice. He was one of the first bishops in Italy to organise retreats for ecclesiastics in his diocese, and these were given in the house of the Missionaries under the direction of the Superior. Father Blatiron kept Saint Vincent regularly informed of the excellent effect produced by these exercises on those who had gone through them. 'I cannot express,' he wrote on one occasion, 'the great consolation they all have received, nor the abundance of graces communicated to them by Our Lord, nor the great modesty and exact silence with which they have been carried out, nor their humility and sincerity in the accounts they have given of their mental prayer, nor the wonderful and almost miraculous conversions that have been effected.' Amongst those converted was a parish priest whose reputation was none too good; he was addicted to vice, an intriguer, a detractor, more particularly of Cardinal Durazzo and the Missionaries. He had acquired a benefice by simony, received sacred Orders on the title of this benefice alone, carried out the duties it entailed, administered the sacraments, and for several years exercised all the functions of a parish priest. He came to make the retreat, not from any love of it, but from interested motives, for he intended to ask the Cardinal for an increase of revenue and hoped that his apparent piety might favourably dispose the Bishop in his regard. This unfortunate priest, moved by the preacher's words, conceived a horror of his state, shed tears, humbled himself, resigned the benefice, and by his conversion, helped to effect that of many others.

After another retreat, Father Blatiron wrote: 'The parish priests left last Friday, all full of fervour and greatly edified; they say wonderful things about the graces God has bestowed on them. . . . I have never seen such good dispositions, nor so many tears shed; I cannot even think of it now without surprise and admiration. . . . I saw thirty of them together in the room, without even one venturing to say a word to another.'

Those on retreat, moved by a desire to humble themselves, publicly confessed their sins. 'We are in the valley of Josaphat,' one of them remarked, whilst listening to these confessions. Cardinal Durazzo's zeal and perseverance had their reward. His priests realised more and more the exalted dignity of their state and the extent of their obligations ; the people, better guided by their pastors, showed themselves more attached to their faith and more observant of their religious duties.

It is to be regretted that all dioceses were not governed by prelates of Cardinal Durazzo's stamp, and that difficulties of a material order limited the activities of the more zealous. If the practice of holding retreats for ecclesiastics was somewhat slow to spread during the seventeenth century, at least the primary impulse had been given, and this impulse, like so many others, had come from Saint Vincent de Paul, who, by his priests, wherever they were established, promoted the reform and sanctification of the clergy. The reform of preaching was also one with which he busied himself, but the importance of this subject demands a chapter to itself.

CHAPTER XXXII

THE REFORM OF PREACHING

FULLY to understand the importance of the reform wrought by Saint Vincent de Paul on Christian eloquence, it behoves us to know what were the abuses with which he had to contend.

'Pulpit eloquence,'[1] wrote du Vair in 1594, ' has remained in such a debased condition that I have nothing to say about it.' Bad taste held undisputed sway : the pulpit resounded with incessant references to mythology ; displays of secular learning ; frequent employment of dry scholastic phraseology ; flowery, over-emphatic, trivial and grotesque language ; a laborious and subtle search of Sacred Scripture for the most unexpected symbolical interpretations ; burlesque grouping of words and ideas ; impudent satire ; violent and contemptuous attacks on political adversaries and on partisans of the reformed religion.

The first characteristic of pulpit eloquence is, or should be, its sacredness ; it is sacred in its sources, for it borrows its material from the Scriptures, the Fathers, the history of the Church and the lives of the Saints ; sacred in its aim and object, for its whole claim is to set forth the truths of Faith, to build up and reform Christian morality.

The exaggerated infatuation for pagan antiquity which was propagated during the Renaissance in all cultivated circles, extended even to Christian orators. Quotations from Plato, Aristotle, Cicero and Virgil were mingled with the words of Jesus Christ, the Evangelists, Saint Paul, Job and Saint Augustine. The faithful heard as much of philosophers, poets and scholars as they did of the Bible and the Fathers. In one homily alone, Camus, Bishop of Belley

[1] *De l'éloquence française et des raisons pourquoi elle est demeurée si basse*, Paris, 1606, oct., au début.

and friend of Saint Francis de Sales, quotes fifty lines in Latin from Virgil, Horace and Lucretius.[2]

Simile and metaphors afforded preachers an opportunity to display the extent of their learning. They appealed to the most fabulous and quaintest elements of history, art and science. As jasper has the property of driving away serpents, so the Church, by her authority, expels heretics. As the phœnix never leaves the mountains of Arabia, so truth ever abides with the Church. The seven gifts of the Holy Ghost are typified by the seven mouths of the river Nile; the virtues by the signs of the Zodiac. The fountain of Albania, to which Pliny attributes the property of relighting extinguished torches and of quenching lighted ones, symbolises the pool of penance ' which extinguishes the torches of sin and rekindles those of virtue.' The *remora*, a small fish powerful enough to bring to a standstill the largest ships flying with all sail spread, is an emblem of sin, ' by which the great ship of humanity sailing on the sea of grace was arrested.'[3]

The taste for fables was strikingly manifested in the way preachers borrowed from the old mythologies. The Jesuit, Gaspard Seguiran, wishing to prove that works do not justify without grace, introduces the gods of Olympus. ' It would seem,' he says, ' as if the poets have in a manner anticipated this truth when in their fables and fictions they tell us that on one occasion all the gods and goddesses assembled in heaven before Jupiter the great to select whatever tree should be the most favourable for each. Jupiter, in the first place, chose the oak for himself, Apollo, the laurel, Juno, the juniper tree, Venus, the myrtle, and so on with the rest. When Minerva observed this selection she burst out laughing and said it would have been better to choose trees that bear fruit rather than fruitless plants which supply nothing but leaves and shade. Jupiter answered and said : " Not so, the gods have not chosen

---

[2] *Collection intégrale et universelle des orateurs sacrés*, par Migne 100 vols., oct., 1844–1892, Vol. I, Coll. 2 ff.

[3] *Conceptions théologiques sur le caresme*, par Pierre de Besse, Paris, 1629, oct., pp. 123, 137, 185, 372, 398. The first edition dates from 1609.

trees on account of their fruits but solely for their own good pleasure and by their sovereign will." [4] It is certainly going very far afield when a preacher selects a remark of Jupiter's from the pagan poets to help us to understand the necessity of grace. However, it was pleasant enough to let a large congregation see that one had read, studied and remembered much. Fashion and vanity fully explain this vogue.

When Camus wished to apologise, before a General Assembly of the three Estates, for speaking after an eminent orator, he felt it necessary to invoke Timotheus, Roscius, the Thebaid, and the Aeneid, Marsyas and Apollo, Protogenes and Timomachus. Here is a specimen of his style. ' Am I not touching the harp after Timotheus, who, of old, with an artistically supple thumb, drew sounds that seem to speak, from lifeless strings? Am I not standing at the bar after the eloquent Roman, or occupying the tribune after the father of Greek fluency? Am I not appearing on the stage after Roscius, that excellent actor, when I now speak from this place, after an orator more admirable than imitable, whose musical numbers, fruitful fecundity and ravishing movement still fill the memories of this audience with astonishment? Is this not rashly to complete the imperfectly perfect verses of the majority of poets, to introduce a cringing Thebaid after an Aeneid, improve on Pindar, whose immeasurable poems forbid emulation and who has been placed by the Roman lyrist in an unattainable position, is this not to follow in the track of that loftily elevated stag, which one is permitted to scent but not to ensnare? Should I not fear the fate of Marsyas who dared to contend in song against Apollo, or that of Arachne who matched her needle against that of Minerva? . . . Do I not see, feel and recognise so many Themistocles incapable of sleep, fascinated by the victory of Marathon gained by this Miltiades? But yet again, Gentlemen, I ask you is it not to retrace a line drawn by Apelles, to complete the Venus of Phidias, the Ialysus of Protogenes and the Medea

[4] *Sermons doctes et admirables des dimanches et festes de l'année preschéz en divers lieux par un docte et célèbre personnage de nostre temps*, Paris, 1617, p. 32.

of Timomachus, for one to follow after such a mind which should have no other rival than itself? Shall it then come to pass that Iris shall be the daughter of Taumanthias, and she, the daughter of Ignorance?'[5]

It would have needed a vast amount of erudition to follow the orator through this mixture of Pagan Antiquity and Fable. And yet, this is only a short extract from the homily of Camus; the rest of his address is in the same vein.

On another page we come across[6] 'those who lived and died with Anthony and Cleopatra,' with Alexander, Cæsar, Sulla, and those who fell at Thermopylae, with 'Thracians writhing and sobbing, weeping and bleeding from the nose,' with Ajax 'who, in his madness, mistook swine for the followers of Ulysses,' with Demosthenes (whose tongue was more efficacious than the lance,) 'the gilded mule of Philip.'

Quotations such as these could be multiplied with the greatest ease, but the reader perhaps has had enough. Imagine the boredom of a modern audience compelled to listen to strings of sentences like these for an hour or more; and yet people flocked in crowds to listen to preachers who followed this fashion. One can only conclude that they were able to interest their hearers who may have found some pleasure in this strange medley of far-fetched and conflicting conceits, inserted at random into these sermons, or perhaps the audience may have wished to seem equally learned by pretending that it enjoyed these amazing productions. It may have been one or either of these causes, or perhaps both.

Christian literature is sufficiently copious to furnish preachers with material without their having to call the pagans constantly to their assistance. But selections taken from the Bible or from Christian authors should be really and not only apparently true, and preachers should not, for example, introduce interpretations of the sacred text merely to display their own more or less ingenious theories which are sometimes utterly foreign to the ideas of the Holy Spirit.

The Sacred Scriptures have in all ages been exploited in a surprising fashion both by exegetes, primarily inter-

[5] Migne, *op. cit.*, col. 37.   [6] Migne, col. 22.

ested in the literal sense, by preachers and ascetical writers chiefly concerned with moral lessons and symbolical meanings. If the pursuit of the mystical sense of the Sacred Scriptures is not bound by the strict rules that govern the interpretation of the literal sense, nevertheless, it should not be left to individual caprice and fancy ; mystical interpretation should be employed with moderation, and only in cases where the sacred text easily and naturally lends itself to such treatment. Many writers, amongst whom must be reckoned Fathers of the Church, such as Saint Augustine, and Doctors, such as Saint Bonaventure and Saint Francis de Sales, yielded too easily to their love of allegory and imagery.

They were persuaded that the Holy Ghost concealed beneath each word, each verse, secret and mysterious meanings which it was their duty to discover and expound for the edification of the faithful. Amazing efforts were made to explore in this way the inexhaustible mine of the Sacred Scriptures, and to disclose all their treasures. Subtlety was added to subtlety in order to arrive at farfetched and more or less imaginary analogies, ingenious and unexpected interpretations, odd and quaint revelations, and forced applications of the text. For example, when after the death of Our Saviour, the holy women went to the sepulchre, they were asked by the Angel : ' Whom seek ye ? Jesus of Nazareth ? ' Now, if a preacher proceeded to develop this passage along the lines that ' we, like the holy women, should seek after Jesus,' there is no doubt that more than one practical lesson might be drawn, without expatiating on the two words ' of Nazareth.' If these words were added, a medieval preacher declares, this was not done without a reason. To find Jesus, one must become a Nazarene like Him, and at once he proceeds to develop complacently the marvellous analogies he has discovered between the law of the Nazarenes and the Christian law ; for instance, the Nazarenes were forbidden to go indiscriminately into the houses of all dead persons ; so, too, Christians should avoid some of the dead, namely, sinners given over to the works of death,'[7] and other analogies of equal value are then set out.

[7] Albert le Grand, *Opera, sermones de tempore*, 1651, Vol. XII, p.70.

Again, in the Book of Genesis, the following sentence may be found : *Germinet terra herbam virentem*, in which the coming of the Messiah would seem to be foretold. But why *virentem* asks a medieval archbishop ?[8] And he makes the following interesting discovery : green is a soft, intermediate colour and therefore well represents the Messiah Who is the middle term between the perfection of the divine essence and the imperfection of our nature. Once more, the red cord hung out by the woman of Jericho to save her house from pillage, was regarded as the symbol of charity, because charity, which is all on fire, draws us to the gates of eternal salvation.[9] Another example ; the Saviour was arrested in the Garden of Olives ; Why ? asks Peter de Besse, and then supplies the answer ; it was because Adam sinned in the garden of Paradise, and chaste Susannah's honour was compromised in a garden. A garden symbolises prosperity and pleasure. The Holy Spirit wishes to teach us that ill fortune will overtake us when everything seems to be going for the best.[10] Again, under the Old Law, a red heifer was sacrificed outside the camp and its ashes employed to sanctify men. The same orator, in the same sermon, preached on Holy Thursday, goes on to say : ' To-morrow, to-morrow this beautiful mystery will be revealed, for the heifer of our sacred humanity will be immolated without the walls of Jerusalem.'[11] The solitary sparrow, like the red heifer, is another symbol in the eyes of Peter de Besse. ' Solitary souls,'[12] he cries out, ' behold the solitary sparrow of which David prophesied : *Vigilavi et factus sum sicut passer solitarius in tecto*. Behold this beautiful bird which loves only desert places, which sings, twitters, imitates the nightingale's song and makes a music of prayer. Sighs serve as the bass part, cries the soprano, tears the tenor, prayers the contralto ; the love of our redemption beats time.'

The Canticle of Canticles is, of course, the favourite book

[8] De Voragine, Archbishop of Genoa († 1292). *Sermones quadragesimales*, Paris, 1518, duodec. Sabbato primae hebdomadis, Sermo I.

[9] Saint Bonaventure, *Opera*, Venice, 1655, duodec. Vol. X, p. 278, in die Pentecostes, Sermo II.

[10] *Premières conceptions théologiques pour le caresme*, p. 556.
[11] p. 565.   [12] p. 556.

THE REFORM OF PREACHING

of preachers who delight in symbols and the most delicate passages, instead of intimidating, seem to attract them. Thus, Seguiran pauses at the words *Venter tuus eburneus* to inform his hearers that baptism is here prefigured. Ivory symbolises the elephant, and this animal, as naturalists tell us, gives birth to its offspring under water ; hence, it is an image of the Church which gives new life to the children of Adam in the waters of Baptism.[13]

Seguiran and his contemporaries were undoubtedly blessed with ingenuity; but they made a singularly unhappy use of it. If preachers desire to show their ingenuity, the pulpit should not serve as the theatre of their exploits, nor the inspired text as the subject on which to exercise a fantastic imagination in pursuit of subtle and elaborate interpretations. Exaggerated symbolism is one abuse ; another is that of regarding the pulpit merely as a professor's chair and not also a chair of eloquence. The preacher's business is not only to instruct ; he should enkindle and move ; hence, the scholastic method is not suitable here. Nevertheless, it was fashionable for a very long time, and was still employed in the first year of the seventeenth century in the sermons of some orators.

They behaved the same way in church as they did in schools ; they defined, divided, demonstrated and refuted. Definitions were formulated in abstract terms ; divisions were followed by sub-divisions ; proofs were set out in syllogistic form ; refutations afforded room for subtle distinctions and sub-distinctions which, instead of bringing light, cast ' an inspissated gloom.' Eloquence lost all its charm under the parching breath of scholasticism with its entities and quiddities ; it became a science and ceased to be an art ; it was still instruction but not an instruction that touched the heart the better to penetrate the mind.

Logic is not everything where man is concerned ; it is in fact of very little value when it comes not to instructing but exhorting. Sinners are quite well aware that their conduct is bad ; it is not by proving with irrefutable arguments that they are doing evil that they can be brought back to the path of duty. A theological lecture and a sermon are two quite

[13] *Op. cit.*, p. 146.

different things. The professor of theology ends with speculation; the preacher urges to action, and a method suitable for one is by no means suitable for the other. The preacher has the faithful before him, and not a class of students. He needs a certain amount of liberty; the impulses of the heart, the outpourings of charity cannot be confined within the prison walls of a syllogism or a dry definition. The articles of the *Summa* of Saint Thomas are masterpieces of dialectic, but no one will claim them as masterpieces of eloquence. They convince but do not stir the emotions; reason is satisfied, but the heart is not touched; when we read them we do not experience those countless, mysterious excitations produced by warm and vibrant speech.

Nevertheless, the scholastic method and its thousand subtleties were introduced into the Christian pulpit. John Menot, Oliver Maillard, John Paulin and many another fell into this deplorable fault. Seguiran seems to have drawn his inspiration from some theological *Summa* or another when he sat down to prepare his sermons. In the wake of learned, medieval theologians and in the same terms, using their language at need the better to imitate his models, he tells us that there are three sorts of prayer: obsecration, oration and postulation; that the virtues have two aspects: the first, *quantum ad affectum*, the second, *quantum ad effectum*; that original sin is defined as *privatio rectitudinis in esse*; and that God is present in the souls of the just *per modum objecti cogniti*. How could formulas such as these move the souls of his hearers, for they are rather calculated to darken than to enlighten, to cool than to inflame men's minds and hearts.

Coton, too, had a mania for employing scholastic language in the pulpit; his sermons are filled with the definitions and divisions employed in the schools. He borrows from Boethus the definition of eternity: *Interminatae vitae tota simul et perfecta possessio*, and of happiness: *Status bonorum omnium aggregatione perfectus*. Works, he informs us, are to be divided into living, dead, deadly, mortiferous, and vivifying works; their causes are efficient, final, meritorious, formal, exemplary or instrumental; living or life-giving works are, at one and the same time, meritorious, satisfactory, impetratory and consolatory. Speaking of death, he points out that one thing can be in another in four different ways : either as the contained in the container, collocated in its natural situation, or the accident in its subject, or the part in the whole ; what is an integral, a potential, and an essential part. He goes on in this way with a dry, pedantic and fatiguing series of distinctions. The essential part leads him to speak of matter and form, and he proceeds to enumerate various sorts of forms and souls which he differentiates from one another by their varying degree of dependence on matter. The soul of an insect is ' not only extracted from matter but also attached to it, and extended according to quantity.'[14] When he speaks of the Blessed Trinity, the Holy Eucharist, the distinction between necessity and infallibility he never ceases to use the language of the schools. Here is his commentary on the words of Jesus Christ : ' If you ask the Father anything in My name, He will give it to you.' ' There is no logician ignorant of the fact that undefined propositions in contingent matters are equivalent to particulars, and in necessary matters, to universals. Man disputes, that is to say Socrates ; man is reasonable, that is to say every man, and whatever is endowed with reason. This being presupposed, we are bound to infer that the hypothetical and undefined preposition : " If you ask anything of the Father in My name, He will give it to you," is universal and without exception, provided it be in a necessary matter concerning our salvation and the glory of God, and that when accidental and contingent, it is not general, and admits of a multitude of exceptions. And this is demanded by the particle *quid*, which means emphatically *something*.'[15] A professor may, perhaps, talk like that to his students, but in a pulpit, it would be much better to quote Our Lord's words without an explanation that deprives the text both of its clarity and charm.

If a preacher is rightly advised to avoid cold, dry scholastic terminology, this does not mean that he should be recommended to adopt a flowery style, aim at a precious or pompous one, or pour out a string of high-sounding words or

[14] Migne, *op. cit.*, col. 550. [15] *Op. cit.*, col. 517.

bombastic phrases. Humility and simplicity are essential to true, Christian eloquence. It will not do for a priest merely to preach the Gospel, he should preach according to the Gospel.

Camus is one of the seventeenth century preachers most blameworthy in this respect; his sermons are filled with such phrases as: 'Lo! I am now about to grasp this intoxicating chalice, replete with so much excellence, to replenish your hearts through the orifices of your ears.' 'May the gentle zephyrs of the Holy Spirit waft the sails of my thoughts over the sea of this great audience to lead and bring it safely home to a fair haven.'[16]

The deputies of the three Estates, on a certain Feast of the Holy Innocents, in an Augustinian Church in Paris, heard this discouraging language: ' Gentlemen, we resemble the she-bear; we have for long licked and relicked the chief points of our remonstrances to bring forth and give shape to the cub of our general recommendations, but so far we are only three rows of jaw-bones which gnaw all men.'[17]

Camus was so far from wishing to cultivate a simple style that he expressed himself with the greatest emphasis when about to tell his hearers that he was going to preach simply.[18]

Coton uses phrases that one might easily imagine had been borrowed from the Bishop of Belley. Thus, he tells us that ' the love of Jesus Christ combined with a stout conscience, produces a certain . . . alexipharmic against the points of all, even the most envenomed, darts of death.'[19] However, Coton, as a rule, is not as pompous and ridiculous as Camus. Although he has a tendency to use scholastic phraseology, his imagination at times gains the upper hand. Paradise he regards as ' a royal palace in which the planets serve as galleries; the firmament, the lower hall; the outermost sphere (*primum mobile*) the chamber, the crystalline sphere, the ante-chamber and the empyrean, the inner room.'[20]

It is all very well for a preacher to strive to paint in vivid language the agony of death, the beauty of Heaven, the torments of Hell or the dreadful splendour of the Last Judge-

[16] *Op. cit.*, col. 35.
[17] *Ibid.*, col. 40.
[18] *Ibid.*, col. 13.
[19] *Ibid.*, col. 559.
[20] *Ibid.*, col. 671.

ment, yet he should not, at the same time, deal with these subjects in a theatrical fashion or advance as true statements that are only symbols of realities. Coton speaks of the Last Judgement as if the Holy Spirit had revealed it to him in all its details. He knows that the end of the world will for fifteen days be preceded by the most terrifying series of events. On the first day, the waters of the deep and the rivers will rise until they overtop the highest mountains by fifteen cubits. On the second, they will subside ' to the deepest caverns of the earth.' On the third, ' sea monsters, dolphins and whales will appear on the sea-shore ; lions, leopards and panthers mingled pell-mell with bulls, wolves and dogs will howl and roar in the most terrifying fashion.' And so on. Beside the Sovereign Judge ' a magnificent throne shall be erected for His most holy Mother ; and all around there shall be seats for the apostles.' The Saviour will appear preceded by His banner ' which is the royal standard of the holy Cross, an oriflamme of marvellous splendour.' The elect will give thanks and the damned will groan. He knows that the Saviour will speak in Syriac, but omits to tell us how we, without learning that language, shall be able to understand it.[21]

It is particularly difficult for a preacher to preserve a just mean when it is his duty to praise. The funeral oration on Crillon by the Jesuit Bening is, from this point of view, a perfect example of bad taste. This is how he proceeds : ' Holy Father, behold your vassal and defender ; King of France, behold your buckler ; noblemen of France, behold your model ; soldiers, behold your father ; poor men and women, behold your benefactor ; Frenchmen, behold your shield ; citizens of Avignon, behold the glory of your town ; religion, behold thy protector ; magnanimity, behold thy paragon ; clemency, behold thy lustre ; liberality, behold thy glory ; sincerity, behold thy pearl. *Abjectus est*, he is dead.'[22] The last few words give him an opportunity to draw breath, and then he starts off once more with : ' La Rochelle, Saint Jean d'Angely, Nîmes, Bréole, behold

[21] *Ibid.*, col. 613 ff.
[22] *Le bouclier d'honneur, où sont représentés les beaux faits de Louys Berton, seigneur de Crillon*, Avignon, oct. s.d.

your thunderbolt ; Calais, Tours, Quillebœuf, behold your fortification ; Dreux, Jarnac, Montauban, behold your Mars ; Paris, La Fère, Boulogne, Laon, behold your Crillon ; Chambéry, Conflans, Charbonnières, Montmélian, behold brave Crillon; Dauphiné, Comtat d'Avignon, behold the bravest of the brave. *Abjectus est*, he is dead.'

He is finished at last, and ' brave Crillon ' may now rest in peace. What did these endless apostrophes convey to those who went to church to be edified ? And what those antitheses so complacently piled up by so many preachers in their sermons ? The fashion persisted for generations, and had not even died out when Boileau was a young man, for he tells us in his *Art poétique* :

> ' *L'avocat au palais en herissa son style*
> *Et le docteur en chaire en sema l'Evangile.*' [23]

If a few well-chosen antitheses serve to enliven a preacher's style, when multiplied to excess they simply become affected and wearisome.

Bening went rather far when, in his funeral oration on Crillon, he said he would speak rather ' of Crillon living than Crillon dead, Crillon on horse-back, than Crillon in the tomb, Crillon at the head of an army than Crillon at the rear of a funeral procession, Crillon living, breathing, fighting, triumphing, than Crillon without strength, life or movement.' It was scarcely worth while repeating the same idea to his hearers when they were already well aware of the fact. He then goes on to speak in the same style of Crillon as he lived : ' If Crillon has his heart in his mouth, he has his mouth in his heart ; if he is the wonder of captains, he is the captain of wonders ; if he is frank in his speech, he is cordial in frankness ; if the recital of his great deeds will be as honey to the ears of my listeners, the tale of his death will be as poison.'

One may judge from this sample that Bening was not the ' wonder ' of preachers.

Sacred eloquence, just because it is sacred, demands a certain dignity of the priest ; it should never be vulgar and

---

[23] ' The lawyer in Court larded his style, and the preacher in the pulpit sowed the Gospel with them (antithesis).'

should avoid the use of language that educated persons, in current conversation, would never dream of employing. It should also abstain from all punning or play upon words. Playing upon words is an intellectual amusement, and the pulpit is not the place to be amusing. Camus frequently falls into this fault. In one of his sermons, he speaks of ' a piercing, present, pressing and oppressing evil' and of Saint Bernard as ' so fruitful and truthful.'[24] Again, ' you have just adored and experienced the fragrance, viewed and admired the body of the Son of God, in the chalice and on the paten of the holy altar.'[25] He was also responsible for the remark that after death the Popes will become butterflies; lords, earth-worms; and kings, wrens.[26] Preachers should not attempt to be clever, for in fact, very few who attempt to do so succeed. Either they are insolent, like the Milanese priest who said one Easter Sunday in presence of Saint Charles Borromeo: ' My brethren, you have a most holy prelate; he resembles an Easter egg; he is red, and has been blessed, but it is also true that he is a trifle hard,'[27] or they simply amuse their hearers with their quaint imagery, like the preachers who said that evil thoughts were ' the matches of vices' or that Jesus Christ was the proxy of Abraham, or the Blessed Virgin the Infanta of the Trinity, or Lucifer the door-keeper of Hell.

Grotesque comparisons and vulgar words and expressions should be banished from the pulpit, but unfortunately too many preachers have compromised the dignity of their office by their unwarrantable freedom of language. In 1614, Camus delivered a sermon before the three Estates in which the following lines occur: ' What would (our fathers) have said if they had seen (judicial appointments) passing as an inheritance to women and infants in the cradle? What now remains but, like the Roman Emperor, to introduce horses into the Senate? And why not, since so

[24] Migne, *op. cit.*, col. 14, ' un mal perçant, présent, pressant et oppressant.' Saint Bernard ' si fécond et si focond.'
[25] Migne, col. 36 ' d'adorer et d'odorer, de mirer et d'admirer.'
[26] *Ibid.*, col. II. ' papes deviennent paillons, sires cirons, et les rois roitelets.'
[27] Bouhours, *Manière de bien penser*, 1696, p. 167.

many asses have secured an entrance ? '[28] To extravagant language such as this should be joined in general condemnation all such buffoonery, grotesque jokes and burlesque remarks as are calculated to provoke laughter in church. The preacher who speaks in such fashion deserves the treatment Our Saviour gave the money-lenders in the Temple when He drove them out with a scourge.

The preacher who had earned the best right to this unhappy type of celebrity in the seventeenth century, was one known to his contemporaries as 'little Father Andrew.' On one occasion, when he noticed several of his hearers on the altar, he stopped to say : ' Behold, behold, the prophecy is now fulfilled : the calves are on the altar, *super altaria vitulos.*' His comparisons were on the same level as his translations or applications of scriptural texts. ' Christianity,' he remarked before a congregation of theologians, ' resembles a large salad in which the vegetables are nations ; the salt, the doctors (*vos estis sal terrae*) ; the vinegar, acts of mortification ; and the oil, the dear, good, Jesuit Fathers. Is there anything sweeter than a good, Jesuit Father ? Go to confession to anyone else and he will say to you : " You will be damned, if you go on like that." A Jesuit will sweeten everything. Again, however small the drop of oil that falls on one's clothes, it will spread, and without being noticed, will produce a large stain ; put one good Jesuit Father in a province, and it will soon be filled with them.' On another occasion, after threatening the divine vengeance on women who imitated the Magdalen's sinful life but not her penitence, he added : ' I see down there a woman very like that sinner ; as she is not amending her life, I intend to point her out and throw my handkerchief at her head.' He then pretended to throw his handkerchief, and all the women, naturally enough, lowered their heads. ' Ha ! Ha ! ' he cried, ' I thought there was only one, and now I see there are more than a hundred.'[29]

A man who perpetrates such acts of buffoonery must surely have forgotten that a church is a holy place. Only

[28] Migne, *op. cit.*, col. 24.
[29] Tallemant des Réaux, *Historiettes*, Paris, 1834–1835, 6 vols., oct., Vol. III, pp. 231 ff.

THE REFORM OF PREACHING

one attitude is becoming before the Tabernacle, that of respect and recollection. The faithful should not be led to imagine they are in a theatre.

Furthermore, the Church of God is not a suitable place for a preacher to leave the domain of religion for that of politics. The pulpit he occupies is placed above the earth in a serene region that should not be disturbed by earthly storms. Passions may rage, parties clash, and clouds pile up below him ; that is not his affair ; he has nothing to do with all that ; it is his business to remain above human contingencies and devote himself to things eternal.

All preachers have not fully understood their duty in this respect, and this was particularly true during the Wars of the League. Preachers attacked the head of the State or the established government, borrowing the taunts, invectives and violent language of journalists and politicians.[30] Many of them, like John Boucher parish priest of Saint Benedict, in Paris, Ponthoise, Canon Theologian of Poitiers, Aubry and Rose, impugned the sincerity of Henry IV's conversion and hence declared that he was not the lawful king. To put some restraint on such preachers of sedition, Parliament issued rigorous edicts and applied them with severity. Nevertheless, there were other forms of indiscreet attacks. Gontier, a Jesuit, preaching before the Court, observed that the Marchioness of Verneuil was trying to make the King smile ; pausing for a moment, he fixed his eyes on the prince, who was surrounded by several ladies, and asked : ' When will you cease from coming with a harem to hear the word of God ? ' Henry IV forgave, and even thanked the priest, but requested him not to repeat the offence.[31]

During the Fronde, the famous Coadjutor could not separate his politics from his religion. His sermons closely resembled his harangues to the people in the Markets when he urged them to revolt, support the faction, and vent their rage on Mazarin.

The minister of God who understands his duty resembles

---

[30] *Sermons de la simulée conversion et nullité de la prétendue absolution de Henri de Bourbon, prince de Béarn*, Paris, 1594, oct.

[31] L'Estoile, *Journal*, collection Michaud, 2ᶜ serie, Vol. I, Part 2, p. 365, note II.

his Divine Master Who was all-loving and merciful; he knows neither hate nor contempt, mockery or insult, and that not only towards Kings and their ministers but towards members of other religious bodies.

For too long a period, during the sixteenth and seventeenth centuries, the bitter, aggressive language employed in the heated and passionate controversies between Catholics and Protestants found an echo in the pulpit. Peter de Besse, for instance, called the Huguenot ministers 'wolves', 'pests', 'furies', and 'ministers of Satan', and said their alleged reform was 'made up of blasphemies, diabolical arts, contradictions, privations, negations, zeros, nothingnesses and geegaws.'[32] Valadier said Calvinists were execrable liars, numbskulls, and satraps of Hell; Coëffeteau maintained that heretics were not our brethren and that we are dispensed from praying for them.[33] When the edict of religious liberty was granted, daring protests re-echoed from the pulpits, even in presence of the Court. On Christmas Day, 1608, Gontier, preaching before the King, called Protestants 'vermin and riff-raff,' and added that Catholics should not suffer them in their midst.[34] This virulent attack enraged Marshal d'Ornano, Lieutenant-General of Guyenne. He said to the King that 'if anyone preached before him in Bordeaux what had been preached in Paris in presence of the King, he would have had the preacher pitched into the river when he came down from the pulpit.' Henry IV, for the sake of peace, forbade Gontier to preach before him in Paris, except in the Louvre, but a few days later, he withdrew the prohibition. The clemency of the King annoyed Sully. 'I am surprised,' Henry replied, 'that you have not noticed that the ministers at Charenton, whom you visit every day, are far worse then he is and preach far more seditiously.'[35]

Such were the chief defects that lowered the dignity of Christian eloquence during the sixteenth and the first years of the seventeenth centuries. We have designedly given

---

[32] *Premières conceptions théologiques sur le carême*, p. 116.
[33] *Sermons catholiques pour tous les jours de l'année*, Paris, 1537, pp. 171, 173.
[34] L'Estoile, *op. cit.*, p. 549.   [35] *Ibid.*, p. 555.

THE REFORM OF PREACHING

quotations from the most popular preachers. Peter de Besse was preacher in ordinary to the Prince de Condé; five editions of his Lenten sermons of 1602 were published inside four years. Coton, Henry IV's confessor, Gaspar Seguiran, confessor to Louis XIII, and Andrew Valadier frequently preached before the Court. Camus, Bishop of Belley, the favourite disciple of Saint Francis de Sales, occupied some of the most important pulpits in the kingdom and was everywhere regarded as a great success. Andrew de Boulanger, ' little Father Andrew,' Provincial of the Augustinians, drew the most fashionable set in Paris to his sermons. Camus and Boulanger, both of whom died in the middle of the seventeenth century, were the last representatives of the old school; they had not either the sense or good taste to allow themselves to be affected by the reform which, under the influence of the Oratory, Bourdoise, Vincent de Paul and the Society of Jesus helped to lead back pulpit eloquence to its true end—the preaching of the Gospel.

The decadence into which preaching had fallen was due to the perversion of the literary and of the moral sense. ' Hence,' writes Jacquinet,[36] ' it was only on condition of a double movement as it were, a double progress, intellectual and moral, literary and religious, that the reform of sacred eloquence could at length be accomplished in the seventeenth century. Such a reform undoubtedly demanded higher standards of art and politeness, a new appreciation of what constitutes good manners, and a fuller cultivation of the mind; but it should above all spring from a salutary awakening of the moral conscience, a revival of the religion of the heart; it was only possible through a renaissance of the old priestly virtues and apostolic labours within the bosom of the Church; it could only increase by the twin progress of the spirit of sacrifice and of love, the sole source of life and power in Christian eloquence.'

The reform of sacred eloquence was, then, the work of

---

[36] *Les prédicateurs du XVIIth siècle avant Bossuet*, Paris, 1863, oct., p. 107. This book is one of the best we know on this subject and has proved of the greatest utility in our treatment of this chapter.

many men, but here we have to speak only of one, Saint Vincent de Paul.

Vincent de Paul was pained to see the preaching of the Gospel pursuing a course that rendered it fruitless. He sorrowfully notes the fact that in Paris the preachers during Advent and Lent, with all their ' affected speech,' ' pompous display,' and ' empty eloquence,' did not convert a single soul.[37] Their words, he says, only fly over the house-tops, stir up a breeze, and touch the outer surface. A little noise and that is all.[38]

If the Christian pulpit was to be restored to the dignity that befits it, it was essential to make priests more fully realise what were their duties, and above all, to inspire them with love, humility and zeal for the salvation of souls. If, instead of striving to edify the faithful and convert sinners, the ministers of God paraded their learning, philosophical knowledge and wit, it was because their sole aim was to win public esteem and the applause of their hearers. This foolish vanity was the source of all the faults referred to above.

Saint Vincent denounced the evil at every opportunity. ' The pride of life : the desire to be always successful, to select new-fangled words, to shine in the pulpit, in discourses to ordinands and catechetical instructions ; what is the reason of all this ? What do men seek for in it ? My brethren, would you like to know ? Self. One wishes to have oneself talked about, one seeks to be praised, one would wish people to say that we have been a great success, that we are working wonders, that we should be lauded to the skies. That is the point, that is the monster, that is the silly fool. O human misery ! O cursed pride ! what evils do you not cause ! In short, it is to preach oneself and not Jesus Christ or souls.'[39] . . . ' Thus to play the peacock by making beautiful discourses '[40] is to commit ' a sacrilege, yes, a sacrilege. . . . Observe, Gentlemen and my brethren, believe me ; we shall never be fit to do the work of God if we are not deeply humble and despise ourselves ; no, if the

[37] *Saint Vincent de Paul*, Vol. XI, p. 270.
[38] *Ibid.*, Vol. XI, pp. 280, 281.
[39] *Ibid.*, Vol. XII, p. 22. [40] *Ibid.*, Vol. XI, p. 85.

THE REFORM OF PREACHING

Company of the Mission is not humble, it will never do any good.'[41]

The preacher, then, is bound, in the first place, to purify and direct his intention. He should consider only one thing—the salvation of souls. Saint Vincent asks, is the Shepherd, standing on a height, who sees wolves ravening the fold, to rest content with ' singing a ditty' ? No, he will cry out : ' Save yourselves, save yourselves, the enemy is at hand, save yourselves, save yourselves.'[42] He will not take time, when giving such a warning, to polish his phrases and round his periods ; he will be quite satisfied if he is understood and will therefore express himself simply and clearly.

Simplicity is one of the chief qualities to be desired in a preacher. In the first place, his matter should be simple. He should ' suit himself to the capacity and intelligence of his hearers' and therefore put aside lofty and elevated subjects, and employ familiar comparisons to explain the truths of the Gospel. Next, his form should be simple : ' all over-decorated preaching,'[43] ' bombastic language and style,'[44] ' ornamental speech,' should be discarded. The Saint asks what fruits will a preacher gather if his aim is ' to carefully select his words, balance his sentences, express simple ideas in an uncommon manner ? ' Will he lead men to love piety and sorrow for sin ? Most certainly not. But people will say : ' Undoubtedly, this man has made a good beginning ; he is eloquent, he has beautiful ideas, he expresses himself agreeably.' That, in fact, is all he was looking for, all he has obtained, and it is doubtful whether he always does obtain it.

Simplicity of form must not be confounded with carelessness ; it is allied to a certain dignity, and the man who employs debased and vulgar language is not simple, but trivial. Lastly, simplicity of tone. ' Avoid,' says Saint Vincent,[45] ' too high pitched a voice, the declamatory tone which passes high over people's heads.' A retired actor was chatting one day with Saint Vincent on the way actors

[41] *Ibid.*, Vol. XI, pp. 258, 274. [42] *Ibid.*, p. 271.
[43] *Ibid.*, Vol. XII, p. 175. [44] *Ibid.*, p. 309.
[45] *Ibid.*, Vol. XI, p. 274.

played their parts in the theatre : ' Formerly,' he said, ' actors recited their verse in a high-pitched tone of voice ; now they speak in a middle tone, and familiarly, and this method has proved more successful than the other.' Vincent was much struck by these words, and after reporting them in one of his letters, he added : ' Should we have less affection and zeal to save souls than these actors have to please the world ? '[46]

The preacher should never forget that he is not merely speaking to make himself understood, but also to persuade. Saint Vincent studied the art of persuasion and laid down rules for doing so with a intuitive skill worthy of the most acute psychologists. What should be done if one wishes to persuade a man to act in a certain way ? First, the advantages of the proposal are clearly pointed out ; next, the exact meaning of the proposal is explained, and finally, the man is told how to attain the end proposed. The Saint himself gives us an example of how we should set about persuading a man eligible for the office of a First President in Parliament, to crave for the position and to take the necessary steps to obtain it. What should be done ? In the first place, one should point out the honour attached to this dignity and the profit that accrues from it. ' A President, Sir, is the foremost man in a city ; everyone gives place to him ; everyone steps off the foot-path when he approaches ; he is honoured by all ; his authority gives him great credit in society ; he can do all things in the Courts of Justice. O Sir ! a President ! he does not yield place even to a bishop ; even sovereigns defer to him, and hold him in the highest esteem. A President ! he can oblige, do an act of kindness to whomsoever he pleases, acquire a large circle of friends, make himself respected in all places. Oh ! Sir, a President ! that is certainly a very high position.' And so he sets out in detail all that can flatter the ambition, and promote the interest and happiness of the man who holds such an exalted position.

But a question naturally rises before the mind of the person who is listening ; what are the duties of a President ? In what does the office consist ? ' Sir, you are the first

[46] *Saint Vincent de Paul*, Vol. VI, p. 378.

THE REFORM OF PREACHING

officer of justice, of a great and honourable body ; you are its head ; you never have to state a case yourself ; you tell others what they have to do ; you collect the opinions of others and deliver judgement yourself.' The man, by now, is quite prepared to become a First President ; a magnificent situation has been conjured up before his eyes, and the desire of attaining it awakened. But there is a great distance between one's desires and reality. ' He would be quite right to be annoyed and to complain of this impertinent adviser who had come along to excite his desire for the office without telling him how to obtain it.' The third stage in the process of persuasion, then, will be to suggest the means, not merely in a general sort of way, but with all essential details. ' Sir, you have so much revenue from that source, so much money from that ; from the former you will take this much and from the latter, that ; in addition, I know Mr. So-and-So who has this office at his disposal, and furthermore Mr. So-and-So is an intimate friend of mine and a friend of his. I will arrange for him to discuss the matter with you. We shall settle it very nicely ; we shall do this and that ; we shall obtain this and that.' The rôle of adviser is now complete. The person advised has adopted the proposal and holds in his hands the means of realising it ; it is for him to act, and he will certainly do so.[47]

Motives, nature, and means, all set out simply and clearly—such is Saint Vincent's ' little method ' which he and his Missionaries had proved to be so efficacious in their apostolic journeys.

It is not necessary to treat these points in the order set out above, or even to make a clear distinction between them. In many cases, there is nothing to prevent the preacher from combining the first two points ; to explain the nature of a virtue is frequently to give the motive for practising it. Every preacher is also quite free to make a different distribution of his matter. The feast of a Saint cannot be dealt with in the same way as a mystery of religion, or a mystery as a parable, an evangelical maxim, or a Gospel text. But, beneath the variety of divisions, we should always be able

---

[47] *Ibid.*, Vol. XI, p. 263.

to discover the three essential features—the motives, the nature and the means.

If sermons composed and delivered according to the 'little method' do not always obtain the results to be expected, the reason is that they have been spoiled by certain defects. There is no place where the practice of the Christian virtues should be more carefully cultivated than in the pulpit. Above all things else, no word contrary to charity should fall from the lips of a preacher. Harsh and injurious language contracts the heart, and even the understanding. As Saint Vincent said so well: 'Bitterness has never served any other purpose than to embitter.'[48] Accordingly, when it is the duty of a preacher to reprove he should be on his guard against directing his reproofs towards particular individuals, and above all, against pointing out offenders to the congregation under only too obviously transparent terms. When confronted with those who profess a different religion or who have none, it is much better not to say anything calculated to hurt their self-love. If we speak to convert, that is certainly not the way to effect our end. 'Never challenge ministers in the pulpit,' was Saint Vincent's advice,[49] 'do not say that they cannot point out any single one of their articles of faith in the Sacred Scriptures, except rarely and then sympathetically, for otherwise God will not bless our work, the poor will be estranged, and think we showed vanity when we did so, and then they will not believe us. We do not believe a man because he is very learned, but because we think he is good we love him. The devil is very learned and yet we do not believe anything he says, because we do not love him. It was necessary for Our Lord first to love those whom He wished to believe in Him. No matter what we do, people will never believe in us if we do not show love and sympathy towards those we wish to believe in us.'

As a result of this principle, Saint Vincent did not advise a frontal attack on errors opposed to the true faith; he believed that an indirect refutation by clear exposition and

[48] *Saint Vincent de Paul*, Vol. I, p. 536; cf. Abelly, *op. cit.*, Bk. III, Ch. XII, p. 181.
[49] *Ibid.*, p. 295.

THE REFORM OF PREACHING

proof of the Catholic religion would prove much more efficacious. When a man feels he is being attacked, the desire to defend himself is at once aroused, and such an attitude of mind is the one most unsuitable for conversion.

A preacher would place himself in a false position if his own conduct were not in harmony with the truths he teaches; he would be pulling down with one hand what he had been building up with the other. If he were not leading a regular life himself, he would scarcely be able to induce sinners to lead one. People would be naturally enough inclined to say : ' Physician, heal thyself.' They would have no more confidence in him than patients in a doctor suffering from the same complaint as that which he professes to be able to cure.

Furthermore, his words would be equally inefficacious were he to mount a pulpit without taking the trouble to prepare a sermon. As a rule, a good sermon is not an improvisation, but the result of long, conscientious labour.

In the Congregation of the Mission, preparation began in the year preceding ordination. The art of preaching had its own place in the syllabus of studies, just as much as liturgy, moral theology, and plain chant. Practice was combined with theory, and those who resided in the Mother House were obliged to practise the art of oratory during vacations ; they preached during the community meals just like the clerical students. In the early days of the Company, ecclesiastics belonging to the Parisian clergy, such as Pavillon, Perrochel and Olier, used to meet at Saint-Lazare to study ' the little method,' and the priests of the house took part in these assemblies. ' A virtue or a vice was proposed as a subject ; each of us took some paper and ink and wrote down a motive for avoiding the vice or embracing the virtue, and then proceeded to look for a definition and means ; finally, all that had been written was collected, and a sermon composed from the material. It was all done without books ; everyone worked out the subject for himself.' In later times, similar meetings were held during vacation, but no extern priests were present. As a rule, Father Portail was always there ; he took notes, arranged and completed them, and in this way, composed a large folio volume on the best method of preaching and catechising. Father Alméras thought the work too long and diffuse ; he made a small abridgment, running to less than ten pages, and sent a copy to each house of the Congregation.

Saint Vincent was anxious that all his confrères, even professors in seminaries, should be able to preach ; hence he advised superiors to send them from time to time to preach the word of God in villages.

The Missionaries availed themselves of their three months vacation to revise their sermons and compose new ones ; to that end they drew upon the holy thoughts with which God had inspired them during prayer. 'Mental prayer,' the holy founder wrote to one of his confrères,[50] ' is *the* great book for a preacher ; by it you will be enabled to draw divine truths from their source, the Eternal Word, and then you will distribute these truths amongst the people.' Saint Vincent's influence was felt outside his Congregation ; it extended to the priests who attended the Tuesday Conferences, that is to say to the élite of the Paris clergy. ' The Company of externs who come to hold conferences in Saint-Lazare,' he said,[51] ' take care that the subjects are treated in a simple way, and as soon as anyone starts ornamenting his language or making too great a display of learning, complaints are at once made to me with a view to applying a remedy.' The subjects usually dealt with at these conferences were the virtue that should animate the clergy, and the members always placed simplicity first, never failing to note that by God's grace, this virtue was manifest in their assemblies.[52]

Saint Vincent also made arrangements that clerics preparing for orders in Saint-Lazare should be taught how to preach.

To advice and teaching he added example. Each of his sermons, each of his conferences might be presented as a model to anyone wishing to know in what the little method consists. We still possess some of his conferences to the Priests of the Mission and to the Daughters of Charity. He is always simple, frequently moving and even eloquent.

[50] *Saint Vincent de Paul*, Vol. VII, p. 156.
[51] *Ibid.*, Vol. II, p. 233.   [52] *Ibid.*, Vol. XII, p. 303.

BOSSUET, BISHOP OF MEAUX

THE REFORM OF PREACHING

As a rule, he deals with practical issues. He was not a man to dwell on mystical considerations. The greatness of God, the states of the Word Incarnate, the privileges of Mary, chiefly held his interest inasmuch as they led him to suggest the taking of good resolutions. The subjects he preferred were the virtues, vows, rules, duties, the reception of the sacraments and prayer. When at times he rose on the wings of speculation, he did not remain there long, but hastened to get back to the field of action where he really felt at home. If we except what he borrows from Holy Scripture, textual quotations are rare enough in his discourses. The *Imitation of Christ*, the writings of Saint Francis de Sales and Louis of Granada are the spiritual books he seems to have known best. He had also read Gerson, the Carthusian writer Molina, Rodriguez and Father Suffren. His addresses abound in delightful little touches, and he had the gift of relating, in a charming and genial manner (though not always sufficiently critical of the validity and truth of some of his stories), whatever he had read or remembered that was applicable to the subject with which he was dealing. Above all, he drew upon what he had learned during prayer. His discourses were the gradual development of ideas that had sprung from intimate contact and union with God.

No one could withstand the charm of his discourses, as Bossuet himself attests in a letter to Pope Clement XI; speaking of the Tuesday Conferences, he says: 'We listened to him with the greatest eagerness, for we felt profoundly that the words of the Apostle were realised in him: "If anyone speak, let his words be as the words of God."'

The great orator took Saint Vincent's teaching at these meetings so much to heart that his most characteristic thoughts frequently recall those of his saintly master. The resemblance occasionally extends even to the form. Think of the beautiful opening of the funeral oration on Henrietta-Maria of France: 'He Who reigns in Heaven, from Whom all empires depend, to Whom alone appertains glory, majesty and independence, is also the only one Who glories in laying down laws for Kings and teaching them, when He so pleases, terrible lessons. Whether He raises up thrones or puts them down, whether He communicates His power to Kings or withdraws it, leaving them to their own weakness, He teaches them their duties in a sovereign manner worthy of Himself.' One might imagine that Bossuet, before pronouncing these words, had read the following lines written by Saint Vincent de Paul :[53] ' God sometimes permits those great agitations which shake the most firmly established states, to make earthly sovereigns remember that they draw their power from Him alone and that they are no more independent of God than the least of their subjects. But when He has done so, He re-establishes them ; to conclude, He raises up and puts down when He pleases and whom He pleases.'

The effect of Saint Vincent's discourses on the Ladies of Charity is well known, especially those concerned with the Foundling Hospital. Manuals of literature reproduce his magnificent appeal to their maternal heart as one of the choicest examples of French eloquence : ' And now, Ladies, sympathy and charity induced you to adopt these poor little creatures as your children ; you have been their mothers according to Divine Grace ever since their mothers according to nature abandoned them. Cease to be their mothers and become their judges ; their life and death is in your hands ; I am now about to collect your votes ; the time has come to pronounce their sentence and to ascertain whether you desire any longer to be merciful to them. They will live, if you charitably take care of them, and on the other hand, they will die and infallibly perish if you abandon them ; experience does not allow you to think otherwise.'[54]

Saint Vincent, in thus letting his heart speak, attained, without thinking of it, real eloquence ; and it was not the only occasion. Let us listen to what he said to his priests about Father Bourdoise in Madagascar : ' M. Bourdoise, my brethren, M. Bourdoise who is so far away and all alone and who, as you know, has won to Jesus Christ, with so much pain and anxiety, a great number of those poor natives of the country where he now is—let us also pray for him. M. Bourdoise, are you still alive, or are you dead ?

[53] *Saint Vincent de Paul*, Vol. V, p. 443.
[54] *Ibid.*, Vol. XIII, p. 801.

THE REFORM OF PREACHING

If alive, May God be pleased to preserve your life, if you are in Heaven, pray for us.'[55]

Abbé Bremond writes; ' Should not such a passage be familiar to us all, even from our college days? Is it not worthy to be compared with the three marvels of this kind : David's lament over Jonathan ; *Montes Gelboe* ; Virgil's *heu! si qua fata* ; and Saint Bernard's funeral oration over his brother.'[56]

Examples such as these could be multiplied. The finest pages of Saint Vincent are those containing his exhortations to zeal and the spirit of sacrifice. Whenever he deals with these subjects, he grows animated and enkindled ; eloquence pours forth as from a fountain.

' Zeal . . . consists in a pure love of rendering oneself pleasing to God and useful to one's neighbour ; zeal to extend the empire of God, zeal to procure the salvation of the neighbour. Is there anything in the world more perfect ? If the love of God is a fire, zeal is its flame ; if love is a sun, zeal is its ray. Zeal is that which is most pure in the love of God[57] . . . Let us ask God to give the Company this spirit, this heart, this heart which will make us go anywhere, this heart of the Son of God, this heart of Our Lord, which disposes us to go as He went and as He would have gone if His eternal wisdom had judged it fitting to labour for the conversion of poor nations. He sent His apostles to do that ; He sends us, like them, to spread the fire in all directions. *Ignem veni mittere in terram, et quid volo nisi ut accendatur.* To spread the divine fire in all places, this divine fire of the fear of God throughout the world, to Barbary, to the Indies, to Japan. . . . When we hear of the glorious deaths of those who are there, O God ! who would not wish to be in their place ! Ah ! who would not wish to be like them ! '[58]

To devote oneself, to spend oneself, to suffer and die for God, such was the ideal Saint Vincent never ceased to hold up before his Missionaries. He put them on their

---

[55] *Ibid.*, Vol. XII, p. 69.
[56] *Histoire littéraire du sentiment religieux en France*, Vol. III, p. 234.
[57] *Saint Vincent de Paul*, Vol. XII, p. 307.
[58] *Ibid.*, Vol. XI, p. 291.

guard against those who, after his death, would strive to lead the Company away from the works it had begun. What kind of men will they be? he asks, and answers, 'Men who cocker themselves.' When he said this, one of his hearers remarked, 'he put his hands beneath his armpits as lazy people do.' He then went on, accompanying his words with gestures of the hands, movements of the head and in a disdainful tone of voice that lent added emphasis to each word: 'Men such as these have a very limited range of ideas; they confine their views and designs within a narrow circle in which they shut themselves up completely. They have no wish to move outside this circle, and if they are shown anything outside it and peep out to have a look at it, they immediately scuttle back to the centre, like snails retiring within their shells.'

Saint Vincent had admirable powers of mimicry; he may quite possibly, at times, have gone a little too far in words and gestures, as indeed he himself admits: 'Last Friday,' he once remarked,[59] 'I gave occasion to the Company to take scandal because I cried out so loudly and clapped my hands; it seemed as if I were annoyed with somebody, and I therefore ask pardon of the Company.'

The Saint, by his teaching, advice and example, succeeded in inspiring all those who were brought into contact with him with his own love for 'the little method.' If to this direct influence be added that which he exercised indirectly by his own priests in missions and seminaries, and the members of the Tuesday Conferences, of whom Bossuet was one, there need be no hesitation in counting him amongst the chief reformers of preaching in the seventeenth century.

We have on this point evidence of the utmost value and that is—his own. Speaking, on August 22, 1655, on 'the little method,' he said: 'If a man now wishes to be regarded as a good preacher in the churches of Paris and at Court, he must preach in this way, without any affectations. People now say of a man who preaches thus, and preaches as well as the best: "this man works wonders, he preaches like a Missionary, like an apostle." . . . He preaches like a

[59] *Saint Vincent de Paul*, Vol. XII, p. 92.

THE REFORM OF PREACHING

Missionary ! O my Saviour ! Thou hast granted to the poor little Company this grace of inspiring it with a method which all desire to follow ; we thank Thee with all our hearts. Ah ! Gentlemen, do not let us render ourselves unworthy of such a grace, so highly esteemed by all, that people say of a first rate preacher : " He preaches like a Missionary." '[60]

It was of the greatest importance to interest the bishops in the little method, because through them it would be much easier to induce the clergy to adopt it. Those who had taken part in the Tuesday Conferences before being raised to the episcopacy, fully realised its worth, but what about the others ? Saint Vincent's appointment to the Council of Conscience enabled him to labour indirectly at the reform of preaching by promoting the still more important reform of the appointment of bishops.

[60] *Ibid.*, p. 268.

CHAPTER XXXIII

THE EPISCOPACY

LONG before Anne of Austria, the Queen Regent, appointed Saint Vincent to be a member of the Council of Conscience, he had availed himself of his opportunities to enlighten those entrusted with the duty of submitting the names of future bishops of France to the Court of Rome. Richelieu and Louis XIII were fully aware of the soundness of his judgement and the wide range of his acquaintances and friends; on more than one occasion they had followed his advice on a matter in which a mistake is bound to lead to the most regrettable consequences. It was on his recommendation that Nicholas Pavillon and Francis Fouquet, in 1637, were appointed bishops, the former to the see of Alet, and the later to Bayonne; in 1638, Anthony Godeau went to that of Vence, and in 1640, Felix Vialard to Châlons. All these prelates had been members of the Tuesday Conferences before they were raised to the episcopal bench.

Their ministry was so fruitful in good that, as we have already seen, when Louis XIII fell ill and was anxious not to leave a single diocese without a pastor on his death, he asked the Saint, through Father Dinet, to draw up a list of ecclesiastics fit to be made bishops. Some days later, Saint Vincent was standing by the King's bedside preparing him to meet his God; the King listened to his words with pleasure, and when the discourse was finished, he said: 'M. Vincent, if I recover, bishops will have to spend three years with you.'

Of all the questions considered in the Council of Conscience, Saint Vincent believed that none, perhaps, equalled in importance the choice of bishops. On this point, more than on any other, he would have regarded himself as a

THE EPISCOPACY

criminal if, deaf to the voice of conscience, he had allowed himself to be influenced by political or personal considerations instead of seeking solely the welfare of the church and the good of souls, or had lightly made up his mind before obtaining, from well informed and trustworthy persons, sufficient grounds for arriving at a sound decision. One of the men on whose judgement he most leaned was Alain de Solminihac who, as may be seen from his letters, often did not wait to be asked but took the initiative ; and the Bishop's suggestions were always received by the Saint with respect and submission.[1]

Thanks to Saint Vincent, many dioceses were governed by pastors animated by an apostolic zeal that formed a striking contrast with the wordliness of their seniors in the episcopacy. Let it suffice to name Lescot, of Chartres ; Perrochel, of Boulogne ; Caulet, of Pamiers ; Habert, of Vabres ; Bassompierre, of Oloron and then of Saintes ; Liverdi, of Tréguier ; Sevin, of Sarlat and then of Cahors ; Bosquet, of Lodeve and then of Montpellier ; and Brandon, of Périgueux.

Saint Vincent believed that for a man to be worthy of the episcopate, he should regard himself as unworthy of the office ; hence he refused to intervene on behalf of those who ventured to seek his assistance. At Saint-Lazare, he was visited by many men anxious to be bishops, all of whom were at one in telling the Saint that in doing so they were not moved by any ambitious consideration ; but beneath the various pretexts alleged to conceal their real motives, he had no difficulty in discerning the true ones. For instance, a member of a religious Order, renowned as a preacher, once wrote to the Saint to say he was thinking of applying for a bishopric in the ecclesiastical province of Reims. His physical strength was well nigh exhausted ; he could not, therefore, observe the rigour of the rule and so was about to seek a position which, by exempting him from fasting and other austerities of his Order, would enable him to work much longer for the salvation of souls. It was not from a love of rank and honour he sought a mitre, but solely from

[1] *Saint Vincent de Paul*, Vol. II, pp. 389, 564, 624 ; Vol. III, pp. 152, 238, 294 ; Vol. IV, pp. 25, 244.

motives of zeal. Saint Vincent saw clearly through this poor pretext and replied like a Saint and an intelligent man. The office of bishop, we read in his reply ' cannot be desired or sought after by a really humble soul such as yours. Your health is failing ; that is a great pity, so do not fatigue yourself too much, and give up the labour of preaching for a while. Your Order is one of the most holy and edifying in the Church ; it needs you ; you are one of its chief pillars ; you sustain and bring credit on it by your teaching and example. Why think of leaving it to avoid an austere life ? Your example would be contagious ; and moreover, do we not go to Heaven by the path of mortification ? ' [2]

A Royal almoner received an equally well deserved lesson. He, too, wished for a more elevated position but, by his own account, not from any personal motives but simply because he was being pestered by his relations. They kept on repeating : ' Just think how long you have been at Court ; anybody else would long since have received a reward for his devotion to the King ; ask for a bishopric and, if recommended by some influential person, you will be sure to obtain one.' Really, he asked, could any man refuse such a satisfaction to his family ? Saint Vincent was not duped by this type of family affection. His answer may be anticipated : put aside human means ; it is God and no other who gives a vocation ; if He pleases to call you to the episcopate, you will be aided by His grace ; if you put yourself forward, you will regret, at the hour of death, that you took the weight of a diocese on your shoulders. [3]

The most astute candidates took very good care not to present their requests to Saint Vincent ; they rightly believed they would have much better chances of success if they approached Mazarin himself, directly or indirectly.

The Saint had a duty to fulfil towards such ambitious men when their names came up before the Council of Conscience—which did not always happen ; he had to point out that they had not the qualities necessary for such an eminent position. He spared the dioceses of Bayonne,[4]

[2] Abelly, *op. cit.*, Bk. II, Ch. XIII, sect. VII, p. 461.
[3] *Ibid.*, sect. IV, p. 448.
[4] *Saint Vincent de Paul*, Vol. III, p. 228.

Périgueux[5] and others from the shame of being governed by bishops unworthy of the name. Without him, Louis Barbier, Abbé de la Rivière, whose morals were deplorable, would have become co-adjutor and subsequently Archbishop of Narbonne.[6] He was, in fact, Bishop of Langres from 1656 to 1670, and that diocese learned to its cost how fatal is the rule of a prelate appointed by favour.

Vincent de Paul, unfortunately, was not all-powerful in the Council of Conscience. In one of Alain de Solminihac's letters to the Saint, he deplores the disedifying conduct of a young prelate, probably Jacques de Montrouge, Bishop of Saint Flour, much more accustomed to hunt after hares than after souls. 'You were perfectly right,' wrote Alain, 'to oppose his promotion, and would to God your advice had been followed!'[7] Saint Vincent also opposed, to the best of his ability, the election of Beaumanoir de Lavardin, nominated, in 1648, to the bishopric of Mans.[8] Rightly or wrongly, this prelate was regarded as having utterly lost the faith. After his death, a rumour spread—some said that they had heard from the Bishop's own lips—that, during his long episcopate, he had never had the intention of conferring the Order of Priesthood on those he ordained. A number of ecclesiastics, rather than remain in an agonising state of doubt, preferred to be re-ordained.[9]

It was Mazarin who, in 1647, for political motives, put forward in person the candidature of Edward Molé for the bishopric of Bayeux. His sole claim to the see was that he was the eldest son of the First President of Parliament. His conduct was not that of a self-respecting priest. Saint Vincent heard the news of his selection from Mazarin who wrote : ' Sir, these lines are to inform you that the First President having come here to ask the Queen for the bishopric of Bayeux . . . for his son, she has bestowed it all the more willingly as he has the necessary qualifications for the office, and Her Majesty has been especially pleased to seize such a favourable opportunity for recognising the

---

[5] *Ibid.*, p. 256.
[6] D'Ormesson, *Journal*, Vol. I, p. 153.
[7] *Ibid.*, Vol. IV, p. 25.   [8] *Ibid.*, Vol. III, p. 351.
[9] Collet, *op. cit.*, Vol. I, p. 473.

services of the father and his zeal for the State in the person of his son. The Queen promised me to write to you on the matter, and I have done so in advance that you may be good enough to see him and give him such instruction as you may deem necessary for the proper fulfilment of this function.' When Saint Vincent read this letter, which confronted him with an accomplished fact, he went to the First President to beg him to withdraw the candidature of his son. Molé listened, thanked him and promised to think it over. After a few days, he paid another visit. ' Oh, M. Vincent ! ' said Molé, ' what sleepless nights you have made me pass ! I am an old man, I am not rich, I have a large family ; my duty as a father is to put them beyond the reach of want by placing them in good positions before I die. If my son has not the requisite qualities for governing a diocese, he will always have some experienced ecclesiastics beside him whose advice he will faithfully follow.'[10]

Happily for the diocese of Bayeux, Edward Molé died after holding the office for only five years.

The friends and relations of rejected candidates did not, as one may easily imagine, cheerfully see their ambitious hopes for the future vanish into thin air. Saint Vincent occasionally felt the brunt of their ill-humour, but this never disturbed him. Some of the disappointed parties, in their desire for revenge, invented odious calumnies which they invested with the most circumstantial details the better to deceive the public. These lies passed from mouth to mouth until they reached the Court and finally the ears of the Queen. ' M. Vincent,' she said to him the next time they met, ' do you know what people are saying about you ? ' To which he simply replied : ' Madame, I am a great sinner.' ' If I were in your place,' Anne of Austria went on, ' I would justify myself.' ' Madame,' he said, ' when Our Lord was accused He did not justify Himself.'[11]

There is a story, for which Canon Maynard[12] made him-

---

[10] *Saint Vincent de Paul*, Vol. II, p. 563 ; Abelly, *op. cit.*, Bk. II, Ch. XIII, sect. V, pp. 451–452.

[11] Abelly, *op. cit.*, Bk. III, Ch. XIII, sect. I, p. 211.

[12] *Saint Vincent de Paul*, 1860 edit., Bk. VIII, Ch. I, pp. 415 ff. Maynard states that he took the incident from a note in Cardinal

self responsible, that a Duchess, enraged at seeing the bishopric of Poitiers eluding the grasp of her son, wounded Saint Vincent, in a momentary fit of rage, by throwing a foot-stool at his head, and that he said to the brother who ran between him and the furious lady : ' You have nothing to do with this : this is my affair ; let us leave,' and that he then added : ' Is not a mother's love for her son wonderful ? ' A touching remark, but it is doubtful if it was ever uttered. History cannot accept an alleged fact for which there is no valid evidence. The silence of Abelly, Collet, and particularly the lay-brother who was his secretary and who has, moreover, left us accounts of other less moving and dramatic scenes, provoked by similar refusals, authorises us to assign to this particular one a place amongst the legends.

When the Queen, after consulting the Council of Conscience, had selected a nominee for a bishopric, Saint Vincent's rôle was not yet finished. He again intervened and spoke to the bishop-elect of his duties. We have already seen how he was commissioned by Mazarin himself to instruct Edward Molé on how a diocese should be governed. Amongst the documents received by the Abbé de Gassion, on his nomination to the see of Oloron, was a letter which says : ' I beg you to be good enough to see M. Vincent, who will be quite pleased to place his knowledge and wisdom at your disposal in all matters regarding this function.'[13] It was, no doubt, the custom to send a similar recommendation to all newly elected bishops.

When the latter arrived in their dioceses, the holy priest did not lose sight of them ; he continued to be their guide

---

Maury's panegyric on Saint Vincent de Paul. The Cardinal would have known of this incident from documents preserved in the Archives at Saint-Lazare. Maynard did not go to the trouble of verifying his statement, for no such note is to be found in the panegyric which was published and annotated by the Cardinal's nephew in 1827. The anecdote was first given in the *Regulae seu Constitutiones communes Congregationis Missionis.* (Lisbon, 1743, p. XXVII.) Maynard learned it from this book and, as usual, modified some of the circumstances to make it more interesting.

[13] Arch. du ministère des Aff. étrang., France, Mémoires et Documents, lettre du 27 Juillet 1647.

and advocate ; he supported their legitimate claims before the Queen, defended them against unjust molestations from the nobility and the encroachments of heretics, freely gave them his advice whenever it was asked, and even without being asked, whenever the good of their dioceses demanded it.[14]

He was extremely discreet on this last point. Whenever he had to advise and, still more, to warn or correct, a battle was waged in his breast between his humility and his sense of duty ; he excused and humbled himself, as if he had done something that needed forgiveness, and then, in a tone of mingled deference and respect, proceeded to the matter in hand, with occasional interruptions to manifest sentiments of affection, humility or admiration. Here, for example, is a letter to a prelate who had submitted some difficulties to Saint Vincent. ' Alas ! My Lord, why do you communicate so many important affairs to a poor, ignorant man, such as I am, hateful in the sight of God and men for the innumerable sins of my past life and my present wretchedness and misery which render me unworthy of the honour that you in your humility show me, and which would certainly constrain me to remain silent if you had not obliged me to speak ! Here, then, are my poor ideas on the points of your two letters ! I put them forward with all the respect due to you and in the simplicity of my heart. I cannot better begin than by giving thanks to God for all the graces He has bestowed on you, begging Him to glorify Himself by the happy results of your labours, to which you devote yourself with a zeal and assiduity that cannot be bettered . . .'[15]

It was always after preliminary remarks such as these, that the Saint, whenever he had to do so, reminded bishops of the duties of their office. He had, as a matter of fact, plenty of opportunities. For example, Henri de Bourbon, Bishop of Metz, one of the worst benefice holders in the kingdom, did not carry out the obligations attached to his benefices. Saint Vincent vainly endeavoured to make him

---

[14] Abelly, *op. cit.*, Bk. II, Ch. XIII, sect. VI, p. 454.
[15] *Ibid.*, Bk. III, Ch. XI, sect. IV, p. 140.

see the error of his ways.[16] Again, Beaumanoir de Lavradin, recently consecrated Bishop of Mans, neglected to have his oath of fidelity registered in the Court of Exchequer. Vincent de Paul had to point out the grave inconveniences resulting from such negligence.[17]

Appeals against episcopal decisions, then very common in France, proved a double-edged sword. If some persons used appeals to remedy real abuses, others, in far greater numbers, saw in them either a means of retarding the effect of just measures taken against lax morals or even of having them annulled; they thereby weakened the authority of the bishops, and a spirit of insubordination was encouraged.

Some prelates, disheartened to see their decisions quashed by the Parliament, ended by shutting their eyes to disorders. They complained to Saint Vincent and to all he replied: 'When you take a certain measure, do not overstep the bounds of your authority; invest your decisions with all the formalities prescribed by law; give the post of Official to tried ecclesiastics, of irreproachable morality, of an integrity above all suspicion, and with a sound knowledge of Canon Law.' He reminded them that Molé had said to him one day: 'We know that decisions taken by the Chancery of Paris are beyond criticism, and hence we dismiss, without even listening to them, all those who beg us to annul its decisions. If all Chanceries were like this, they would be treated in the same way.'[18]

There were also some bishops in France much inclined to go to law and perpetually quarrelling with their canons or parish priests. To all such Saint Vincent recommended a settlement; he begged them to strive for a friendly agreement rather than prolong, without any certainty of success, quarrels that embittered hearts and were ruinous to a diocese.[19]

He succeeded, by an ingenious arrangement, in putting

---

[16] Arch. du ministère des Aff. étrang., France, Mémoirer et Documents, t.855, f⁰ 12, lettre de M. Gaudin, du 20 Janvies 1646.
[17] *Saint Vincent de Paul*, Vol. III, p. 491.
[18] Abelly, *op. cit.*, Bk. II, Ch. XIII, sect. VI, p. 455.
[19] *Ibid.*, Bk. III, Ch. XI, sect. IV, pp. 141–142.

an end to a famous law-suit between René de Rieux and Robert Cupif regarding the bishopric of Saint Pol-de-Léon. René de Rieux had to fly the country for political reasons. On May 31, 1635, after several years of voluntary exile and as the result of a canonical enquiry held by four bishops, he was deposed by the Holy See. Four years later, Robert Cupif was presented by the King and appointed by the Pope to the bishopric. René de Rieux appealed. The ensuing law-suit deeply disturbed the diocese and provoked passionate controversies, even outside France. Saint Vincent effected a settlement in 1648 by which Robert Cupif renounced the see of Saint Pol and accepted that of Dol. De Rieux was thereby enabled to resume the government of his diocese, and both prelates expressed their entire satisfaction with the result.[20]

Furthermore, Saint Vincent de Paul had no love for rigorous measures; and when consulted on this point, he deprecated them. He told a Vicar General that it was not by imposing censures, pronouncing interdicts, launching excommunications, forbidding the hearing of confessions, preaching and the collecting of alms, that prelates would extend the kingdom of Christ. These are grave measures that should be reserved for exceptional cases, after all milder methods have been tried in vain. In his eyes, preaching by example was the best of all methods; if that did not suffice, then mild and charitable remonstrances should be employed, which, if necessary, should later become firm and severe. As a general rule, to go too far seemed to him to do more harm than good.[21]

Saint Vincent sought to combat another abuse: the love of pomp and splendour. Bishops, as a rule, were selected from wealthy and noble families; they had formed luxurious habits which it would have seemed paradoxical to abandon, for they imagined their episcopal rank, by raising them to a still higher position in society, obliged them all the more to play the part of great noblemen. They devoted far more attention to the respect with which episcopal dignity should be surrounded than to their obligation of waiving

[20] Abelly, *op. cit.*, Bk. II, Ch. XIII, sect. VI, p. 453.
[21] *Saint Vincent de Paul*, Vol. II, p. 5.

THE EPISCOPACY

their superiority the better to attract their flocks. Saint Vincent, on the contrary, was convinced that a bishop is a father and that the title of father, instead of repelling, should tend to establish a certain family equality, for the goods of a father belong, in some sort, to his children. ' The world,' he wrote to the Bishop of Boulogne,[22] ' thinks and says that the holy poverty of a bishop who conforms his life to that of Our Lord, the Bishop of bishops, is more to be esteemed than the riches, retinue and pomp of a bishop with great possessions.'

If we turn over the pages of the correspondence between Saint Vincent and the French episcopacy, we shall find that he was consulted on the most varied matters. Now we meet with a prelate who, thinking he is too weak to rule a diocese, asks if it would not be wiser to resign; again, another determined to retire into private life, does not know in whose favour he should resign his see, and therefore places the matter in the Saint's hands.[23] Other bishops have recourse to him to know where they could find good co-adjutors,[24] suitable Vicars General,[25] or how they should act in the midst of political troubles[26] or when confronted with the plague.[27]

Vincent de Paul never left one of these letters unanswered. He was always willing to take the lead and be the first to write when matters of administration or, indeed, any others that called for his intervention, supplied him with a sound reason. If he heard anything edifying about a bishop, he wrote to congratulate him;[28] if told that a prelate, as the result of excessive zeal, was injuring his health, he begged him not to overwork.[29]

To him was chiefly due the transference of the episcopal see of Maillezais to La Rochelle,[30] for he hoped that the

---

[22] *Ibid.*, Vol. III, p. 94.
[23] Abelly, *op. cit.*, Bk. III, Ch. XI, sect. IV, p. 139.
[24] It was, thanks to Saint Vincent, that Nicholas Sevin, Bishop of Sarlat, became co-adjutor of Alain de Solminihac, Bishop of Cahors.
[25] *Saint Vincent de Paul*, Vol. VII, p. 299.
[26] *Ibid.*, Vol. IV, p. 335. [27] *Ibid.*, pp. 520–523.
[28] Abelly, *op. cit.*, Bk. III, Ch. IX, sect. IV, p. 143.
[29] *Ibid.*, p. 145. [30] *Ibid.*, Bk. II, Ch. XIII, sect. VI, p. 453.

presence of a bishop would greatly contribute to the spread of the Catholic religion in a city so long delivered over to heresy. On his advice, the Queen gave the archbishopric of Bordeaux to the Bishop of Maillezais, the bishopric of La Rochelle to the Bishop of Saintes, the bishopric of Saintes to the Bishop of Oloron, and established Canons in the cathedral of La Rochelle by uniting the simple benefices of the Chapter of Maillezais, which had then fallen vacant, to the Chapter of La Rochelle.[31]

Saint Vincent's influence over the episcopacy of France deserved to be made known ; it was essential if his labours for the reform of the clergy were to bear fruit. If those who by their office are constituted guardians of ecclesiastical discipline had themselves continued to lead irregular lives, it could hardly be expected that they could have efficaciously combated laxity in their clergy or animated them with a love for the apostolic life.

Laxity had spread everywhere, amongst the regular as well as the secular clergy. We have already shown how Saint Vincent collaborated with zealous bishops in restoring the real spirit of the priesthood amongst the pastoral clergy ; it would be a serious omission in this work if we said nothing about the help he gave religious reformers in their restoration of the primitive rule.

[31] Abelly, *op. cit.*, p. 453.

CHAPTER XXXIV

THE REFORM OF THE MONASTIC ORDERS

IF we are to understand the position of the Monastic Orders when Saint Vincent became a member of the Council of Conscience, we must retrace our steps for some years.

In 1619, Louis XIII, during a visit to the Abbey of Marmoutier, was painfully affected by the sight presented to his eyes during the Mass at which he assisted, and by his subsequent inspection of the Abbey. On his return to Paris, the King conveyed his impressions to the Bishop of that city. ' Sire,' Richelieu replied, ' the evil is, in fact, very great and most monasteries are suffering from it ; a genuine reform is essential ; Cardinal de La Rochefoucauld seems to me to be the man best qualified for such a delicate task ; why does Your Majesty not obtain from the Holy See the necessary faculties for him to carry out the work ? '[1]

The King highly approved of the suggestion. At this time, the Abbey of Sainte Geneviève had just lost its head and the Cardinal was nominated Abbot. A petition was also forwarded to Rome asking that all necessary faculties for the reform of all the ancient Orders of France, as well as the post of Vicar General, should be granted to La Rochefoucauld. The Brief of nomination was signed on April 8, 1622. As soon as this was made known in Paris, two commissions were appointed : one by the Cardinal, to work out a general set of regulations ; and the other by the King, to obtain information on the difficulties that were bound to

[1] Robillard d'Avrigny, *Mémoires chronologiques* (Paris), 1720, 4 vols., duodec. Vol. I, p. 314 ; La Morinière, *Les vertus du vrai prélat représentées en la vie de Mgr l'Eminentissime cardinal de La Rochefoucauld*, Paris, 1646, quarto, pp. 146–147 ; Bibl. de Ste-Geneviève, Ms. 712, f⁰ 36 v⁰.

arise. The first commission was composed of a Carthusian, a Dominican, a Jesuit, a Benedictine, a monk of the Order of Saint Bernard (a Feuillant) and a monk of the Order of Saint Francis of Paula (a Minim) ; the second consisted of four bishops, six Councillors of State and two Masters of Requests.[2]

The reforms was advancing very slowly, or rather seemed to be at a standstill, when Louis XIII handed over the direction of the affairs of the kingdom to Cardinal Richelieu. The iron hand of the Prime Minister was needed to crush the forces of opposition that had risen on all sides. In order to bring more easily the members of religious Orders under his authority, he lost no opportunity of adding other benefices to those already in his possession. He became Abbot of La Chaise-Dieu, Cluny, Cîteaux, Marmoutier, Redom, Saint-Pierre-au-Mont, Ham, Saint-Riquier, Notre Dame de Vaulleroy, Saint-Lucien de Beauvais, Signy, Saint-Maxient, Saint-Arnoul de Metz, Saint-Benoît ; Prior of Saint-Germain-des-Champs, of Coussay, etc., etc.[3]

Monastic reform could only come from within. The two Cardinals would have wasted all their energies if they had not found in the old Orders themselves the instruments they needed, that is to say, men of tried virtue and consummate wisdom.

The Benedictine Reform, transplanted from Lorraine to France by Dom Didier de la Cour, founder of the Congregation of Saints Vanne and Hydulph, changed its name to that of the Congregation of Saint Maur, and on French soil, remained, up to 1648, under the jurisdiction of a man of the greatest worth, Dom Gregory Tarrisse, who modified the Constitutions and affiliated a considerable number of monasteries. The Order of Saint Augustine took on a new lease of life under the vigorous action of two virtuous religious : Charles Faure, who was the first Superior-General of the Congregation of France or the ' Génovéfains,' and Alain de Solminihac, at first Abbot of Chancelade and

[2] Gabriel de La Rochefoucauld, *Le Cardinal François de La Rochefoucauld*, Paris, 1926, oct., pp. 196–201.
[3] Paul Denis, *Le Cardinal de Richelieu et la réforme des monastères bénédictins*, Paris, 1913, quarto, pp. 464–465.

later Bishop of Cahors, who raised up the Abbey from a state of material and moral ruin and made it the headquarters of a new branch of the Augustinian family. The Third Order of Saint Francis was restored by Mussart. God gave Father Michaelis to the Dominicans to raise them up from the state of laxity into which they had fallen ; to the Premonstratensians, Saint Peter Fourier, in Lorraine, and Father Layruels in France ; to the Canons Regular of Saint Anthony, Father Sanejehan ; to the Carmelite friars, Fathers Louis de Genouillac-Vaillac and Denis of the Mother of God. The Feuillants, Recollets and Trinitarians also found in their own Orders zealous leaders who, not content with regretting the past and deploring the present, succeeded in inspiring their brethren with a desire to lead a more perfect life, and guided them in the way.

The Tarrisses, Faures and their emulators would certainly have failed in the work of reform if fear of Richelieu had not kept the malcontents in check, and when the Prime Minister died on December 4, 1642, they raised their heads. Louis XIII was ill and on the point of death ; Cardinal de La Rochefoucauld, old and infirm, was only a shadow of his former self. Circumstances seemed favourable to those who preferred a free and easy life to a regular one. The reformed monks and friars were crushed under a hail of libels ; they were spared no pang, and from more than one monastery were expelled ignominiously after being despoiled of all they possessed. There were even armed contests ; blood flowed and the police were compelled to interfere.

At Blancs-Manteaux, the Maurists managed to secure Dom Faron de Chalus, the head of the cabal, confine him in a room at Saint Germain-des-Prés and from thence send him to the Abbey of Saint Faron at Meaux.[4] Dom Lemperière, the leader of the mitigated order, re-entered the Abbey of Cluny in triumph during Holy Week of 1643, and the reformed, who refused to leave, were expelled in 1644.[5] ' When the day arrived,' wrote D'Ormesson, ' the reformed, having refused to leave, were attacked by the older monks,

[4] François Rousseau, *Dom Grégoire Tarrisse*, Paris, 1924, oct., pp. 64–66.
[5] *Journal*, Paris, 2 vols., quarto, Vol. I, p. 229.

and after being driven out from three strongholds where heads were broken, they were compelled to depart that evening.' At Marmoutier, the adversaries of the Maurists ' seized on the Chapter Room and the great refectory of the Abbey, broke down the doors and seized the furniture and utensils . . . To put an end to their violence, it was necessary to summon the Governor and Lieutenant-General of Tours who arrived with an armed band.' Scenes of disorder broke out again a few days later. The fourth Sunday after Easter, whilst the Prior, vested in alb and stole, was kneeling in prayer in the sacristy, preparing to celebrate Mass, two monks fell on him, threw him on the ground, loaded him with insults, calling him a rascal, a scoundrel, a ragamuffin, a traitor, and a rogue. On May 12, the Feast of Saint Martin the helper, whilst the reformed were taking part in a procession, their opponents endeavoured to shut the Abbey gates and prevent them from re-entering, but the servants and some monks who had remained within the house were on the watch and prevented the execution of the plan.[6]

Almost all the monasteries that had accepted union with Saint Maur had to suffer similar scenes of disorder.

The mitigated order had a powerful friend at Court in the person of the Prince de Condé. The first prince of the blood, who was so physically weak that he could not walk and had to be carried about on a litter, was constantly on the move in furtherance of his plots and intrigues. The death of Richelieu left a large number of Abbeys and Priories without a titular head. Condé's protection was of great assistance to a number of petitioners who were either indifferent or hostile to all ideas of reform. His second son, Armand de Conti, a lad of thirteen years still at school, undergrown, sickly and lame, and already provided with the wealthy Abbey of Saint Denis, now received that of Cluny, to which those of Lerins and Molesme were soon added.[7]

Moreover, the reformers did not always receive the support from Rome on which they relied. Richelieu had too

[6] Paul Denis, *op. cit.*, p. 242.
[7] *Ibid.*, pp. 378–379 ; Rousseau, *op. cit.*, p. 114.

REFORM OF THE MONASTIC ORDERS

often acted independently, thinking that his own authority was all-sufficient; his work lacked the solid foundations that papal approbation and the fulfilment of canonical formalities would have given it.

After Richelieu's death, appeals to the Court of Rome were multiplied. The irregularities committed either by him or by Cardinal de La Rochefoucauld were denounced to the Holy See; the high handed proceedings of the two reforming Cardinals and their encroachments on episcopal rights were bitterly resented. Rome, when requested to pronounce on the validity of a particular act, looked at it from the juridical standpoint; it did not consider whether such an act was favourable to the reformers or their opponents, but only if all the conditions for validity had been fulfilled, and unfortunately, in only too many instances, a juridical examination revealed the non-observance of forms which obliged the Court to declare these proceedings invalid.

In this contest against laxity and want of discipline the reforming party could scarcely rely on Mazarin, who was always ready to subordinate the interests of religion to his political plans; the Prince de Condé, as we have seen, was not favourable, and Parliament itself seemed only to take pleasure in destroying the work of Richelieu. The only one left was Vincent de Paul, then a member of the Council of Conscience, and the reformers found in him their stoutest defender. All that Anne of Austria did to assist the party of reform was due to the efforts of Saint Vincent, who never ceased to throw the whole weight of his influence on their side.

It was, perhaps, at his suggestion that a decision was reached in 1644 to bring litigants before a special commission composed of Brulard, Prior of Léon, d'Ormesson, Laisné, Dominic Séguier, the Bishop of Meaux, and Bignon and Verthamon, Councillors of State, to whom were added, on September 13, 1645, de Villarceaux, Pinon, Lamoignon, Marcillac, Thomel and La Marguérie, Masters of Requests.[8]

When it looked as if trouble might arise at a General Chapter, Saint Vincent used to beg the Queen to send a distinguished prelate, furnished with the necessary powers,

[8] Paul Denis, *op. cit.*, p. 241.

to reduce the promoters of disturbance to powerlessness, facilitate free and full discussion, and assure freedom of deliberation and election. Once he had the delegate's report in his hands and was certain that everything had been carried out according to the regulations, he turned a deaf ear to all malcontents.[9]

The support given to Dom Gregory Tarrisse by Saint Vincent, and through the latter's efforts, by the Queen, did not prevent the Maurists from losing the Abbeys of Cluny, Citeaux, and Prémontre, but it did enable them to hold those of Blancs-Manteaux and Saint Germain-des-Prés in Paris, Saint Denis, Marmoutier, Chezal-Benoît, Montmajour, La Chaise-Dieu, Saint Martin of Séez, Saint Ouen of Rouen, Fécamp, Saint Sever, Saint Germer of Flay and many others. Saint Vincent and Dom Tarrisse were united together by the bonds of close friendship and reciprocal esteem. 'The mere thought of his exterior modesty and recollection,' says the Saint of the Benedictine, 'gently recalls me to the presence of God whenever the necessity of transacting external affairs has distracted me a little.'[10] Saint-Lazare once possessed four letters from the celebrated Benedictine reformer to the Founder of the Mission[11] and amongst those of the Saint's now extant, there is one addressed to the Superior of Saint Maur, but it is not quite certain whether it was written to Dom Tarrisse or to his successor, Dom John Harel.[12] However, it is quite certain that the two friends frequently met and corresponded. The introduction of reform into the monasteries of Saint Benedict, the deplorable conflict that arose between the monks of Saint Méen and the Bishop of Saint Malo, and finally, the office of Vicar General of the Abbey of Saint Ouen in Rouen, which Saint Vincent was forced to accept and hold for some

---

[9] Abelly, *op. cit.*, Bk. II, Ch. XIII, sect. VII, pp. 459–460.

[10] Dom Martène, *Histoire de la Congrégation de Saint-Maur*, Dom G. Charvin's edit., 5 vols., oct., Paris, 1928–1931, Vol. III, p. 125. This work, still in course of publication, is full of valuable information on the Benedictine reform of the seventeenth century.

[11] Dom Martène, *Histoire de la Congrégation de Saint-Maur*, Ms. 3 vols. folio, Vol. III, p. 412.

[12] *Saint Vincent de Paul*, Vol. IV, p. 192.

R.P.D. GREGORIVS TARRISSE SVPERIOR.
GENERAL CONG. S. MAVRI.
Obijt An. 1648. Die 25. Sept Ætatis Suæ 74.

B. Moncornet excd.

GREGORY TARRISSE
SUPERIOR OF THE CONGREGATION OF SAINT MAUR

REFORM OF THE MONASTIC ORDERS

years whilst the Abbot was under detention, as well as many other causes, frequently brought together these two men, so well fitted to understand and esteem one another.

Saint Vincent was also the friend, guide and counsellor of another great reformer, Cardinal de La Rochefoucauld.[13] On February 3, 1644, the Cardinal, foreseeing the difficulties that were bound to arise after his death in connection with the Monastery of Sainte-Geneviève, of which he was Abbot, proclaimed before all the professed religious of the Abbey and of the Congregation of France, that he intended to resign in favour of his coadjutor, Charles Faure, and to alter the period of tenure of office from that of life to one of three years. The realisation of this plan necessitated the intervention of the civil authority. The preliminaries were long, difficult and delicate. An attempt was made to impose on the monks a clause stating that the King reserved to himself the right of confirming the Abbot-elect, and this the monks refused to accept. To put an end to the difficulty, the Cardinal sent Father Boulart to Saint Vincent on June 23, at ten o'clock in the evening. The Saint consented to speak to the Queen on the subject, but only on condition that he was summoned by her, and that she was unaware of his desire to speak on the matter. Madame de Sénecey, the Cardinal's niece and a Lady in Waiting to Queen Anne of Austria, arranged things so well that on the following day, and for a reason completely foreign to that which had dictated Father Boulart's step, Saint Vincent was summoned to Court.[14] He had the happiness of being successful. All difficulties were removed from that quarter; Rome was petitioned for Bulls which arrived in Paris before the end of the year.

It was just in time, for Cardinal de La Rochefoucauld died on February 14, 1645, assisted by his holy friend who took part in the prayers for the dying and remained until the Cardinal's last breath.[15]

---

[13] Postulatory letter of the Abbot of Sainte-Geneviève, John de Montenas, to the Pope (May 21, 1706).

[14] Bibl. de Ste-Geneviève, Ms. 712, f⁰ 81–85; Ms. 613, f⁰ 235; *Saint Vincent de Paul*, Vol. II, p. 463.

[15] Bibl. de Ste-Geneviève, Ms. 712, f⁰ 82.

Saint Vincent was also acquainted with Father Faure and endeavoured by various acts of kindness to induce the latter to forget the annoyance caused to the Order of Saint Augustine by the cession of Saint-Lazare, but it would seem that he never completely succeeded.[16]

Saint Vincent's relations with Alain de Solminihac were far more intimate and cordial, and he contributed with all his might to the erection of the Congregation of Chancelade. He removed obstacles created by the Court, procured protectors on the great Council of State, furthered its interests, both in Paris and Rome, with all who could be of any assistance, pointed out the easiest methods and those most certain to succeed, encouraged its delegates, and in short, displayed so much zeal for the establishment of the new Institute that he could not have shown more in favour of one of his own undertakings.[17] This conduct was all the more praiseworthy inasmuch as by supporting Alain de Solminihac, he was opposing the Superior of the Augustinian Congregation of France, with whom it was important for the Saint to remain on good terms, for the influence of the Superior and some of his friends was being exerted against him.

Other Canons Regular of Saint Augustine formed a distinct branch known as the Congregation of Saint Anthony of Vienna, in which also there was fortunately a movement in favour of reform. In 1618, Louis XIII ordered a reform which gradually extended, despite occasional violent resistance. In 1630, the various houses received new Constitutions, drawn up by the General Chapter and approved by Urban VIII. Saint Vincent had on more than one occasion to defend the reformed ' Antonines ' against their adversaries.[18]

He also played some part in the reform of the Order of Grandmont, of which Father Frémont was the chief author. Their friendship dated from the days when the latter was Prior of the College of Grandmont in Paris. They met frequently, and held conversations on the spiritual life,

[16] *Saint Vincent de Paul*, Vol. I, p. 278.
[17] *Ibid.*, Vols. II, III, IV, *passim*.
[18] Abelly, *op. cit.*, Bk. II, Ch. XIII, sect. VII, p. 456.

REFORM OF THE MONASTIC ORDERS

from which they each departed still more firmly resolved to live for God, and for Him alone.

In 1642, Frémont was sent to Epoisses (Côte-d'Or), on Richelieu's personal intervention, to establish a reform, in which he succeeded, notwithstanding the opposition of the older religious. He even extended the Order by establishing a monastery at Thiers in 1650, in which he took up his residence and established a novitiate. On July 1, 1651, he received a letter from Saint Vincent requesting him, without entering into details, to come to Paris for a matter of great consequence concerning the glory of God, the general welfare of the Order of Grandmont, and, in particular, the promotion of the reform. Both men were charmed to meet again and to be able to discourse at length, as of old, on the interior life. Saint Vincent, after hearing Frémont, expressed his delight in the following words: *Nunquam locutus est homo sicut hic homo.* He fell at the monk's feet for a blessing, saying: 'Bless me, Father; I see clearly that the Holy Spirit speaks by your lips.' Frémont was taken aback and vainly endeavoured to raise up the Saint. 'You have before you,' he said, 'only a poor little religious, full of faults and most unworthy of your esteem. It is you who should bless me, you in whom the Holy Spirit abides, you whom He has filled with apostolic zeal, and of whom He has made use to convert a million souls to the true faith.' He waited, but all in vain, and both arose without receiving the desired blessing. Saint Vincent then told his friend why he had asked him to come to Paris. 'The Priory of Saint Michel of Lodève, which belongs to your Order, is without a titular; the Queen offers it to you and asks you to establish a reform there; you will not, Father, refuse Her Majesty's request, because it is for the glory of God.' 'I am most grateful to the Queen,' said Frémont, 'for this noble gift, but as I have renounced all ecclesiastical dignities, I regret I cannot accept it.'

The two friends met again. Francis de Bosquet, Bishop of Lodève, was present at one of these interviews and pointed out that several persons were seeking for the Priory and that, all things considered, it would be better to rest content with offering Father Frémont a pension of one hundred crowns from the benefice. The latter consented to this, subject to the permission of his Superior General. Saint Vincent and de Bosquet undertook to ask Father Barny for the necessary authorisation. Their letter remained unanswered. Some months later, Frémont, happy to see his community increased by two novices, wrote to the Saint and the Bishop that he was now in a position to send disciples to the Priory at Lodève, and that he would do so as soon as he was informed of the General's consent.[19] The latter still remained silent. Saint Vincent wrote to him again on January 24, 1652. 'There is reason to hope,' he said,[20] 'that our good God wishes to employ you, Most Reverend Father, in raising up an Order as holy as yours is. . . . The King wishes to assist, and it seems as if it were the will of God, for He has given you this good religious as a most suitable instrument to be employed by Your Reverence; you can do so most usefully if you will be good enough to grant him the powers of a Grand Vicar to rule the houses of Epoisses, Thiers and Lodève, with faculties to admit novices and professed religious in the aforesaid ancient observance, the whole being subject to your authority and holy guidance.'

When Father Barny received a letter under the King's private seal commanding him to grant his subordinate the title of Vicar General and permission to introduce the reform in Saint Michel of Lodève, he was convinced that Frémont was intriguing to escape from his jurisdiction. Accordingly, he submitted outwardly, but did all in his power to raise obstacles. Lodève, as a matter of fact, was not reformed until 1679.

The Dominicans in France had not escaped the general process of monastic decline. They had fallen very low indeed in the early years of the seventeenth century, when a contrary movement began to make itself felt. It was at this time that Father Michaelis established in the Faubourg-Saint-Honoré, Paris, the Convent of the Annunciation, from which the reform spread rapidly to all the provinces.

[19] Pierre Legay, *Histoire de la réforme de Grandmont, contenant la vie du très Révérend Père Charles Frémont*, 1718, Ms. bibl. nat. fr. 19,682, pp. 155–160.
[20] *Saint Vincent de Paul*, Vol. IV, p. 309.

The new branch of the Dominican Order took the name of the Congregation of Saint Louis. Unfortunately, a division broke out amongst its members, and two very distinct parties were formed—the Gascons and the Parisians, as they were called, or more properly the Southern and the Northern Fathers. The convents in Paris and Toulouse were the chief centres of disturbance; there was also another centre at Saint-Maximin, but here the movement was in favour of autonomy. The Parisians complained that most of the Superiors, even in the North, were Gascons. They disliked ' being sent to the South, where,' as their records state, ' there is nothing to eat but garlic, onions and rancid oils; which is extremely repugnant to the refined temperament of Parisians and of all those who esteem a good education.' To use Father Mortier's phrase, this was ' the garlic battle.' There was a shower of letters, memoirs, bitter, biting and frequently amusing pamphlets. The Gascons were quite willing to dwell with the Parisians, but the latter would not tolerate the former at any price. ' Every man to his own home,' was their battle-cry.[21]

Master General Ridolfi was strongly opposed to separation, and the debates were continued under his successor, Master General Turco. On the Parisian side, Father John of Saint Mary, Superior of the Annunciation Convent, even went so far as to demand, in insulting and violent pamphlets, that the houses should be placed under the immediate jurisdiction of the bishops. The matter was brought before the Council of Conscience which decided that the evil should be remedied by the Master General, and this view was shared by the Queen. Saint Vincent was ordered to communicate Anne of Austria's opinion to Father Turco and the Master General's reply reveals how deeply uneasy he felt about Father John of Saint Mary's line of action. On April 9, 1645, Father Turco wrote: ' I urgently beg Your Most Reverend Paternity to act in such fashion that, by the authority of the most Christian Queen, this Father may be compelled (all possibility of his making a petition being removed) to submit to the order by which I am

[21] P. Mortier, *Histoire abrégée de l'Ordre de Saint-Dominique en France*, Tours, 1920, oct., pp. 231-247.

transferring him from the convent at Paris to that at Avignon. This measure is dictated for several motives: the approach of the day on which the Assembly of the Clergy of France is to be held, for in that body he might find many supporters; his hot-headed character; his tendency towards novelties; his nature, so prone to insolence and insubordination; his crafty cleverness . . . in infecting the minds of others with his own obstinate designs for a separation. He would flout any authority if the most Christian Queen, in her goodness and piety, does not deign, through the influence of Your Most Reverend Paternity, to employ her power for the execution of the measures that should be taken.'[22]

This letter had not reached Paris before Father Turco decided to place both Gascons and Parisians under the authority of two distinct Commissaries who were themselves placed under the jurisdiction of the Vicar General. The Master General did not conceal the opposition which the execution of his design was bound to encounter in Paris, and therefore, when writing to Saint Vincent to inform him of the decision arrived at, he asked for the help of the Queen Regent. 'If what I have decided,' he wrote,[23] ' meets with her approbation, I beg Your Most Reverend Paternity to induce her to support the Reverend Father Vincent Bosside, Vicar General, and to use her power to such effect that brethren sent from Paris shall withdraw to the convents assigned them, and be not tolerated elsewhere. If it were otherwise, the latter would find means of despising my authority, for from what I learn, even here in the heart of the Curia itself, they have supporters who have been deceived by their dissimulation and false pretexts. . . . I implore your support in which I put my whole trust.'

In the eyes of the Parisians, Father Turco had not gone far enough in the policy of separation, and they refused to support him. The Council of State next intervened and erected the Congregation into a province, but this solution did not prove to be any more successful than the preceding one.[24]

[22] *Saint Vincent de Paul*, Vol. III, pp. 509–510.
[23] *Ibid.*, p. 512; Mortier, *op. cit.*, p. 247.
[24] P. Mortier, *op. cit.*, p. 247.

The Master General then resolved to visit France in person and hold an enquiry into the whole situation. He had several long interviews with Saint Vincent in Paris, heard the grievances of the Gascons at Toulouse, and visited all the houses (even those that had not accepted the reform) of the whole province of Toulouse. What he saw in these last houses deeply distressed him, and he refers, in a letter to Saint Vincent, to ' the pitiful state ' in which he found them ' both in temporals and spirituals,' to the ' wretched condition of the houses which were falling into ruins at Marciac, la Réole, Port-Sainte-Marie, etc.,' to the ' quarrels,' ' differences ' and ' factions that were disturbing the peace,' to ' the general complaints of seculars who were neither ministered to nor edified,' and lastly, to the desire that all the Fathers had expressed for assistance ' seeing themselves without novices, students or any means or hope of securing more, on account of the cramped condition and poverty of their convents.'[25]

At the conclusion of his investigation, the Master General decided that it was necessary to separate the Parisians and Gascons; he declared that the river Loire should form the boundary; only convents north of the river were assigned to the Congregation of Saint Louis; the others, united to the convents of the non-reformed province of Toulouse, under the authority of the same Provincial who should always be selected from the observants, were to form the new province of Toulouse. He hoped by the infusion of new blood to restore life to the non-reformed convents which seemed to be on the eve of dissolution.[26] The Fathers attached to these last monasteries protested against a decision which placed them in an inferior position; they did not wish to unite with the reformed, and still more strongly objected to submit to one of the reformed. If a union was to be effected, they demanded equal rights and refused to be treated as religious of a lower rank, unworthy to hold the office of Provincial. The spirit of revolt spread and captured all the convents.[27]

[25] *Saint Vincent de Paul*, Vol. III, pp. 394–395.
[26] Mortier, *op. cit.*, p. 247.
[27] *Ibid.*, p. 253.

Saint Vincent had an interview in Paris with the ringleaders; he begged them to live peacefully together, urged them to seek some common ground of agreement and added that he would examine their proposals when submitted to him. On December 21, 1648, he wrote to Father Turco to inform him of the result of the interview.[28]

In the course of the Master General's reply, he says : ' I cannot make a single concession until they have first obeyed and made reparation, by their obedience and submission, for the evil seeds of rebellion and want of respect which their acts of violence and deceit have sown in the minds of their brethren, and which would give rise to dangerous consequences and bad example if I now yielded to them in the slightest degree, even if my duty and conscience allowed me to do so. In conclusion, Sir, I beg you to agree with me that they should obey, and afterwards, I will let them see that I am their father, always prepared to forgive when they are prepared to be forgiven, that is when they have done their duty.'[29]

Peace was not established until 1656 when, by the constitution of the congregation of Aix, the seventeen convents of the non-reformed were brought under the authority of a Vicar General.

Besides these extensive movements for reform which affected entire Orders, there were also lesser reforms concerned with particular monasteries. When trouble arose in a convent, Saint Vincent was accustomed to employ a means which he regarded as most efficacious for the discovery of the roots of the evil and the application of the most suitable remedy, namely, the despatch of a prudent and clear-sighted ecclesiastic to the convent or monastery, provided with the necessary powers to hold a canonical visitation.[30] As a general rule, this expedient proved admirably successful. There were, moreover, cases of individual reforms in which the Saint, whenever an opportunity arose, collaborated zealously. During several years, he helped to support an Italian religious who had been propagating false doctrines.[31] In his voluminous daily correspondence, letters

---

[28] *Saint Vincent de Paul*, Vol. III, p. 392. [29] *Ibid.*, p. 394.
[30] Abelly, *op. cit.*, Bk. II, Ch. XIII, sect. VIII, p. 466.
[31] *Ibid.*, Bk. III, Ch. XI, sect. V, p. 153.

from members of religious Orders may be found; some sought advice, others consolation; he induced some to abandon the disastrous resolutions to which discouragement or the attractions of an easier life had led them. To those who wrote to say they intended to leave their Order to join another, his usual reply was a recommendation to persevere in their state of life and an assurance that by amending their lives they would find the interior tranquillity of which they felt the need.

Writing to a religious who was cross-grained, held obstinately to his own views and found the yoke of obedience almost intolerable, he says: 'You should give yourself once more to Our Lord by renouncing your own judgement and fulfilling His most holy Will in the state to which Providence has called you.' Another, a doctor of theology, considered that the rule of his Order, which was all very well in former days, was an anachronism in the seventeenth century; he wanted a reform, but in the direction of making the rule easier, and begged Saint Vincent to intervene to this effect with the Holy See. The Saint reminded him of Our Lord's words: 'Blessed are those who suffer for justice,' and added: 'There are crosses everywhere, and your advanced age should cause you to avoid those which you might find in a change of state.'[32] A celebrated preacher, a Doctor and Professor of Theology, also considered his rules were a little too severe. He had heard of an Order in which the life was more easy, and to which he felt attracted. Saint Vincent pointed out that he would endanger his salvation in such a community. 'It is,' he wrote,[33] ' a disorder and not an Order, a body without any consistency or real head, in which the members live without any government or common bond . . . a chimera of a religious Order which serves as a refuge for unruly and dissolute religious.' He concluded: 'I beg Our Lord to preserve you from such folly.'

Convents of nuns were not exempt from the failings and

[32] Abelly, *op. cit.*, Bk. III, Ch. XI, sect. V, pp. 156–157.
[33] *Ibid.*, Bk. II, Ch. XIII, sect. VII, p. 460. (*Libertine*, in Saint Vincent's time, was generally understood to mean a freethinker; but the idea of a loose-liver was also connoted.)

defects to be found in those of men. Relaxation was often introduced by those very persons whose duty it was to prevent it; the rule became relaxed when the Superior and the priests charged with the spiritual guidance of the nuns were members of a decadent Order. In the fifteenth century, a worldly spirit penetrated the celebrated royal Abbey of Longchamp in this way, and two centuries later, Saint Vincent was able to measure the extent of its ravages when he observed how little the nuns respected the obligations of their vows and rules; the orders of the Abbess were not obeyed; the nuns sought to be beautifully and richly dressed, were over-familiar with their confessor, conversed frequently and at length with young men in the convent parlours, and broke the rules of enclosure. There were, of course, violent antipathies and divisions amongst them. Saint Vincent saw that a reform was essential, and as only the Sovereign Pontiff could impose it, he begged the Queen to petition Rome for a reform.[34] The Prefect of the Congregation of Regulars, before coming to a decision, ordered a private investigation which was entrusted to Saint Vincent himself. His report is still extant.[35] He decided that it was necessary to withdraw the Abbey from the jurisdiction of the Order of Saint Francis and place it under the authority of the Ordinary. At the very moment he was writing this letter, the evil had grown even greater, for the nuns, driven from their convent by the civil wars, had taken refuge in Paris, and as they kept making ceaseless rounds of visits, they had lost whatever little remnants of the religious spirit they once possessed.

Circumstances occasionally demanded severe penalties. An Abbess of noble birth, interned in a monastery of another Order for scandalous conduct, thought that Adrian Lebon's influence would prove strong enough to induce Saint Vincent to mitigate her punishment. The former Prior of Saint-Lazare was acquainted with the Abbess, to whom indeed he was under some obligations. He went to the Saint and asked for her pardon, but to no effect. 'Is that the way you treat me?' said the former Prior, 'have you so

[34] *Saint Vincent de Paul*, Vol. IV, p. 269.
[35] *Ibid.*, p. 500.

REFORM OF THE MONASTIC ORDERS

quickly forgotten all I have done for you and your Company?'[36] These words hurt Saint Vincent deeply and he replied : ' It is true we have been loaded with honours and benefits ; we owe you all that children owe a father. Pray, Sir, be good enough to take back all you have given us, as we are not worthy to keep it.' The Prior withdrew in high dudgeon. Some time afterwards, when more fully informed of the faults with which the Abbess was charged, he threw himself at the Saint's feet and said : ' Pray forgive the hasty words I uttered the other day ; your severity is only too well justified ; I myself now beg you to continue the punishment.'

There was another class of nuns to which Saint Vincent devoted much attention ; these were wandering religious, who, driven from their convents by war or famine, resided with their relations or friends and were liable to contract in the world habits scarcely reconcilable with the monastic life. He sought a refuge for these lost sheep without a fold. Those whom he could not place in convents of their Order, because he could not find an Abbess or Prioress willing to receive them, were brought together by him in houses which he rented and in which they had to lead a community life, under the rule of a Superioress sometimes supplied by another Order.[37]

If we were to give a detailed account of the innumerable services which Saint Vincent rendered to members of religious Orders of both sexes, either in the Council of Concience or by his own personal efforts, by his intercessions, during the unhappy years of the Fronde, on behalf of those who had ceased to receive from the royal domain the revenues lawfully due to them,[38] by revising their Constitutions,[39] obtaining royal Letters Patent by which they were granted an existence in the eyes of the law, or in any

---

[36] Abelly, *op. cit.*, Bk III, Ch. XXII, p. 318.
[37] *Ibid.*, Bk. III, Ch. XI, sect. V, p. 157.
[38] *Ibid.*, Bk. II, Ch. VIII, sect. VII, p. 462.
[39] Saint Vincent revised the Constitutions of the Nursing Nuns of the Charity of Notre-Dame. (See, *Constitutions des religieuses hospitalières de la Charité-Notre-Dame, de l'Ordre de Saint Augustin*, with a prefatory letter by the Bishop of Saintes).

other way, a volume would not suffice.[40] He sent his priests into parishes that depended on the Knights of Malta to preach missions ;[41] he put an end to a conflict between the nuns of Saint Elisabeth of Paris and the penitent religious of the reformed Third Order of Saint Francis, who were their spiritual guides, by determining, in a set of regulations in which Father Faure and Father de Condren collaborated, the respective rights and duties of both parties ;[42] and induced the dissenting Carmelite nuns to submit to the Papal Brief which stated that only apostolic visitors had a right to make visitations of the houses of their Order.[43]

Abelly says quite truly that Saint Vincent seized every opportunity ' to honour, help, serve and protect ' members of the various religious Orders, and these four words sum up all.[44]

[40] Saint Vincent secured Letters-Patent for the Congregation of Saint Anne of Arras. (De Marte, *La vie meslée ou la vie de Damoiselle Jeanne Biscot*, Valenciennes, 1692, p. 132. There are further references to Saint Vincent at pages 288–289.)
[41] *Saint Vincent de Paul*, Vol. I, p. 389.
[42] Bibliot. de Ste-Geneviève, Ms. 712, f⁰ 86 v⁰.
[43] *Saint Vincent de Paul*, Vol. VIII, pp. 61, 166, 187, 335, 395, 413, 414, 422.
[44] Abelly, *op. cit.*, Bk. III, Ch. XI, sect. V, p. 158.

CHAPTER XXXV

THE FOUNDLINGS

THANKS to the efforts of Saint Vincent de Paul, the Church in France had taken on a new lease of life; but the religious reforms studied in the preceding chapters, were far from exhausting his amazing activity. A number of charitable institutions, created and maintained by his exertions, formed a powerful barrier to the spread of public misery due to war, pestilence, famine and crime fostered by the culpable negligence of the civil power.

As the youngest deserve pride of place, we shall begin with the children.

We know very little of what was done for foundlings before the seventeenth century. They were first taken to the Church of Notre-Dame, where a woman was always in waiting to receive them, and then, after certain formalities, they were sent to the Trinity Hospital in the Rue Saint Denis.[1] The Masters of the establishment then confided the babies to women of good character who undertook to nurse and rear them.[2] The necessary funds were provided partly from a tax and partly from alms.[3] By a decree of August 11, 1552, the Parliament enforced an annual contribution of

[1] This hospital disappeared in 1789.

[2] Decree of the Parliament, August 11, 1552. Leo Lallemand has collected some fifteenth and sixteenth century notices in the first few pages of his excellent book: *Un chapitre de l'histoire des enfants trouvés. La maison de La Couche à Paris.* Paris, H. Champion, 1885, oct., pp. 5-9.

[3] The Lords High Justices were the Archbishop of Paris, the Chapter of Notre Dame, the Abbot of Saint-Germain-des-Prés, the Abbot of Saint-Victor, the Abbot of Sainte-Geneviève, the Grand Prior of France, the Prior of Saint-Martin-des-Champs, the Prior of Saint-Denis de la Charte, the Abbess of Montmartre, the Chapters of Saint-Marcel, Saint Merry, and Saint Benoît, etc. They were sixteen in number.

960 *livres* from the Lords High Justices of the city and suburbs for the support and education of all children abandoned within the territory over which they exercised jurisdiction.[4] Public sympathy for the foundlings was excited in an original and ingenious fashion : the faithful entering Notre-Dame on Sundays and Holidays, saw on the left-hand side of the porch several babies lying in a cradle fixed to the pavement, whilst two or three nurses stood by with plates for alms beside them crying in pitiful tones : ' Help the poor foundlings.'[5]

A foundling might not be picked up by the chance passer-by ; in 1615, Bouchel wrote : ' Whenever a child is left exposed in the streets of Paris, it is not lawful for anyone to take it up except the commissary of the district or a person going in his direction.'[6] A formal report was drawn up in which the place where the child was found was stated and also the state of its health at the time.[7] If the commissary, fearing lest people might think he was the foundling's father, did not act, it was the duty of the woman in charge of the foundlings to go and seek it, and for this she was paid five *sols*.[8]

The rules laid down by Parliament were as a rule ignored. In 1654, the Canons complained that children were usually brought by the mothers themselves, or by others who accompanied them, or by officers of justice who had not received a mandate from the Provost of Paris or his civil or criminal lieutenant. To put an end to these disorders, they demanded, and their demand was granted, that the Administrator should be empowered to imprison all who exposed infants, including the mothers, and to keep them in gaol until the guilty parties were discovered.[9]

The Chapter of Paris, which had supreme charge of this work, decided that it would be well to place all foundlings

---

[4] Bibl. Nat., ff. 18,605.

[5] A decree of October 16, 1411, speaks of ten children who had been abandoned, and of two plates ; Bouchel says there was only one plate in 1615. (*Bibliothèque ou Trésor du droit français*, éd. de 1671, Vol. I, p. 1014.)

[6] *Op. cit.*, p. 1013.   [7] Abelly, *op. cit.*, Ch. XXX, p. 142.

[8] Bouchel, *op. cit.*, p. 1013.

[9] Decree of May 27, 1564.

in a home close to the Chapter House, and selected some houses at the Gate of Saint Landry, near the Bishop's palace, at the end of a lane running down towards the Seine. The Parliament, after visiting the property, approved of the project in 1570; they gave orders that certain repairs should be made, and decreed that the Lords High Justices of Paris should meet at a place and at times fixed by the Bishop ' to confer and to draw up reports and such police regulations as they considered . . . should be observed for the government and administration of the work.[10]

Five persons were placed in charge of *La Couche*, which was the name given by the public to this new establishment; three women and a burgess, charged with the care, maintenance and nourishment of the children, and a treasurer to receive and take care of the funds.[11]

What became of this organisation during the troubled days of the League? Political circumstances did not encourage either the Parliament or the Chapter to render much assistance. One remark of Saint Vincent's is of more value than if we were to give a long description of the wretched condition of these children during the first half of the seventeenth century : ' After fifty years, not a single one of them is now alive.'[12] Of the three or four hundred children brought to *La Couche* every year there was not a single survivor after half a century.[13] Such was the state of affairs in the city of Paris itself. No doubt, a large number, perhaps more than half, were almost on the verge of extinction when found, but how had the others come to die? Saint Vincent himself supplies the answer : ' These poor little creatures were badly looked after; one nurse for every four or five children!' ' They were sold at eight *sols* apiece to beggarmen who broke their arms and legs so that passers-by might be induced . . . to bestow an alms; they

[10] Lallemand, *op. cit.*, p. 8.
[11] Félibien et Lobineau, *Histoire de Paris*, preuves, Vol. II, p. 831.
[12] *Saint Vincent de Paul*, Vol. XIII, p. 798.
[13] Abelly, *op. cit.*, Bk. I, Ch. XXX, p. 142; *Saint Vincent de Paul*, Vol. XIII, p. 807. This last does not refer elsewhere to more than two to three hundred; but, in this discourse, it seems as if only those who survived are referred to.

were allowed to die of hunger; they were dosed with laudanum to put them to sleep.'[14] And that was not all; Saint Vincent grieved over another evil that might easily have been avoided; these poor babies, deprived of all earthly happiness, had not even the joys of Heaven after death, for the widow in charge of *La Couche* allowed them to expire without a thought of having them baptised.[15]

The buying and selling of foundlings was carried out on a large scale, and the woman in charge was all in favour of this traffic, because she had not the means to feed and support the children. The buyers were either beggarmen, anxious to profit by the pity aroused at the sight of these babies, or women whose interest it was to be regarded as their mothers, or nursing mothers whose health was impaired, or even wizards prepared to immolate human victims in the course of their diabolical operations.[16] It should be added that there were also some good folk who were only too happy to introduce an adopted child into an empty home.[17]

Vincent de Paul was aware of these abuses; he deplored them and sought for means to end them. He asked some Ladies of Charity to visit *La Couche*, hoping that the sight of these poor, wretched little creatures would arouse their pity and induce them to lend a helping hand. The Ladies, yielding to their own sympathies and at the urgent request of the Chapter, placed themselves at Saint Vincent's disposal. Later on, he reminded them how Providence had led them to undertake the work. ' Firstly, it caused these Gentlemen of Notre-Dame to seek your help for two or three years; secondly, you held a number of meetings with that object in view; thirdly, you prayed long and fervently to God on the matter; fourthly, you took the advice of wise and prudent persons; fifthly, you made an attempt; and sixthly, you at length decided to undertake the work.[18]

---

[14] *Saint Vincent de Paul*, Vol. XIII, p. 798.
[15] Abelly, *op. cit.*, Bk. I, Ch. XXX, p. 142.
[16] Abelly, *op. cit.*, Bk. I, Ch. XXX, p. 142; *Saint Vincent de Paul*, Vol. XIII, pp. 775, 798; *Abrégé historique de l'établissement des Enfants trouvés*, Paris, 1753, quarto (Arch. Nat. S. 6160).
[17] Bouchel, *op. cit.*, p. 1014.
[18] *Saint Vincent de Paul*, Vol. XIII, p. 798.

THE FOUNDLINGS

The first attempt was very modest. On January 1, 1638 Saint Vincent wrote to Saint Louise de Marillac :[19] ' At the last meeting, it was decided to request you to make an attempt to do something for the foundlings, to make enquiries as to whether there is any way of feeding them on cows' milk, and to that end, to take charge of two or three.' The meeting was not quite so peaceful as this letter might lead one to suppose, for, though the ladies were agreed in principle, they were divided on the plan to be adopted. Mademoiselle Hardy thought that the Company should take charge of *La Couche*, and that neither the house should be changed nor the way in which it was managed. Such was not Saint Vincent's opinion. ' My idea,'[20] he said, ' is that it would be better to relinquish the funds of this establishment rather than submit to the necessity of rendering so many accounts and overcoming so many difficulties ; a new establishment should be begun and that one left as it is, at least for a time.' Mademoiselle Hardy was immovable ; several ladies promised to support her ; she urged Saint Vincent to call a meeting, and the latter, seeing that he would be compelled either to annoy her or to abandon what he thought the better plan, decided to risk the lady's displeasure.

The attempt was begun in January, in Saint Louise de Marillac's own home, and was carried on during the following months in a rented house in the Rue des Boulangers, outside the gate of Saint-Victor. Twelve children, chosen by lot, were removed from *La Couche* and taken there, whilst a number of Daughters of Charity took up residence near by with a view to looking after the children.[21] From the start, the new establishment was beset with difficulties of every sort ; first, from Madame Pelletier, the superioress of the house, a woman of great independence of character, better fitted for the world than for a community in which, as a matter of fact, she did not remain ;[22] second, from the military authorities who requisitioned one or more rooms

---

[19] *Ibid.*, Vol. I, p. 417. [20] *Ibid.*, Vol. I, p. 433.
[21] Abelly, *op. cit.*, Bk. I, Ch. XXX, p. 143.
[22] *Saint Vincent de Paul*, Vol. I, p. 437.

and billeted soldiers there;[23] and third, from the wet nurses, for it proved very difficult to find any, and in many cases, cows' or goats' milk had to be substituted.[24]

The number of children was increased from twelve as resources permitted. Finally, after a two years' trial, Saint Vincent de Paul decided that the time had come to take over the whole work. On January 17, 1640, he held a meeting of the Ladies of Charity and told them what God expected of them. Never before had they responded in such numbers to his appeal; the Princesse de Condé and the Duchesse d'Aiguillon were present; like the others, they approved the plan proposed and promised to contribute liberally to the expenses.[25]

The notes of Saint Vincent's address to this meeting are extant.[26] He pointed out the excellence of the proposal, refuted objections, anticipated difficulties and submitted a plan of organisation. These brief notes, as Mgr Baunard rightly says,[27] ' give us Saint Vincent's ideas, if not his very words, and it is not difficult for the reader to imagine them rising to the lips of the man of God, enkindling them with the fire of charity, animating them with his voice, and then seeing them pour forth in simple, devout, ardent, penetrating language, that is yet not as eloquent as the example of his life and the sanctity that radiated from his whole person.' The children must be assisted because God loves the praises that issue from their mouth, because they are in extreme necessity and to leave them in such a state would be to expose them to destruction. *Non pavisti, occidisti.* Who knew if several amongst them might not grow up to be great men and women, great saints! Melchisedech, Moses, Romulus and Remus were foundlings. But the expenses will be heavy! If it takes 550 livres to support six or seven babies, apart from the rent of the house, what will it not take for the hundreds that are brought in every year, and the numbers will undoubtedly increase? And all we have is 1200 livres. To all this he answered in a few, simple words:

[23] *Saint Vincent de Paul*, pp. 440-445.
[24] *Ibid.*, pp. 421-433.   [25] *Ibid.*, Vol. II, p. 6.
[26] *Ibid.*, Vol. XIII, p. 774.
[27] *La Vénérable Louise de Marillac*, Paris, 1898, oct., p. 208.

THE FOUNDLINGS

'The only remedy is to do all that we can.' The Ladies of Charity were deeply moved and were unable to resist eloquence such as this that came straight from the heart. It was only on March 30 that the plan was put into execution. As the house in the Rue des Boulangers was too small, Mademoiselle Le Gras took some of the children into her own house at La Chapelle, which at this time was the Mother-House of the Daughters of Charity. She received the children who had been boarded out in the city, and from the very first day, began to send those brought to her out to be nursed. On March 30, there were three children as may be seen from a list drawn up by Saint Louise de Marillac herself: ' a girl named Simonée put out to nurse at Villers, otherwise called Saint-Sépulcre,' with ' Mary Parsin, wife of James Prévault ; . . . a girl named Madeline Lebon . . . put out to nurse with Thomasina Patrue, wife of Denis Boucher, residing at Denville, close to Montfort-Lamaury ; . . . Joseph Lheureux, put out to nurse' with ' Margaret Plassière, wife of Peter Hallard, dwelling at La Folie, near Gif.' We have been at pains to employ the exact phraseology of this document. On the margin, next to the names in order, Saint Vincent appended the names of the places : ' Villers-Saint-Sépulcre, Denville near Montfort, La Folie near Gif.' On March 31 there was another case ; little Nicholas who was ' lent ' to the wife of a street-porter close to the Gate of Saint Landry. The list goes on until April 20. Twenty children all told. Sometimes their Christian names are given and sometimes another, perhaps the family name, is added ; Peter Martin, Samson Lefort, Toinette Ricier, Frances Pratuque ; sometimes both names are missing. Occasionally a special title is added, for instance, ' Joan of the Resurrection ' put out to nurse on the 10th, two days after Easter Sunday. Occasionally Mademoiselle adds a comment of her own, as for instance, ' Charles, who is said to be of noble birth.' Out of the sixteen children boarded out in April only three were placed with the nurses in the Rue des Boulangers. Two remained in Paris ; a washer-woman and the wife of a sculptor had asked to have them. The others were sent to Châtre-sous-Montlhéry, Rocourt-lez-Meulan,

Villers-Saint-Sépulcre, Bourdonnet, Doublinville and Méru. A child named John is simply said to have been handed over to ' Michelle Damiette known to Madame de Souscarrière,' a Lady of Charity, but the name of the place is not given. Between March 30 and April 20, five babies died.[28]

Faithful to Saint Vincent's instructions, two Ladies of Charity in turn daily visited the two refuges for foundlings. From time to time, Daughters of Charity paid a visit of inspection to the children in the country. In 1649, a lay-brother from Saint-Lazare was sent to do so, in all probability because just then it was not safe to travel;[29] he was absent for six weeks. From the very beginning, they were on the look-out for a young man who would undertake this work.[30]

Saint Vincent loved these innocent creatures with the heart of a father, as may be seen from every page of his correspondence. He took an interest in their health and grieved over those who died, consoling himself with the reflection that the number of little angels in Heaven would thereby be increased. When Saint Louise de Marillac sent him a picture painted by herself, he wrote in reply : ' The picture of the Virgin and Saint Joseph holding the Child Jesus by the hand seems to me to be just the very thing for your little foundlings.'[31]

It is not uncommon to find legends intermingled with historical facts. There are some minds who are incapable of resting content with the beauty of reality and who feel a need of transcending it ; they are not satisfied with facts ; they demand romance. Certain phases in the life of Saint Vincent, his relations with the galley slaves and the foundlings, lend themselves in particular to the pleasures of imagination, and imagination has not been slow to seize upon them. Stories are told of how he often went out at night, even in winter, heedless of frost and snow, seeking

[28] *Pensées de Louise de Marillac*, ed. aut., pp. 199–202.
[29] Abelly, *op. cit.*, Bk. II, Ch. XIII, sect. II, p. 127.
[30] *Saint Vincent de Paul*, Vol. II, pp. 295, 296, 301, 509 ; Vol. X, p. 649 ; Vol. XIII, pp. 600, 780 ; *Lettres de Louise de Marillac*, pp. 227, 1059 ; *Supplément aux Lettres de Louise de Marillac*, lettre 181 bis.
[31] *Saint Vincent de Paul*, Vol. I, p. 455.

THE FOUNDLINGS 263

through the worst quarters of the city for abandoned babies, pressing them to his heart the better to warm them and carrying back those whom he had found to the Daughters of Charity. It is related that in the course of one of these nocturnal excursions, just when a band of brigands was about to fall on him, he told them who he was, whereupon the bandits fell at his feet, bent down and received his blessing.[32] Maury first, and then Maynard tell,[33] a story that has often been repeated : Saint Vincent, they say, returning on one occasion from a mission in the country,[34] found himself before the walls of Paris in presence of a beggar-man engaged in deforming the limbs of a child with the intention of using it to excite public sympathy ; horror-stricken, he cried out : ' Oh ! wretch ! you have indeed deceived me ; in the distance I mistook you for a man.' After which, he rescued the victim, traversed the streets of Paris bearing his beloved burthen in his arms, gathered a crowd, related what he had seen, and then, with the crowd all around him, entered *La Couche* in the Rue Saint-Landry.

Capefigue asserts that he had the good fortune to skim through the pages of a diary kept by one of the Sisters in charge of the foundlings and gives some extracts.

' January 22, M. Vincent arrived about eleven o'clock at night ; he brought us two children ; one may be six days old, the other is older. The poor little things were crying. The Lady Superioress has handed them over to the nurses.'

' January 25. The streets are full of snow ; we were expecting M. Vincent ; he did not come this evening.'

' January 26. Poor M. Vincent is chilled to the bone ; he came to us with a child which is already weaned. It is pitiful to see it ; it has fair hair and a mark on its arm. How hard must be the heart that came thus to abandon a poor little creature ! '

' February 1. His Grace the Archbishop paid us a visit ; we need some public assistance ; the work is progressing

---

[32] Capefigue, *Vie de Saint Vincent de Paul*, Paris, Martial Ardant (1827), oct., p. 40.
[33] See *Collection intégrale et universelle des orateurs sacrés de premier ordre*, ed. Migne, 100 vols., quarto, Vol. 67, col. 1021.
[34] *Op. cit.*, 3rd ed., Vol. III, p. 400.

slowly ; M. Vincent only takes into account his own ardent love for these poor children.'

'February 3. Some of our poor children have come back from the nurses ; they seem quite well. The eldest of our little girls is five ; Sister Victor has begun to teach her the catechism and how to ply her needle. The eldest of our little boys, who is called Andrew, is learning remarkably well.'

'February 7. It is very cold. M. Vincent paid a visit to our community ; this holy man is always on foot. The Superioress asked him to rest, but he hurried off at once to his little children. It is marvellous to listen to his beautiful words of kindness and consolation. These little creatures listen to him as to a father. Oh! what does not this kind, good Monsieur Vincent deserve! I have seen his tears flow to-day. One of our little ones died. " It is an angel now," he explained, " but it is very hard not to see it any more." '

It is much to be regretted that the diary in which the touching recital is given was never seen by other eyes than those of M. Capefigue, and that the style and some of the expressions smack much more of the nineteenth than the seventeenth century.

However, there are other documents whose authenticity is beyond dispute which attest in no less expressive fashion Saint Vincent's affectionate interest in the little family of the Rue des Boulangers, an interest not merely in their bodies but also in their souls : these were his letters to Saint Louise de Marillac, his conferences to the Ladies and Daughters of Charity and the regulations drawn up for Sisters in charge of the foundlings.

An address given on December 7, 1643, is entirely devoted to this work, which was so dear to him. His heart expands freely as he speaks to the Sisters, pointing out what a glorious patent of nobility it is to be servants of the foundlings. ' If persons of the world,' he says, ' consider themselves honoured by serving the children of the great, how much more should you who are called to serve the children of God.' These poor little ones are, in truth, children of God, ' for He takes the place of father and mother and provides for their wants. He takes pleasure in their little prattlings, nay, even in their little whimperings and complaints.'[35] And it is to the Sisters He has confided His own children, to the Sisters who have remained virgins the better to belong to Him and who, by accepting the duties of motherhood in regard to these little foundlings ' are virgins and mothers at the same time.'[36] In this way, they may be proud of resembling the Blessed Virgin, and also the angel guardians who look upon themselves as fortunate in being constantly close to these children. ' When they see God . . . when they glorify Him . . . they do so standing beside the children . . . when they receive His commands, they are in the same place ' ; ' they offer up to God the glory rendered to Him by the little cries and prattlings of these tiny creatures.'[37]

After thus exalting, in presence of the Sisters, the nobility of their duties, he goes on to speak of the advantages that will accrue, for God will certainly reward them. ' If God had not called you to serve Him, if He had left you amidst the cares of the world, you would have been mothers, and your own children would have given you far more trouble and anxiety than these. And to what profit ? Like most mothers, you would have loved them with a natural love. What recompense would you have had ? Merely a natural one ; your own satisfaction. . . . If they were children of . . . good position, you would have much trouble and anxiety, perhaps more than these give you ; and what reward ? A very small salary, and you would be looked on as servants. But for serving these poor little children abandoned by the world, what shall you receive ? God, for all eternity.'[38] Yes, God for all eternity, but before that, there are great consolations even here on earth ; for is it not a consolation to see these little creatures snatched from certain death, brought up in the fear of God and in the hope that later on some of them may become the founders of Christian families ? Is it not a consolation to know that others, purified in the holy waters of baptism, are singing the praises of God amidst choirs of angels ?[39]

[35] *Saint Vincent de Paul*, Vol. IX, pp. 131–132.
[36] *Ibid.*, p. 133.   [37] *Ibid.*, p. 136.   [38] *Ibid.*, pp. 134–136.
[39] *Ibid.*, pp. 138–140.

It was by considerations such as these that Saint Vincent inflamed the hearts of his Daughters and stimulated their courage. When he had magnified the beauty of their vocations in their eyes, he hastened to add: '*Noblesse oblige*, you have great duties to perform.' First, the duty of affection. 'Feel,' he kept on repeating, 'feel like mothers towards these children.' Mothers 'have no greater consolation than that of seeing how their little children behave; they admire and love everything they do . . .; they expose themselves to all sorts of evil to shield them from the least pain.'[40] Next, the duty of giving good example. 'You should fear above all lest you might scandalise these poor little ones, by doing or saying anything wrong in their presence. If Mademoiselle Le Gras could have angels, she would give them to serve these innocent creatures. A rumour has been going around that only those are sent here who are of no use for anything else. It is quite the contrary; the most virtuous are needed here; for such as is the " aunt " (that is what they call you) such will be the children. If she is good, they will be good; if she is bad, they will be bad because they easily do what their " aunts " do. If you get vexed, they will; if you behave frivolously before them, they will do likewise; if you complain, they will complain.'[41] Finally, the duty of giving the children a Christian education. 'My Daughters, strive to imprint firmly in their minds a knowledge of their obligations to God, and a great desire for their salvation. . . . Take care that from the very moment they begin to lisp they will pronounce the name of God. Teach them to say: " O my God." Induce them to talk to one another often about our good God; tell them about Him yourselves in simple little words, according to their capacity; whenever you give them anything they think nice or good, let them know and let them say that it is God who gives it to them.'[42]

Saint Vincent saw the soul through the body; Heaven through earth. The charity of a mere religious neutrality would have seemed very narrow in his eyes; he would have thought himself guilty of a second act of abandonment

---

[40] *Saint Vincent de Paul*, p. 133. [41] *Ibid.*, Vol. X, p. 47.
[42] *Ibid.*, Vol. IX, p. 140.

towards these little creatures, already rejected by their mothers, if he had not taken thought of their spiritual interests.

His anxiety to inculcate the truths of Faith and habits of piety in these children is revealed in every line of the rules drawn up for the Sisters to whom they were entrusted.

'When in the morning the Sisters enter the children's room, they shall kneel down and offer up to God all the services they are about to render the infancy of Our Lord in the person of these little children, and shall recite the *Veni Sancte Spiritus*, sprinkle them with holy water, and lead them to raise up their hearts to God.'

'They shall make acts of adoration, love and thanksgiving, and petition that they may not offend Him during the day or during their whole lives.'

'They shall then assist the girls who accompany them to take up the children and dress them properly.'

'As soon as they are dressed, they shall place them on their knees to pray to God, and lead them to recite acts of the love of God, of adoration and thanksgiving.'

'They shall then give them their breakfast, namely, for the youngest aged from three to four, some soup that has been slowly cooked, and for those who are older, from five, six, seven to eight years of age, a slice of bread.'

'At ten o'clock, they shall see that they are placed on benches in front of the tables for their dinner, after making them say the *Benedicite*; at the end of dinner, grace after meals.'

'At one o'clock, they shall bring together those who are older and teach them the Catechism and their lessons. After which, they shall give them a little bread and some sweets, if they have any.'

'At four o'clock, supper shall be prepared for the children.'

'At five, they shall begin to put them to bed, and the bigger boys and girls shall offer up their prayers to God. They should all be in bed at six o'clock, because they rise, in summer and winter, at five.'

'When the children are in bed, care shall be taken to see

that they again raise their hearts to God, and that they are sprinkled with holy water, as in the morning.'[43]

It certainly seems cruel to take little children from their cots at five o'clock in the morning, winter and summer; this, however, was soon realised, for the hour for rising was fixed at seven, and for those under four, even later. This is the hour set down in the second set of rules, which are more detailed; they also were drawn up by Saint Vincent and, before they were finally drafted, sent to Mlle Le Gras and altered and completed in accordance with her suggestions; thus they were the result of their joint collaboration. This set of rules is a veritable hand-book, full of admirable advice.[44]

Educationalists, instead of training children, only too often encourage their faults; they flatter their vanity, allow them to contract habits that will later lead to impurity, foster hypocrisy, arouse jealousy and close their hearts to sentiments of confidence and affection. There was nothing like that in the Foundling Hospital. The Sisters are begged ' not to waste their time decking the children out, curling their hair, or placing little badges on them to show that some are better than others.' They shall not, the rule goes on, ' allow them to rise in the morning quite naked . . . walk bare-footed or bare-headed or uncover themselves.' They shall avoid ' combing the children's hair in open places such as the court-yard or in front of an open window ' and shall not allow boys and girls to play together. The rules also state that the Sisters should treat the children ' equally and uniformly ' in all that concerns food, clothing, bedding, and even marks of endearment. Only children who are sick are to have preferential treatment. Gifts from outsiders were accepted, but only on condition that they

[43] Arch. Nat. S. 6160.
[44] We are referring here to the set of regulations for foundlings inserted in the manuscript volume of the *Common Rules and Constitutions of the Daughters of Charity*. There can be no doubt that this set of regulations was drawn up by Saint Vincent himself, for the amendments suggested by Mlle Le Gras (see *Pensées de Louise de Marillac*, éd. aut., pp. 196 ff.) are to be found there word for word. Father Alméras may, however, have slightly modified the form.

were to be distributed amongst all the children. These precautions against jealousy were accompanied by safeguards against idleness. When the children were about five years old, they were to be taught their catechism and letters. All were taught how to read, and the boys, in addition, how to write. There were also lessons in handwork ; the boys were taught knitting and the girls lace-making. If any child wasted linen, silk, or wool they were to be reprimanded for committing such a fault.

The foundlings did not always pay attention to all this good advice ; they sometimes ' fought, told lies, were stubborn and greedy,' etc., etc. They had to be corrected, and the Sisters were advised to punish them, if they thought it advisable, but without passion and according to a scale of penalties. First, silent correction, to be given by a cold, severe look ; next, verbal correction, addressed to the reason, the feelings and even self-interest ; to the reason, by pointing out the gravity of the fault ; to the feelings, by words and signs of affectionate encouragement, and to self-interest, by the promise of a little reward, in case of improvement. If the child fell into the same fault, it was to be warned ; if it offended again, it was punished by being told to kiss the ground, or made to wear a badge of ill-conduct, or deprived of sweetmeats or a little toy. When warnings and punishments such as these proved unavailing, the Sisters informed the Sister Servant and then only did the great punishment heave in sight—the cane. The rule says that the culprit should be caned without passion, some time after the fault has been committed and never on the head.[45] The culprit, however, did not always experience the avenging rod. Just when the cruel instrument was about to descend, someone arrived, as if by chance, asked for forgiveness and induced the criminal to promise he would never offend again. Forgiveness then followed ; the pardon was gratefully received, and most often accompanied by a sincere desire to redeem the past by exemplary conduct.

The moral training of the children was completed by a religious formation. The establishment had its own chapel

[45] Whipping was very common in the seventeenth century in families, orphanages, educational establishments and prisons.

and chaplain. Every child admitted was at once baptised conditionally, unless a paper was attached stating that it had received Baptism. A number of devotional exercises, such as morning and evening prayers, grace before and after meals, the daily recitation of the Rosary, not all at one time, but in three parts, reminded them during the day of their duties to God, their Creator and Benefactor. On Sundays and Holidays, they assisted at morning Mass, and in the afternoon, listened either to a sermon or a reading from some devotional work. At Easter, all children over five or six years old went to Confession; those who were seven or more also went to Confession on the great church festivals of the year, and on such days, the older ones received Holy Communion.

The Sisters also carefully attended to the health of the children. Before a nurse was accepted, they took great pains to find out whether she was fitted for her work. They were not always able to secure a sufficient number of wet nurses and it was only then that babies were bottle-fed. The laws of hygiene, at least as far as they were known at that time, were scrupulously observed. The Sisters ' will take care,' says the rule, ' that in winter children do not remain too long by the fire; they shall rather encourage the little ones to warm thenmselves by taking a little exercise, though from time to time it is necessary to bring them near the fire. They shall also prevent them from sleeping in the sun or in any unhealthy place.' In case of infectious diseases, the rule goes on, children shall be divided into three classes, the healthy, those under suspicion, and the sick.

The boys left the Hospital at twelve years of age or thereabouts and were handed over to masters to learn a trade. The girls remained longer. Those over fifteen worked all day. If a girl were observed to be exceptionally devout, she was given permission to rise every day at four so as to have time for mental prayer. Many of them became nuns, and positions were secured for the rest. In 1646, there were ten or twelve Sisters who looked after and trained the children.[46] They were frequently visited by Saint Vincent and even still

[46] *Saint Vincent de Paul,* Vol. II, p. 550; III, 55.

THE FOUNDLINGS

more frequently by Mlle Le Gras. One may imagine the smiles of delight that lit up the countenances of these two great servants of God and the kind and gentle words that fell from their lips as they walked amongst the cots or came upon the elder children in the midst of their play.

It was no easy task to carry on the administration of such a vast and complex undertaking. The good will of Saint Vincent and of the Ladies of Charity was frequently paralysed by adverse influences. They had to take into account the demands of the Chancellor, the Chapter, the Lords High Justices, all of whom regarded themselves as in some sense masters of the house. Another source of trouble came from the nurses, the mothers and benefactors who had undertaken to defray the expense of one or more of the children. The Ladies of Charity were often discouraged, and on more than one occasion, threatened to abandon the work entirely : if Saint Vincent had not been at hand to hearten them the whole undertaking would have quickly collapsed. He settled the question of a home for the foundlings by building a row of thirteen houses on the field of Saint Lawrence, a little to the north of Saint-Lazare, and leased them to the Ladies of Charity, on August 22, 1645, at a rent of 300 livres.[47] The greatest difficulty was, of course, where to find the money. On December 7, 1643, Saint Vincent reckoned that the number of children assisted by the Daughters of Charity since 1638 was about twelve hundred.[48] The cost of providing for such a number was by no means negligible ; even in 1644, the annual outlay exceeded 40,000 livres.[49] The fixed income of 1200 livres, which was all they could rely on to carry on the work, even when supplemented by the heavy pecuniary sacrifices made by Saint-Lazare, was obviously utterly insufficient.[50] Saint Vincent called the attention of Louis XIII to the state of the foundlings, and the King, by letters-patent of July, 1642, granted an annual income of 4000 livres from the Crown lands de Gonesse ; 3000 for the children and 1000 for the

[47] Arch. de l'assistance publique, hôpital des Enfants-trouvés, liasse 10.
[48] *Saint Vincent de Paul*, Vol. IX, p. 138.
[49] Abelly, *op. cit.*, Bk. I, Ch. XXX, p. 143.
[50] *Ibid.*, Bk. III, Ch. XI, sect. II, p. 127.

Sisters.[51] In June, 1644, Anne of Austria made an additional grant of 8000 livres to be levied on the revenues of the 'great farms,' but that was not to come into force until January 1, 1646.[52] The alms and collections of the Ladies of Charity made up the balance. In those hard times, when money was scarce, it required all the unwearied tenacity of Saint Vincent, his eloquence and the ascendancy due to his sanctity to balance the annual budget. After 1640, all his addresses to the Ladies of Charity have the same theme : perseverance in the works already undertaken. He was always able to find words that went straight to the heart.

His most famous address was delivered in 1647.[53] Vincent de Paul enquires : Should the Company of the Ladies of Charity continue or abandon the work on behalf of the foundlings ? He examines the reasons for and against and reminds them of the good that has so far been accomplished : five or six hundred children snatched from death and brought up as Christians ; the elder ones apprenticed or about to be. If such has been the commencement, what does the future not promise ? Then, raising his voice, he concluded : ' So now, Ladies, sympathy and charity led you to adopt these little creatures as your children, you have been their mothers according to grace, ever since their mothers according to nature abandoned them ; reflect now whether you, too, intend to abandon them. Cease to be their mothers and now become their judges ; their life and death are in your hands ; I am now about to collect your opinions and votes ; the time has come to pronounce their sentence and to see if you still desire to have mercy on them. They will live if you continue to take charitable care of them, and, on the contrary, they will infallibly die and perish, if you abandon them ; experience does not allow you to think otherwise.'[54]

The Ladies pronounced sentence, and it was a sentence

[51] Arch. Nat. S. 6160 original.
[52] Abelly, *op. cit.*, Vol. I, p. 143 ; Léon Lallemand, *Un chapitre de l'histoire des enfants-trouvés*, Paris, 1855, oct., pp. 5 ff.
[53] *Saint Vincent de Paul*, Vol. XIII, p. 801, note 1.
[54] Abelly, *op. cit.*, Bk. I, Ch. XXX, p. 144.

of mercy. They unanimously resolved to continue to assist the foundlings. Abelly says that as a result of this meeting, they obtained the Castle of Bicêtre from the Queen as a residence for children who were weaned.[55] This huge and unused Castle had become a haunt of malefactors and evil-doers. The Ladies had coveted it for four years, and if they had not obtained possession of it sooner, this may possibly have been due to Saint Louise de Marillac's objections. Saint Louise was, in matter of fact, utterly opposed to the transfer of the foundlings to Bicêtre ; she was afraid of the dangers to be encountered on the roads, the distance from Paris, and the evil reputation of those who frequented the Castle.[56] However, she had to bow to the inevitable. One Saturday in July she received a note from Saint Vincent asking her to have four children, two boys and two girls, in readiness, for the Ladies who would call for them next day and take them in a carriage to Bicêtre. The Ladies went to study the details of organisation on the spot.[57] The arrangements which they made were not calculated to dissipate Saint Louise de Marillac's fears ; quite the contrary. ' Experience will show us,'[58] she wrote to Saint Vincent, ' that it was not without reason I feared Bicêtre as a residence. These ladies intend to try to make our Sisters perform impossibilities. They have selected little rooms for them in which the air will immediately become foul, and have left the large rooms empty ; but our poor Sisters dare not do anything. They do not even want to have Mass said in the house but wish the Sisters to go to Gentilly to hear it. And what will the babies do in the meantime ? And what will become of the work ? ' She ends her letter sadly : ' I am very much afraid we shall have to abandon the service of these poor little infants.'

She was, however, spared this sorrowful extremity, Some days later M. Leroy, the director and administrator of the Foundling Hospital, appointed by the Chapter of Paris. paid her a visit. He came to complain that he had not been

---

[55] *Lettres de Louise de Marillac*, p. 135.
[56] *Ibid.*, pp. 198, 321.
[57] *Saint Vincent de Paul*, Vol. III, p. 210.
[58] *Lettres de Louise de Marillac*, p. 321.

informed of the move to Bicêtre and that his rights had been ignored. ' He claims that he can go there and preach whenever it seems good to him, place a priest there and take entire charge of the spiritual administration,' Saint Louise wrote to Saint Vincent, adding : ' he was more jealous of his rights than of a bishopric or a cardinal's hat.'[59] She was astonished at his complaints, for the Ladies had, as a matter of fact, always looked after the spiritual side of the work, as they were persuaded that the Chapter had left their hands free in the matter, and until now, no one had ever protested. They had made all arrangements for Baptisms, Paschal Confessions, instructions for first Communion, Masses and funerals, and hence were quite surprised to see M. Leroy arriving with his grievances. Leroy was quite right in his desire to have a chaplain appointed as soon as possible for the Castle of Bicêtre, and in this Mlle Le Gras fully agreed with him, for she had planned to have a chaplain to teach the small boys, whilst the Daughters of Charity would look after the girls ; a very elementary sort of instruction, no doubt, since it was not judged expedient to teach them how to write.[60]

At this period in the history of the Foundling Hospital, Mlle Le Gras took a much more prominent part. She was frequently at Bicêtre, where she kept herself fully informed of the details of administration and was far more competent than anybody else to form a judgement on the needs of the work. Her letters are heart-breaking. ' Fifty-two children have died since the move to Bicêtre, and there are fifteen or sixteen who are not much better. I hope that when everything has been settled according to the wishes of these good ladies, the children will not die off so fast.'[61] Later on, she grieves over the inadequate supply of alms : ' When people see this magnificent place and are told it is for little children and that all the ladies in charge are persons of high rank, most of them believe we have plenty of

[59] *Lettres de Louise de Marillac*, p. 327.
[60] *Ibid.*, pp. 329–330.
[61] *Ibid.*, p. 347 ; deposition of Sister Geneviève Doinel, the seventeenth witness at the process of Beatification of Saint Vincent.

THE FOUNDLINGS 275

money, and yet we have to borrow the price of provisions and all those other necessities of which you are aware.' Her crowning misfortune was that when she wished to make a little money by selling the wine obtained from the Castle vineyards, the tavern keepers of Paris rose in rebellion and so insulted and maltreated the Sisters that the officers of the law had to intervene and, if Saint Vincent had not taken action, they would have been severely punished.[62] Matters went from bad to worse until in 1649 there was not even enough bread. Mlle Le Gras could not stand it any longer; she took up her pen and asked the Chancellor to send her some.[63] Paris, at the moment, was boiling over with excitement; Saint Vincent had left for the provinces early in January after a visit to the Court which had enraged the Frondeurs against him, and he was unable to return until June; several Ladies of Charity, and those not the least influential, had also left the capital. Even the wealthiest felt the effects of the hard times. From Fréneville, the Saint wrote to his Assistant, Lambert aux Couteaux, to send wheat to Bicêtre; to Madame de Lamoignon, to obtain from the Sheriffs, through her son's influence, an escort to guard the wheat; and to the Ladies of Charity, to hold a meeting to decide on what steps should be taken to assist the foundlings.[64] Another danger promptly arose. The environs of Paris, where bands of lawless soldiers were wandering about in all directions, were no longer safe. The Sisters were living in mortal terror of their lives. Mlle Le Gras recommended the Sister-Servant, Geneviève Poisson, and her companions to take the most rigorous measures to avoid the danger that might arise from the ruffianly conduct of the soldiery. ' Take the greatest care to keep all the Sisters together,' she wrote,[65] ' and take the utmost care that the young ones, whom you should always have under your eye, are confined to the school.' Things became so bad that the Castle had to be evacuated.[66] We do not know when the children were removed from Bicêtre;

[62] *Lettres de Louise de Marillac*, p. 349.   [63] *Ibid.*, p. 363.
[64] *Saint Vincent de Paul*, Vol. III, p. 408.
[65] *Lettres de Louise de Marillac*, p. 394.
[66] *Saint Vincent de Paul*, Vol. III, p. 428.

they were not there on May 14,[67] but they were certainly there in November.[68]

One of Saint Vincent's chief preoccupations, on his return to Paris, was to ensure the existence of the Foundling Hospital. It was a difficult problem to settle, for it was a very unsuitable time to ask the Ladies of Charity to make further sacrifices, and yet the children could not wait. Mlle Le Gras wrote to him : ' I am very much afraid lest Madame de Herse may have kept the ladies away from the meeting by the suggestion which she made that they should take money with them. I think, Sir, it will be necessary for her to let them know that she did not intend them to subscribe personally or wished to force anyone. The more I reflect on what should be done the more I fear the whole affair will be left to ourselves. The nurses are beginning to threaten and are bringing back the children, and debts are multiplying to such an extent that there is no hope of paying them.'[69] To these cries of distress all Saint Vincent replied was : ' The care of the foundlings is in the hands of Our Lord.'[70] It certainly was, and the less human effort made itself felt, the greater appeared the sustaining hand of God. Matters were in a very bad state at the end of 1649. There was no bread, linen, blankets or money ; debts were piling up and charity growing cold. Mlle Le Gras knocked at every door but all in vain. She began to lose courage, and in her letters during November, suggests that they should no longer accept any more foundlings and even speaks of abandoning the whole work if help does not soon come.[71]

Saint Vincent gathered the ladies together and, with tears in his eyes, begged them to save these little creatures from death. Only the plan of this address is now extant ;[72] it is touching in its eloquence and how much more so must not the actual discourse have been ! The pretexts alleged by the ladies could not withstand his downright replies. ' We

[67] *Saint Vincent de Paul*, Vol. III, p. 436.
[68] *Lettres de Louise de Marillac*, p. 437. The letter was written in November, not October.
[69] *Ibid.*, p. 443.
[70] *Saint Vincent de Paul*, Vol. III, p. 524.
[71] *Lettres de Louise de Marillac*, letters 263, 266, 273.
[72] *Saint Vincent de Paul*, Vol. XIII, p. 797.

THE FOUNDLINGS

have no money,' they said. ' How many little comforts have you not at home that serve no useful purpose ? ' was his answer. ' Ah ! Ladies ! how far removed are we from the piety of the children of Israel whose women contributed their jewels to make a golden calf ! ' His confidence was rewarded by a large number of valuable gifts.[73]

The children were removed back to Paris from Bicêtre, where the air was too sharp, and the Saint asked for a refuge for them in a hospice known as ' Les Enfermés.'[74]

Whilst those who were weaned had been living in Bicêtre, the babies had been petted by the Daughters of Charity in ' The Thirteen Houses,' where they led a fairly peaceful life until nearly the end of the Fronde. In May, 1652, the troops of Turenne and Condé fought a battle quite close to the establishment, and soldiers were killed at their very door. The nurses, terrified at the sound of fighting, ' all ran off with the girls, each one with her own baby,' leaving the other children asleep in bed. The alarm was happily of brief duration ; the danger rapidly disappeared and order was once more restored.[75]

During the following years, there are fewer and fewer references to the foundlings in the correspondence of Saint Vincent and Mlle Le Gras. This silence shows that former difficulties had by then disappeared. The Ladies of Charity, the Sisters and the Missionaries of Saint-Lazare,[76] to whom the spiritual side of the work had been entrusted, rivalled each other in their care of those little creatures who were eminently worthy of sympathy.

In 1654, ' The Thirteen Houses ' began to admit children born in the maternity wards of the Hôtel-Dieu, of mothers who had died there in child-birth or who had left without their babies.[77] On July 11, 1657, Saint Vincent gave an address to the Ladies of Charity which throws some light on the state of affairs at that time. He says that the number of

[73] Saint Vincent refers to one of these gifts in his address (*Ibid.*, p. 800).
[74] *Saint Vincent de Paul*, Vol. IV, p. 21.
[75] *Ibid.*, p. 382.
[76] *Ibid.*, Vol. IX, pp. 193, 194 ; Vol. XII, p. 90.
[77] *Origines de la maternité de Paris*, par Henriette Carrier, Paris, 1888, oct., p. 64.

children was 395, that about 365 children were abandoned every year, and that in the preceding year, the income was 16,248 livres and the expenses 17,221. He then went on : ' It is to you, Ladies, that God has given the grace of keeping alive a number of these children and of helping them to lead a good life. When they learn to talk, they learn to pray to God, and little by little they are kept occupied according to their power and capacity ; they are carefully supervised so that their little habits may be well regulated and evil inclinations corrected in good time. They are happy to have fallen into your hands and would be wretched in those of their parents, who are, as a rule, poor and vicious. It is quite sufficient for me to see how they spend their days to realise the fruits of this good work which is so important that you, Ladies, have all the reason in the world to thank God for having entrusted it to you.'[78]

The Ladies did not abandon the foundlings when, in 1670, the establishment was placed by the King under the administration of the General Hospital. The Daughters of Charity also remained at their post until driven out, on account of their religious habit, first in 1792, and afterwards on March 31, 1886.

The memory of Saint Vincent is still recalled by a statue in the Hospice in Rue Denfert-Rochereau, by Stouf, one of the greatest sculptors of the eighteenth century, and by an interesting eighteenth century picture representing Vincent de Paul seated with Mlle Le Gras and the Ladies of the Court who are offering him their jewels for the Foundling Hospital.

Alhoy, in a poem published in Paris in the year XII, mentions the statue in his poem : *Les Hospices*.[79]

' *Dans ce lieu, par Vincent du ciel même inspiré,*
A l'abandon s'élève un autel consacré,
Propice à la misère, indulgent même au crime ;
De tous deux il reçoit le fruit ou la victime,
Et la nuit et le jour l'accès en est ouvert.
A peine déposés, la Pitié les accueille ;
De Vincent, leur ami, la fille les recueille.

[78] *Saint Vincent de Paul*, Vol. XIII, p. 807.
[79] Oct., p. 18.

THE FOUNDLINGS

Sur eux, du haut du ciel étendant son manteau
Je vois son ombre sainte abriter leur berceau.
L'enfance à ses genoux dans son temple l'implore.
Sous le ciseau de Stouf il y respire encore.
Son oeil doux, attendri, brûlant de charité
Prolonge son regard sur la postérité.
De ce temple à jamais le seuil est tutélaire ;
Et dès qu'il l'a franchi, l'orphelin trouve un père.[80]

[80] 'Here stands an altar consecrated to the weak and helpless by Vincent, the inspired of Heaven, the friend of the wretched, indulgent even to crime itself ; here he receives the fruit and victims of both. Day and night it is open to them and scarcely have they been put down than they are welcomed by Pity ; the daughter of Vincent, their friend, raises them up. I see his holy shade from the height of Heaven spreading his mantle of protection over their cradle. Childhood, on its knees, here begs his aid in his temple. He breathes again under Stouf's chisel. His mild, pitiful eye, aflame with charity, looks forward to another age. The threshold of this temple is a sanctuary for ever, and once the orphan has crossed it, he finds a father.'

CHAPTER XXXVI

MENDICANTS

WHILST Saint Vincent was thus engaged in protecting the interests of the foundlings, he did not lose sight of poor old people unable to earn their daily bread and reduced to beggary or death by starvation. The problem of beggars and begging had long exercised public opinion. Saint Vincent had solved it in 1621 at Mâcon, but in Paris the evil assumed far greater proportions, and it was much more difficult to discover a remedy.

The establishment of public workshops had failed ; the drafting of beggarmen to the army to increase the number of effectives only cleared the streets of Paris of the young and strong, and that only for a time. It was suggested that if beggarmen were confined in mendicity institutions with a well-planned system of work, better results might be attained, and this solution was envisaged by the civil authority in the first years of the seventeenth century. In 1611, everything was ready for its application. Letters Patent were obtained, verified by Parliament, posted up at street corners, and read by the clergy in church whenever they preached. All mendicants born within the Provostship or Viscounty of Paris were commanded to seek for work or to go, on the day and hour appointed, to the fair-ground of Saint-Germain, thence to be despatched to their respective depôts : sturdy beggars to the hospice in the Faubourg-Saint-Victor ; women, girls and sick children under eight years of age to the hospice in the Faubourg-Saint-Marcel ; and such poor as were unable to work, through age or infirmity, to the hospice in the Faubourg-Saint-Germain. All beggars born in the provinces were ordered to leave Paris within eight days. These measures were completely successful ; the face of Paris changed almost in a night ; not one of the nine

LA SALPÊTRIÈRE

or ten thousand mendicants who had hitherto pestered the public was to be seen in the streets. And yet, only ninety-one had presented themselves for confinement. The rest had preferred to fly from a city that no longer afforded them hospitality, or to live in ease and idleness on the money they had amassed ; as soon as their savings were spent, they had either to leave Paris, to work, or to renounce their liberty. In less than six weeks, eight hundred, overcome by hunger, were knocking at the doors of the hospital. Strong and healthy men were set to various kinds of work ; they ground corn in hand-mills, brewed beer, made cement and sawed timber ; the girls and women spun yarn, knitted, made stockings and buttons. A free and easy life was far more attractive than this, and hence, once their first fears were over, the beggars ventured out again into the open.

In 1612, it became necessary to issue a warning that the orders promulgated in the previous year were still in force ; a larger hospital was built which, under the name of Our Lady of Pity, was intended to serve as a place of internment for all classes of beggars. The Queen Regent, Marie de Médicis, the Parliament, the Clergy, the Municipality united their efforts to overcome this formidable plague which was ever ready to burst out anew. Severe punishments were threatened : men who refused to obey were to be whipped, have an iron collar placed round their necks and sent to the galleys ; women were to be whipped and have their heads shaved. All citizens were forbidden, under penalty of prosecution, to give alms in the streets or hospitals, or to afford lodgings to vagabonds. For four years these threats proved availing ; from 1612 to 1616, very few beggars ventured to appear in the streets of Paris, but in 1617 they began to appear again in large numbers. The author of a pamphlet published in that year, groans over the new invasion. ' The hospices,' he writes, ' may be seen filled with poor people, mostly there of their own accord ; the churches and streets are packed with soldiers, blackguards, lackeys, men and women, all begging, and to such an extent that a man cannot find a corner to transact business or to say a *Pater Noster* without three or four interruptions, ceaseless importunities, blasphemies of the name of God, outrageous and insulting language, which is the reason why people murmur in surprise at the numbers there are to be seen ... When one sees collection-boxes for those interned, or for the blind and others, asking for assistance, it is said that these are mockeries and lies, without a shadow of piety and that there are no longer any beggars interned.'[1] This false rumour spread all the more rapidly as some beggars pretended they had been ejected from the hospices.

The failure of the measures taken in 1611 and renewed in 1612 was due to a number of causes : the want of agreement amongst the governors of the General Hospital, their restricted powers, excessive indulgence towards delinquents, and finally, bad organisation. A Parisian craftsman who had taken an apprentice from *La Pitié* could get nothing out of the young man. ' I was three years in the hospice doing nothing,' said he, ' and now I am not going to start working.'

Mendicants in the provinces were not slow to hear that supervision of the streets of Paris was relaxed, and at the good news, they flocked to the capital in crowds. The number of poor persons living in the five hospitals that went to make up the General Hospital, dropped from 2200 in 1616, to 1300 or 1400 in 1622, and the great majority of these consisted of children, old men, or sick persons. The Parliament from time to time in 1629, 1630, 1632, called attention to the prohibitions issued in 1611 and 1612, but nobody took any heed. A rigorous application of the laws would have been far more effective in attaining the desired end than all these repeated prohibitions. Furthermore, the Thirty Years War, by spreading famine and desolation throughout entire provinces, was instrumental in driving the hunger-stricken to Paris, where the number of beggars became so great that it was found impossible to intern them all, and the public authorities had to fall back on the distribution of alms. This last measure entailed a further inconvenience, for it attracted crowds to Paris from less favoured localities. About 1640, there were nearly 40,000 beggars in the capital,

[1] *Mémoires concernant les pauvres que l'on appelle enfermez.* Archives curieuses de l'histoire de France depuis Louis XI jusqu'à Louis XVIII, par MM. L. Cimber et F. Danjou, première série, t. XV, p. 256.

where they spread fear and terror by their misdemeanours.[2]

The Company of the Blessed Sacrament did not remain idle when confronted with this disorderly rabble. In 1631, it deliberated on the best means of dealing with this plague of mendicancy, and in 1636, the matter again came up for discussion. A committee of eight was formed to study the question and send in a report. The Company, as its annalist tells us, came to the conclusion that this should be ' one of the most important objects of charity.' ' That which chiefly aroused its sympathy,' he goes on to say, ' was the desolate state of the souls of these mendicants . . . the assistance the Company desires to procure for them is primarily concerned with their eternal salvation, rather than with their temporal relief, which, as a matter of fact, is not neglected.'[3] The annalist's statement here in regard to the corporal assistance rendered to mendicants is quite true. The First President, the Procurator General and other magistrates in high position, met frequently to deliberate on this important matter; charitable associations gave generously; houses of religious orders fed all who went to their doors; Saint-Lazare distributed food three times a week, and this was accompanied by a few words of devout exhortation so that corporal and spiritual alms might go hand in hand.[4] ' The poor,' wrote Sauval, ' are supplied in abundance whilst families that are not very well off are often in want of the necessaries of life.'[5] Then came the Fronde with its own crop of miseries. It was certainly no time to renew the regulations of 1611; the number of beggars was so great that it was impossible to intern them all and so nothing remained but to assist them by alms. Peace was not restored until 1653 and then only was Paris able to take steps to suppress public begging.

[2] Christian Paultre, *De la suppression de la mendicité et du vagabondage en France sous l'ancien régime*. Paris, 1906, oct., p. 154. The preceding pages have been largely based on this excellent book (3rd part, Ch. I).

[3] *Annales de la Compagnie du Saint-Sacrament*, p. 26.

[4] Arch. Nat. M. 212, liasse 7, déposition de Claude de Chandenier.

[5] *Histoire et recherches des antiquités de la ville de Paris*, Paris, 1724, 3 vols. in f⁰, t. I, p. 526.

Saint Vincent, on his part, was seeking to solve the problem ; faithful to his usual tactics, he proceeded to do so slowly, continuously and perseveringly. At first, he made a very modest attempt, and then went forward as far as Providence and the resources at his command allowed. Before making a beginning, he waited as usual for a manifestation of the divine Will which came in the following manner. A citizen of Paris called on him and said : ' I intend to expend 100,000 livres on good works ; keep them in trust for me and find out what is the best use you can make of them. I make one condition—my name must remain unknown.' Saint Vincent thanked the man, prayed, reflected, thought of the poor old people who were without food, and began to envisage the realisation of a project that had long appealed to him, namely, the erection of a home in which some of those unfortunate people, who had been handed over to the loving care of the Sisters of Charity, might be sheltered from want and enabled to lead a Christian life, whilst engaged in some form of work proportioned to their strength and capacity.[6] Just at that time, a house called ' The Name of Jesus,' from a plaque over the door, was up for sale. The proprietor, Noël Bonhomme, sold it in 1644 or 1645, to Saint-Lazare for 11,000 livres, and then had adopted all sorts of tricks in order to continue to live in it with his family ; he had to be brought before the Courts[7] and the trial ended in a verdict for the plaintiffs on September 28, 1647.[8] Saint Vincent now had the building at his disposal ; nothing was easier than to adapt the house to its new purpose, turn one of the rooms into a chapel and procure the requisite furniture. He approved of these suggestions, and the work of alteration began. With the modest funds at his disposal, it was not possible to afford accommodation in the new hospice for a large number of poor persons ; it was decided to take forty, twenty men and twenty women.

If the work was to prove a success, it was essential to make

[6] Abelly, *op. cit.*, Bk. I, Ch. XLV, pp. 211–212.
[7] *Saint Vincent de Paul*, Vol. II, pp. 628, 633 ; Vol. III, pp. 633, 637.
[8] Arch. Nat. S. 6601.

a careful selection, and the Saint therefore consulted a number of persons, amongst them, of course, Mlle Le Gras. The paper in which she replied to his queries is still extant. ' Desiring,' she says,[9] ' to consider the matter before God, it occurred to me to regard it from every angle, namely, its beginning, continuation and end.' In the first place, the work appealed to her because it was according to the divine plan, God having said : ' Thou shalt eat thy bread in the sweat of thy brow ' ; next, because the old people would find means in the home to live and die like Christians. Who should be selected ? To this she replied : ' It is to be wished that those chosen should be decent folk, by no means beggars.' She also suggests that, at least at first, in addition to the really poor, artisans ' of fairly good condition ' should be admitted, who would consent to ' pass for poor people ' and remain for six months to teach their crafts to the others. She would not have married persons or those with children dependant on them. However, she adds, if some of these propose ' to come and spend some time in the home,' leaving their families for a time, they might be admitted, but in small numbers, if their presence was of such a nature as ' to supply a solid foundation for this work.' There was, it is true, one considerable drawback : ' it might perhaps be necessary ' to supply some of the inmates ' with a little wine or beer ' and the thought of such an expense caused her to hesitate. She attached the utmost importance to the idea that the first group of inmates should contain some men and women capable of teaching the others trades or crafts that would help to defray expenses. She wished to have a silk-weaver, a cloth-weaver, a serge-maker, shoe-makers, cobblers, button-makers, worsted-workers, lace-makers, glove-makers, seamstresses and pin-makers. She then goes on : ' Having a sufficient number of good workmen to make a good start and to carry on the work, we should not worry about the expense that must be gone to for tools, implements and materials, or the difficulty in discovering the addresses of places where they can be purchased easily and

[9] Arch. des Filles de la Charité, Ms. *Écrits de Louise de Marillac*. This document is published in *Pensées de Louise de Marillac*, pp. 265-267.

at a fair price. Divine Providence will not fail us in any respect, and we shall find out the proper addresses by experience. We must fully make up our minds that there will be very little profit the first year.' Saint Vincent certainly benefited by these very judicious observations.

In March, 1653, everything was ready. The old people were notified, and on the appointed day all arrived except two, a man and a woman. New clothes had been prepared for them, and on the following day when Saint Vincent was to inaugurate the work, they were present in all their finery. Mlle Le Gras had asked him to say a few words on the Passion and to request them to venerate the Holy Cross; it was most probable that he followed her advice.[10]

After a few month's trial, which proved to be very successful, the benefactor and Saint Vincent, or rather the Priests of the Mission, entered into a contract to set the new foundation on a solid basis. The contract is dated October 29, 1653, and supplies valuable information on the expenses actually incurred or to be incurred, as well as on the organisation of the work.[11]

Out of the 100,000 livres supplied by the founder, 11,000 had gone to the purchase of the house; furniture, ecclesiastical vestments and plate, and alterations accounted for 5400; reckoning on the moneys spent during the last six months, it was estimated that the cost of food and maintenance for the first year would amount to 3600 livres; 20,000 livres were set aside for extensions, in case the house proved too small; Saint-Lazare borrowed the balance, say 60,000 livres, to wipe out certain debts, and in return, paid down 3000 livres a year which it was estimated would ultimately be the current annual expenses of the hospice. Saint-Lazare reserved to itself the right of discharging this debt in six instalments on condition of being allowed to devote the capital sum to the purchase of annuities or interest-bearing bonds to private individuals. An administrative council of three was appointed; it was to consist of the Superior General of the Congregation of the Mission and two citizens chosen by the latter. Saint Vincent co-opted

[10] *Saint Vincent de Paul*, Vol. IV, pp. 552–553.
[11] The contract may be found in the Arch. Nat. S. 6601.

Desbordes-Goder, King's Councillor and auditor of the Exchequer, and Lobligeois, a merchant draper of Paris. The Superior General occupied an important place in the Council, for, on the death of one of his colleagues, he was empowered, after consulting the survivor, to nominate a successor, and also, after taking the advice of his two fellow-members, to make new, or modify the old, regulations. The Council decided on the admission and removal of the old people and also on the steps to be taken against those whose conduct left anything to be desired.

The hospice of the Name of Jesus had not corporal assistance solely in view. The founder had said to Saint Vincent: 'Sir, I am making this gift not merely to solace the wretchedness of the poor ; I also desire that they should be instructed and taught all that is necessary for their salvation.'[12] There is a clause in the contract stipulating that a Priest of the Mission should take charge of the religious services, and the anonymous founder was so insistent on this point that if unexpected obstacles were to interfere with its execution, he says he would prefer to abandon the foundation. The contract was approved by the Archbishop of Paris on March 15, 1654, and confirmed by Letters Patent in the following November. The King, in return for the favours accorded to the hospice, asked that the *Exaudiat* should be daily recited by the poor for his welfare and that of his successors, and for the ' preservation and peace ' of his State.[13]

With the 20,000 livres at his disposal, or with part of the sum, Saint Vincent purchased,[14] on September 5, 1654, an adjoining house and a fairly large plot of ground, and was thus enabled to make better arrangements for the separate accommodation of the men and women. The Chapel, situated between the two buildings, was common to both ; so was the refectory ; the inmates therefore assisted at the same Mass and listened to the same reading at table, though they could neither see nor speak to each other.[15]

[12] *Saint Vincent de Paul*, Vol. XIII, p. 157.
[13] Arch. Nat. S. 6601.
[14] *Ibid.*
[15] Abelly, *op. cit.*, p. 213.

Mlle Le Gras herself kept the accounts ;[16] we learn from her notes that the current expenses of the first year exceeded by 585 livres what had been anticipated. The sum total of the workers' earnings in one year was not very large—only 51 livres. The workers had a right to the fourth part of their earnings, but, as the price of their ration of wine was deducted, these diminished in proportion, and indeed, in the case of hearty drinkers, to such an extent that a negative result was reached, and they owed money to the house. However, such cases were rare ; Mlle Le Gras' account-book mentions only one case in the first year.

As Saint-Lazare was not far distant, Saint Vincent never failed to visit his poor old people as often as he could ; it was he who gave them their first Catechism lesson. Thanks to the notes taken by someone present, a Sister or one of his secretaries, we are able to assist at it ourselves. It is ' the little method ' in action, with its clarity, simplicity and persuasive power.

When the Rosary had been recited, Saint Vincent began : ' My children, I think we would be doing something very pleasing to God if we chatted together on Christian doctrine, and I will therefore ask you some questions on the principal mysteries of Faith and on the Sign of the Cross. But you should not be surprised if all of you do not know how to make it properly ; Oh ! no, my children, but you should do your best to learn.' There were two reasons why they should do so ; first, a general motive, the knowledge of the principal mysteries is necessary to salvation ; and the second, a particular motive ; the hospice of the Name of Jesus was established for that end. ' I am going to ask you a few questions,' he went on, ' and even if you do not know the right answers, do not let that disturb you. I will ask you if you know how to make the Sign of the Cross, and if you don't, do not worry over that. You are not the only ones. How many persons are there at Court, and even great magistrates, perhaps, who do not know how to do so ! Now that should encourage you to overcome the shyness we usually feel when unable to answer questions we have been asked.' He then asked each in turn to make the Sign of

[16] *Pensées de Louise de Marillac*, pp. 272 ff.

the Cross, and whenever it was not made correctly, he instructed the individual by making it himself.

When his hearers seemed to have been sufficiently instructed on this point, he went on to the mystery of the Trinity. All were questioned and it was clear from the replies that some were not quite sure and others wrong. He was not a bit surprised. It is an abstract subject, and so he brought it to the level of his audience by the well-known comparison of the sun : ' Just as there are three things in the sun, and these three things do not make three suns, so, too, in the Holy Trinity, there are three Persons who are only one God. Well, then, there are three things in the sun, namely, the sun itself and its light, its heat. The sun itself is that beautiful orb we see in the sky. The light is that which shines on us and on all things that are on earth ; it banishes the darkness of night and brings joy to all the world, for if we were in darkness, how could we be happy ? The third thing in the sun is warmth which proceeds from the sun itself and from its light. This is the great warmth that ripens the fruits and all things else on earth. When we have very warm weather, stifling, such as we had when we first came here, well, that comes from the sun. You see by this comparison that there is only one God and three Persons in God, and the three Persons are inseparable from God Himself, just as the sun is inseparable from light and the light from the warmth. These three things are inseparable, as you know from experience. Why will it not be so warm this evening as it is just now ? Because the sun will have gone down, and as warmth is inseparable from the sun, we shall not feel its effects any longer, for the sun will have set.'

There was a small boy in the room ; Saint Vincent had not selected him by chance or brought him without a motive ; he relied on the boy's replies to engrave the lessons of the Catechism on the memories of the old folk who did not know how to read, and also, perhaps, to rouse feelings of emulation. ' My child, who is God ? ' he asked. ' Sir, He is the Creator of Heaven and earth and Lord of all things.' ' Very good, that is an excellent answer. He is the Creator of Heaven and earth. What do you mean by the words : Creator of Heaven and earth ? ' ' I mean He Who has made all things.' Saint Vincent called special attention to the word ' all.' 'There is not the smallest little creature that He has not made, not even a flesh-worm, which is very small indeed; He created even that. But, Sir, is it possible He created that? Yes, it is quite true He created the flesh-worm which moves between the flesh and the skin, and also those little ants you may have seen running about; He created all these.' The small boy was waiting for more questions, all of which he answered with the same ease and correctness. 'My child, how many Gods are there?' 'There is only one God, Father.' 'And how many Persons in God?' 'There are three, but all three are only one God.' 'Will you please give me an example to explain that?' 'Sir, the example of a candle will do, because three things are to be found in a candle : the wax, the wick and the flame, and all three make only one candle.' Saint Vincent then told the little boy to sit down, and turning to a woman he asked her : 'Who is God?' 'He is the Creator of Heaven and earth.' 'What is the meaning of that? Creator? What does it mean to create something?' 'It is to make something that is nothing.' Saint Vincent was not quite satisfied with the reply and altered it without appearing to do so. 'Oh! you are a great scholar, my dear ; you wish to say that to create is to make something out of nothing and that it is God alone Who can make something out of nothing. Men can certainly make things ; but that means they can make one thing out of another as, for example, to make this house, and that is to make something ; but as stones, cement and other things are needed, that is not called creating but making. . . . To make, one must have material, but for creation nothing is required but the omnipotence of God Who can create all that He pleases.'

Doctrine entails practical consequences and it was to these that the downright mind of Saint Vincent immediately turned. God has made all things ; hence it is from Him that the inmates of the Name of Jesus have received all they enjoy, and they certainly have received much. 'What more can you desire?' he asks. 'You are supplied with food, not indeed such as great magistrates have, but enough for your wants. How many poor people are there in Paris and elsewhere who are not so well off as you ? How many poor noblemen who would think themselves very lucky if they had the food you have ! Think of all the labouring men, working from morning till night, who are not as well fed as you ! All these considerations should oblige you to work with your hands as much as you can, according to your strength, without thinking : " Oh ! I need not bother to do anything as long as I am sure I shall not want for anything." Ah ! my children, you must be very much on your guard against that state of mind, and rather say we are bound to work for the love of God since He Himself gives us the example, working continually for us.' He ended with the recitation of the prayer, *Sancta Maria, succurre miseris*.

It is probable that he often went to instruct his poor. In his old age, incapable as he was of going on a mission, he had close at hand, a few steps from Saint-Lazare, an opportunity of indulging the passion of his life ; how could he have resisted the pleasure of speaking to his poor about God and their duties ?

Notwithstanding certain drawbacks, such as not being at liberty to go in and out as they chose, the old people in the hospice of the ' Name of Jesus ' were peaceful and happy. Abelly says :[17] ' A marvellous peace and unity reigned there ; grumbling and back-biting were banished with other vices. The poor busied themselves at their little employments and acquitted themselves of all the religious duties appropriate to their state. It was, in fine, a little replica of the life of the early Christians and a house of religious rather than a hospice of seculars.'[18] Hence places were in demand several years in advance. If Saint Vincent showed any preference, it was in favour of the relations of his priests and Daughters ; amongst those who were inmates of the house were a sister of Father Tholard's and an aunt of Father Gorlidot's,[19] both Priests of the Mission, and possibly Sister Carcireux's father.[20]

[17] *Saint Vincent de Paul*, Vol. V, p. 153.
[18] *Op. cit.*, Bk. I, Ch. XLV, p. 214.
[19] *Saint Vincent de Paul*, Vol. VIII, p. 64.   [20] *Ibid.*, p. 343.

The paucity of funds at his disposal compelled him to admit only forty poor persons, and to defer applications for a considerable time ; this, of course, saddened the Saint who would gladly have extended the work. He could only see one remedy for the situation : to increase resources by accepting whatever gifts were offered. This was his state of mind when approached by Abbé Brisacier, who desired, on his brother's behalf, to make a foundation in favour of six old persons. The number was too large and the accommodation too restricted ; only four could be admitted, one of whom died shortly afterwards. The anonymous founder then learned of the arrangement made for adding four new inmates to the hospice ; he was very much annoyed and complained to Saint Vincent who expressed his regret, yielded to the founder's wishes and returned his money and his poor to Abbé Brisacier.[21]

The hospice of the Name of Jesus as founded, was, no doubt, in Saint Vincent's eyes a rudimentary undertaking destined to develop ; his heart must have bled at the thought that by the decision of a man whom he was bound to respect, he was compelled to abandon its further extension. But was there no means of establishing in another place, with other funds, a second home for the poor over which Saint Vincent would have greater authority ? The Ladies of Charity had already asked themselves that question in 1653.

The sight of the good order and regularity reigning in the hospice of the Name of Jesus combined with the happiness that shone on the faces of its inmates, had fortified the conviction of the Ladies that Saint Vincent was capable, by the creation of a model general hospital, of solving the problem of mendicancy. They discussed the matter amongst themselves, decided to bring forward a proposal at the next meeting, and, to anticipate all objections on the financial side, arranged in advance the sums they proposed to contribute. The Duchesse d'Aiguillon promised 50,000 livres ; another lady, 3000 livres a year, and each was fully resolved to add her name to the list of subscribers. When the day for the meeting arrived, great was their enthusiasm

---

[21] *Saint Vincent de Paul*, Vol. VIII, p. 290.

MENDICANTS

and also their confidence; they thought the whole affair was settled. Saint Vincent listened, praised their zeal, but added that it would be rash, in such an important affair, to come to any decision until they had reflected more deeply on the matter and had recourse to God in prayer. They could not obtain anything more from him, and some present openly manifested their discontent at his slowness.[22]

The question was not debated only at their meetings; the Company of the Blessed Sacrament was also concerned with the proposal. At a meeting on June 5, 1653, they relieved M. du Plessis-Montbar ' of the various works of piety with which he was overwhelmed' to devote his attention 'solely and absolutely' to 'the question of a great hospital.'[23]

Mademoiselle Le Gras was quite aware of the fact that each party, with perhaps a secret desire to be first in the field, was working at a plan for a general hospital. We have proof of this in one of her writings dated August, 1653.[24] To the question whether an undertaking like that of a general hospital is better suited for men or for women, she answers: 'If the work is regarded as merely secular, then it seems to me that men should take it up, but if it is regarded as a work of charity then women can undertake it, just as they have undertaken other great and difficult works of charity on which God has set His approval by the blessings He has in His goodness bestowed on them.'

She goes on to say that God has in all times made use of women to show forth His power: Judith, Saint Ursula, Saint Catherine, Saint Teresa and many, many others; she then sets out the conditions to which the Ladies of Charity should submit if they are to render their action fruitful and useful: to allow themselves to be guided by

---

[22] Abelly, *op. cit.*, Bk. I, Ch. XLV, p. 214; *Discours funèbre pour Madame la Duchesse d'Aiguillon* (par l'abbé Brisacier), 3rd ed., Paris, 1675, p. 24.

[23] *Annales de la Compagnie du Saint-Sacrement*, p. 136.

[24] *Pensées de Louis de Marillac*, p. 286. The Daughters of Charity still possess, in the Mother-House, the original of this document which is dated 1653 and not 1659.

Saint Vincent; not to bring any passion into their discussions but to state their views simply; to get in touch with devout personages, either to benefit by their advice or to secure support from the judges and magistrates in case of law-suits, which no doubt would be inevitable if thousands of poor persons, so different in temperament, character and humour, were to be made to perform their duty. She excluded the Company of the Blessed Sacrament from collaborating with the Ladies of Charity because the rule of the Company was that its members ' should lie concealed in all their charitable actions' and hence should not be requested ' to undertake public works.' Their spirit is opposed to that of the Ladies who are accustomed to appear in public and to act in broad daylight.

Saint Vincent had probably read these lines when, at another meeting, the Ladies urged him to come to a decision; they pointed out, with figures in their hands, that money would not be wanting, for they had received further promises of help. Although he did not think the time for action had yet arrived, he promised to reflect on the matter. It was generally agreed that a beginning should be made at once and the Queen asked to hand over the house and grounds of La Salpêtrière, then lying idle, for the new enterprise. Saint Vincent himself saw Anne of Austria who willingly consented. The patent of donation was contested, and as a law-suit would have put off the execution of the project indefinitely, one of the Ladies, to buy off opposition, made an offer of 100 livres a year which was accepted. The Ladies were in a great hurry to get to work, but the Saint was much less inclined to proceed so rapidly. It was a very complicated question; before beginning, it should be examined from every angle, all difficulties should be foreseen and ways and means sought either to divert or to overcome them. Whilst they grew more and more impatient with his want of decision, he deplored their thoughtless ardour. His addresses are full of appeals to moderate their zeal. ' The works of God,' he kept on telling them, ' come into being little by little, by degrees and progressively.' Instances from Sacred Scriptures sprang to his lips in support of his statements. He reminded them that it took a century to build Noah's Ark, that the children of Israel had to wait for forty years before entering the Promised Land, that three or four thousand years rolled on before the coming of the Messias, ' because God does not hasten in His works and does all things in their time.' He found the same lessons on turning over the pages of the Gospels. Our Lord might have appeared on earth in the fullness of His manhood and at once worked out our Redemption. He preferred ' to be born a little child, to grow in age, like other men, to arrive little by little at the consummation of this incomparable benefit.' When He said : ' My hour has not yet come ' it was to teach us ' not to advance too rapidly in those matters that depend much more on God than on us.' He might, in His lifetime, have established the Church on earth ; He was content with laying its foundations, leaving to His apostles and their successors the work of completing the edifice. ' Accordingly,' said Saint Vincent, ' it is not expedient to wish to do everything all at once and at one blow, or to think that all is lost if everybody else does not hurry along with us to co-operate with the small amount of good-will we possess. What then should be done ? Go quietly, pray to God a great deal and act together.' The words ' act together ' were not added without a reason, for the Saint and the Ladies did not see eye to eye on all points : they envisaged great plans and schemes to be carried out immediately ; he preferred to begin in a small way and proceed by stages ; they were for shutting up the beggars by force, he detested all forms of violence. ' Let us just make an attempt at first,' he said, ' let us be satisfied with admitting one or two hundred poor people ; let us accept only those who come of their own accord ; let us not force anybody ; such persons, being well treated and quite content, will attract others, and so, little by little, the numbers will increase with the resources Providence will send. Nothing will be spoiled by acting in this way ; haste and force are, on the contrary, hindrances to God's designs. If the work is from Him, it will succeed and last ; if not, it will simply vegetate and perish.'[25] His prudence prevailed over their zeal ; they waited, and in the mean-

[25] Abelly, *op. cit.*, pp. 214 ff.

time, La Salpêtrière was in the hands of the workmen who rapidly transformed the building.

This undertaking of the Ladies of Charity was not approved of by all ; many thought that so vast and complex a work was beyond their powers. With perhaps a few exceptions, all Court Officials, Members of Parliament and associates of the Company of the Blessed Sacrament, were fully persuaded that men, and men endowed with official authority, were absolutely necessary to begin and carry on the work. From criticism they proceeded to action. On November 9, 1653, Saint Vincent wrote to the Duchesse d'Aiguillon, who was then at her country seat : ' The Grand Master has forbidden your masons who are building at La Salpêtrière to go on with the work, under threat of imprisonment. . . . The enterprise will come to an end, if your charity does not effectively intervene.' He concludes by begging her to return to Paris ' to see the Grand Master and consult on what steps should be taken.'[26] He had a number of friends in the opposition camp, and was well aware of the fact that they were all-powerful in Court and Parliamentary circles ; he was under no illusions as to their gaining the upper hand at last. Their scheme, however, did not appeal to him ; they meant to suppress all begging, and consequently, to intern, whether they liked it or not, all poor people who refused to work ; hence, lodging, food, occupation and discipline had to be provided for thousands of individuals. Such an undertaking far surpassed the Ladies' powers ; in the circumstances, it was useless to oppose the plan and hence he advised the latter to yield. But in their eyes, to yield meant to sacrifice the whole undertaking, for they were fully convinced that only Saint Vincent could make it a success, and accordingly they showed some opposition. On October 17, 1654 or 1655, the Duchesse d'Aiguillon wrote to him : ' As for the hospital, I respect your ideas, but allow me to tell you mine before you come to a definite decision. The Ladies will gladly drop it whenever you please, but they have control of the funds of the house, and it is only just first to see what is going to become of it, for they will be accused perhaps

[26] *Saint Vincent de Paul*, Vol. V, p. 47.

before God and most certainly before men of having ruined the whole affair by abandoning it. They have no idea of mixing themselves up with the matter after it has become a great work, but they do wish to see that it is established under proper management, with a permanent system of government. Otherwise, matters will turn out as they have at La Pitié, and that is what they and I believe you could prevent, with the grace of God.'[27] The Duchess forgot, when writing these lines, that Saint Vincent was not free to apply his own methods, and would not have the means of carrying out the work in accordance with the ideas of those in high places.

In the end, the Ladies submitted ; they made a generous, nay, a heroic sacrifice. They had already expended 50,000 livres ; 12,000 for cabinet-makers who had made wooden beds :[28] 12,000 for cloth ; 10,000 for linen, bed-clothes and utensils ; they had, moreover, entered into contracts to spend 100,000 livres on feeding the poor. They were quite prepared to hand over all this to the administrators appointed by the King and even to continue their assistance as far as it might be deemed useful. In this way those who the administrators themselves referred to as ' the first promoters ' of the General Hospital gave an admirable example of disinterested conduct.[29]

In March, 1656, the edict of the King suppressing mendicity was promulgated. La Pitié, La Salpêtrière, Bicêtre, The Refuge, Scipion, and La Savonnerie were selected as houses of residence for all mendicants. Bellièvre de Pomponne, First President of the Parliament, Fouquet, the Procurator General, the Governors of La Pitié and some other laymen were appointed members of the Administrative Council.

The new hospital was not open to all classes of mendicants. It was decided that ' vagabonds and vagrants '

[27] *Ibid.*, Vol. VI, p. 110.
[28] Several of the beds were made in the upholsterers' workshop in Saint-Lazare. (Abelly, *op. cit.*, p. 217.)
[29] *L'hôpital général charitable*, Paris, 1657, oct., p. 9. This is certainly the work of the directors of the Hospital, or, if it be preferred, of one of them speaking for all.

should be expelled; married beggars and honest poor people should be assisted; persons suffering from contagious diseases confined to hospital; mendicant priests sent home to their bishops; wounded and disabled soldiers advised to return to their garrisons from which they would be despatched to their final destinations. In the case of beggars from the provinces, it was first thought they should be expelled from Paris, but such a solution raised weighty objections. It was in Paris that the poor inhabitants of Picardy and Champagne, driven from home by the recent movements of the military forces who wrecked all that they encountered on their line of march, had found sufficient food to prevent them from dying of starvation. Peace had not yet been concluded between France and Spain. The chances of war might, by causing fresh disasters, multiply the number of its victims, and the question arose as to what was to become of these poor people if the gates of Paris were shut in their faces and there was no possibility of obtaining a refuge and of securing admission.

Saint Vincent was much preoccupied with these considerations. One day, during the summer of 1655, whilst on his way to Villepreux to see Father de Gondi, he stopped at an inn at Saint-Cloud. After the midday meal he spent half an hour conversing with his secretary, Brother Robineau, and spoke at length on the future of the General Hospital. ' In the course of which,' writes the latter, ' he requested me to take pen and paper and dictated to me at great length the reasons why, in his opinion, poor people should not be shut up, at least during the war . . . and also, on the other hand, the reasons to the contrary. . . . We remained there for nearly three hours working at this plan.' They would have worked even longer were it not that they had to take the road again to Villepreux if they were to reach it before nightfall, but the General Hospital was still the only topic of conversation on the journey. ' I am deeply pained,' said Saint Vincent, ' to see that they desire to exclude poor country folk from the hospital; what will become of these poor people? To establish a General Hospital, shut up in it only the poor of Paris and do nothing for those in the country is certainly not to my liking. Paris is the sponge of the whole of France; it attracts most of the gold and silver of the country. If they cannot enter Paris, what is to become of them, especially those poor people of Champagne, Picardy and other provinces ruined by the wars?'[30]

Saint Vincent submitted his reflections to others besides his secretary, and they perhaps may have had something to do with the final draft submitted to the King by which only those beggars were expelled who had come from places already provided with an alms-house for poor old folk, or that were otherwise in a position to come to their assistance. He must have uttered a sigh of relief when he learned that the royal proclamation was not as rigorous as might have been feared.

He was, on the other hand, taken completely by surprise, on reading Article XXIII which entrusted the Priests of the Mission with the spiritual care of the General Hospital, for the authorities had omitted to consult him on the point.[31] 'As we have long known,' said the King, 'the blessings which God has bestowed on the labours of the Missionary Priests of Saint-Lazare, the great fruits they have hitherto gathered by the assistance they have rendered the poor, and the hope we entertain that they will continue to do so and even increase these fruits in the future, it is our wish that they shall take charge of their spiritual aid and instruction so that they may assist and console the poor of the General Hospital and those other houses over which it has authority, and that they be entrusted with the administration of the sacraments, under the authority and jurisdiction of the Lord Archbishop of Paris, to whom they shall be presented by the General of the said Missionaries, and by him approved.' The schedule of regulations annexed to the edict laid down the rights and duties of the chaplains in the following terms : ' The Missionary Priests of Saint-Lazare are entrusted with the spiritual instruction of the poor. They are empowered to accept their testamentary dispositions. In regard to questions of order and temporal discipline, they shall be

[30] Remarks on the virtues of Saint Vincent. (Ms. Robineau, pp. 151–153.)
[31] *Saint Vincent de Paul*, Vol. VI, p. 239.

subject to the government of the General Hospital. The Superior of the said Missionaries shall have a deliberative vote at the Council in matters concerning spiritual affairs.'

The royal edict was not brought into force for nearly a year, as local arrangements had not yet been completed. In the interval, a great mission was given to all the mendicants of Paris during February, 1657 ; it was preached in all the hospitals that went to make up the General Hospital, by forty ecclesiastics, all of whom were either Priests of the Mission or members of the Tuesday Conferences.[32] There are reasons for thinking that Bossuet was one of those who took part in this mission, in which the preachers exercised their zeal and ability to the utmost. Their labours were crowned by a large number of conversions.

The mission was hardly over when the Parliament published a decree forbidding public begging and commanding ' all poor mendicants, able-bodied or otherwise, of all ages and of both sexes, to appear, from Monday, May 7, at eight o'clock of the morning until the thirteenth day of the said month inclusive, in the court-yard of Our Lady of Pity . . . to be despatched by the directors to the houses dependant ' on the General Hospital. A company of archers was formed at the same time to seek out and expel all delinquents. Of the 40,000 poor people who used to beg in the streets of Paris, four or five thousand[33] complied with the decree ;[34] the others disappeared. Many reached the provinces and a few resigned themselves to the necessity of work. There were thousands of sudden cures ; the blind recovered their sight ; the maimed and crippled the use of their limbs ; the paralysed their power of movement. Never did medicine effect so many and such rapid cures as the decree of the Parliament.

Quite a large number of the poor got it into their heads that it was Saint Vincent's fault that they were no longer

[32] *L'hôpital général charitable*, p. 10.
[33] This is the figure supplied in 1657, by the governors of the General Hospital themselves in a letter to Mazarin (Arch. du Minist. des Aff. Etrang., France, Vol. 902, f⁰ 296).
[34] *Saint Vincent de Paul*, Vol. VI, p. 296.

MENDICANTS

free to beg. One of them said to him one day at the gate of Saint-Lazare : 'May I tell you what people are saying about you ? ' 'Yes, pray tell me,' was the reply. 'Well, Father, everyone in Paris is abusing you because they think you are the cause of the poor people being shut up in the big hospital.' To this all Saint Vincent said was : 'Oh, very well, I will pray for them.'[35]

In the hospital the beggars did not find the chaplains who had been nominated. Saint Vincent was placed in a dilemma by which he had either to decline the King's request for the twenty priests who had been asked for, or to close some houses and leave the Madagascar Mission without assistance for a long period.[36] To refuse to obey the King's command would have seemed, in his eyes, to be resisting the Divine Will, but on the other hand, the houses were already established, engagements had been entered into, and to violate one of his promises would be an act of injustice. After long hesitations, Saint Vincent assembled the priests of Saint-Lazare for a consultation ;[37] they were unanimously opposed to the royal proposal. The Duchesse d'Aiguillon and M. de Mauroy, Superintendent of Finances, had been particularly urgent in favour of acceptance ; the Saint wrote to both to express his regret based on his inability to supply the priests required.[38] As a result of this refusal, a deed was drawn up by which the Priests of the Mission renounced all rights conferred on them by the Letters Patent. This resolution, taken on the very eve of the opening of the hospital, would have placed its administrators in a most embarrassing position were it not that Saint Vincent himself undertook to supply a band of chaplains composed of some priests of the Tuesday Conferences and others belonging to the diocese of Paris, under the direction of Louis Abelly who was to be given the title of Rector. Abelly accepted, out of kindness, a post which, in the circumstances and considering his state of health, he could not long retain. After a year or two he resigned and his place

[35] Abelly, *op. cit.*, Bk. III, Ch. XI, sect. VII, p. 176.
[36] *Saint Vincent de Paul*, Vol. VI, p. 251 ; Vol. XIII, p. 179.
[37] *Ibid.*, Vol. VI, pp. 239, 245 ; Vol. XI, p. 368.
[38] *Ibid.*, Vol. VI, p. 256.

was filled by M. Régnoust, another member of the Conference.[39]

The XXVIIth Article of the royal edict left the administrators free to choose the women who seemed to them best fitted to take charge of persons of their own sex. They asked for the Daughters of Charity and Sisters Joan Lepeintre and Magdalen Ménage were appointed.[40] They were, however, only allowed to go on condition that they 'would merely make an attempt' and render as much assistance as they could to start the work. The only references to their presence at La Salpêtrière are to be found in a letter of Saint Louise de Marillac, dated August 8, 1657,[41] and in the deposition of a witness at her process of Beatification.

The Ladies of Charity were placed at the head of the staff in charge of all girls and women interned in the hospitals; their authority was not restricted merely to the moral and religious side of the work, they had also to deal with the temporal; they ordered materials for the women engaged in various employments and selected men and women from outside who were to teach and train them.[42]

Saint Vincent, whilst co-operating with the governors of the General Hospital by procuring helpers of whom they stood in need, also gave an example of obedience to the royal edict. He ordered the daily distribution of bread and soup at the gate of Saint-Lazare to be discontinued. Despite the fact, the poor still kept coming and waited around, complaining that they had not received anything. Their complaints must have wrung his heart-strings, but he never yielded. 'Father,' they said to him, ' didn't God command that alms should be given to the poor?' 'That's quite true, my friends,' he used to reply, 'but He also commanded us to obey the magistrates.' However, as the number of these unfortunate people had considerably increased, owing to a very severe winter, he thought the

---

[39] Abelly, *op. cit.*, Bk. I, Ch. XLV, p. 218; *St. Vincent de Paul*, Vol. VIII, p. 128.
[40] *L'hôpital général charitable*, p. 4.
[41] *Lettres de Louise de Marillac*, p. 865.
[42] *Saint Vincent de Paul*, Vol. VI, pp. 376–377.

prohibition should not, in the circumstances, be enforced, and shortly afterwards, the distribution of bread and soup was resumed.[43]

After his death, the Ladies of Charity carried on their work for the poor in the General Hospital. The immense services which they rendered far surpassed the rôle that had been assigned to them, for without their generous assistance and co-operation, the General Hospital of 1657 would not have lasted any longer than that of 1612.

The famine of 1662 forced up the price of wheat to such a height that the Governors had not enough money to purchase food for the inmates; it seemed inevitable that the latter would have to be dismissed, but the Ladies undertook to prevent such a calamity. Madame de Miramion and Mademoiselle de Lamoignon went to Madame Martinozzi, the Princesse de Conti, and implored her to come to their help; to Madame de Miramion she gave 100,000 francs and to Mademoiselle de Lamoignon a pearl necklace and other jewels that fetched 40,000 crowns. These sums were abundantly sufficient to tide over the crisis.[44]

In 1695, Madame de Miramion again intervened to prevent the Board of Governors, which owed 100,000 crowns, from sending away 700 girls. These poor creatures, if thrown on the world without any means of support, could scarcely have avoided shoals and shipwreck. The Duc d'Orléans, the Duc de Bouillon, Madame de Maintenon, the Chancellor of France, the Dowager Princesse de Conti, the Duchesse de Guise and many other personages of the Court and City generously came to the assistance of Madame de Miramion. She received more than 50,000 francs in a week and was thus enabled to support the poor girls for two years.[45]

The activities of the Ladies of Charity, as we have seen, were extensive; they were real mothers to the poor and a sort of Providence for the Governors of the Hospital. It was thanks to their co-operation that the work was estab-

---

[43] Abelly, *op. cit.*, Bk. III, Ch. XI, sect. III, p. 133.
[44] *La vie de Madame de Miramion*, par l'abbé de Choisy, Paris, 1706, p. 77.
[45] *Ibid.*, p. 341.

lished, and it was owing to their efforts that it succeeded in tiding over formidable difficulties. Their rôle has not been sufficiently insisted on by the historian of the General Hospital, and the great names of Saint Vincent de Paul and his two noble helpers, the Duchesse d'Aiguillon and Madame de Miramion, should not be forgotten in works dealing with the suppression of mendicancy in the seventeenth century.[46]

[46] It is to be regretted that M. Paultre, in the admirably documented and detailed pages devoted to the General Hospital in his work *De la répression de la mendicité et du vagabondage en France sous l'ancien régime*, does not even once refer to the part played by Saint Vincent de Paul and the Ladies of Charity, Raoul Allier does mention it (in *La cabale des dévots*, p. 63) but only to deny or minimise its importance. Abelly, no matter what may be said, was not a forger nor his history a legend. All that he tells us is in perfect harmony with the account given in *L'hôpital général charitable*, a work written by the first Governors. The Company of the Blessed Sacrament did certainly play a part in the foundation of the General Hospital, but it is an exaggeration to state that the Company was the first to whom this idea occurred ; for it was being discussed before the Company even existed. On the other hand, it was undoubtedly the Ladies of Charity, as Abelly states, who made the first attempt to carry out the plan.

CHAPTER XXXVII

PRISONERS

THE compassionate heart of Saint Vincent de Paul made no distinction between one class of unfortunate creatures and another; he embraced them all in the same charity, not excepting those who, if they had led orderly lives, would have escaped punishment. His heart went out to prisoners and galley-slaves, just as it did to the poor and the sick. If God's loving kindness extended to all the wretched, why should he impose a limit to his? To whom should he not be kind, if not to prisoners? The loss of liberty, by putting them in a state of absolute dependence on cruel and rapacious men guided too often only by their own selfish instincts, entailed a thousand other privations on prisoners. Prison officials, through negligence or avarice, left them without the necessaries of life; contractors cheated them in the quantity and quality of the goods supplied; registrars and warders demanded sums of money for the most trifling services, even those they were bound to perform.[1]

Prisons, far from contributing to the moral betterment of their inmates, were rather schools of corruption and irreligion. Harlots were just as free to enter a prison as any other visitor. 'Instead of being places of penance and sorrow,' writes the annalist of the Company of the Blessed Sacrament,[2] 'they were cess-pools of prostitution and scandal.' The sexes were not separated, men and women lived together in a state of deplorable promiscuity. Decent folk, whose sole crime was that of bankruptcy, were compelled to herd together with public malefactors and wretched creatures who delighted solely in dirt and filth. It seemed

[1] *Annales de la Compagnie du Saint-Sacrement*, p. 65.
[2] *Ibid.*, p. 28.

as if religion had nothing whatever to do with these unfortunate men and women. They never saw a priest ; they never heard Mass or received the Sacraments ; they never prayed, for devotion, if it is to flourish, needs stimulation. If a prison contained heretics, one may imagine to what dangers the faith of Catholics was exposed.

The Company of the Blessed Sacrament, of which Saint Vincent was a member, did not merely bewail this unfortunate state of affairs ; it sought for remedies, and, with the authorisation of the authorities concerned, applied them or at least indicated them to others in a better position to do so. The members were accustomed to visit the prisons. Each member went on his appointed day ; the eves of the feasts of the Church were set apart for priests who were thus enabled to offer their ministrations.[3] Heretics who were a source of danger were isolated.[4] Solid, iron barriers separated the men from the women.[5] Female visitors had to be satisfied with conversing through a grille, and only female relatives of the prisoners and virtuous ladies who came out of charity were admitted.[6] Those imprisoned for debt were separated from the other prisoners.[7]

In 1640, the Company of the Blessed Sacrament appointed three of its members to receive and examine petitions from poor prisoners in the Conciergerie, to hasten the settlement of their business affairs and to have sentence pronounced on their cases. The multitude and complexity of these cases obliged the members to co-opt three collaborators, and in order to secure a wider field from which to select, it was decided to establish a new, independent, autonomous association.[8]

Good example is contagious. Ladies illustrious for their station in life as well as for their virtues were filled with a noble spirit of emulation ; they, too, went down into the dungeons, conversed with the prisoners, took an interest in their lot and sought for means to lessen their sufferings.

In 1643, Father Amable Bonnefons, S.J., in his book

---

[3] *Annales de la Compagnie du Saint-Sacrement*, pp. 26, 33, 39, 64.
[4] *Ibid.*, p. 59.   [5] *Ibid.*, p. 40.   [6] *Ibid.*, pp. 26, 28, 39.
[7] *Ibid.*, p. 59.   [8] *Ibid.*, pp. 65, 235.

PRISONERS

The Charitable Christian,[9] mentions four different groups engaged in prison-work : the Congregation of the Gentlemen of Notre-Dame, established in the professed house of the Society, the Company of the Blessed Sacrament, the Association specially created to look after the interests of those imprisoned for debt, and the Ladies of Mercy. There are no documents extant dealing with the activities of the Gentlemen of Notre-Dame. The two last groups continued their charitable labours up to the end of the seventeenth century, and perhaps later. They did not cease from their labours until the State, arriving at a better knowledge of its duties, had undertaken to provide prisoners with the necessaries of life, to look after their health, protect them from acts of injustice, send magistrates periodically to listen to their complaints, taste their food, examine their quarters and, in short, obtain a full account of all their needs. Whilst waiting for the Prisons Board to function, it was only fitting that private charity should be allowed to act, and introduce some little improvement and consolation in the lives of the prisoners. The Ladies of Mercy at first dealt with only four prisons ; the Conciergerie, the Grand Châtelet, the Little Châtelet and Fort-Lévesque.[10] Later on, they took charge of the Abbey, the Temple, Saint Germain-des-Prés, Saint-Martin, Saint-Éloy and the Hôtel de Ville.[11]

It would seem as if such an interesting work must have attracted the Confraternities of Charity. The rules laid down by Saint Vincent for Montmirail[12] and Folleville[13] expressly refer to prisoners. In Paris, the Ladies of Charity only took charge of galley-slaves, and there is no indication before 1660 of the members of the parochial Confraternities of the capital visiting other prisoners. The Confraternities of both men and women were gradually drawn into the

[9] 1643 edition, pp. 124 ff.
[10] Bonnefons, *op. cit.*, p. 125.
[11] *Mémoire des prisons de Paris dont la Compagnie des dames, où Madame la première présidente de Lamoignon est supérieure, prend soin depuis longtemps.* (Bibl. Maz. A 10,694, 91ᵉ pièce.) This seems to have been printed about the year 1675.
[12] *Saint Vincent de Paul*, Vol. XIII, p. 462.
[13] *Ibid.*, p. 477.

movement—which induced charitable associations to do something for these unfortunates. The Ladies of Charity also followed the current; one of them, Madame de Lamoignon, wife of the First President, was for long President of the Ladies of Mercy;[14] another, Mademoiselle de Pontcarré, with the help of some of her lady friends, procured an additional supply of food every Wednesday for the prisoners in the Conciergerie.[15]

When the prisoners saw the attention paid them and heard the words of help and consolation falling from the lips of their visitors, they felt better able to endure their sufferings. The succours of religion were no longer lacking. The chapel was suitably furnished; Mass was celebrated and a sermon preached on Sundays and Holydays; Confessions were heard on certain days; a printed leaflet pasted on a piece of wood, a scrap of linen, or cardboard, was placed in each cell thus enabling the prisoners to read their morning and night prayers; less blasphemous language was heard; quarrels were not so frequent, and if an individual forgot himself in this respect he was excluded from the help rendered his companions in misfortune. Enquiries were made as to whether the prisoners were receiving sufficient wholesome food, whether the straw was renewed, whether fire-wood was supplied, whether the sick were nursed, and whether the elementary rules of hygiene were being observed. At the Conciergerie, the Ladies maintained two Sisters of Charity to supply soups and medical requisites to the sick.[16] They made it a rule not to interfere in criminal cases and to respect the decisions of the Judges, but if a verdict seemed to them to be manifestly

---

[14] *Réglement des Assemblées de Madame de Lamoignon, première président du Parlement de Paris, pour assister les prisonniers, les pauvres honteux et les malades.—Réglement des Assemblées d'hommes à cette fin de diverses paroisses de Paris.—Réglement des Assemblées qui accordent aussi les procez et les querelles.* (Bibl. Maz. A 10, 694, 94ᵉ pièce.) This document at least dates from 1672.

[15] *Mémoire des prisons de Paris* . . . ; *Instructions utiles pour les dames qui désirent rendre la charité aux pauvres prisonniers.* (Bibl. Maz. A 10, 694, 92ᵉ pièce.)

[16] *Annales de la Compagnie du Saint-Sacrament*, pp. 64, 211; *Réglements des Assemblées.* . . .

unjust, they conveyed 'a gentle and humble remonstrance' to the magistrate who had delivered it, by a person of rank and upright life, and then let the matter rest.[17] In the case of those imprisoned for debt, they worked hard to have them set free as soon as possible. If prisoners were penniless, alms were collected for them, and if the amount subscribed was not sufficient, urgent requests were made to the creditor to be satisfied with what had been collected. If prisoners possessed any money or property, various proposals were made to the creditor until an agreement was reached; creditors, as a rule, abandoned legal proceedings as soon as they had received part of their due and a date had been fixed on which the balance should be paid.[18]

Saint Vincent was delighted to see prisoners thus assisted and encouraged, but his heart was grieved at the thought that prisoners of State, confined in the Bastille, were rigorously deprived of all contact with the outside world. As an inevitable result, there were no prayers, no exercises of piety, and hope in God was replaced by despair and perhaps hatred. He pleaded their cause at the Council of Conscience and succeeded in having a discreet and reliable priest appointed as chaplain whom he selected himself from the members of the Tuesday Conferences.[19]

As Prior of Saint-Lazare, Saint Vincent had special authority over certain prisons. These were, in the first place, prisons within his own bailiwick, namely, those inside the Priory enclosure close to the Court in which the Bailiff administered justice, and those in the Rue de Cléry, in Villeneuve-sur-Gravois, now called Bonne-Nouvelle.[20] The Saint's virtue and character does not permit us to doubt that he saw to the corporal, moral and religious welfare of the prisoners who came under his seignorial jurisdiction. Unfortunately, documentary evidence is wanting on this aspect of his work and we can only just refer to it.

We have fuller information as to another prison that lay within the walls of the Priory itself. This prison, or, to use

---

[17] *Mémoires des prisons de Paris.*
[18] *Réglement des Assemblées.* . . .
[19] Abelly, *op. cit.*, Bk. II, Ch. XIII, sect. IX, p. 467.
[20] Arch. Nat. S. 6627.

a milder term, house of correction, which was almost empty in 1632 when the Priests of the Mission took possession of Saint-Lazare, soon came to be well known over all Paris. Children of the nobility and of the citizens of Paris who were not giving satisfaction to their parents were sent there. We should like to have discovered a complete list of those admitted by Saint Vincent, but we must rest content with three or four names.[21] In December, 1634, John de Montholon was sent to Saint-Lazare, at the request of his guardian, for having secretly married a woman whose social position did not correspond with his own.[22]

Paternal authority was then far greater than it is to-day and occasionally was exercised tyrannically. Family reasons had far more weight in deciding the future of children than their capacities or tastes. A young man intended for the ecclesiastical state by his father, a certain M. Demurard, Treasurer of Lyons, preferred to get married. By doing so, he had to resign a benefice, and instead of resigning in favour of his brother as he had been ordered, he handed it over to a person who, in his eyes, was more capable of fulfilling its obligations. The paternal anger was not slow to fall on the youth and he was forcibly carried off to the prison of Saint-Lazare, there to expiate his act of disobedience. Saint Vincent at first did not know why he had been sent there, but as soon as he learned, he informed the family that if they did not remove the prisoner the Parliament would set him free.[23] On another occasion, a young libertine who had made up his mind to change his mode of life went to Saint-Lazare to make a retreat in which he hoped he would gain strength to resist the temptations of the flesh. His mother heard of it and thought it an admirable opportunity of getting hold of the young man and confining him with the others in the house of correction. She made the proposal to Saint Vincent who promptly and energetically refused.[24] Why, he asked, punish a repentant sinner who,

[21] See P. Coste's *Les détenus de Saint-Lazare aux XVIIe et XVIIIe siècles* in the *Revue des études historiques*, July–September, 1926.
[22] *Saint Vincent de Paul*, Vol. I, p. 291.
[23] *Ibid.*, Vol. VII, p. 605.
[24] *Ibid.*, Vol. VIII, p. 178.

of his own accord, was taking the right step to return to the path of duty? The Marchioness of Pransac had probably better luck with her eldest son, who was leading a life of debauchery, a blasphemer, foul-mouthed, and in short, as she said, ' in a state of extreme disfavour and abandonment by Our sweet Saviour and His most holy Mother,' and who had not given the same signs of repentance.[25] Saint Vincent very probably granted her request.

At the suggestion of the Archbishop (1637) and with financial assistance from the Company of the Blessed Sacrament, he admitted vagabond mendicant priests who dishonoured their sacred ministry. After a year's detention they were set free, but almost immediately again began to give scandal and had to be interned once more.[26]

The number of lunatics and persons of vicious character confined in Saint-Lazare, for both categories were represented, oscillated, in 1659, between fifty and sixty.[27] Saint Vincent always charitably referred to them as his ' boarders.' His discourses to his community and recommendations to the priests and brothers employed in their service, sufficiently reveal the place they held in his heart. To encourage priests and brothers to love their very trying duties, he was accustomed to remind them that in ancient Rome, the Popes had been condemned by Emperors to guard wild beasts, that Jesus Christ had consented to be regarded as mad, and that He had lived surrounded by lunatics, demoniacs, fools and the possessed. He threatened his community with the vengeance of God if they ceased to treat the ' boarders ' well.

Having learned one day that they were not being properly fed, he took occasion at the next repetition of prayer to manifest how deeply he felt on this matter. ' A propos of the boarders,' he said in a tone of legitimate indignation,[28]

[25] *Ibid.*, Vol. VIII, p. 348.
[26] *Annales de la Compagnie du Saint-Sacrement*, par le Comte René de Voyer d'Argenson, éd. Beauchet-Filleau, Marseille, 1900, oct., p. 74.
[27] Report on the advantages of the union with Saint-Lazare ; Claude de Chandenier's evidence (Arch. Nat. M 212, n. 7).
[28] *Saint Vincent de Paul*, Vol. XI, p. 331.

'I have learned that they are sometimes given most unappetising and very badly prepared dishes, and even meat or wine that was left over from the evening before.... That is wrong. These are persons whose relations pay us a good pension; is it not just that they should be given food that is appetising and has been properly prepared? In the name of God, my brethren, do not let that occur again, but give them what you give us, what you give the priests. For, observe, brothers, you are committing an act of injustice against these poor people, some of whom are poor innocents who have to be confined and who cannot even see you to complain of the injustice you do them. Yes—I call it an act of injustice. If you behaved like that towards me or anybody else, we are in a position to ask you to behave justly in our regard, and to treat us like anybody else; but those poor folk who are not able to do so and who, what is worse, do not even see you so that they could ask you to do so. Oh! surely, it is a very grave offence not to act justly towards them of your own accord. I often see their relations and they ask me how they are treated. I tell them that they are treated exactly like ourselves. And now, it seems this is not so, and that you are doing the contrary.... I beg those in charge to insist that these dear people shall be supplied exactly with what the priests are supplied. I say, moreover: it is a further injustice committed against those who pay a larger pension not to be supplied with something more than those who pay less.... I would far prefer you should deprive me of it in order to give it to them than fail to carry out my instructions.' Saint Vincent not only insisted on the duty of supplying his boarders with good food; he was also anxious that their oddities, laziness or silly conduct should be borne with the greatest patience.

All sorts of vicious characters were to be found in the house of correction. Libertines and spendthrifts formed the largest group, but there were also public blasphemers, atheists, drunkards and even actual brigands. Some of them had robbed their relations; others had maltreated or even attempted to murder them. In the circumstances, it was essential for discipline to be stringent. No one was admitted to the house of correction unless on a magistrate's warrant. A priest was placed in charge of the whole work; another priest, subject to the authority of the first, attended to the spiritual welfare of the inmates, whilst lay-brothers were in charge of the discipline and maintenance of the establishment. The inmates were not allowed to receive visitors save with the consent of those who had sent them to Saint-Lazare, and were neither seen by nor known to any of the community, except the staff of the house of correction.

Under the influence of the good advice they received, the edifying books they read, the devotional exercises at which they were occasionally bound to assist, most of them improved and promised to amend. They were not set at liberty until they had given such a promise, shown solid proof of amendment and prepared themselves by a retreat, a general confession and the reception of Holy Communion to make a better use of their freedom.

In Paris, the house of correction at Saint-Lazare was regarded as one of the best managed in the city. On one occasion a magistrate said to a man of rank who was weary of the insolent behaviour of his nephew, a young debauchee who kept demanding money from him under threats of murder: 'Shut him up in Saint-Lazare; there is no better place to cure him of his faults.' 'I was not aware,' said the unfortunate uncle, 'that such characters were admitted to Saint-Lazare. I am very glad to hear it; Paris is in need of three or four such houses of correction.' On another occasion, a devout ecclesiastic who was well aware of the methods employed to bring vicious young men to their senses, remarked: 'They are received and treated there with so much kindness and attention that they live almost like religious, in a separate building, and punctually carry out all their exercises of piety at stated times.' 'Many of them,' he went on to say, 'have profited so well by their sojourn there, that on leaving, they withdrew to the cloister and embraced the religious state.' Several were attracted by the most austere religious Orders whilst others chose communities devoted to the service of their fellow-men or joined the ranks of the secular clergy. Amongst those who remained laymen many attained positions of great dignity and trust. The house of correction, then, fully deserved its name. Amendment, and not punishment, came first; the future rather than the past was borne in mind.

A lady of rank one day congratulated Saint Vincent on the astounding transformations effected in the prison of Saint-Lazare. 'You are,' said she, 'the refuge of sinners.' At these words, he could not refrain from showing that his feelings had been hurt. 'Pray reserve that title,' said he, 'for Jesus Christ and His merciful Mother. I don't deserve it.' And yet he actually did, for the invocation *Refugium peccatorum* in the Litany of the Blessed Virgin was not inapplicable to Saint Vincent.[29]

Two years before he died, he asked his priests to continue, after his death, the works that had been established in Saint-Lazare, including the lunatic asylum and the house of correction. 'A day may come,' he said,[30] 'when men with warped minds will decry the good works which God led us to embrace and carry on with His blessing. . . . Say to these false brethren courageously: "Gentlemen, allow us to follow the laws of our fathers; leave us in the state in which we are; God has placed us in it and it is His will that we should abide there."' The holy founder's recommendation was faithfully observed by his disciples; as long as the Priests of the Mission remained in Saint-Lazare, that is to say, until the French Revolution, unfortunate men whose reason had been affected or whose heart had been corrupted were still admitted.

[29] Abelly, *op. cit.*, Bk. II, Ch. VI. The chapter is entitled 'Les pensionnaires enfermés à Saint-Lazare.'
[30] *Saint Vincent de Paul*, Vol. XII, pp. 90–92.

CHAPTER XXXVIII

THE GALLEY-SLAVES

CONVICTS, perhaps, more than all other classes of the unfortunate had a right to Saint Vincent de Paul's attention, for his office of Chaplain General to the galleys imposed special obligations on him in their regard. To render his charity wider and more efficacious, he associated his priests with this work. The spiritual assistance of galley-slaves is one of the duties stipulated in the contract that gave birth, on April 17, 1625, to the Congregation of the Mission.[1]

At that time, criminals condemned to the galleys were brought to Paris and placed in a special prison situated close to the Church of Saint Roch. Every six months, when the chain-gang set out for Marseilles, the prison was emptied and then gradually re-filled. It would be hard to imagine the physical and moral sufferings of these unfortunate men in their narrow, filthy and badly ventilated dungeons from which they never emerged, and in which, to employ Count René de Voyer d'Argenson's energetic phrase, ' they rotted alive.'[2]

Their death, regrettable in itself, also deprived the King of the services they might have rendered him. It would have been easy to bring the convicts out into the courtyard, where they would of course have to be under surveillance, but want of money did not permit of a sufficient number of gaolers. In the last months of the year 1630, the Company of the Blessed Sacrament, touched with compassion, defrayed the expense of four additional warders,

[1] *Saint Vincent de Paul*, Vol. XIII, p. 201.
[2] *Annales de la Compagnie du Saint-Sacrement*, par le Comte René de Voyer d'Argenson, éd. Beauchet-Filleau, oct., Marseilles, 1900, p. 18.

with the result that these confined in the lower dungeons were able to breathe fresh air for a few minutes every day. The prison of Saint Roch, established in a rented house, was incapable of being altered and repaired to such a degree as the health of the galley-slaves demanded. In 1632, Saint Vincent obtained, from the King and the Sheriffs of Paris, permission to remove them to the parish of Saint Nicholas-du-Chardonnet where they were placed in a square tower that formed part of the old walls of Paris and stood, flanked by two small towers, between the Gate of Saint Bernard and the Seine, on the Quay de la Tournelle, a few minutes' walk from the Collège des Bons Enfants. The work of the Missionaries was thereby greatly facilitated. However, no matter what Abelly may say,[3] the Fathers at that time had little or nothing to do with the convicts. The Company of the Blessed Sacrament, after making enquiries in 1634, made it clear that the prisoners were in need of everything, and in particular of the succours of religion. René de Voyer d'Argenson says :[4] 'They have neither Mass nor any religious instruction whatever, and the Company begged one of its ecclesiastical members to assist the convicts in both these respects ; this was done faithfully enough for some time.'

This member was in all probability the parish priest, George Groger, who approached the diocesan authorities and obtained on September 2, 1634, an order from the Archbishop, by which religious worship was established in the galley-slaves' Tower. In this document, the prelate

[3] *Op. cit.*, Bk. I, Ch. XXVIII, p. 127. This is what he says : 'He solicited the late King Louis XIII both directly and indirectly . . . to consent . . . that this old tower between the Gate of Saint Bernard and the river should be set apart to serve as a place of retreat for those poor men in chains ; this was granted in the year 1632 ; they were subsequently brought there and for some years only subsisted by the alms of some charitable persons. M. Vincent, on his side, not to be importunate to others, himself provided for their spiritual welfare, sending them the priests of his Congregation who resided at the Collège des Bons Enfants, to celebrate Holy Mass, to instruct, confess and console them.'

[4] *Op. cit.*, p. 56.

TOWER AND GATE OF SAINT-BERNARD

enjoins the parish priest or his delegates to erect ' a chapel in the most suitable part of the Tower,' ' to place therein a portable altar,' to bring there the necessary altar vessels and vestments, to celebrate Mass there on Sundays and Holydays, to visit sick galley-slaves, to administer the Sacraments, and in general to devote the same care and attention to convicts as a parish priest is bound to show his other parishioners.[5] Hence it would seem that Mass had not been celebrated in La Tournelle before September 2, 1634. This is certainly surprising when one thinks of the zeal of Saint Vincent de Paul, but it is quite certain that the state of affairs was not due to any negligence on his part, but was rather the result of circumstances over which he had no control.

The prison of La Tournelle, like all other prisons in Paris, was under the control of the Procurator General and not the General of the Galleys; the Chaplain General therefore was not, as such, in charge of the spiritual welfare of convicts imprisoned in the capital. This was the duty of the parish priest who, as a matter of fact, claimed it, and hence, as we have just seen, when the diocesan authorities organised religious worship at La Tournelle, it was to George Groger, the parish priest of Saint Nicholas du Chardonnet, that the order was sent. If Saint Vincent had attended to the galley-slaves in their former prison he had done so out of kindness, with the consent and perhaps at the request of the parish priest of Saint Roch.

Fresh obligations, in virtue of a contract to which we shall later refer, were added in 1639 to those set out in the Archbishop's first decree.[6] The Chaplain of La Tournelle arrived regularly every morning at the chapel about half-

---

[5] Ms. MM 492 of the Arch. Nat. supplies (f⁰ 185) the official translation of this document.

[6] In 1633, the Company of the Blessed Sacrament must have ceased from providing the religious services for the prisons of Paris, which, in default of others, it had undertaken, on account of the protests of the parish priests who considered this intervention as ' an insult to their pastoral dignity.' (*Annales de la Compagnie du Très-Saint-Sacrement*, p. 39.) It would seem, therefore, that the cession of prison chaplaincies to the parochial clergy was a general measure.

past seven; he presided over morning prayers, celebrated Mass, visited the sick, and returned at the end of the day for evening prayers. He preached every Sunday and taught catechism twice a week, or, if he thought it necessary, he substituted a sermon. Before the departure of the chain-gang for Marseilles, a short mission was given to the galley-slaves to prepare them for the reception of the Sacraments of Penance and of the Blessed Eucharist, and to assist them to bear their sufferings in a Christian manner; sufferings, indeed, of such a nature that many of them frequently died on the journey.[7] The funerals of galley-slaves who died in La Tournelle were carried out with a certain amount of solemnity, and, according to custom, six ecclesiastics assisted at the funeral service. The chaplain was also a vigilant guardian of morality at La Tournelle into which women of evil life tried to secure an entrance on any and every pretext. He was on the alert against abuses and reported them.[8] His task was rendered all the more easy by the support given him by the Company of the Blessed Sacrament which took a marked interest in all that concerned convicts.

These unfortunate men certainly deserved sympathy. Maltreated by their gaolers, and compelled to buy food at exorbitant prices, most of them suffered from sickness, and every year more than one fell a victim to privations. The sick were treated no better than those in health. They were supplied with the same bread and water as was given to those who were well, and prisoners who had no money were forced to subsist on this meagre pittance. Another abuse was that the clerk, whose duty it was to write down the names of the galley-slaves on their arrival, did not state the duration of the sentence, and hence the period of detention depended on the caprice of the officials. The Company of the Blessed Sacrament waged a vigorous war against these deplorable abuses; it denounced them to the Procurator General, deputed several of its members to pay regular visits to La Tournelle, voted funds to supply the sick with soups and medicines, had copies made of the list

[7] We learn from a letter that, in 1662, eighteen convicts died on the journey. (Arch. Nat. Marine B⁶ 77, f⁰ 342.)
[8] Arch. Nat. MM 492, f⁰ 187 v⁰.

THE GALLEY-SLAVES

of judicial sentences, one of which was given to the convicts and the other to the branches of the Company at Aix and Marseilles so that, the length of the period of detention being known, the release of the prisoner could not be deferred after his sentence had been served.[9]

It is probable that Saint Vincent had a part, perhaps the chief part, in these decisions of the Company. No one had displayed as much interest as he in the work for convicts. On the one hand, as Chaplain General to the Galleys, he could not remain indifferent to their lot ; on the other, his biographers and his own writings show that he was constantly preoccupied with the thought of assuring them all the physical, moral and religious assistance of which they stood in need. To attain this end, he appealed to the organisations he had established : the Ladies of Charity in the parish of Saint Nicholas, the Ladies of the Hôtel-Dieu, who brought alms and sympathy to the convicts, the Daughters of Charity, who became their servants as they already were the servants of the parochial poor, the priests of the Tuesday conferences, who frequently gave missions to those unfortunate men during the days preceding their departure in the chain-gang.

As soon as the prison had been transferred to La Tournelle, Saint Vincent wrote to Saint Louise de Marillac, the Superioress of the Charity of Saint-Nicholas : ' Charity towards these poor convicts is of incomparable merit in the sight of God ; you have done well to assist them and you will do even better if you continue to do so in whatever way you can, until I shall have the happiness of seeing you, which will be in two or three days' time. Reflect a little as to whether your Charity of Saint-Nicholas would be willing to undertake this work, at least for a time. You might help them with whatever money remains over. It is indeed a difficult task, and it is that very fact which makes me throw out the suggestion to you on the spur of the moment.'[10] The Charity of Saint-Nicholas subscribed what it could and Saint-Lazare followed suit ; but these alms, added to those of the Company of the Blessed Sacrament, were far from

---
[9] *Op. cit.*, pp. 54–56.
[10] *Saint Vincent de Paul*, Vol. I, p. 166.

meeting all the requirements. One can then well imagine Saint Vincent's joy when, one day in 1639, he heard that a wealthy financier, M. Cornuel, who had died recently, had bequeathed an annual sum of 6000 livres to the convicts. His joy, however, did not last long, for Cornuel's daughter, acting under the influence of her husband, instead of carrying out her father's wishes, claimed the whole sum. Saint Vincent brought every means into play that his heart and his diplomacy could suggest; he was supported by persons of rank and position, and the intervention of Mathew Molé, the Procurator General, proved decisive. The lady, when handing over the capital sum, asked that its temporal administration should be entrusted in perpetuity to the Procurators General. This gift enabled the Daughters of Charity to be employed in the service of the convicts. Saint Vincent, supported by the Ladies of Charity, suggested to the Procurator General that 300 livres of the revenues should be earmarked for the improvement of religious worship, under conditions which would enlarge the scope of the duties of the chaplain of La Tournelle beyond those prescribed by the decree of 1634 of the Archbishop of Paris.[11]

The Daughters of Charity began to work for the convicts in 1640. Saint Vincent gave them a set of rules which manifest his solicitude both for the Sisters and for their charges; for the Sisters, because he did not conceal the dangers to which they would be exposed in such corrupt surroundings; for their charges, because their sufferings filled his compassionate heart with grief. The corporal and spiritual assistance of galley-slaves was the two-fold employment assigned by the Saint to his Daughters. Corporal assistance extended to all matters concerning food, linen and the care of the sick. They were to purchase provisions, and if money were wanting, even to beg alms from the charitable.[12] They prepared the convicts' meals, and once a day carried to each prisoner 'his little ration' for the entire day, aided by a gaoler in case the soup-pot was too

[11] Arch. Nat. MM 492, f⁰ 189 v⁰; Abelly, *op. cit.*, Bk. I, Ch. XXVIII, p. 128.
[12] *Saint Vincent de Paul*, Vol. IV, p. 426.

heavy. The sick were the object of quite special attention. Nothing was neglected to cure, to console or to prepare them to meet their God : visits, medicines, food more carefully prepared and fresh for every meal, encouragement, and suggestions to lead those in danger of death to receive the Last Sacraments. In case of death, the Sisters supervised the funeral and burial. They also had charge of the linen, and the convicts received a bundle of fresh linen every Saturday, and before the departure of the chain-gang, enough to last them for the journey.

The few days that elapsed between the departure of one group of galley-slaves and the arrival of another were not days of rest for the Sisters ; on the contrary, the work was harder than ever, for bedding had to be renewed, the main hall washed and scrubbed, and order restored throughout the prison. Such were the occupations of the Daughters of Charity in La Tournelle. It was Saint Vincent's wish that they should not only be the servants but the angel guardians of the convicts. He asked them to turn away from the prison all evil-doers and those who would give the convicts bad advice, to induce Ladies of Charity to visit, and at the approach of the departure of the chain-gang, to make discreet arrangements for the customary mission to be preached.

Contact with the galley-slaves and even with their gaolers presented more than one inconvenience ; hence the Saint urged such of his Daughters as were employed at La Tournelle to take every suitable precaution against the dangers to which they were exposed. He recommended them never to appear save when they were actually wanted, not to remain alone with the convicts except in case of necessity ; to be modest, reserved, discreet and cautious ; not to take part in idle conversations ; to appear deaf, in case frivolous remarks were addressed to them, or if too much liberty was shown, even to reply coldly or to walk away ; to offer up every day a special prayer to the Holy Spirit to obtain grace to remain pure, to have great confidence that their prayer would be heard, as God heard that of the three children in the fiery furnace, for God will never deprive those of His grace who expose themselves to danger out of charity and obedience. 'Resemble,' he adds, ' the light of the sun which passes continually over filth without being soiled in the slightest.' He also recommended gentleness and patience, virtues they were frequently called on to practise, for unruly, insolent and even violent characters were not rare amongst the convicts. 'They shall be on their guard against affording even the smallest ground for complaint, and therefore shall never speak to them rudely, reproach them for the annoyance they have caused or even defend themselves if falsely accused; on the contrary, they shall strive not to utter an unnecessary word, and win them by kindness and sympathy, seeing the pitiable state in which these men usually are both in mind and body, and that even in this condition they do not cease to be members of Him who made Himself a slave to redeem us from the servitude of the evil one.' The holy founder permits and even recommends his Daughter to take vengeance, but it is the vengeance of Christians who pray to God for convicts that insult them 'as did Saint Stephen for those who stoned him.'

The Daughters of Charity carried out his advice, but none perhaps as perfectly as Sister Barbara Angiboust. After her death, in the course of a conversation between the Sisters and the Saint in which her virtues were recounted one by one, her patience was loudly praised. Let us listen to the moving dialogue between Saint Vincent and Barbara's companion, Sister Joan Luce.

'Father, I lived with her amongst the galley-slaves. She was wonderfully patient in bearing the sufferings she encountered there through the evil temper of these men. For, though they were sometimes so angry with her as to throw the soup and meat on the ground, and said whatever their impatience suggested to them, she bore it all without saying a word, and quietly picked up the meat, looking just as pleasant as if they never had said or done anything to her.'

'Oh! that's wonderful! to look just as pleasantly at them as before.'

'Father, not only that, but on five or six occasions she prevented the gaolers from beating them.'

'Well, well, Sisters, if there are any present who spent

some time with the galley-salves and who wished to hold their own against these poor men, rendering them evil for evil, insult for insult, let them grieve deeply, seeing that one of your Sisters who wore the same habit as you, when the food she was carrying was thrown at her, never said a word, and when people wanted to punish them, would not allow it.'[13]

The devotedness of the Sisters employed in the service of the galley-slaves was all the more meritorious as their duties were less attractive to nature. Saint Vincent frequently had need to encourage them. On one occasion, after speaking to the Sisters on their work for the Foundlings, he went on to ask them to thank God because He had given them charge of galley-slaves. ' Yes, Sisters, it is God Who has given you this work, without your ever having thought of it, or Mademoiselle Le Gras, or, indeed, myself ; for that is how God's works are accomplished, without men thinking of them. When a work has no author, one should say that it is God who wrought it. But what is this particular work ? It is helping poor criminals or convicts. Ah ! Sisters, what a happiness to serve poor convicts delivered into the hands of those who have no pity on them ! I have seen them, these poor men, treated like beasts ; it was this that touched God with compassion. They made Him have pity on them. And so His goodness has done two things on their behalf ; first, it has caused a house to be bought for them, and second, it has so arranged matters that they are served by His own Daughters, for to say a *Daughter of Charity* is just the same as saying a *Daughter of God.*'[14]

In this way Saint Vincent de Paul ennobled employments that are basest in the eyes of the world by revealing their grandeur in the eyes of Faith. His Daughters found in these frequently repeated exhortations the strength and courage they needed if they were not to succumb ; they were happy to be servants of the convicts ; they gloried in the title and thanked God for it as a special mark of His favour.

Let us now follow the convicts to Marseilles. The life they led here was not, like that at La Tournelle, a life of

[13] *Saint Vincent de Paul*, Vol. X, p. 645.
[14] *Ibid.*, Vol. X, p. 125.

inaction. Two hundred and seventy-five men, with eighty soldiers, were placed on board each galley. Here they were fastened to their benches by chains, bound two by two to the same cannon-ball, their shoulders naked and their heads covered with a red linen bonnet. They were compelled to row strenuously under pain of being scourged until the blood flowed, sometimes until they died. The galleys were long, flat vessels, defended by five cannon and a dozen swivel-guns. In the second half of the seventeenth century there were more than forty galleys stationed at Marseilles. The captain took his station on the poop; close by stood the overseer, the head of the galley-slaves, who took and transmitted the captain's orders. Two assistant overseers stood, one in the middle of the galley, the other near the bow, and threatened the shoulders of the rowers with their scourges.

Even in Marseilles itself the galley-slaves had two great protectors : John Baptist Gault, of the Oratory, Bishop of the city, and Gaspard de Simiane, Chevalier de la Coste, a member of the Company of the Blessed Sacrament.

John Baptist Gault was consecrated bishop in the Church of Saint Magloire, Paris, on October 5, 1642, and was in all respects worthy of that high position to which he had been called. The time he spent in the capital after his consecration was not wasted, as far as his episcopal city was concerned, for he made such arrangements as he thought profitable for the good of souls, and in particular, he reflected deeply on the most useful means of helping the convicts. In Paris, none were so deeply interested in this matter as Saint Vincent de Paul, Chaplain General to the Galleys, and the Duchesse d'Aiguillon, aunt of Armand John du Plessis, Duke of Richelieu, who was then General of the Galleys. The bishop met Saint Vincent and the Duchess and all three agreed that a mission should be given to these unfortunate prisoners. They also discussed what could be done for sick convicts, and together explored all means that could be taken to alleviate their lot.

John Baptist Gault made his official entrance into Marseilles on Januray 9, 1643, and immediately revealed his charity for the poor and sick. He visited the hospitals, sought out the most wretched hovels and left behind him an abundant supply of alms. He was about to begin a mission at Aubagne, of which the Bishops of Marseilles were Lords, when he heard that five priests from Saint-Lazare had arrived in Marseilles to preach a mission to the convicts. This was in the month of March, and as there was a rumour that the galleys were leaving for Catalonia, very little time remained; the mission at Aubagne was accordingly deferred and preparations at once begun for the mission to the convicts. In the first place, more Missionaries were needed, for those sent by Saint Vincent under the direction of Father du Coudray were far too few. D'Authier, the founder of the Priests of the Most Blessed Sacrament, lent eight; a number of Oratorians volunteered, and the Jesuits, who were chaplains to certain galleys, agreed to look after their own. A number of Italian priests in the city were about to return to Italy, but at the Bishop's request, they remained to hear the confessions of Italian convicts.

A plan was drawn up. Each galley was to take two or three priests on board for twenty days. The first week should be devoted to teaching the principal points of Catholic doctrine, and for the rest of the time, convicts should be prepared for the reception of the Sacraments. When the first group of galleys had been evangelised, the priests would move on to a second and then to a third, and in this way it was hoped the immense work would be completed in two months.[15] The mission was possibly begun in the second half of March.[16] The Bishop moved from galley to galley, catechising, preaching, hearing confessions, consoling and promising his support to those who complained of unjust treatment. The Missionaries, stimulated by his example, showed marvellous zeal and kindness; they ignored both fatigue and the fact that their hearers were poor convicts, and refused to pay any attention to the opposition which at first they encountered.

---

[15] Marchetty, *Vie de messire J. B. Gault*, Paris, 1650, quarto, p. 247.
[16] In a letter written to Fr. d'Arcy on May 5, J. B. Gault says that the mission began a month and a half ago (Marchetty, *op. cit.*, p. 264; see also p. 246).

They deserved to succeed and did so. An eye-witness writes :[17] 'The most strange and extraordinary sights were now to be seen; men who had not gone to confession for ten or twenty years and who had obstinately made up their minds not to do so as long as they were on the galleys, nevertheless fulfilled this duty; many Turks asked and received the grace of Baptism; numbers of heretics abjured their errors;[18] there were also large numbers of other conversions that might be regarded as miraculous. The grace of God was so efficacious during this mission that there was scarcely a galley-slave who did not make a General Confession and with such great sentiments of contrition that some might have been seen expressing a wish to die at the feet of their Confessor. Ever since the mission, all the convicts have gone to Holy Communion, whilst formerly only three or four were accustomed to make their Easter duty. They have never been so obedient; no longer are they to be heard cursing, blaspheming and denying the name of God. . . . As soon as they are awakened, they all recite together the prescribed prayers, and in the evening, after chanting the Litany of the Blessed Virgin, one of them reads out aloud an Act of Contrition so that the others . . . may make it with him. . . . At midday, a bell is rung to remind them to say the angelical salutation. . . . On Sundays and Holy days they chant Vespers at two o'clock and with such great devotion that those who come to hear them go away more pleased with their singing than with the melody of the trumpets and the sweetness of the hautboys which they intermingle with the chant in order to render the service more solemn. For the rest of the day, whole benchfuls may everywhere be seen assembling and forming groups in which some read the lives of the Saints and others various devotional works.'

Peter de Bausset, Provost of Marseilles, adds that only six of the Catholic convicts refused to approach the Sacraments;[19]

[17] Marchetty, *op. cit.*, p. 256.
[18] Thirty, according to Father du Coudray (*Saint Vincent de Paul*, Vol. II, p. 395).
[19] *Tableau de la vie et de la mort de Monseigneur Jean-Baptiste Gault, évêque de Marseille*, par Pierre de Bausset, Paris, 1643, in 8°, p. 42.

THE GALLEY-SLAVES 327

and even these men might possibly have done so if the mission had lasted longer. Unfortunately, the galleys were unexpectedly ordered to proceed to Catalonia ; on May 11, the only galley remaining in the harbour was the *Monréale*.[20] Now, if the other Missionaries had no further duties to perform, the same did not hold good of the five Priests of the Mission. Several Turks had resolved to embrace the Catholic religion and they had to be instructed and encouraged to persevere in their good resolutions. In order to impress the Turks who had remained faithful to Mahomet, it was decided that the baptism of the neo-converts should be carried out with all possible solemnity. There were ten converts, one of whom lay ill on board the *Monréale* ; he was received into the bosom of the Church a week before the others ; this step was dictated by prudence for it seemed as if he were about to die.[21] On Sunday, May 31, the Feast of the Blessed Trinity, the city of Marseilles gave itself up to public rejoicings ; an immense crowd filled the cathedral and the purifying waters of Baptism flowed over the heads of the nine catechumens. The liturgical ceremonies were carried out in all their majesty and the desired result was produced. Two Turks went to Father du Courday to say that they also renounced their errors.[22] On June 13, Chevalier de la Coste wrote to say that three or four more wished to follow the example of their companions.[23]

The Duchesse d'Aiguillon, by her generosity and influence over the General of the Galleys, had done so much for this mission that the Bishop of Marseilles felt bound to inform her of the miracles of grace that had been worked on the hearts of the galley-slaves. He wrote to her some time in May,[24] on the very day he was about to reconcile four

[20] Ruffi, *op. cit.*, p. 125 ; Marchetty, *op. cit.*, pp. 270, 290.
[21] *Saint Vincent de Paul*, Vol. II, p. 395.   [22] *Ibid.*, p. 398.
[23] *La Compagnie du Très-Saint-Sacrement de l'autel à Marseille*, par Raoul Allier, letter to M. du Coudray, p. 156.
[24] And not March 6 as given by Abelly (*op. cit.*, p. 36). On one hand, the letter to the Duchesse d'Aiguillon takes it for granted that the mission had been going on for some time ; on the other, it was written at least twelve days before that to Father d'Arcy (May 5).

heretics, to invite her to offer up thanks to God for the fruits of the mission. In another letter, written on May 5, to Father D'Arcy, an Oratorian, he also manifested his joy at the results obtained. Nobody indeed had contributed more to the success of the mission than the Bishop himself. Always at work, notwithstanding his feeble health, his ardent zeal inspired him with sufficient energy to conquer all fatigue. His strength, however, at length gave way; on May 11 he had haemorrhage of the lungs and fears began to be entertained for his life. Father du Coudray and his four companions went to ask the Bishop for his blessing; he enquired about the progress of the mission and urgently requested them to continue to labour zealously for the convicts.[25] He declared he was very glad ' to have contracted his illness in the galleys' and ' to die in the service of His Master'; 'that,' said he, ' is to die on the true field of honour.'[26] The saintly bishop expired on May 23, 1643. Death did not take him by surprise; he was awaiting it. The fame of his holiness, increased by the reports of miracles which, as it was said, God multiplied at his intercession, led the King and the Assembly of the Clergy of France to ask for a canonical enquiry into his virtues with a view to his Beatification.

The amelioration of the lot of the galley-slaves was one of the dominating ideas of his episcopate. In 1618, Philip Emmanuel de Gondi, then General of the Galleys, had, most probably at Saint Vincent's suggestion, begun to build a small hospital for convicts which was not completed from lack of funds.[27] John Baptist Gault resolved to make another attempt; in a letter to Father d'Arcy he says that he was moved to do so on account of the slight amount of assistance which sick convicts received ' in body and soul.' He added that ' almost all of them die in a state of abandonment and despair, and they never receive the Sacraments of the Eucharist and Extreme Unction.' The situation, unfortunately, was by no means new, nor was its cause—want of funds. The prelate appealed to the Duchesse

[25] Marchetty, *op. cit.*, p. 289; Bausset, *op. cit.*, p. 42.
[26] Marchetty, *op. cit.*, p. 292.
[27] Ruffi, *La Vie de Monsieur le chevalier de la Coste*, Aix, 1659, in 8⁰, p. 123.

THE GALLEY-SLAVES

d'Aiguillon for help, and she promised 9000 livres. A mere promise, even though he was certain that it would be fulfilled, was not enough to provide the Bishop with the funds he needed for immediate action, and yet he was most anxious to begin at once. All that he could do was to borrow money, but he was terrified at the thought that he might die in debt. The Bishop was anxious to see the Duchess play her part and hence sent Father d'Arcy to pay her a visit. She sent him a bill of exchange for 2000 livres, but the money arrived after his death.[28] If regret that he was dying in debt saddened the Bishop's last moments, the thought that the work, now entrusted to Chevalier de la Coste, could not have been placed in better hands, was his greatest consolation.

Count d'Argenson states that the hospital was completed in two years, thanks to the generosity of the Duchesse d'Aiguillon and the zeal of Saint Vincent de Paul.[29] As soon as the first patients were admitted to the hospital, de la Coste conveyed the good news to both. A few days later,[30] he wrote again to Saint Vincent to give fuller details : ' I cannot express the joy experienced by the poor convicts when they were transferred from this hell to what they call a paradise. The mere arrival in hospital cures them of half their sickness because they are relieved of the vermin with which they are covered ; their feet are washed and they are then put in a bed somewhat softer than the wood on which they are accustomed to lie. They are absolutely delighted to find themselves lying in a bed, tended and treated with a little more charity than they ever had on the galleys, to which we have sent back a large number of convalescents who would have died there.' All that the hospital now needed was official recognition by the King, and this was despatched in July, 1646.[31]

Circumstances did not permit of the Priests of the Mission

[28] On May 29, the Duchesse d'Aiguillon wrote to the prelate who she thought was alive. Her letter is given in Marchetty, *op. cit.*, p. 209.
[29] *Annales de la Compagnie du Saint-Sacrement*, p. 91.
[30] *Saint Vincent de Paul*, Vol. II, p. 526.
[31] There is a copy of this document in the National Archives, Navy section, B⁶ 77, f⁰ 231 ff.

going to Barbary. After the mission to the convicts, Father du Coudray was forced to remain in Provence to negotiate with M. d'Authier on the projected union of the Company of Priests of the Most Blessed Sacrament with the Congregation of the Mission. This, in all probability, was the reason of his departure to Brignoles where he received a letter from Chevalier de la Coste dated June 13 : ' I beseech the Lord . . . that we may always have here three or four of your valiant champions to wage war against the devil, and prevent him from gaining possession of those poor convicts who have been ransomed by Jesus Christ at the price of His blood.'[32] The Chevalier's wish was soon realised. On July 25, after Father du Coudray's return to Paris, the Duchesse d'Aiguillon and Saint Vincent signed an agreement in virtue of which the Congregation of the Mission received 14,000 livres on condition of maintaining four Missionaries in Marseilles. These priests, it is stated, ' shall have authority over the chaplains, whom they may dismiss and replace according as they find it more advantageous for the glory of God. Every five years they shall go aboard each of the galleys at Marseilles and other ports of the kingdom to instruct poor convicts and others on the said galleys in the love of God. They shall also take charge of the hospital for poor galley-slaves at Marseilles.' Saint Vincent also undertook to send Missionaries to Barbary, ' as soon as he shall decide that the time has come to console poor captive Christians there and to instruct them in the faith and in the fear and love of God.'[33]

The Missionaries arrived at Marseilles in the course of the year 1644, under the direction of Francis Dufestel. This new foundation enabled the Saint to discharge more easily his obligations as Chaplain General to the Galleys. This post, hitherto personal, was attached by an edict dated January 16, 1644, to the office of the Superior General of the Mission, and by the same edict, the King allowed the Superiors General to delegate their powers to the Superior of the house at Marseilles.[34] The duties of Chaplain General were very extensive : in the first place he had to

---

[32] Raoul Allier, *op. cit.*, p. 156.
[33] *Saint Vincent de Paul*, Vol. XIII, p. 298.   [34] *Ibid.*, p. 302.

deal with all matters concerning morality and religion; he was also bound to call attention to abuses and acts of injustice, even in temporal matters, of which the convicts might have been victims. He had full authority to visit the galleys to see that all on board were carrying out their duties; convicts, chaplains, gaolers and even physicians. The details into which he was to make enquiries were numerous and varied. Were morning and evening prayers recited regularly and in a becoming manner? Was the name of God blasphemed, and did the officers punish blasphemers? Was loose conduct tolerated on Sundays and Holy days? Was gambling allowed on these days before Mass, and was merchandise sold? Were there any Turks or heretics prepared to enter the Church? Did their co-religionists visit them with the intention of confirming them in their errors? Had the sick, if any, been to Confession? Were they visited and treated by the doctors and surgeons? Did they receive soup, wine and bread? Were women and young boys allowed on board the galleys? Had each convict his shirt, pair of drawers, jacket and thick woollen, hooded cloak? Was the bread of good quality and was there enough of it? Were broad beans served every day? Had each galley a double tent?[35]

If the Missionaries encountered convicts who were particularly miserable and unhappy, or if they came across recently converted Turks or heretics, they paused to console the former and encourage the latter. They returned to the galleys on the vigils and the day before the vigils of the principal Feasts to exhort the convicts to approach the Sacraments, and on these occasions, procured confessors who were able to hear confessions in different languages. Twice a year, in March and October, commissaries visited all the galleys to hold a sort of court of enquiry. All who were found to be actually disabled were set free. The Chaplain General never failed to be present on these occasions to protest in case of need on behalf of such unfortunate men as were wrongly adjudged to be still capable of

[35] *Règlements relatifs aux devoirs des prêtres de la Mission, tant envers les aumôniers des galères qu'envers les forçats.* (Arch. Nat. S. 6707.)

service. The mission was repeated every five years and, as in 1643, infidels might again be seen asking for Baptism, heretics abjuring their errors and hardened sinners throwing themselves at the feet of a priest to obtain forgiveness for their sins.

The spiritual welfare of the convicts demanded as many chaplains as there were galleys, and even some more, for five priests had been added to hear the confessions of Germans, Italians, Irish, Bretons and converted Turks. The chaplains were appointed by the Commissary, approved by the Bishop, and presented by the Chaplain Royal who exercised the authority of a superior, supervised their conduct and, if he were not satisfied with it, dismissed them. The King's Letters Patent declare : ' We decree and most expressly enjoin on our aforesaid Chaplain Royal to insist on having a good priest as chaplain for each galley ; he should be learned, of exemplary life, and experienced in the direction of souls, approved by the Ordinary . . . and that all the said chaplains shall live together in community under the direction and government of our said Chaplain Royal ; and in case the said chaplains are found not to have the necessary qualifications, or do not live as good priests, the said Chaplain Royal shall provide the said galleys with another good priest in place of those not judged suitable, in virtue of the authority conferred on him by these presents.'[36]

Every fortnight, from All Saints to Trinity, conferences were held for the chaplains, in the House of the Mission, on moral and dogmatic theology, spirituality and clerical discipline. Whenever the King gave orders that the *Te Deum* should be chanted, all chaplains assembled on board the *Réale*. The chaplains also put to sea with the galleys, and when the latter were in port, paid three visits a day, to recite morning and evening prayers and to instruct ignorant convicts. On Sundays and Holy days they said Mass on board, chanted Vespers and taught catechism. Each chaplain, in turn, was on duty for a day on the principal galley—the *Réale*—and in case of accidents, it was to this vessel that messengers were to apply for the succours of

[36] Arch. Nat. S. 6707 ; MM 534. f⁰ 239.

THE GALLEY-SLAVES 333

religion. Moreover, each chaplain in turn visited the sick in hospital.[37]

The Superior of the Mission at Marseilles was much concerned about his staff of chaplains. Even with the help of Saint Vincent, who, on more than one occasion, appealed to the good-will of the priests at the Bons Enfants, he found it very difficult to fill vacancies. Moreover, the officers of the galleys, ignoring his rights, selected chaplains as they thought fit.[38] Finally, arrears in the payment of salaries provoked complaints, threats of resignations in a body and an almost general state of laxity. The money allotted to maintain the Convict Hospital and to pay chaplains' salaries came from three sources : revenues from coaches, an annual grant from the King and a very small subscription, three *sols* a day for each patient, to be paid by the Commissaries. For a long period, owing to the troubles caused by the Fronde, the coaches ceased to pay a dividend and the King to keep his promise ; as for the Commissaries, they thought very little about paying their debts. When the chaplains, tired of demanding their salaries without any result, seemed fully determined to leave, the Superior drew on the community funds and Saint Vincent appealed for help to his friends. Peace was restored, but shortly afterwards the trouble began all over again.

To the services rendered by the Missionaries at Marseilles a new one was added in the course of time ; the Fathers gladly acted as intermediaries between the galley-slaves and their families. Saint Vincent encouraged them to do so by his example, for messages and parcels often passed through Saint-Lazare on their way to Marseilles. ' It is very hard,' he wrote to the Superior, ' for poor people to send those small sums to the convicts, by which they assist them from time to time, by any sure way except by us, and it is hard for us to refuse them this act of charity, for it is only a slight inconvenience.'[39] In almost all his letters to Marseilles, between the years 1657 and 1660, we

---

[37] *Saint Vincent de Paul et ses œuvres à Marseille*, par H. Simard, Lyon, 1894, in-8⁰, pp. 178 ff.
[38] *Ibid.*, pp. 193 ff.
[39] *Saint Vincent de Paul*, Vol. VI, p. 316.

come across references to some little commission or another, now he is sending two or three crowns, again a few books, and occasionally only a few coppers. At times, a few lines from the convict's relations are sent with the money.

The Missionaries of Marseilles walked in the footsteps of their holy founder. One of the first arrivals, Louis Robiche, died on January 27, 1645, aged thirty-five; his great charity for the galley-slaves was so well known in the city that the news of his death caused general grief. The people of the city, wrote Saint Vincent, ' flocked to the house in such large numbers that it was feared the floors would give way beneath them; it became necessary to remove the body from the room in which he died and place it in the chapel of the large room on the ground-floor, so that all might have the satisfaction of seeing him. . . . Although the room was very spacious and more than a hundred persons could see him at the same time, nevertheless some clung to the windows outside whilst others mounted on ladders and pieces of timber which they chanced to find. . . . A man of rank got hold of a cushion and actually tore it to pieces with his teeth to have some of the blood that had fallen on it; others scraped the chair on which he was seated; others again took the wax that fell from the tapers, and indeed, if they had been allowed to do so, they would have carried off and broken up everything he had used, even to breaking the statues that were there. . . . People go with great devotion and pray at the place where he is buried.'[40]

In January, 1647, Saint Vincent's first associate, Father Portail, on his return from Italy, made a visitation of the house at Marseilles. Community affairs, and the complicated nature of the questions which he had to settle with the administrators of the galleys, kept him in that city for a long time. He was still there in 1649 when the plague, which carried off eight thousand inhabitants in a few weeks, threw the whole city into a state of grief and consternation. Amongst the victims were Father Brunet, a Vincentian, and Chevalier de la Coste. Father Brunet had been a member of the Congregation since 1627 and so was one of the oldest confrères. Saint Vincent grieved over him as ' a

[40] *Saint Vincent de Paul*, Vol. II, p. 519.

THE GALLEY-SLAVES 335

good labourer of the Lord,' 'a great friend of the poor' and 'a light of the Company.'[41] De la Coste was a 'great servant of God,'[42] a man whom the convicts might justly call their father and protector. He had established, under the title of 'The Gypsy Women,' a cloistered community of penitents who had been accustomed, before their conversion, to follow the galley-slaves for no good purpose. The rule of life was borrowed from that of the Priests of the Mission: rising at four o'clock; the invocation of the Blessed Trinity customary in the Congregation; an hour's mental prayer; reading from the New Testament, kneeling and with the head uncovered; half an hour's spiritual reading; a visit to the Blessed Sacrament before and after leaving the house, in addition to a regular visit every evening before supper; a monthly retreat and an annual retreat of eight clear days to begin every year on October 10. His favourite maxims remind us of those of Saint Vincent de Paul: 'Nothing, however good it may be, should be undertaken with an inordinate desire to succeed, because at the first difficulty our soul will be disturbed; let us leave the result to whatever Divine Providence may ordain.'[43] 'We should work as if we hoped for nothing from God's Providence, and when we have not omitted the smallest detail, the whole success of our efforts should be expected from the same Providence, as if we had done nothing.'[44] De la Coste bequeathed 16,000 livres to the Priests of the Mission at Marseilles for the maintenance of a seminary in that city or in any other place in Provence, or, if the seminary had not been established when he died, to give missions and receive ordinands.[45]

The plague of 1649 drove the galleys from Marseilles; they took refuge in Toulon where they remained by government orders for fifteen years.[46] The chaplains accompanied the galleys, and it became necessary to send one of

[41] *Ibid.*, Vol. III, p. 471.   [42] *Ibid.*, p. 474.
[43] *La vie de Monsieur le chevalier de la Coste*, par le sieur de Ruffi, 1659, in-8⁰, p. 331.
[44] Ruffi, *op. cit.*, p. 308.   [45] *Ibid.*, p. 198.
[46] One of the chief reasons why the galleys were kept for so long at Toulon was the frequent insurrections that broke out in Marseilles. (Arch. Nat. Marine B⁶ 77, f⁰ 388.)

the Fathers of the house at Marseilles to reside with them. Saint Vincent did not like his priests to live alone, but he would have liked even less to abandon the galley-slaves. Charity for these wretched men was of greater importance than the drawbacks of a situation that accorded ill with the ideals of community life. The Priests of the Mission continued to labour for galley-slaves up to the end of the eighteenth century. The plague of 1720, far from diminishing their zeal, did but increase it. Even after seven of their number had fallen in a few days on the field of honour, those spared by the scourge remained courageously at their post. Both the living and the dead were worthy to bear the name of sons of Saint Vincent de Paul.

MARSEILLES IN THE XVIIth CENTURY

CHAPTER XXXIX

SLAVES

SAINT VINCENT'S labours for those in captivity were not confined to Marseilles. Beyond the horizon, on the far side of the Mediterranean, lay the shores of Barbary where wretched men were suffering under the cruel dominion of Turks and occasionally even of renegades. They often turned their eyes towards their native land hoping for assistance, and assistance at length arrived. The man who had stretched out a hand in kindness to the galley-slaves did not forget them.

In the seventeenth century, the word Barbary designated all those lands of North Africa washed by the Mediterranean Sea. Morocco, Algeria, Tunis and Tripoli formed parts of Barbary. The Turks had extended their dominion over this vast territory, and from it defied the nations of Christendom and interfered with their commerce and navigation by incessant piratical raids. In their fast and well-armed vessels they sailed the seas, chased the ships they fell in with, plundered them, massacred those who put up a fight and led the survivors into slavery. They frequently raided the coasts of Spain, France and Italy, marched into the country, plundered houses and broke into convents where devout young women had sought shelter from the dangers of the world; they then returned to their ships, laden with booty and driving before them, like a herd of cattle, the unfortunate inhabitants who had not had time to escape. Neither men, women, children nor the aged were spared. They were pitilessly torn from their homes to be transported to a foreign land and sold at some seaport town in the marketplace, where on the previous evening cattle and horses had been bought and sold. There was little difference between the two scenes, for the slaves were treated like animals;

they had ceased to be human beings and were now simply articles of merchandise. Stripped naked, they stood waiting for inspection; the buyers arrived, examined them, made sure that they were physically sound and then made a selection. The slave had to submit to the most minute and degrading examination; he opened his mouth to show his teeth, trotted, ran, and carried loads to exhibit his strength and agility. The Calvary of these wretched creatures had, however, only begun. Most of them were to continue it in the convict hulks where, fettered in irons and closely supervised by cruel gaolers, they languished away amidst indescribable conditions of filth and squalor. There were twenty convict hulks in Algiers, fourteen in Tunis, five in Bizerte, each of which could accommodate two, three or even four hundred slaves.

Any place, even a stable, was good enough for a slave. In a letter from Bizerte to Saint Vincent[1] the writer says: 'Amongst the slaves here, apart from those in the hulks, I found forty shut up in such a small and narrow stable that they could scarcely move. The only air they can breathe comes from a vent-hole closed with iron bars which is placed high up in the wall. They are chained together in pairs, kept perpetually in confinement, and yet have to work at grinding coffee in a small hand-mill; every day they are bound to grind a fixed amount which far surpasses their strength. These poor people certainly eat the bread of sorrow, and it may well be said that they eat it in the sweat of their brow in this stifling hole, over-burthened with work. Shortly after I had entered to pay them a visit, as I was embracing them in their pitiable plight, I heard cries of women and children mingled with tears and sobs. Raising my eyes to the vent-hole I saw there five poor young Christian slaves, three of whom had each a little child and all were in a state of the most dire want.'

When slaves were removed from these cattle-sheds, to employ the phrase of Saint Vincent's first biographer, it was to cultivate the soil, hew marble in the quarries, row in the galleys or serve on board vessels that pursued Christian ships. As a rule, whilst slaves were at work, they

---

[1] Abelly, *op. cit.*, Bk. II, Ch. I. sect. VII, § 9, p. 127.

wore only a pair of drawers, no matter what the temperature. Blows rained down on their backs, and sometimes with such violence that death supervened, or at least the poor victim was left crippled for life. When the day's work was done, they were led back to the hulks, where, instead of a well earned rest, they had to suffer new agonies and frequently contracted an epidemic disease that put an end to their painful existence. Death was longed for and greeted with joy; many had not even patience to wait for it but anticipated its arrival by suicide.

The slaves were employed as rowers on the galleys, and when, exhausted with fatigue, they slackened speed or rested, the boatswains scourged them without mercy. In certain cases, if, for example, an enemy ship was being pursued or if the galley itself was in flight, woe to those who relaxed : the boatswains cut off an ear or a nose or clove in a man's head with a hatchet. A few mouldy biscuits or a handful of rice with a little fresh water was the only food supplied to the captives, and hence, when the galleys returned to port, they were crowded with sick men.

The lot of those who remained on shore was not much more enviable. 'If these poor men,' wrote an eye-witness,[2] 'endure the utmost misery when at sea, those who remain behind suffer almost as severely; they are compelled to hew marble daily, exposed to the burning rays of the sun which are so strong that I can only compare them to a fiery furnace. It is amazing to see what work and excessive heat they can endure, for the heat is enough to kill horses, and yet these poor Christians do not cease to bear it, and lose only their skin which they yield up as a victim to these devouring flames. One may see them with their tongues hanging out, like poor dogs, on account of the unendurable heat in which they must breathe. One winter's day, a poor old slave, overcome with sickness and no longer able to work, asked leave to withdraw, but the only answer he received, was that he must go on working even if he were to perish on the stone.'

It is true that not all the slaves were so badly treated. Many lived with their masters and were employed on work

[2] Abelly, *op. cit.*, § 7, p. 118.

of an easy nature. The most fortunate even selected their own type of work and deducted part of their wages every month for their masters.

The number of slaves was very great. Abelly speaks of twenty thousand and more in Algiers and its environs, and of five or six thousand in Tunis.

Bad as was their physical condition, their moral state was worse. The Turks endeavoured to make them apostatise, for they believed that every Moslem who converted a Christian was certain to attain Paradise, no matter what heinous crimes he had committed. If the slave was a young girl or a young woman whom her master desired to marry, the poor victim had to battle continuously to preserve her faith, for by the law of Mahomet, a Moslem may not marry a Christian. Moreover, for all slaves there was the attraction of liberty which they regained on the day they put on the turban; it was, no doubt, a relative liberty, for by renouncing their faith they renounced the right of ever again seeing their family and native land. The presence of priests amongst the slaves, far from keeping the latter in the right path, only turned them from it, so pernicious was the example of the former. 'The great dissoluteness,' wrote Saint Vincent,[3] 'reigning amongst these ecclesiastics, discouraged the Christians and caused many to go over to the religion of Mahomet, whilst encouraging the Turks who saw these disorders.'

Such was the deplorable state of the poor slaves in Barbary when Saint Vincent de Paul sent them his Missionaries. The Kings of France had not indeed forgotten the fate of those of their fellow-country-men who groaned in the convict hulks of Barbary; they had vainly attempted, by means of treaties, to put an end to Turkish piracy. The Barbary corsairs paid no attention whatever to such engagements. Louis XIII, towards the end of his reign, asked Saint Vincent to send his priests to Barbary for the corporal and spiritual assistance of Christian captives, and gave him, to that end, from 9,000 to 10,000 livres. The Duchesse d'Aiguillon also wished to share in this good work and on July 25, 1643, signed a contract by which she established a

[3] *Saint Vincent de Paul*, Vol. V, p. 85.

house for Missionaries at Marseilles. It is stated in the contract that the Founder of the Mission would send priests of his Congregation to Barbary, when he judged the time had come, ' to console and instruct poor captive Christians . . . in the faith, love and fear of God and also to give . . . missions, catechetical and other instructions as they are accustomed to do.'[4]

It was a praiseworthy plan but one that seemed difficult to realise, for the Turks, so it was thought, would only tolerate the presence of priests who were slaves. Saint Vincent got round the difficulty. The treaties entered into between France and the Grand Turk allowed the King of France to be represented by consuls in the maritime cities of Turkey and all countries dependent on it, and authorised these consuls to keep a chaplain in their houses. Hence it was as chaplain to Lenge de Martin, consul at Tunis, that Julian Guérin, Priest of the Mission, arrived in that city on November 22, 1645, accompanied by a lay-brother, Francis Francillon.

Before Father Guérin could arrive at an accurate knowledge of his environment he was bound to use the greatest prudence. At first he exercised his ministry in secret, but little by little, encouraged by the friendly attitude of the Moslems, he grew bolder, allowed them to see what he really was, established chapels in the hulks, and celebrated divine worship in public. ' You would be delighted,' he wrote,[5] ' to hear the *Exaudiat* and other prayers for the King of France chanted in our churches and chapels on all Sundays and Holy days ; even foreigners show marks of respect and affection for him ; and you would rejoice to see with what devotion these poor captives offer up prayers for all their benefactors who, they know, either live in France as a rule or come from France, and it is no small consolation to see how men of all nations, in their chains and irons, pray to God for the King of France.'

On the approach of Easter, Father Guérin redoubled his efforts so that every Catholic slave might be able to make his Easter duty. He was not afraid of the dangers to be

---

[4] *Ibid.*, Vol. XIII, p. 300.
[5] Abelly, *op. cit.*, Bk. II, Ch. I, sect. VII, par. 7, par. 122.

encountered on the roads, and frequently went without an escort to the place on which he had decided, trusting to Providence which, on more than one occasion, protected him from the attacks of brigands. Hearing, on Easter Sunday, 1647, that an Algerine galley, with a crew of three hundred slaves, lay anchored in the port of Bizerte, he at once set off to visit it. For ten days, helped by another priest, he catechised these poor men, several of whom had not practised their religion for twenty years, and had the happiness to hear their confessions and give Holy Communion to them all, with the exception of a few Greek schismatics. Every morning the slaves laid aside their chains, left the galley and assisted at Mass in a private house. Father Guérin's zeal attracted the admiration even of the Turks who went to embrace him and kiss his hands. The master of the house where he lodged refused to accept payment, for, as he said, ' he was happy to do an act of charity to those who were charitable to others.' Even the Dey of Tunis proved benevolent ; Father Guérin was aware of this and hence he went and told the Dey quite freely that he needed another helper in his work for the slaves. ' Not only,' replied the Dey, ' do I give you permission to bring another Missionary from France, but if necessary, two or three. You are here, I know, to do good and not evil. Do not be afraid to come and see me whenever you need my protection ; I will never refuse it.' Father Guérin at once wrote to Saint Vincent who selected a young priest remarkable both for his exceptional ability and admirable zeal, John Le Vacher, whose life and martyrdom have recently been recounted by a retiring scholar, Father Gleizes, of the Congregation of the Mission.[6] Father Le Vacher landed at Tunis on November 22, 1647. The two Missionaries were worthy of each other, and if only Divine Providence had left them long enough together, no one could tell what good they might not have effected. Father Le Vacher had barely time to become acquainted with Father Guérin and to profit by his advice and experience. Early in 1648 the plague broke out and raged with particular violence in the hulks. The two priests went from one dying man to another pre-

[6] *Jean Le Vacher*, Paris, 1914, in-12.

pared to sacrifice their lives, if such was God's Will, in the performance of their duty.

Father Le Vacher was attacked in May, and for a moment, all hope seemed lost. However, he recovered, and Father Guérin sent the good news to Saint Vincent that he might share in it. ' It is impossible,' he wrote, ' for me to tell you how great were the sighs, groans, and tears of the poor slaves, of the merchants, of the Consul, and how much they consoled us. Even the Turks visited us in our affliction, and the most eminent persons in the city of Tunis sent to offer me their help and assistance. To conclude, Sir, I see clearly that it is well to serve God faithfully since He raises up, in the midst of our tribulations, even His enemies to succour and assist His poor servants. We are afflicted by war, famine and pestilence, even to an excessive degree, and as well as that, we are without money ; but as far as courage is concerned, we have plenty of it. God be thanked, we no longer fear the plague any more than if it had never existed. The joy our brother and I feel at the recovery of our dear Father Le Vacher has rendered us as strong as the lions in our mountains.'[7] Saint Vincent's joy was not of long duration ; a few days later, he had a letter from Father Le Vacher to say that Father Guérin had died on May 25, a victim of his zeal for the plague-stricken. Two months later, the French Consul died of the disease, and Father Le Vacher and Brother Francillon were left all alone. At the request of the merchants, and by command of the Dey, Le Vacher was forced to act as temporary consul.

Two years previously, the Duchesse d'Aiguillon had purchased the consulate of Algiers for the Congregation of the Mission and obtained from the King for its Superior General the right of nomination to the post. The death of Lange de Martin gave her the idea of also purchasing the consulate of Tunis, which she did. Her idea was to prevent any rivalry or even disagreement, at least of a permanent nature, between the consuls and the Missionaries, by placing both under the sole direction of the holy founder of the mission. Saint Vincent selected a cleric of his Congregation, one Benjamin Huguier, formerly a procurator of the

[7] Abelly, *op. cit.*, Bk. II, Ch. I, sect. VII, § 1, p. 95.

Châtelet in Paris, for the post of Consul at Tunis. Father Le Vacher was impatiently expecting the nomination, and was grievously disappointed to hear that the Dey insisted on his remaining at his post. He courageously resumed the yoke, aided until 1652 by Huguier, whom he appointed Chancellor. He was by no means pleased to carry out the duties of consul, for it was a heavy burden owing to the responsibilities and worries it entailed. France was, in the eyes of the Turkish authorities, the official protector of all Christians, whether Italians, Greeks, Spaniards, Portuguese, Flemings or Germans. Only the English were excepted. Hence it was his duty to put forward all claims made by Christians whose rights had been violated. He had also to deliver letters of clearance to vessels setting out from the ports of Barbary, to protest against captures made by pirates and to demand restitution, to negotiate the redemption of slaves, to act as arbitrator in all disputes between merchants and their slaves, to prevent merchants from importing into Turkish dominions all such goods as were prohibited by ecclesiastical law and the royal edicts, such as sails, ropes, iron, lead and military equipment. As a Missionary, Father Le Vacher had other and no less absorbing occupations. As Vicar General of the Archbishop of Carthage, he had jurisdiction over all Christians residing in Tunis, both merchants and slaves. Priests and members of religious Orders who were slaves received all their faculties through him. It was his duty to organise religious worship, administer the Sacraments, strengthen the faithful in their religion, bring back wandering sheep to the fold, preach, instruct and console. In a word, he was a pastor, and as there was no other priest residing within the territory of the Dey of Tunis, one may judge of the crushing burden of work he had to get through daily if he was to carry out all his duties. It was perfectly clear that it would have been much better if the office of consul was in the hands of another, but as long as the Dey, Hadji Mahammed, was in authority, he had to endure it. The death of the Dey removed the sole obstacle which had kept Father Le Vacher at this post ever since 1648.

The new consul, Martin Husson, a young lawyer of the

Parliament, arrived in Tunis in July, 1653. Saint Vincent had a high idea of his virtue and character as may be seen from the letter he then wrote to Father Le Vacher : ' Here at last is M. Husson. . . . I beg you to give him a gracious welcome for he is one of the most accomplished men of his profession with whom I am acquainted. His virtue will soon be revealed to you, I do not say in all its actual extent, for it surpasses what one may imagine, but quite enough of it to oblige you to treat him with the utmost consideration. He is not only wise, courteous, active and devout, but also a thoroughly good man of business, always ready to do what he can for the good of his neighbour. He is leaving here to serve God and the poor in Barbary, notwithstanding its remoteness and the dangers to be encountered by sea and land. He is leaving Paris, where he is a Parliamentary lawyer, and his relations who love him tenderly and who have striven to keep him at home by many tears, remonstrances and contrivances. Such detachment is most certainly admirable at his age and so, too, is the purity of intention with which he now undertakes this journey ; hence he will not only lead a community life with you, but will not make any arrangement save with your consent. Furthermore, he is so gracious to all, so courteous to his friends and so obedient to his spiritual guide that when you see what he will be to you, you will feel obliged to be the same to him. And hence I need not recommend you, Sir, to take the initiative in showing him honour, confidence and kindness, or in deferring to him as much as possible, especially in all consular affairs, because, with the help of God, both of you will be of one heart and mind.'[8]

Husson would not leave Paris without paying a visit to Saint-Lazare where Saint Vincent saw him on Easter Sunday and gave him written instructions as to his future line of action.[9] This document, also intended for Father Le Vacher, is full of excellent advice, one piece of which should be especially noted : ' Let them obey the laws of the country, except those that concern religion, on which subject let them never dispute or say anything in contempt

[8] *Saint Vincent de Paul*, Vol. IV, p. 625.
[9] Abelly, *op. cit.*, Bk. III, Ch. XXIV, p. 335.

of it.'[10] Saint Vincent had advised them to be of one mind and one heart, and seldom has advice been better followed. During the four years they lived together, they were united by bonds of friendship that never relaxed; they had the same joys, and the same sorrows.

They had many opportunities to exercise patience. The Dey, who was credulous and easily offended, was inclined to listen to false accusations. He summoned Father Le Vacher one day and said: 'I have been pained to hear that you are preventing Christians from embracing the law of Mahomet; I command you to leave the city and never return.' The Missionary obeyed, went to Bizerte and wrote to Saint Vincent to know what he should do. There were two vessels full of Christian slaves lying in the harbour, and instead of simply waiting for the Superior General's reply, Father Le Vacher made good use of his enforced leisure: he interviewed the slaves and disposed them by his exhortations to receive the Sacraments. The Dey, in the meantime, was convinced by Husson that he had made a mistake; thoroughly frightened at the possible consequences of his action, he expressed his regret and sent word to the Governor of Bizerte to send Father Le Vacher back to Tunis within a month. The slaves in Tunis bewailed Father Le Vacher's departure; they were deeply distressed at the thought of losing him; they prayed, fasted and heard Masses to obtain from God the grace of seeing their beloved Father once more. His return filled them with joy; those who were able to do so went to meet him and ran to embrace him. This touching sight showed Father Le Vacher how deeply he was loved and attached him still more strongly to the flock committed to him by the Shepherd of Souls. Shortly after this incident, another affair had to be settled. Although the importation of cotton sail-cloth into Turkish dominions was forbidden by French laws and even by the Holy See, under pain of excommunication, the Dey had hopes that the Consul would, at his request, have some imported from France, but in this he was disappointed. Husson gave a polite refusal to this impertinent request. The Dey, failing on this side, turned to another and succeeded in corrupting

[10] *Saint Vincent de Paul*, Vol. XIII, p. 364.

a merchant from Marseilles, then in Tunis, by a very heavy bribe. The Consul, after vainly endeavouring to induce the merchant to abandon his evil designs, informed the King of France so that every precaution might be taken in all the sea-port towns of Provence and Languedoc to prevent the despatch of cotton sail-cloth. As a result the Dey was greatly annoyed both with Husson and Father Le Vacher, who had acted in concert with his colleague. As an opportunity of avenging himself was slow in coming, the Dey seized on a pretext to summon the Missionary to his palace. ' Chevalier de la Ferrière,' he said, ' owes me seventy-five piastres ; I want you to pay me, because by your religion, you share alike in good and bad fortune.' Father Le Vacher had no difficulty in disposing of such a puerile pretext, but the Dey was not thinking so much of the pretext as the money. He simply replied : ' You may say what you like ; I mean to have the money.' As he took violent measures, the seventy-five piastres had to be paid down. Saint Vincent, after relating this incident to his community, added : ' And that is only a beginning ; for if God does not change the Dey's disposition, they are on the eve of suffering even still greater acts of oppression. Now indeed they may say they are really beginning to be Christians, for they are beginning to suffer for serving Jesus Christ, as Saint Ignatius the Martyr said when he was being led to martyrdom.'[11]

Not only did God not change the Dey's disposition, but he even allowed it to become more threatening. The capture of a Barbary vessel by a French ship, and the sale at Leghorn of thirteen Turks who had been captured, renewed his desire for revenge. He sent for the Consul and in harsh language threatened him with expulsion if he did not promise to obtain the release of the prisoners. ' You are asking me for what is impossible,' said Husson, ' for the masters to whom the slaves now belong are not subjects of the King of France but of the Duke of Tuscany.' ' That is nothing to me,' replied the Dey, ' I withdraw your authorisation to remain in Tunis and even in all places under my authority ; depart, let me never see you again.'

So Father Le Vacher was left alone with Brother Francis

[11] *Ibid.*, Vol. XI, p. 335.

Francillon. It was feared he, too, might experience the effects of the Dey's anger, but nothing happened. He was ordered by the Dey to take up the duties of Consul until Husson's successor should arrive.

The difficulty of replacing Husson, the plight of M. Barreau, a cleric of the Congregation of the Mission who was Consul at Algiers and laden with debts, together with Rome's refusal to allow priests to act as consuls, led Saint Vincent to ask himself whether it would not be better to sell or farm out the consulates. He was personally inclined to this solution, and if he did not adopt it, this was due to the influence of the Duchesse d'Aiguillon, who thought otherwise. She brought forward some excellent reasons.[12] ' She thinks,' writes Saint Vincent, ' that our priests would have no certainty of being able to assist the poor slaves if they were living under consuls who had private interests to look after, who would be governed by other principles than those of charity and the public good, and who consequently might hinder the fruition and continuance of their priestly functions, cause them to be insulted, if not worse, in order to get rid of them so that there might be no one to keep an eye on their own conduct or offend them in any way.' There was also another solution : to recall the Missionaries, sell the consulates, and leave the Christian slaves to be attended to by priests who were in captivity. Saint Vincent would not entertain this idea for a moment ; to abandon the slaves would have seemed to him an act of base cowardice ' A Missionary,'[13] he wrote to someone who made this proposal, ' is, as it seems to me, needed in that country both to assist the slaves when they are ill and to strengthen them in the Faith at all times. It is true that priests and members of religious Orders who are slaves could supply the need, but they don't. They themselves are so badly conducted that someone in authority is needed to keep them in order ; moreover, there is reason to doubt whether sacraments administered by many of them to the poor captives would be valid. Now, if the salvation of even one soul is of such importance that we are bound to risk our life to procure it,

[12] *Saint Vincent de Paul*, Vol. VI, p. 315.
[13] *Ibid.*, Vol. VII, p. 117.

how can we abandon such numbers of souls through fear of incurring expense? And even if there were no other good result from our holding these positions than that of revealing the beauty of our holy religion to this accursed land, by sending thither men who gladly cross the seas, leave home and comfort, and expose themselves to a thousand insults and outrages for the consolation of their brethren in affliction, I think that both men and money would be well spent.'

So Father Le Vacher remained at his post and continued to fulfil the double rôle of Consul and Missionary from 1657 to 1666. He was greeted as a saviour by the slaves in Tunis, Bizerte, and wherever he went all over the country; although chiefly preoccupied with the care of their souls, he did not forget the body, and his arrival was usually the occasion of a little feast in which he shared with the slaves. Once the poor captives had seen him, they were touched to the heart by his kindness, treasured his words of wisdom, and felt strengthened in the faith and better prepared to face their trials. If we wish to form some idea of these visits we cannot do better than listen to Saint Vincent telling his Missionaries of one of Father Le Vacher's journeys to Bizerte where a galley full of slaves had just arrived from Algiers. ' As soon as ever he could be seen from the galley and recognised by his dress, these poor folk with loud cries began to manifest their joy, crying out : " There is our liberator ; our pastor, our father, etc." Scarcely had he gone aboard the galley than all these poor slaves threw themselves on him, weeping with joy and tenderness at the sight of their liberator in body and soul, and they even fell on their knees, some of them clinging to his cassock, others to his great-coat, in such fashion as to tear it, so greatly did they desire to get close to him. It took him more than an hour to make his way through the galley to pay his respects to the captain, because they hindered his passage and he could not move, so great was the cheering and delight of those poor men. The captain gave orders for every man to take up his position, and most courteously welcomed this good priest ; he told him that he had the highest esteem for the charity and behaviour of Christians in thus helping each other in their afflictions. Afterwards, dear Father Le Vacher bought three bullocks, the fattest he could find, and had them slaughtered and distributed the meat amongst them; he also had plenty of bread baked, and in this way gave the slaves a feast for the body whilst also doing his best to supply them with spiritual food (which is much more necessary for the glory of God), catechising and instructing them in the mysteries of our most holy Faith, and in fine, comforting them with the greatest charity. This lasted for eight days and brought a multitude of blessings and consolations on those poor convicts who called him their liberator and consoler, for he had in truth replenished them with food for both body and soul.'[14]

This zeal on behalf of the slaves charmed not only Saint Vincent, but even the Dey expressed his admiration and congratulated Father Le Vacher on his return to Tunis. When the Missionary in his modesty said that the congratulations were really due to those who, by their alms, had enabled him to perform such acts of charity, the Dey replied that the merit of others did not in any way detract from his own. ' O my Saviour,' cried Saint Vincent, when relating this incident, ' O Gentlemen! What good can a priest not do? You see how he makes even infidels respect our religion.'

Whilst John Le Vacher was thus devoting his life to the slaves in Tunisia, his brother Philip was showing similar apostolic zeal by the services he was rendering the slaves of Algeria amidst even greater difficulties. The first Missionaries arrived in Algeria in 1646. There were two, a priest and a cleric; the priest, Boniface Nouelly, attended to the spiritual welfare of the slaves, whilst the cleric, John Barreau, formerly a lawyer of the Parliament of Paris, took over the consulate which the Duchesse d'Aiguillon had just purchased and presented to Saint Vincent. Father Nouelly seemed by his rare qualities to be just the man for the work to which he had been appointed; he had a great fund of devotedness and self-sacrifice; he was prepared to offer his life for the slaves, and actually did so. The plague of 1647-1648 was one of the most disastrous in the history of

[14] *Saint Vincent de Paul*, Vol. XI, pp. 447 ff.

the city of Algiers, in which plague was almost endemic. Father Nouelly's zeal was only increased by the danger; the slaves were dying; he was their pastor, and if he did not visit them, who would prepare them at their last hour? As he was constantly to be found amongst the plague-stricken he could not possibly escape and was carried off by the disease on July 22, 1647.

He was succeeded by James Lesage, who also fell a victim to the plague after he had been only two months in Algiers. John Dieppe took his place and expired in the flower of his young manhood, for he arrived in Barbary only to die. These three holy Missionaries might have prolonged their lives by avoiding danger, but Saint Vincent had taught them too well the beauty of sacrifice. Instead of their temporal life they preferred the eternal welfare of the dying to whom they bore, with the grace that cleanses from sin, the Bread that gives strength against the last assaults of the enemy of man.

From May 2, 1649, to the end of 1651, John Barreau remained alone. Saint Vincent's hesitation as to which of his priests he should send and the hostile attitude of the Turks, who had kept the Consul in prison for seven months, were the chief causes of the delay. At length, after two long years of waiting, Barreau had the joy of embracing Philip Le Vacher. Both these men thoroughly understood and loved each other. 'I have learned,' wrote Saint Vincent to them some time later,[15] ' of the close friendship and intimate charity that reigns between you; I have thanked God for it ever since, and I will do so as often as I think of it, so deeply has my soul been moved with gratitude for so great a blessing which rejoices the heart of God Himself; all the more so as from this union He will bring about an infinite number of good results for the advancement of His own glory and the salvation of souls. In the name of God, Gentlemen, let you, for your part, do all that in you lies to render this union more firm and more cordial even unto eternity, remembering the Roman maxim that by union and taking counsel success is finally achieved. Yes, united you will make a success of God's work which nothing can

[15] Abelly, *op. cit.*, Bk. II, Ch. I, sect. VII, § 2, p. 100.

destroy but disunion, and this work is the practice of the most exalted, though the least sought after form of charity that can possibly be exercised on this earth. O Gentlemen! would that we had a clearer intuition of the excellence of apostolic labours so that we might have an infinite esteem of our good fortune, and correspond with the duties of our state! All that is needed to produce the most wonderful fruits in the Church is simply ten or twelve Missionaries so enlightened. Heaven and earth regard with pleasure the happy lot that has fallen to you of honouring, by your labours, the incomprehensible charity that brought Our Lord to earth to succour and help us in our slavery. I do not think there is an angel or saint in Heaven who does not, as far as the state of glory permits, envy you this good fortune, and although I am the most hateful of all sinners, I confess nevertheless that if I were permitted, I would envy you myself. . . . Seldom is anything good done without pain; the devil is too subtle and the world too corrupt not to make every effort to stifle such a good work in its cradle; but courage! Gentlemen, it is God Himself Who has placed you in your present position and employment; having His glory as your end, what can you fear, or rather, what may you not hope for?'

Missionaries who had not been forewarned might easily be shipwrecked on certain reefs, and compromise the work of God. Saint Vincent pointed out three special dangers to Father Le Vacher. The first is a too rigorous exercise of his rights as Vicar General of Carthage. 'I beg you,' wrote the Saint,[16] ' to condescend as much as you can to human frailty; you will win slaves who are ecclesiastics far more by sympathising with them than by rebuffs and reprimands. They are not wanting in light but in strength which secures an entrance to the heart by the external unction of kind words and good example. I do not say that their disorderly conduct should be either authorised or condoned, but I do say that the remedies to be employed should be mild and gentle, seeing the state in which they are, and applied with the utmost discretion, both on account of the locality and of the harm these men cause you should

[16] *Saint Vincent de Paul*, Vol. IV, p. 120 ff.

you displease them, and not only you, but the Consul also and the work of God; for they will be able to convey impressions to the Turks which may lead the latter not to tolerate you in that country in the future.' The second danger lay in his relations with the Turks and renegades. ' In the name of Our Lord,' Saint Vincent says, ' have no intercourse with these people; do not expose yourself to the dangers that may arise from doing so, for by exposing yourself, as I have said, you would expose the whole work to peril and would do a great wrong to the poor Christians, inasmuch as they would no longer receive any assistance and you would close the door for the future to the liberty we now enjoy of rendering some service to God in Algiers and other places. . . . It is easier and of greater importance to prevent a number of slaves from apostatising than to convert a single renegade. A doctor who preserves us from illness is far better than one who effects a cure. You have not been charged with the souls of Turks or renegades, and your mission does not extend to them, but to poor Christian captives.' Philip Le Vacher fell into another fault, excessive zeal, for which Saint Vincent gently chided him. ' We have great reason,' he wrote, ' to thank God for the zeal He has given you for the salvation of poor slaves; but such zeal is not good unless it is discreet. It would seem as if you are trying to do too much in the beginning, such as wishing to give a mission in the hulks, to go and live there and to introduce new devotional exercises amongst these poor people. And that is my reason for begging you to follow the customs of our dead priests who went before you. Good works are often spoiled because we go too fast, for then we act according to our own inclinations which hurry away the mind and reason, and make us think that the good which we see there, to be done is actually feasible and opportune; such is not the case, and we recognise the fact subsequently by our ill success. What God effects is effected almost of itself, without our thinking about it. . . . Be passive rather than active, and then God will effect by you alone what all men together cannot effect without Him.'

' If what God effects is effected almost of itself,' still it is not always effected without difficulty, especially in the surroundings in which the Missionaries were living at Algiers. Of this John Barreau had bitter experience. A religious of the Order of Mercy, Father Sebastian Brugière, in order to obtain the release of some slaves, had borrowed 40,000 livres which he was unable to repay. He was thrown into a dungeon and fell ill; on that account he was allowed to retire to the Consul's house, after giving a promise not to leave the country. Barreau, who had just arrived in Algiers, was a soft-hearted man; he was touched by the lot of the poor religious, and in an outburst of generosity, he guaranteed to pay his debts. This kind act was also an imprudent one, and Barreau, who was just as insolvent as Father Sebastian, was thrown into prison on June 26, 1647. He was still there on July 20 when he heard that his confrère, Father Nouelly, was gravely ill of the plague. He asked for and obtained his liberty.

He was imprisoned again in 1650, for refusing to pay out of his own private funds the debts of a Christian who had absconded. After five months, as he had not yet been set free, official steps were taken to secure his release. On January 15, 1651, Saint Vincent wrote to him: ' The King was away from Paris for the last six or seven months, and on his return, we did our best to procure you this boon. It was finally decided to write to Constantinople and that the King would make a formal complaint to the Porte about your imprisonment, and ask that the articles of peace and alliance entered into between Henry IV and the Grand Signor, in the year one thousand six hundred and four, should be carried out, and that therefore the Turks should cease from their attacks on the French and hand over the slaves in their possession; otherwise, His Majesty would see that justice should be done. We shall, with the help of God, do our best to see that this is carried out quickly, and, it will be for Providence to do the rest. . . . Perhaps It will be propitious in our regard and deliver you from prison and distress by some shorter road than that of Constantinople.' The ' shorter road ' was the removal of the Pasha. About two months later, Pasha Murath was succeeded by Pasha Mahomet. Before Murath left his post, he preferred not to give his successor an opportunity of laying hands on the money demanded from the prisoner, and he became conciliatory; he was satisfied with 10,000 livres which the Consul gave him.[17]

After six years of relative tranquillity, Barreau was subjected to another hard experience, occasioned by the bankruptcy of a Marseilles merchant, which proved to be far more severe than any that had preceded. The man's creditors brought the case before Pasha Ibrahim II, and as usual, the French Consul was called on to pay the absconding merchant's debts. He refused to do so and the Pasha ordered him to be thrown down and bastinadoed; the agony was so intense that the victim lost consciousness. The Pasha, however, was not satisfied, for his determination to gain his end had stifled every sentiment of pity in his heart. He ordered the executioner to drive in pointed awls between the flesh and the finger-nails; the consul, maddened with pain, promised to pay twelve thousand livres.. Whereupon he was allowed to leave, or rather to be carried home, for he was unable to move. Scarcely had he been put to bed than four satellites arrived for the money with an order that if it was not produced at once, he was to be brought back to the Pasha to be tortured to death. The consul had only a hundred crowns, but the slaves, hearing of his danger, came in crowds, and taking from their pockets the money they had so painfully amassed, made up the amount demanded.

The post of consul, as may be seen, was not an enviable one; he was the scapegoat on whom the Turks wreaked their anger whenever the Christians had given them any grounds for complaint. In the beginning of 1658, Barreau was again maltreated for the same reason as before; a Marseilles merchant refused to pay his debts. A few months later, a far graver incident rendered Saint Vincent seriously uneasy. The governor of the French fort was obliged to pay an annual tax, but neglected to do so. The Pasha, after summoning him in vain to appear, resolved to send a troop of a thousand soldiers against him. Faced with this danger, the Governor put on board a ship all that he most valued, as well as sixty Arabs and four horses and set sail for Leghorn. The news provoked a riot amongst the Algerians, who seized

[17] *Saint Vincent de Paul*, Vol. IV, p. 140.

on the property of all French merchants, and the consul was again thrown into prison. Vincent de Paul feared for his life, but the Saint's mind was soon relieved, for the news of the consul's release arrived almost as soon as that of his imprisonment.

Philip Le Vacher was less exposed to outrages on the part of the Turks; his greater prudence may have afforded fewer opportunities for their malice. He converted Moslems and reconciled renegades, thus exposing himself to severe punishments; but he always managed to surround the conversions with such a veil of mystery that the Turks never knew what had really happened. The approach of Easter meant exceptionally heavy work, because, as he could not hear the slaves' confessions during the day, he had, every year, to spend seven or eight nights amongst them, preparing them for the Festival. There was an abundant harvest; not only did hardened sinners return to God, but heretics also abjured their errors.

It is a great pity that the story of the African Church in the seventeenth century has never been written. It would have contained thousands of edifying details, worthy of the early days of the Church, revealing both the devotedness of the Missionaries and the glorious heroism of the slaves. The little that remains deserves to be recorded.

We have already spoken of the sad fate of the Barbary slaves and the absolute necessity of the work undertaken by Saint Vincent. Those of his sons whom he sent there showed themselves fully deserving of his confidence. Their first care was to make arrangements for divine worship; they set up chapels in the hulks and suggested to the priest-slaves that they should exercise their ministry there. The latter, freed from all work and from their fetters, thanks to a pecuniary indemnity paid to their masters, were quite pleased to fulfil an obligation more in conformity with their sacerdotal office. The slaves themselves contributed to the maintenance of worship and the support of the chaplains. 'High Mass and divine service were celebrated on Sundays and Holy days,' writes Abelly, 'with as much solemnity as in a parish in Paris.' A small lamp burned day and night before the Blessed Sacrament. Every year, on the Feast of Corpus

Christi, the Blessed Sacrament was exposed and even carried in procession within the walls of the chapel between two rows of the faithful who followed It devoutly bearing tapers in their hands. When the Viaticum was carried to a sick man in the hulks Our Divine Saviour received similar tokens of reverence. If a priest had to go through the city to administer Holy Communion to the sick he was preceded by a Christian; the only external sign of their errand was that they saluted no one on the way. The Christian slaves who were at liberty and free to do so, then followed in silence, except in Algiers, where such processions would have led to riots. Apart from the chapels in the hulks, there was a larger and more beautiful chapel in the consulate; this was the consul's chapel as well as that of the Christian merchants. The chapel in Tunis was dedicated to Saint Louis of France; that in Algiers to Saint Cyprian, Bishop of Carthage.

The Missionaries in Barbary carried out most of the religious exercises observed in the parish churches of France. They erected Confraternities, some of which, and especially those of the Blessed Sacrament, of the Holy Rosary, of Our Lady of Mount Carmel, of the Holy Souls in Purgatory, had large numbers of members. On the patronal feast of each Confraternity there was a sermon and the traditional procession. The Forty Hours were devoutly celebrated, and the Jubilee attracted as many to the Sacrament of Penance as Easter Sunday.

The religious practices of the Christian slaves helped to preserve them in the faith of their fathers, and even exercised a salutary influence on heretics, apostates and Turks; as may be seen from the following letter written to Saint Vincent: ' We have a great harvest in this country, and it has grown even greater on account of the plague; for, apart from the Turks who were converted to our faith, and whose conversion we keep secret, there are many others whose eyes have been opened, at the hour of death, and who have recognised and embraced the truths of our holy religion. We have had in particular three renegades who, after receiving the Sacraments, have gone to Heaven. There was another some time ago who, after being absolved from apostasy, was surrounded at the hour of death by Turks. The latter urged him to utter some blasphemies, as they are wont to do on such occasions, but he would never consent, and keeping his eyes raised to Heaven and holding a crucifix to his breast, died a true penitent. . . . His wife who also had denied the faith and who was once a professed nun, has likewise been absolved from her twofold apostasy, having manifested all the necessary good dispositions. At present she always remains at home, never goes out, and we have told her to make two hours' mental prayer daily, and perform some bodily acts of penance, in addition to those prescribed by her rule ; but of her own accord she performs many more in addition, so deeply does she regret her former sins, and she would willingly expose herself to martyrdom to expiate them, if she had not two little children whom we have baptised and whom she is now rearing devoutly, like a true Christian mother. . . . Another renegade died who was living near us and he too ended his days like a true Christian penitent. I am waiting from day to day to baptise some other Turks who are well instructed and most fervent for our religion. They often come to me at night in secret. There is also another of them, a man of rank in this country.'[18] If the letter, as seems probable, was written by Fr. Guérin, this important personage was none other than the son of the Dey of Tunis who, as a matter of fact, became a convert and fled to Sicily to practise Christianity freely. If the Turks had laid hold of this letter, the writer would have paid for his imprudence with his life. The Missionaries, as a rule, showed themselves much more reserved ; they preferred either to say nothing to their correspondents about the conversions of Turks or expressed themselves in such veiled language as the following : ' Our Lord has given us the grace to recover two lost precious stones ; they are of great value and of quite celestial splendour ; this has caused me much pleasure.'[19]

In 1646 Fr. Guérin had the happiness of converting three English slaves, one of whom, a lad eleven years old, was remarkable both for his fervent piety and good looks. The child used to pray every day to the Blessed Virgin for the

[18] Abelly, *op. cit.*, Bk. II, Ch. I, sect. VII, § 10, p. 134.
[19] Abelly, *ibid.*, p. 135.

grace of holding fast to the faith. His master, in order to win him to Mahomedanism, used promises and threats alternately, gifts and blows. ' Cut off my head, if you like,' said the child, ' I am a Christian and intend to remain one.' Fr. Guérin ends the letter, in which these facts are related, with the following remark ; ' At such a young and tender age, his whole life is really wonderful ; I can truly say he is a little temple in which the Holy Ghost abides.'[20]

The young English slave had imitators. John Le Vacher, in one of his letters, recounts the touching story of two children, about fifteen years old, one English and one French, who were slaves of different masters in Tunis. They met frequently, played together, and after the English lad, a Protestant, had been converted by the French boy, who was a Catholic, they encouraged each other in the faith they held in common. Some English Protestant merchants, who arrived in Tunis to ransom their fellow-countrymen, put the boy's name down on their list, but rather than be regarded as a Protestant, he preferred slavery to liberty. Slavery, was, however, very painful, for both boys belonged to fanatical Turks who were prepared to go any lengths to force them to apostatise. One day, the English boy secretly entered the house where his friend dwelt and found him lying on the ground, beaten black and blue. As he could not see any sign of life in the body, he was afraid his companion was dead ; he ventured to call out his name and the French boy answered : ' I will remain a Christian all my life.' The English child knelt down to kiss the bleeding feet of his friend and whilst he was doing so, the Turks entered the room. ' What are you doing ? ' they asked in astonishment. They received the following moving reply : ' I am honoring those limbs that have just suffered for Jesus Christ, my Saviour and my God.' He was insulted and driven out of the house, but walked away quite peacefully. A few days later, a similar scene was played, but the rôles were reversed. It was now the English boy who was lying half-dead in the midst of his torturers when the French child entered. The sight of his friend gave the latter courage. ' Which do you

[20] Abelly, *op. cit.*, Bk. II, Ch. I, sect. VII, § 1, p. 135.

choose,' he asked the poor victim, 'Jesus Christ or Mahomet?'—'Jesus Christ,' replied the young martyr, 'I am a Christian and intend to die one.' The Turks were enraged and one of them who had two large knives in his girdle said to the courageous French boy: 'Do you want me to cut off your ears?'—'I am not a bit afraid of you,' was the reply and, snatching the knife from the Turk, he cut off an ear which he handed to the stupefied man, saying: 'Take this; do you want the other one?' The knife was taken away from the boy to prevent him repeating the deed. After this, the Turks gave up all hope of converting the two boys and ceased to maltreat them. This world was not made for such angels; both died of the plague in the following year.

The grace of martyrdom, denied to them, was granted to a young man, twenty-one years old, named Peter Borguny, a native of Majorca. Threatened with being sent to the galleys at Constantinople, from which he would never return, he lost heart and went to implore mercy of the Pasha who, taking advantage of his fears, induced him to apostatise. Remorse followed close after his fall, and to repair the scandal, Peter Borguny, in the presence of any who cared to listen, vehemently abused the Mahomedan religion, with which he contrasted the beauty of the Christian faith. At times, he trembled at the fear of being tortured, but quickly recovered when he thought that Jesus Christ would be there to help him. 'He died for me,' he reflected, 'it is only just that I should die for Him.' At last, urged by grace, he went to the Pasha and said: 'You led me astray; I declare I am a Christian; I abjure your belief and religion; I hate you and cast aside the turban you gave me.' Suiting the action to the word, he threw down and trampled on the turban, adding: 'I know what I am exposing myself to; don't delay; Jesus Christ will support me in my torments.' The Pasha, scarlet with rage, condemned him to be burnt alive. The courageous martyr left the Pasha's house clad in a pair of drawers, an iron chain around his neck, carrying on his shoulders the stake to which he would be bound, and so walked to the place of execution. He cried out to the crowd that surrounded him: 'Long live Jesus Christ and may the Catholic, Roman and Apostolic faith triumph for ever!

There is no other in which one can be saved.' Philip Le Vacher was present; he absolved the man from his excommunication and imparted absolution; the fire then did its work. The bones of the martyr were gathered together, brought to Saint-Lazare and subsequently to his native place, Palma. His cause was introduced at Rome in the eighteenth century.

Chastity, also, had its martyrs amongst those Barbary Christians. A young slave, solicited and outraged by his master, wounded the latter whilst struggling with him: he was condemned to death for attempted murder. In Tunis, a young Portuguese, Anthony de la Paix, suffered in the same cause. His lewd mistress tempted him for more than a year to commit sin; under the lying pretext that she herself had been solicited, she called for vengeance and was the cause of the young man's receiving, on various occasions, more than five hundred strokes on the soles of the feet. This unmerited punishment did not shake the martyr's courage; he continued to resist. On July 26, 1646, he was bastinadoed so violently that he died of the effects, protesting his innocence to his last breath. The husband of the liar and calumniator was present at the execution and the tone of conviction in which Anthony de la Paix spoke led the man to guess the truth; he went home and strangled his wife. It was said that through the intercession of this martyr, miracles were wrought, and he now bears the title of the 'Venerable Anthony de la Paix.'

The martyrology of Barbary contains many other names known only to God. John Le Vacher, in one of his letters, refers to two Frenchmen who, urged to deny their faith, were cruelly bastinadoed by the Dey's orders, and died with constancy under torture rather than consent to deny their religion. Another Frenchman was impaled; at the moment of execution, his torturers trembled[21] 'like a leaf' so much did they marvel at his intrepid courage. Women showed themselves just as brave as men. 'Not long ago,' writes Fr. Guérin,[22] 'these cruel men gave a woman more than five hundred strokes on the soles of the feet to force her

[21] Gleizes, *op. cit.*, p. 19.
[22] Abelly, *op. cit.*, Bk. II, Ch. I, sect. VII, § 12, p. 139.

to deny Jesus Christ, and not content with that, as she was lying half-dead on the ground, two of them stamped so violently with their feet on her shoulders that her breasts broke asunder.'

The best remedy to preserve the faith and virtue of the slaves was ransom. As young women were more exposed than others, attention was chiefly devoted to them, but the Missionaries would have needed mountains of gold to save them all from the hands of their lewd masters. If they were forced to abandon many to their wretched fate, they nevertheless did succeed in saving a large number. 'We have,' wrote Father Guérin,[23] 'rescued one of those poor French women who had fallen into the hands of a renegade Frenchman. All the merchants contributed, and my own share amounted to seventy crowns; there are others who are young and beautiful and who are in very great danger unless they are helped; one of them would already have been lost were it not that I had with great difficulty obtained a respite of three months for her ransom, and if I had not placed her where her master could not violate her.' Another Frenchwoman, long subject to the tyranny of a brutal master, aroused Father Guérin's pity; at length he succeeded in ransoming her and thus announced his joy to Saint Vincent who had sent him the necessary funds: 'It is a real miracle to have saved her from the claws of this tiger, who was unwilling to release her either for gold or silver. He took it into his head to send for me one morning and when I went to him we agreed on a sum of three hundred crowns, which I paid down on the spot. I had this woman's order of release executed and placed her in a safe place. Two hours later, the wretch was sorry and almost went mad with regret. It is really a direct divine intervention.' He added another piece of good news: 'I have also rescued that young Sicilian woman who was a slave in Bizerte, whose husband had turned Turk. She has endured unutterable tortures for three years rather than imitate her husband in his apostasy. I wrote to you about last Christmas of the pitiable state in which I found her, wounded from head to foot. I paid two hundred and fifty

[23] Abelly, *op. cit.*, Bk. II, Ch. I, sect. VII, § 12, p. 139.

crowns, which I received as an alms, for her ransom, to which I partly contributed myself.'[24]

The price fixed for ransom sometimes proved to be beyond the Missionary's resources, and he had then to resign himself to the inevitable, his heart pierced with grief. John Le Vacher writes :[25] ' Some time ago a young woman from Valencia, twenty-five years old, was brought to this city of Tunis. She had been captured near her native city and was very well made. She was sold by public auction ; I bid up to three hundred and thirty crowns, lent to me by the merchants, but a ruffianly Moor, bidding still higher, secured her because I had not sufficient money ; he had already two wives and now here is a third. The poor creature has not stopped crying for three days and was only forced to lose the faith after her honour had been violated.' At this same auction, several nuns captured by pirates in their convent which was close to the sea-shore, almost suffered the same fate as the young woman from Valencia.

At Algiers, Philip Le Vacher showed an equal solicitude for young women who, after losing their liberty, were in danger of losing their innocence and their faith. The Governor of the city fell in love with a young girl from Vence ; he bought her, had her clothed in costly apparel and made up his mind to marry her, but the Missionary succeeded in purchasing herself and her two sisters for a thousand crowns. Another instance was that of a young Corsican girl who, with her mother and little brother, was ransomed, after every effort had been made to induce her to apostatise so that she might marry a Turk. Philip Le Vacher also rescued a Marseilles boy, eight years old, whom they hoped to make a little Mahometan. Another child from Marseilles, five years older, showed heroic courage in maintaining the faith. He was knocked down and beaten ; the flesh was torn from one arm, ' as one makes a carbonado to put it on the grill ' ;[26] but as these tortures did not alter his resolution, he was condemned to receive four hundred blows. This was certain death. ' So,' writes Father Guérin, ' I promptly went to seek his master, threw

[24] Abelly, *ibid.*, p. 140.   [25] Abelly, *ibid.*, p. 138.
[26] Abelly, *ibid.*, p. 140.

myself three or four times at his feet with my hands joined and begged for the child. He gave him to me for two hundred piastres; as I had not the money I borrowed a hundred crowns at interest and a merchant gave me the balance.'

Most ransoms were effected by correspondence. The Missionaries were in that case simply agents, whose rôle consisted in receiving money sent from Christian countries and paying it to the owners who then handed over the slaves in exchange. Abelly reckons that the number of captives delivered by the Missionaries, between 1645 and 1661, was more than 1200, and that the money paid as ransom was not far from 1,200,000 livres.

The centre of this eminently Christian work was Saint-Lazare, to which all offers and demands were conveyed. The money was sent to the Superior of the house in Marseilles who undertook to have it sent by sea to Barbary. Saint Vincent frequently added something to the money of which he was only the depositary; he did so either in cases in which he was particularly interested, such as priests, members of religious Orders, Christians whose faith was in the greatest danger, or to help the poorest Christian slaves with a little money. The Ladies of Charity frequently supplied him with funds for these unfortunate prisoners, and here as everywhere else, the Duchesse d'Aiguillon was the most generous; she even defrayed the expenses of a small hospital in Algiers for poor sick slaves abandoned by their masters.

Great was the joy of the Ladies of Charity when they heard, in 1658, that a naval expedition against Algiers was in preparation; in their mind's eye they already saw the Dey forced to negotiate and to set free all French slaves. Chevalier Paul, of Marseilles, was to be Commander-in-Chief. Saint Vincent urged him to begin the campaign as soon as possible, and as the chief cause of the delay was want of money, he promised 20,000 livres to be deducted from the alms collected for the ransoming of slaves. In 1660, this celebrated Naval Commander, on his return from the Ionian Islands, where he had gone to support the Venetians who were at war with the Turks, sailed for

Algiers at the head of a fleet of forty ships. He was unable to land, owing to the violent gales that were blowing, and after remaining five days in front of the city, grew tired and sailed away, having picked up forty slaves who had swum out to the ships.[27]

The service, organised by Saint Vincent, between Paris and Barbary and Barbary and Paris, enabled families to obtain news of the slaves, and the slaves to hear what was going on in their native countries, which was a great help and comfort for them in their affliction. A letter from relations was a bond attaching them to their friends and country; it frequently prevented them from apostatising, which would, indeed, have put an end to their captivity, but only at the price of remaining for ever on those infidel shores and separating them once for all from all they loved.

If Vincent de Paul had any regrets, they were that he was unable to take a direct part in this work of charity and to extend it to Morocco and Tripoli. At one time it seemed as if divine Providence was about to call his Missionaries to Salé, but, rather than enter into competition with another congregation, he preferred to break off negotiations that were already well advanced. His Missionaries laboured courageously despite the rigours of the climate and the hatred and cruelty of those in power. The thought of their labours and sufferings inspired the Saint whenever he spoke of them to his community. It was after mentioning the names of John and Philip Le Vacher that he uttered the noble words, worthy to be recalled to mind in this context: ' Zeal consists in a pure desire of rendering oneself pleasing to God and profitable to one's neighbour. Zeal to spread the empire of God, zeal to procure the salvation of one's neighbour! Is there anything in the world more perfect? If the love of God is a fire, zeal is its flame; if love is a sun, zeal is its rays. Zeal is that which is most pure in the love of God.'[28]

[27] *Saint Vincent de Paul*, Vol. VII, pp. 130, 139, 160, 165, 171, 174, 192, 197, 211, 218, 249; Vol. VIII, pp. 25, 268, 439, 449.
[28] *Ibid.*, Vol. XII, p. 307.

CHAPTER XL

SAINT VINCENT AND LORRAINE

WHEN in 1639 Saint Vincent went to the assistance of Lorraine, the province was crushed by the weight of ten long years of suffering; a sort of fatality seemed to weigh on that unfortunate land. In 1628, 1629 and 1630 the harvests proved a failure and were succeeded by a dreadful famine; from 1629 to 1637, Lorraine was ravaged by the plague; in 1632, it was invaded by French soldiers, who were joined, in 1635, by Hungarians and Swedes. One hundred and fifty thousand men, divided into seven army corps of different nations, wandered about in every direction within the narrow confines of the Duchy, dragging behind them fifty thousand women and camp-followers.

Wherever the troops went, they pillaged, burned and massacred: army commanders requisitioned corn, crushed whole districts under the weight of heavy taxation, seized whatever they thought their troops needed, and behaved as if there were no civil population whatever. The Lutheran Swedes, exasperated at the sight of buildings reminding them of the Catholic religion, burned down or demolished churches and monasteries wherever they went. In such circumstances, one can readily understand that the land was left untilled; why sow if there was to be no harvest, and if a man was not to enjoy the fruits of his labours? Famine was the inevitable consequence of war, and so too was pestilence, for the movement of troops rendered sanitary measures impossible.

The greater part of the population died of starvation; men and women might have been seen wandering about from place to place with haggard eyes looking for anything to eat, fighting with domestic animals for acorns and grass, and with carnivorous beasts for the flesh of horses, dogs and cats. The repugnance usually experienced at the sight of putrid bodies and the disgusting odour they exhaled, was not strong enough to overcome the tortures of hunger. The corpses of men either killed or dead from want of nourishment were not spared, and children were seen digging up the corpse of a father or mother to devour it. Even the living were attacked and men were hunted like hares. A woman was condemned to death at Mirecourt for having eaten the flesh of a child she had strangled.[1] 'One mother made a bargain with another to eat her own child on condition that the other would afterwards do likewise. A man was hanged at the gate of Nancy for having killed his sister for a loaf of army bread. The most terrible incidents of the famines of Samaria and Jerusalem were not as horrible as what men then witnessed.'[2] Villages were depopulated either by death or emigration; Frouard, which contained a hundred families in 1633, had only five or six inhabitants in 1635; Buissoncourt, Parey-Saint-Césaire and the country round Vermois were completely deserted. At Art-sur-Meurthe, the population dropped from 42 to 6; at Crévic, from 256 to 10; at Lay-Saint-Christophe and Eulmont, from 181 to 12; at Neuville, from 75 to 10; at Malzéville, from 228 to 46; at Mangonville, from 24 to 1; at Roville, from 33 to 1; at Richardménil, from 29 to 5; at Vandoeuvre, from 57 to 14, but it is useless to go on with such lists. The average number of losses was no less in other districts, and in some even greater.

It seemed difficult for the level of human existence to sink lower, and yet Lorraine had to endure even greater evils. The renewal of hostilities, which had been interrupted for a time, the acts of brigandage perpetrated by Croatian troops, the depredations of the soldiers, and an exceptionally severe winter, continued the work of death and destruction. Caussin, Louis XIII's confessor, was not exaggerating when he said that the misfortunes that befell

[1] Abram-Musgotus, Ms. de la bibl. de Nancy.
[2] Collet, *op. cit.*, Vol. I, f. IV, p. 287. Countless such details may be found in the Memoirs of the Marquis of Beauvau, the register of John Conrard and the Journal of Claude Guillemin.

Jerusalem did not equal those of Lorraine ; *Sola Lotharingia Hierosolymam calamitate vincit.* Lorraine needed peace and war was unending. Charles IV, driven out by the French in 1638, returned to the Duchy at the head of his army in January, 1641. We may see from the tax-collectors' accounts that, at this date, famine was increasing, the death rate mounting and the current of emigration running more strongly. Almost the entire population of Nancy consisted of persons who had fled from the surrounding districts. Workmen, weary of prolonged unemployment, went elsewhere to offer their services and earn a livelihood. The rich in their splendid castles were, as far as food and clothing were concerned, on the same footing as those who lived in hovels. It was an egalitarian regime, as far as hunger and privations were concerned. Priests shared the common lot ; many had sold the sacred vessels of their churches in order to live and assist their flocks ; when the money was spent—which did not take long—they, like everybody else, had to fly from a country that could no longer support them. Cloistered nuns remained in their convents as long as they could, preferring to bear privations as long as possible rather than violate the law of enclosure. For months at a time, convent bells implored the charity of the public by prolonged peals. It was, of course, impossible to receive help from those who had nothing to give, but at length their appeal reached the ears of the King, who supplied the nuns with black army bread, consisting of equal parts of oats and rye.

The treaty of Saint-Germain, signed on April 2, was followed by a short truce. The Lorrainers, dissatisfied with the heavy sacrifices of territory imposed on them, took up arms again at the end of three months, but their courage failed before the weight of numbers, and as a punishment for rebellion, a pitiless Governor, the Marquis de la Ferté-Senneterre, was appointed, who thoroughly deserved the name of ' the butcher of Lorraine.' The province known as that of the Three Bishoprics, annexed to France in 1552, experienced, after some years' delay, the back-wash of the calamities that had befallen the Duchy. Plague and famine crossed the frontiers and began their dread work ;

here, too, the rate of mortality was appalling and destitution became general.

The Priests of the Mission, called to Toul in 1635 to take charge of the Hospital of the Holy Spirit, in place of a religious Order no longer acceptable to the city, were sad witnesses of the universal state of misery.[3] It was from them, and also from persons who had fled to Paris, that Saint Vincent heard, in all its horror, the lamentable situation of the people of Lorraine. His thoughts went first of all to Him who is the source of all good, and he strove to obtain the divine forgiveness by prayer and penance. In 1636, when the Spaniards were besieging Corbie, he suppressed a dish at table which was never afterwards supplied. In 1639, he asked something more : ' This is a time to do penance,' he said to his priests, ' since God is afflicting His people. Should we not be at the foot of the altar bewailing their sins ? We are obliged to do so ; but in addition, should we not retrench some of our usual food for their relief ? '[4] And for three or four years the community of Saint-Lazare had to be content with black bread.

Supernatural means would have been inefficacious if not accompanied or followed by natural ones. Saint Vincent was not one of those mystics who, with eyes raised to Heaven, are satisfied with saying : ' Act, O my God, I have confidence in Thee ' ; he was well aware of the truth that if we are right to rely on the Almighty, the Almighty also relies on us. He asked himself : ' What can I do to put an end to these scourges, or at least, to lessen their disastrous effects ? ' And it occurred to him that he should pay a visit to Richelieu. When he met the Cardinal, he threw himself on his knees, drew a touching picture of the evils that were afflicting Lorraine and pointed out their deplorable effects on morals and religion. ' My Lord,' he cried, ' let us have peace ; have pity on us ; give peace to France.' Richelieu

---

[3] Abbé Deblaye, *La charité de Saint Vincent de Paul en Lorraine* (1638–1647), Nancy, 1886, in 8⁰, pp. 11–20 ; Collet, *op. cit.*, Bk. IV, pp. 285–288 ; Abelly, *op. cit.*, Bk. II, Ch. XI, sect. I, p. 374.
[4] Abelly, *op. cit.*, Bk. III, Ch. XIX, I, p. 298.

replied with a sigh :[5] 'Ah ! Monsieur Vincent, I desire peace just as much as you ; but peace does not depend on me alone.' The man who pleaded the cause of Lorraine lost his suit, but was not discouraged ; as he could not reach the roots of the evil, he set about remedying its effects. To fight famine and help the sick and wounded, funds were required.

Money was provided probably by someone who had been moved by the Saint's words ; it was sent to the Superior of the house in Toul and at once utilised.[6] Father du Coudray and his confrère, Father Boucher, took into their house forty poor people, many of whom were ill, and secured lodgings in the suburbs for one hundred and fifty more. On February 3, 1639, Saint Vincent wrote : ' They are feeding and assisting them with a charity that draws tears from the eyes of those who hear of it, but it is very much to be feared that they will succumb.' Father du Coudray, invited to take things more quietly and not spend too rapidly the money placed at his disposal, replied in these or equivalent words : ' Either help me, recall me, or let me die with these poor people.'[7]

Every good work, to be permanent and fruitful, demands organisation. Saint Vincent held a meeting of the Ladies of Charity to explain the situation in Lorraine and to ask them to come to its assistance. A plan was drawn up and regulations drafted. They would collect or furnish funds of which they would supervise the employment, set down the moneys received and expended and receive accurate reports, at these monthly meetings, on the progress or decline of the famine and of the action taken by those who were combating it.[8] Personal generosity would not have sufficed and the Ladies approached the Queen and the King ; Louis XIII gave a grant of 45,000 livres to help men and women belonging to religious Orders, and make

---

[5] Abelly, *op. cit.*, Bk. I, Ch. XXXV, p. 169. This incident occurred sometime between 1639 and 1642 ; no more definite date than that can be assigned.
[6] Abelly, *op. cit.*, Bk. II, Ch. XI, sect. I, p. 375.
[7] *Saint Vincent de Paul*, Vol. I, p. 538.
[8] *Ibid.*, Vol. II, p. 61.

further generous gifts.[9] A few days before his death, he drew once more on his personal funds to assist the famine-stricken people of Lorraine through the agency of Saint Vincent de Paul.[10] The Queen sent the mourning tapestries and beds that had been used at the King's funeral, and the Duchesse d'Aiguillon did the same after the death of her uncle, Cardinal Richelieu.[11]

Saint Vincent entrusted his Missionaries with the distribution of relief. The Fathers at Toul as we have seen, attended to the poor of that city and its environs. John Bécu and Rondet, who were priests, and Gaillard, Aulent, Delestoile and Bourdet, who were clerics, set out, during April, 1639, and visited in pairs three different sections of the unfortunate Duchy: Bar-le-Duc, Verdun, and Nancy. Another group saw that Metz and its neighbourhood was fed, and then two new posts were established: one at Saint Mihiel (about January, 1640) and the other at Pont-à-Mousson (May, 1640). Hence there were in all seven different districts provided for, each of which regularly received every month 500 livres brought from Paris by a lay-brother, Mathew Régnard.[12] Charity, however, began to grow cold after some time, and the Saint seriously asked himself, on February 28, 1640, how he could keep the supply of alms at this level.[13] To those well supplied with this world's goods, he handed letters from his Missionaries in the hope that by reading these pages, their hearts would be touched. He frequently received an offering in reply and sometimes a letter of sympathy.[14] ' Having seen the letters from Lorraine,' an ecclesiastic wrote to him. . . . ' I could not read them without shedding tears which flowed so abundantly that I frequently had to interrupt my reading. I praise God for the paternal providence He extends over all His creatures, and beg Him to continue His graces to your priests who are engaged in this divine work.' A few

---

[9] *Ibid.*, p. 80.
[10] Jacques Dinet, *Idée d'une belle mort ou d'une mort chrétienne dans le récit de la fin heureuse de Louis XIII*, Paris, 1656, in-f⁰, p. 42.
[11] Abelly, *op. cit.*, Bk. II, Ch. XI, sect. I, p. 388.
[12] *Saint Vincent de Paul*, Vol. I, pp. 552, 590 ; Vol. II, p. 80.
[13] *Ibid.*, Vol. II, p. 32.
[14] Abelly, *op. cit.*, Bk. II, Ch. XI, sect. I, p. 378.

crowns would have been more useful than tears, but perhaps he may have supplied both. The alms sent by Saint Vincent saved thousands of Lorrainers from death. The sick, found scattered in the woods or in streets and squares, were gathered together and nursed; the hungry were fed, and the naked clothed.

Saint Vincent did not allow his Missionaries to depart until he had given them instructions; he composed a set of regulations that bear the mark of his wisdom, experience and unbounded charity.[15] As soon as his envoys arrived at their destination, the first thing they were to do was to visit the Blessed Sacrament, and then proceed from the Church to the presbytery. After a consultation with the parish priest, a list was drawn up of poor persons, beginning with the very poorest who could not earn a living; this list was provisional and was to be followed by an enquiry which might lead to modification both of the numbers and the localities on the list. No attention was paid to special recommendations or petitions on behalf of individuals; the equitable distribution of assistance was regarded as an act of justice towards the poor. Next, the amount of food required in each particular instance was calculated as closely as possible. Flour was purchased, taken to the house of the parish priest or of a charitable lady, and the amount of bread needed for a week was baked. At the end of a week a fresh batch was baked, but as bread did not agree with every stomach, soups were also prepared and the Missionaries set aside a little money to defray that source of expense.

After the first distribution of food, or a little later, the Missionaries continued their journey, remaining for a longer period in those places that had suffered most. They returned to every place they had visited to see that their instructions had been faithfully carried out, brought new supplies of wheat, and revised the first list so that any

---

[15] Collet says (*op. cit.*, Vol. I, Bk. IV, p. 290, note d) : 'The original of this set of regulations, dated April 15, 1639, was in the Seminary at Toul in the beginning of this year 1747. There is a copy in the manuscript history of this seminary pp. 71, etc.' Abbé Deblaye has utilised this document in his work, pp. 26–27.

necessary modifications might be made. The poor still remained poor; all the gold of the capital would not perhaps have saved them from want, but at any rate, the needy were not dying of hunger, and that, as far as the body is concerned, was the chief end of these charitable journeys.

The passing life of the body was not the Missionaries' sole care; the salvation of the soul, especially in those unhappy days in which the gates of eternity were opening to such multitudes, was of far greater importance in their eyes. They gathered the poor together and preached to them; catechised the children; prepared the sick for death; and advised all to make general confessions. The Missionaries had another duty: that of gratitude to the benefactors of the poor. They were not importunate; they did not ask for anything; they contented themselves with simply describing the misery before their eyes, with recounting the manner in which they had dealt with it, with stating what remained to be done, and then left it to God to inspire their readers to renewed acts of generosity. Saint Vincent asked them to send regular reports that could be communicated to the Ladies of Charity, and with them to enclose receipts of the money expended signed by the civil or ecclesiastical authorities or by the Superiors of monasteries that had received assistance. Father du Coudray, the Superior at Toul, thought he was falling in with the Saint's wishes by requesting the Vicar General of the diocese, in December, 1639, to supply him with a written attestation of the charitable activities of the Missionaries. The Superiors of the monasteries in the city were also invited to certify in writing that they had had their due share of alms.

Saint Vincent received and read the documents; one of them stated: 'I, John Midot, Doctor of Theology, Archdeacon, Canon and Vicar General of Toul, the episcopal See now being vacant, do certify and solemnly declare that the Priests of the Mission residing in this city have continued for about the past two years, with much edification and charity, to comfort, clothe and supply the poor with medicines: in the first place the sick poor, sixty of whom they have admitted to their own house and provided lodgings for one hundred in the suburbs; secondly, a number of other poor, decent persons, reduced to the utmost extremity and refugees in this city, to whom they have given alms; and in the third place, numbers of poor soldiers, returning sick and wounded from the King's armies, who have also been admitted either to the house of the said Priests of the Mission or to the Charity Hospital where they have been fed and nursed. With which charitable actions and with their conduct in general all persons of good will have been greatly edified.'[16] After reading this letter, he turned to another from the Dominican Nuns of a large convent in Toul : ' We may and do say with the whole diocese of Toul : " Blessed be God for having sent us these angels of peace, in such calamitous times, for the good of this city and the consolation of its people, and for ourselves in particular to whom they have done and continue every day to do, acts of charity, supplying us from their possessions with corn, wood, and fruit, thus assisting us in our extreme necessity." An inner feeling urges us to render this testimony and we do so most willingly.'[17]

Saint Vincent, quite taken aback by such eulogies, folded up the papers and most probably the Ladies of Charity never set eyes on them. He wrote and begged Father du Coudray not to send any such documents in future, adding : ' It is quite enough for God alone to know what we are doing, and that the poor are being helped without our wishing to provide any further testimony of it.'[18] His idea was that Father du Courday should simply forward receipts and not laudatory testimonials, but du Coudray must have misunderstood the Saint for he now took refuge in complete silence which after some months earned him reproaches of another nature. The dominant trait in Father du Coudray's character was independence; he found it hard to be guided by anybody, and when he believed that help would be more useful to one class of person rather than another, he was quite prepared to act according to his own ideas, despite the instructions he had received. This line of action

[16] Abelly, *op. cit.*, Bk. II, Ch. XI, sect. I, p. 375.
[17] Collet, *op. cit.*, Vol. I, Bk. IV, p. 291.
[18] Abelly, *op. cit.*, Bk. II, Ch. XI, sect. I, p. 375.

was not at all to the liking of the Superintendent of the Three Bishoprics, Anne Mangot, Lord of the Manor of Villarceaux, who complained to Saint Vincent, and the latter sent further instructions to Father du Coudray. On June 17, 1649, he wrote: 'As for the two thousand livres you received from M. de Saint-Nicholas for the nuns, in the name of God, Sir, do not use it for any other purpose, under no matter what pretext of charity. Charity is not charity if it is not accompanied by justice, or if it suffers us to do more than we can reasonably effect.'[19] A few days later another letter arrived begging him to carry out exactly de Villarceaux's orders. On July 10, the Saint wrote to the same effect, adding some practical advice: 'I very humbly beseech you . . . to obtain a receipt for all that you supply to each monastery. As for the distribution of alms in cities where there are members of the Congregation, you should point out to them that they are bound to carry out exactly the orders given you by the said Lord of Villarceaux, and obtain receipts for all they give, for we should bear in mind that on no pretext whatever should even a farthing be allocated or applied to other purposes. And you will please send me by Brother Mathew a copy of M. de Villarceaux's inventory and orders, if any, and let me know every month what sums you have expended or ordered to be expended in other places. Never was there greater need of right order than there is now and, in fact, it is being observed. You said nothing to me about the number of poor country people who have taken refuge in the city or the suburb, to whom you are giving alms. Every month I supply such an account to these good ladies for all the other districts; Toul is the only place of which I have not given an account for quite a long time; and the Ladies are greatly consoled by these accounts. Last Saturday we spent two or three hours reading the other letters with which they were delighted and consoled.'[20] Saint Vincent was not satisfied with these remonstrances; he sent his Assistant, Father Dehorgny, to Lorraine to bring his fellow-missionaries advice, sympathy and encouragement.

[19] *Saint Vincent de Paul*, Vol. II, p. 54.
[20] *Ibid.*, Vol. II, p. 60.

At Toul, the visitor met Father Julian Guérin, the future founder of the Tunis Mission, who was then showing the same zeal for the famine-stricken as he was later to show for the slaves. Father Dehorgny wrote:[21] 'All in general have an unparalleled esteem for the Missionary here who both instructs and comforts them. . . . He is devoting himself with the greatest charity and energy to these frontiers. He even allowed himself to be so overwhelmed by hearing general confessions and neglecting to eat, that he fell sick.' Father Guérin had desired and gladly accepted the duty confided to him at Saint Mihiel. Scarcely had he arrived in that city than he set to work with a zeal stimulated by the extent of its poverty and wretchedness. 'I began, as soon as I arrived, to distribute alms. I find there is such a large number of poor people here that I cannot give something to each; there are more than three hundred in very great necessity, and more than three hundred in the direst need. . . . More than a hundred . . . look like skeletons covered with skin and . . . they present such a horrible appearance that if Our Lord did not give me strength, I would not dare to look at them. Their skin is like black marble and is so shrunken that their teeth are dry and uncovered, and their eyes and whole countenance have a scowling appearance. . . . It is the most dreadful sight that can ever have been seen. They hunt about in the fields for roots which they cook and eat. . . . Several girls are dying of hunger; some of them are young and I fear lest despair may bring upon them greater misery than that of this world.' One may imagine the impression produced on the tender heart of Saint Vincent when he read this letter, which was shortly followed by others. 'The last time we distributed bread, it was found that there were eleven hundred and thirty-two poor people, not counting the sick, of whom there are great numbers and whom we assist with food and suitable remedies. . . . The gentlemen of the city are loud in their praises of these acts of charity and openly declare that many would have died without this help, and proclaim the obligations they are under to you. A poor Swiss, a few days ago, abjured his Lutheran

[21] Abelly, *op. cit.*, Bk. II, Ch. XI, sect. I, p. 382.

BARON GASTON DE RENTY

heresy, and after receiving the sacraments, died in a most Christian fashion.'[22]

A large supply of bread was needed for eleven hundred and thirty-two hungry men and women, but the money from Paris seemed to multiply in the Missionary's hands. People were astonished and inclined to believe that God was renewing, at Saint Vincent's prayers, the miracles of the multiplication of the loaves and the manna in the desert. ' I recalled to mind,' wrote Father Dehorgny,[23] ' what the Sacred Scriptures tell us of the manna, namely, that each family took what it required and that this proved sufficient for all, whether the number of those who collected it was great or small. I observe something similar here, for our priests, who are looking after a large number of poor, do not give less than the others and still they have enough.' He also bore testimony to the fact that Father Guérin's statements to Saint Vincent were in no way exaggerated ; he wrote : ' I could tell you, Sir, some extraordinary things about this city, which would seem incredible if we ourselves had not witnessed them. . . . The majority of the citizens and especially of the nobility are enduring such extremes of hunger as can scarcely be imagined, and what is still more deplorable, they do not venture to beg. . . . A few summon up courage to do so, but others would rather die, and I myself have spoken to persons of rank who do nothing but weep.' In these circumstances, the people went to any length to satisfy their hunger. If a horse died, no one enquired what it had died of ; its carcase was quickly cut into pieces which were carried away. A woman would fill her apron with such diseased flesh and barter it with other poor women for pieces of bread. A young girl of rank, on the point of ' selling what she regarded as the dearest thing in life for . . . a piece of bread ' was deterred from doing so just in time. For want of horses, the tillers of the soil yoked themselves to the plough, and so, too, did the clergy, for there was no other means of earning a livelihood.

From the religious point of view, a certain amount of consolation was to be derived. ' Our Lord seems . . . to have bestowed the special privilege of a spirit of patience

[22] *Ibid.*, p. 380.   [23] *Ibid.*, p. 382.

and devotion on Saint-Mihiel, even in its extreme poverty, for the people are so greedy for religious instruction that nearly two thousand people have been attending the lessons in catechism. . . . This is a very large number for a small city in which most of the large houses are empty. Even the very poorest are most careful to be present and also to receive the Sacraments.'[24] Father Guérin's health began to give way under the double burthen of fatigue and privation; he was compelled to return to Paris in September, 1641, and neither did Father Dupuis, who took his place, remain very long. We may gather from Saint Vincent's letter of recall, dated January 12, 1642, that he was just then hesitating about continuing the work. ' If you should have any advice to give me as to your leaving the city for good and all, and not providing a successor, you might do so as soon as possible Your remark that your absence would spare sixty livres a month for the poor has deeply moved me, and God knows how tenderly I shall embrace you on your arrival here.'[25]

Saint-Mihiel, like the other cities in Lorraine, was not abandoned until 1643. At that time there were very few sick left, and as the garrison had been reduced in numbers at Saint Vincent's request, the inhabitants were again able to set about earning a living. The departure of the Missionaries, however, was a source of grief to the entire city. The King's Lieutenant, the Provost, the Sheriffs and Governor, begged the Saint in a joint petition to continue his good work on behalf of the citizens. They reminded him of what had been done by himself and his associates : the distribution of alms, the help given to the sick and the utterly destitute poor, both those who had publicly proclaimed their condition and those who concealed it, whether of high or low degree, consecrated to God or living in the world ; they declared that his charity had saved the lives of an infinite number of persons, expressed the most humble thanks and begged him, as the needs remained the same, to continue his protection and assistance, of which ' this poor, desolate city ' they go on to say, ' is in as great need as ever . . . if

[24] Abelly, *op. cit.*, Bk. II, Ch. XI, sect. I, p. 380.
[25] *Saint Vincent de Paul*, Vol. II, p. 213.

help is retrenched or entirely stopped, then of necessity a great number of inhabitants will die of hunger, or go elsewhere to seek a livelihood.'[26]

Saint Vincent withdrew his priests, as he had already decided, but continued his charitable assistance as we shall see later.[27]

He selected Fr. de Montevit and Brother Levasseur to help the unfortunate people of Bar-le-Duc where the state of affairs was also heartrending. A mere walk through the streets sufficed to show the visitor poor people ' stretched in great numbers on the pavements and thoroughfares, and before the gates of the churches and the citizens' houses, dying of cold, hunger, sickness and want.' About eight hundred received bread every time it was distributed, and twenty or thirty were supplied with clothing.[28]

The Missionaries worked without ceasing, and their zeal was in fact excessive. Fr. de Montevit collapsed, exhausted by fatigue, and died after a prolonged illness on January 19, 1640, in the Jesuit College where he edified all by his patience, piety and docility to the doctor's orders. The Rector of the house, Fr. Roussel, wrote to Saint Vincent: ' He died as I wish and pray to God to die. The two Chapters of Bar-le-Duc and the Augustinian Fathers attended his funeral, but that which lent greatest honour to his obsequies were the six or seven hundred poor people who were present, each with a taper in hand, and weeping as bitterly as if they were attending their father's funeral. The poor certainly owed him this display of gratitude, for he fell ill whilst healing their diseases and comforting their poverty ; he was always in their midst and breathed no other air than the fetid atmosphere in which they lived. He heard confessions with such great assiduity both morning and evening that I could never once induce him even to take a walk.'[29] The Rector thoughtfully gave orders that Fr. de Montivet should be buried close to the confessional where he had reconciled so many souls to God.

Whilst Fr. de Montevit lay ill and unable to work, Saint Vincent sent Fr. Boucher from Toul to replace him. Fr.

[26] Abelly, *op. cit.*, Bk. II, Ch. XI, sect. I, p. 388.
[27] *Ibid.*, p. 388.   [28] *Ibid.*, p. 383.   [29] *Ibid.*, p. 384.

Boucher, on Christmas Eve, remained twenty-four hours in the confessional, without taking time either to sleep or eat and only pausing to say Mass. This was certainly excessive zeal. On January 17, whilst his confrère lay dying, he experienced the first shiverings of an attack of fever that kept him hovering between life and death for over a week. ' Your priests,' wrote Fr. Roussel, ' are gentle and amenable in all things save in taking the advice given them to give their bodies a little repose. They think that bodies are not made of flesh and blood or that life should last only a year.' He adds that the Brother is ' a very devout young man who nursed the two priests with all the patience and attention that could be desired even by the most troublesome patient.' Saint Vincent was not the man to forget the Rector's kindness ; a conference was held at Saint-Lazare on the duty of gratitude, and mention was made of what the Congregation of the Mission owed to the Society of Jesus.[30] Scarcely had Fr. Boucher recovered than he set to work as hard as ever, despite Fr. Roussel's charitable remonstrances. We may judge of his zeal from the following lines which he sent to Paris a month later : ' Quite recently I . . . have clothed . . . two hundred and sixty poor people. But should I not rather tell you, Sir, how I clothed every one of them spiritually, by means of a general confession and Holy Communion ? I have administered the Sacraments to more than eight hundred within the space of a month, and I trust to do better during the coming Lent. We give the hospital a pistole and a half a month for the poor we send there, and as there are about eighty who are worse than the rest, we give them soup, bread and meat.'

Every week an ample supply of linen, especially shirts, was distributed. Old shirts were not thrown away ; they were washed and mended and thus helped to make other unfortunates happy ; when completely worn out, they were torn up and used as bandages for the wounded and for those suffering with ulcerated sores. At that time, Lorraine was afflicted from an epidemic of ringworm of the scalp, and the Missionaries at Bar daily attended to about twenty-five cases ; they employed a remedy which showed its efficacy

[30] Abelly, *op. cit.*, Bk. III, Ch. XVII, p. 268.

by the number of cures effected. Passing tramps completed their clientèle ; Bar-le-Duc, the gate of Lorraine, was a thoroughfare for crowds of poor people who were dying of hunger in their own districts, and had left them to reach France. These emigrants, directed to the Missionaries at Bar by their friends in other parts of Lorraine, were given food, shelter and a little money to help them on the way.[31]

Fr. Boucher left Bar in July, 1640, a few days after Fr. Dehorgny's visit and was replaced by one of his young confrères, Fr. Dupuis, ' as yet without experience, but very devout and docile.'[32]

The Missionaries encountered the same types of poor people at Pont-à-Mousson as they had at Bar-le-Duc ; habitual mendicants, to the number of four or five hundred ; poor men and women who had come in from the country ; tramps ; about sixty decent poor persons who received special treatment according to their state of life ; poor nursing mothers ; young girls exposed to loss of honour through youth and indigence, and finally, about a hundred sick poor. Some of these were given bread ; others, flour, meat, vegetables, money, farming implements, tools, shoes, and clothes, according to their respective needs. The Missionaries paid the surgeons and bought medical requisites ; they bandaged sores, procured lodgings for the sick, and places of refuge for young girls.

To food for the body they added nourishment for the soul in the shape of religious instruction, sermons and lessons in catechism. The dying were prepared for the last Sacraments, and departed from this life in the most admirable dispositions.

The poor frequently arrived in such an exhausted state that they died whilst eating a mouthful of bread. Very few came in from the surrounding country, for the people were afraid to travel owing to the number of wolves in the neighbourhood.[33] It is stated, and the account rests on the episcopal official report, that a child was approached by a

[31] *Ibid.*, Bk. II, Ch. XI, p. 383.
[32] *Saint Vincent de Paul*, Vol. II, p. 62.
[33] Abelly, *op. cit.*, Bk. II, Ch. XI, sect. I, p. 378.

few others slightly older than himself who seized, slew and devoured him.[34]

In December 1640, it was rumoured in Pont-à-Mousson that the Missionaries were about to leave, and the people were greatly perturbed. The Mayor, Sheriffs, law officers and Town Council met and decided to send a joint letter to Saint Vincent begging him to alter his decision. ' The apprehension which we now feel,'[35] they state, ' of seeing ourselves shortly deprived of the charitable assistance which your goodness has been pleased to bestow on our poor, has induced us to have recourse to you, Sir, in order that, if you will be so good, the same assistance as was hitherto given may still be continued, because the need for it is just as great as ever. The harvest has failed for the past two years ; the troops have eaten our rising crops of corn, and the constant presence of soldiers in garrison have left us objects of compassion ; those who were formerly well off are now reduced to beggary ; such, then, are motives, as strong as they are true, to stir your tender heart, already so full of love and pity for us, to continue its benignity towards those five hundred poor people who would die within a few hours if, by misfortune, your kindness were to fail. We beseech your goodness not to suffer such a desperate state of affairs, but to give us the crumbs that fall from other, better provided cities ; you will not only do a charity to our poor people, but will snatch them from the claws of death.'

Nancy was in a similar condition and met with like assistance. Fr. John Bécu daily provided for the needs of five hundred individuals and assisted a hundred and eighty ' decent poor,' about thirty of whom were ecclesiastics or persons of rank. He provided accommodation for the sick wherever he was able ; in his own house, in the hospital of Saint Julian and in various houses in the city.[36]

Metz suffered even more from famine than Nancy and Pont-à-Mousson. The army of beggars in that city amounted at times to from four to five thousand persons. Every morning ten or twelve corpses, more or less eaten by wolves,

[34] Deblaye, *op. cit.*, p. 54.
[35] Abelly, *op. cit.*, Bk. II, Ch. XI, sect. I, p. 379.
[36] *Ibid.*, p. 377.

were picked up in the streets. The wolves showed as little fear of the living as of the dead; they invaded hamlets and villages and even entered the city at night through breaches in the walls. There was so little safety in Metz that the Parliament thought it prudent to move to Toul, where it remained for twenty years (1638-1658). The Bishop, Henri de Bourbon, an illegitimate son of Henry IV, though immensely wealthy, was far more concerned with his own pleasures than the needs of his flock. The bishopric was, in his eyes, a benefice and nothing more; a source of revenue and not a charge implying duties; he had, as a matter of fact, only taken the first step towards Holy Orders which gave him the right to enrich himself from the goods of the Church, and hence, without violating any sacred obligation, he was free to marry Charlotte Séguier in 1668. Metz deserved a better prelate than this worldling who showed himself so indifferent to the needs of his people, but what the bishop did not supply was provided by a poor, simple priest, a stranger to the diocese. The Sheriffs and 'the Thirteen' of the city felt obliged to express their gratitude to Saint Vincent and did so in a letter written in October 1640.[37] 'Sir,' they wrote, 'you have put us under such a strict obligation by relieving, as you have done, the poverty and extreme necessity of our poor, both those who are sick and those who keep in the background, and especially the poor monasteries of the nuns of this city, that we should be ingrates if we refrained any longer from manifesting our gratitude to you. We can assure you that the alms you sent could not have been sent to a better place or put to a better use than for our poor, who are so numerous; and especially is this true of our nuns who are destitute of all human help; some of them have not received any of their little revenues since the war, and others no longer receive the assistance formerly given by well-to-do citizens who now have lost the means of doing so. Hence, Sir, we are constrained to beg you, as we do very humbly, to be good enough to continue the assistance you have already supplied, both to the said poor and to the monasteries of this city. It is most meritorious both for those who carry on this good work and for you,

[37] *Ibid.*, p. 376.

Sir, who have charge of and administer it with so much prudence and skill.'

Verdun, like Metz, had nothing to expect from its bishop, Francis of Lorraine, who was on the same footing as Henri de Bourbon, and in 1661 abandoned the ecclesiastical state and married Christine de Marsanhe, Baroness de Saint-Menges. Every day, for at least three years, the Missionaries were at their post, succouring 400, 500 or even 600 poor people, fifty or sixty sick, and thirty ' modest poor ' without counting other unfortunates. They could not always prevent Death from claiming his victims, but their exhortations prepared the dying for their last hour. ' O, Sir,' wrote one of them,[38] ' how many souls are going to Paradise on account of poverty ! Since I came to Lorraine I have assisted more than a thousand poor persons to die, all of whom seemed to have been perfectly disposed for death. There are surely many intercessors in Heaven praying for their benefactors.' The Sheriffs of Verdun, in their gratitude, wrote a letter of thanks to Saint Vincent which unfortunately has been lost.[39] Early in the nineteenth century, the inhabitants of the city showed their gratitude in another form by erecting an altar in the Cathedral dedicated to the great benefactor of Lorraine.

Toul, Saint-Mihiel, Bar-le-Duc, Pont-à-Mousson, Nancy, Metz and Verdun, are the only places in Lorraine where the Missionaries took up permanent quarters to assist the poor and the sick. As it was impossible for them to settle permanently everywhere, they selected the chief centres because the poor were to be found there in the greatest numbers, and hence their charity could be exercised most advantageously. Saint Vincent, however, did not neglect other cities and villages ; he sent periodically from Paris a travelling Missionary who supplied the monasteries or local authorities with the funds collected for them. For such a delicate and dangerous mission he needed a strong, intelligent, clear-sighted man on whom he could fully rely, of

[38] Abelly, *op. cit.*, Bk. II, Ch. XI, sect. I, pp. 376-378.
[39] The registers of the Town Hall at Verdun, dated January 21, 1640, mention the resolution adopted by the Sheriffs to write to Vincent de Paul to thank him for his generous assistance.

robust health, a stout pedestrian with a wary eye and exceptional presence of mind, for Lorraine was infested with bandits and soldiers; synonymous terms in those days. Saint-Lazare was fortunate enough to possess such a man in the person of Brother Mathew Régnard, who was nicknamed Reynard on account of his skill in extracting himself from difficult situations. Between 1639 and 1649 he made fifty-three expeditions to Lorraine and was never once robbed, although after some time it became known who he was and what he was carrying; his arrival was announced and expected and men lay in wait for him. He carried in a torn, old wallet, such as beggar men use, a purse usually containing twenty thousand livres, and sometimes twenty-five or thirty thousand; occasionally even more. He had certainly enough money to excite cupidity, but an angel seems to have guided his footsteps, and what God protects is well protected. He nearly lost his purse or his life on eighteen different occasions, and eighteen times providentially escaped. The story of his adventures, written by himself, was still extant in 1748 in the archives of Saint-Lazare, It is not known whether the document was lent, went astray, or disappeared in the famous pillage of 1789, but Collet read it and the following details are taken from his work.

If Brother Mathew was with a convoy and the band was attacked and carried off, he always managed to escape; if he were travelling with others he left them just before they were set upon and robbed. The woods through which he passed were frequently full of disbanded soldiers lying in wait for their prey; if he saw them, he dropped his purse in a bush or in the mud and walked straight up to them like a man who had nothing to fear. In this way he averted suspicion and most often nothing was said to him, though at times he was beaten. When the soldiers moved off, he retraced his steps and recovered his treasure. One day he was seized by some bandits, taken into a wood and carefully searched. 'Give us fifty pistoles,' they said, 'or we will not let you go.' He replied: 'To whom are you talking? I am a poor man and if I had fifty lives, I could not purchase them with a single Lorraine farthing.' He spoke with such sincerity that the robbers released him. On another occasion, he was walking along, carrying a purse containing 34,000 livres, when a horseman suddenly appeared at his side, pistol in hand, who shouted : ' Walk on before me or I will shoot you.' He walked quietly along to the solitary spot to which the soldier directed him so that the Brother might be robbed more easily. Mathew kept an eye on the bandit all the time, without appearing to do so, and observing that his captor turned his head for a moment, he dropped the purse. About a hundred yards further on, he reached some muddy ground, and digging his heels well into the soil, he began to make a series of profound bows to the horseman who probably thought that the Brother was mad. They set off again until they reached the edge of a precipice where the bandit searched Mathew thoroughly, but only found a knife which he took and then disappeared. The Brother retraced his steps until he reached the spot marked by his heels, and thanks to this clue, he soon recovered his wallet. Another day, as he came out on a wide-spreading plain, he saw in the distance some Croats who had already observed him. Despite his imminent danger, Mathew did not lose his head ; in front of him were some high bushes ; he walked towards them and dropped his purse ; a few yards farther on, he dropped his stick. The wily traveller then tranquilly went his way, passing through the midst of the dreaded Croats. When evening fell, he returned and spent the whole night looking for the wallet, but in spite of his fervent prayers to Heaven, there was no sign of it. He knew, however, that he was not far from it, and at last, as day broke, he saw his stick. The rest was only child's play to a man like Brother Mathew.

His fame soon became legendary throughout the whole of Lorraine, and of course, the wider his reputation spread, the greater grew the dangers and the need for taking precautions. Close to Saint-Mihiel, a Captain recognised him and without reflecting on the consequences of his words, said : ' There goes the famous Brother Mathew.' When the soldiers heard the well-known name, they looked at each other, the same sentiment of greed filled every heart and inspired them all with the same resolution. The Captain quickly recognised his imprudence, and seeing his men moving away, he drew a pistol, placed himself before them and cried out firmly : ' Stop ! I will blow the head off any man who is so mad as to injure a person who is doing so much good.' At Nomédy, the Croats, recognising the Brother whose wallet was stuffed with crowns, were on the watch at every exit from the city. Mathew was on his guard ; he went into the Castle, left by a secret door and followed a path known only to a few. He was in Pont-à-Mousson whilst the Croats were still waiting for him. When they learned the truth, they manifested their rage by oaths and blasphemies ; they said that God, or rather the devil, must have carried him up in the air over the woods. Incidents such as these led the public to believe that a special Providence was watching over Brother Mathew and people felt at their ease when travelling in his company. The Countess of Montgomery, for instance, hesitated about travelling from Metz to Verdun, for she still remembered the unlucky day when, without any respect for her dignity or that of the King of France, the King of Spain and the Duke of Lorraine, all of whom had given her passports, she was robbed by highwaymen of her money and baggage. Hearing that Brother Mathew was going on the same journey, she offered him her carriage, saying : ' Come with me ; your company will be a better safeguard than all the passports in the world.' Her hopes were not deceived ; Brother Mathew's guardian angel saved them both from all mishaps. Queen Anne of Austria took the liveliest interest in the lucky Brother's adventures and was delighted to listen to his own picturesque accounts of his travels. ' I owe the invisible protection that accompanies me everywhere I go to the prayers of M. Vincent,' he said modestly, and the Queen was of the same opinion.[40]

Brother Mathew was a veritable Providence for the monasteries of Lorraine whose situation, especially those of women, was heartrending ; Saint Peter Fourier, in his letters, gives us a harrowing picture of their condition. The departure of their boarders and the loss of revenue from their

[40] Abelly, *op. cit.*, Bk. I, Ch. XXXV, p. 165 ; Bk. II, Ch. XI, sect. I, p. 390 ; Collet, *op. cit.*, Vol. I, Bk. IV, pp. 320–322.

farms deprived some monasteries of every means of subsistence; others were sacked, like the other buildings of the cities in which they were situated. The nuns were not merely afraid of extreme poverty; they were still more afraid of the soldiery who were as hungry for debauchery as for pillage. The nuns of Nancy, Metz, Epinal, Saint-Nicholas-du-Port, Noményy, Mirecourt and other places, experienced all sorts of privations and mental distress.[41] At the sight of their misery, good Brother Mathew was moved to tears. 'Sir,' he wrote to Saint Vincent,[42] 'the grief of my heart is so great that I cannot express it without weeping when I think of the extreme poverty of these good nuns who have been assisted by your charity; and I cannot tell you even the least part of what they have to endure. One can scarcely recognise their habits which have been patched all over with pieces of green, grey and red cloth, in fact, with anything they can lay their hands on. They have had to wear wooden shoes!' The Carmelite nuns of Nancy lived for a long time on barley and oaten bread; a few herbs and vegetables cooked as a rule without fat or butter completed their meal; their only drink was water, and for the sick, a little sour wine. On fast days their evening meal consisted solely of wild fruits. The Visitation nuns at Nancy were not much better off. They reduced the consumption of bread to the least possible amount for a year and a half, lest they should have to leave their enclosure; half an ounce of meat three times a week was all that could be supplied. The cook employed only salt and water when preparing soup and the usual dishes of herbs, and on Sundays, as a treat, they were given a meat soup. Their drink consisted of a little sour liquid made from the juice of wild apples, water and the skins of pressed grapes. The rest was in keeping; patched habits and veils; shoes with soles that could not be seen from the number of nails, no firewood for heating, or oil or candle to give light; in winter, the baker out of charity used to bring them a few coals from his oven and this was the sole source of heat for months at a time. 'What has most distressed us,' wrote the Superioress of Saint Chantal, 'is

[41] Deblaye, *op. cit.*, p. 83.
[42] *Saint Vincent de Paul*, Vol. IX, p. 84.

that when our garden was well stocked, the soldiers came and took everything away, even pulling up the roots. . . . They also carried off a goat and a calf.'

In such conditions one can well understand that the question of leaving the enclosure to go to other places where life was not so hard was continually arising. A score of convents were founded between 1633 and 1664 by nuns driven from their own by famine. From Saint Nicholas they went to Munster, Châtellerault, Brussels and Paderborn; from Dieuze, to Toul, Marsal and Saverne; from Nancy, to Verdun-sur-Seine, Montfort-l'Amaury and Châteaudun; from Bar, to Mantua; from Noményto Bonne; from Mirecourt, to Aosta and Port-Beauvoisin.[43]

The King, as we have seen, took pity on the monasteries of Lorraine by giving them a grant of 45,000 livres and issuing orders that they should receive a regular supply of army bread. They also received veils, shoes, and large bales of cloth from which the nuns might make their habits.[44] The gifts varied according to the needs. The Carmelite nuns of Neufchâteau and Pont-à-Mousson required bedclothes of which they received a supply. The nuns of the Annunciation at Vaucouleurs, on returning to their convent after a prolonged absence, were supplied with furniture by Brother Mathew. The Friars Minor of Vic, who were in great distress, were given a large part of the seven hundred livres presented to Saint Vincent as stipends for Masses to be said for the repose of the soul of Richelieu.[45] A letter of thanks from Fr. Felician, Vicar General of the Capuchin Fathers of Lorraine, shows that they, too, like the others, had received a share of the Saint's alms.[46] Brother Mathew was accustomed to ask for a receipt from the monasteries to which he brought money, and the fifty-three still extant, all dated in the early months of 1647, resemble each other in

---

[43] Deblaye, *op. cit.*, pp. 84–87.
[44] Abelly, *op. cit.*, Bk. II, Ch. XI, sect. I, p. 388.
[45] Collet, *op. cit.*, Vol. I, Bk. IV, pp. 306–307. Collet says that he took these details from letters preserved in the Seminary at Toul.
[46] Collet consulted this letter (May 20, 1643) in the Seminary at Toul (*op. cit.*, p. 306, note 1).

their general tenor. Here is the first : ' We the undersigned humble Sister Servant of the Annunciation of Neufchâteau, certify that we have received from the hands of Brother Mathew seventy livres of the alms given by His Majesty to the poor religious of Lorraine ; and this obliges us, with our whole community, to redouble our vows and prayers for His said Majesty. Neufchâteau, this 28th of January, 1647. Sr. Elisabeth Herbin of Saint-Gabriel, humble Sister Servant of the Annunciation at Neufchâteau.'[47]

Saint Vincent also assisted the nuns by facilitating the removal of those who could no longer remain in their convents. At his request, Catharine de Bar, driven from Bruyères, where there was an Annunciation Convent, and then from Rambervillers, where, under the name of Mechtild of the Blessed Sacrament, she had embraced the Benedictine Rule, and finally, from Saint-Mihiel, where she lived in a most frightful state of misery, was received into the Abbey of Montmartre, Paris, as well as two other nuns of Rambervillers, whilst ten others were placed in various other convents. Mother Mechtild established a new branch of the Benedictine Order in Paris ; the Benedictine nuns of the Perpetual Adoration of the Blessed Sacrament.[48]

Saint Vincent suffered most keenly whenever he learned that an ecclesiastic, obliged to work for a living, was forced to abandon or neglect his priestly duties. A canon of Verdun who had become a farmer, wrote one day to his brother, a refugee in Paris, that worn out by excessive labour and want of food, ' he could no longer work or live, if he did not soon receive some assistance.' ' As a matter of fact,' he wrote, ' I do not know where to turn for help save to you, dear brother, who have been happy enough to have received and enjoyed the favour of one of the holiest and most charitable persons of our unfortunate century. And hence, through you, I hope for this favour from M. Vincent.' Saint Vincent was approached, and shortly afterwards Brother Mathew brought the venerable canon enough to live on without having to till the soil.[49]

[47] Archives of the Mission.
[48] Abelly, *op. cit.*, Bk. II, Ch. XI, sect. I, p. 388.
[49] Abelly, *op. cit.*, Bk. I, Ch. XI, sect. I, p. 386.

The indefatigable Brother Mathew still kept travelling through the whole of Lorraine, handing over large sums of money to all who were in need : members of Religious Orders of men and women, ruined noblemen and citizens, unemployed workmen and agricultural labourers. On each of his journeys, in addition to the bales of cloth supplied to religious communities of women, he clothed one hundred men and women.[50] He visited Château-Salins, Dieuze, Marsal, Moyen-Vic, Épinal, Remiremont, Mirecourt, Châtel-sur-Moselle, Stenay, Rambervillers, Lunéville and other places. We should like to have all the letters of thanks that flowed into Saint-Lazare after Brother Mathew's visits, but only one remains ; we shall now give it as it probably expressed the feelings of all.

'Sir,' wrote the Sheriffs of Lunéville to Saint Vincent, in 1642,[51] ' during all these many years in which this poor city has been afflicted by war, pestilence and famine, which have reduced it to its present state of utter misery, we have received instead of consolations, nothing but harsh treatment from our creditors and cruelty from the soldiery who have forcibly deprived us of the food we possessed ; in suchwise that it seemed as if Heaven itself had nothing in store for us but chastisements, when one of your children in the Lord arrived here laden with alms which greatly tempered our excessive evils and raised our hopes for God's mercy. As our sins have provoked His anger, we humbly kiss the hand that smites us and also welcome the effects of His divine graciousness with sentiments of extraordinary gratitude. We bless the instruments of His infinite clemency, both those who comfort us by such opportune acts of charity and those who procure and distribute these alms, and in particular you, Sir, whom we believe to be, after God, the principal author of so great a boon. It is more fitting that the Missionary whom you sent here should inform you that these alms have been well employed in this poor city, in which the chief citizens are reduced to nothingness, than to learn it from us who are more interested parties ; he has observed our state of desolation, and you will see before God the eternal

[50] *Ibid.*, p. 389. [51] *Ibid.*, p. 385.

obligation under which we are to you for having come to our relief in these circumstances.'

These statements were unfortunately only too well justified. The Archives of the Lorraine Chamber of Accounts enable us to follow year by year, from 1635 to 1645, the progress of want and misery in Lunéville and its environs. It is a sad list of villages burned, ruined or plundered by bands of soldiers ; to such an extent, indeed, that in most places the population either fell to zero, or at best to one, two, three or four inhabitants. After 1645, matters began to improve gradually but very slowly, as may be seen from the note concerning the years 1652–1653 : ' No payments have been made, on account of the poverty of the localities, at Laneuville-aux-Bois, Embermenil, Azerailles, Flin, Verdenal and Mehoncourt. Jolivet and Marainviller are utterly deserted.'[52]

Large sums of money were certainly needed for Lorraine, and yet it became necessary to diminish the supplies, for other provinces were also suffering from famine. The Queen summoned Saint Vincent one day and pointed out the critical situation that had arisen in the province of Artois. Arras, Bapaume, Hesdin, Landrecies, Gravelines, recently conquered by the King, were in ruins, as were the neighbouring villages, and the province was in such a state of distress as to recall that of Lorraine. So Brother Mathew bent his steps towards the north, travelling from village to village, from house to house, accompanied by the parish priest or his delegate, distributing, according to their recommendations, clothes, money and other alms. Artois was assisted for two years, and Lorraine for ten. ' In these two provinces,' says Abelly, ' Monsieur Vincent came to the assistance of twenty-five cities and their suburbs, all of which were in a state of extreme necessity, and he also relieved a large number of towns and villages.' He distributed ' up to fifteen or sixteen hundred thousand livres,' not to mention ' fourteen thousand ells of cloth of various kinds,' almost all of which was purchased in Paris, besides furniture for houses and vestments and sacred vessels for churches.[53]

[52] Deblaye, *op. cit.*, pp. 75–77.
[53] Abelly, *op. cit.*, Bk. II, Ch. IV, sect. I, p. 388–389.

SAINT VINCENT AND LORRAINE

Even that was not all, for poor Lorrainers who had fled to Paris also had experience of Saint Vincent's generosity. The depopulation of Lorraine was not solely due to the number of deaths ; the chief cause was emigration. Saint Vincent and the Ladies of Charity, touched by Brother Mathew's accounts, resolved to bring to Paris young girls of the Duchy who, on account of their poverty, were exposed to danger, and also orphans and even children of families that had lost their all. Brother Mathew, seeing it was impossible to take all the members of this triple category along with him, selected those who deserved most pity. For several months in succession he returned to Saint-Lazare, accompanied by large numbers of young travellers, the expenses of whose journey he defrayed. One hundred and sixty young girls thus escaped the dangers that awaited them, and Saint Vincent procured a means of livelihood for them in Paris. Small boys were admitted to Saint-Lazare and young girls to the Foundling Hospital. Positions in accordance with their condition were secured for the latter ; some as ladies' companions, others as housemaids or manual workers. The boys, who were well looked after, remained in Saint-Lazare until they were sufficiently grown up to earn their own living.[54]

The current of emigration from Lorraine swept a multitude of others into Paris who had no need of Brother Mathew's escort. These refugees threaded their way through the armies, with their little bundles on their backs, perhaps at the risk of their lives, but in no greater danger than if they had remained at home. As soon as they reached Paris, they made straight for Saint-Lazare, perfectly certain that they would there receive both help and assistance. In 1643, Fr. Fournier, Rector of the College at Nancy, wrote to Saint Vincent :[55] ' Your charity is so great that all the world has recourse to it. Everybody here regards you as the refuge of the poor and afflicted, and hence many have come and asked me to recommend them to you, that they may thus experience the effects of your goodness. Here are two whose

[54] *Ibid.*, p. 386 ; Bk. III, Ch. XX, p. 307 ; *Saint Vincent de Paul*, Vol. I, p. 591.
[55] Abelly, *op. cit.*, Bk. II, Ch. XI, sect. I, p. 387.

virtue and rank will rightly incline your charitable heart to come to their assistance.' The Saint welcomed them all, sought out lodgings for them, tried to secure them position and provided them with food and clothing. People in Paris said : ' Monsieur Vincent must have come from Lorraine himself, since he does so much for poor Lorrainers.'[56] He also provided for their spiritual needs. Either from indifference or perhaps from the want of priests, driven away by the famine, many had not approached the Sacraments for a long time. At his request, some ecclesiastics of the Tuesday Conferences gave missions at La Chapelle near Paris, in 1639, 1641 and 1642, to prepare them for their Easter duty.[57] Perrochel preached the last of these missions, which the Ladies of Charity and some devout laymen helped to make a success by good example and personal attendance.[58]

The greater number of the nobility of Lorraine had fled from their province where there was nothing to keep them, for their castles had been demolished or razed to the ground and their estates were uncultivated or utterly deserted ; they went to Paris like the rest, simply not to die of hunger. Their distress was all the greater as they were most unwilling to beg for alms ; they formed the category known as ' the decent poor ' who received no assistance because no one was aware of their poverty. Saint Vincent knew this and replied to someone who pointed it out to him : ' Ah ! Sir, what a pleasure you have given me ! Yes, it is right to help and comfort these poor noblemen in honour of Our Lord who was both very noble and very poor.' He began at once to cast about for means to remedy this particular evil. At first he thought of asking the Ladies of Charity to do so, but as he was only too well aware of all they were doing he did not entertain this idea for long. Moreover, if he asked them, some of the money that they were sending to Lorraine would be needed in Paris. He made up his mind not to ask anything more of the Ladies, to create a new association, and

[56] Evidence of Mary Dessert, the 39th witness at the Process of Beatification.
[57] *Saint Vincent de Paul*, Vol. I, p. 552.
[58] Abelly, *op. cit.*, Bk. I, Ch. XXXV, p. 166 ; Bk. II, Ch. XI, sect. I, p. 386 ; Collet, *op. cit.*, Bk. IV, p. 309.

as it was gentlemen who were to be helped, he would turn to gentlemen for assistance. He looked around on that group of great Christian men whose lives were devoted to works of charity, and none seemed better fitted for his purpose than Baron Gaston de Renty. This devout nobleman really loved the poor whom he served and instructed in his castle at Beny which he had turned into a hospice. Whenever he resided in Paris his happiest hours were those spent every day with the sick in the Hôtel-Dieu and with tramps in the Hospice of Saint-Gervais, encouraging the former to die well or bear their sufferings patiently, and teaching the latter the truths of religion. He was equally interested in seminaries, missions to Barbary, Canada, the Levant, and religious communities. He took part in every enterprise for the good of religion and mankind.

As soon as Saint Vincent explained his project to the Baron, the latter at once agreed. It was not difficult to find seven or eight other noblemen of the same way of thinking, and there was no desire to have a larger number. A meeting was called ; Saint Vincent explained the object he had in view, and it was decided, in the first place, to draw up as complete a list as possible of those who were to form the habitual clientèle of the new association, and then to give beside each name an indication of the degree of poverty, so that grants might be made in proportion to the sums at their disposal. De Renty himself took charge of collecting the money. At the next meeting, after the report was read, the noblemen present contributed as much money as was thought necessary for a month. They met on the first Sunday of the month and proceeded in the same fashion ; they continued to do this for eight years with a perseverance that never wearied. The members themselves distributed the funds, preserved the most absolute discretion, and strove, by the delicacy of their methods, to remove from the word ' alms ' any touch of humiliation ; they dealt on a perfect footing of equality with those whom they assisted and conveyed the impression that they were paying a debt. Saint Vincent always added his own contribution to those of the noblemen ; when the subscriptions did not reach the total anticipated, he supplied the balance. On one occasion, there was a deficit of three hundred livres which happened to be the exact sum he had received to purchase a horse instead of the old one which carried him and which was, in fact, so worn out that it frequently collapsed. The money went to the nobles of Lorraine, and the poor beast had to continue its increasingly feeble and broken-winded career.

On another occasion, two hundred livres were wanting; he called the Procurator and the following dialogue ensued :

' How much money have you in the chest ? '
' Just enough to feed the community for one day.'
' How much is that ? '
' Fifty crowns.'
' What ! Is that all ? '
' Yes, that's all ; I haven't another farthing.'
' Very well, then, bring it to me ; I want it.'

The Procurator did what he was told and the fifty crowns went to swell the monthly budget of the Lorrainers. Somebody overheard the dialogue and mentioned it to the noblemen of the Association ; one of them sent a purse of a thousand francs to Saint-Lazare on the following day. When Saint-Lazare had nothing to give, Saint Vincent borrowed rather than deprive himself of the pleasure of doing an act of charity. ' It is necessary,' he wrote one day to one of his confrères,[59] ' for us to borrow in these hard times both to feed ourselves and to assist the poor.'

The noblemen of De Renty's Association would have thought it far too little merely to secure the subsistence of those of Lorraine ; they were accustomed to visit and render them every service a friend can expect from a friend. When peace was restored to the Duchy, some of the refugees began to think of returning ; Saint Vincent supplied them with all the money they needed to take them home and even to support them for some time afterwards.

The Association of the Lorraine nobility became the Association of the English and Scotch nobility, when many representatives of the aristocracy of both these countries sought refuge in Paris during Cromwell's persecution ; it

[59] Collet, *op. cit.*, Bk. IV, p. 315, note M.

ANGÉLIQUE ARNAULD

assisted them for more than twenty years with the same zeal and according to the same methods.[60]

The relief of Lorraine ceased in 1649. The civil wars of the Fronde, the general condition of impoverishment that ensued, and Saint Vincent's absence from the capital for five months, hardly permitted the collection of further alms. This was the most sombre epoch for all works of charity. In the following years, it was necessary to come to the relief of provinces in a still greater plight; Lorraine, moreover, was beginning gradually to recover and henceforth was able to fend for itself. The eyes of Vincent de Paul, ever on the watch for those in need, were now turned in another direction.

---

[60] Abelly, *op. cit.*, Bk. I, Ch. XXXV, pp. 167–169; Bk. II, Ch. XI, sect. I, p. 387.

CHAPTER XLI

SAINT VINCENT AND THE RELIEF OF PICARDY AND CHAMPAGNE

THE Thirty Years' War, with its dreadful train of ruin, murder, misery and famine, will always constitute one of the saddest epochs in history. ' The history of man,' wrote Michelet,[1] ' seems to have come to an end when we enter on this period ; we are dealing no longer with men and nations ; only with the brutality of war and its rude instrument, the soldier. . . . It is his reign, and the people, their property, lives, bodies and souls, men, women and children, are delivered into his hands. Whoever carries a foot of steel at his side is king and does what he wills. Hence an orgy of crime and unlimited licence ; the horrors of cities besieged and the dreadful joys that follow a victorious assault ; horrors that were daily renewed in the case of open villages and defenceless families. In all directions, the vanquished, the wounded and the slain ; women passing from hand to hand. Everywhere tears and outcries.'

The Peace of Westphalia, signed on October 24, 1648, did not bring back to France the complete tranquillity of which she was in need. Though secure on her Eastern frontiers, she was always on the defence against the Spanish armies that threatened her from the North. The war in Flanders, begun in 1635, was only ended in 1659 by the Peace of the Pyrenees. These twenty-four years were years of unbelievable suffering for Picardy and Champagne, traversed by the belligerent armies and often the scene of battles. Acts of pillage and rapine were multiplied wherever the soldiers went, and Mazarin's troops inspired as much terror in the civil populations as those of the Archduke Leopold, the Governor of the Low Countries. At

[1] *Histoire de France*, Paris, 1857–1862, Vol. XII, p. 1.

times they inspired even more, for Germans, Swiss and Poles were recruited by the Cardinal Minister after the Peace of Westphalia and placed under the command of a Swiss, John Louis, Baron d'Erlach. These adventurers, or rather bandits, felt for the most part a hearty detestation of the Catholic religion ; they were utterly ignorant of the laws of honour and morality ; theft, rapine, murder even without a motive, had become habitual ; they rejoiced in the sufferings of others and delivered themselves up, for the sheer pleasure of it, to refinements of cruelty that surpass all the imagination can conceive or the pen set down.[2]

In one village, they seized a goat, put the bonnet of an old woman who had fallen into their hands on the animal's head, placed it in a bed and then went for the priest to administer the last sacraments. When the priest saw the animal he was indignant, and refused to lend himself to the whims of these ruffians. He paid for his refusal with torture and death. In other places, they fastened cats to the shoulders of the inhabitants and then scourged the poor creatures, which in their agony clawed the bodies of their victims till the blood flowed. In the village of Tourelle, near Rheims, an unfortunate peasant, pursued by these wretches, took refuge in his pig-sty, where he remained for three days without food. He was discovered by some soldiers who set fire to bundles of straw, the smoke of which smothered the man as he lay within. If a peasant refused to say where his money was hidden, they burned the soles of his feet or other sensitive parts of the body.[3]

One may imagine the dangers to which young girls were exposed. Near Rozoy, a gentleman named d'Arboy offered a large sum of money to avoid the pillage with which he was threatened. His proposal was accepted when the soldiers, perceiving his sister, demanded that she should be handed over with the money. Upon d'Arboy's refusal, they hanged him, carried off everything in the house on which they could lay their hands, and also his sister.[4] Little girls

---

[2] Feillet, *La misère au temps de la Fronde et Saint Vincent de Paul*, 5th ed., Paris, 1886, Ch. III, p. 73.
[3] Feillet, *op. cit.*, Ch. VI, p. 143.
[4] *Ibid.*, Ch. VIII, p. 191.

of eight and ten were subjected to the most abominable outrages under the eyes of their manacled parents.[5] After shamefully abusing their victims, these monsters—the word is not too strong—sprinkled them with gun-powder and set them on fire. Abominable scenes such as these were not confined to the provinces of Picardy and Champagne; they were reproduced in Anjou, Normandy, Maine, and, in fact, almost everywhere.[6] The terrified villagers fled into the cities, driving their flocks and herds before them; they thronged the streets and slept in outhouses.

The Spaniards, strengthened by the troops who had followed Turenne, now Mazarin's enemy, took the offensive in June, 1650. They captured Ribemont, Catelet and Guise (which they were forced to abandon on July 2), La Capelle, Vervins, Rethel and Château-Porcien, and crossed the Aisne and the Vesle. Turenne ventured even as far as La Ferté-Milon and Dammartin, with the intention of pushing on to Vincennes to liberate the captive princes, but as the Spaniards would not venture so far he contented himself with fomenting intrigues in Paris with the object of promoting popular risings. As his efforts failed, the Franco-Spanish army fell back on the Meuse and besieged Mouzon, which held out until November 6.

This marching and counter-marching occasioned new disorders. Ribemont, already traversed and pillaged by the royal armies of Du Plessis-Praslin, and De Rose, or Rosen-Worms, the successor of Baron d'Erlach, was handed over to the Archduke's forces. The latter pushed into the Church of Saint Peter, cruelly tortured many who had taken refuge there as a sacred asylum, stripped a monk, who had hidden beneath the arches, of his habit, suspended him from a beam by the arm-pits, pitilessly scourged him with their stirrup-leathers and, after a thousand other barbarous indignities, left him lying half-dead.[7] The resistance of Guise angered the Spaniards, who, compelled to retreat to escape the royal army which was pursuing them, signalised their passage with arson and pillage. The Castle of Vadencourt, the Abbey

---

[5] Feillet, *op. cit.*, Ch. VI, p. 143.   [6] *Ibid.*, Ch. VIII, p. 191.
[7] *Ibid.*, Ch. VIII, p. 190.

of Boheries, where their own sick and wounded had been nursed, Flavigny-le-Grand, Montreux, the Castle of Sart, Etreaupont, Sorbais, Luzoir, Gergny and many other places bore horrible traces of their savage vandalism. Almost all the inhabitants of Mont-Notre-Dame sought refuge in the towers of the church, taking with them their most precious possessions. The Archduke's soldiers, seeing that they could not get at them, piled up at the foot of the tower all the wooden materials they could find in the church, the pulpit, benches and confessionals, and set fire to them, with the result that the bells melted and the towers crashed down. Braine was demolished. The Abbey of Saint-Cloud, in which some members of the royal family were buried and which possessed inestimable art treasures, was badly damaged and the treasures destroyed or dispersed. Most families either took refuge in the towns or hid themselves in the woods, where their only food was roots.

Between July 28 and August 6, 1650, from fifteen to sixteen thousand of Du Plessis-Praslin troops marched through Merle. The amount of damage done within a radius of from three to four leagues was enormous : ten houses were burned down in the chief suburb and a number of others demolished by the soldiers to make huts. On the 12th, the Spaniards under Fuensaldaño arrived and carried off all the corn and cattle that remained, demanded 1600 livres not to plunder the church and 3000 to leave the Governor at liberty. Scarcely had Fuensaldaño's men departed than the Count de Sfondrat's soldiers appeared and started to pillage and plunder once more ; the women fled with their furniture, and this exodus cost the town another 8000 livres. The people of Saint-Gobain, with their cattle, fled to the forest to which they removed their furniture and provisions ; they were pursued and plundered by the soldiers ; they then hid in quarries or subterranean caves, where they remained for three months in a state of utter destitution. At Mayot, seventy houses were burned and the rest demolished ; the twenty survivors were unable to make out a livelihood. Versigny lost almost all its inhabitants ; they died of hunger in the forest of Monteau-les-Loups, from which they were afraid to venture on account of skirmishers who were watching at the edge of the woods and who murdered anyone they could lay hands on. All the houses in Juvincourt were destroyed by fire. In August the soldiers reaped the harvest, wasting and destroying by their carelessness and lack of skill three-quarters of the crops and carrying what was left into the cities to be sold, as well as the contents of all the granaries which they emptied completely. The vineyards were also ravaged and destroyed.

Almost everywhere famine was accompanied by sickness. At Montcornet, death carried off two-thirds of the inhabitants and 'of those who remain,' said the parish priest in 1650, 'half are ill and in danger of death.' The wisest fled the country and took refuge in the Palatinate.[8] As a matter of fact, this dreadful state of affairs was widespread in France, but nowhere was it so lamentable as in Picardy and Champagne. When the royal troops left the neighbourhood of Guise, even the soldiers were not strong enough to undergo the fatigue of a march, heightened as it was by burning rays of a July sun which darted beams on faces made gaunt by famine and revolting by sickness. Many fell by the way never to rise again.

The state of affairs was known in Paris; word was brought to Saint-Lazare and Vincent de Paul shuddered. He went to see the wife of President de Herse; as a result of their conversation he sent two Missionaries to Picardy with a horse laden with provisons and about five hundred livres in cash. When the supplies of food were exhausted (which did not take long, so great was the number of soldiers lying by the roadsides) the Missionaries went into the nearest towns to purchase more. Where they had expected to find plenty of provisions, they saw nothing but misery; foodstuffs were scarce and prices exorbitant. There was nothing left but to write to Paris. Saint Vincent at once called together the Ladies of Charity, read the letters from Picardy, and begged them to take up the work of assisting the wretched inhabitants of these unhappy provinces. The Ladies clearly recognised the necessity of increasing the number of Missionaries and the amount of assistance, but

---

[8] Edouard Fleury, *Le diocèse de Laon pendant la Fronde*, Laon, 1858, pp. 50–51.

the burthen was heavy, for they were already attending to the Hôtel-Dieu and the Foundling Hospital, and moreover, the troubles occasioned by the Fronde had diminished their own revenues. It was incumbent on them to find further large sums of money for this new undertaking, and they felt powerless to do so ; it was absolutely necessary for them to look for help elsewhere.[9] The next point was how precisely this should be effected. To assist the famine-stricken population of Lorraine they had disseminated amongst their wealthy friends copies of letters from Missionaries who had been sent to that province. They now resolved to use the same method, but to do so more thoroughly ; hitherto, they had distributed a few copies of the letters amongst their friends ; in future, they would print leaflets, thousands of copies of which would be struck off and despatched every month to the chief cities of France to let the public know how others were suffering and dying of hunger.[10]

The success of these small pamphlets would depend to a great extent on the ability of the man who edited them ; it was of the utmost importance that extracts should be well chosen and skilfully presented, if necessary, with a short introduction, a brief commentary, and in conclusion, an urgent appeal for charity. The choice fell on Charles Maignart de Bernières, a well-educated man of rank with an excellent knowledge of the Sacred Scriptures and the Fathers, and, in addition, animated by the fire of charity, for in 1649 he had resigned his post as Master of Requests to devote his life to the assistance of the poor and unfortunate.[11] Bernières, it is true, was a Port-Royalist, but what was wanted from him now was not doctrine but skilled assistance,

---

[9] Abelly, *op. cit.*, Vol. I, Ch. XL, p. 187 ; Vol. II, Ch. XI sect. II, p. 391.

[10] See in the *Recueil des Relations* the introduction to the *Relation* of September, 1650.

[11] *La vie et les œuvres de Charles Maignart de Bernières* (1616–1662) by A. Féron, Rouen, 1930, in-8°. Féron has a weakness for the Company of the Blessed Sacrament of which de Bernières was treasurer ; he is inclined to think that M. Vincent's first biographer unduly exalted the saint to the detriment of his emulators in charity. We cannot share his views and will state later on why Abelly deserves the confidence we place in him.

and the Ladies were convinced, and perhaps had a promise, that he would confine himself to the domain of charity and not digress into the fiery fields of polemical discussion. Such an appeal for assistance to a Jansenist made by Saint Vincent and the Ladies who surrounded him may seem strange, but there cannot be the slightest doubt about the part played by de Bernières.

In May 1651, that is to say, only nine months after the creation of this periodical, Anthony Lemaistre, who was thought to be the author of the preface to the book called *L'Aumône Chrestienne*,[12] attributed the *Relations*[13] (for such was the title given to the publication of the Ladies of Charity) to ' a most devout and most charitable magistrate.'[14] He wrote the following account, exaggerating in one or two instances (so at least we think) the part played by the latter : ' As miseries that are remote are often unknown to many because they have not been published in print, this magistrate, combining prudence with zeal, has thought that he should make them known to the whole of Paris and even to the chief cities of France by means of most true and exact *Relations*, which he has taken the trouble to set down himself by writing an account composed of several extracts from the letters sent to him every week by those who are assisting the poor in these places.'[15] The name of the anonymous editor, whose modesty Lemaistre respected, was made known in 1738 by the annotator of Lancelot's *Mémoires*.[16]

De Bernières' account-book is still in existence ; it may be found amongst the papers of Count de Montholon,[17] and has been published by M. Féron. The entry for February 15, 1651, runs as follows : ' Paid Savreux (the name of the bookseller) for the 4,000 *Relations* for the month of January and for the reprinting of old ones and other matters : 66 livres.'[18]

[12] Paris, 1651, 2 vols., oct.
[13] Each *Relation* was as a rule made up of eight quarto pages.
[14] P. 3.   [15] P. 16.
[16] Cologne, 1738, 2 vols., oct., Vol. II, p. 208, note. The notes are not by Lancelot.
[17] At the Castle of Rivière-Bourdot, Quevîllon, near Rouen.
[18] See Féron, *op. cit.*, p. 21.

The amounts expended on the *Relations* for the following months are also given in their respective places.[19]

Was it De Bernières who took the initiative in starting this publication ? As the first *Relation* was issued on the day after the Ladies of Charity had decided to add to their already heavy burthens those of relieving the unfortunate provinces and of appealing to the wealthy for further subscriptions,[20] there certainly seems to be a link between their deliberations and the creation of this monthly organ.[21] The Ladies, moreover, following Saint Vincent's example,[22] were ardent propagators of the leaflets which they were accustomed to take to ' suitable houses,'[23] and de Bernières himself stated that he was working for the Ladies' fund, or rather for that of the poor whom they assisted, in the following words which formed the conclusion of each issue : ' Those who feel inclined to contribute should communicate with the priests of the parishes or with Mesdames de Lamoignon and de Herse.' When Madame de Lamoignon, the President of the Ladies of Charity, was no longer at her post, two other names

---

[19] The *Relations* were reprinted in 1655 with a preface, some extracts from the book entitled *L'Aumosne Chrestienne* and an instruction on how to comfort the poor. In the preface, the author of this *Recueil* admits that he is the author of the *Relations* published for the past five years.

[20] Saint Vincent himself states that the first assistance rendered by the Ladies to Picardy was given on July 15, 1650 (*Saint Vincent de Paul*, Vol. XIII, p. 804). The facts related above explain why the publication of the first *Relation* was delayed two months.

[21] This is true only of the interval between September, 1650, and February, 1651. Shortly before Easter a special number of the *Relation* appeared. De Bernières' zeal then seems to have cooled, unless, perhaps, he had received no further letters. March and April form one number and so do September and October, whilst May and August have each a number to itself. There are only three *Relations* for 1650 : March, October and November-December ; three also for 1654 : January-February-March, April-May, and June-December ; 1655, one : January-April, before the *Recueil* was printed, and then one more for December.

[22] *Saint Vincent de Paul*, Vol. IV, p. 148.

[23] *Ibid.*, Vol. VI, p. 52. People did not subscribe to the *Relations ;* they were distributed gratis.

were given, namely, her daughter's and Madame de Traversay's, both of them members of the same Company. In 1655, in the preface to *A Collection of the Relations*, which was then reprinted by de Bernières, he again states : ' The respectable poor are no less afflicted now than they formerly were ; the same provinces are still in a state of desolation and the same Company, that of the Ladies of Charity, still continues to distribute amongst them all that is sent to them in charity.' On the other hand, it is quite possible that in this matter of assisting the provinces, the Company of the Blessed Sacrament and that of the Ladies of Charity may have constantly collaborated, at least at first, and this, in fact, would have been easy, for Saint Vincent was a member of the former and the director of the latter Association. This hypothesis, which allows us to believe that the idea of the *Relations* was first suggested at a meeting of the Company of the Blessed Sacrament, easily explains why the editorship was entrusted to de Bernières, and why the list of expenses is to be found amongst his accounts. Whatever may be thought of this theory, the first *Relation* appeared under the heading : ' The month of September 1650. State of the poor on the Picardy frontier. Selections from several letters written by ecclesiastics and other devout and trustworthy persons who were sent from Paris expressly to help them.'

Almost all these ecclesiastics were Saint Vincent's Missionaries. Anthony Lemaistre states in the preface to the *Aumosne Chrestienne* that their letters, from which extracts were taken for the *Relations*, had been addressed to de Bernières.[24] Abelly alleges that they were sent direct to Saint Vincent.[25] Which of them is right ? The preface to the *Aumosne* was written in 1651 by a man who knew de Bernières, and indeed frequented his society. On the other hand, Abelly, whose book, it is true, was published in 1664, utilised the notes and documents supplied to him by Saint-Lazare, and we know that when preparing his Chapter on the relief work carried out in Picardy and Champagne, he had before him the memoirs prepared by the Missionaries

[24] P. 16. M. Féron (*op. cit.*, p. 33, note 2) holds the same view.
[25] Abelly, *op. cit.*, Vol. II, p. 393, 397, 398 and 402.

who had been sent to these provinces.[26] It is clear, therefore, that the authority of each of these writers is high, but which of them should we prefer ? Everything would seem to favour Abelly's statement. The Missionaries in Picardy and Champagne were sent there by Saint Vincent ; they were subject to his authority and to his alone ; hence it was to him they were bound to give an account of their stewardship, to state their needs and those of the people amongst whom they were working. Why should they have written to de Bernières who was unknown to them ? Saint Vincent could do all that they required ; it was he who brought their letters to the meetings of the Ladies of Charity who then proceeded to apportion the funds ; it was only afterwards that de Bernières received letters to be inserted in the *Relations*. Such was the usual method of proceeding, and everything leads us to think that no other line of action was adopted. A direct correspondence between the Missionaries and de Bernières, especially with a view to publicity, would not have been at all to Saint Vincent's taste, and he would certainly have put an end to it. The *Relations* did not print only letters from Missionaries ; it is quite possible that some letters, or even the majority of the others, were sent direct to de Bernières from his own correspondents. Lemaistre's statement, therefore, may be, and we believe is, partly true and partly exaggerated.

During this dreadful period of public misery, the *Relations* were not the sole publications that urged the duty of assisting the unfortunate inhabitants of the two provinces. There was also a pastoral letter of the Archbishop of Paris, the *Aumosne Chrestienne*, published by Anthony Lemaistre (1651), the *Exhortation to the people of Paris*, by Godeau (1652), not to mention others better known.

What was needed above all was an intense propaganda and a strong charitable organisation. Saint Vincent set everything in order. The Ladies of Charity met every week to hand over to their treasurer all the alms they had

[26] Brother Robineau's Ms. p. 143 ; Father Berthe, at that time assistant to Father Alméras, had, as general director, control of the work of relief in which he collaborated ; he had, no doubt, the chief part in the preparation of these memoirs.

collected, to hear the correspondence read to them, and to proceed to an equitable distribution of the funds.[27] Saint Vincent, in order to give greater solemnity to the meetings, from time to time offered the position of chairman to some ecclesiastical dignitary ; the Archbishop of Reims on at least two occasions accepted his invitation.[28]

During the early years the Ladies received and despatched ten, twelve, fifteen and even sixteen (this was the highest figure) livres a month, for flour was then very dear and the number of poor people greatest. At the end of 1652, poor parish priests received one hundred crowns a month. Abelly reckons the sum total expended by the Ladies of Charity, between 1650 and 1660, at more than six hundred thousand livres, in money, provisions, clothes, linen, bedding, shoes, medicines, tools, corn and church vestments.[29] Hard and constant work was needed to amass such resources, and Saint Vincent, as usual, employed both natural and supernatural means. He celebrated Mass once a month in Notre-Dame that God might inspire the wealthy to give, and to give generously, and the Ladies who assisted at his Mass went to Holy Communion for the same intention. He also worked hard himself by begging from house to house ; sometimes he returned home bent down under the weight of crowns collected ; on some occasions he brought back as many as 1800. It was heavy work but not fatiguing, for joy lightened the burthen. He had also at times disappointments which he cheerfully endured ; he remarked on one occasion : ' To-day after I had preached very well to a lady, I thought she would give me a large contribution. Do you know what I got ? Four white crowns. Now, what use is that ? '[30]

De Bernières' account-books show that the Jansenists, especially the Dukes of Luynes and Liancourt, gave liberally.

[27] Abelly, *op. cit.*, Bk. II, Ch. XI, sect. II, p. 397 ; *Saint Vincent de Paul*, Vol. VI, p. 53.
[28] *Saint Vincent de Paul*, Vol. IV, pp. 197, 398.
[29] Abelly, *op. cit.*, Bk. I, Ch. XL, p. 188 ; Bk. II, Ch. XI, p. 397 ; *Saint Vincent de Paul*, Vol. IV, pp. 197, 499 ; Vol. VI, pp. 53, 614.
[30] Brother Robineau's Ms. p. 144. (A ' white crown ' was worth three francs.)

In addition to the sums handed over to Mlle Viole and Madame de Herse, amounting to 24,000 livres from January, 1651, to September, 1652, there were also direct contributions to the provinces which would easily reach double that figure. In addition, the Company of the Blessed Sacrament instituted a system of collection from its members that resulted ' in very considerable sums.'[31]

The gulf of misery was so deep that even such splendid gifts as these were unable to fill it. Furthermore, nothing palls so rapidly as open-handedness, unless it is devoted to one's own pleasure and amusement. Saint Vincent showed anxiety even as early as 1651. ' May God grant,' he wrote to one of his confrères,[32] ' that they may be able to continue ! How difficult it is for these Ladies to bear the weight of such great expenditure ! ' It became necessary to lessen the amount given in alms, and this at a time when the need was greater than ever.[33] The Missionaries were filled with grief and so, too, was their holy Founder. In March, 1652, the author of the *Relations* called attention to the fact that public charity was growing cold, which, no doubt, was due to the fact that famine and misery were on the increase, and had now reached even Paris and the Ile-de-France, thus diminishing the resources of those who had been hitherto the chief contributors. There were fresh complaints of the hard-heartedness of the wealthy in the *Relations* for December, 1654 and 1655 ; in 1657, Saint Vincent wrote :[34] ' Charity has grown very cold in Paris because everyone now feels the effects of the general state of public misery, so that . . . instead of sending sixteen thousand livres every month to the ruined provinces, it is very difficult just now to send a thousand.' In order to spread the distribution of alms over a longer period, he reserved money and supplies for the most necessitous cases, and frequently called attention to those engaged in the work of relief to the necessity of doing so. ' As long as any man is strong enough to work, the tools of his trade or craft

---

[31] Beauchet-Filleau, *op. cit.*, pp. 67, 126, 143, 190.
[32] *Saint Vincent de Paul*, Vol. IV, p. 197.
[33] *Relation* (July–August, 1651).
[34] *Saint Vincent de Paul*, Vol. VI, p. 614.

should be purchased for him, and he should not be given any further assistance. . . . Alms are not for those able to work . . . but for the poor enfeebled sick, poor orphans or old people.'[35]

The men to whom these instructions were sent were bound to Saint Vincent by the closest ties, for they were in fact his own Missionaries. We have already stated that at first he sent two priests, and then, when more fully informed of the ravages caused by the famine, he added to their number. On December 29, 1650, we find seven priests and six brothers,[36] on March 8, 1651, sixteen or eighteen of both categories,[37] and on May 22, 1652, ten or twelve.[38] On the approach of Easter, some additional priests were sent.[39]

The Missionaries were allotted to different dioceses,[40] and laboured in those of Laon, Noyon, Soissons, Châlons and Reims. A director general was authorised to supervise the work of his confrères ; he travelled about from place to place to discover local needs, to regulate expenses, and to nominate distributors of alms in all places to which the Missionaries could not go ; Saint Vincent was kept fully informed by the director as to how things were going. Father Berthe occupied this post for nearly two years (1651-1652) until sickness necessitated his recall.[41] Those of his collaborators whose names have come down to us are James Le Soudier at Saint-Quentin, Donald Crowley at Rethel, John Francis Mousnier, John Henry, Edmund Deschamps, Louis Champion, John James Mugnier, all priests ; Francis d'Hauteville, a cleric ; Mathew Regnard, John Parre, John Pascal Goret, John Dubourdieu and John Proust, lay-brothers. The Missionaries in Sedan and Montmirail are not included in this list. It is scarcely necessary to mention Father Alméras, who was sent to Picardy in 1652, fell ill there after three months and had to be recalled to Paris for medical treatment.[42] Saint Vincent

[35] *Saint Vincent de Paul*, Vol. IV, p. 183.   [36] *Ibid.*, p. 127.
[37] *Ibid.*, p. 156 ; Cf. p. 451.   [38] *Ibid.*, p. 392.   [39] *Ibid.*, p. 339.
[40] Abelly, *op. cit.*, Bk. II, Ch. XI, sect. II, p. 397.
[41] Abelly, *op. cit.*, Bk. II, Ch. XI, sect. II, p. 397 ; *Saint Vincent de Paul*, Vol. IV, pp. 183, 463, 465, 498.
[42] *Saint Vincent de Paul*, Vol. IV, pp. 433, 542 ; Vol. V, pp. 72, 92, 94, 132, 144.

was not even satisfied with all these ; when he reflected on the sad state of the provinces of Picardy and Champagne, he decided that his Daughters also were bound to lend their assistance. They nursed the sick and wounded and fed the hungry. In this way, he mobilised all his forces in the fight against human misery ; to the destructive energy of those who were instruments of famine and death, he opposed the beneficent energy of those who had consecrated themselves to God to combat evil and bring life to others.

The Missionaries, especially in the beginning, encountered a certain amount of difficulty in carrying out their work of charity. Disbanded soldiers fell on them and the alms collected to help the poor fell into the hands of their oppressors. Saint Vincent applied to Queen Anne of Austria, and on February 14, 1651, he obtained from the Court a public official Act, expressly recommending all civil and military authorities to respect and protect all who were carrying supplies to the ruined provinces so that their inhabitants might not perish of hunger.

' His Majesty, having been fully informed that the inhabitants of the majority of the villages of his frontiers of Picardy and Champagne are reduced to beggary and to a state of extreme destitution through having been exposed to acts of plunder and hostility by the enemy and by the movements and billetings of all the armies ; and furthermore, that many churches have been pillaged and despoiled of their sacred vestments, and that in order to sustain and feed the poor, several persons of this good city of Paris have contributed large and abundant alms which are most carefully employed by the Priests of the Mission and other charitable persons despatched to places that have suffered most ruin and evil, with the result that a large number of these poor people have been comforted in want and sickness ; yet whilst they have been doing so, the military, passing through or sojourning in these places where the said Missionaries are at work, have seized and robbed sacred vestments, provisions, clothing and other objects intended for the poor, so that if they have not His Majesty's protection, it will be impossible for them to continue so charitable and important a work ; both for the glory of God and the comfort and relief of His Majesty's subjects ; and His Majesty desiring to contribute to this work as far as he possibly can, with the advice of the Queen Regent, his mother, strictly forbids all his Governors, Lieutenant-Generals in his provinces and armies, Marshals and Camp Commandants, Colonels, Captains and all other leaders and officers commanding his troops, both cavalry and infantry, Frenchmen, and foreigners of no matter what nation, to billet or allow to be billeted any soldiers whatsoever, in the aforesaid villages of the said frontier provinces of Picardy and Champagne on behalf of which the said Priests of the Mission may ask them to provide a safeguard to assist the poor and the sick and there distribute the provisions which they are taking to the said villages, in such wise that they shall have full and complete liberty to exercise their charity in these places and in whatsoever manner as may seem good to them.'

' His Majesty likewise forbids all troops to take anything whatsoever from the said Priests of the Mission and those persons employed with or by them, on penalty of death, taking them under his special protection and safeguard and expressly enjoining all bailiffs, seneschals, judges, and provosts of merchants, to whom it may appertain, to see to the execution and publication of these presents and to prosecute all who may contravene them so that their punishment may serve as an example.'[43]

The Royal proclamation produced its effect. The Missionaries, now freer in their movements, redoubled their zeal in their mission of charity. Extracts from the letters reproduced in the *Relations* and the special reports collected by Feillet enable us to see to what a frightful degree of misery the unfortunate people of Picardy and Champagne had sunk. The same sights were to be witnessed again as had been seen in Lorraine, and Missionaries who were in a position to make comparisons, declared that the new situation was even more lamentable than the old.[44]

Wherever the armies passed the same scenes of horror were enacted : burnings, requisitions, domiciliary visits,

[43] *Saint Vincent de Paul*, Vol. XIII, p. 324.
[44] *Relation*, Oct., 1650.

plunderings, thefts, murders and acts of insolence and cruelty of every description. A Missionary newly arrived in Champagne thus gives his first impressions : ' No tongue can utter, no pen express, no ear dare listen to what we have seen in the early days of our visits. . . . All the churches and the most sacred mysteries profaned, vestments stolen, baptismal fonts broken, priests slain, maltreated or put to flight, all the houses demolished, the whole of the harvest carried off, the fields left without seed or tillers, almost universal famine and death, corpses without burial and for the most part exposed as a prey to wolves. The poor who have survived this state of misery are reduced (after losing all their possessions) to gathering corn or barley in the fields that has just begun to sprout and is half rotten. The bread they bake resembles mud and is so unwholesome that the life they lead is a living death. Almost all of them are sick ; they lie concealed in roofless cabins or holes into which one can scarcely enter, stretched for the most part on the bare ground or on rotten straw, without linen or clothes save a few wretched rags. Their faces are black and disfigured, and they resemble ghosts rather than men.'[45] Not only did the officers allow the soldiers to do as they pleased, they encouraged and even set them an example. They often set off to sack a village with as much display as if about to storm a stronghold. Infantry and cavalry marched in battalions of 1500 men, with their officers in front, drummers before and cannon behind. There was only one means of avoiding pillage : the payment of a fixed sum. If any inhabitant dared to resist, he was beaten ; if he murmured or remonstrated, he was maltreated and threatened with death ; if a complaint were lodged with the Generals, the same reply was always given : ' What can you expect ? The soldiers are not paid and they have to live.'

Hundreds of villages were completely destroyed by fire. Houry was wiped out with the exception of one house and a mill ; Marle lost one hundred houses ; at the end of 1653, Mouchy-le-Gache had only five houses standing out of sixty.[46] The débris of the houses supplied the soldiers with

[45] *Relation*, Jan., 1651.   [46] *Ibid.*, Nov.-Dec., 1653.

firewood and material for hutments.[47] The inhabitants, driven from their homes, sought refuge in the woods, hid in cellars, hunted around for caverns and concealed themselves under the ground like wild beasts. They were hunted, captured, suffocated, massacred or smoked out 'like foxes.'[48] One may imagine what girls and young men had to endure from the soldiers. The man disappeared to give place to the brute; reason surrendered to the basest and grossest instincts. It would be easy to dilate on such a sad theme but there are some things better left in the shade, and a veil should be thrown over such horrors.

Rosen's soldiers signalised themselves above all others by their barbarity and savagery. A contemporary states that one cannot refer to them 'without tears of blood.'[49] Their leader stated at a dinner party: 'The villages between the Aisne and the Marne have been handed over to me to be pillaged.' His men obeyed him so thoroughly that de Noirmoutiers and de Bussy became indignant and ordered their own troops to treat de Rosen's as enemies. On January 3, 1651, both generals added their names to those of Fabert and de Montaigut in a joint letter in which they requested Mazarin to interfere.[50] De Rosen, however, had not waited until January 3 to complain to the Cardinal of the line of conduct adopted by the four Generals in his regard. Mazarin, thus prejudiced, imagined that the Generals' letter was dictated from motives of jealousy, and on the 14th he replied to Fabert that de Rosen's troops had been despatched to hinder the enemy's entrance into Luxembourg to rest and re-form there, or to enter that Duchy itself and drive out the enemy. In these circumstances, he could not be superseded.[51] Notwithstanding the complaints that still kept pouring in, Mazarin continued to confide in de Rosen. It was all in vain, for Souyn, the Bailiff of Reims, had to go to Paris in June, at the head of a deputation to beseech the Queen to give orders for de

---

[47] Nicolas Lehault, *Recueil concernant les désordres qui se sont passés dans le comté de Marle pendant la guerre* (1635 à 1655), Vervins, 1851, in-12, p. 42.
[48] *Relation*, Oct., 1650.   [49] *Ibid.*, March-April, 1651.
[50] Feillet, *op. cit.*, p. 294.   [51] *Ibid.*, p. 554.

Rosen's troops to leave the province or to cease from plundering; it was also in vain that letters written by Lieutenant-General Audry, in which the excesses of the military were described, were printed in Paris to be submitted to the Royal Council.[52]

The people, abandoned by the Court, were forced to organise themselves against their oppressors. A body of two hundred peasants, raised and commanded by Charles Oudard, a tiler, nicknamed 'Captain Grind-Iron,' undertook the defence of the country between Damery and Châtillon, on the Marne. Oudard became the terror of all pillagers; concealing himself in the outskirts of a wood or by the side of a road, he awaited their coming, fell unexpectedly on them and murdered them without pity. Unfortunately, he found this line of business remunerative, and no longer made any distinction between robbers and honest men. He was greatly helped in his marauding expeditions by a nephew, a youth of eighteen; both of them were torn from their beds one day by armed peasants and hanged by the road-side; their bodies were long left exposed there as a terror to evil-doers.

The troops of Charles of Lorraine were scarcely any better than those of de Rosen. When complaints were made to the Duke, he replied cavalierly: 'Everyone of my soldiers is possessed by a devil who, at the mere sight of pillage, multiplies himself by three or four so that afterwards it is impossible to tame him.' Wherever the soldiers went there was nothing to be seen but wounded and dying, corpses transfixed by spits or sharp stakes, or the charred remains of men and women whose houses had been burned over their heads. A farmer near Braine, who refused to give the soldiers a sum of money he did not possess, was fastened by the feet to the tail of a mettlesome horse; the animal was violently beaten and darted off through winding paths, leaving the bleeding limbs of its victims behind it.[53] But the unfortunate people, even when the soldiers had gone, were not left in peace; tax-collectors and their creditors

[52] Lacourt, *op. cit.*, fol. 144.
[53] Stanislas Prious, *Histoire de Braine et de ses environs*, 1846, p. 57.

next came on the scene. The taxes were cruelly heavy;[54] the collectors of the tax on salt, wrote a missionary,[55] ' carry off even the shirts and . . . the earthen pots ' of the poor ; and he rightly added : ' It is amazing that persons are forced to take salt from those who have not a morsel of bread.'

In July, 1650, Mazarin resolved to order the General Assembly of the Clergy, whose opposition he feared, to follow the King to Guyenne. The expenses of the journey were to be defrayed by a sum of 200,000 livres levied on the benefice-holders of the kingdom. On the reception of this command, the Archbishop of Reims protested and the clergy of the diocese of Soissons resisted. They said that it was unjust to reckon amongst holders of benefices, parish priests who received nothing whatever from their cures.[56] In 1651, the inhabitants, exempted for ten years from the tax on serfs, were afraid lest they might be forced to pay up arrears, and the Sheriffs of Rethel begged the Ladies of Charity to secure the remission.[57] In 1652, it was the turn of the creditors. There was promise of an excellent harvest ; there seemed to be no prospect of an immediate passage of an army, and at last it looked as if the granaries would be filled. But there was a fresh disappointment. During the famine the peasants had borrowed in order to live, and now when better days were drawing near, the creditors pitilessly claimed their dues. Famine was again in sight. Parliament took action and published a decree on June 13 that put an end to the seizures.[58]

Requisitions, plunder and devastation inevitably brought about famine conditions. A great portion of the land was left uncultivated, and where people did sow seed they had very little hope of crops arriving at maturity because the soldiers would in all probability seize them in order to sell them in the nearest towns, or in places further off, if those

[54] *Relation*, April-May, 1654.
[55] *Relation*, May-June, 1651.
[56] Fleury, *op. cit.*, p. 68.
[57] *Saint Vincent de Paul*, Vol. IV, p. 227 ; cf. *Relation*, July-August, 1651.
[58] Feillet, *op. cit.*, p. 364.

CARDINAL MAZARIN

first approached refused to purchase.[59] The most fortunate lived on barley or rye bread, and the meat that was left after it had been boiled to make soup ; and they had not always even that. The father of a family one day went to a Missionary and asked him to be kind enough to give some preserves for his sick daughter. ' I am sorry,' said the priest, ' but you are one of the wealthiest men in Saint-Quentin and what we receive is intended only for the poor.' ' And am I not poor ? ' replied the unhappy father, ' my daughter has had nothing for the past two days but a little water.'[60] Most families had to be content with roots, decayed fruits and bread made from bran. People hunted for snails, frogs, mice, lizards and other reptiles ; they fell on the carcases of dogs and horses and devoured what had been left by the wolves ;[61] they browsed on grass, like the beasts of the field ; they tried to support life on the bark of trees and tore up their rags to devour the fragments.[62] A parish priest declared that he ' had buried three of his flock who had died of hunger ; others have lived on chopped straw mixed with earth from which they compose a food that cannot be called bread, since it is not made of any species of corn.' Others devoured five putrid carcases of horses. ' An old man entered the presbytery to have a piece of horse-flesh roasted ; the animal had died of mange fifteen days previously, was infected with worms and had been thrown into a stinking pit.'[63] Even human flesh was not excepted. If we are to believe the author of an anti-Mazarin pamphlet,[64] two children at Mareuil-en-Dôle had devoured the corpses of their father and mother. This may perhaps be fictitious, but one can scarcely disbelieve this passage from a letter published in the *Relations* : ' A fact we

[59] *Relation*, November, 1650.
[60] Feillet, *op. cit.*, p. 297 ; *Relation*, December, 1650.
[61] Lacourt, *op. cit.*, f⁰ 145 ; *Relation*, January, 1651.
[62] *Relation*, January, 1652.
[63] *Nouvelle Relation*, January, 1652.
[64] An eight-page pamphlet, published in 1652 by Simon Le Porteur, a Parisian bookseller, entitled : *Le récit véritable du funeste accident arrivé dans la Picardie, au village de Mareuil-sur-Deules, entre Soissons et Fismes, où deux enfants ont été trouvés se nourrir des cadavres ou corps de leurs père et mère.*

should not dare to relate, if we ourselves had not seen it, and one that inspires horror is that they (the famine-stricken) eat their own arms and hands and die in despair. We have done our best to hinder this evil as far as our alms will allow.'[65]

Living accommodation, like food, was scarce either as a result of the flight of the country-folk into the towns or on account of the large number of houses that had been burned down or destroyed. The sick were to be seen lying in the streets and the squares and in the woods; lodging was sought anywhere it could be found, in caverns, holes and cellars. Even the thatched cottages themselves did not afford much shelter; the rain came in through the roof, and it was neither pleasant nor healthy to paddle about in the water by day and sleep on damp, rotten straw by night.[66] There was no firewood, no shoes, no bed-clothes, no clothing, save a few tattered rags. In such circumstances, there was no hope of enduring the severe winter weather.

Sickness found easy victims in exhausted bodies exposed without defence to all sorts of weather conditions. There were invalids in every house. 'It is pitiful to see them,' wrote a Missionary,[67] 'some covered with scabs, others spotted with purpura; some with boils all over them, others with abscesses; one with the head swollen, another with the stomach; one with the feet, and another swollen all over from head to foot; when the swelling bursts pus flows out in large quantities and the stench is so great that nothing more horrible or pitiable can be looked on.' To these evils was added a formidable type of epidemic which spread from whatever places the armies had pitched their camp. The sickness began with violent pains in the head, accompanied by fever and diarrhoea; the crisis occurred on the tenth, eleventh or twelfth day and after that the fever ran its course, sometimes lasting a month. Its chief victims were the obese, the middle-aged and those exhausted by privations.[68] The *Relation* for September, 1650, states that

[65] *Relation*, January, 1652.
[66] *Relations*, October and November, 1650.
[67] *Relation*, November, 1650.
[68] *Particularités pour servir à l'histoire de Reims*, par Lacourt, Ms. Bibl. nat., fonds Champagne, t. XXXIII, f⁰ 142 v⁰.

there were a hundred and fifty ill at Ribemont and five hundred at Guise. In two months, the latter town lost five hundred of its inhabitants. Between August 15 and December 31, 1650, eight hundred died at Marle.[69] At Bazoches, fifty were buried in one day. Corpses were discovered in houses half eaten by wolves that had been attracted by the smell.[70] The greater part of the inhabitants of the country round Rethel and Thierache had died of the famine before May, 1651.[71] There were two thousand victims of the epidemic in the city of Reims alone.[72] In February, 1652, famine carried off more than two hundred a day in the provinces.[73] By 1656, sickness and emigration had transformed one hundred and twelve parishes in the diocese of Laon into deserts.[74]

Matters were in a bad state from the point of view of religion, for most parishes had lost their clergy who had either died or been driven away by famine.[75] The churches that had not been burned down were in a deplorable condition; rain fell into the sanctuary and even on to the altar. There were no vestments, missals, chalices or ciboriums. The Sacred species had disappeared, carried off and profaned by the soldiers. When a priest celebrated Mass he had to protect the Host lest it be carried away by the wind.[76] Hunger, moreover, was a danger to the faith, for in Sedan and its environs, Catholics yielded to the solicitations of members of the Reformed Churches who promised to assist them.[77]

Such were the evils; what were the remedies? It was not in Saint Vincent's power to deliver Champagne and Picardy from the troops that overran and ravaged them or to turn wolves into lambs, but wherever the emissaries of destruction were accomplishing their accursed work, he sent

---

[69] Lehault, *op. cit.*, p. 46. [70] *Relation*, December, 1650.
[71] *Relations*, March–April, May–June, 1651.
[72] Lacourt, *op. cit.*, p. 47. [73] *Nouvelle Relation*, January, 1652.
[74] Fleury, *op. cit.*, p. 89.
[75] Fleury, *op. cit.*, p. 89; *Relation*, December, 1650.
[76] *Relation*, October, November, December, 1650; April–May, 1654.
[77] *Relation*, July–August, 1651.

his messengers to bring back life. To the destructive armies of the King and of the Fronde he opposed his own armies of Ladies and Daughters of Charity, of Priests and Brothers of the Mission to alleviate the miseries of war and famine. The Ladies collected the funds; the priests and brothers wisely expended the money provided by the Ladies of Charity, in food, clothes, corn and various other ways, and his Daughters nursed the sick and wounded.

Contemporary evidence is not wanting by which we may see the part played by the Priests of the Mission in the relief of the devastated provinces; the chief source is their letters to Saint Vincent published in the *Relations* where they tell of their journeys to the various towns and villages, give an account of what they have seen and done, and state their needs. The enquiries held at Laon in 1651, 1653, and 1656 on the losses incurred since 1648 also supply valuable material. The depositions of witnesses, as Fleury tells us,[78] refer to the presence in the villages around Laon of the Missionaries of 'Monsieur Vincent,' who by their alms 'were the providence of the district.'

Nicholas Lehault, a notary at Marle, has left us a contemporary account of the calamities that befell his native place.[79] 'For the last two years or so,' he wrote in 1652, 'the Priests of the Mission have been distributing much charity amongst the poor of Marle and the surrounding districts; they have gone to their houses, to the Hôtel-Dieu and other places, to dress wounds and nurse the sick; their gifts, attention and diligence have saved a large number of persons from death. . . . Many respectable families both in this city and elsewhere, who from shame did not dare discover their utter poverty, have also received quite a special assistance, as have also several priests and members of the parochial clergy, who, not receiving any revenue from their benefices nor from their patrimonial possessions, also felt the pressure of the common and public calamity.' The

---

[78] Fleury, *Le diocèse de Laon pendant la Fronde*, Laon, 1858, in 8-vo., p. 58.

[79] *Recueil concernant des désordres qui se sont passés dans le comté de Marle pendant la guerre* (1635–1655), Verviers, imp. de Papillon, 1851, in-12, p. 73.

preponderant part taken by Saint Vincent and his helpers in the relief of the devastated provinces is also attested by letters addressed to him by the ecclesiastical and civil authorities thanking him for his assistance and begging for its continuance : for example, the Sheriffs of Rethel,[80] who wrote frequently, though only eight of their letters are extant.[81] On May 22, 1651, they wrote to Saint Vincent :[82] ' Nobody up to the present, except Your Reverence and members of your Company, has had compassion on our miseries.' Again, on September 8, 1653, they thus express their gratitude : ' For the last two years, Champagne, and especially this city, subsists solely on the charities you have despatched to them. And at present the whole country would remain abandoned and all the surviving inhabitants would have died of hunger if you had not prevented it by sending a person from your house who . . . by your orders, exercises great charity in their regard, thus rescuing them from the most utter misery and giving them life. The whole country is under the greatest obligations to you.'[83] In other letters, addressed to the Ladies of Charity, the Sheriffs state that their alms ' have rescued from the grave an infinite number of necessitous persons ' ;[84] and they also pay homage to the intelligent zeal of the Missionaries.[85]

Their pitiful appeals for help touched Saint Vincent, but how many others were stretching out their hands to him ! We have only one of his replies, dated May 20, 1651 : ' Nothing can be added,' he tells them,[86] ' to the two hundred and fifty livres sent from here every week. May God grant

[80] They say so themselves ; writing to Saint Vincent they say (*Saint Vincent de Paul*, Vol. IV, p. 226) : ' It is with regret that we have to inform you so frequently of the miserable state to which we are reduced ' ; and to the Ladies of Charity : ' The reception of so many benefits should impose a truce on our importunities.'

[81] Six to Saint Vincent and two to the Ladies of Charity. There are seven in the collection *Saint Vincent de Paul*, Vol. IV, V and XIII ; the eighth was published in part in the *Relation* for February, 1652. It is not absolutely certain that this last was addressed to Saint Vincent.

[82] *Saint Vincent de Paul*, Vol. IV, p. 200.
[83] *Ibid.*, p. 8.   [84] *Ibid.*, Vol. XIII, p. 831.
[85] *Ibid.*, p. 829.   [86] *Ibid.*, Vol. IV, p. 197.

that we may be able to continue them ! You can imagine what difficulty these ladies experience in bearing the burthen of such a heavy expense which amounts to more than a thousand livres a month for Champagne and Picardy. I very humbly beg you to believe, Gentlemen, that I will do all in my power to satisfy you and to assist your poor, both in the city and the neighbouring villages ; for the benefactors desire that both one and the other shall be visited by the priest of our Company who is there, and assist as far as what has been given to him can stretch, selecting by preference the sick poor and the most abandoned to the less necessitous.' Further appeals were added to those of the Sheriffs of Rethel ; for instance, that of President and Lieutenant-General Simonnet : ' We may without fear of contradiction observe in the charity you practise the earliest form of Christian devotion, for, in the primitive Church, Christians had but one heart and would not suffer that one amongst them should go without succour and assistance. . . . You, too, Sir, will not suffer it, for you provide for their needs with as much order as zeal, by the priests of your Congregation. . . . They have saved the lives of innumerable people and consoled and assisted others to die. These, in truth, are the effects of your charity.'[87]

The Sheriffs[88] and the Lieutenant-General of Saint-Quentin, in several letters, interpreted the grateful thanks of their fellow-citizens. The Lieutenant-General, after thanking Saint Vincent for his alms which ' had restored life to thousands reduced to the utmost extremity by the calamities of war,' added, ' and hence I am obliged by the office I hold and my knowledge of the duties it entails, to beg you to continue to be the father of our country by preserving the lives of many, many more poor sick and dying assisted by your priests who acquit themselves of their duties in the noblest fashion.'[89] Nor was Reims indifferent or ungrateful for the help it had received ; two letters are extant, one

[87] *Saint Vincent de Paul*, p. 233.
[88] *Relation*, February, 1652. It is very probable, but not certain, that the letter quoted in this *Relation* was addressed to Saint Vincent.
[89] *Saint Vincent de Paul*, Vol. V, p. 377.

from the Chief Magistrate[90] and the other from a member of the Chapter who subsequently became Archdeacon.[91] Ham also expressed its gratitude through its parish priest.[92]

These letters, which we shall not quote in full in order to avoid wearisome repetition, prove that history in no way exaggerates the services rendered by Saint Vincent de Paul to Picardy and Champagne, when war, pestilence and famine were rendering these unhappy provinces desolate. We should undoubtedly have many further expressions of gratitude if we still possessed the documents employed by Abelly, but these, unfortunately, are not now extant.[93] We shall now consider in greater detail the work done by Saint Vincent's children in their fight against famine and death.

The Missionaries found that the best means at their disposal in their fight against famine was the establishment of soup kitchens. A nourishing soup was made for seventy persons from a dozen of twopenny loaves and two pounds of various fats.[94] In all probability recipes for soup varied, for in time of famine, the chief point was to provide a good, substantial soup as cheaply as possible. Bernières suggests one in his *Instructions for the relief of the poor* (1649), republished in 1652 and 1654 as an introduction to his *Collection of Relations*. Another was given in *The way to make soup and what it costs for a hundred persons*; and still another in an *Instructive memorandum on how to assist the sick poor, to make soups for them and on how to distribute them*. Mother Angélique Arnauld herself was moved to a holy rivalry. ' Tell him,' she wrote[95] on January 17, 1649, to the Sister-cellarer of Port Royal, referring to de Bernières, ' tell him I have discovered a better way than his for making soup for the poor. . . . Instead of the bushel, which costs fifty *sols*, I take a little mutton or some hearts, livers and giblets which do not cost so much. I have the meat cooked and then taken and cut into small pieces, and the bread also is cut into very

---

[90] *Ibid.*, Vol. IV, p. 260.   [91] *Ibid.*, Vol. V, p. 385.
[92] *Ibid.*, p. 333.   [93] *Op. cit.*, Bk. II, Ch. XI, p. 407.
[94] Feillet, *op. cit.*, p. 365.
[95] *Letters* of Mother Angélique Arnauld, Utrecht, 1742–1744, 3 vols., in-12, Vol. I, p. 401.

small fragments. The whole thing is boiled again, after the cabbages have been cooked ; these were put in after the meat had been taken out and the boiler filled with water. During Christmastide and yesterday, on account of the weather, ten or twelve such pail-fulls were made in this way. But only forty *sols* worth of bread was used ; and thus a sufficient supply was secured for a hundred and fifty people who have nothing whatever.'

The paucity of funds at the Missionaries' disposal did not permit them to extend the distribution of food to every village or to repeat it daily. Only orphans under ten and those in extreme need were provided for, and that only twice a week.[96] In almost all districts the work was carried on thanks to the help rendered by devout girls or charitable women, who in this matter gladly helped the Missionaries.

Real, true charity looks to the future ; it is not content with remedying the miseries of the present, but considers those of the future in order to anticipate them. The Missionaries supplied the farmers with seed for corn crops, and also agricultural implements for the cultivation of the soil. They secured supplies of peas, beans and barley, ploughs, reaping hooks, flails and winnowing fans ; these gifts were accompanied by bill-hooks, axes and spinning-wheels ; in a word, everything that could help men and women to earn a living.[97] The Missionaries did not forget to exercise their charity towards young girls. 'An extra grant of fifty livres sent last week,' wrote one of them,[98] ' has saved several girls from shipwreck.' Another added : ' They have begun to send them to the Community of the Daughters of Saint Martha (at Reims) were they are instructed in the fear of God and taught to spend their time at some little employment.'[99] The Missionaries also collected foundlings, despite the heavy expenses incurred by so doing. In December, 1650, those at Saint Quentin took charge of thirty-five orphans still at the breast.[100] The special number of the

[96] Fleury, *op. cit.*, p. 76.
[97] *Relation* (special number for March, 1651 ; *Relation*, March–April, 1652).
[98] *Relation*, March–April, 1651.
[99] *Saint Vincent de Paul*, Vol. V, p. 95.
[100] *Relation*, December, 1650.

RELIEF OF PICARDY AND CHAMPAGNE

Relation for March, 1651, refers to five hundred orphans under seven who were both fatherless and motherless. The *Relation* of April-May, 1654, states that there were six hundred orphans under twelve in the environs of Laon all ' in a shameful state of nakedness ' ; that of December reckons that there were more than six thousand in the villages visited by the Missionaries in their journeys through the diocese. Cloth was brought from Paris and charitable women gratuitously undertook to make clothes for them. The sick were even more numerous than the orphans. Saint Vincent's envoys were deeply pained because they could not come to the relief of all who were in distress ; even if there had been fifty or even a hundred of them they would not even then have been able to cope with the situation. Nursing the sick was only part of their task ; first of all they had to look for them in the streets and in their own homes, and they did so every day. Wherever they went they encountered most pitiful sights. A Missionary at Saint Quentin related that whilst passing through a suburb, he went into twenty-five hovels, in each of which there were two or three sick people ; in one, two poor widows and their eight children were lying on the floor, without linen, and in a state of complete destitution. On the same day, another priest, passing through Saint Quentin or the neighbourhood, found several doors shut ; he knocked in vain, no one came to open. He sent for a locksmith and found the sick lying on a pile of half-rotten straw ; they had had nothing to eat for two days.[101] The Fathers frequently came across similar cases.

When the sick had been discovered, the next thing to do was to provide them with accommodation. The Missionaries reorganised several hospitals and established others. Thanks to their efforts, Guise, Laon, Marle, La Fère, Rethel, Donchéry, Boult-sur-Suippes, Sommepy, Vandy, Saint-Étienne-à-Arnes and other places were enabled to provide lodgings for the shelterless sick in plainly furnished houses that were at any rate better than the streets, caverns or tumbled-down hovels in which they had been

[101] *Relation*, September, 1650.

discovered.[102] 'Refuges such as these,' we read in a contemporary document,[103] 'which charity and devotedness have thrown open to the sick will save many from death.'

The Daughters of Charity acted as nurses in the hospital at Rethel and Saint-Étienne-à-Arnes.[104] At Bazoches, they visited the sick in their homes, brought them soup and medicine, and if necessary, bled the patients.[105] There was such a multitude of sick that the Sisters were greatly overworked, so much so that Saint Vincent feared lest their spiritual life might suffer; hence he recommended his Daughters not to forget themselves whilst working for others. On March 8, 1651, he wrote to the Daughters of Charity at Saint-Étienne :[106] 'There is one thing,' he told them, ' which can do much to bring down God's graces on yourselves and your work, and that is the observance of your devotional exercises, such as morning mental prayer, even if only for half an hour, particular examination of conscience, spiritual reading, the raising of your hearts to God, and purity of intention in all your thoughts and actions. To be faithful in this is to be true daughters of Our Lord; it will render you worthy of His love and will help you to advance with certainty in the way of perfection. . . . I do not know if, on your departure, I recommended these holy practices to you; if I did not, I do so now, even though I am well aware you never omit any of them willingly and that, amidst all your work and worry, you frequently place yourselves in the presence of God and this presence enables you every day to find time to carry out all the rest, as far as the place and the service of the poor will permit. So continue, my dear Sisters, to fulfil the divine Will in all things, place your confidence in God, offer yourselves to Him, call upon Him, and do not doubt that He will be your strength, your consolation, and one day, the glory of your souls.'

[102] *Relations*, February, March–April, 1651; Lacourt, *op. cit.*, f° 143 v°.
[103] Lacourt, *op. cit.*, f° 142 v° and 143 v°.
[104] *Relation*, February, 1651; *Saint Vincent de Paul*, Vol. VIII, p. 205.
[105] *Relation*, December, 1650; *Saint Vincent de Paul*, Vol. IV, p. 161.
[106] *Saint Vincent de Paul*, Vol. IV, p. 161.

God was indeed their strength, and hence they never were afraid of the epidemic, notwithstanding its ravages. The doctors did not know how to combat it ; the Missionaries made use of a powder, the efficacy of which they loudly proclaimed in their letters, whilst a Jesuit Brother, John Roch, preferred to use emetics, by which, it is said, he effected some wonderful cures.

Sanitary precautions greatly contributed to the amelioration of public health. At Reims, ' care was taken to keep the streets very clean ; every day, a bell was rung at the city-gate at one o'clock of the afternoon to warn the people to clean up.'[107] The burial of the dead was even more important than scavenging the streets. Turenne's army, defeated by the King's forces in December, 1650, near Saint Étienne-à-Arnes and Saint-Souplet, had left more than 1500 dead on the field. The bodies were left to rot without burial, and the air was filled with the germs of infection. As soon as Saint Vincent learned this, he wrote to the Missionary who was assisting the poor in that district, Father Edmund Deschamps, asking him to leave aside all other work and bury the dead. The work of the grave-diggers, which was rendered easier by an exceptionally heavy frost, was almost finished when a thaw set in. The last days were the hardest owing to the difficulty of digging graves in a muddy and sticky soil. When the last blow of the pick had been struck, Edmund Deschamps was pleased to announce the fact to Saint Vincent and to add that the entire province blessed those charitable persons who by their alms had contributed to this good work.[108]

The question of the parochial clergy was, in the Saint's opinion, the most important of all, not only from the point of view of religion, for in the absence of priests public worship would cease, souls would be abandoned, and as a consequence, the dying would be in peril of their eternal salvation ; but also from the point of view of the relief of the poor and sick, because in every parish, it was chiefly on the priest that Saint Vincent relied to organise all charitable works, because his Missionaries could not be everywhere at

[107] Lacourt, *op. cit.*, f° 142 v°.
[108] *Saint Vincent de Paul*, Vol. IV, p. 143.

once. In order to keep the priests in their parishes, for they were threatening to leave, he assured them of a salary of five or six *sols* a day, provided them with cassocks, body-linen and all things necessary for divine service; altar-cloths, altar linen, chasubles, stoles, burses, surplices, chalices and cruets, holy water fonts and sprinklers, lights for the church, maps, censers, torches and lanterns to accompany the Blessed Sacrament when carried in procession, bells and devout pictures.[109] The Missionaries, at every visitation, stimulated the zeal of the parish clergy. It is greatly to be desired that we had a complete history of each of the men who were placed by the Saint at the service of the poor of Picardy and Champagne. Heroic deeds must surely have abounded. Saint Vincent, in a letter to Father Lambert, tells how Father Crowley, who, with two priests and a lay-brother, was in charge of Rethel and the surrounding district, 'crossed rivers, travelled bare-footed, and undertook dangerous journeys in the midst of the troops.' He was told one day that the soldiers had just carried off the cattle of some poor people, that is to say all their possessions; he pursued the robbers and caught up with them in a wood; he pleaded so well that the cattle were restored and he himself had the joy of bringing them back to their lawful owners.[110] In August, 1652, Father Crowley, like most of his confrères, was recalled to Paris. Saint Vincent had resigned himself to this measure through force of necessity, for the capital, besieged by the armies of Condé and Charles of Lorraine and suffering from the direst want, absorbed the alms of charitable persons. On the other hand, as the harvests were good and the day seemed to be at hand when the two unfortunate provinces would be able to fend for themselves,[111] relief was suspended for the time being.

The situation, however, rapidly changed. Paris recognised the King's authority; Condé and Charles of Lorraine, seeing there was no hope of capturing the capital, withdrew to the Eastern and Northern frontiers, pursued by Turenne,

[109] Fleury, *op. cit.*, p. 78.
[110] *Saint Vincent de Paul*, Vol. IV, p. 381.
[111] *Ibid.*, p. 433.

then in the King's service, whilst the Spaniards advanced as far as Vervins and took that town. Once again, Champagne and Picardy became a prey to the military, and similar scenes of disorder, the disgrace of armies, were renewed. The situation rapidly grew worse. On January 3, 1653, the Duchesse d'Aiguillon and Madame de Herse, deeply moved by the news that had reached them, hastened to inform Saint Vincent and begged him, as they were unable to travel, to come and confer with them. He was expected at the Mother-House of the Daughters of Charity for a conference and he was preparing to go out. Picardy and Champagne were, however, of far greater importance. The carriage was at the door; he got in and drove off to the Ladies. What took place at this meeting will never be known. It was quite clear that help must be sent to the people of Champagne and Picardy as soon as possible, but the question was where to find the money? It seemed an insoluble problem and Saint Vincent wrote that same day:[112] ' I fear we cannot make any great efforts because a great deal of expense has been already incurred for the relief of this diocese which needs seven or eight thousand livres a week.' It is probable that a General Assembly of the Ladies of Charity was decided on, and that as no suggestions were forthcoming from the deliberations, they separated after recognising their powerlessness. On January 11, Saint Vincent wrote to the Superior at Sedan : ' I am deeply afflicted at the wretched state of affairs on your frontier as well as at the large number of the poor who are overwhelming you ; however, I can only pray to God to help them, and that, indeed, I do, for nothing in addition to the hundred livres a month that you receive is to be expected. Sedan is the only place on the frontier to which Paris still continues to send alms ; it has been compelled to withdraw them from almost everywhere else in order to cope with cases of extreme necessity in this diocese where the armies have remained so long.'[113]

The *Relations* again begin to refer to Picardy and Champagne in March, and alms began once more to be

[112] *Ibid.*, pp. 419, 537.   [113] *Ibid.*, p. 542.

despatched ; a few Missionaries were sent to distribute them, and in October they were at work at Rethel and Saint-Quentin.[114] The state of affairs was by then very bad ; in many parishes there were no longer any priests to supply the poor and sick with the consolations of religion ; those who had not yet deserted their posts were threatening to leave and to go and seek elsewhere for means of subsistence. It was of the utmost importance to remedy this evil as quickly as possible, and Saint Vincent resolved to send Father Alméras to Laon. In a letter addressed to the Canon Precentor of that city he thus sets out his idea of the mission entrusted to his confrère : ' We are sending a priest of our Congregation to visit the poor parish priests and other clergy of your diocese who are in need of assistance, and also to strive to bring them together, with the consent of the Vicar General, so that he may confer with them on the best means of coming to the relief of parishes that have been deserted and to act in such a way that none is left without spiritual assistance. He will afterwards distribute clothes and determine what sum shall be allotted every month. He will also see the poor, especially those in country places ; in which he will follow your advice.'[115] Father Alméras assembled the clergy by deaneries, strongly urged them not to desert their posts and even to adopt neighbouring parishes that had been left without pastors. He distributed cassocks, provided sacristies with all that was needed for public worship, and supplied the clergy with sufficient money to repair churches which had been destroyed.[116] After three months' toil, either in the diocese of Laon or in the neighbouring bishoprics, Father Alméras, whose delicate health was unfitted to endure such great fatigue, fell gravely ill in Laon, and Saint Vincent had to recall him to Paris some time in May.[117] After this recall, apart from the staffs of the house of the Mission at Montmirail and Sedan, only three lay-brothers were left in Picardy and Champagne :

[114] *Relations*, October, November–December, 1653.
[115] *Saint Vincent de Paul*, Vol. V, p. 72.
[116] *Ibid.*, p. 92 ; *Relations*, April, May, 1654 ; Fleury, *op. cit.*, p. 78.
[117] *Saint Vincent de Paul*, Vol. V, pp. 132, 144.

Brother John Parre, at Laon ; Brother John Proust at Noyon ; and Brother Mathew at Rethel.[118]

There are no documents extant to supply us with information on the work done by the two last Brothers, but there is a fair amount of material at our disposal in regard to the first. We can follow Brother Parre as he moved from place to place by means of the letters written to him by Saint Vincent. Acting for the Ladies of Charity, he distributed amongst the parish priests money to repair their churches, stipends for Masses, vestments for their sacristies and cassocks ;[119] he supplied tillers of the soil with seeds and agricultural implements ;[120] workmen, with spinning-wheels and tools ;[121] clothes to those who were worst clad,[122] and bed-clothes to hospitals.[123] He established Confraternities of Charity at Rethel, Rheims, Château-Porcien, La Fère, Ham, Saint-Quentin, Rocroi, Mezières, Charleville, Donchéry and other places, procured good directors for them, and superintended their working by periodical visits.[124] The Bishops of Noyon entrusted him with the building of a church at Fieulaine, where a statue of the Blessed Virgin had just been discovered and rendered famous by miracles, and which was called Our Lady of Peace.[125] He called Saint Vincent's attention to any cases of religious vocations which he encountered on his journeys,[126] as well as to the needs of churches, parish clergy and private individuals.[127] His letters were taken to the meetings of the Ladies of Charity, read aloud, commented on and discussed ; the state of the treasury was

[118] *Ibid.*, Vol. VI, p. 92.
[119] *Ibid.*, pp. 394, 547, 616, 622 ; Vol. VII, pp. 366, 557, 571 ; Vol. VIII, pp. 20, 21, 109, 319, 321, 324, 329, 339, 340, 371.
[120] *Ibid.*, Vol. VIII, pp. 72, 109, 324.
[121] *Ibid.*, Vol. VIII, pp. 21, 73.
[122] *Ibid.*, Vol. VI, pp. 376, 394 ; Vol. VII, p. 404.
[123] *Ibid.*, Vol. VI, p. 622.
[124] *Ibid.*, Vol. VII, pp. 557, 599; Vol. VIII, p. 21 ; Vol. XI, p. 339.
[125] *Ibid.*, Vol. VII, p. 559 ; Vol. VIII, pp. 20, 21, 38, 51, 63, 72, 129.
[126] *Ibid.*, Vol. VII, p. 119 ; Vol. VIII, p. 325.
[127] *Ibid.*, Vol. VI, p. 486 ; Vol. VIII, p. 109.

examined to see what help could be given, and as a general rule, the amount voted was less than what he had asked for. Saint Vincent, along with the money, sent him advice replete with wisdom, which Brother Parre always treated with the deepest respect.

The Saint frequently recommended economy. The Ladies, from much giving, were now beginning to grow tired, and so too were those whom they asked to subscribe. The *Relations* bewail the fact;[128] Brother John groaned over it[129] and Saint Vincent notes it with sadness.[130] Hence, there should be no waste in the distribution of funds; nor even liberality; only just what is necessary and nothing more. Here are Saint Vincent's own words: 'A small amount has been set aside to help some poor persons to sow a little patch of land; I mean, the poorest, those who without such assistance could do nothing. And even so, nothing is quite ready as yet, but an effort will be made to get together at least one hundred pistoles for that purpose, whilst waiting until it is time to sow. Nevertheless, they beg you to find out in what parts of Picardy and Champagne the poorest people are to be found, those, namely, who are in need of such help; I repeat, the greatest need. You might recommend them, in passing, to prepare a little patch of ground, to dig and manure it, and also to pray to God to send them some seed to put into it, and without promising anything, give them hope that God will provide. Moreover, we should like to make arrangements by which all the other poor people, both men and women, who have no land, may earn their living, by supplying the men with tools and the girls and women with spinning-wheels and flax or wool to spin, but only to the poorest. When peace arrives everyone will have something to do, and as the soldiers will no longer take away what the people possess, they will easily be able to make some little savings and will gradually recover; now, to that end, the Assembly has decided that they should be helped to make a beginning, and also informed that no further help is to be expected from Paris. So find out then,

[128] *Relations*, December, 1654, and December, 1655.
[129] *Saint Vincent de Paul*, Vol. VII, p. 366.
[130] *Ibid.*, Vol. VII, pp. 387, 519, 545, 599.

my dear Brother, in what places are poor persons in the greatest need of assistance for the last time, and roughly the amount of money needed for that purpose ; as also to cover roofless and ruined churches, but only the part over the altar so that Mass may be said with some decency : I mean churches in places where the people themselves are unable to do so, and which do not depend on any Chapter, Abbey or Lord with a right to tithes, who are obliged to maintain them, for it is their duty to effect repairs, and if you let us know who are those patrons who hold benefices and those communities, together with the names of the parishes containing ruined churches which they are bound to maintain, we shall see that they are requested to do so.'[131]

Saint Vincent did not leave it to others to put the matters before benefice-holders whom he personally knew. On July 12, 1659, he wrote to Charles de Saveuses : ' Your very humble servant Vincent . . . now very humbly requests you, on behalf of the Ladies of Charity and especially on the part of Madame the Duchesse d'Aiguillon and Madame Fouquet, who have heard, Sir, that you are about to proceed to Rheims to visit the churches that depend on your Abbey of Saint Nicholas, to be kind enough to pay particular attention to the needs of the church at Avançon, which is completely destroyed, so that you may afterwards induce the Gentlemen of the Holy Chapel to make such contribution as will place it in such a condition that Mass may be said there, and the sacraments administered with some decency.'[132]

To his advice on the need of economy Saint Vincent added recommendations on discretion. As he was well aware of the ingenious methods adopted by some to appear poor, he advised Brother Parre to be on his guard and suggested two means : first, to acquire exact information, and second, to keep secrets. ' The Ladies have expressed a wish that I should request you, as I now do, to find out skilfully, in each canton and village through which you pass, the number of poor persons who need to be clothed during the coming winter, either wholly or in part, so that an estimate may be made of the probable expenses and also that you

[131] *Ibid.*, Vol. VIII, p. 72.   [132] *Ibid.*, p. 22.

may be able to have the clothes ready as soon as possible. It is thought that it will be better to buy linsey-woolsey than serge. Hence you should write down the names of those poor people so that when the time for distribution arrives, the alms may be given to them and not to those who can do without them. Now, to make a proper selection, it is essential that you should see them in their own homes, so as to see with your own eyes who are most in need and who are less so. Now, as it is impossible for you to pay all these visits yourself, you might employ some devout and prudent persons who will do their work honestly and give you accurate information of the state of each individual. But this information must be obtained without the poor knowing anything about it, for otherwise those who have already some clothes would conceal them so as to appear naked.'[133] Brother Parre was, as a matter of fact, an intelligent man, well able to detect even the most skilful tricksters, and both Saint Vincent and the Ladies of Charity knew that they might safely rely on his zeal, intelligence and powers of penetration. On one occasion, during a meeting of the Ladies, a letter most flattering to the Brother was read in public in which it was stated that he had established a Confraternity of Charity in Reims consisting of its most notable women to attend to the poor and of the orphans of the city and its environs : it was also stated that he had formed a similar confraternity at Saint-Quentin. Madame Talon, mother of the Advocate-General, who was present at the meeting, had returned from Reims only a few days previously, and several persons had spoken to her of the Brother in the most laudatory terms. Full of what she had heard, she repeated his praises. ' Not only,' said she, ' did the good Brother establish a Charity at Reims but he is still busy organising it, and at his request, a virtuous Canon of the city has accepted its direction.' She then went on to state a number of facts which went to show how charitably and intelligently he was carrying on his mission. A lady interrupted her with the remark : ' If the Brothers of the Mission have received all those graces by which they have been able to accomplish all the good we have just heard, what will not

[133] *Saint Vincent de Paul*, Vol. VI, p. 367.

the Priests do ? ' When Vincent de Paul heard these words, he experienced a feeling of pleasure, as he publicly confessed that evening during a conference.[134]

The praises of Brother Parre and his confrères reached beyond the walls of the room in which the Ladies of Charity held their meetings. Somewhat later, a Missionary travelling through Champagne met the local parish priest, who asked : ' Who are you ? ' ' A Priest of the Congregation of the Mission,' replied the other, whereupon the parish priest fell on the traveller's neck and publicly embraced him. He then took the Missionary to his own house and told him of all that Saint Vincent had done for the country. ' I personally,' he added, ' owe him a deep debt of gratitude. Look at the cassock I am wearing : *et hac me veste contexit.*'[135]

In addition to those who were ground down by the invading armies, there was another class of unfortunates to whom the Saint's heart went out, namely, the soldiers themselves who were in hospital suffering from either sickness or wounds. Hence, he gladly complied with the Queen's commands when she asked for Sisters to nurse them. We find Daughters of Charity at Châlons, Sainte-Menehould, Sedan, La Fère, Stenay, Calais, spending themselves on those victims of war, nursing back to life those who had taken up arms to deal death to their fellow-men. He willingly reminded them, the better to attach them to their new duties, that they had been sent by the Queen : ' It is the Queen who has asked for you. Just think, Sisters ! who are we to be remembered by the greatest Queen in the world, we who are but poor, wretched creatures, or to speak more truly, simply beggars. Yes, my Daughters, you and I. Consequently, we have great reason to be humble,'[136] It was certainly a great honour, yet one not to be published on the highways and by-ways. ' Humble yourselves,' he repeated,[137] ' do not say at the inns where you will put up, that the Queen sent for you, that she preferred you to many others ; say nothing at all about that. If people ask

[134] *Ibid.*, Vol. XI, p. 339.
[135] Abelly, *op. cit.*, Bk. III, Ch. XI, sect. V, p. 154.
[136] *Saint Vincent de Paul*, Vol. X, p. 2.
[137] *Ibid.*, p. 552.

" Where are you going ? " just say " We are going where God calls us," or, at another time, " We are going to such a place." " To do what ? " " Just whatever God may be pleased we should be told to do." ' Saint Vincent loved to repeat the words : ' We are going where God calls us,' and to draw from them the consoling consequences : ' How happy you are, my dear Sisters, that God has chosen you to assist the poor wounded ! From the moment you leave here, your good angels will count your footsteps ; all that you will say, do or think will be reckoned for you before God. Oh ! Sisters, how happy will you not be to have helped so many poor people when you appear before Our Lord ! '[138]

The Queen's first request was for Sisters for the Hôtel-Dieu at Châlons. This was early in 1653, and Mlle Le Gras selected Sisters from various houses, thus imposing sacrifices on each community which she hoped would be of short duration. The Sisters did not, however, return home until the following year.[139] In December, the Queen, who was passing through Châlons with the young King, paid a visit to the Hôtel-Dieu where she received the Sisters and expressed her satisfaction in affectionate terms. ' By God's grace,' wrote Barbara Angiboust, after speaking of the Royal visit,[140] ' the gentlemen of the city were very much edified at the good order which our dear Sisters have succeeded in establishing in the hospital. . . . If they had not come here, I do not know what the whole Court would have said.' Sister Barbara's presence at Brienne, on February 16, 1654, would seem to indicate that by then the Hôtel-Dieu at Châlons no longer needed the Sisters.[141] Sister Hardemont was on the staff of the Hôtel-Dieu at Châlons, but left in November, 1653, to nurse those who had been wounded at the siege of Sainte-Menehould,[142] and it was here, assisted by a number of her companions[143] (perhaps five, for that was the number for which the Queen had

[138] *Saint Vincent de Paul*, Vol. X, p. 5.
[139] *Letters* of Louise de Marillac, March 18, 1653, p. 605 ; November 13, 1653, p. 641 ; *Saint Vincent de Paul*, Vol. V, p. 59.
[140] Arch. Mother-House of the Sisters, an autograph.
[141] *Letters* of Louise de Marillac, Feb. 16, 1654, p. 659.
[142] *Ibid.*, Nov., 1653, p. 641.
[143] Cf. *Saint Vincent de Paul*, Vol. X, p. 648.

expressed a wish),[144] that she accomplished her mission of charity until December.[145]

Scarcely had the Sisters left Châlons than the Queen made a fresh appeal to Saint Vincent for help; this time for Sedan where the unfortunate soldiers in hospital were piled on top of each other and were suffering severely. Anne Hardemont was sent to Sedan with three companions,[146] but after two or three months, that is to say in September or October, 1654, they went elsewhere to nurse the sick and wounded.[147]

In 1656, two Daughters of Charity, Mary Martha Trumeau and Elisabeth Brocard, were sent to the hospital at Le Fère[148] to which the Queen had summoned the Sisters, not for a definite period of time, but until the close of military operations. By their skill, tact and devotedness they remedied, to a certain extent, the deplorable condition in which they had found the hospital.[149] On June 17, 1656, Saint Vincent said: ' They are edifying the whole city, and the civil authorities have written not only to me to express the highest esteem for them, but also to the whole Court, which is astonished at the good they are effecting.'[150]

In 1657, Sister Prévost was sent expressly from Sedan to the hospital at Stenay;[151] Sister Hardemont was present before Montmédy whilst the siege was going on; she received an injury from a fall, and as a result, was an invalid for the rest of her life.[152]

In the following year, the Daughters of Charity were again sent to nurse sick and wounded soldiers at Calais, after the Battle of the Dunes and an epidemic had filled all the hospitals. Anne of Austria had asked for six but only four could be spared. Saint Vincent, speaking to the assembled

---

[144] *Letters* of Louise de Marillac, no date, p. 661.
[145] *Saint Vincent de Paul*, Vol. V, p. 59.
[146] *Ibid.*, Vol. X, p. 1.
[147] Sister Hardemont was at La Roche-Guyon about this time. *Letters* of Louise de Marillac, January 27, 1655, p. 694.
[148] *Saint Vincent de Paul*, Vol. X, pp. 197–198.
[149] *Ibid.*, Vol. VI, p. 137.
[150] *Ibid.*, Vol. X, p. 289.
[151] *Ibid.*, Vol. VI, p. 382; Vol. X, p. 289.
[152] *Ibid.*, Vol. X, p. 475.

community before the Sisters went, said :[153] ' My Daughters, the Queen is asking for some of you to go to Calais to bind up the wounds of the poor soldiers. What a motive for humbling yourselves when you see how God wishes to employ you for such great ends ! Oh, my Saviour ! men go to war to kill their fellow-men, and you, you go to war to repair the evil they have done ! . . . I am well aware that, by God's grace, there are many of you quite prepared to go wherever you are sent.' He then went on to encourage these dispositions with the following words : ' Do you all really know that not only those who shed their blood for the faith are martyrs ? For instance, those Sisters who are going to the Queen are going to martyrdom ; for even though they may not die, they are exposing themselves to the danger of death and are doing so for the love of God, like so many other dear Daughters who have spent their lives in the service of the poor, for that too is a martyrdom. And I think that if they had been alive in Saint Jerome's day, he would have reckoned them amongst the martyrs.'[154] Several Sisters volunteered, and the most robust were selected. The Queen placed them under the orders of the young King's governess. All four fell ill a few days after their arrival, and two of them, Frances Manseaux and Margaret Ménage, died.[155] Anne of Austria asked for four more, and again there was a batch of volunteers. On August 2, whilst Saint Vincent was in the Hôtel-Dieu, he was told that a Sister wished to speak to him. It was Henrietta Gesseaume, one of the oldest Sisters in the Company. ' I have learned,' she said, ' that two of our Sisters died at Calais ; I now offer myself to continue their work, if you are willing.' Sister Henrietta was fifty years of age and seemed to be too old for such work. ' I will think about it, Sister,' said Saint Vincent. She went on Saturday to Saint-Lazare for his reply, and was over-joyed to hear that her request was granted. Sisters Mary Joan and Frances were to be her companions.[156] Their departure was fixed for Monday, August 5, and on the 4th Saint Vincent met the four travellers in private and gave them some parting advice. His mind went back to the idea of martyrdom.

[153] *Saint Vincent de Paul*, Vol. X, p. 507.   [154] *Ibid.*, p. 510.
[155] *Ibid.*, Vol. XI, p. 39.   [156] *Ibid.*, p. 40.

'It was thought that owing to the great number of the martyrs, the Church would be exhausted, and that there would be nobody left to sustain it; but I say to you what was once said on this matter: *Sanguis martyrum est semen christianorum*. For one who may suffer martyrdom, there will be multitudes of others; the martyrs' blood will be, as it were, a seed which will produce fruit, aye, in abundance. The blood of our Sisters will induce others to join them and will merit God's grace for those who remain unto their sanctification.'[157]

On August 3, the two Sisters who were ill at Calais, Mary Poulet and Claudia Muset, wrote to Sainte Louise de Marillac. The former had been confined to bed for one week and the latter for three. They sent word of the misfortune that had befallen them, gently complained that they had received no news from Paris, conveyed the last wishes of their dead companions, and asked forgiveness from Saint Vincent, Fr. Portail, Sainte Louise de Marillac and all the Sisters, as if their last hour had come. This letter was accompanied by another from their confessor, a Capuchin Father, Francis de Coulommiers, in which he said that the sick Sisters were being carefully nursed by the Superintendent's order, and on their behalf begged a letter in reply from Mademoiselle Le Gras herself.

The new nurses set out with Sister Henrietta Gesseaume at their head, and on the 8th, although the little band was still twenty-four leagues away from Calais, Henrietta wrote to Sainte Louise de Marillac: 'We chanced to meet the mistress of the Calais coach who told us of the death of our dear Sisters and of the others who are ill. But that is far from discouraging us; on the contrary, we are impatient to arrive in order to assist the others. We are quite comfortable in the coach; there are only our four selves inside. . . . Great numbers of lay-folk are lying on the ground or on straw, and that is a great pity.' She wrote again on September 10 to announce the recovery of the two sick Sisters, the illness of the three who had gone with her, and her fears of the condition of one of them. She added: 'I think that in a fortnight at the latest, we shall be able to take the road

[157] *Ibid.*, Vol. X, p. 551.

home, because just now there is very little that can be done for the soldiers. We thought to return this week, but the good Gentlemen in charge of the hospital made us remain, and they have written to the King's governors to find out what is to be done about our return. I beg you to let us know what you are pleased to think we should do. These good Gentlemen are very anxious that two of us should remain here for some months, but I do not think it is worth while for us to separate, because the roads are in a very bad state during the winter.'[158]

Sister Henrietta and her companions were on the way back to Paris in October. The Queen did not forget the two dead Sisters; a monument was erected at her expense over their graves; the inscription recalled their sacrifice and the name of her who had sent them to Calais.

The Battle of the Dunes has taken us far away from the provinces with which this chapter is concerned, but as the war in Flanders was a continuation of the fight waged in Picardy and Champagne between the army of the King and that of the Spaniards supported by Condé, we thought we might for a moment cross the frontiers which we had fixed for ourselves as boundaries.

In conclusion, let us listen to Saint Vincent himself, ' the great Minister of the liberated regions,' as a recent writer has called him, giving us a striking account of the immense work he had undertaken, with the help of the Ladies of Charity, in an address which he gave them on July 11, 1657 :

' Since July 15, 1650, up to the day of the last General Assembly three hundred and forty thousand livres have been sent and distributed amongst the poor ; and since the last General Assembly until to-day nineteen thousand five hundred livres, a sum that is almost as much as that of the preceding years. These sums were spent on feeding the sick poor, on collecting and supporting about eight hundred orphans from the ruined villages, both boys and girls, who have been set to learn a trade or sent out to service after they had been taught and clad ; in supporting a number of priests in their devastated parishes, who would otherwise

[158] These letters are in the Mother House of the Daughters of Charity.

have been compelled to abandon their parishioners, as they could not have lived amongst them without assistance ; and lastly, in reparing, at least to some extent, some churches which were in such a pitiful condition as one cannot describe without a shudder of horror.

' The places where money was distributed are the cities and environs of Rheims, Rethel, Laon, Saint-Quentin, Ham, Marle, Sedan and Arras. This is apart from the clothes, cloth, bed-covering, shirts, albs, chasubles, missals, ciboria, etc., the price of which would amount to a considerable sum if it were reckoned up.

' Undoubtedly, Ladies, one cannot reflect without surprise on the large quantities of clothes supplied to men, women and children, and also to priests, as well as the various vestments provided for churches that were despoiled and reduced to such poverty that it may be said that without this charity, the celebration of the Holy Mysteries could not have taken place, and that these sacred buildings would have only served for profane uses. If you had ever visited the homes of the Ladies who took charge of these various articles, you would have seen that their houses were like places of business and shops of wholesale merchants.

' Blessed be God, Ladies, who has given you the grace to clothe Our Lord in His poor members, most of whom had nothing but rags, and many of the children were as naked as one's hand ! Such was the nakedness of the girls and women that a man with even a slight sense of modesty did not venture to look at them, and they were all likely to die of the cold during the severe winter weather. Oh ! how deeply you are indebted to God for giving you the inspiration and the means of providing for such great needs ! And how many lives have you not also saved of those who were sick ! For they were abandoned by all ; they lay there on the ground, exposed to the weather and reduced to a state of extreme necessity by the military and the high price of corn.

' In truth, there were some years when their misery was even greater than it is now, and at that time up to sixteen thousand livres a month was sent to relieve them. All hastened to contribute at the sight ·of the danger in which the poor were of perishing if not promptly assisted, but for the last year or two, as times have been a little better, alms have greatly diminished. And yet there are still nearly eight churches in ruins and the poor are obliged to travel a long distance to hear Mass. . . .

'Ladies, has not the recital of all these things touched your hearts ? Are you not moved to gratitude for God's goodness towards you and towards those poor afflicted people ? His Providence turned to some ladies of Paris to help two devastated provinces ; does that not seem to you a singular and novel fact ? History does not tell us that anything like it ever happened to the ladies of Spain, Italy or any other country. That was reserved for you, Ladies, who are here present, and for some others who are with God, in whom they have found an ample recompense for such perfect charity.'[159]

It was certainly an amazing fact that some ladies, under Saint Vincent de Paul's guidance, had been able to raise from their ruins Lorraine, Champagne and Picardy, and even that was not all : in the famine period both Paris and Ile-de-France also experienced the effects of this unbounded charity, and we shall now follow them in this new sphere of action.

[159] *Saint Vincent de Paul*, Vol. XIII, p. 184.

CHAPTER XLII

THE RELIEF OF L'ILE-DE-FRANCE

IN 1648 a financial dispute brought the Court and the Parliament into conflict. The Queen, after a pretence of falling in with the Parliament's proposal, was emboldened by the victory of Lens and gave orders on June 26 to have a *Te Deum* sung in Notre-Dame for the victory, and to have the leaders of the opposition arrested. Broussel, the idol of the people, was apprehended, and a riot broke out ; chains were stretched across the streets and barricades erected. On the following day, the City Guards rebelled, crying out : 'Long live Broussel.' The Parliament, in a body, with Molé at its head, went to petition the Queen to have the prisoners released. Anne of Austria yielded, but only on condition that the Parliament would in future concern itself only with legal matters. Broussel, who was being escorted by soldiers to Sedan, turned back and was received with the acclamations of the people when he arrived in Paris on June 28.

The ashes of the conflagration were still warm and the slightest incident might cause the fire to break out afresh. Mazarin thought it wiser to leave the city and take up his residence with the Court at Rueil, intending to wait there for Condé and his troops, after which he would starve out the capital and punish the guilty. Condé s complete change of front, due to the efforts of de Retz, compelled the Queen to sign the declaration of October 12, by which the Parliament received almost all that it had asked for. The royal family returned to Paris, but public agitation still continued. On the night of January 5-6, the Court fled in secret, and on the following day Paris learned that Mazarin, now at Saint-Germain-en-Laye with the royal family, was planning to starve it out so as to put an end to all opposition from the

Parliament and force the people to beg for mercy. The Sheriffs of the City, faced with the impending misfortune, sent delegates to the Queen to beg her to intervene, but Anne of Austria would listen to nothing. ' Let the Parliament leave by one gate,' she said, ' and we will immediately re-enter the city by another.'

The Parliament did not leave Paris ; supported by the nobility, who were jealous of Mazarin's influence over the Queen, it organised public resistance. The Bastille, taken on January 13, 1649, was placed under the command of Broussel, and another councillor was entrusted with the command of the Arsenal. The Chambers met daily, both morning and evening, not excepting Sundays and Holy Days. The citizens were armed and preserved order throughout the city ; the gates were guarded and neither man nor baggage was allowed to leave Paris. As part of Mazarin's plan to acquire control over the capital was to starve it out, every possible precaution was taken to secure it on this head. The mills were requisitioned ; domiciliary visits were paid to all establishments in which corn was suspected to be stored ; all foodstuffs necessary for life were taxed ; the supplies to bakeries and slaughter-houses carefully supervised ; the number of market officials increased ; precautions were taken against the possible pillage of provision stores or of communities, such as Saint-Lazare,[1] which had considerable supplies of wheat, either for its own needs or for those of others ; and convoys of food were escorted by soldiers. It was debated whether all beggars who were not Parisians should be banished, and if this measure was not adopted the chief reason was fear of an insurrection amongst the crowds who lived in the various ' Courts of miracles.'

These wise precautions preserved Paris from the loss of life that ensues during a famine ; but the suburbs were by no means so well off, for there the soldiers of the Royal army abandoned themselves to their usual excesses. Each

---

[1] On January 11, 1649, a resolution was adopted at a meeting in the Hôtel-de-Ville that four men should be sent to Saint-Lazare on the following night ' to guard Father Vincent's wheat.' (*Registres de l'Hôtel-de-Ville de Paris*, Paris, Jules Renouard, 5 vols., oct., Vol. I, p. 119.)

victory, each conquest was accompanied by scenes of murder and pillage. Prisoners were treated without mercy; they were stripped and left naked, notwithstanding the rigours of an exceptionally severe winter; all would have died of the cold were it not for the kind heart of the King's sister who provided them with clothes at her own expense. At Charenton, they were brutally thrown into the Seine; the soldiers shouting as they threw in their victims : ' Now go and have a look at your Parliament.'

All who were living in the neighbourhood of the city suffered severely. A few extracts from the letters of Mother Angélique Arnauld on the condition of Port Royal-in-the-Fields and its environs will enable the reader to form an opinion on the general state of affairs, for what happened in that district is a sample of what was going on elsewhere in the environs of Paris.

' January 7 : This poor district is in a horrible condition; everything here has been plundered; the soldiers enter the farms and destroy the corn; they will not even give a single grain to the poor owners who ask for some as an alms that they may have it ground. The people are no longer working . . . all the horses are gone and everything has been stolen. . . . It will be impossible to send you any bread or to provide any for ourselves. We shall be quite satisfied with peas and milk-foods and we shall be very happy if they are left to us.'[2] A few days later, she writes : ' If everything is taken from us, as has happened to others, we shall not know where to turn for food, as there is none left in this countryside. . . . On the highways, there is nothing but pillage. . . . If we were reduced to sleeping in the wood, like the peasants, who are happy to find a quiet spot to avoid being beaten to death, I know not how we could endure it. If these poor people have half as much bread as they really need, they still think themselves lucky.'[3] April. ' Our horses and asses are dead. It is very distressing to think of all the misery. War is a terrible scourge. It is a wonder that all the people and cattle are not dead from having been shut up for so long together. We had horses under our room, and opposite us,

[2] *Lettres*, Utrecht, 1742–1744, 3 vols., in-12, Vol. I, p. 402.
[3] *Ibid.*, p. 404.

in the Chapter Room ; there were forty cows belonging to us and to our poor people in a cellar. The farm-yard was full of hens, turkey-cocks, ducks and geese, both inside and outside, and when the people asked us to take charge of them they used to say : " Take them for yourselves if you like ; we would prefer you to have them than the soldiers." Our church was so full of wheat, oats, peas, beans, kettles and all sorts of rags, that we had to walk over them to reach the Choir, the floor of which was quite filled up with the books of our Gentlemen. Furthermore, there were ten or twelve girls who sought refuge with us. All the servant-maids who work in barns were inside, and all the servant-boys outside. The barns were full of cripples ; the wine-press and the lower part of the farm-yard were full of cattle. . . . We suffered from the cold, for, as the supply of firewood gave out, no one ventured to look for more. . . . Everything here has become excessively dear. . . . It is, in fine, a heartrending sight to look at this poor district.'[4] May 14. 'We have been constantly surrounded by the cruellest troops in the whole world who have ravaged our whole countryside committing all sorts of cruelties, sacrileges and evil deeds. . . . All our dear hermits have again put on their swords to protect us and have erected such stout barricades that it would be difficult to force an entrance.'[5] If we generalise this picture, we shall have an exact idea of the state of the whole country round Paris during the first half of 1649.

One can easily imagine the discomfort experienced in the capital from the loss of free communication with the outside world ; commerce had ceased ; there were no coaches, posts, or fairs. A general state of weariness ensued which was increased by the rivalries that were now beginning to appear between the nobility and the Parliament and by the bad news from England of the death of Charles I on the scaffold on February 9.

All felt that peace was absolutely necessary, and Molé, who was sent to negotiate one with the Court, signed, on March 11, the Treaty of Rueil, which was made definite on April 1 under the title of the Peace of Saint-Germain. The

[4] *Lettres*, Utrecht, 1742–1744, 3 vols., in-12, Vol. I, p. 416.
[5] *Ibid.*, p. 424.

Court promised not to punish those who had taken part in the revolt, to lessen the taxes, to disband its troops, and to pay the generals and their lieutenants; it also authorised the meetings of the Parliament. When peace was concluded, the Court, to the general disappointment, did not return to Paris. The people began to distrust the sincerity of its promises, and the general vexation and rage were manifested in a series of violent pamphlets. The printer of one of the most scurrilous, *La custode de la reine qui dit tout*, was sentenced to death by the Parliament, but the people attacked the executioner and released the culprit. The Court at length decided to return, and on August 18, they entered Paris amidst the enthusiastic cheers of a fickle mob that was quite prepared to attack, on the following day, the very persons it was now acclaiming.

What line of conduct did Saint Vincent de Paul pursue in the midst of these political events? After the Court had left the city for the second time, moved by the unhappy spectacle before his eyes and the thought of what was likely to follow, he made up his mind to profit by his influence over the Queen. His departure from the capital, at this particular moment, might lead to serious consequences; if he went to Saint-Germain without mentioning the fact to anybody, it would be generally believed in Paris that he was secretly in league with the Court; if he went to see the First President before leaving the city, the Court would be offended and might suspect him of being an envoy of the Parliament. He thought the matter over and decided, in spite of everything, to go, after telling Molé of what he proposed to do. On January 14, 1649, he left Saint-Lazare before daybreak,[6] accompanied by Brother Ducournau. The inhabitants of Clichy, who had been plundered on the previous evening by German cavalry, had posted guards, armed with pikes and guns, at the chief cross-roads to protect themselves if necessary from brigands. As soon as the noise of the two horses' hooves was heard in the darkness, the guards rushed out with their weapons turned against the travellers. The result might have been serious if one of the guards had not recognised his old parish priest. At Neuilly,

[6] *Saint Vincent de Paul*, Vol. III, p. 402.

the Saint and his companion had to face another danger; the Seine had risen in flood and now covered a portion of the bridge.[7] They plunged gallantly into the stream, reached the opposite bank safely, and arrived between nine and ten o'clock at Saint-Germain.

One may guess the nature of his interview with the Queen. He spoke to her for an hour on the dreadful misery with which Paris was threatened and begged her to apply the only efficacious remedy—the dismissal of Mazarin. From Anne of Austria's apartments he proceeded to those of the Cardinal Minister, to whom he made much the same suggestions, only putting them in a more moderate form. ' Submit,' he concluded, ' to the present evil state of affairs; throw yourself into the sea to appease the storm.' Mazarin seemed to listen with interest. ' Very well, Father,' he replied, ' I will go and see if Le Tellier is of your opinion.' A council of state was held that day; the question was debated; Le Tellier was not of Saint Vincent's opinion, and Mazarin remained. Saint Vincent attributed his failure to the forcible language he had used when speaking to the Queen. On the following day, he remarked: ' I have never, never succeeded when I have spoken with the faintest suspicion of harshness; I have always noted that if one wishes to move the mind, one must be ever on one's guard against embittering the heart.'[8] He left Saint-Germain on the 17th provided with a passport and furnished with an escort, but he had no intention of returning to Paris; prudence dictated that he should keep away from the capital for some time. He made up his mind to pay a visit to Father de Gondi, at Villepreux, and then to move on to Le Mans,

[7] The flood of 1649 was considered to have been one of the severest that Paris ever experienced. Several quarters of the city were flooded; the bridge at the Tuileries was partly carried away and several houses collapsed. ' People are obliged to go about the streets in boats ' according to the *Gazette* of January 14. (See Maurice Champion, *Les inondations en France depuis le VIe siècle jusqu'à nos jours*, Paris, V. Dalmont, 1858–1864, 6 vols., oct., Vol. I, p. 76.)

[8] Abelly, *op. cit.*, Bk. I, Ch. XXXIX; Collet, *op. cit.*, Bk. V, pp. 467–470; Abelly and Collet utilised an account written by Brother Ducournau.

Angers, Saint-Méen, Nantes, Luçon, Richelieu, Saintes, Cahors, and Marseilles, stopping at each of these cities to make a visitation of the establishments entrusted to his religious families.[9]

He stayed a week at Villepreux. He had left it and was riding towards Le Mans when a messenger overtook him to say that the farm at Orsigny, which supplied Saint-Lazare with nearly all its foodstuffs, was about to be pillaged; the Brothers employed on the farm were awaiting his instructions. The news was serious and this was not the moment for him to proceed any further. Not far from Étampes, at Valpuiseaux, Saint-Lazare possessed another farm, that of Fréneville. He remained there waiting to see what would happen.[10] He had thought to stay there only a few days, but heavy falls of snow and the exceptional severity of the weather compelled him to remain for over a month. It was a cold and hungry time; he had only a little green wood for fuel and some mouldy bread and fruit for food.[11] The two Daughters of the Charity who looked after the poor in the village, did their best for him, sending him some of their own brown bread and apples. 'We will send them some wheat in return,' wrote the grateful old man.[12] Privations such as these did not lessen his zeal. On more than one occasion he preached in the parish church on the good use of sufferings, on the necessity of reforming one's life to avert the anger of God, adding that it was necessary above all else to purify one's conscience by a devout reception of the Sacraments. Saint Vincent, with one of his confrères and the parish priest, heard the confessions of the whole parish. In Valpuiseaux, he was easily able to obtain information as to what was happening at Saint-Lazare, and the news was anything but good. On the pretext of taking stock of any supplies of corn that might be in the house, the place was searched from top to bottom. All the flour and corn stored in the granaries were carried off to the public markets by order of a councillor who falsely

---

[9] *Saint Vincent de Paul*, Vol. III, p. 417.
[10] *Ibid.*, Vol. III, p. 412.
[11] Abelly, *op. cit.*, Bk. I, Ch. XXXIX, p. 183.
[12] *Saint Vincent de Paul*, Vol. III, p. 405.

alleged that he was acting on behalf of the Parliament. Shortly afterwards, the buildings were requisitioned as billets for six hundred soldiers. The Missionaries were no longer masters in their own house ; their keys were taken away ; everything was turned upside down and the woodpile was set on fire, thus depriving them of their supplies of fuel.

Fr. Lambert, who was acting as Superior in Saint Vincent's absence, had recourse to the Parliament. Shortly afterwards, the soldiers received orders to depart and to hand over the keys, and a guard was sent by the city authorities to watch over ' the safety and preservation of the house ' ; but the evil had been done, and Saint-Lazare never received an indemnity for the damage inflicted. As the community was deprived of its revenues from the public coaches and the provisions usually sent from the farm at Orsigny, it became impossible to keep on the staff and at the same time feed the two or three thousand poor people who came to the door every day for food. Fr. Lambert, acting on Saint Vincent's advice, preferred to empty Saint-Lazare and the Bons Enfants[13] rather than cease from giving alms. The priests and students were sent either to Richelieu, Le Mans or elsewhere, and on March 4, there were only seven or eight priests, eighteen or nineteen students, and a few brothers left in Paris.[14] At Fréneville, Saint Vincent took over all that had been saved from the pillage of Orsigny : two hundred and forty sheep and two horses, but even here the animals were not safe. A quarter of a league from Fréneville, some soldiers had entered a farm and emptied all the stables. When the Saint heard this, he hastened off with his flock of sheep, intending to bring them to Richelieu. It was now February 23, and after walking some miles through the snow and seeing that his sheep could go no farther, he halted at a walled village, four or five leagues from Étampes, and entrusted them to a lady with whom he was acquainted.[15]

[13] Abelly, *op. cit.*, Bk. III, Ch. XI, sect. III, pp. 133-134.
[14] *Saint Vincent de Paul*, Vol. III, p. 417 ; Abelly, *op. cit.*, Bk. I, Ch. XXXIX ; *Registres de l'Hôtel-de-Ville de Paris, pendant la Fronde*, ed. Le Roux de Lincy et Douet d'Arq, Paris, 1846-1848, 3 vols., in-8°, Vol. I, pp. 119, 149, 153, 156, 163, 204.
[15] *Saint Vincent de Paul*, Vol. III, pp. 412, 416.

MADELEINE DE LAMOIGNON

On March 2 he reached Mans and stayed in the Seminary directed by the Priests of his Congregation. Here he learned to his surprise that the Bishop-elect, Philibert de Beaumanoir de Lavardin, had not waited to obtain his Bulls before entering his episcopal city. At the Council of Conscience, Saint Vincent had vigorously opposed de Lavardin's candidature, and the latter, as the Saint was well aware, still bore a grudge against him. He was bound in good manners to call on the prelate, but was doubtful if a visit would be agreeable to de Lavardin. He hesitated for some time and then decided to send two of his priests to announce his arrival in the city, to present his respects and to ask for permission to remain at Le Mans for a week. The Bishop was flattered by this step and was most cordial. ' M. Vincent,' he told the Fathers, ' may remain in Le Mans as long as his business here may keep him, and if he had not gone to stay with you, I would have gladly offered him hospitality in my house.' This friendly reply encouraged the Saint; he perceived that the Bishop would willingly receive him, and the interview would have taken place had not political events compelled de Lavardin to beat a hasty retreat from the city. He was afraid of being captured by the soldiers of the Marquis de la Boulaie, who was by no means tender towards Mazarin's partisans.[16] The Saint was not disturbed, although news of his presence in the Seminary had spread through the city and several of the chief inhabitants had called on him.[17] On March 17, he left Le Mans after a sufficient enquiry into the state of the establishment and the dispositions of his confrères.[18]

Half a league from Durtal, he nearly met with a fatal accident when fording the Loire. His horse stumbled and fell in the river before the Saint was able to free himself, and if the priest who was with him had not promptly come to the rescue, the accident might have had tragic consequences. He was taken, dripping with water, into a small cottage, and here, in front of a good fire, whilst his clothes were drying, he carried on a friendly conversation with the owner who

[16] Abelly, *op. cit.*, Bk. III, Ch. XVI, sect. I, p. 257.
[17] Collet, *op. cit.*, Vol. I, p. 473.
[18] Abelly, *op. cit.*, Bk. III, Ch. XVII, p. 267.

lamented his troubles, complaining especially of the sufferings he endured from hernia. ' I will send you a bandage that will give you some relief,' said the traveller.[19] He re-mounted his troublesome steed and continued his journey, until at nightfall he reached an inn, where he ate a meal with a good appetite as he had not tasted food the whole day. When dinner was over, he gathered the servants together to instruct them in the truths of religion. The mistress of the house, surprised at his zeal, collected the children of the village and brought them to her home ; delighted to see such a little flock around him, he separated them into two groups, over one of which he took charge, and the other he handed over to the priest who was with him ; both then gave a lesson in catechism which was followed with interest and profit.[20]

The children of this village were not the only ones who benefited by this journey ; wherever Saint Vincent stopped, he spent his leisure time in the same manner. His whole life was devoted to manifesting charity towards body and soul ; he felt constrained to do good, and the gift of himself was the pleasantest way in which he could find repose.

He remained five days at Angers. The Daughters of Charity in the Hôtel-Dieu, delighted to see their father again, poured out their hearts to him during the interviews he held with each in turn. ' Things are going on so well here,' he wrote to Saint Louise de Marillac, ' that my heart is filled with consolation.'[21] On March 24, he left for Saint-Méen. Just before entering Rennes, the horse had to cross a small wooden bridge on one side of which was a mill and on the other a very deep pool. The horse was frightened by the revolving wheel and suddenly backed ; one of its hind legs was already over the bridge, and in another moment, both horse and rider would have been into the pool. The horse stopped just as it was about to lose its balance, and once again the Saint's prayers were offered up in gratitude to God who was watching over his footsteps in such a fatherly fashion. That evening he reached a small,

---

[19] Abelly, *op. cit.*, Bk. III, Ch. XVII, p. 267.
[20] *Ibid.*, Bk. I, Ch. XXXIX, p. 184.
[21] *Saint Vincent de Paul*, Vol. III, p. 422.

THE RELIEF OF L'ILE-DE-FRANCE

dirty inn where he meant to pass the night. The best room was not very good, but it was given to him. Scarcely had he settled down to rest than the innkeeper came in to ask him to give it up to some friends of his who had just arrived ; he willingly agreed, and satisfied himself with the narrow little spot that was then assigned him. His patience was often severely tested in the inns where he stayed ; on one occasion, the room next door was invaded by a group of peasants who drank for part of the night and then kept on talking until morning. Instead of complaining to his host, he gave them, when leaving, a present of some beautiful ' *Agnus Dei,*' which, says Collet,[22] ' he might have presented with perfect propriety to the Duchesse d'Aiguillon.'[23]

In the course of his travels, Saint Vincent had hitherto refrained from paying mere visits of courtesy, and he did so for excellent reasons, for in the Western provinces, as in Paris, passions were running high. He hoped to pass through Rennes without being noticed, but in this his hopes were deceived. Scarcely had he arrived in the city than he was told that his relations with the Court had rendered him suspect in the eyes of Mazarin's enemies and that if he did not leave at once orders would be issued for his arrest. He was not, however, frightened by this warning. He had, as a matter of fact, some business to transact with the Canon Theologian of Saint Brieuc whom he had already arranged to meet. Whilst the Saint and the Canon were conversing together in an inn, he was recognised by a gentleman who angrily cried out : ' M. Vincent will be very much surprised when he gets a pistol bullet in his head two leagues from here.' After uttering this threat the man quickly went out and all present were under the impression that he meant to carry out his threat. The Canon Theologian, not wishing to abandon the travellers, accompanied them to Saint-Méen, where they arrived on March 29, Monday in Holy Week.[24] It was in this city that Saint Vincent spent the Easter holidays after he had carried out his visitation. He would have departed immediately after his work was done, were it

[22] Collet, *op. cit.*, Bk. V, p. 475.
[23] Abelly, *op. cit.*, Bk. III, Ch. XXII, p. 320.
[24] The date is mentioned in Brother Ducournau's Ms.

not that the bad weather and the floods kept him at Saint-Méen. He spent his enforced leisure in attending to the pilgrims who came in crowds to pray to the great patron saint of the district. He spent long hours in the confessional bringing more than one soul back to God, or at least stirring up the fervour of the tepid.

On April 16 or 17 he left for Nantes. The Sisters in the hospital were impatiently awaiting his arrival, for they were being persecuted and calumniated, and, far from receiving any help from the Bishop, were well aware that he rather supported their accusers. The City Council, the Chapter and the Presidial Court had met to enquire into the charges and to debate whether the Sisters were to be sent away or to remain. Although the Sisters had been unanimously declared innocent, the Bishop, nevertheless, had begun another enquiry, and this was the state of affairs when Saint Vincent arrived at Nantes. His advice to the Sisters, the measures he took, and his conversations with the Bishop, the Governors of the hospital and other persons in authority, partly dissipated prejudices and restored peace. When the Sisters bade him good-bye on the 29th, on his departure for Luçon, many eyes, perhaps all, were wet with tears.

From Luçon he went to Richelieu, and this proved to be the last stage of his journey. An order from the Queen awaited him there, ordering him to return to Paris. On May 11 he wrote to Fr. Portail, who was expecting him at Marseilles,[25] ' I do not see how I can do the will of God if I do not obey, for I have always believed and taught that princes must be obeyed.' His ' tiny, little fever,' and the visitations of two houses, those of the Missionaries and the Sisters, kept him in Richelieu longer than he had anticipated.

As soon as Fr. Lambert heard of Saint Vincent's illness, he sent the brother-infirmarian of Saint-Lazare to Richelieu. The patient was not expecting him, and when good Brother Alexander appeared, he looked surprised and perhaps slightly annoyed. ' My illness is not very severe,' he thought, ' was it necessary to send a brother from Saint-Lazare ? ' This thought was followed by another. ' I have

[25] *Saint Vincent de Paul*, Vol. III, p. 434.

not cordially welcomed the brother; I have caused him pain,' and he went down on his knees to ask forgiveness; in order to remove completely the tacit reproach of his reception of Brother Alexander, he repeated the act of humility, on his return to Paris, in presence of Fr. Lambert.

The sight of the brother-infirmarian was not the only disagreeable surprise Saint Vincent encountered at Richelieu; he experienced another, and probably an even greater one when he was told that a carriage, drawn by two fine horses, and driven by the Duchesse d'Aiguillon's own coachman had arrived from Paris to take him home. The carriage was in fact his own; it had been presented to him a few years previously by the Ladies of Charity who had selected a very unpretentious one in the hope that he would consent to make use of it. Unpretentious as it was, he would have nothing to do with it. A carriage was quite well for 'the great,' but he was the son of a poor peasant. However, it was not so easy to refuse a gift at Richelieu as it had been in Paris. The carriage was there and so, too, were the horses and coachman; they had travelled leagues and leagues to reach him and if he were to allow it to return empty, it would be a slight that could not but hurt the Duchesse d'Aiguillon. He submitted; after all, once he was back in Paris, he could send back the horses and confine the carriage for evermore to the stables at Saint-Lazare. The Duchesse, on her side, was expecting a little opposition; but her mind was made up. When she learned that Saint Vincent, after his return to Saint-Lazare, had sent back the horses, she refused to accept them. For a month, he begged and insisted; she refused to yield. 'You know quite well,' she told him, 'that your legs swell and that they are growing feeble from age; the day seems at hand when you will no longer be able to walk or to ride a horse.' 'When that day comes,' he replied, 'I will no longer leave the house.' The dispute continued until the Queen and the Archbishop of Paris gave him formal orders to accept the carriage and use it to pay visits. The Duchesse d'Aiguillon emerged victorious from the fray.[26] However, Vincent de Paul had his

[26] Abelly, *op. cit.*, Bk. I, Ch. XXXIX, p. 186; Bk. III, Ch. XIII, sect. I, p. 207; Collet, *op. cit.*, Bk. V, pp. 477-478.

revenge in the way taken by the saints. The carriage, always contemptuously referred to as 'my shame' or 'my disgrace,'[27] became the carriage of the poor; any weak or infirm person whom he saw walking with difficulty along the street, was taken in and driven home.[28] The horses also had to suffer humiliations for, when not in the carriage, they were yoked to ploughs or carts.[29]

It was on June 13 that Saint Vincent, after five months' absence, reappeared in Paris, two months in advance of the Queen.[30] One of his first visits was to Anne of Austria, but what took place at that interview will never be known to history. He did not forget his promise to the man at Durtal; he bought a bandage and requested the lady of the place, the wife of a Marshal of France, to see that it reached its destination accompanied by a letter. The priest who had rescued him from the Loire did not persevere in his vocation, but once he had left the Congregation he was overcome with remorse. He wrote letter after letter, begging to be allowed to return; Saint Vincent, who knew his grave defects of character, thought it useless to reply, but at last one day he took up his pen and asked the priest not to insist any further. The poor man only begged the more: 'Sir,' he wrote, 'I once saved your body from death, do you now save my soul.' Such a petition could not be resisted. 'Come to Saint-Lazare,' was the reply, 'and you will be received with open arms.'[31] When Saint Vincent was home again in Saint-Lazare, he found, after his long absence, that the house was not in the same state as when he had left it. Wheaten bread had given place to barley loaves, which were in turn to give place to oatmeal. This was a result of the civil wars of the Fronde. He suffered privations, like the others, and had the joy of seeing his confrères, aided by his words and example, gaily take their share in the public distress. The poor, especially numerous in Paris, suffered much more:

[27] *Saint Vincent de Paul*, Vol. V, p. 344; Vol. XII, p. 251; Abelly, *op. cit.*, p. 186.
[28] Abelly, *op. cit.*, Bk. III, Ch. XI, sect. III, p. 136.
[29] Collet, *op. cit.*, p. 478; Abelly, *op. cit.*, p. 186.
[30] *Saint Vincent de Paul*, Vol. III, p. 454.
[31] Abelly, *op. cit.*, Bk. III, Ch. XVII, p. 266.

'That,' he wrote on October 8, 'is my burthen and my sorrow.'[32]

Another of his burthens and sorrows was the fact that abominable acts of sacrilege had been committed in several districts in the neighbourhood of Paris, such as Limeil, Beaubourg, Férolles, Ville-Abbé, Antony, Châtillon-sur-Marne ; churches had been defiled, tabernacles forced open, vestments carried off, and ciboriums containing the Sacred Species stolen. The Company of the Blessed Sacrament invited all its members to fast and perform penitential exercises as a reparation. On August 12 it decided that missions would be given at its expense by the Priests of Saint-Lazare in each of these parishes ; that it should be represented by ecclesiastics and lay-men at the procession which brought the missions to a close, that each member should carry a candle weighing two pounds, and that artistic representation of the Blessed Sacrament in richly ornamented frames should be hung in the six churches in a prominent and elevated position. The Missions began after All Saints, and, owing to the circumstances that had called them into being, were carried out with special solemnity. Saint Vincent supplied eight priests for Antony, four for Châtillon, three for Ville-Abbé, and two for Beaubourg. In addition, two clerical students were sent to Antony and one to each of the other parishes. The Mission at Férolles was combined with that at Brie-Comte-Robert which was to have been given at that time.[33] People thronged in from all around to make reparation ; Saint Vincent himself went and also sent his confrères. During these solemn celebrations in honour of the Blessed Eucharist, the people showed a noble ambition to make the reparation, as far as that was possible, equal to the offence.

The year 1649 ended in turmoil. Mazarin and Condé were fighting to see which would get the upper hand. Condé proudly relying on his rank as first prince of the blood and on his victories over the Spaniards, behaved as if he were

[32] Collet, *op. cit.*, Vol. I, Bk. V, p. 479.
[33] Beauchet-Filleau, *op. cit.*, pp. 107–110.

master and acted as if everything was his due. Mazarin listened and made promises, but whilst yielding outwardly, he was secretly plotting to detach from Condé all who might be useful to the Prince in time of need. Like a crafty politician, he bided his time. He had not long to wait, for on January 18, 1650, before any hint had been given of his plans, Condé, Conti and de Longueville were arrested in their houses and sent to prison. Mazarin had judged correctly ; in Paris, no one made the slightest move, not even the Co-adjutor, de Retz, who had been won over to Mazarin's side by the promise of a Cardinal's hat.[34] Matters did not pass off so quietly in the provinces, for there were revolts, although very superficial, almost everywhere. The sight of the Queen and the young King, paraded in military fashion by Mazarin through every part of France, sufficed to restore peace. The revolt in Guyenne, the gravest of all, ended in October by the capitulation of Bordeaux. Turenne, at that moment allied with the Spaniards, was beaten at Rethel on October 20 ; Mazarin had triumphed everywhere and on his return to Paris he was publicly cheered. The moment had now arrived for him to redeem the promises which he had made to both parties ; he did not trouble his head to do so, thus making a grave mistake, for those who had hitherto supported him against the Princes, now formed a coalition against him. He recognised the weakness of his position, left Paris during the night of February 6-7, 1651, and after a journey through Normandy, he fled to Germany. When Mazarin had departed, Condé was again master, but once more his haughty and imperious conduct turned men's minds against him, and those who had just summoned him to their side now proceeded to reject him. He left Paris, took refuge in Guyenne, of which he was Governor, and raised troops there, but he was driven back by the Royal army, first beyond the Charente and then beyond the Dordogne.

At the end of December, an exciting piece of news spread through Paris : Mazarin, at the head of an army recruited in Germany, was marching on Poitiers, where the Court was then in residence. There was an outburst of public fury ;

[34] Collet, *op. cit.*, Vol. I, p. 479.

Parliament decreed that his furniture and library should be sold and a sum of 150,000 livres, to be deducted from the proceeds of the sale, should be given as a reward to whoever handed him over, alive or dead. The late King's brother and Condé were reconciled and bound themselves reciprocally not to lay down their arms until they had driven him out of the Kingdom. Mazarin, despite these threats, marched through France unimpeded, and the news soon spread that he had reached the Queen at Poitiers on January 29. The Princes stirred up the provinces; the Duc de Rohan, Governor of Anjou, declared for them and was attacked by the Royal forces under d'Hocquincourt; he was beaten at Angers, and capitulated on February 28. From Angers, d'Hocquincourt moved on Orléans; Nemours and Beaufort tried to reach that city before him; each side made forced marches to be there before the other, but the honour fell to Mademoiselle (the King's aunt) who had started from Paris. When she arrived before Orléans, she had no troops, but was plentifully supplied with money; she gave large sums to the ferrymen who effected a huge breach in one of the walls through which she entered. In this way, Orléans was captured without bloodshed by a young girl of twenty-five, who, with the full consent of the city magistrates, concentrated all power in her own hands. When the Royal army arrived, the gates remained shut, and she moved on towards Jargeau and Sully. Beaufort pursued her so hotly that she was forced to beat a retreat, which, if Turenne had not come up in time, would have turned into a rout.

The Court halted at Gien, whilst the two Generals of the opposing side, Nemours and Beaufort, fruitlessly endeavoured to arrive at an agreed plan of military operations. They were still seeking for one when Condé arrived from Guyenne. Under his command, the army of the Fronde marched against d'Hocquincourt and defeated him at Blénau, but once again was confronted with Turenne and beaten. Condé, unable to make headway on the banks of the Loire, set off to try his fortune at Paris where his partisans were awaiting his arrival. He was welcomed by Gaston d'Orléans who presented him to the Parliament, but he met with a cold welcome from that body. President Bailleul told him plainly that the Assembly would have preferred not to see him ' in the sanctuary of justice in the state in which he now was, condemned by a council and with his hands still bloody from battles waged against His Majesty.' The Prince had to listen to even harsher language, at the Court of Aids, from the mouths of President Amelot and Fouquet, the Procurator General. Neither did the Hôtel-de-Ville spare him; the notables declared, on April 20, ' that for no cause whatsoever would a union be effected or a single penny contributed to assist their Royal Highnesses the Princes against the King on the pretext of Mazarin.' Condé suffered from no illusion; he was neither loved nor wanted; he was being supported for the sole reason that once he was gone Mazarin would take his place. He felt more and more the need of support from his army and ordered his officers to approach Paris. Tavannes obeyed, but Turenne, after attacking Arpajon and placing the Court in Saint-Germain, fell on him as he was about to enter Étampes, captured or killed 3000 of his men and carried off a rich booty. This notable feat of arms earned for the victor the office of Commander-in-Chief of the Royal army, in place of the incapable d'Hocquincourt, who was sent back to Péronne, of which he was Governor. His soldiers camped at Étrechy, then at Palaiseau and a contingent was sent to occupy Saint-Denis.

Paris was being gradually encircled; the shops were closed; the streets resounded with seditious cries, for the people were discontented with the Parliament, Mazarin and the Princes. The gates of the city were closely watched, and a citizen's guard, posted close to the gate of Saint-Denis, stopped Saint Vincent one day and, amidst insults and threats of death, compelled him to descend from his carriage. His frankness and courtesy succeeded in saving him on this occasion, but, as a precaution he asked the Duke of Orléans for a pass, which was readily granted.[35]

Condé realised that it was essential to re-establish his prestige. The Royal army was driven back from the bridge at Saint-Cloud, which it had attacked, and was forced to

[35] Abelly, *op. cit.*, Bk. III, Ch. XXI, p. 315.

THE RELIEF OF L'ILE-DE-FRANCE

retreat. Emboldened by this slight success, he placed himself at the head of 10,000 citizens, marched on Saint-Denis, which was defended by 300 Swiss, surprised them and brought them back as prisoners to Paris. On the following day, Saint-Denis was again taken by the King's army, which pursued the forces of the Fronde beneath the walls of Paris and caused consternation in Saint-Lazare and the Foundling Hospital.[36] Both sides now began to mark time. Mazarin transferred the Court to Corbeil, and then to Mélun, whilst Turenne besieged Étampes. Both were awaiting assistance from Charles, Duke of Lorraine, who was moving rapidly on Paris with an army of 8000 men, but Charles, whilst allowing each of the opposing factions think he was coming to its aid, had not made up his mind which side to support. He preferred to wait until he was actually on the spot and then throw in his lot with whoever paid him most. His soldiers, already masters of Coucy, had just camped at Dammartin; after a month of conferences, he made up his mind and decided to support the enemies of Mazarin.

Paris threw open its gates to the Duke of Lorraine, and on June 2, at ten o'clock in the evening, he entered the city riding between Condé and the Duke of Orléans, whilst his troops were advancing on Lagny. On the following day he began negotiations with the Court, with the result that a treaty was arranged on the 6th by which he promised to leave the Kingdom within a fortnight if the Royal army raised the siege of Étampes on June 10. Both parties carried out their engagements. One element of Condé's plan was based on the release of an army that had been shut up within Étampes for two months; he relied on it to strengthen his own authority by bringing troops closer to Paris. Large numbers of soldiers, disguised as working men, were taken from the army to mingle with the crowds, and they were prepared to go wherever Condé required a riot to intimidate the Assemblies and to secure votes favourable to his designs.

[36] *Saint Vincent de Paul*, Vol. IV, p. 382. See *Choses mémorables de l'abbaye de Saint-Denis en France pour l'année* 1649 ff. in the *Registres de l'Hôtel-de-Ville de Paris pendant la Fronde*, ed. Le Roux de Lincy et Douet d'Arcq, Paris, 1846–1848, 3 vols., oct., Vol. III, p. 374.

An occasion for employing such a band of seasoned soldiers was not slow in appearing; on June 25 the Parliament deliberated on the means of obtaining peace and union, and the question naturally arose as to whether the Court or the Princes should be the first to offer pledges. After a long and fruitless debate, the meetings adjourned. A large and impatient crowd was waiting without, and when it was announced that no resolution had been taken, there were loud shouts of indignation, followed by scenes of violence; the magistrates were mobbed and beaten and compelled to resume the debate. When Parliament met again, it decided to suspend its sittings until means had been taken ' to guarantee justice,' and each member looked after its own safety. The Duke of Orléans himself was attacked one day; two pistol shots, fired close to him, probably without any intention of assassination, rendered him a docile instrument of Condé who thus attained his object; every source of authority in Paris had now submitted to him, and by inspiring terror, he had become master of the situation.

In the meantime, Turenne, who was outside the walls of Paris, remained inactive, or rather bided his time. Marshal de la Ferté was to bring him a contingent of 3000 men, and with this reinforcement he hoped to strike a decisive blow. As soon as Turenne heard that the troops had arrived, he conducted the Court to Saint-Denis; when Condé learned this he ordered his soldiers, who were then at Saint-Cloud, to march by night around Paris on Charenton. Turenne was informed of the stratagem and moved his forces across the plain of Saint-Denis, where he met Condé's troops as they were marching close to the gate of Saint-Antoine and fell on them with the intention of cutting their lines of communication. Luckily for Condé, the barricades erected by the Parisians in the preceding months as a protection against the Duke of Lorraine's marauding soldiers, were still in position; they now served to protect Condé and gave him time for reinforcements to come up. The arrival of six pieces of artillery and a band of Parisian volunteers, led by Beaufort, enabled him to hold out. A heroic resistance was made, but gradually it became clear that the Royal troops were winning. Suddenly, the cannon in the Bastille were heard thundering, the gate of Saint-Antoine was thrown open, Condé's soldiers passed through, and were safe within the walls of the capital. Turenne had thus failed to gain a decisive victory; he failed through the intervention of the young King's aunt who had issued the necessary orders.

The passage of Condé's army along the boundary walls of Saint-Lazare during the night of July 1-2, was marked by an annoying incident. Eight soldiers broke into the seminary of Saint Charles, which was situated at the extreme end of the enclosure, and threatened the Superior, Fr. Alméras, who, to placate them, 'offered food and money.'[37] They ransacked every room, broke open every box and chest and carried off everything that took their fancy. As they were about to cross the threshold to rejoin their comrades, they were seen by a Swiss soldier and the Duc de Bouillon's coachman who fell on them with one accord, sword in hand, and compelled them to abandon their booty. After this feat of arms, the two brave defenders asked leave to remain to protect the house against pillagers, and their offer was gratefully accepted. Saint Vincent,[38] writing three days later, says: 'These two men were unknown to us and we to them. . . . God sent them most opportunely to defend this house, and they did so, as they told us, out of sympathy. They left on the next day to rejoin their master, the Duc de Bouillon, at Saint-Denis. . . . As things are rapidly growing worse, we have been advised to keep some armed men on the premises, and in fact, we have had them this very night and intend to keep them to protect us, by God's grace, during these stormy times. I myself remained up with them one night, with six or seven members of the Company, and the same number of domestics remain up every night in Saint-Charles, and in the enclosure and grounds of Saint-Lazare, from which we have removed all the furniture.'

Condé, rescued by a young girl, had not come very well out of his adventure, and his ambition was destined to bring him still lower. A great meeting was summoned at the Hôtel-de-Ville for the 4th; it was widely rumoured that a proposal would be made for an unconditional return of the

[37] *Saint Vincent de Paul*, Vol. IV, p. 418. [38] *Ibid.*, p. 420.

King. The Princes, the Governor, the Provost of the Merchants, the Archbishops, representatives of the Parliament, of the City Council, of the clergy, of the religious communities and of the city guilds (310 persons in all), were invited to attend the meeting. Fr. Le Gros, a Priest of the Congregation, was delegated by Saint Vincent. From early morning groups began to gather in the Place de Grève; as the hour fixed for the meeting drew nigh, the crowds became more and more tumultuous. As the deputies passed in they were questioned. 'If you do not give us what we want,' cried the mob, 'we will slaughter you.' 'What we want' really meant that the Duke of Orléans should be the King's Lieutenant-General, and Condé, Commander-in-Chief of the armies. The Princes were slow to arrive. The King sent a trumpeter with a message which was read in public and produced an uproar amongst some of the deputies. He complained that the gates of the city had been thrown open to Condé, but gave his word that, notwithstanding this act of treason, he would continue to send corn for those in want. The Procurator of the King and of the City next spoke and proceeded to enumerate a list of grievances to be laid before the King. They demanded peace, the return of the Court, and the removal of him who was 'the cause and subject of all the evils.' The last words were obviously directed at Mazarin, but those who were present pretended not to understand the Procurator and reproached him because he had not mentioned the Italian. At last the Princes arrived and were received with all the ceremony due to their rank. After an exchange of commonplace remarks, expressions of gratitude and warning, they withdrew without having placed any proposals before the meeting. Outside, in the square, the mob became threatening. The rioters occupied all the corridors of the Hôtel-de-Ville; the lurid light of houses on fire now became visible, and the cracking of firearms was heard. After the Princes had departed, the Assembly-hall was made a target and bullets began to fly through it from all directions. There was a general scramble for safety; the rioters strove to break open the doors of the Hôtel-de-Ville and, as they failed to do so, they burned them. Once within the building, they sacked, plundered and slew without a pause. Fr. Le Gros managed to conceal himself, but did not get back to Saint-Lazare until the following day.[39]

Condé was regarded by many as having been responsible for these massacres, and the least that can be said is that he did nothing to prevent or stop them. Excitement and helpless amazement had paralysed men's minds, and hence the Princes were able to gather the fruits of their unhappy victory. Some days later, Broussel was elected Provost of the Merchants, the Duke of Orléans, Lieutenant-General of the Kingdom, Condé, Leiutenant-General of the armies, and Beaufort, Governor of Paris. They were now the masters, but masters universally despised, and in these conditions, their domination could not last long.

Saint Vincent was one of those who desired such a result, but he preferred to see it brought about by conciliatory measures rather than by deeds of violence. His friendly relations with the leaders of both parties enabled him to play the part of an intermediary between Condé and the Princes. Despite his extreme repugnance to interfering in affairs of State, he did make an attempt, as we know from one of his letters to Mazarin :

'I very humbly beg your Eminence to forgive me for returning here yesterday evening without having had the honour of receiving your Eminence's commands; I was compelled to do so because I was unwell. His Highness the Duke of Orléans has just informed me that he will send M. d'Ornano to me to-day with a reply which he desired to concert with His Highness the Prince. I informed the Queen yesterday of the conversation which I had the honour to hold with each of them separately ; in both instances, it was most gracious and respectful. I told His Royal Highness that if the King were re-established in his authority and a decree of justification granted, your Eminence would supply the desired satisfaction ; that such an important matter as this can with difficulty be settled by deputies and that it needed persons who have reciprocal confidence in each other to deal with these matters in a friendly way. He manifested both in word and in deed that he agreed with this and told me he

[39] *Registres de l'Hôtel de Ville*, Vol. III, pp. 51–73 ; *Saint Vincent de Paul*, Vol. V, p. 421.

would confer with his Council. I trust with God's help to be able to convey his reply to your Eminence to-morrow morning.'[40] The negotiations did not produce the result that the Saint had expected. Mazarin would not agree to the King's return to the capital as long as the Princes remained in Paris, and as long as the *Frondeurs* occupied the chief position ; it was probably on this point that the negotiations broke down.

Saint Vincent, overwhelmed with grief at his failure, made up his mind to write to the common Father of all the faithful, Pope Innocent X. His letter is dated August 16 :

' Most Holy Father, may I dare, full of confidence in that fatherly kindness which welcomes and gives ear to the least of your children, to set before you the lamentable state of our country, France, which is certainly most deserving of pity ? The Royal Family, torn by dissensions ; the people, split into factions ; the cities and provinces, afflicted by civil war ; the villages, hamlets and towns, overthrown, ruined and burned ; tillers of the soil placed in such a position that they cannot reap what they have sown and no longer sow for the following year. Soldiers deliver themselves up with impunity to all manner of excesses. The people, for their part, are exposed not only to acts of rapine and brigandage, but also to murder and all forms of torture. Such of the inhabitants of the country districts as have not perished by the sword are dying of hunger ; the priests, who are not spared any more than others, are inhumanly and cruelly treated, tortured and put to death. Virgins are dishonoured and even nuns themselves exposed to their licentiousness and rage ; the temples of God are profaned, plundered or destroyed ; the churches that still remain are for the most part abandoned by their pastors so that the people are almost deprived of the Sacraments, Mass, and all other spiritual helps. Finally, a thing horrible to think of and still more horrible to mention, the Most August Sacrament of the Body of Our Saviour is treated with the utmost indignity, even by Catholics, for, in order to carry off the sacred vessels, the Blessed Eucharist is thrown on the ground and trampled under foot. Now, in these circumstances, how do heretics who do not believe in these mysteries behave ? I neither dare nor can express it.

[40] *Saint Vincent de Paul*, Vol. IV, p. 423.

It is but little to hear or read of such things; one must actually see them.

'I am well aware that your Holiness may rightly accuse me, who am but a private nameless individual, of great temerity for venturing to expose such evils to the head and common Father of Christians, who is so well and so fully instructed on the affairs of all nations and especially of all Christian nations. But I implore you, Holy Father, not to be angry with me if I do speak. I will speak to my Lord, even though I be but dust and ashes. In truth, Most Holy Father, no other remedy remains for our evils than that which can proceed from the paternal solicitude, the affection and the authority of your Holiness. I know how deeply your Holiness is afflicted by our afflictions and how very often you have already attempted to stifle these civil wars, even at their birth, and that to this end your Holiness has despatched pontifical letters and enjoined the Most Illustrious and Most Reverend Apostolic Nuncio to intervene efficaciously in your name; and he has done so, I know, with the zeal of an apostle, and also that he has laboured, as far as in him lay, although fruitlessly until now, in the service of God and of your Holiness. But, Most Holy Father, there are twelve hours in the day, and he who has not succeeded once may by a fresh attempt obtain better success.

'Why should I say more? The arm of the Lord is not shortened and I firmly believe that God has reserved to the care and solicitude of the Pastor of His universal Church the glory of at length obtaining for us rest after fatigue, happiness after so many evils, peace after war, the re-establishment of union in the Royal Family, so deeply divided, relief for peoples crushed by prolonged wars, the restoration of life to the poor, beaten down and almost dead from famine, relief for entire countrysides that are utterly devastated and for ruined provinces, the restoration of temples that have been overthrown, security for virgins, the return of priests and pastors of souls to their churches, and finally, the restoration of life to us all.'[41]

This letter had not reached Rome before the Fronde had begun to show signs of collapse. The discontent produced

[41] *Ibid.*, p. 455. The text is in Latin.

by increasing taxation and the outrages of the military, the anarchy brought about by the rival Parliaments of Paris and of Poitiers which combated each other by issuing contrary edicts, the demand for help addressed by the Princes to two foreigners, the Archduke Leopold and the Duke of Lorraine, the divisions amongst the leaders of the Fronde, the defection of large numbers, the death of Nemours, killed in a duel with Beaufort, and the retreat of the Duke de La Rochefoucauld, all concurred in rendering Condé still more unpopular. Two acts of the King at length succeeded in turning the people of Paris away from the men who had led them astray ; these were the dismissal of Mazarin, who was sent in exile to Bouillon, and the promise of a complete amnesty for all who had taken part in the Fronde, provided they made a full and complete submission within three days. It was quite easy to guess that the first of these measures was only of a temporary nature and of a purely political character, but the people, who were not over-suspicious, did not look into the matter too closely, or may perhaps have feigned not to see it. Public manifestations of attachment to the King and of hostility to the Princes were multiplied in Paris. A display of fireworks on the evening of September 5 reminded the populace that this was the birthday of Louis XIV. A Royalist league was formed which adopted a scrap of white paper as a cockade and chose as its leader Le Prévost, a Councillor of the Parliament and Canon of Notre-Dame. Deputations were sent to the Princes to complain of the excesses of their soldiers and Condé's troops were disbanded.

De Retz, the co-adjutor, always ready to play a part in great political affairs, was anxious that he himself should administer the finishing stroke to the Fronde now in its death-agony. He called a meeting of the Canons, parish priests, superiors of religious Orders, and noblemen, placed himself at their head, and on September 9, they set off to Compiègne to petition the King to hasten his return to the capital. He knew that the long-expected Cardinal's hat had arrived from Rome, and thought that the King, flattered by the step he had taken, would himself confer on him the insignia of the Cardinalate. The King did not even take the trouble to give de Retz an audience ; he sent two supporters of Mazarin, Servien and le Tellier, to present the co-adjutor with a few words in writing to the effect that he would be pleased to return to Paris if the Parisians did ' something to hasten this return by no longer tolerating the violent authority of those who wished to prolong public disturbances.'

This reply became known in Paris almost immediately; it was discussed in all quarters and produced a general state of misunderstanding in which Saint Vincent shared. On the following day, the Saint, thinking that the Court had been deceived as to the state of public opinion in Paris, wrote a letter to Mazarin in which he stated the exact state of affairs :

' I venture to write to your Eminence ; I beg you to allow me to do so and to say that I now see the city of Paris again returned to its former condition, asking for the King and Queen with its whole heart and soul ; furthermore, that wherever I go and to whomsoever I speak, I find the same things are being said. Even the Ladies of Charity, who are some of the most distinguished persons here, tell me that on their Majesties' approach, they will go out, a regiment of ladies, and given them a triumphant reception.

' Accordingly, My Lord, I think your Eminence will perform an act worthy of your goodness if you advise the King and the Queen to take possession of their city and of the hearts of Paris.' After these introductory remarks, Saint Vincent proceeds to take up, one by one, the objections which Mazarin might bring forward in favour of his temporising attitude and endeavours to point out their worthlessness. Why does the King delay his return to Paris ? Is it because he thinks that many of its citizens are still opposed to him ? Very, very few, replies the Saint, are of that way of thinking ; ' at least, I do not know of any . . . ; the neutral, if there are any, will be carried away by the crowd and the vigour of those who are warmly in favour of it (i.e., the King's return), and they are the majority of Paris, except, perhaps, those who ' are not ' re-assured by the amnesty.' Does the presence of the Duke of Orléans and of Condé in Paris open up the possibility of further massacres ? No, the former ' will be delighted at the opportunity of putting himself once more on good terms with the King,' and ' the latter, seeing Paris obedient to the King, will submit, and I have good authority for not having any doubts on that point.' It may, perhaps, be said ' that Paris should be chastised for its own good.' History shows that this method has never proved successful with Parisians. ' Charles VI, after he had chastised a large number of rebels, disarmed and removed the chains of the city, only poured oil on the flames and so angered the rest that they kept up a rebellion for sixteen years, withstood the King more than they ever had done before, and to that end, leagued themselves with all the enemies of the State.' Henry III and Louis XIV himself, during the first epoch of the Fronde, ' did not obtain very much result' from ' having blockaded Paris.' 'Your Eminence may, perhaps, intend to make peace with Spain and then come here in triumph, to fall upon Paris and teach it a lesson.' Such a plan would have fatal results. ' Your Eminence would be hated more than ever, if perchance you gave back the Spaniard all that you now hold of his possessions, as it is said your Eminence intends to do.' If you prefer to defer the King's entry until peace has been concluded not only with Spain but also with the Princes, that is a bad policy, for, ' in this case, Paris will be comprised in the articles of peace and will acquire the benefit of its amnesty from Spain and from the said Lords and not from the King, with the result that the city will be so grateful to them that it will declare for them at the first opportunity.' Your Eminence may, perhaps, be told that it is in your own interest to re-enter Paris with the King ' to produce a disturbance and to maintain war in order to show that it is not you who are stirring up a tempest, but evil-minded persons who do not intend to submit to the will of their Prince.' To act in such a fashion would not be wise. ' It is not of much importance one way or the other whether your Eminence returns either before or after the King, provided you do return . . . ; once the King is re-established in Paris, His Majesty can bring your Eminence back whenever he pleases ; of that I am assured.' ' Furthermore, if your Eminence . . . contributes to the re-union of the Royal house ' and leads back ' Paris to the King's obedience, you will assuredly, My Lord, win back men's minds in your favour, and you will, in a very short time, be recalled and in the best possible manner'; but as long as 'men's minds are in revolt' peace can only be made 'on this condition, because the foolishness of the people consists in this' and experience shows that 'those who have fallen sick of this malady are never cured by the causes' which have 'thrown the wheels of their minds out of gear.'

'If your Eminence,' as it is said, 'refuses passports to the Princes to proceed to Court ; if you do not permit the King to hear them or their delegates or any other representative body'; if ' to this end, your Eminence has placed foreigners around the King and the Queen, and your own domestics . . . to prevent access to Their Majesties, it is, My Lord, greatly to be feared . . . that the opportunity will be lost, and the hatred of the people turn to fury. . . ' 'On the contrary, if your Eminence advised the King to go and receive the acclamation of the citizens, you will win the hearts of all those in the kingdom who are well aware of your influence over the King and the Queen, and all will attribute this favour to your Eminence.' . . . ' I take courage, My Lord, to represent these matters to you in the hope that your Eminence will not take it amiss, above all when you know that I have not told a single person, save one of your Eminence's servants, that I am doing myself the honour of writing to you, and that I have had no communication with my old friends who hold sentiments contrary to the King's wishes, that I have not communicated the present letter to anybody whomsoever, and that I shall live and die in the obedience due to your Eminence, to whom Our Lord has committed me in a special way.'[42]

Frankness such as this, admirable as it was, did not please Mazarin, who showed his annoyance by acquainting Saint Vincent with the fact that he was no longer a member of the Council of Conscience.

The greater number of projects attributed by Saint Vincent to Mazarin in this letter, either as a simple hypothesis or as a hearsay, had never entered the Cardinal's mind. He had no intention of treating for peace either with

[42] *Saint Vincent de Paul*, Vol. IV, p. 473.

the Spaniards or the Princes ; nor did he intend to chastise Paris. What he aimed at above everything else was that the King should not fall under the influence of the leaders of the Fronde in his own absence, and hence, before allowing the Court to re-enter the capital, he insisted on the departure of some and the resignation of others.

Mazarin was successful ; Broussel resigned his post as Provost and Beaufort that of Governor ; then, after an interval of two days, the Duke of Lorraine and Condé left Paris. The ground was almost but not quite swept clean, for the Duke of Orléans and Mademoiselle were still there. On October 21 the King, accompanied by Turenne, left Saint-Germain ; he sent a messenger, from the Bois-de-Boulogne, ordering his uncle to leave Paris, and the Duke replied in writing that he would leave the city on the following day, which he did. A few days later Mademoiselle, in her turn, departed.

The Parisians loudly manifested their joy at the sight of the young King who had thus returned to them ; they pursued him with their cheers up to the Louvre, his new residence, and one more easily defended than the Palais Royal. ' The King ' as we may read in the *Gazette*, ' is in his Louvre ; the soldier is at the barrier ; and the sound of the drum and the fanfare of the trumpet which in the past but served as a melancholy warning to the citizens to hold themselves in readiness to preserve and defend their property and lives, now serves but to excite transports of joy.' Mazarin, in order to let popular excitement subside a little, had the wisdom not to appear in Paris until February.

The Fronde was at an end, but the state of public misery which was its melancholy result, still persisted. The political events, of 1652 especially, had plunged Paris and its environs into an abyss of evils of which no description can give an idea. In every place through which the soldiers passed, and especially wherever they pitched their camp, they destroyed the crops and plundered the houses. Before these hordes of barbarians, the people fled in crowds to the capital, followed by a long procession of cattle and carts in which were piled up their most precious possessions. It was a lamentable exodus ; all did not reach the end, for corpses lay scattered by the way : carcases of animals, that had died of hunger and fatigue, and the bodies of little children lying on the breasts of their lifeless mothers.

Port-Royal in Paris was filled with refugee nuns who had fled from their convents ; on May 16 there were one hundred and sixty ;[43] on June 12, two hundred and forty ; and the numbers kept on increasing until the parlours had to be transformed into dormitories.[44] The streets and squares of Paris, already overcrowded and insufficiently supplied with food from the suburbs, were filled with more than 100,000 mendicants. These unfortunate people were merely one division of the grand army of beggars ; there were the ' modest poor ' of whom there was a considerable number : 1800 families of the working-classes in the Saint Médard district ; 12,000 in the Faubourgs Saint-Marcel, Saint-Jacques, Saint-Laurent and Villeneuve-sur-Gravois.[45] ' I am sending you a morsel of the bread for the poor,' wrote Mère Angélique to Port-Royal-in-the-Fields,[46] ' to let you see to what extremity they are reduced. We see none but poor people who come here to tell us that they have had nothing to eat that day ; others who have not had food for two or three days, and some who have had nothing to eat but cabbage boiled in water without salt. I beg you to show this bread to our Sisters and to tell them that I beseech them for the love of God to reflect on the state of extremity to which He has reduced . . . those whom He has pleased to treat in this way without their having any right to complain ; and let them meditate on the thoughts with which He may inspire them as to what they owe both to His justice and His love ; let them consider, as I often told them, that we are being helped with many alms that might have been given to the poor, and are hence obliged to retrench as much as possible.'

These lines were written in March, but as the year went by, bread became blacker and dearer. The King had given permission for wheat to be brought into Paris, but the troops had to be reckoned with, and the soldiers were simply

---

[43] *Lettres de Mère Angélique*, Vol. II, p. 113.
[44] *Ibid.*, p. 130.   [45] *Relations*, March–April, 1652.
[46] *Lettres de Mère Angélique*, Vol. II, p. 67.

brigands who paid no attention to Royal edicts; they seized wheat and corn wherever they found it, in the fields, in granaries and in mills.[47] Saint Vincent wrote to the Queen for help and protection. 'The military,'[48] he said, 'do not cease from coming in bands to carry off the corn, not only from the plain of Saint-Denis, as I myself have seen, but also from the district lying between La Chapelle, and La Villette, which are two villages about a quarter of a league distant from Paris, where they have attacked the owners of farms who venture near them to reap their harvest. I very humbly beg your Majesty to allow me to acquaint you with this fact because your Majesty did me the honour to inform me that the King has not forbidden those who have sown their land to gather its fruits.'

A series of fights, such as that on July 2, would not have displeased the Parisians. The poor artisans of the Faubourg-Saint-Antoine hurled themselves on some horses that had been killed and sold them at a good round sum.[49]

It was impossible for people who had to pay exorbitant prices for food to pay their rent also. Petitions were addressed to Parliament from all parts of the city asking for a moratorium for rents due at Easter, and the Feasts of Saint John and Saint Remy. The Parliament granted the petition for the Easter term, but decided that each case should be examined for the second term.[50] It was a wise decision, for the condition of all tenants was by no means the same. Apart from those who had a hard struggle to earn their daily bread, there were others living in luxury, going to the theatre and places of amusements and spending money recklessly. 'People are still going to the Hôtel de Bourgogne' (the Theatre),[51] wrote Mère Angélique to the Queen of Poland on July 22, 'and those who are enduring the present state of agony have so little compassion for the sufferings of their neighbour that they are hunting for amusement just as much as in times of peace; and what is

[47] *Lettres de Mère Angélique* Vol. II, pp. 153, 161.
[48] *Saint Vincent de Paul*, Vol. IV, p. 430.
[49] *Relation*, June–July, 1652.
[50] Feillet, *op. cit.*, p. 408.
[51] *Lettres de Mère Angélique*, Vol. II, p. 157; cf. p. 143.

the most horrible feature of all is that they will not suffer the preachers to preach penance.' Then come expressions of gratitude to the Queen for her charity, which is indeed necessary if the severe but true words of the Holy Spirit are not to be applied throughout eternity, ' the great and powerful shall be mightily punished.'

Saint Vincent was not one of those who were wont to squander money. The Fronde, by depriving Saint-Lazare of its revenues from public coaches and subsidies, reduced its income by twenty-two or twenty-three thousand livres.[52] To this should be added the losses arising from thefts by the soldiers who plundered the farms on which the house subsisted. On August 30 he wrote :[53] ' We shall lose this year about 26 to 30 *muids* of corn at least, even if we shall be able to keep the little that has been left to us, for that, as a matter of fact, is in great danger as most of it is still in barns in the country.' As early as the beginning of 1652 the pinch of want began to be felt, for it was then debated whether the novices or students should not be sent to Mans, where the cost of living was not so high.[54]

Sickness, that inseparable companion of famine, was causing great havoc amongst the poor ; in Paris alone, during each of the summer months, the number of deaths mounted to 10,000.[55] The Hôtel-Dieu supplied the largest proportion, a hundred a day. Despite the vacancies caused by deaths, the transformation of two large apartments into wards, and the detestable practice of putting several patients into one bed to economise room, the Hôtel-Dieu was far from meeting all requirements. The authorities were compelled to place the sick on straw mattresses and to send wounded soldiers to the Hospital of Saint Louis, which was usually reserved for cases of contagious diseases.[56] Outside the walls of Paris, the state of public misery was even more dreadful. On May 4, the *Relations* tell us there was awful news from Chastres and Linas ; ' Nothing is to be heard of

[52] *Saint Vincent de Paul*, Vol. IV, p. 327.
[53] *Ibid.*, p. 463. A *muid de Paris* (the measure varied in different districts) was equivalent to 18 hectolitres.
[54] *Ibid.*, p. 307.   [55] *Ibid.*, p. 463.
[56] *Lettres de Mère Angélique*, Vol. II, p. 142.

in these parts but murders, acts of pillage and theft, violations and sacrileges ; the churches here are plundered just as much as those on the frontier ; the Blessed Sacrament here has also been cast on the ground so that the sacred vessels might be looted ; the villages are deserted ; most of the corn-crops have been cut down ; the priests are in flight and without their flocks ; the peasants have taken to the woods where they are suffering from famine and from the legitimate fear of being slain by those who pursue them.'[57] It seemed as if one could not descend to still lower depths and yet Etampes and Palaiseau proved that this was not the case. The Missionaries sent to the relief of these places were horrified at the ghastly spectacles that met their eyes. Everywhere houses in ruins, pale emaciated countenances of men and women stricken with prolonged hunger, the sick abandoned and deprived of the necessaries of life, even of a cup of water to quench their thirst ; corpses of men and women lying about in all directions, carcases of horses and other animals more or less devoured by wolves and exhaling an insupportable stench. In the village of Etréchy, where the armies had encamped, there was nothing to be seen but the dying, and putrefying corpses. The sick lived alongside them, for they were too weak and feeble to move away from such dangerous proximity.[58]

The *Relations* for October add still more sombre details to this picture of horror. A visit to twenty-two villages situated in the environs of Villeneuve-Saint-Georges led to the discovery of 347 people on the point of death, without beds, clothing or food. In Villeneuve itself, from twelve to fifteen hundred dead horses were lying on the ground as well as several soldiers and victims of the famine.[59] Corbeil and the surrounding district were no better off. The reports given in the *Relations* enable us to apply to the inhabitants of this district some remarks to be found in a contemporary pamphlet. ' Persons have been seen at night lying like animals on dung-heaps, and in the day time exposing themselves to the sun to enjoy its warmth, quite covered over and crawling with worms, dead before they had even expired . . .

[57] *Relation*, March–April, 1652.   [58] *Ibid.*, June–July, 1652.
[59] *Le Magasin charitable*, p. 15.

others have been seen crawling, like lizards, over manure-heaps; others again lying on straw, motionless through complete physical exhaustion; and still others in sewers and stables.'[60] Étioles was in ruins; no houses standing, only tottering walls. 'At Étioles,' we read in the *Summary Description*,[61] 'the houses are so many stables, the inhabitants so many sick, the sick so many dying; the Missionaries bury them daily.' The letters forwarded from Lagny make one shiver. At Nully, a live child was thrown into a heated furnace and a husband and wife beaten to death with bundles of thorns. At Daumar, a poor beadle, a victim to his sense of duty, was the sufferer; all his limbs were mutilated, his stomach slit open, his entrails torn out and placed in his hands to force him to tell where the sacred vessels of the Church were hidden.[62]

Although Mère Angélique had fled to Port-Royal in Paris, she was kept informed of all that was passing at Port-Royal-in-the-Fields and its environs; from her correspondence we can share with her in the news she received. May 1. 'The barbarity of the soldiers is such that Turks could do no worse. . . . What deeply afflicts us is that they have been compelled to remove the Blessed Sacrament from our Church so as to keep it in safety. It has also been removed from almost all the parishes because these wretched soldiers have in many places trampled it under foot; in others, they have sold it; and when, after previously pillaging all they could lay their hands on and when money could not be found to redeem it, they have trampled it under foot.[63] It is said that it is Poles and Germans who commit this horrible sacrilege.' This letter was addressed to Louise-Marie de Gonzague, Queen of Poland. On May 16, Mère Angélique continues: 'The licence of the soldiers is so horrible and the country between here and Port Royal so devastated that not a single soul is to be found in the villages; so that, as they cannot obtain any bread, they break into any places where it can be found. Never

[60] *Estat sommaire des misères de la campagne et besoins des pauvres aux environs de Paris*, 20, 22, 24 and 25 October, 1652, p. 3.
[61] P. 5. [62] *Relation*, September–October, 1652.
[63] *Lettres de Mère Angélique*, Vol. II, p. 101.

have such dreadful disorders been witnessed.'[64] On June 28 : 'All the villages in the neighbourhood are entirely deserted and any of the inhabitants that were left have fled to the woods, the others having died of famine or been murdered by the soldiers. Almost all the Abbeys have been plundered, and what is still more horrible, even nuns who were unable to escape have been shamefully abused. A soldier who died in the Hôtel-Dieu confessed with great sorrow all the abominable crimes he had committed, but what grieved him most was that once, when he had pursued a nun she climbed up by means of the grille to the crucifix which she embraced, and when he saw this, filled with rage, he had murdered her with a bullet. The house of my brother d'Andilly[65] was not only plundered by Lorrainers but almost demolished, the trees were torn up and all the poor peasants mutilated. The same thing happened in one of our own villages,[66] and in fact everywhere else. . . . It seems as if all the soldiers were possessed by the devil. Up to the present, God has protected our house in the Fields by the extreme charity of the Duc de Luynes who would not abandon it, though urged by his friends to do so. He has had eight towers built to defend it and supplied a quantity of weapons to all the solitaries. Moreover, a number of country gentlemen and a number of poor people and working men have also retired there so that over a thousand persons are now living there by the charity of this good nobleman.'[67]

Let us turn away from this dreadful picture of public misery and see what remedies were being applied.

In the first place, prayer. In that century of profound faith, it was the most natural thing in the world to have recourse to God, the fountain-head of all good, to obtain from Him the cessation of war, the source of all evils. The Archbishop of Paris ordered public prayers to be held to which all public bodies were invited. Processions passed through the streets ; the great patron saints of the city were invoked and their relics exposed. On June 11, the last and

[64] *Lettres de Mère Angélique*, Vol. II, p. 113.
[65] D'Andilly Pomponne.   [66] Mondeville.
[67] *Lettres de Mère Angélique*, Vol. II, p. 014.

most solemn of the public processions was held ; the shrine of Saint Geneviève was carried from her Church to Notre-Dame, in the midst of an immense crowd of the faithful. The Princes and the nobility of the Court followed the shrine ; then came the members of Parliament in their red robes, and the other city bodies in their robes of state.[68]

At Saint-Lazare, Saint Vincent never grew weary of recommending prayer and acts of penance. The thought of the privations which the poor were enduring led him to say on one occasion : ' Whilst they are suffering and battling against extreme privation and all the other miseries they endure, it behoves us to act like Moses, and following his example, lift up our hands unceasingly to Heaven on their behalf ; if they are suffering for their sins and ignorance, we should be their intercessors with the Divine mercy.' He addressed these exhortations to prayer and penance to appease the wrath of God to all with whom he was brought into contact ; to those who came to see him, to his Priests, and Daughters, to the ecclesiastics of the Tuesday Conferences and to the Ladies of Charity. When at the end of morning prayer the Litany of Jesus was recited, on reaching the words *Jesus, God of peace*, he pronounced this invocation with even more than his usual air of grave devotion and repeated it, the better to emphasize his prayers.[69] In the list of the subjects for conferences held at Saint-Lazare during 1652, there were three on public calamities and one, on June 10, ' on the procession of the reliquary of Saint Geneviève.'[70] After stating the points to be dealt with, the following words were added : ' Two priests or clerics and two lay-brothers shall fast ; this custom was continued for nine years and only ended when peace was restored.' Three members of the community, according to Abelly,[71] ' fasted daily in turn ; a priest, a cleric and a brother ; the priest said Mass for peace and his two companions in penance offered up Holy Communion for the same intention.'

[68] A detailed account of this ceremony was inserted in the *Registres de l'Hôtel-de-Ville de Paris*, Vol. II, pp. 370-377.
[69] Abelly, *op. cit.*, Bk. I, Ch. XLIII, p. 201.
[70] *Saint Vincent de Paul*, Vol. XII, pp. 456-459.
[71] Abelly, *op. cit.*, p. 199.

Whilst expecting much from God's Providence, Saint Vincent never forgot that it was his duty to make himself its instrument. It was absolutely necessary to establish charitable organisations, but before doing so, money had to be collected. With the help of the Ladies of Charity who were accustomed to meet daily, when the situation was at its worst,[72] he sought for and obtained funds, thanks especially to the wide circulation attained by the *Relations*.

A large sum of money, the gift of the Queen of Poland, gave rise to a misunderstanding which was quickly removed. Louise-Marie de Gonzague had sent 12,000 livres for the poor to Mademoiselle de Lamoignon and Mère Angélique Arnauld, through her usual intermediary, Madame des Essarts. Mère Angélique had no sooner heard the good news than she wrote to thank her illustrious friend and to submit her plans. On May 16 she wrote :[73] ' The alms cannot be better employed than on poor country folk who are utterly ruined, and on agricultural labourers who will never recover unless they are helped. A sum of money might be lent to some of them for a fixed period and then afterwards lent to others, as soon as the first are able to re-pay. I have also another idea and that is to have some cows bought which could be let out on loan to our poor people ; if they can pay, then the money would be given to others. A cow can support a whole family in the country, especially the poor little babies whose mothers are so badly nourished that they have scarcely any milk. Mademoiselle de Lamoignon may perhaps have other ideas just as good as ours. I shall be very pleased if Your Majesty will settle all this.' A letter from Poland, dated June 9, informed Mère Angélique that the Queen agreed to her proposals. At a meeting of the Ladies of Charity, they were told of the state of utter misery of Étampes and its environs and they sought for some means of rendering immediate assistance to that unfortunate district. Saint Vincent thought of the 12,000 livres and told them that in case they wished to borrow a third of this sum, the Queen of Poland would send them enough to pay their debt. Louise-Marie de Gonzague did

[72] *Saint Vincent de Paul*, Vol. IV, p. 392.
[73] *Lettres*, Vol. II, p. 115.

HIPPOLYTE FÉRET,
VICAR GENERAL OF PARIS

in fact approve of the Saint's idea, but a rumour began to circulate that the Queen was taking away the distribution of alms from Mère Angélique and entrusting it to the Ladies of Charity.[74] The Abbess of Port-Royal was surprised, and asked Mademoiselle de Lamoignon for an explanation. She wrote : 'As I have learned, Mademoiselle, that M. Vincent has received a letter from the Queen of Poland in which it is said that she intends that the twelve thousand livres which she sent are to be distributed by the Ladies of his Company, I wish to inform you as soon as possible that I will carry out this new order of the Queen as gladly as that formerly conveyed to Madame des Essarts and subsequently confirmed by Her Majesty in a letter of June 9, in reply to one I had written giving my ideas about the distribution of the alms, and in which she did me the honour to inform me that I might employ it as I thought best for the welfare of the poor. It is true, my dear Sister, that this alteration has somewhat surprised me, especially as I know it is not the Queen's intention that the gift should be made known to the public and talked about ; I think I knew her well enough not to be mistaken when I persuade myself that she would have been just as pleased if this alms were employed in assisting persons whose needs are all the greater and more deserving of pity inasmuch as they are known only to few, rather than in coming to the aid of public necessities, which, indeed, are very great, but which, being known to all, can more easily be assisted by the charity of kind-hearted persons who, by stripping themselves of portion of their luxury and superfluities . . . could, as I think, remedy such cases without overmuch difficulty. It seems to me that if Her Majesty had no other design than that of employing these alms on the kind of good works undertaken by the Ladies, and not on others of which I know the need, she would not have indicated a wish that I should take part in the distribution of this charity. Nevertheless, as it is said that this new order has come from Poland and is in closer conformity with the Queen's intentions than the former, I have no intention of opposing it, and shall be quite happy if Madame des Essarts hands you over the balance to be disposed of as

[74] *Saint Vincent de Paul*, Vol. IV, p. 445.

you please.'[75] Mère Angélique had good reason to be surprised. Mademoiselle de Lamoignon questioned Saint Vincent who replied in a letter : ' I very humbly request you to disabuse the Ladies of the idea that the Queen of Poland offered them the distribution of this alms, and I can assure you that I certainly did not say so.'[76] The matter rested there ; it was a simple misunderstanding which was removed by one word of the Saint.[77]

It was of very little importance in the eyes of the Ladies of Charity whether it was by themselves or by others that the poor were assisted, provided they were actually helped.

They had many other holy rivals in the exercise of Christian charity all around them, and in particular the members of the Company of the Blessed Sacrament ; and they rejoiced at the fact. The money they received was quickly spent. The needs were, in fact, immense, but charitable organisations were not wanting. The chief and most urgent need was soup-kitchens. A multitude of hunger-stricken men and women received food at the gate of Saint-Lazare every morning and evening ; in June, 1652, the Mother-House of the Daughters of Charity fed 1500 of the ' modest poor ' and 800 refugees ; the Sisters in the parish of Saint Paul looked after 5000 poor persons and from 60 to 80 sick ; in the other parishes of the capital, the Sisters attached to Confraternities of Charity were overwhelmed with the number of poor and sick who needed their care.[78] Food for the soul was supplied with food for the body and the poor did not depart without hearing a few words about God and about their duties.

Saint Vincent was not content even with this two-fold

---

[75] *Lettres*, Vol. II, p. 165.
[76] *Saint Vincent de Paul*, Vol. IV, p. 445.
[77] We regret that Raoul Allier, when referring to this incident, has seen in the action of the Ladies of Charity ' a significant haste,' ' an anxiety to secure for scrupulously orthodox works of charity ' funds that they regarded as in bad hands seeing that they were entrusted to Jansenists.'
(*La cabale des dévots*, Paris, 1902, p. 85.) That is not history but an expression of opinion which is anything but historical.
[78] *Saint Vincent de Paul*, Vol. IV, p. 406 ; Abelly, *op. cit.*, Bk. III, Ch. XI, sect. III, p. 33.

THE RELIEF OF L'ILE-DE-FRANCE

charity. On June 13, 1652, during a meeting of the Ladies over which the Archbishop of Reims presided, he proposed that missions should be given to the refugees. To this there was one obvious objection; his priests, by their statutes, should confine their work to country places, and here it was the city of Paris that was in question. He put this objection himself and supplied the answer: 'There is an excellent proverb that says one should take whatever is good wherever one finds it. We are bound to go and serve the refugees in the country when they are there; they are our portion; and now that they have come to us, driven away by the rigour of war which has made the country a desert, it would seem that we are even more strictly bound to labour for their salvation in the afflicted conditions in which they now are.'[79] This idea was approved by all the Ladies, and two missions were begun simultaneously on June 21; one at Saint-Lazare and the other at Saint Nicholas du Chardonnet. Saint Vincent took part in the first. After the sermon, at which 800 refugees were present, the men were taken inside the cloisters of Saint-Lazare and divided into nine or ten groups; and whilst one priest was instructing the women in the church, each of the groups listened to catechetical and moral lessons from a priest, lessons which many of those present had no doubt long forgotten.[80]

Saint Vincent paid special attention to certain classes of refugees; for instance, he extended the hospitality of Saint-Lazare to ecclesiastics who had been forced to leave their dioceses. On June 21, he wrote: 'They are arriving here every day to be fed and instructed in those matters which they are bound to know and practise.'[81] He also devoted particular care to nuns who had fled from their convents. 'Some of them,' we read in the same letter,[82] 'are on the streets, some are lodging in places of doubtful reputation, and others with their relations.' All sorts of dangers awaited these nuns, the least of which was the loss of the spirit of prayer and recollection. A house was rented

[79] *Ibid.*, Vol. IV, p. 405.
[80] Abelly, *op. cit.*, Bk. I, Ch. XLII, p. 195.
[81] *Saint Vincent de Paul*, Vol. IV, p. 407.
[82] *Ibid.*, p. 406.

to enable them to lead a cloistered life ; they were collected together, and Saint Vincent lent some Visitation Nuns to take charge of this temporary convent. There was also much to be feared for country girls who were now compelled, through the evil days through which the country was passing, to live in cities. To allow them to wander about the streets was simply to expose them to all forms of temptation. He collected a hundred and placed them in a house in the Faubourg-Saint-Denis, procured all that they needed to sustain soul and body, and even had a special mission preached in order to induce them to make a general confession of their past life and, in the case of those who were not in the state of grace, thus to be reconciled with God.[83]

Similar and no less important houses of refuge were established in other Parisian parishes. The first, as Mère Angélique tells us, [84] was in the parish of Saint-Merry ; this was due to the energy of the ladies of the parish, who were urged to do so by their pastor, M. du Hamel. The refugees did not remain idle ; their time was spent in spinning, and they were thus enabled to lay by some money for the day in which they would return to their homes. Courses of religious instruction and devotional exercises also formed part of the daily routine. The Company of the Blessed Sacrament also took an active part in all works instituted for the refugees, either by voluntary contributions which the members undertook to pay, or by initiating some admirable schemes of their own. The project of grouping homeless nuns in a convent for themselves and refugee priests in Saint-Lazare was first mooted at a meeting of the Company, of which, it should not be forgotten, Saint Vincent was a member ; it is quite possible these resolutions were taken as a result of his suggestions ; in any case, it was he who was deputed to carry them out.[85]

However wretched was the situation in Paris, it gave only the faintest idea of the deplorable conditions of the environs. Here, it is scarcely possible to exaggerate ; the presence of the armies interfered with the supply of relief in most of the

[83] Abelly, *loc. cit.*
[84] *Lettres*, Vol. II, p. 141, June 28, 1652.
[85] *Annales de la Compagnie du Saint-Sacrement*, p. 128.

THE RELIEF OF L'ILE-DE-FRANCE

places that had suffered the greatest privations. When peace was concluded and Paris more fully informed of the dreadful truth, a shiver ran through the citizens, and, indeed, every class of society made vigorous efforts to relieve the sufferings of their neighbours. The Archbishop of Paris headed the movement ; by his orders, all parish priests held meetings for the relief of the poor in their parishes, made frequent collections in their churches, and urged their flocks from the pulpit and in the confessional not to forget the starving ; all confessors and preachers were recommended to speak on the theological principles governing the duty of alms-giving.[86]

Leaflets and pamphlets were published to stir up public sympathy. In October, 1652, three *Relations* and one pamphlet were issued, the title of the latter being : *A summary statement of the state of misery in country places and of the needs of the poor in the environs of Paris* ;[87] in November, *Notes on the needs of country places in the environs of Paris* ;[88] and in January, 1653, *The Charitable Store.*[89]

The title of this last pamphlet recalls an ingenious arrangement that had first occurred to Christopher du Plessis, Baron de Montbar, an advocate in the Parliament. All the parish priests of the capital had established in their presbyteries a sort of magazine or store-house which was constantly being replenished, without incurring any expense, by the generosity of the faithful. Every gift was accepted, good and bad, new and old, superfluities and necessities :

[86] *Estat sommaire*, p. 8.
[87] 12 pages, octavo, dated October 20, 22, 24 and 26, 1652. It is not signed by Feret, as some have alleged who thought mistakenly that the signature of the last document was the signature of the whole pamphlet. (Cf. Raoul Allier, *La cabale des dévots*, p. 90.)
[88] This pamphlet (8 pages octavo) is dated November 20, 1652.
[89] 27 pages, octavo. This pamphlet, as well as the two preceding, may be found in the Bibl. Nat., Recueil Thoisy, T. 318. Maynard, in his *Life of Saint Vincent* (1860 ed., Vol. IV, pp. 194-199), refers to several pamphlets inspired by the famine that rendered desolate certain Western provinces, such as Berry and Poitou ; we do not refer to them here, because these pamphlets are later than 1660.

medicine, food-stuffs, clothes, linen, furniture, utensils, workmen's tools, sacred vessels and linen, devotional objects, books ; anything that could be used in a sacristy, church, house or hospital.

From the presbyteries, the gifts were taken either to the town-house of Madame de Bretonvilliers, which had the advantage of being situated at the end of the Ile-Saint-Louis, close to the banks of the river and therefore handy for loading boats, or to the Hôtel de Mandosse, quite close to the Hôtel de Bourgogne. The various objects collected were then conveyed, either by boats or carts, to other depots established right in the heart of the devastated areas : at Villeneuve-Saint-Georges, Juvisy, Gonesse and other places, to be thence transferred, under the superintendence of the Missionaries, to various special store-houses (there was one for each district) and finally to be taken to the homes of the poor. During the months of October, November, December and January, from five to six thousand pounds of meat, two to three thousand eggs, and all sorts of provisions and utensils were distributed weekly.

The zeal of those who became beggars to relieve the poor was worthy of admiration ; they went from house to house, seated on carts, to collect all that the inhabitants were willing to give. They approached associations as well as individuals ; the Company of Butchers of Saint-Sulpice, Sainte-Geneviève, Place-aux-Veaux and Saint-Nicolas-aux-Champs, each gave from five to six thousand pounds of meat ; the Hosiers Company gave money, vestments and articles of their own manufacture. A barrel large enough to hold from eight to ten bushels of salt was constantly being emptied and replenished. In these store-houses one might come on silver plate bearing the crests of famous families, time-pieces, and all manner of interesting objects. A lady of rank sent the dress she was wearing ' to clothe,' as she said, ' the members of Jesus Christ.' Some, for the sake of the poor, handed over the wheat they had painfully amassed as a provision for a rainy day. There were moving incidents of charity such as that of a poor woman who arrived with her bundle of clothes, put it down, took off her shoes and departed bare-footed.

The efficient organisation of charitable relief required a large staff, for surgeons were needed, and also gravediggers, or, as they were then called, ' air-renewers ' ; nurses were also required and ecclesiastics as well. The religious Communities showed praiseworthy zeal in their response to appeals addressed to them ; each of them was offered a section of the environs of Paris : Villeneuve-Saint-Georges was first taken over by the Jesuits and then by Nicolaites, and Juvisy at first by the Vincentians and afterwards by Recollets ; Corbeil was entrusted to Capuchins, Lagny and Étampes to Vincentians ; the Picpus Fathers took charge of Brie and its environs ; the Discalced Carmelites, Tournon ; the reformed Dominicans, Gonesse and Luzarches ; the Recollets, Saint-Denis and the priests of M. Charpentier, Mont-Valérien.[90] The Mission confided to these religious Communities was not solely spiritual ; they had to be at their posts and organise the distribution of alms ; make arrangements for the division and distribution of relief sent from Paris, for distributing soup, helping orphans, managing hospitals and burying the dead. As they were unable to do all this by themselves, they looked around for helpers. Paris supplied them with grave-diggers ; the charitable store with ladders on which to carry the bodies and with picks and hoes to dig the graves. One may imagine what the Missionaries had to endure before these gifts arrived, when they were reduced to scooping up the earth with their hands.[91]

The Priests of Saint-Lazare had already showed what they could do before the other communities set to work ; several had laboured in Picardy and Champagne ; they were men of experience and their methods served as a model.[92] Early in May, Saint Vincent was informed by the Ladies of Charity that the village of Palaiseau, where the armies had encamped for three weeks, was losing from ten to twelve inhabitants a day and that half the population was ill ; he hastened to send four priests, a surgeon and provisions. On May 29, the first cart set out by his orders ; it

[90] *Le Magasin charitable*, pp. 3–12.
[91] *Etat sommaire*, p. 9.
[92] *Le Magasin charitable*, p. 13.

contained sixteen large loaves of bread, fifteen pints of wine, and large baskets filled with eggs. The same process was repeated on the following days ; meat was sometimes added and occasionally sacks of flour instead of bread.[93]

Saint-Lazare soon succumbed beneath the weight of this expense. In July, Saint Vincent was forced to confide his woes in the Duchesse d'Aiguillon, the President of the Ladies of Charity. ' Sickness,' he wrote,[94] ' still continues to rage at Palaiseau. The first who fell ill and did not die are now in need of convalescent treatment, and those who were well are now ill. One of our priests came here expressly to tell me that the military have cut down all the corn and that there is no harvest to be gathered. And yet, we are now no longer in a position to meet this expense. We have already supplied them with 663 livres in money, in addition to the provisions and other articles we sent them in kind. I very humbly request you, Madame, to call a little meeting at your house and to settle on all we have to do. I shall be there, if I can. I have just sent off the priest with a Brother and fifty livres. The epidemic is so dangerous that our first four priests there fell ill, as also the Brother who was with them. They had to be brought back here and two of them now are at death's door. O Madame ! What a harvest to be gathered for Heaven in these days when such great wretchedness and misery is at our doors ! ' Those who were sent to replace the sick also fell victims to the epidemic ; on July 24, eight Missionaries had already succumbed and others begged to set out at once.[95] Despite the devotedness with which he was surrounded, Saint Vincent was soon in an embarrassing position, for it was his duty to see that two other districts were assisted, namely, Lagny and Étampes. In the latter place, the contagion raged even more fiercely than at Palaiseau. On July 15, Father David died of the plague. ' He did,' wrote the Saint,[96] ' all that a man from Heaven could do in regard to hearing confessions, teaching catechism, rendering bodily

---

[93] *Saint Vincent de Paul*, Vol. XIII, p. 362 ; Abelly, *op. cit.*, Ch. XI, sect. II, p. 124.
[94] *Ibid.*, Vol. IV, p. 424.
[95] *Ibid.*, p. 435.   [96] *Ibid.*, p. 438.

assistance, and burying the dead, whose corpses had long since putrefied. He had twelve corpses buried at Étréchy, that were infecting the whole village, after which he fell ill and died of it.' An appeal was made to Saint-Lazare to fill the vacant places; everyone wished to go but only three were selected: a priest, James de la Fosse, a cleric, Claude Ferot, and a lay-brother. A month later the first was brought back to Saint-Lazare on a stretcher, and on August 30, another sick man arrived from Palaiseau to rejoin his confrère in the infirmary.[97] In other places too they fell victims to the pestilence. In September, Saint Vincent learned that all his Missionaries at Étampes, Fathers Deschamps, Labbé, Desvignes, des Jardins, a cleric, de Nelz, a lay-brother and a domestic servant were ill, and that William de Lamoignon had generously afforded them an asylum in his castle at Basville. The Saint sent a priest, Thomas Goblet, and a cleric, Michel Caset, to nurse them, and four other members of his community to carry on relief work for the poor. On October 2, he wrote: 'We have still seven or eight scattered here and there in that diocese[98] seeking out and serving parishes abandoned by their pastors and clergy, and especially attending to the sick poor who have no one to console them and to administer the last Sacraments or to bury them when they die.'

Some of the patients were brought back to be nursed at Saint-Lazare.[99] Fathers Deschamps and Watebled were carried off by the plague; Saint Vincent wept over them and found in his heart words that fittingly expressed his sense of grief and loss. Of the former,[100] he wrote: 'We have lost more than I can express, that is if one can really lose by being deprived of those whom Our Lord has taken to Himself,' and of the latter: 'He showed great zeal and gave the poor the provisions we sent to him. He has left behind him a sweet perfume of the grace that ever accompanied him.'[101] Saint Vincent was not discouraged by these losses, yet they placed him in an embarrassing situation. On October 25, he wrote sadly: 'We no longer have anybody to send to the country to render assistance to parishes

---

[97] *Ibid.*, p. 463. [98] *Ibid.*, p. 488. [99] *Ibid.*, p. 513.
[100] *Ibid.*, p. 514. [101] *Ibid.*, p. 515.

that have been abandoned.'[102] Nevertheless, he still resolved to maintain Missionaries at Lagny and Étampes; at Lagny, Father Gaucher, Nicholas Sene, a cleric, Leonard Lamirois, a lay-brother, and probably Father Hennin and some others;[103] according to a report drawn up on December 26, they were attending to 180 sick, 89 orphans and 296 cases of dire poverty.[104] The author of the *Charitable Store*, writing of Étampes on January 2, 1653, says: 'The poor and sick in this locality are so numerous that it is impossible to supply a list of them, as all, generally speaking, are ill or poor and in a state of utter destitution. . . . These good Missionaries have re-established the hospital and are nursing the sick together with the Sisters of Charity; they have also a soup-kitchen for nearly two hundred of the poor at Étampes. In other places they have set up four soup-kitchens, one at Etrechy, another at Villeconin, a third at Saint-Arnoult, and a fourth at Guillerval. The soup-kitchen at Etrechy is for thirty-four poor widows and orphans; twelve loaves at eight *sols*; and sixty *sols* a week; and so in proportion for the others. They are also helping the poor at Boissy-le-Sec, Saclas, Fontaine, Boissy, Buillerval, Dormoy, Marigny, Champigny, petit Saint Marc, and Brières; the cost amounts to one hundred crowns a week and more.'[105]

This quotation from the *Charitable Store* mentions the fact that there were Daughters of Charity at Étampes. They had arrived there in July and worked hard, braving all dangers and scorning fatigue. One of them, Sister Mary Joseph, had served the poor for two years in Picardy and Champagne before going to Étampes where she fell sick. Whilst on her death-bed, a poor woman, ignorant of the Sister's illness, came to be bled. The dying Sister, with an amazing display of energy, rose up and carried out the woman's request; then, exhausted by her effort, she died immediately she was back in bed.[106] 'This good

---

[102] *Saint Vincent de Paul*, p. 512.   [103] *Ibid.*, p. 530.
[104] *Le Magasin Charitable*, pp. 3-4.   [105] *Ibid.*, p. 12.
[106] *Vie de Mademoiselle Le Gras*, par Gobillon, p. 118; *Saint Vincent de Paul*, Vol. X, p. 510; *Relations*, September–October, 1652.

THE RELIEF OF L'ILE-DE-FRANCE

Daughter,' said Saint Vincent, ' may rightly be called a martyr of charity.'[107]

As the number of deaths increased, so did the number of orphans ; they were collected together in a house of which Sister Joan Frances was placed in charge. The Ladies of Charity, by their alms, enabled the Sister to carry on the work. Saint Vincent had only allowed her to go provisionally and intended to withdraw her when times grew better ; hence she was recalled on September 20, 1653,[108] but in response to urgent requests, he allowed her to continue for a time her services ' to Our Lord in these little creatures.'[109] In 1654, the Ladies of Charity, seeing that the town was not perhaps showing much inclination to adopt the orphanage, ceased to contribute. Sister Joan Frances, placed in a delicate position, procured situations for such of the children as were able to earn a living, and Saint Vincent came to her assistance for the others by appealing to the Ladies of Charity to have pity on them.[110] The letter from which we learn these facts was written on June 25, 1654 ; after that, there is complete silence as to what happened to Sister Joan Frances and the orphanage at Étampes, but she probably was removed shortly afterwards.

Étampes long remembered its great benefactor. M. Feillet wrote in 1862 ; ' When the city rose from its ruins, it erected, out of gratitude to Saint Vincent and his disciples, an iron cross not far from the Church of Saint Basil, on a spot called *Le Carrefour des Ormes*, which was still to be seen a few years ago.'[111]

---

[107] *Saint Vincent de Paul*, Vol. X, p. 510.
[108] *Ibid.*, Vol. V, pp. 15, 18.
[109] *Ibid.*, p. 67.   [110] *Ibid.*, Vol. V p. 158.
[111] *Op. cit.*, p. 414.

CHAPTER XLIII

THE SICK ; LUNATICS ; ORPHANS

THE list of the various classes of persons who benefited by the sympathetic charity of Saint Vincent de Paul is already very long and yet it is not complete. His heart went out to all who were in distress, and his sympathy was always translated into acts of kindness that were carried out in a liberal and intelligent manner.

Consider his work for the sick. His whole life was preoccupied with the idea of obtaining their cure or in case all his labour having proved vain, of preparing them for a happy death. In the early stages of his apostolic career, after his arrival in Paris, he was frequently to be seen in the wards of the Charity Hospital. At Clichy, the sick were the best loved members of his flock. His short sojourn at Châtillon-les-Dombes was marked by the foundation of the first Confraternity of Charity which, thanks to his efforts, spread throughout the whole of France with marvellous rapidity. By means of this Confraternity, the poor were nursed in their own homes, and had not to leave their families, at a time when hospitals, insufficient in number and organised without any attention to the rules of hygiene (which were, moreover, very badly understood) instead of helping patients to recover, frequently only hastened their end.

It was in order to assist the sick poor in the Hôtel-Dieu of Paris that he established the Company of the Ladies of Charity, which subsequently undertook so many other charitable works. The Daughters of Charity were, in the first instance, placed at the disposal of the Confraternity of Charity to which they lent their aid by visiting and nursing the sick poor in their own homes. The idea of introducing

Sisters into hospitals came later, and then Saint Vincent sent his Daughters to those at Angers, Nantes, Saint-Denis, Montreuil-sur-Mer, Châteaudun, Belle-Isle, Ussel and Cahors.

In 1655, the Sisters took charge of the hospice known as *Les Petites Maisons* which was situated in Paris, on the ground now occupied by the Carrefour des Ménages or the *Bon-Marché*. This large establishment, also known as the *Hospice-des-Ménages* or the Hospice for those suffering from ring-worm of the scalp, contained nearly four hundred patients of both sexes, old men, lunatics, and those suffering from diseases of the skin. When the General Council for the relief of the poor asked Saint Vincent to supply Sisters for this work, he did not hesitate for long ; the thought of the lunatics confined there helped to shorten the time he usually took before arriving at a decision. His joy was accompanied by a certain pride, a noble and a supernatural pride, at the idea that no community of women had hitherto devoted themselves to the relief of poor lunatics, and that Our Lord had allowed Himself to be regarded as mad, ' to sanctify this state as well as all others ' having ' willed to be regarded as a scandal to the Jews and a folly to the Gentiles.'[1] He recommended his Daughters to rejoice with him and to be proud that they had such a noble vocation, which indeed was shared by his priests, for ever since he had taken possession of the Priory of Saint-Lazare, the Congregation of the Mission had an asylum for lunatics in the Mother-House.

Other forms of work had opened up for the Daughters of Charity. When they had been entrusted with the management of *Les Petites Maisons*, Alain de Solminihac, the saintly Bishop of Cahors, began to treat with Saint Vincent for Sisters to take charge of an orphanage for girls. He had to wait four years before he could induce the Saint to undertake this work. Saint Vincent alleged, though in vain, that he had no Sisters at his disposal ; the prelate insisted and even ' grew angry.'[2] He may, perhaps, have thought that the plea of insufficiency of numbers was rather an excuse

---

[1] *Saint Vincent de Paul*, Vol. X, p. 126 ; cf. p. 114.
[2] *Ibid.*, Vol. X, p. 578.

than the real motive, and in this he may not have been far wrong. It was a new type of work and would probably entail other foundations of the same nature ; it was to enter on a road that might lead them away from the sick poor, and a road, moreover, that would be pleasanter, for youth has attractions not to be found in other periods of life. In the end, Saint Vincent yielded to the urgent requests of his friend. The bonds of friendship, the high opinion he had formed of the other's sanctity, and in addition, the eminent dignity of the prelate, decided him to submit ; if he had offered any further resistance, he would have feared that he was disobeying God's will, which in his eyes was made manifest in a special way through the Bishops.

The Sisters appointed for the orphanage left Paris on November 5, 1658. Saint Vincent gathered them around him on the eve of their departure to give them some advice and instructions. He took care to direct their attention to the novelty of the work : ' You are going go teach orphan children and to instruct them in all things necessary to their salvation ; not only to teach, but also to train them, so that this is one of the greatest works yet undertaken by your fellow-Sisters. You have Sisters in hospitals and in the parishes of Paris, Sisters with the convicts and in the Foundling Hospital, but, so far, you have had no employment similar to this.'[3] Saint Vincent had certainly not forgotten that one of his Daughters had been in charge of the orphanage at Étampes ; if he did not refer to her now it was because this Sister had remained at her post just long enough to give those in charge of the establishment time to organise it. It was not, therefore, a foundation properly so called, and the provisional character of the establishment explains why it scarcely counted in his eyes.

The National Archives[4] contain the draft of a set of rules dated July, 1657, ' for orphan girls about to be entrusted to the care of the Sisters of Charity at Cahors.' The document bears the stamp of Saint Louise de Marillac and she was, in fact, its author. ' The little Sisters,' for so the orphans were

---

[3] *Saint Vincent de Paul*, Vol. X, p. 578.
[4] S. 6173. This set of rules is given in the *Pensées de Louise de Marillac*, p. 259.

styled, are treated seriously, quite as much so as nuns. Amongst the religious exercises prescribed are daily Mass, the Rosary, spiritual reading, half-an-hour's visit to the Blessed Sacrament, three examinations of conscience, and an almost constant union with God whilst rising, dressing, working, and at meals. There was very little time allotted to conversation : silence at meals, silence at work ; one period of recreation and that for half-an-hour after the meal at ten o'clock, ' in honour of the infancy of Jesus.' They are also advised ' to eat only from necessity.' The 'little Sisters' are, in addition, invited to sanctify each of their actions by a special intention ; for instance, for universal peace and Christian union, for the new-born, for the sick, the afflicted, those in their last agony, prisoners, priests, superiors and the members of religious Orders. Every morning they should select a soul in Purgatory and attribute to it all the fruits of the prayers and work of the day. This was a rather top-heavy scheme, especially for the orphan girls of Cahors, but no doubt before this draft was embodied in a regular set of rules, more than one alteration was made. Alain de Solminihac, for his part, did not spoil the children ; the food he supplied was on the rough side : black bread and sometimes a little dripping or beef. Although the Sisters were not subjected to such an austere regimen, they could not make up their minds to take any other food than that supplied to the children. Their Superiors were informed of this fact, and it is probable that they were ordered to adopt a more nourishing dietary.[5]

Saint Vincent never ceased to look after the interests of the orphanage of Mademoiselle Marie Delpech de l'Estang, Foundress of the Daughters of Saint Joseph or of Providence which, after a preliminary trial of some months at Bordeaux, was transferred, on February 11, 1639, to Paris, to a house in the Rue du Vieux-Colombier owned by M. Gontier, Councillor to the Parliament, in which there were already some nuns from Charleville, driven from Lorraine by famine.[6] At first, three orphan girls were admitted ;

[5] Letter of M. Fournier to Mlle Le Gras, December 21, 1659 (Arch. Daughters of Charity).

[6] Interesting information on this community may be found in the National Archives S. 4735, L. 1061, H. 4120.

after six months the number rose to seventy ; after a year, to a hundred ; after six years, to two hundred and twenty-six. Development such as this required larger and larger premises. In the middle of the year 1639, Mademoiselle de l'Estang took up residence in a house close to the Jesuit novitiate ; in 1640, she purchased a house in the Rue Saint-Dominique, close to the Esplanade des Invalides, and in 1645 new buildings were erected.

The brethren of the Blessed Sacrament took an interest in the French islands of America : Martinque, Guadeloupe and Saint-Christopher, where the numerical superiority of men over women produced, from the moral point of view, deplorable results. They thought that Mademoiselle de l'Estang's orphanage might supply an easy remedy to this state of affairs, if orphan girls of a marriageable age were sent to these islands. Eight left in 1642, fourteen in 1643, sixteen in 1644, and the work seemed so useful that branches were established at Rouen and Abbeville.

Saint Vincent was the chief support of this orphanage ; he secured for it the protection of Anne of Austria and alms from the Ladies of Charity. Thanks to his efforts, the King gave his approval to the new foundation by Letters Patent, and the Archbishop of Paris endorsed its statutes or regulations, on which the Saint himself had worked, at the request of Pope Innocent X, in collaboration with the Bishops of Lisieux, Senlis, Meaux and Chartres.[7] He also nominated M. Gambart, a member of the Tuesday Conferences, to the post of spiritual guide of the community and suggested to the foundress that she should frequently see Mlle Le Gras to whom she should submit her difficulties. He believed he could find no better means of giving her a practical lesson on how to govern than by inviting her to attend a Council of the Daughters of Charity at which a question was discussed in her presence. ' Out of your two hundred Sisters,' said Saint Vincent to her before she left the meeting, ' select three or four of the wisest ; hold a meeting with them from time to time and also consult your spiritual guide. Look upon any tendency to act only by your own lights as a temptation.' This was, in fact,

[7] Brief of March 12, 1645 (Arch. Nat. L. 1061).

Mademoiselle de l'Estang's chief fault and the principal cause of her failures.[8] In 1791, the Convent of the Daughters of Providence consisted of only fifty members, amongst whom there were twenty nuns, two novices and one postulant.

Amongst other difficulties that Saint Vincent had to struggle against were the disastrous effects of floods, of which that of 1652 was one of the worst. Several districts in Paris resembled parts of Venice, but Gennevilliers, in the suburbs, suffered most. The Seine overflowed its banks, flooded the streets, and inundated the ground floors of houses and buildings. The people, imprisoned in their houses, could not obtain supplies of food, for the river ran with such force that no one would venture on the water. Saint Vincent was not intimidated by the danger; he was too old and too infirm to be of much help himself, but he sent two lay-brothers on a wherry, laden with provisions, and with orders to call first on the parish priest for directions as to how the food should be distributed. The curate joined the brothers on the wherry and supervised the distribution of provisions. Every day, as long as the floods lasted, the boat returned with a plentiful supply of food. When the waters had subsided, the chief citizens of Gennevilliers paid a visit to Saint-Lazare to thank the Saint, in the name of the whole population, for all he had done for them.[9]

The misfortunes of the Irish nation were of a different and more terrible nature than those of Gennevilliers. Cromwell's persecution led to a large exodus of penniless Irish Catholics to France, and Saint Vincent could not remain indifferent to their hard fate; he regarded them as not merely poor but persecuted, and in a sense as martyrs. The higher the rank of those members of the ecclesiastical hierarchy whom he assisted, the greater the precautions he took that his gifts should remain unknown. The amount of assistance he gave the exiled Bishops will never be known. Occasional references to gifts in his letters[10] allow us to infer

[8] Collet, *op. cit.*, Vol. I, p. 426.
[9] Abelly, *op. cit.*, Bk. III, Ch. XI, sect. II, p. 126; Collet, *op. cit.*, Bk. V, p. 500.
[10] *Saint Vincent de Paul*, Vol. V, p. 414; Vol. VI, pp. 133, 252.

that he frequently intervened in order to assist the venerable prelates to maintain their rank with dignity in a foreign land.

Irish priests also had a liberal share in his alms. His heart bled to see them stretching out their hands to passers-by for help and also to see them spending their days in idleness. He feared lest, after they had shown such courage in the maintenance of their faith, they might fall victims to laziness and evil ways. It was essential, in his eyes, to establish an organisation, to induce these ecclesiastics to earn a living by some form of work, and as most of them were not sufficiently instructed to do so, a preliminary series of instructions should be provided. One of their fellow-countrymen, a Priest of the Mission, was appointed to gather them together and to train them, but such an arrangement was not appreciated by all. Certain malcontents, by their remarks, stirred up distrust and jealousy. Saint Vincent was insulted and calumniated ; he was bluntly told that if he minded his own business and let that of others alone, things would not go so badly, and he was even denounced to the Holy See. The opposition party intrigued so skilfully that the meetings were less and less well attended, and ultimately no one at all put in an appearance. The Saint humbled himself before God ; the sins of his past life rose up before his mind and he accused himself as being the cause of the failure. However, though pained, he was not discouraged. Some time afterwards, whilst talking with the Irish confrère who had assisted him in this ungrateful work, he said : 'Let us make another effort ; go and see your fellow-countrymen and try to persuade them that it is to their own interest to abandon this life of idleness which is such a danger to their souls ; at any cost, the meetings must be resumed. We will begin to help them again when we see them prepared to make themselves more useful and more exemplary than they are at present. I beseech you, Sir, to work hard at that.' This language astonished the Irish priest, who replied : 'And yet you know, Sir, what their past conduct has been. Their ingratitude deserves that you should do nothing for them in future.' At these words, the Saint cried out : 'No, no, that is just the very reason they

THE SICK; LUNATICS; ORPHANS

must not be abandoned.'[11] As a matter of fact, he did most for those who were most hostile and most unfortunate. One of the latter class was a blind priest who had had all his needs provided for, including a guide; he frequently called at Saint-Lazare, and was never allowed to depart without sharing a meal with the Community.

Despite the privations imposed on them by their poverty, the young Irish ecclesiastics could not resign themselves to interrupting their studies; they attended lectures at the University of Paris, were satisfied with little, and may, perhaps, have managed to exist by begging. Saint Vincent had pity on them and sought out kind friends in provincial University towns, where the cost of living was not so high, who helped the young Irishmen to continue their studies.[12]

A large number of laymen had also fled from their native land to Paris, and it was not easy to provide for them owing to their ignorance of the language. Saint Vincent came to their assistance; he placed at their disposal one of his Irish confrères who helped to maintain them in the love and practice of their religion by frequent reunions, at which he addressed them on their duties as Christians.[13] Quite a considerable body of Irishmen solved the problem of making a living by joining the Army. At the siege of Bordeaux, in 1651, there were five Irish regiments, and after the capture of the city, they marched North to join the troops who were fighting against the Spaniards around Arras. When they were no longer required, they received orders to move to Troyes and were accompanied by more than five hundred and fifty orphans and a hundred poor widows when they arrived in that city. It was pitiful to see these poor creatures, bare-footed and covered with the rags of those who had fallen in battle; they straggled through the streets, looking for food and often contented themselves with what the dogs had disdained to eat. Saint Vincent, informed of this by the Superior of the house at Troyes, told the Ladies of Charity of the wretched plight of these unfortunate women and children, and the Ladies sent money, provisions and

[11] Abelly, *op. cit.*, Bk. III, Ch. XI, sect. VII, p. 172.
[12] *Ibid.*, Bk. III, Ch. XI, sect. V, p. 154.
[13] *Ibid.*, sect. III, p. 134.

clothes. The girls and widows were admitted to the Hospice of Saint-Nicholas where they were provided with easy and remunerative work, such as sewing and spinning. Father Henry, an Irish Vincentian, was sent to them and acted as their chaplain; he preached two sermons a week to prepare them for the reception of their Easter Communion.[14]

The wealthy citizens of Troyes had remained only too long indifferent to the spectacle of human misery that lay before their eyes, but the alms sent by the Ladies of Charity from Paris succeeded in rousing them from their state of apathy. The *Relation* for April–May, 1654, tells us : ' The relief of the poor Irish is still being carried on with good results . . . ; the six hundred livres that were forwarded to them has stirred up the charity of this city, and not only in regard to the Irish, but also to the other poor of the town.' It was a happy form of contagion of which the results were an increase in the practice of alms-giving, the bringing of some slight comfort to the afflicted, and additional spiritual joy to those who had come to their relief.

Bodily misery is not the only form of human suffering; man also has a soul that is not exempt from pain and grief. Created for eternity and placed in a world of corruption that turns him aside from his last end, he needs, as Saint Vincent well knew, help of another nature, and hence he established the preaching of retreats and missions.

[14] Abelly, *op. cit.*, Bk. II, Ch. XI, sect. III, p. 403 ; *Relations* for January–February–March, and for April–May, 1654 ; January–April, 1655.

END OF VOLUME II

The Mayflower Press, Plymouth. William Brendon & Son, Ltd.